WHERE IT'S AT

RADICAL PERSPECTIVES
IN SOCIOLOGY

WHERE IT'S AT

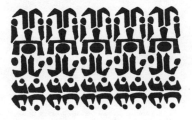

RADICAL PERSPECTIVES
IN SOCIOLOGY

EDITED BY

STEVEN E. DEUTSCH
UNIVERSITY OF OREGON

AND

JOHN HOWARD
RUTGERS,
THE STATE UNIVERSITY

HARPER & ROW, PUBLISHERS
NEW YORK, EVANSTON, AND LONDON

WHERE IT'S AT: **Radical Perspectives in Sociology**
Copyright © 1970 by **Steven E. Deutsch and John Howard**

**Library of Congress Catalog
Card Number: 70-91253**

CONTENTS

PART TWO   STRUCTURAL PROBLEMS
IN AMERICAN SOCIETY

PART THREE   THE UNITED STATES AND THE THIRD WORLD

PREFACE

Where It's At we are making the assumption that we know where
it is at, or at least how to get there.[1] We do know where sociology is at the present time, and we strongly believe that it should
be somewhere else. That belief prompted us to assemble this
collection of readings.

It would be difficult at this point in time to write a text in
radical sociology. Five or ten years may be required for the full
dimensions of the perspective to be defined. We felt, however,
that a collection of articles reflecting that perspective could be
assembled; they themselves would perhaps aid in the formulation
of a sharper definition of radical sociology.

Fundamentally, we are challenged by Noam Chomsky's questions about "The Responsibility of Radical Intellectuals." In deciding to assemble materials which would contribute to a radical
sociology, we were sensitive to those whose personal and intellectual commitments have contributed to outlining such a perspective. We are encouraged by the growth of radical professional associations such as the New University Conference and by
the organization of radical caucuses within the traditional academic disciplines. While the sterility of most social science jour-
nals persists, magazines such as *Liberation* offer radical commentary on the contemporary American society.

[1] See John R. Howard, "Notes on the Radical Perspective in Sociology"
in this book; and Steven E. Deutsch, "The Radical Perspective in Sociology," *Sociological Inquiry*, forthcoming.

Along with the growth of the radical spirit, symbolized inside academia by the development of radical caucuses and outside it by the increase in the number of young people who are willing to try a radically new way of life, we see the development of a spirit of repression. Radicals have experienced physical and legal attack. But in essence, there can be no real choice but to do work which one believes has importance and integrity.

We are in agreement with the call to resist illegitimate authority, and we have sought in this book to present work which documents the exercise of that authority and then pieces which suggest radical alternatives. This we hope will enable the reader to better assess the world in which we live and gain a perspective of the world as it might be.

The book is intended for use in the introductory course in sociology, and for certain advanced courses such as social problems, American society, industrial sociology, and race and ethnic relations. It might also find use in certain courses in related academic disciplines such as political science, and professional fields such as social work. As with any reader, the instructor has the alternative of assigning the pieces within the framework in which the text book authors present them or of integrating them into a framework which he himself develops in his lectures.

The organizing framework employed in the book reflects the basic strains and tensions in the society. Within that framework we have dealt first at the level of description and analysis, identifying sources of structured strain, and then with the more complex problems of alternatives and change. Specifically, each Section of Part II has descriptive-analytical pieces and then a corresponding section of articles on alternatives. We believe that such a framework is an important feature of this collection. The rationale for this structure explains both the selection of pieces and the intent of the total work. Given the phenomena focused upon, we anticipate that, in the next few years the book will become more relevant rather than less relevant.

We have been intellectually challenged and stimulated over the years by our students; to them we owe a debt of gratitude for keeping our sociology relevant, critical, engaging, and exciting. We dedicate this book to those who will develop and employ a radical framework in the future. Mary Howard has been helpful as a commentator and on occasion as a willing conscript. Harper

& Row has been supportive throughout the enterprise; Michael Mattoon has been a cooperative and understanding editor; and we are especially grateful for the enthusiasm, sustained support, and interest shown by Anthony Mellor of Harper & Row.

STEVEN E. DEUTSCH
JOHN HOWARD

INTRODUCTION

NOTES ON THE RADICAL PERSPECTIVE IN SOCIOLOGY*

JOHN HOWARD

CONTEMPORARY AMERICAN SOCIOL-
ogy is probably viewed by many persons as being a radical discipline. In an article appearing in *The New York Times Sunday
Magazine*, Irving Kristol suggested that much of the unrest on
college campuses across the nation during the Fall of 1968 had
been inspired by sociologists—graduate students and faculty;[1] and
even Vice President Spiro Agnew was quoted during the 1968
election campaign as stating that policy with regard to urban
problems should be guided by the hard-headed knowledge of the
businessman and the engineer rather than the dubious nostrums
of the sociologist.

In truth, sociology's reputation for daring is hardly deserved.
Like the fake priest played by Humphrey Bogart in the movie
The Left Hand of God, the discipline is not what most people
think it is. It has neither posed a radical analysis of the society nor
consistently concerned itself with alternatives and change.

In the last few years an increasing number of sociologists have
begun to question the orientation of the discipline. In a piece
appearing in *Trans-action* magazine Herbert Gans criticized his
colleagues for not choosing to do research having greater relevance for policy—particularly with regard to poverty.

* For a complementary piece, see Steven E. Deutsch, "The Radical Perspective in Sociology," *Sociological Inquiry*, forthcoming.
[1] Irving Kristol, "A Different Way to Restructure the University," *The New
York Times Sunday Magazine*, 4, No. 13:3, 50–53, 162–180, December 8,
1968.

1

Sociology has long limited itself to describing and explaining human behavior, using methods and concepts not easily adapted to the needs of policy. As a result, sociologists find it easier to catalogue behavior (and misbehavior) of the poor than to suggest experiments that would test ways of eliminating poverty.[2]

Many published studies, Gans commented, "are still small and narrow, often intended more for colleagues than for application to current social problems."

Alvin Gouldner,[3] Maurice Stein,[4] and Thomas Hoult[5] have also questioned some of the basic dicta of the discipline, particularly the principle of "ethical neutrality."

Discontent is to be found among graduate students as well as faculty. The November, 1968, issue of *The Human Factor*, the journal of the Graduate Students Union at Columbia University, was devoted to a self-proclaimed radical critique of the discipline. We quote from the conclusion of Albert Syzmanski's "Toward a Radical Sociology." Whatever the dismay felt by the elders of the sociological tribe, Syzmanski's article represents the thinking of at least some of the people who will play a role in shaping the future of the discipline.

We maintain that radical sociologists must have an integral conception of their role as radical-sociologists, and avoid the schizophrenic dissociation of their academic and political activities. Radical sociology should not mean contributing money to radical causes, nor should it mean dropping out to organize slum dwellers, draft resisters, or guerrillas. The goal of radical sociologists should be above all the formulation and propagation of a sociology relevant to the practical problems facing man. We must conceive of our contribution to the building of a decent society in terms of (1) the development of an understanding of the organization and dynamics of our society; (2) the development of an understanding of how that society can be

---

[2] Herbert Gans, "Where Sociologists Have Failed," *Trans-action*, October 1967, p. 2.

[3] Alvin W. Gouldner, "Anti-Minotaur: The Myth of a Value-Free Sociology," *Social Problems*, 9, No. 3:199–213, Winter, 1962.

[4] Maurice R. Stein, "Value Sterility, Value Neutrality, or Value Advocacy: The Choice Before Us," *The Human Factor*, 8, No. 1, November 1968.

[5] Thomas Ford Hoult, "Who Shall Prepare Himself to the Battle," *The American Sociologist*, 1, No. 1:3–7, February 1968. See p. 21 in this text.

changed and a human social organization substituted; and (3) the dissemination of these understandings to our fellow social scientists, our students, and to men in general.[6]

The elders of the discipline probably view sentiments of this sort as the aberrations of youth, or as an expression of outrage at the multiple indignities of graduate student life—some academic equivalent of the Freudian drama of the slaying of the father. It is possible, however, that they bespeak more than momentary madness or infantile leftism.

This book forms a part of the dissent from the discipline as traditionally constituted. In this brief essay we shall explore the meaning of the term "radical sociology." Is it possible, in any scholarly sense, to speak of a radical sociology? Some might argue that it makes no sense to link words such as these: that on one level it is verbal magic, while on another level, it is like speaking of "Baptist sociology" or "Stalinist sociology"—that is, it connotes an ideological bias which precludes the objective analysis of behavior.

In the remainder of this essay we shall attend to these questions.

RADICAL SOCIOLOGY: NOTES FOR A DEFINITION

Radical sociology rests upon a certain conception of the social role of the sociologist. We are in accord with Thomas Hoult's observation that "it is both logical and necessary for sociologists to become involved in at least certain aspects of building the 'good society.' " That

It is appropriate for sociologists *acting as such*, to "take sides" relative to those controversial social issues which are functionally related to conditions that seem likely to enhance or undermine the development of the social sciences.[7]

Hoult argues that a sociology having any degree of integrity cannot exist except in a society with libertarian values. Therefore,

[6] Albert Szymanski, "Toward a Radical Sociology," *The Human Factor*, 8, No. 1:21, November 1968.
[7] Hoult, *op. cit.*, p. 3.

involvement in the actions and passions of the times, in the continuing struggle to maintain and extend those values should be part of the professional role of the sociologist.

In this sense, radical sociology tends to focus on what might loosely be termed "social problems." It is not the case, however, that all sociology dealing with social problems is *per se* radical. A number of attributes identify the radical perspective.

First, it is assumed that certain of the questions with which sociologists concern themselves are more important than others. Certain questions bear on deep and enduring cleavages in the society and on complexes of values which have great portent in terms of its character. Thus, issues and questions of class, race, and generation, of the distribution of power, and the management of dissent bear on what kind of society now exists and what kind of society it will become.

Second, even when important phenomena are studied, the manner in which questions are put may preclude radical analysis. Put somewhat differently, attendance to important issues is not *per se* radical; it is also, in part, a matter of how one asks one's questions. C. Wright Mills in "The Professional Ideology of Social Pathologists" indicated that many sociologists and social workers tended to view the difficulties of people as personal and psychological in nature rather than as consequences of social structure.[8] The radical raises questions with regard to social structure and whether it generates and sustains the problems of individuals.

There is an extensive literature in sociology which acknowledges the existence of certain kinds of social problems—poverty, racism, powerlessness—but often there is the accompanying assumption that these problems can be understood in terms of the characteristics of their bearers rather than in terms of system defects. For example,

—Regarding education, a vast literature attempts to account for the inferior performance of slum children in the public schools in terms of their "cultural deprivation," "impoverished home lives," "lower aspiration levels," and the like. The radical would at least raise questions as to whether the school system itself generates failure. Are there systematic differences in the quality of physical

[8] C. Wright Mills, "The Professional Ideology of Social Pathologists," in Irving Louis Horowitz (ed.), *Power, Politics, and People.* New York: Oxford University Press, 1967.

plant between slum and nonslum schools?[9] Do teachers expect
lower-class children and nonwhite children to be stupid and therefore react to them as if they were in fact stupid?[10]

—Regarding the disproportionately high percentage of households among blacks headed by a female, does one seek an explanation in terms of the "self image of the Negro male" and the "historical legacy of slavery" or in the persistent exclusion of blacks
from the job market by employers and trade unions?[11]

The radical perspective has important consequences for the
formulation of policy. It is not simply a matter of preference or
prejudice, but a question of how one accurately accounts for certain problems. Explanation governs the formulation of policy.
Some of the work of E. White Bakke on unemployed whites
during the depression revealed the same kind of family breakdown that the Moynihan report indicated for blacks.[12] The
disintegration of the family among whites was directly and
clearly a consequence of the breakdown of the economy and
of course had nothing to do with "self-image" or "historical
legacies." The radical perspective suggests that system analysis
not only is likely to generate sounder explanations for the phenomena in question, but also holds more promising possibilities
for the formulation of effective policy.

In short, then, radical sociology has recourse to the distinction
which C. Wright mills made between "the personal troubles of
milieu and the public issues of social structure."[13] In other words,
if a few people are poor, one may look to "case factors." If masses
are poor, one has grounds for asking questions about social structure.

Radical sociology asks whether the problems generated by
social structure are inherent within it (a consequence of "internal
contradictions," if one will) or simply "mistakes" or unintended

[9] Patricia Sexton, *Education and Income*. New York: Viking Press, 1961. *See* p. 241 in this text.
[10] See for example, Robert Rosenthal and Lenore Jacobson, *Pygmalion in the Classroom: Teacher Expectation and Pupils' Intellectual Development.* New York: Holt, Rinehart & Winston, 1968.
[11] See the section on "The Distribution of Work Opportunities," p. 283 in this text.
[12] E. White Bakke, *Citizens Without Work*. London: Oxford University Press, 1940.
[13] C. Wright Mills, *The Sociological Imagination*. New York: Oxford University Press, 1959, pp. 8–13. *See* p. 15 in this text.

consequences? Poverty, for example, can be seen as simply a residual category, i.e., the poor are those people who have *not yet* been raised up in standard of living by the dynamic of an expanding economy. Alternatively, it may be viewed as an inevitable consequence of a certain kind of economy. The policy implications of these alternatives are quite profound. If problems are seen simply as accidents, then one poses policies which leave the fundamental structure of the system intact (in terms of education, for example, bonus pay for teachers willing to work in slum schools). On the other hand, if defects are discerned to be an integral part of the way the system normally operates, then policy calling for more fundamental kinds of restructuring becomes necessary (again, in terms of education, something such as "community control" of schools by ghetto people).

Further, the radical perspective generates its own definition of problems and system defects. It deals in an area where there is broad consensus—poverty and inequality, for example—but it does not assume that conventional definitions exhaustively identify what is. As John Seeley indicated in "The Making and Taking of Social Problems," one needs to ask who is doing the defining. Seeley commented on the inadequacy of conventional definitions.

. . . the table of contents of almost any "social problems" text shows a notable bias in the predictable direction. The text I have momentarily at hand lists among "Deviant Behavior" only Crime, Juvenile Delinquency, Mental Disorders, Drug Addiction, Suicide, and Prostitution; and among "Social Disorganization" Population Crisis, Race and Ethnic Relations, Family, Work, Military, Community and Traffic Disorganization and Disaster. The presence of the military chapter is unusual and somewhat happenstantial, but otherwise this pretty well is the "mix as usual," representing our study of categories of persons sufficiently powerless to offer small resistance to violation by enquiry.

. . . on the Social Disorganization side also we have a more or less customary collection of relatively unresistant units that could be disorganized and could be enquired into. Note no business disorganization, religious disorganization, intellectual anomie, political breakdown, or disorganization, debasement and degradation of the most eminent candidate: post primary education.

Safe. Safe. Safe.[14]

[14] John Seeley, "The Making and Taking of Social Problems: Toward an Ethical Stance," *Social Problems*, 14, No. 4:382–389, Spring 1967.

Radical sociology generates its own definition of social problems partly by asking questions about system defects and about the possible role of social structure in perpetuating problems and defeating the intentions of meliorative policy.

Lest it be said that the radical perspective involves the sociologist in making judgments which are properly foreign to any science, let us point out that there is no such thing as being "above the battle." A number of persons have indicated that the social scientist who refuses to take sides opts by default for the status quo. Beyond this, there is a respected body of theory in sociology which rationalizes and justifies the status quo. One need only mention Talcott Parsons's "Revised Analytic Theory of Social Stratification"[15] or the Davis-Moore theory of stratification.[16] The logical shortcomings and analytic insufficiencies of the functionalist approach to stratification and inequality have already been commented upon at length in other places, and there is no need to discuss them here. As Howard Becker suggested, no matter how one approaches it, ultimately it is a question of "Whose Side Are We On?"[17]

Finally, radical sociology is a sociology of *engagement*. Traditionally the role of the sociologist in the field has been that of observer. He has confined himself to watching others do their thing. The radical perspective suggests that it is legitimate (in a scholarly sense) for the sociologist to play a vigorous role in the situations and organizations which he studies. Etzkowitz and Schaflander in their article "A Manifesto for Sociologists" gave several illustrations of engaged social science.

One social scientist who has gone beyond the non-involved, observer-participant category is Robert Coles, a psychiatrist. He went to study the Student Non-Violent Coordinating Committee in Mississippi during the Summer of 1964. Once down there he found that no one in SNCC was interested in talking to him. To them he seemed to be just another social scientist asking what they thought were ir-

15 Talcott Parsons, "Revised Analytic Approach to the Theory of Social Stratification," in Reinhard Bendix and Seymour Lipset (eds.), *Class, Status, and Power*. Glencoe, Ill.: Free Press, 1953.
16 Kingsley Davis and Wilbert Moore, "Some Principles of Stratification," *American Sociological Review*, 10:242–249, 1945.
17 Howard S. Becker, "Whose Side Are We On?," *Social Problems*, 14, No. 3:239–248, 1967.

relevant questions. But instead of just asking his questions and getting "put on" answers, he decided to stay for the summer and offered to become their doctor. Gradually he came to be trusted by them enough to begin group psychotherapy.

Coles came to occupy a key position in their organization. As part of the inner circle, he helped to make decisions and then participated in the action they took. He thus knew what was going on from the inside. The insight and knowledge he gained thereby was far greater than that of the sociologist who flies down on the "Civil Rights Special" to ask Stokely Carmichael "How's it going, baby?" over a one-night scotch-and-steak quiz session.

SNCC trusted Coles and he was able to tape record and take notes without having to ask any questions. He was interacting in a real life situation. His resources and materials were drawn from his daily life. He learned more about what was happening that summer than any sociologist could learn by any other sociological method. No outside observer, no one coming in with a questionnaire, or sending a questionnaire down, or coming down there to do depth interviewing, could learn as much as he did as part of the decision-making apparatus. Like any other social scientist, when he returned North he scientifically checked and evaluated his research.[18]

It can be questioned, then, whether the purposes of scholarship are necessarily served by lack of involvement. Indeed, under some circumstances scholarly purposes may be properly attended to *only* if the sociologist becomes involved.

Etzkowitz and Schaflander go beyond this; they suggest that the sociologist should play a positive role in the creation of institutions which embody humanist and libertarian values. They suggest that this is necessary both in terms of the professional obligation of the sociologist to use his skills in the alleviation of social ills, and in terms of the superior quality of the data which emerges when the sociologist has been deeply involved in a situation rather than riding the coattails of people who are involved.

We have tried, in this brief essay, to touch on some of the defining characteristics of radical sociology. This text brings together a number of articles which both enlarge on the definition and provide illustrations of the radical perspective in the analysis of the social system.

[18] Henry Etzkowitz and Gerald M. Schaflander, "A Manifesto for Sociologist Institution Formation—A New Sociology," *Social Problems*, 15, No. 4:399–408, 1968. *See* p. 34 in this text.

Most of the articles are by social scientists, but many are not. Indeed, one piece is by Senator J. William Fulbright who might best be described as a "Southern Gentleman." But it is the case, however, that while his manner is always courtly his approach is not always conservative.

It would be difficult at this point in time to write a text on radical sociology. An anthology, however, goes part of the way toward defining the perspective. If the idea is brought into higher articulation for the reader, then this work will have served its purpose.

PART ONE

THE COMMITMENT OF THE SOCIOLOGIST

THE COMMITMENT
OF THE SOCIOLOGIST

INTRODUCTION

THERE ARE SIX ARTICLES IN THIS section. Each contributes to defining the radical perspective in sociology. Although the articles need not be read in the order presented, nevertheless there is a rationale underlying the ordering.

The piece by C. Wright Mills, taken from *The Sociological Imagination*, develops the distinction between the "personal troubles of milieu and the public issues of social structure." This distinction is crucial for grasping the nature of the radical perspective. In that sense, the Mills work precedes the remaining pieces.

Thomas Ford Hoult's "Who Shall Prepare Himself to the Battle?" cogently discusses the social role of the sociologist and raises questions about the meaning and relevance of "ethical neutrality." Hoult's line of argument suggests that it is both logical and necessary for the sociologist, in his professional capacity, to become involved in public issues.

"A Manifesto for Sociologists," by Henry Etzkowitz and Gerald Schaflander, extends this discussion and advances the position that the sociologist should play a positive role in "institution formation." In confronting the malfunctioning of social structure, sociologists should go beyond mere diagnosis and undertake the formation of organizations which will allow people to cope more effectively with the problems generated by a breakdown in social structure.

Martin Luther King, Jr.'s article focuses on the role of the social scientist in a particular setting—the civil rights movement—

a setting, of course, in which a sociology of *engagement* will inevitably have meaning.

The section concludes with articles by the historian Staughton Lynd and the sociologist Richard Flacks. They discuss whether the radical intellectual can function meaningfully within the context of the university. Is it necessary for the radical intellectual to drop out—to go into the ghetto to organize slum dwellers, to work with draft resisters? Lynd argues that the radical may find it necessary to desert the university in order to engage in radical action. Flacks suggests that radical scholarship and radical action are both meaningful components of a professional role which can be played out within the university.

The selections in this section, then, cover a variety of perspectives. All have in common an implicit rejection of the passivity of traditional social science, an explicit challenge to the notions of value-neutrality in sociology,[1] and a call for a radical sociology in place of what Mills calls "abstracted empiricalism" or "grand theorizing." The writings which follow present the reader with a composite view of where sociology might and, in the editors' view, ought to go. As such, this section will help in the examining of the trends that might lead us toward a radical sociology.

[1] On this theme see Alvin W. Gouldner, "Anti-Minotaur: The Myth of a Value-Free Sociology," *Social Problems*, 9, No. 3:199–213, Winter 1962.

PERSONAL TROUBLES
AND PUBLIC ISSUES

C. WRIGHT MILLS

PERHAPS THE MOST FRUITFUL DISTINCTION WITH WHICH THE SOCIO-
logical imagination works is between "the personal troubles of
milieu" and "the public issues of social structure." This distinction
is an essential tool of the sociological imagination and a feature of
all classic work in social science.

Troubles occur within the character of the individual and
within the range of his immediate relations with others; they
have to do with his self and with those limited areas of social life
of which he is directly and personally aware. Accordingly, the
statement and the resolution of troubles properly lie within the
individual as a biographical entity and within the scope of his
immediate milieu—the social setting that is directly open to his
personal experience and to some extent his willful activity. A
trouble is a private matter: values cherished by an individual are
felt by him to be threatened.

Issues have to do with matters that transcend these local environments of the individual and the range of his inner life. They
have to do with the organization of many such milieux into the
institutions of an historical society as a whole, with the ways in
which various milieux overlap and interpenetrate to form the
larger structure of social and historical life. An issue is a public
matter: some value cherished by publics is felt to be threatened.
Often there is a debate about what that value really is and about

From C. Wright Mills, *The Sociological Imagination*, pp. 8–13. Copyright
© 1959 by Oxford University Press, Inc. All rights reserved. Reprinted by
permission of Oxford University Press, Inc., New York.

what it is that really threatens it. This debate is often without
focus if only because it is the very nature of an issue, unlike
even widespread trouble, that it cannot very well be defined in
terms of the immediate and everyday environments of ordinary
men. An issue, in fact, often involves a crisis in institutional
arrangements, and often too it involves what Marxists call "contradictions" or "antagonisms."

In these terms, consider unemployment. When, in a city of
100,000, only one man is unemployed, that is his personal trouble,
and for its relief we properly look to the character of the man, his
skills, and his immediate opportunities. But when in a nation of
50 million employees, 15 million men are unemployed, that is an
issue, and we may not hope to find its solution within the range of
opportunities open to any one individual. The very structure of
opportunities has collapsed. Both the correct statement of the
problem and the range of possible solutions require us to consider the economic and political institutions of the society, and
not merely the personal situation and character of a scatter of
individuals.

Consider war. The personal problem of war, when it occurs,
may be how to survive it or how to die in it with honor; how to
make money out of it; how to climb into the higher safety of
the military apparatus; or how to contribute to the war's termi-
nation. In short, according to one's values, to find a set of milieux
and within it to survive the war or make one's death in it meaningful. But the structural issues of war have to do with its causes;
with what types of men it throws up into command; with its
effects upon economic and political, family and religious institutions, with the unorganized irresponsibility of a world of nation-
states.

Consider marriage. Inside a marriage a man and a woman may
experience personal troubles, but when the divorce rate during
the first four years of marriage is 50 out of every 1,000 attempts,
this is an indication of a structural issue having to do with the
institutions of marriage and the family and other institutions that
bear upon them.

Or consider the metropolis—the horrible, beautiful, ugly, mag-
nificent sprawl of the great city. For many upper-class people,
the personal solution to "the problem of the city" is to have an
apartment with private garage under it in the heart of the city,

and forty miles out, a house by Henry Hill, garden by Garrett Eckbo, on a hundred acres of private land. In these two controlled environments—with a small staff at each end and a private helicopter connection—most people could solve many of the problems of personal milieux caused by the facts of the city. But all this, however splendid, does not solve the public issues that the structural fact of the city poses. What should be done with this wonderful monstrosity? Break it all up into scattered units, combining residence and work? Refurbish it as it stands? Or, after evacuation, dynamite it and build new cities according to new plans in new places? What should those plans be? And who is to decide and to accomplish whatever choice is made? These are structural issues; to confront them and to solve them requires us to consider political and economic issues that affect innumerable milieux.

In so far as an economy is so arranged that slumps occur, the problem of unemployment becomes incapable of personal solution. In so far as war is inherent in the nation-state system and in the uneven industrialization of the world, the ordinary individual in his restricted milieu will be powerless—with or without psychiatric aid—to solve the troubles this system or lack of system imposes upon him. In so far as the family as an institution turns women into darling little slaves and men into their chief providers and unweaned dependents, the problem of a satisfactory marriage remains incapable of purely private solution. In so far as the overdeveloped megalopolis and the overdeveloped automobile are built-in features of the overdeveloped society, the issues of urban living will not be solved by personal ingenuity and private wealth.

What we experience in various and specific milieux, I have noted, is often caused by structural changes. Accordingly, to understand the changes of many personal milieux we are required to look beyond them. And the number and variety of such structural changes increase as the institutions within which we live become more embracing and more intricately connected with one another. To be aware of the idea of social structure and to use it with sensibility is to be capable of tracing such linkages among a great variety of milieux. To be able to do that is to possess the sociological imagination.

What are the major issues for publics and the key troubles of private individuals in our time? To formulate issues and troubles, we must ask what values are cherished yet threatened, and what values are cherished and supported, by the characterizing trends of our period. In the case both of threat and of support we must ask what salient contradictions of structure may be involved.

When people cherish some set of values and do not feel any threat to them, they experience *well-being*. When they cherish values but *do* feel them to be threatened, they experience a crisis —either as a personal trouble or as a public issue. And if all their values seem involved, they feel the total threat of panic.

But suppose people are neither aware of any cherished values nor experience any threat? That is the experience of *indifference*, which, if it seems to involve all their values, becomes apathy. Suppose, finally, they are unaware of any cherished values, but still are very much aware of a threat? That is the experience of *uneasiness*, of anxiety, which, if it is total enough, becomes a deadly unspecified malaise.

Ours is a time of uneasiness and indifference—not yet formulated in such ways as to permit the work of reason and the play of sensibility. Instead of troubles—defined in terms of values and threats—there is often the misery of vague uneasiness; instead of explicit issues there is often merely the beat feeling that all is somehow not right. Neither the values threatened nor whatever threatens them has been stated; in short, they have not been carried to the point of decision. Much less have they been formulated as problems of social science.

In the 'thirties there was little doubt—except among certain deluded business circles—that there was an economic issue which was also a pack of personal troubles. In these arguments about "the crisis of capitalism," the formulations of Marx and the many unacknowledged re-formulations of his work probably set the leading terms of the issue, and some men came to understand their personal troubles in these terms. The values threatened were plain to see and cherished by all; the structural contradictions that threatened them also seemed plain. Both were widely and deeply experienced. It was a political age.

But the values threatened in the era after World War Two are often neither widely acknowledged as values nor widely felt to be threatened. Much private uneasiness goes unformulated; much public malaise and many decisions of enormous structural relevance never become public issues. For those who accept such inherited values as reason and freedom, it is the uneasiness itself that is the trouble; it is the indifference itself that is the issue. And it is this condition, of uneasiness and indifference, that is the signal feature of our period.

All this is so striking that it is often interpreted by observers as a shift in the very kinds of problems that need now to be formulated. We are frequently told that the problems of our decade, or even the crises of our period, have shifted from the external realm of economics and now have to do with the quality of individual life—in fact with the question of whether there is soon going to be anything that can properly be called individual life. Not child labor but comic books, not poverty but mass lesisure, are at the center of concern. Many great public issues as well as many private troubles are described in terms of "the psychiatric"—often, it seems, in a pathetic attempt to avoid the large issues and problems of modern society. Often this statement seems to rest upon a provincial narrowing of interest to the Western societies, or even to the United States—thus ignoring two-thirds of mankind; often, too, it arbitrarily divorces the individual life from the larger institutions within which that life is enacted, and which on occasion bear upon it more grievously than do the intimate environments of childhood.

Problems of leisure, for example, cannot even be stated without considering problems of work. Family troubles over comic books cannot be formulated as problems without considering the plight of the contemporary family in its new relations with the newer institutions of the social structure. Neither leisure nor its debilitating uses can be understood as problems without recognition of the extent to which malaise and indifference now form the social and personal climate of contemporary American society. In this climate, no problems of "the private life" can be stated and solved without recognition of the crisis of ambition that is part of the very career of men at work in the incorporated economy.

It is true, as psychoanalysts continually point out, that people do often have "the increasing sense of being moved by obscure forces within themselves which they are unable to define." But it is *not* true as Ernest Jones asserted, that "man's chief enemy and danger is his own unruly nature and the dark forces pent up within him." On the contrary: "Man's chief danger" today lies in the unruly forces of contemporary society itself, with its alienating methods of production, its enveloping techniques of political domination, its international anarchy—in a word, its pervasive transformations of the very "nature" of man and the conditions and aims of his life.

It is now the social scientist's foremost political and intellectual task—for here the two coincide—to make clear the elements of contemporary uneasiness and indifference. It is the central demand made upon him by other cultural workmen—by physical scientists and artists, by the intellectual community in general. It is because of this task and these demands, I believe, that the social sciences are becoming the common denominator of our cultural period, and the sociological imagination our most needed quality of mind.

". . . WHO SHALL PREPARE HIMSELF TO THE BATTLE?"

THOMAS FORD HOULT

THE CENTRAL PURPOSE OF THIS PAPER IS TO DEMONSTRATE THAT IT is both logical and necessary for sociologists to become involved in at least certain aspects of building "the good society." To accomplish this purpose, the paper has three sections: the first section presents arguments to support the proposition that—

> It is appropriate for sociologists, *acting as such*, "to take sides" relative to those controversial social issues which are functionally related to conditions that seem likely to enhance or undermine the development of social science.

—hence the section is concerned with providing empirically-minded and discipline-oriented sociologists a logical basis for declaring themselves on selected public issues and policies; the second section is a plea to American sociologists to face up to the implications of the fact that they are, at least theoretically, the best qualified people available to lead others in building the kind of society where there would be optimum opportunity for the greatest numbers to achieve happiness; and in the final section, the various illegitimate uses of the "ethical neutrality" position are illustrated and commented on. Underlying the discussion at every point is the writer's conviction that the future welfare of society and of sociology are interlocked—that the special knowledge and

From Thomas Ford Hoult, ". . . Who Shall Prepare Himself to the Battle?" *The American Sociologist*, 3: 1:3–7, February 1968. Reprinted by permission of American Sociological Association and the author.

empirical methods of modern sociologists are two of the most crucial tools needed for development of the "good society," and that sociology's very existence is dependent upon preservation of those aspects of the good society that we symbolize by the term "liberalism."

SOCIOLOGY, SOCIAL ACTION, AND THE LIBERAL SOCIETY

It is a hopeless task, some assert, to attempt to rally any significant number of today's sociologists to the cause of the general welfare. Such a cause is too reminiscent of our ministerial past; it smacks of dogooderness. "The dominant drift in American sociology is toward professionalization, the growth of technical specialists, toward the diffusion of the value-free outlook. . . ," Alvin Gouldner has observed.[1] I agree. It is true, I believe, that most modern sociologists are profession-oriented. But, this fact does not *automatically* mean that the majority of sociologists will not contribute their services to any cause; it means—to put the best face on it—that he who wishes to obtain the help of sociologists in general must show that the help sought is fairly directly related to the good of the discipline. It was with this point in mind that the introductory proposition was phrased in such a way as to put total stress on sociology's development—however, it will be seen from subsequent discussion that, in large part, the same social conditions which contribute to sociology also contribute to the general welfare, hence the proposition's focus is not nearly as narrow as it may seem.

The introductory proposition will, it is hoped, appeal to the many sociologists who do not "take a stand" on controversial public issues primarily because, being profession-, not cause-, oriented—and being aware of the long-standing disagreement among honorable men about the implications of ethical neutrality—they have not been conscious of any discipline-related logical reasons for taking such stands. But there *are* such reasons, the proposition asserts—there are social conditions which enhance the development of sociology, and there are others which undermine it, and

[1] Alvin W. Gouldner, "Anti-Minotaur: The Myth of a Value-Free Sociology," *Social Problems*, 9, No. 3:199–213, Winter 1962; see p. 210.

it is a perfectly proper aspect of the professional role of the sociologist to contribute to the former and work against the latter.

In effect, thus, the proposition recommends two things: 1) that in some respects it is not only *logically* necessary to dispense with the Lundbergian idea of differentiating between citizen role and scientist role—it is *wise* to dispense with the idea; and, 2) that we view the status "sociologist" as calling for a dual role involving interdependent a) research-teaching activity, and b) selected social action activity.[2] Such a view of the sociologist role is simply an assertion that particular types of social action, in addition to other kinds of action, are as proper for the sociologist as is laboratory building for the chemist; neither activity is "pure science," but each is essential to its respective profession.

There may be those who will accept the idea of the dual role outlined, but who will object to the implication that *all* sociologists should engage in both of the role activities described. "What is the objection to specialization?" it might be asked. "Why would it be improper for a sociologist to specialize in either 'a' (research-teaching) *or* 'b' (social action)?" The answer to the second part of the query (dealing with the proposed social action specialty) may be phrased in the form of a question: Is there anyone in sociology today who would seriously contend that an individual engaging in social action only, and doing no research-teaching, is—on the basis of his activity—qualified for the title "sociologist"? I doubt it. On the other hand, with regard to the proposed research-teaching specialty, it is logically impossible to take a "non-position" relative to social issues. As will be indicated in the third section of this paper, the man who attempts to stay "above or beside" the battle by not taking sides on social issues, actually, by the consequences of such "non-choice," becomes an ally of the existing power structure—and has, thus, taken sides after all. In other words, there is no alternative to playing *both* parts of the dual role—which is not to say that all sociologists must become soap box orators (effective tactics may more often call for quiet analysis rather than flamboyant preaching); nor does it deny that some individuals may be more in-

2 A suggestion that is mildly reminiscent of Lester F. Ward's "pure" and "applied" sociology.

terested in the research-teaching aspects of the role while others may be more aroused by the role's social action aspects. But the important point is that it is illogical to speak of a *sociologist* who does research-teaching only or who participates in social action only—if an individual confines his activities to the former, then it is more to the point to title him "apologist for the status quo" or "non-rocker of boats"; and if he does only the latter, then he is appropriately termed a politician or administrator.

Among the sociologists who would agree with the foregoing, there may be a sizable number who would still feel concern for one or both of two reasons—namely, that if we follow the recommendation to support particular social conditions, we: 1) thereby reject Max Weber's logically sound observation that ". . . it can never be the task of an empirical science to provide binding norms and ideals from which directives for immediate practical activity can be derived"[3]; and/or, 2) sociology might degenerate into a plethora of competing sectarian movements led by a never-ending series of prophets and messiahs who will cry, "Follow *me*—I *alone* have the truth, the light, the way to the peace that passeth understanding."

In answer to those who may feel concern for the first reason, I believe I am on defensible logical grounds in saying that there is no necessary contradiction between Weber's observation, on the one hand, and the recommendation, on the other hand, that we support particular social conditions. While engaging in the latter activity we would *not* be saying, "Sociology indicates we 'should' hold to these ideals"—that *would* be a rejection of Weber. We would just be saying, "We adopt these (given) ideals because they appear to promise the most for our discipline."

For those who are concerned that sociology might break down into sectarian movements, the answer lies in several aspects of the nature of the discipline and in one of its prime needs. Its "nature" includes a strong emphasis on cultural relativity, on the importance of adequate empirical data, and on the value of dispassionate, objective examination of evidence and alternatives; when people are trained in terms of such emphases, they generally become particularly resistant to would-be charismatic leaders. As

[3] Max Weber, *The Methology of the Social Sciences*, translated and edited by Edward A. Shils and Henry A. Finch (Chicago: The Free Press of Glencoe, Illinois, 1949), p. 52.

for the relevant prime need of the discipline, Professor Parsons has pointed out that we ". . . have a vested interest in what is in some sense a 'liberal' society"[4]—that is, we can function effectively, as sociologists, only in a society where equalitarianism and social justice are basic values, and where democratic controls, due process, free inquiry, and free speech and press are meaningfully supported. Such social conditions are not only needed by sociology—they are ideals toward which American sociologists— despite their general inaction—have a strong positive orientation. This is the well-known "liberal bias" of sociology; it is a bias which is common among social scientists because such people, in the course of their training, almost uniformly learn that in Western countries, at least, there is a strong historical and current association between a liberal society (as defined by implication above) and the type of society where there are optimum chances for the greatest number to achieve happiness (i.e., the "good society"). This type of learning, and the resulting liberal bias—along with the scientific training of sociologists—suggests that, no matter how politically active sociologists may become, it is most unlikely that a multitude of sectarian ideological movements will develop in American sociology.

If the question arises as to *how* the needed and desired goal of creating and supporting a liberal society can best be achieved, Weber—our man for all seasons—supplies a handy answer:

> The question of the appropriateness of the means for achieving a given end is undoubtedly accessible to scientific analysis. Inasmuch as we are able to determine (within the present limits of our knowledge) which means for the achievement of a proposed end are appropriate or inappropriate, we can in this way estimate the chances of attaining a certain end by certain available means. In this way we can indirectly criticize the setting of the end itself as practically meaningful (on the basis of the existing historical situation) or as meaningless with reference to existing conditions. Furthermore, when the possibility of attaining a proposed end appears to exist, we can determine (naturally within the limits of our existing knowledge) the consequences which the application of the means to be used

[4] Talcott Parsons, "The Editor's Column," *The American Sociologist*, 2, No. 2:62–64, May 1967; see p. 64.

will produce in addition to the eventual attainment of the proposed end, as a result of the interdependence of all events.[5]

To those who would argue that social science's need for a
liberal society is not an established fact, I would call attention to
the state of social "science" in authoritarian environments. Anyone who has read the "sociological" literature produced in Stalinist Russia knows what a travesty social science becomes when its
practitioners are forced to cleave to sectarian dogma.[6] Under such
conditions, even purely physical science can suffer, as indicated
by Lysenkoism in Russia and by the Hitlerian dichotomy of
"Aryan science" as opposed to "Jewish science." It was chilling
to read, in the *American Sociological Review*, about the fate of
one of mainland China's greatest sociologists:

> In reply to a letter to Dr. Sun Pen-wen asking for a set of
> his works, he wrote, "I have come to understand that all my
> books are only good for burning and hence I have none to
> send you. I have also learned that I formerly neglected to study
> the works of Karl Marx which I am now doing many hours
> a day. Please don't write again.[7]

KNOWLEDGE FOR MAN

If I could be granted a wish, I would wish that a sizable number
of sociologists would go much further than suggested in the
opening proposition. I fully accept Robert S. Lynd's thesis[8] that
social and psychological scientists are, by far, the theoretically
best qualified people in the land to sketch the dimensions of, and
to lead others toward, the "good society" (as defined above).
We are the specialists in the principles of human behavior; *we*,

[5] Weber, *op. cit.*, pp. 52–53; but note that the passage quoted is taken from
a section of Weber wherein he is stressing his belief that scientists, while
acting as such, should not recommend courses of action *except* in terms of
efficiency for reaching defined ends.
[6] See, for example, M. Baskin, "Soviet Evaluation of American Sociology,"
translated by John K. Musgrave, *American Sociological Review*, 14, No.
1:137–143, February 1949.
[7] Albert R. O'Hara, "The Recent Development of Sociology in China,"
American Sociological Review, 26, No. 6:928–929, December 1961; see fn. 2,
p. 928.
[8] Robert S. Lynd, *Knowledge for What? The Place of Social Science in
American Culture* (Princeton: Princeton University Press, 1939).

THOMAS FORD HOULT 27

better than anyone else, can properly assess previous faltering attempts to improve the general welfare; *we*, above all—as put so forcefully in *Can Science Save Us?*[9]—know how to create and apply the measuring techniques and devices which can pinpoint the real sources of social discord and dissatisfaction and thus reduce to a minimum the supposed need for "educated guesswork" on the part of leaders of vital human affairs.

"But," some will object, "the 'new sociologist' merely measures, counts, observes—he does not judge." This has been our own popular stereotype, but it is now appropriate to ask: Is the supposedly non-judging type of "new sociologist" truly up-to-date? Or is he so "out of it" he does not realize that, in terms of knowledge and status, we have passed beyond the era of the thirties and forties when sociologists in general were so insecure about their standing as scientists that many of them, trying to play it safe, concentrated on developing a "science of that which is not worth knowing"?[10] We're big boys now! And, like other "real scientists" such as physicists and biologists, we're qualified to make judgments about what apparently will and what won't contribute—given particular sociocultural conditions—to the betterment of man.

And what are we doing, we "naturals" for leaders of the age? As a group, we are spending a good share of our time and energies making out grant applications and collecting and analyzing mountains of trivial data on superficial subjects. We also play a mean game of faculty politics, and we party well, especially when publishers pay the liquor bill. Meanwhile, the planet teeters on

[9] George A. Lundberg, *Can Science Save Us?* Second Edition (New York: David McKay Company, Inc., 1961).
[10] Quoted by Karl Mannheim in his review of *Methods in Social Science*, edited by Stuart A. Rice (Chicago: University of Chicago Press), 1931; review reprinted in Karl Mannheim, *Essays on Sociology and Social Psychology* (New York: Oxford University Press, 1953), pp. 185–194; the fragment quoted appears in Mannheim's volume, p. 192, in the following context:

> In the introduction to the volume under discussion (p. 10), the question is asked whether Marx and Carlyle would have been unable to envisage their problems had they known the statistical method. If the answer is in the affirmative, then we do not hesitate to confess that we would rather renounce statistical exactness than forego seeking answers to those questions which seem important to us. Should it not be possible to save these questions, then the cruel name of a 'science of that which is not worth knowing,' which was originally applied to academic, dry classical philology, would befit our science.

the brink of World War III. It is enough to make one weep to think that almost three decades after Lynd published his indictment we are still hawking status quo sociology. *Knowledge for What?* Lynd asked, and, clinging to the line followed by Nazi medical experimenters—and by developers of atomic, chemical, and bacteriological weapons—we quote Aristotle as our authority that knowledge is a good in itself and cannot be judged on external grounds:

> All knowledge is obviously good because the good of any thing is that which belongs to the fullness of being which all things seek after and desire . . .[11]

It is perhaps monstrously presumptuous of me to do so, but I am here asking others who are concerned to join me in building, at long last, a *meaningfully* new sociology. (I say "presumptuous" and "at long last" because I too am guilty of having been apathetic —if not cowardly.)[12] Such a sociology would begin and end with the advice of Francis Bacon:

> I would address one general admonition to all: that they consider what are the true ends of knowledge, and that they seek it not either for pleasure of the mind, or for contention, or for superiority to others . . . but for the benefit and use of life, and that they perfect and govern it in charity. . . .[13]

The meaningfully new sociology would teach its recruits that it is not an indication of scholarly detachment for a sociologist to refuse to indicate which of a variety of alternatives seems most likely, on the basis of available evidence, to contribute to the good society (as defined); it is a cheap avoidance of responsibility. The

[11] Aristotle, interpreted by Thomas Aquinas, in Hans Jonas, "The Practical Uses of Theory," as reprinted in *Philosophy of the Social Sciences*, edited by Maurice Natanson (New York: Random House, 1963), pp. 119–142; see p. 119.

[12] Although I finally decided to include this and one other note of self-denigration, I remain unsure about the wisdom of making such observations. I would agree with N. J. Demerath III, who wrote (see p. 77 of his "In a Sow's Ear: A Reply to Goode," *Journal for the Scientific Study of Religion*, 6, No. 1:77–84, Spring 1967): "There is a certain arrogance in pointing at the weaknesses of ones' own work since modesty is easily labelled false, and nothing is hollower than the implied promise of greater works to come."

[13] Natanson, *op. cit.*, p. 120.

recruits would also be taught that the so-called apolitical scientist is not *just* irresponsible; he is always a Frankenstein who can quite easily engage in activities that threaten to destroy man himself. As Tom Lehrer puts it with bitter humor, the politically non-committed scientist, having no significant human group loyalties, is motivated by expedience only and can therefore be *expected* to choose the side of the highest bidder regardless of the nature of the job requirements:

"Don't ask me where the bombs come down"—says the ex-Nazi missile expert, now working for the United States—"That's not my department. . . ."

The logical opposite of the apolitical scientist described is not —at least for present purposes—the "political man" who is almost totally lacking in objectivity. Neither is he the teacher who carelessly, and without labeling, presents *evaluations* of facts as if they were *empirical* observations. The politically-responsible sociologist I envisage would cling tenaciously to the generally accepted canons of science. He therefore would not think of supporting or opposing given issues, controversial or not, without having a defensible (i.e., "scientific") basis for his stand. He would, whenever possible—in line with his training and responsibility—insist upon having adequate empirical, and even experimental, knowledge before drawing conclusions. Where such knowledge is lacking—because of the pressure of time or because of the inherent complexities of any given case, as in international affairs—then he would feel that the *minimum* requirement is to be as certain as possible that sources of information are reliable (in accordance with *generally* accepted standards, not Pentagon, pacifist, or other specialist point of view) and that judgments which appear tentatively justified are properly qualified and labeled.

THE USES OF ETHICAL NEUTRALITY

The philosophical position which is usually termed "ethical neutrality" may seem to some to be a major obstacle to this paper's "call to commitment." However, the *legitimate* use of ethical neutrality constitutes no such obstacle; it is only when it appears in what may be called its "illegitimate" forms that it is a block to decision and action. It is a perfectly legitimate application of the ethical neutrality principle when an investigator, while gathering and analyzing data, temporarily suspends his culture- and time-bound values for the purpose of doing his work as objectively as possible. But it is clearly an illegitimate application of the principle when an individual, strictly for personal reasons, cites it as a rationalization for inaction, as a cover, a disguise.

Since arguments for the illegitimate uses of ethical neutrality often have a certain surface plausibility, it is wise to become familiar with the relevant characteristics and tactics of those who use the arguments. One such tactic is illustrated by the individual who says, "Sociologists should not take sides on controversial issues because they are scientists and scientists should not draw conclusions until they are 'absolutely sure' "—an interpretation which amounts to a permanent abrogation of responsibility be- cause, of course, in the complex affairs of mankind we can be *absolutely* sure of nothing of importance. Another approach is that of the individual who says, "I believe in taking a stand *as a man;* but it is not appropriate to take a stand *as a sociologist*"—a differentiation which is illogical but which, if acted on, might yield defensible practical results. But it is notable that people who say "I only take a stand as a man, not as a social scientist," are almost always the very same people who take no stands at all. Hence, in such cases, it appears that the careful differentiation between "men" and "sociologists" has, at best, an unintended ironic meaning.

Those who use ethical neutrality or similar arguments as an excuse for inaction, for not "choosing sides," are, it should be remarked, adopting a philosophical stance that was undermined decades ago. It is *impossible*, as it has been shown repeatedly, to take a "non-position" relative to social issues. Even Max Weber, often cited—in a kind of "If it was good enough for old Max, it's good enough for me" spirit—as the granddaddy of the ethical neutrality approach to data, clearly saw the logical fallacy of the "non-choice" position:

> . . . all action and naturally, according to circumstances, in- action imply in their consequences the espousal of certain values—and herewith—what is today so willingly overlooked— the rejection of certain others.[14]

[14] Weber, *op. cit.*, p. 53.

THOMAS FORD HOULT   31

Then almost thirty years ago, Lynd wrote his "portrait in acids" of American social science in general and of sociology in particular.[15] Said one reviewer:

> His colleagues won't like what he bids them see. They will refuse to face the fairly patent fact that the "detachment" and "objectivity" that they have exacted of themselves have been excuses for keeping quiet, dodges to avoid thinking, devices for saving their skins.[16]

Much more recently, Alvin Gouldner gave us "Anti-Minotaur: The Myth of a Value-Free Sociology."[17] As Gouldner and a host of others have made clear, value neutrality is a myth because the man who does not self-consciously take a "side" on any given issue has—whether he means to or not—declared for entrenched forces. Politics enmesh us nowadays, said Mahatma Gandhi, ". . . as with serpent's coils from which there is no escape however hard one may try."[18] In the words of Karl Popper:

> . . . anti-interventionism is untenable—even on purely logical grounds, since its supporters are bound to recommend political intervention aimed at preventing intervention.[19]

There are a variety of reasons which may be cited to account for the "no stand as a sociologist" position. One of the more obvious is avarice; this would appear to be the motive of those who have sold out—to industry, to the military, or to the hope for the next grant—and who make use of the seasoned bureaucrat's stock answer. "That's not my department." In addition, there are the many who are just plain lazy—the ones who, for example, say the only reason they haven't made up their minds about the Vietnam war is because they haven't taken the time to do any systematic reading on the subject: "I feel sort of guilty," they

15 Lynd, loc. cit.
16 Max Lerner, "The Revolt Against Quietism," The New Republic, 99, No. 1283:257–258, July 5, 1939; see p. 257.
17 Gouldner, loc. cit.
18 Paraphrased by Martin Buber in "Letter to Mahatma Gandhi," as reprinted in The Pacifist Conscience, edited by Peter Mayer (New York: Holt, Rinehart and Winston, 1966), pp. 269–282; see p. 279.
19 Karl R. Popper, The Poverty of Historicism (Boston: The Beacon Press, 1957), pp. 60–61.

say, "but with term papers to grade, and all—you know—I just don't seem to get around to it. And anyway, the situation is so confused that a really *objective* person can't make any firm decisions. So why bother to try?"

Although greed and sloth may account for a significant number of those who choose to remain on what they *think* is dead center so far as controversial social issues are concerned, I am personally convinced that *cowardice* is the most important single explanation. That is, I hypothesize that among the sociologists who refuse to declare themselves pro or con on such questions as nuclear weapons, civil liberties, racial discrimination, etc., the majority are motivated by fear—they are, I hypothesize, consumed with fear of those who hold power and/or fear that they may commit the supposedly cardinal sin of the academic (i.e., doing or saying something that may turn out to be wrong or foolish).[20]

There are, so far as I am now aware, no "hard" data to support the proffered hypothesis—it remains to be tested. But its plausibility is suggested by a multiplicity of small signs and events: the sociologists who refuse to sign a petition until they see who else is signing; the ones among us who say they are "above the battle," but who eagerly lead the charge when they are personally touched by some safe issue such as the allocation of faculty parking space; the seeming correlation between taking a stand and having tenure; the apparent readiness with which so many of our "greats"— excepting the rare George Lundbergs among us—openly, and frequently *as sociologists,* espouse a variety of causes, while those of us who have not "arrived" are so often the ones to shout about making sociology a "pure" science.

In conjunction with the foregoing, it is intriguing to speculate on *why* sociology, in comparison with the other behavioral disciplines, is seemingly so overloaded with "scientismists"—many of whom, I have asserted, are sheep in scientists' clothing. The American Anthropological Association has gone on record in opposition to the Vietnam war on the grounds that "genocide is not

---

[20] The poor souls who are being taught that "if it can't be said in numbers, it's not worth saying" should be exempted; to the degree that they are well integrated into their academic subculture, they are just plain uninformed about what is of permanent importance in human affairs—therefore, they cannot logically be held accountable for their actions or the lack thereof.

in the interests of the AAA." It seems doubtful that enough support could be mustered to pass such a resolution in the ASA. Why? Is it, perhaps, because so many of us, in our classes and elsewhere, stress scientism to such a degree that we tend to "pull" a superfluity of the frightened and the unsure who find our ranks attractive *because* being a sociologist means (they think) that one is safe from the world's controversies—means, indeed, that one can, with in-group approval, spend one's life fiddling with trivia while Hanoi burns?[21] And on the other hand, do students who have some faith in themselves, and therefore the courage of their convictions, leave us in disgust and go into other fields? I don't know—but I see here the makings of some provocative dissertations in the general field of the sociology of sociology.

· · ·

Those who agree with the foregoing points—that it is logically impossible to be neutral about values; that the very existence of our discipline is dependent upon "liberalizing" social conditions; that the so-called apolitical scientist is likely to be a cad or a coward; and that we sociologists are, at least theoretically, particularly well qualified to point the way to the good society—will see the logic of the proposition with which this paper begins. They may also wish to play a part in building a meaningfully new sociology, one of the norms of which would be that practitioners must, relative to significant political and ideological issues, speak out fearlessly—

> For if the trumpet give an uncertain sound, who shall prepare himself to the battle?[22]

---

[21] Having published my own share of frivolous nothings, I do not exempt myself from the implied accusation; but note footnote 12.
[22] 1 Corinthians XIV, 8.

INSTITUTION FORMATION—
A NEW SOCIOLOGY

HENRY ETZKOWITZ
GERALD M. SCHAFLANDER

ALMOST ALL OF AMERICAN SOCIOLOGY HAS ABDICATED THE RESPONSI-
bility for finding solutions to the most urgent problems facing
our society. What sociologists usually do is merely observe and
ask questions as "objective" outsiders. They come to the people
who are actually doing things in the world when they have a
few moments to spare from doing laboratory-manipulated studies
of students paid for by foundations and government and then use
various techniques to find out what these people are doing in their
groups or institutions, always looking in from the position of a
neutral non-involved observer.

We are nauseous over the continual replication of meaningless,
microscopic quantifications of "what's wrong or right with American society" from sterile, neutral, non-involved, objective re-
search-sociologists!

We believe, as human beings and as sociologists, that we have a
deep moral responsibility to go far beyond mere objective analyses
of society (away from Parsonian-Mertonian Structural-Function-
alism and Vidich-Stein Radical Nihilism).

From Henry Etzkowitz and Gerald M. Schaflander, "A Manifesto for Sociologists: Institution Formation–A New Sociology" *Social Problems*, 15: 4:399–
408, 1968. Reprinted by permission of The Society for the Study of Social
Problems and the authors.
Written in April, 1967, as the first paper prepared by members of the Community Cooperative Center Research and Development Corporation, 1310
Atlantic Avenue (Bedford-Stuyvesant), Brooklyn, New York. Because
events have moved so rapidly, some revisions have been made in the paper
since it was first written.

34

Marshall Clinard, in his 1966 Presidential Address to the Mid-Western Sociological Association on the responsibility of sociologists, said that they should go beyond routine survey research, get out into the world, get involved in crucial problems, and come back with recommendations for policy makers.

Although this is a significant call for sociologists to transcend their usual bounds, it still limits the area for sociological solutions to what might be accepted by government or policy makers, and does not consider the possibility of sociologists themselves organizing new institutions to implement their own proposals.

We believe it is imperative for sociologists to analyze precisely what is sick in American society and then to act to try to change and heal American society.

We call upon young sociologists and old sociologists (who are dying of "microscopic ennui") to join us in a macroscopic effort to return American sociology to a fundamental and basic institutional involvement in American society by exploring the life and death problem of slave-ridden Americans in the ghetto.

With race riots increasingly rampant in inner cities; with white-Negro cooperation at its lowest point in the civil rights movement; we moved to 1175 Bedford Avenue, Bedford-Stuyvesant (America's number one ghetto with nearly half a million residents) on January 9, 1967; and proceeded to build a Community Cooperative Center with a fifty-fifty white-Negro integrated Board of Directors. We put up our own money from our teaching salaries at Hunter and Brooklyn Colleges and rented a 20,000 square-foot building at 1310 Atlantic Avenue, Brooklyn; proceeded to renovate it with 30 young drop-outs and delinquents and opened March 1, 1967, as a new Institution in Bedford-Stuyvesant.

As researchers we have found that when tape is used as an unobtrusive recorder of real-life interactions between people (building an institution together), the resources and materials are usually genuine and truthful.

When a sociologist is accepted as a partner by the people he is working with and studying, the taping is rarely a barrier or proscenium separating the sociologist from the respondent. In fact, most people tend to forget the recorder is on. The involvement and life-heat of the interaction consume the attention of both parties and insure an accurate reproduction of the responses of all the actors. Thus the Heisenberg principle is overcome in this type of sociological research because the research instrument rarely influences the process being studied! Isn't this one ultimate object of scientific research?

When an actor routinely acts, the proscenium in the theatre is the barrier between the actor and the audience. When the actor, however, breaks through the proscenium and becomes a person or character who is believable, identifiable, and full of verisimilitude, he and the audience are bound together in a common living experience and each forgets the presence of the proscenium. It's not artificial or stagey or contrived. It's real, genuine interaction!

It is our contention that routine survey research questions are generally unnatural; they set up a proscenium behind which the respondent acts out a role on cue (role plays) and in front of which the sociologist generally asks artificial, contrived questions. The resulting barrier often prevents truthful, believable interaction, i.e., did most people really admit sexual inadequacy to Kinsey; religious non-observance to Lenski?

Some sociologists go beyond survey research and become participant observers, taking sociology a giant stride beyond the neutral quantifiers. Some become members of the institutions or groups they are studying, as for example, Erving Goffman, who went into an asylum in Washington, D.C. as a recreation director, watched the doctors and patients, and concluded that no one was sane! He found out how they role-played in their institution and how they got along.

A New School graduate sociology student, Gerald Levy, worked in the Welfare Department of New York City and came out with a fine report on how the bureaucratic system unconsciously worked to hurt and put clients off. In this instance a sociologist became part of an existing institution, but with no commitment to try to change what he saw as "sick."

C. Wright Mills will go down in sociological history as a brilliant and perceptive analyst of the power elite. He analyzed the power structure of the U.S. in the late fifties but, like Malcolm X, who also "told it like it is," Mills neither had a program for social change nor any hope at all for any coalition that could effectuate a change in the bureaucratic growth of the power elite.

In the final analysis, Mills saw no hope of changing present institutions nor did he believe new institutions could be built to stop the drift towards war and to restore democracy at home.

The pseudo-heirs to C. Wright Mills—Coser, Vidich, and Stein, leaders of the radical nihilists—write with vigor and refreshing passion about what's wrong with the Structural-Functional School of Parsons and Merton and the bureaucratic evils of American society. But Vidich tells his students to make the best deal they can within American society. He tells them to remain cool, detached, and objective—not to try to change or alter or fight bureaucracy, because if they do, they'll be corrupted through having to use the same tactics as the very bureaucrats they're struggling against. This non-prescription perpetuates the status quo because it serves as an ideology to rationalize and legitimate inaction for young sociologists, and graduate students (who come to sociology through Mills' perceptive critique—and are turned off by Vidich and Stein at the height of their desire to participate in social change).

We cannot opt out of American organization life with the analysis that bureaucracy inevitably corrupts. As the radical nihilists argue, if we do adopt this analysis it is likely to act as a self-fulfilling prophecy in influencing us to make deals or sell out to those organizations which we cannot avoid or must participate in.

To try to be an omniscient, rigidly objective, or value-free observer from afar is not only to abdicate from one's responsibilities as a citizen but to condemn oneself to be an essentially irrelevant critic; for it is only by participating in the most important and macroscopic areas of life in one's society (and in our society that means large and complex organizations) that one will have the relevant resources, data, and materials to develop a proper analysis of that society.

One social scientist who has gone beyond the non-involved observer-participant role is Robert Coles, a psychiatrist. He went to study the Student Non-Violent Coordinating Committee in Mississippi during the summer of 1964. Once down there he found out that no one in SNCC was interested in talking to him. To them, he seemed to be just another social scientist asking what they thought were irrelevant questions. But instead of just asking his questions and getting "put-on" answers, he decided to stay for the summer and offered to become their doctor. Gradually he came to be trusted by them, enough to begin group psychotherapy.

Coles came to occupy a key position in their organization. As part of the inner circle, he helped to make decisions and then participated in the action they took. He thus knew what was going on from the inside. The insight and knowledge he gained thereby was far greater than that of the sociologist who flys down on the "Civil Rights Special" to ask Stokely Carmichael "How's it going, baby?" over a one night scotch-and-steak quiz session.

SNCC trusted Coles and he was able to tape record and take notes without having to ask any questions. He was interacting in a real life situation. His resources and materials were drawn from his daily life. He learned more about what was happening that summer than any sociologist could learn by any other sociological method. No outside observer, no one coming in with a questionnaire, or sending a questionnaire down, or coming down there to do depth interviewing, could learn as much as he did as part of the decision-making apparatus. Like any other social scientist, when he returned North he scientifically checked and evaluated his research. Yet he didn't innovate or initiate any basic institutional changes and SNCC's "Black Power" deterioration is history.

Many action sociologists (such as A. Shostak) counsel the poor and become grantsmanship experts within the government anti-poverty structure—thus becoming co-opted into a bureaucratic government program.

The expansion of the Viet Nam war and the accelerated growth of a Pax-Americana foreign policy has severely curtailed anti-poverty funds as well as disrupted normal organizational expectations with sporadic "start and stop" funding. Moreover, social change was seriously inhibited because the Federal Government never could withstand the pressure from the big city political machines, and the local Congressmen who represented economic and political interests violently opposed to poor and grass roots organization which threatened their very economic and political control.

The experience of Mobilization for Youth in New York City, local congressional opposition to the grape workers' organizing struggle in California, and the cut-off of the independent Head Start Program in Mississippi are but a few of the many examples which illustrate the political schizophrenia of the government anti-poverty program.

Another unique approach is that of Saul Alinsky, who left academic sociology to organize the poor. In the Woodlawn area of Chicago he connected existing organizations to each other in a new structure, The Woodlawn Organization. He gave it operational and tactical direction and prepared to confront Mayor Daley. Under Alinsky's leadership the residents of Woodlawn as members of T.W.O. marched on City Hall and demanded a say in urban renewal plans for their neighborhood. They were able to stop the proposed plans imposed from City Hall and get a reconsideration of urban renewal planning in the area so that they would be included in the planning process. However, after the initial confrontation with City Hall, the momentum of the T.W.O. slacked off. The marches to City Hall stopped and even the demonstrations in front of stores to lower prices dissipated.

Woodlawn is basically the same now as it was before Alinsky started. No fundamental institutional changes were achieved in Woodlawn nor in Syracuse, Rochester, or other communities where Alinsky's highly creative confrontations excite and motivate poor people, yet leave them in the same slums, with the same high cost of living and unemployment as when they started. They may have more self-esteem and self-identity but jobs, lower cost foods, and a decent place to live are no closer in any community served by Alinsky's non-institutional approach to social change.

Many church, labor, and sociological groups have been attracted to Alinsky because of the dynamic excitement of his program and the potential increase in self-identity and self-esteem he develops among the poor. But we wonder if relative deprivation and disillusionment are not the end result of the Alinsky program when no fundamental institutional change occurs among the Alinsky-trained poor.

In the summer of 1948 Sol Tax, an anthropologist from the University of Chicago, took some of his students to study an Indian community in the Middle West. The students were appalled at the Indians' living conditions and wanted to change them. Tax, the anthropologist, first felt that they should remain outside as observers, but later, back at the University, changed his mind and the next time he brought the students back to the Indian community he was determined to act to change the situation.

In the Indian community there were two opposing factions and thus two views of what this situation was. One faction wanted to return to the old ways while the other wanted to discard the old ways and modernize. Tax's group proceeded to develop alternate solutions based on the views of these two Indian factions. Since they were committed to deriving their program for change from the ideas and wishes of the Indians, rather than suggesting new programs, the Tax group ended with a project to produce Indian *trinkets* for sale. This satisfied both factions: those who wanted to keep the old as well as those who wanted to act for economic improvement.

Thus, the Action-Anthropologist, feeling bound by the definition of the world of those he would help, was no more able to overcome the situation of debilitating poverty than the Indians.

The major difference between the program of the Tax Action Anthropologists and those of us who are "new" Institution-Formation sociologists[1] is that we feel that we must propose and/or develop new and unique institutional solutions to the situations people are in because there is no guarantee that poor people alone know how to solve their own problems—or that red or black voices necessarily speak with truth or clarity on the nature of their own appalling condition.

We cannot necessarily derive programs for social change from the very people who are victimized and desire change. They are usually limited in both knowledge and experience.

A social scientist who has recognized this is the late Allan Holmberg, a Cornell anthropologist, who went to the Indian community in Vicos, Peru, as a participant-intervener with a plan of action. In 1952, Cornell University, in association with the Indigenous Institute of Peru, rented Vicos, a hacienda of 2,000 Indians, and initiated a program for social change in education, community development, and involvement of the people in making decisions about what should be done. Yet Holmberg retained final veto power as an anthropological landlord.

---

[1] Or "Involved Observers"; see Kenneth B. Clark, *Dark Ghetto*, New York: Harper, 1965, Introduction.

Once people had a taste of modern life and education they often decided to leave for the cities while, with improvement of conditions in Vicos, some returned home. This can only be a temporary halt in the movement of people to cities, given the sociohistorical thrust towards urbanization.

Although Holmberg instituted a worthwhile effort to improve the lot of people in a rural area of Peru, he neglected consideration of macroscopic analyses of the long term trend towards the urbanization of Latin America. This would have shown him the difficulties of achieving significant changes in a traditional rural Institution and perhaps have led him to devote his efforts for social change towards urban Latin America.

Today in the ghettos we see a strong parallel between our sociological attempt to build new institutions and the CIO organizing drive in the late 1930's.

The CIO organizers didn't come to workers and ask them: "What's troubling you?" "What is your problem?" What they did was to say: "Look, you're getting picked off one at a time; you're being speeded up because you haven't got a union; because if one of you gets kicked around the rest of you don't go out. Here's a program we've got for you. . . . Sign this card. We're going to form an organizing committee; we'll sign everybody up that's inside the shop; we'll pull the shop out, and I'll tell you when to pull the shop out because that's what I'm an expert at. Here's the program we've got—if you don't like it, don't sign the card. If you like it, sign the card and we'll organize the plant."

People signed it or they didn't. If they did, the union organized. They wrote the leaflet, went out in front of the plant, pulled them out or sat down inside the plant until they got their contract.

When we came into Bedford-Stuyvesant (an area where more than one-half of the women are husbandless or unwed mothers; most of the rest of the population are unemployed, on welfare, narcotized or drunk; and young people are bitterly screaming for "black power" while they roam the streets) everybody said: "ask the community what they need." What community? Were we supposed to sit down and try to find some kind of consensus when Roy Wilkins doesn't agree with Martin Luther King and Martin Luther King rarely talks to Wilkins or agrees with Stokely Carmichael? They seldom get together, as Robert Penn Warren says, on any one issue. There is no one voice for the Negro—at the national or local level—as we have observed.

Therefore, it seemed very clear that it was up to us—because we have the knowledge and training—to propose new solutions. We could say, as did the CIO organizers, "This is the idea that *we* think is right. This is the program; we're going to come in as whites on a fifty-fifty basis. If you don't like it, OK!! If you do like it, come on and join us."

What we are proposing as sociologists is that we should initiate and organize totally new institutions where old ones are ineffective, and then study the institutions that we organize, as well as their relationships to other institutions that they will affect.

THE COMMUNITY CO-OP CENTER: A NEW AND UNIQUE INSTITUTION

As a first step, we analyzed what was essentially lacking in Bedford-Stuyvesant—an independent economic base for the Negro community. Without this economic base, Negroes could not build their own political power base or any other institution in the community, but instead were left dependent on the outside bureaucracy coming in—the welfare, the schools, the police, etc. They could present no defense against such bureaucracy without an economic base from which they could struggle. Because of plantation oppression and economic and educational discrimination, Negroes could not, through hard work alone, build up private enterprise as the Jews have done. Obviously, it's now too late! Economic opportunities and areas are no longer technologically open.

We felt it would take a new institution to accomplish this. So, we took an old institution, the co-operative, from another part of society and made basic and fundamental changes in it to make it effective in ghettos such as Bedford-Stuyvesant.

Excerpts from the following presentation to foundations and private individuals on January 25, 1967 started the fund raising and organization.

> The proposal to create a new and unique Community Cooperative Center in Bedford-Stuyvesant is designed to achieve the following purposes:

Organize and study the effects of introducing a unique Community Cooperative Center in the slums of Bedford-Stuyvesant as a potential model for other urban ghettos to begin to solve their own economic, social, and political problems . . . through a SELF-GENERATING and repetitive generating effort.

AS AN INITIAL OPERATIONAL SERVICE PROGRAM TO THE COMMUNITY
Simultaneously, the Project would initiate several levels of research to culminate in Ph.D. theses and/or books, as blueprints for the "Institution-Formation Sociology"—via foundation support (one time only) across the U.S.A.—with major concentration in ghettos of Boston, Philadelphia, Baltimore-Washington, Chicago, Detroit, Cleveland, Los Angeles, Oakland-San Francisco, Memphis, New Orleans, and Harlem in New York City.

Market Research to determine precisely the "what and how much," daily consumption patterns of a validated cross-section of Bedford-Stuyvesant's ghetto community. Also what effects the mass media and the "outside consumer-oriented" society have on individual aspirations, desires and values.

An exhaustive continuing study of the effects existing institutions in the community have on Co-op members (churches, schools, police, welfare services, etc.) and what effect membership in a successful Co-op might have re institutional (long-range) influence on old and new members of the Community Cooperative Center.

UNIQUE INSTITUTIONAL PHILOSOPHY
The Project basically involves the transfer of an old, respected, and successful (rural and union-oriented) institution, the Co-op, from "developed" American society to the "underdeveloped," anarchic sub-society of the ghetto.

The venerable institution, the Co-op, is being drastically restructured and altered in order to become a SELF-GENERATING source of continuing capital . . . to meet the continuing and growing needs of the specific ghetto . . . by *reinvesting profits in sorely needed community services.*

The basic and radical changes to be instituted are:

1) No membership fee will be charged to new members. The original organizing capital will be provided by foundation grants.

2) *Drastically reduced prices* (not competitive) on drugs, milk, butter, bread, meat, underwear, shoes, etc.; rather than the traditional "meet-competition" pricing approach of the old Co-op movement. Therefore, needless and often wasted time will be saved from recruiting large (absent) original member-

ship fees; and endless educational efforts will be eliminated to keep members of the Co-op buying at competitive prices . . . in order to guarantee FUTURE "divvies" and/or individual members dividends.

3) Total elimination of individual divvies or profits. A basic policy of reinvestment of the profits in social services to the membership and community will be substituted for the age-old (Rochdale) Co-op "divvy." Credit unions, camp and social scholarships, and job-training are early objectives of the project.

4) As services expand, more and more jobs at the CCC itself will be created—totally new and unexplored job and career images and opportunities will be fostered to develop dignity, self-respect, and to give hope and faith to the ghetto—to replace alienation.

Above all, this Project should be supported because there is confusion and anarchy in the civil rights movement itself; there are arguments and deep differences over strategy and tactics and priorities and feuding between SNCC, SLC, NAACP, CORE, and the government and foundations. Here is a program that cuts through factionalism and ideological hang-ups.

In August of 1967, seven months after crankup, the new socio-economic Institution, the CCC, presented itself in the following brochure:

The Community Cooperative Center is a non-profit, tax-free (filed for), bi-racial corporation at 1310 Atlantic Avenue in Bedford-Stuyvesant (Brooklyn, New York), the number one ghetto in the U.S.

THE COMMUNITY COOPERATIVE CENTER OPERATES A GASOLINE STATION, PARKING LOT, DRUG STORE, AND CHILD CARE CENTER.

The basic purpose of the Community Cooperative Center is that the profits from the business services—with drastically lower prices—are turned over to support the largest Child Care Center in New York City (107 children now attending, ranging from 3 months to 5 years) from 7:30 a.m. to 7:00 p.m. They are supervised by 4 certified teachers, 12 trained unwed mothers, 5 graduate nurses and 6 volunteer college students.

Other health and social services will be added as profits increase.

THE COMMUNITY COOPERATIVE CENTER HAS BEEN ORGANIZED AS A SELF-HELP, SELF-GENERATING, SELF-PERPETUATING, INTEGRATED INSTITUTION THAT HAS RECEIVED ITS ORIGINAL FINANCING FROM

TEACHERS, STUDENTS, WEALTHY INDIVIDUALS, AND SMALL FOUNDA-
TIONS COMMITTED TO INTEGRATION.

The July 16, 1967, *New York Times* editorial puts it quite grimly and bluntly when it says: "As the trend towards violence grows among Negroes, so does its counterpart among frightened whites. More and more cries of black power evoke the echo of white power. . . . But it must be recognized that the threat of confrontation between Negro and white in the U.S. today is the most serious problem this nation faces, more serious even than Viet Nam . . ."

THIS RARE BRIDGE BETWEEN BLACKS AND WHITES IS WORKING
HERE, AND, THIS UNIQUE DIALOGUE MUST BE MAINTAINED AND
SOLIDIFIED WITH NEWARK AND DETROIT SMOLDERING AND WATTS
STILL FESTERING.

This totally new and different institution might just be the key answer to the crises of our inner cities which, according to the New York Times, could tear this country apart.

The Bedford-Stuyvesant Community Cooperative Center is a model and, when successful, can be duplicated in your community.

IF YOU WANT TO JOIN WITH US BY CONTRIBUTING, OR HELPING IN
ANY WAY, WRITE TO CCC RESEARCH AND DEVELOPMENT CORPORA-
TION, 1310 ATLANTIC AVENUE, BROOKLYN, NEW YORK (467-1220).

Sincerely; ANNA COPELAND, Chairman (Girl Scout leader and youth religious leader); GERALD SCHAFLANDER, President (Instructor of Sociology, Boston University); JOHN BRYAN, Vice President (Graduate Student, Howard University); CLIFFORD ETHERIDGE, Vice President (Former Gang Leader); RUPERT VAUGHAN, Vice President (Brooklyn College Student); ELLIOTT JEFFRIES, Vice President (Contractor); and HENRY ETZKOWITZ, Treasurer (Instructor of Sociology, Northeastern University, Boston).

From a sociological research standpoint, the living proof of the correctness of this Institution-Formation or Involved Observer approach is what we have learned first hand about unwed mothers, drop-out students, narcotics, unemployment, and the terrible void in verbal communication and interaction between Negroes and whites, through actually living and working together.

We have voluminous tape recordings of personality and organizational conflicts; hundreds of hours of tapes indicating significant, repetitive behavior patterns of young men and women involved in a life style and culture totally unknown to white America, which is only vaguely hinted at in Claude Brown's *Manchild in the Promised Land*.

Though Negroes in the ghetto aspire to achieve material possessions—status and educational goals—similar to those of white middle-class society; nevertheless their constant and repetitive failures to achieve these goals leave them alienated, frustrated, and then aggessive (J. Dollard). This inevitably leads to internal aggression of Saturday night knifings and cuttings; and external aggression of rioting, looting, intense exploitive sex (unwed mothers), alcohol, and narcotic gratification—all part of a secondary ghetto culture. For the dominant white middle-class culture— ever present through T.V.—stimulates a new, acute frustration level right in the ghetto apartment—every 15 minutes. They are tantalized, restimulated and refrustrated every 15 minutes with visual and auditory symbols of the white middle-class culture that they can never really "make."

So they turn inward in gratification and outward in aggression and establish a unique life style—a truly secondary culture. They are in schizoid conflict between the dominant culture they desire —and the secondary culture they are in.

Now, for the first time, white students and teachers have recorded sociologically the daily interaction, anxieties, fears, and hopes of a group of whites and Negroes together building a new Institution and a new way of life.[2]

Does anyone really believe this kind of material and resources could ever be derived from objective, neutral interviewing? It came through the confidence and trust we established by raising money, meeting payrolls, working in the cold together, and sharing mutual hopes, fears, and conflicts as this Institution is being built.

Only through naked confrontation, through daily living and working together could these conflicts be resolved and could we, as sociologists, begin to define the scope and true nature of the sociological and social psychological problems that threaten to erupt into race riots this summer unlike anything witnessed in America before.

---

[2] These tapes with analyses will be presented in a forthcoming book, *The Way It Really Is: A Socio-Historic Narrative Documentary*, Doubleday.

We say nonsense to all of the separatist experts in the civil rights movement—when there's no "real" black power movement; when SNCC is going down the drain; when CORE is near dead; when the NAACP is ineffective in the ghetto, and when we've got more Negroes and whites working together in the CCC than anywhere else in the U.S.

Now we may run out of money and we may flop; but we've got a 20,000-square-foot building; we've got Negroes and whites working together. We refuse (truculently and belligerently) to let Negroes stereotype us as members of the "White Society" power structure.

We refuse to assume the guilt of white people who think like members of the White Citizens' Council and the KKK. We will not allow any Negro to judge us merely as whites. We are human beings and we'll judge them as human beings. There'll be no stereotypes. We will not accept it. We do not think that because they are Negroes they are good or bad. They are good or bad (just as whites) because they produce and they perform or they don't. And that's our program; that's the institution we have, and this is a way to heal ghetto society.

We are acting in the tradition of the old CIO organizers. And we believe this is one way in which inner city slums in American society can be changed.

The information and data we have on sex, narcotics, educational insufficiency, family disintegration, and how Negroes respond to money or the lack of money is direct and personal and bears the imprint of the way it really is—which, we believe, can only flow from naturalistic field research.

We call for a return to the Chicago tradition of Albion Small's conception of the sociologist as "social agitator." We must form new institutions to heal the sickness in the ghettos through Community Cooperative Centers that are self-generating; new schools bereft of bureaucratic ponderousness; new social aid and protective institutions, free of spying but full of preventive social therapeutic tools; and other new institutions where the best elements in the so-called white society—artists, scientists, professionals, teachers, and students join hands with Negroes in the ghetto to re-build American society from the heart of our key cities.

THE BEHAVIORAL SCIENTIST IN THE CIVIL RIGHTS MOVEMENT

MARTIN LUTHER KING, JR.

IT IS ALWAYS A VERY RICH AND REWARDING EXPERIENCE WHEN I CAN take a brief break from the day-to-day demands of our struggle for freedom and human dignity and discuss the issues involved in the struggle with concerned friends of good will all over the nation. It is particularly a great privilege to discuss these issues with members of the academic community, who are constantly writing about and dealing with the problems that we face and who have the tremendous responsibility of moulding the minds of young men and women all over our country.

THE CIVIL RIGHTS MOVEMENT NEEDS THE HELP OF SOCIAL SCIENTISTS

In the preface to their book, *Applied Sociology* (1965), S. M. Miller and Alvin Gouldner state: "It is the historic mission of the social sciences to enable mankind to take possession of society."[1] It follows that for Negroes who substantially are excluded from society this science is needed even more desperately than for any other group in the population.

From Martin Luther King, Jr., "The Role of the Behavioral Scientist in the Civil Rights Movement," *The Journal of Social Issues*, 24: 1:1–12, January 1968. Reprinted by permission of The Southern Christian Leadership Conference, Atlanta.

[1] S. M. Miller and A. Gouldner, *Applied Sociology*. New York: The Free Press, 1965.

For social scientists, the opportunity to serve in a life-giving purpose is a humanist challenge of rare distinction. Negroes too are eager for a rendezvous with truth and discovery. We are aware that social scientists, unlike some of their colleagues in the physical sciences, have been spared the grim feelings of guilt that attended the invention of nuclear weapons of destruction. Social scientists, in the main, are fortunate to be able to extirpate evil, not to invent it.

If the Negro needs social sciences for direction and for self-understanding, the white society is in even more urgent need. White America needs to understand that it is poisoned to its soul by racism and the understanding needs to be carefully documented and consequently more difficult to reject. The present crisis arises because although it is historically imperative that our society take the next step to equality, we find ourselves psychologically and socially imprisoned. All too many white Americans are horrified not with conditions of Negro life but with the product of these conditions—the Negro himself.

White America is seeking to keep the walls of segregation substantially intact while the evolution of society and the Negro's desperation is causing them to crumble. The white majority, unprepared and unwilling to accept radical structural change, is resisting and producing chaos while complaining that if there were no chaos orderly change would come.

Negroes want the social scientist to address the white community and "tell it like it is." White America has an appalling lack of knowledge concerning the reality of Negro life. One reason some advances were made in the South during the past decade was the discovery by northern whites of the brutal facts of southern segregated life. It was the Negro who educated the nation by dramatizing the evils through nonviolent protest. The social scientist played little or no role in disclosing truth. The Negro action movement with raw courage did it virtually alone. When the majority of the country could not live with the extremes of brutality they witnessed, political remedies were enacted and customs were altered.

These partial advances were, however, limited principally to the South and progress did not automatically spread throughout the nation. There was also little depth to the changes. White America stopped murder, but that is not the same thing as ordaining brotherhood; nor is the ending of lynch rule the same thing as inaugurating justice.

After some years of Negro-white unity and partial successes, white America shifted gears and went into reverse. Negroes, alive with hope and enthusiasm, ran into sharply stiffened white resistance at all levels and bitter tensions broke out in sporadic episodes of violence. New lines of hostility were drawn and the era of good feeling disappeared.

The decade of 1955 to 1965, with its constructive elements, misled us. Everyone, activists and social scientists, underestimated the amount of violence and rage Negroes were suppressing and the amount of bigotry the white majority was disguising.

Science should have been employed more fully to warn us that the Negro, after 350 years of handicaps, mired in an intricate network of contemporary barriers, could not be ushered into equality by tentative and superficial changes.

Mass nonviolent protests, a social invention of Negroes, were effective in Montgomery, Birmingham and Selma in forcing national legislation which served to change Negro life sufficiently to curb explosions. But when changes were confined to the South alone, the North, in the absence of change, began to seethe.

The freedom movement did not adapt its tactics to the different and unique northern urban conditions. It failed to see that nonviolent marches in the South were forms of rebellion. When Negroes took over the streets and shops, southern society shook to its roots. Negroes could contain their rage when they found the means to force relatively radical changes in their environment.

In the North, on the other hand, street demonstrations were not even a mild expression of militancy. The turmoil of cities absorbs demonstrations as merely transitory drama which is ordinary in city life. Without a more effective tactic for upsetting the status quo, the power structure could maintain its intransigence and hostility. Into the vacuum of inaction, violence and riots flowed and a new period opened.

URBAN RIOTS

Urban riots must now be recognized as durable social phenomena. They may be deplored, but they are there and should be understood. Urban riots are a special form of violence. They are not insurrections. The rioters are not seeking to seize territory or to attain control of institutions. They are mainly intended to shock the white community. They are a distorted form of social protest. The looting which is their principal feature serves many functions. It enables the most enraged and deprived Negro to take hold of consumer goods with the ease the white man does by using his purse. Often the Negro does not even want what he takes; he wants the experience of taking. But most of all, alienated from society and knowing that this society cherishes property above people, he is shocking it by abusing property rights. There are thus elements of emotional catharsis in the violent act. This may explain why most cities in which riots have occurred have not had a repetition, even though the causative condition remain. It is also noteworthy that the amount of physical harm done to white people other than police is infinitesimal and in Detroit whites and Negroes looted in unity.

A profound judgment of today's riots was expressed by Victor Hugo a century ago. He said, "If a soul is left in darkness, sins will be committed. The guilty one is not he who commits the sin, but he who causes the darkness."

The policy makers of the white society have caused the darkness; they create discrimination; they structured slums; and they perpetuate unemployment, ignorance and poverty. It is incontestable and deplorable that Negroes have committed crimes; but they are derivative crimes. They are born of the greater crimes of the white society. When we ask Negroes to abide by the law, let us also demand that the white man abide by law in the ghettos. Day in and day out he violates welfare laws to deprive the poor of their meager allotments; he flagrantly violates building codes and regulations; his police make a mockery of law; and he violates laws on equal employment and education and the provisions for civic services. The slums are the handiwork of a vicious system of the white society; Negroes live in them but do not make them any more than a prisoner makes a prison. Let us say boldly that if the total violations of law by the white man in the slums over the years were calculated and compared with the law-breaking of a few days of riots, the hardened criminal would be the white man. These are often difficult things to say but I have come to see more and more that it is necessary to utter the truth in order to deal with the great problems that we face in our society.

VIETNAM WAR

There is another cause of riots that is too important to mention casually—the war in Vietnam. Here again, we are dealing with a controversial issue. But I am convinced that the war in Vietnam has played havoc with our domestic destinies. The bombs that fall in Vietnam explode at home. It does not take much to see what great damage this war has done to the image of our nation. It has left our country politically and morally isolated in the world, where our only friends happen to be puppet nations like Taiwan, Thailand and South Korea. The major allies in the world that have been with us in war and peace are not with us in this war. As a result we find ourselves socially and politically isolated.

The war in Vietnam has torn up the Geneva Accord. It has seriously impaired the United Nations. It has exacerbated the hatreds between continents, and worse still, between races. It has frustrated our development at home by telling our underprivileged citizens that we place insatiable military demands above their most critical needs. It has greatly contributed to the forces of reaction in America, and strengthened the military-industrial complex, against which even President Eisenhower solemnly warned us. It has practically destroyed Vietnam, and left thousands of Americans and Vietnamese youth maimed and mutilated. And it has exposed the whole world to the risk of nuclear warfare.

As I looked at what this war was doing to our nation, and to the domestic situation and to the Civil Rights movement, I found it necessary to speak vigorously out against it. My speaking out against the war has not gone without criticisms. There are those who tell me that I should stick with civil rights, and stay in my place. I can only respond that I have fought too hard and long to end segregated public accommodations to segregate my own moral concerns. It is my deep conviction that justice is indivisible, that injustice anywhere is a threat to justice everywhere. For those who tell me I am hurting the Civil Rights movement, and ask, "Don't you think that in order to be respected, and in order to regain support, you must stop talking against the war." I can only say that I am not a consensus leader. I do not seek to determine what is right and wrong by taking a Gallup Poll to determine majority opinion. And it is again my deep conviction that ultimately a genuine leader is not a searcher for consensus, but a molder of consensus. On some positions cowardice asks the question, "Is it safe?" Expediency asks the question, "Is it politic?" Vanity asks the question, "Is it popular?" But conscience must ask the question, "Is it right?" And there comes a time when one must take a stand that is neither safe, nor politic, nor popular. But one must take it because it is right. And that is where I find myself today.

Moreover, I am convinced, even if war continues, that a genuine massive act of concern will do more to quell riots than the most massive deployment of troops.

UNEMPLOYMENT

The unemployment of Negro youth ranges up to 40 percent in some slums. The riots are almost entirely youth events—the age range of participants is from 13 to 25. What hypocrisy it is to talk of saving the new generation—to make it the generation of hope—while consigning it to unemployment and provoking it to violent alternatives.

When our nation was bankrupt in the 30's we created an agency to provide jobs to all at their existing level of skill. In our overwhelming affluence today what excuse is there for not setting up a national agency for full employment immediately?

The other program which would give reality to hope and opportunity would be the demolition of the slums to be replaced by decent housing built by residents of the ghettos.

These programs are not only eminently sound and vitally needed, but they have the support of an overwhelming majority of the nation—white and Negro. The Harris Poll on August 21, 1967, disclosed that an astounding 69 percent of the country support a works program to provide employment to all and an equally astonishing 65 percent approve a program to tear down the slums.

There is a program and there is heavy majority support for it. Yet, the administration and Congress tinker with trivial proposals to limit costs in an extravagant gamble with disaster.

The President has lamented that he cannot persuade Congress. He can, if the will is there, go to the people, mobilize the people's support and thereby substantially increase his power to persuade

Congress. Our most urgent task is to find the tactics that will move the government no matter how determined it is to resist.

CIVIL DISOBEDIENCE

I believe we will have to find the militant middle between riots on the one hand and weak and timid supplication for justice on the other hand. That middle ground, I believe, is civil disobedience. It can be aggressive but nonviolent; it can dislocate but not destroy. The specific planning will take some study and analysis to avoid mistakes of the past when it was employed on too small a scale and sustained too briefly.

Civil disobedience can restore Negro-white unity. There have been some very important sane white voices even during the most desperate moments of the riots. One reason is that the urban crisis intersects the Negro crisis in the city. Many white decision makers may care little about saving Negroes, but they must care about saving their cities. The vast majority of production is created in cities; most white Americans live in them. The suburbs to which they flee cannot exist detached from cities. Hence powerful white elements have goals that merge with ours.

THE ROLE FOR THE SOCIAL SCIENTIST

Now there are many roles for social scientists in meeting these problems. Kenneth Clark has said that Negroes are moved by a suicide instinct in riots and Negroes know there is a tragic truth in this observation. Social scientists should also disclose the suicide instinct that governs the administration and Congress in their total failure to respond constructively.

What other areas are there for social scientists to assist the civil rights movement? There are many, but I would like to suggest three because they have an urgent quality.

Social science may be able to search out some answers to the problem of Negro leadership. E. Franklin Frazier, in his profound work, *Black Bourgeoisie*, laid painfully bare the tendency of the upwardly mobile Negro to separate from his community, divorce himself from responsibility to it, while failing to gain acceptance into the white community.[2] There have been signifi-

[2] E. Franklin Frazier, *Black Bourgeoisie*. New York: Macmillan, 1962.

cant improvements from the days Frazier researched, but anyone knowledgeable about Negro life knows its middle class is not yet bearing its weight. Every riot has carried strong overtone of hostility of lower class Negroes toward the affluent Negro and vice versa. No contemporary study of scientific depth has totally studied this problem. Social science should be able to suggest mechanisms to create a wholesome black unity and a sense of peoplehood while the process of integration proceeds.

As one example of this gap in research, there are no studies, to my knowledge, to explain adequately the absence of Negro trade union leadership. Eighty-five percent of Negroes are working people. Some 2,000,000 are in trade unions but in 50 years we have produced only one national leader—A. Philip Randolph.

Discrimination explains a great deal, but not everything. The picture is so dark even a few rays of light may signal a useful direction.

POLITICAL ACTION

The second area for scientific examination is political action. In the past two decades, Negroes have expended more effort in quest of the franchise than they have in all other campaigns combined. Demonstrations, sit-ins and marches, though more spectacular, are dwarfed by the enormous number of man-hours expended to register millions, particularly in the South. Negro organizations from extreme militant to conservative persuasion, Negro leaders who would not even talk to each other, all have been agreed on the key importance of voting. Stokely Carmichael said black power means the vote and Roy Wilkins, while saying black power means black death, also energetically sought the power of the ballot.

A recent major work by social scientists Matthew and Prothro concludes that "The concrete benefits to be derived from the franchise—under conditions that prevail in the South—have often been exaggerated," . . . that voting is not the key that will unlock the door to racial equality because "the concrete measurable payoffs from Negro voting in the South will not be revolutionary" (1966).[3]

[3] Donald R. Mathews and James W. Prothro, *Negroes and the New Southern Politics*. New York: Harcourt, Brace, & World, 1966.

James A. Wilson supports this view, arguing, "Because of the structure of American politics as well as the nature of the Negro community, Negro politics will accomplish only limited objectives" (1965).[4]

If their conclusion can be suppported, then the major effort Negroes have invested in the past twenty years has been in the wrong direction and the major pillar of their hope is a pillar of sand. My own instinct is that these views are essentially erroneous, but they must be seriously examined.

The need for a penetrating massive scientific study of this subject cannot be overstated. Lipsit in 1957 asserted that a limitation in focus in political sociology has resulted in a failure of much contemporary research to consider a number of significant theoretical questions. The time is short for social science to illuminate this critically important area. If the main thrust of Negro effort has been, and remains, substantially irrelevant, we may be facing an agonzing crisis of tactical theory.

The third area for study concerns psychological and ideological changes in Negroes. It is fashionable now to be pessimistic. Undeniably, the freedom movement has encountered setbacks. Yet I still believe there are significant aspects of progress.

Negroes today are experiencing an inner transformation that is liberating them from ideological dependence on the white majority. What has penetrated substantially all strata of Negro life is the revolutionary idea that the philosophy and morals of the dominant white society are not holy or sacred but in all too many respects are degenerate and profane.

Negroes have been oppressed for centuries not merely by bonds of economic and political servitude. The worst aspect of their oppression was their inability to question and defy the fundamental precepts of the larger society. Negroes have been loath in the past to hurl any fundamental challenges because they were coerced and conditioned into thinking within the context of the dominant white ideology. This is changing and new radical trends are appearing in Negro thought. I use radical in its broad sense to refer to reaching into roots.

Ten years of struggle have sensitized and opened the Negro's eyes to reaching. For the first time in their history, Negroes have

[4] James A. Wilson, "The Negro in Politics," *Daedalus*, Fall 1965.

become aware of the deeper causes for the crudity and cruelty that governed white society's responses to their needs. They discovered that their plight was not a consequence of superficial prejudice but was systemic.

The slashing blows of backlash and frontlash have hurt the Negro, but they have also awakened him and revealed the nature of the oppressor. To lose illusions is to gain truth. Negroes have grown wiser and more mature and they are hearing more clearly those who are raising fundamental questions about our society whether the critics be Negro or white. When this process of awareness and independence crystallizes, every rebuke, every evasion, become hammer blows on the wedge that splits the Negro from the larger society.

Social science is needed to explain where this development is going to take us. Are we moving away, not from integration, but from the society which made it a problem in the first place? How deep and at what rate of speed is this process occurring? These are some vital questions to be answered if we are to have a clear sense of our direction.

We know we haven't found the answers to all forms of social change. We know, however, that we did find some answers. We have achieved and we are confident. We also know we are confronted now with far greater complexities and we have not yet discovered all the theory we need.

And may I say together, we must solve the problems right here in America. As I have said time and time again, Negroes still have faith in America. Black people still have faith in a dream that we will all live together as brothers in this country of plenty one day.

But I was distressed when I read in the *New York Times* of August 31, 1967, that a sociologist from Michigan State University, the outgoing president of the American Sociological Society, stated in San Francisco that Negroes should be given a chance to find an all Negro community in South America: "that the valleys of the Andes mountains would be an ideal place for American Negroes to build a second Israel." He further declared that "The United States Government should negotiate for a remote but fertile land in Equador, Peru or Bolivia for this relocation." I feel that it is rather absurd and appalling that a leading social scientist today would suggest to black people, that after all these years of suffering and exploitation as well as investment in the American dream, that we should turn around and run at this point in history. I say that we will not run! Professor Loomis even compared the relocation task of the Negro to the relocation task of the Jews in Israel. The Jews were made exiles. They did not choose to abandon Europe, they were driven out. Furthermore, Israel has a deep tradition, and Biblical roots for Jews. The Wailing Wall is a good example of these roots. They also had significant financial aid from the United States for the relocation and rebuilding effort. What tradition does the Andes, especially the valley of the Andes mountains, have for Negroes?

And I assert at this time that once again we must reaffirm our belief in building a democratic society, in which blacks and whites can live together as brothers, where we will all come to see that integration is not a problem, but an opportunity to participate in the beauty of diversity.

The problem is deep. It is gigantic in extent, and chaotic in detail. And I do not believe that it will be solved until there is a kind of cosmic discontent enlarging in the bosoms of people of good will all over this nation.

There are certain technical words in every academic discipline which soon become stereotypes and even clichés. Every academic discipline has its technical nomenclature. You who are in the field of psychology have given us a great word. It is the word maladjusted. This word is probably used more than any other word in psychology. It is a good word; certainly it is good that in dealing with what the word implies you are declaring that destructive maladjustment should be destroyed. You are saying that all must seek the well-adjusted life in order to avoid neurotic and schizophrenic personalities.

But on the other hand, I am sure that we will recognize that there are some things in our society, some things in our world, to which we should never be adjusted. There are some things concerning which we must always be maladjusted if we are to be people of good will. We must never adjust ourselves to racial discrimination and racial segregation. We must never adjust ourselves to religious bigotry. We must never adjust ourselves to economic conditions that take necessities from the many to give luxuries to the few. We must never adjust ourselves to the madness of militarism, and the self-defeating effects of physical violence.

In a day when Sputniks, Explorers and Geminis are dashing through outer space, when guided ballistic missiles are carving highways of death through the stratosphere, no nation can finally win a war. It is no longer a choice between violence and nonviolence, it is either nonviolence or nonexistence. As President Kennedy declared, "Mankind must put an end to war, or war will put an end to mankind." And so the alternative to disarmament, the alternative to a suspension in the development and use of nuclear weapons, the alternative to strengthening the United Nations and eventually disarming the whole world, may well be a civilization plunged into the abyss of annihilation. Our earthly habitat will be transformed into an inferno that even Dante could not envision.

CREATIVE MALADJUSTMENT

Thus, it may well be that our world is in dire need of a new organization, The International Association for the Advancement of Creative Maladjustment. Men and women should be as maladjusted as the prophet Amos, who in the midst of the injustices of his day, could cry out in words that echo across the centuries, "Let justice roll down like waters and righteousness like a mighty stream"; or as maladjusted as Abraham Lincoln, who in the midst of his vacillations finally came to see that this nation could not survive half slave and half free; or as maladjusted as Thomas Jefferson, who in the midst of an age amazingly adjusted to slavery, could scratch across the pages of history, words lifted to cosmic proportions, "We hold these truths to be self evident, that all men are created equal. That they are endowed by their creator with certain inalienable rights. And that among these are life, liberty, and the pursuit of happiness." And through such creative maladjustment, we may be able to emerge from the bleak and desolate midnight of man's inhumanity to man, into the bright and glittering daybreak of freedom and justice.

I have not lost hope. I must confess that these have been very difficult days for me personally. And these have been difficult days for every civil rights leader, for every lover of justice and peace.

They have been days of frustration—days when we could not quite see where we were going, and when we often felt that our works were in vain, days when we were tempted to end up in the valley of despair. But in spite of this, I still have faith in the future, and my politics will continue to be a politic of hope. Our goal is freedom. And I somehow still believe that in spite of the so-called white backlash, we are going to get there, because however untrue it is to its destiny, the goal of America is freedom.

Abused and scorned though we may be, our destiny as a people is tied up with the destiny of America. Before the Pilgrim fathers landed at Plymouth, we were here. Before Jefferson scratched across the pages of history the great words that I just quoted, we were here. Before the beautiful words of the "Star Spangled Banner" were written, we were here. For more than two centuries, our forebears laboured here without wages. They made Cotton King. They built the home of their masters in the midst of the most humiliating and oppressive conditions.

And yet out of a bottomless vitality, they continued to grow and develop. If the inexpressible cruelties of slavery could not stop us, the opposition that we now face will surely fail. We shall win our freedom because both the sacred heritage of our nation, and the eternal will of the almighty God, are embodied in our echoing demands.

And so I can still sing, although many have stopped singing it, "We shall overcome." We shall overcome because the arch of the moral universe is long, but it bends toward justice. We shall overcome because Carlysle is right, "No lie can live forever." We shall overcome because William Cullen Bryant is right, "Truth crushed to earth will rise again." We shall overcome because James Russell Lowell is right, "Truth forever on the scaffold, wrong forever on the throne, yet that scaffold sways a future." And so with this faith, we will be able to hew out of the mountain of despair a stone of hope. We will be able to transform the jangling discords of our nation into a beautiful symphony of brotherhood. This will be a great day. This will not be the day of the white man, it will not be the day of the black man, it will be the day of man as man.

THE RESPONSIBILITY OF
RADICAL INTELLECTUALS

STAUGHTON LYND

I ASK THAT WE CONSIDER CAREFULLY WHETHER THE AMERICAN UNI-
versity is realistically likely to become, in the words of the conference call, a place where "we may freely express the radical
content of our lives" and a "base" which will export "humane
values" to other institutions in the society. Asking that question
also means not accepting unthinkingly the equation of radical
intellectual and fulltime academic. Even in America this equation
is inaccurate; surely we have had as much to learn from Paul
Sweezy, who was thrown out of the academic world, and Herbert
Aptheker, who was never permitted to enter it, and Issac Deutscher,
who first taught at a university the last year of his life, as from
say, C. Wright Mills and William Appleman Williams. What is
far more striking is that of the principle luminaries of the intellectual tradition to which most of us in some degree are drawn,
namely Marxism, not one—not Marx, not Engels, not Plekhanov,
not Lenin, not Trotsky, not Bukharin, not Rosa Luxemburg,
(who had a particular contempt for professors), not Antonio
Gramsci, not Mao Tse-tung—put bread on his table by university
teaching. Please observe that I am not quoting the eleventh thesis
on Feuerbach. I am not arguing (for the moment) that we should
act rather than think. My point is that without exception the most
significant contributions to Marxist thought have come from men

From Staughton Lynd, "The Responsibility of Radical Intellectuals," *New
University Conference Newsletter*, May 24, 1968, pp. 5–6. Reprinted by
permission of New University Conference, Chicago, and the author.

and women who were not academics, who passed through the university but did not remain there.

An exceedingly modest inference from that momentous fact is that whatever else it means to be a radical intellectual in America today, one thing requisite is an experimental attitude with respect to life-styles. Conferences all over the country this past year have explored the possibilities of radical vocation and radicalism in the professions. Just as some of us in the years past chose to teach in Southern Negro colleges, so now adventurous souls are seeking out junior colleges and public high schools in white working-class neighborhoods. Are they not also radical intellectuals who are sweating out inner-city teaching, or researching police brutality and local power structures, or attempting to clarify current tactical dilemmas in the Movement, or painstakingly documenting trends in American imperialism at some local equivalent of the British Museum? If we believe in what Marx called "praxis," or practical, critical activity, and in a future society in which the barriers between manual and intellectual labor will be broken down, we should at least not permit our present society narrowly to define what the life of the mind, or better, the use of the mind, must mean.

We ought to take very seriously the fact that the university corrupts radicals more often than it destroys them. Whatever our social origins, the university is a marvellously effective instrument for making us middle-class men. First it sets us in competition one with another. As undergraduates, graduates, and very often as professors, we are not working together on a common task, not —like children in a Soviet kindergarten—rolling a ball too large for any one of us to roll alone. We are competing in the performance of tasks little significant in themselves to see which ones of us will be permitted to realize the upwardly-mobile fantasies which the university requires us to entertain. You cannot work at a university as a factory worker labors at the bench. In the university it is up or out; hence, simultaneously scornful of tenure and attracted to it, we are unable matter-of-factly to conceive the university as a source of livelihood, a kind of work in which (like baseball umpiring) "you can't beat the hours"; no, we become emotionally engaged in the upward scramble and, whatever our rhetoric, in fact let the university become the emotional center of our lives. Neither the first nor the second halves of the academic career curve—the frenzied struggle for position, the economic assurance which follows—seem exactly the contexts from which radicalism may be expected to emerge. It is a very peculiar sort of radicalism which permits one to be arrested only in summertime, or obliges one to hurry home from Hanoi to be on time for a seminar. But that is the kind of radical one has to be so long as one's first commitment is to university life. If it is symbolic, one-shot, moral-gesture radicalism, that may be not so much because of our ideological orientation as because of the academic schedule. The point is that whatever we may think, or think we think, university life requires us to act as if our radicalism were episodic and of secondary importance. The conference call says: "we are committed to the struggle for a democratic university." We are unlikely to do much in the direction even of that objective, let alone make an American revolution, so long as we are not prepared to be fired at any moment. The most hopeful recent happening in American intellectual life is that last fall so many graduate students and professors were arrested along with undergraduates in demonstrations against Dow.

But what is required to stand up against the blandishments and threats of academia is not merely courage, but clarity. If I am not mistaken, most of us simultaneously half-believe in two contradictory images of the university and the teacher. On the one hand, we are inclined to conceive the university as an oasis of pure thought where Veblenian intellectuals set their idle curiosities to work. Together with this image goes the notion of the university as a privileged corporation, governed by laws different from those applicable to society at large, immune from kinds of harassment which the off-campus citizen must expect. On the other hand, however, we are attracted to the vision of the university as a power house for social transformation, a counter-society dedicated to the *Aufhebung* of its institutional environment. The first projection leads to socialist scholars' conferences which seem to wish to convey the implicit message: We too have panels with speakers and discussants; we too meet in expensive downtown hotels; we too, whatever the content of our papers, are scholars. The second projection finds Martin Duberman writing *In White America*, Staughton Lynd directing freedom schools, Howard Zinn freeing pilots in Hanoi, Noam Chomsky arrested at the Pentagon.

From such intellectual confusion springs tactical inconsistency. Which of us objected when SNCC was the "institutional client," when intense young men in blue jeans walked onto college campuses, scorned debate as bull-shitting, and recruited students for illegal activities in the larger society? Is it not the case that before we sought to get the military off the campus we did our darndest to get the civil rights movement on it? It would seem that, intellectuals though we may be, we change our definition of the university every year or two just as we change our attitudes toward decentralization or the Supreme Court. We should be able to do better than that. We need to recognize, if we cannot resolve, the tension between the rhetoric of truth-seeking and the rhetoric of ethical commitment.

Consider the position of the American Association of University Professors toward obstructive demonstrations on campus. The Association states: "action by individuals or groups to prevent speakers invited to the campus from speaking, to disrupt the operations of the institution in the course of demonstrations or to obstruct and restrain other members of the academic community and campus visitors by physical force is destructive of the pursuit of learning and of a free society." This is not an illogical position if the university is conceptualized as an oasis of freedom in a hostile environment, a conception we often espouse. However, the position of many Dow demonstrators was that they were obstructing that portion of the Dow Chemical Company's activity most accessible to them. They obstructed Dow not because it invaded the campus sanctuary but because its off-campus activities are nefarious. Dow does not cleanse itself in the eyes of these demonstrators if, while on campus, it observes academic decorum and agrees to debate its views. Were it in the power of these demonstrators, they would put Dow out of business.

This too is a stance many of us have adopted. But where does it leave us when right-wing demonstrators seek by non-violent obstructive means to interfere with projects ethical in our eyes but nefarious in theirs?

The tension between the rhetoric of truth-seeking and the rhetoric of ethical commitment was exhibited during the recent contretemps between myself and the Board of Governors of Chicago State College. Among the professors who formed an *ad hoc* defense committee there were three positions. One was that a teacher necessarily teaches the whole of what he thinks and is, and therefore should have the right to say anything he wishes in the classroom.

A second position held that whatever considerations of academic appropriateness might apply to on-campus utterances, off-campus a teacher should be free to advocate like any other citizen.

My own attitude was different from both the foregoing. In contrast to the first position, it seemed to me there was a difference between the low-keyed presentation of intellectual alternatives and the attempt to kindle in an audience an awareness of some indignity. Both seemed to me important things for the man of intellect to do; yet they are different; and my instinct was to accept the proposition that a classroom is a place where one's purpose should not be persuasion, but an opening-up of possible new ways of seeing things.

In contrast to the second position, I felt that a teacher should be free not only to talk as he wishes outside the classroom but to act as he wishes. It seemed and seems to me that when and if a teacher is arrested, prosecuted, convicted, sentenced, and put in jail, he will be unable to meet his classes, and at that point his academic employer may with some justice put him on leave or, if uncharitably inclined, dismiss him. Until that point is reached I believe a teacher should not be penalized, nor obliged to answer questions concerning his public life. Like any other citizen he should be considered innocent until proven guilty. Academic employers should eschew appointing themselves as judges and convicting a man before the courts have acted.

Perhaps many of you experience moments when such questions seem real. One characteristic answer to which we turn in such moments is: "Yes, but I am less a scholar than a teacher. The college has shown itself an instrument not only of bourgeoisifying those who stay there permanently, but of radicalizing those who pass through it for four years. As a radical faculty member I can at least protect, perhaps in part produce, radical students. I too am in one sense an organizer, dealing with a constituency, less concerned with paper than with the eager, frightened young human beings whom the campus, like the factory as Marx described it, brings together and subjects to common experiences."

The fundamental problem for the full-time teacher is that he sends his students forth to confront problems which he himself has not encountered. Whether as drop-out or graduate, the student leaves the campus but the teacher does not. The teacher's life does not speak to the problem of how to "make it" as a radical off the campus. I suspect our students learn this lesson well. We may imagine that we are contributing to the revolution by teaching Marxism or socialism or radicalism to a new generation of activists. We may overlook the possibility that those whom we thus indoctrinate will become teachers in their turn, justifying their existences as radicals with the argument that they are readying for action a new generation of radicals—namely, their students—who, however, are all too likely also to become teachers, speaking, just as we do, of the splendid young people to whom they lecture who need only a solid intellectual grounding—and so on.

The fact that we ourselves as full-time academics cannot provide models of off-campus radical vocation is the more frustrating this spring because the draft has forced so many of our students, as we have not been forced, to say Yes or No to the demands of the larger society.

After all these distressingly negative and essentially preliminary words, let me briefly attempt to answer the questions: What is a university? And what is a radical intellectual? The purpose of the foregoing has been to insist that, as radicals, we should take neither the institution nor the role for granted but attempt to approach them with fresh eyes. The way to do that, I think, is to begin with the reality of the Movement and observe how an intellectual function crystalizes out from its activity; or alternatively, how in the mildest of the Movement's so-called mindless activism, obviously necessary intellectual tasks fail to be performed.

By now we have a certain stock of experience. SNCC, for instance, established an educational institute in Waveland, Mississippi, in the fall of 1964. The Free University of New York has existed almost three years. SDS attempted last summer to run three schools for campus organizers in Boston, Chicago and San Francisco. Teach-ins, educational conferences, at least two new national newspapers and three nationally-circulated periodicals, all testify to the seriousness with which the Movement, charges of mindless activism notwithstanding, has tackled the function of internal education.

Different observers will assess this experience differently. Some feel that what is lacking is a systematic body of general theory. My own conclusion, perhaps predictably, is almost the reverse. Having been personally involved in several of these experiments, my impression is that their characteristic weakness has been remoteness from action. This expresses itself in two different ways. At Waveland, for example, the most educational experience for the SNCC staff people assembled there was to travel into a New Orleans courtroom where, I believe, the precedent-establishing Bombrowski case was being argued, and then return to Waveland to discuss its implications with the lawyer, Arthur Kinoy; almost everything else in the program presented at Waveland by distinguished guest speakers passed the students by, because not linked to their immediate experience. Similarly, the Free University of New York struck me as different from the usual bull sessions of campus radicals mainly in locale. Those who talked together were not acting together. What was exhilarating about Vietnam teach-ins, it seems to me, was that students and teachers together addressed a problem in relation to which all were amateurs. Although action was not always explicitly projected, in the atmosphere of such occasions was a serious search for means of protest. Subsequent teach-ins at which this element was lacking, as at Ann Arbor last September, appear to me to have been sterile by comparison.

Remoteness from action in such educational ventures reflects the fact that those commonly called in as teachers, namely ourselves, are ourselves thus remote. There is no getting away from the fact that universities combining theory and practice, like the University of Havana whose students work together in the cane fields, or the University of Yenan where students grew their own food, wove their own clothes, and graduated together to fight the Japanese, can only be created by individuals who combine theory and practice personally. I have been at too many embarrassing occasions when full-time activists and full-time intellectuals were brought together in the naïve hope, on the part of the activists, that the intellectuals could give them a magical something which they somehow lacked. A more hopeful model in my own experience was the Mississippi Freedom Schools. There Northern white college students and Southern black teen-agers had first to encounter one another as whole human beings, to establish trust. This happened in the process of finding a church basement together, deciding on a curriculum together, improvising materials together, that is, in a context of common work; and it matured in that context, too, as those who talked together in the morning registered voters together in the afternoon. Please note I am not advocating a narrow pragmatism. What was read togther in the mornings was often James Joyce, what was talked about may have been French or algebra as well as Negro history. But I must simply testify that the context of shared experience (which meant, too, that teachers characteristically boarded in their students' homes) made all the difference.

Do I mean, then, that in the protesting words of the rector of Charles University in Prague the social sciences must become "a mere tool of propaganda and agitation"? No, my point is that if we take Marx, or Freud, or Veblen seriously we must understand that a man's view of the world grows out of—I did not say "reflects"—his socially conditioned experience. You and I as intellectuals do not merely observe this phenomenon. It is exhibited in our lives, too. Many intellectuals will not and should not become activists. The intellectual's first responsibility is, as Noam Chomsky says, "to insist upon the truth," "to speak the truth and to expose lies." But what truth we discover will be affected by the lives we lead. There is no such thing as "working-class truth" or "bourgeois truth" or "the truth of the anal personality." Yet that portion of the truth to which we are led, the truth which seems to us significant, is not independent of our experience as whole human beings. Moreover, to hope that we can understandingly interpret matters of which we have no first-hand knowledge, things utterly unproved upon the pulses—to hope, for instance, that upper-middle class white professors can have much illumination to shed upon black power—is intellectual hubris. Another way to phrase what I am saying is the following. It is easy for us to see that the factory does more than oppress the worker, it also assimilates him to its hectic pace, its system of material rewards, its hierarchical decision-making. Similarly we are not merely oppressed by the university but conditioned, too. The grotesquerie of this university, elucidating Aquinas with the left hand while with the right hand it uproots poor Negro families in Hyde Park and Woodlawn, is too much the grotesquerie of our own lives as well.

Again, it is easy for us to see that liberal intellectuals tacitly assume a division of labor between themselves and democratic politicians. They can restrict themselves to cloistered thought because, in their view of things, somewhere out there in the world of action is a democratic political process which in the long run will assimilate their thinking and be guided by it. But does it not also affect us that, as Professor Morgenthau wrote last fall in *The New Republic*, "the great national decisions of life and death are rendered by technological elites, and both the Congress and the people at large retain little more than the illusion of making the decisions which the theory of democracy supposes them to make"? Do we not also justify our intellectual labors by assuming the existence of a political *deus ex machina*, whether that be the Party, or the proletariat, or the youth? I think the times no longer permit this indulgence, and ask us, at the very least, to venture into the area where political parties, and working-men, and young people do their things, seeking to clarify that experience which becomes ours as well, speaking truth to power from the vantage-point of that process of struggle.

To do this, we ourselves must have a foot solidly off the campus. More of us, like Joe Tuchinsky at Roosevelt, should teach part-time and supervise the training of draft counselors with the remainder; or like Sid Peck and Bob Greenblatt of the National Mobilization Committee alternate years of full-time intellectual work with years of full-time work for the Movement. The economic problems in living thus more adventurously are not insuperable. Nothing in the Communist Manifesto or for that matter the New Testament assures us that at age thirty-five or forty we should expect to achieve economic security for the rest of our lives. Disgorge the bait of tenure, and the problem of making a living can solve itself year by year. Face the problem of livelihood as husband and wife, accepting the possibility that sometimes one of you, sometimes the other, will be the main breadwinner, and you will have taken a long step toward solution of the so-called woman question. Face the problem of livelihood together with your friends in the Movement, recognizing that at some times you may support them, at others they you, and that you can all take greater risks because of this assurance, and you will have taken a long step toward the overcoming of alienation. The great hindrance is not in the objective world but in our heads. The hindrance is the notion that real intellectuals—unlike Thucydides, Machiavelli, Milton, Locke, Hamilton, Jefferson, Trotsky, Lenin, and unlike what Marx would have been if he could—do nothing but think. The first constituency we need to radicalize is ourselves. Our path of honor is to live so as to be able to tell the truth about the hopes and sufferings of mankind in our generation.

RADICALS IN THE
UNIVERSITIES

RICHARD FLACKS

LET ME START BY RECALLING AT RANDOM CERTAIN RECENT IMPRES-
sions and observations.

Consider the following: It seems likely that at least half a million college students have participated in one way or another in
what has come to be called a student movement; a large proportion of these in serious demonstrations, acts of civil disobedience,
and activity requiring considerable commitment; a considerable
proportion becoming quite astonishingly revolutionary in their
sentiments in the process. When you examine who these people
tend to be, you find that overwhelmingly they are the sons and
daughters of those with the highest educational attainment in the
society.

Consider this. Seemingly parochial campus uprisings become
dramatic and newsworthy events with surprisingly marked political effects. The Free Speech Movement at Berkeley not only
had the effect of catalyzing similar outbursts on campuses all
across the country; it also had the effect of shaking California's
political structure and cultural climate in fundamental ways. On
a smaller scale, two years ago five hundred students from this
University took over the Administration building for two and a
half days in protest against university complicity with Selective
Service. This action produced a wave of similar ones on other
campuses, and these demonstrations led directly to a national

From Richard Flacks, "Radicals in the Universities," *New University Conference Newsletter*, May 24, 1968, p. 4. Reprinted by permission of New
University Conference, Chicago, and the author.

debate on the draft which led to a new draft law, which so
threatens the nation's universities as to generate a mood of universal disgust with the national administration.

Or consider this. Academic revulsion at the President and his
policies contributes significantly to an historic split in the Democratic Party. Not one but two opposing candidates arise, intend-
ing to build their organizations by recruiting college youth.
Meanwhile the President of the United States can make no announced trips to American cities because he fears hostile demonstrations—organized largely on the campuses.

It is obvious that the present crackup of the American Establishment is most fundamentally due to the success of the National
Liberation Front and to the ghetto rebellions. But it should also
be clear that the grassroots anti-war movement created the constituency and the energy for politicians like McCarthy and Kennedy, shaped their rhetoric and analysis, and had much to do with
affecting the attitudes of that large segment of the communications industry which now seems intent on getting Johnson. And
that grass-roots movement started on the campus, and gets its
main impetus still from students and from faculty.

I do not believe that the emergence of a mass radical movement among the children of the educated middle class is accidental. Nor do I believe that the striking political impact of
events on the university campus is accidental or ephemeral. I
want to argue that they are signs of a new social and cultural
situation, which we cannot yet fully understand, but which we
as radicals must take seriously, because we have a decisive role to
play in it.

The United States has been and is a capitalist society, which
means not only that its economic system is organized for capitalist relations of production, but also that its culture has been
and is capitalist. The classic radical faith, of course, was that an
alternative culture would emerge in such a society as the working
class began to realize itself as an exploited class and as an agency
for social transformation.

It is perhaps true to say that this analysis was wrong not because the industrial working class was not exploited or did not
have a consciousness of exploitation, but because for a variety
of very good reasons it did not have the capability of creating
an alternative culture—that is a new ideal for individual character.

Another part of the radical analysis assumed that the university in capitalist society functioned to promote, elaborate and enrich the culture of capitalism. The integration of the university into this culture always presented some difficulty, since most academics undoubtedly chose their careers because they were either incapable of success within the productive system or repelled by it; moreover the official values of the academy were somewhat at variance with those of the culture at large. To a large extent, this problem was averted by insuring some freedom for criticism and especially for engagement in tasks without any immediate social usefulness, by providing modest but secure material comfort, and by giving academics the privilege of coming into intimate contact with the minds of the future elite.

Despite the fact that the university was undoubtedly a bourgeois institution, a minority of its graduates have for a variety of reasons, become people who have rebelled against the culture of capitalism in large part because of their university experience. Over the years, a certain anti-capitalist, humanist sentiment has been carried by assorted intellectuals, bohemians, reformers and radicals and has fed back into the university, thereby influencing new generations. Thus despite itself, the university and the educated middle class have been a major source for whatever alternative to capitalist values have persisted in the society.

No one can doubt that the postwar years have seen a major transformation of the university and its role in the society. Alongside the traditional system of elite higher education, vastly overshadowing the tradition of disinterested scholarship is the emergence of the knowledge industry, a system of research and training, housed in the university, which services the needs of the state and the corporations, especially their planning and development functions. In the process, the old bases of university-society integration have been replaced by a newer and more naked integration; i.e., direct and massive subsidation of public and private institutions by the state, the corporations and the foundations. Thus the universities no longer serve only the somewhat luxurious function of socializing elites and invigorating the going value system; they are now far more closely integrated into the political economy. They are as indispensable to its functioning as the factory, the bank, and the government agency.

On this analysis, many of us would undoubtedly say that such an institution is not either an honorable or a practical place within which to do one's work as an intellectual, a scholar, a teacher, or a serious radical. And yet it is a remarkable fact that, just when the universities as institutions seem most fully absorbed into capitalism and its culture, there should simultaneously break out the most intense and serious radicalism in history. The fact that this occurs should prompt us to find out why; the reasons for its occurrence, I believe, provide both the imperative and the opportunity for us to be revolutionary within the university.

•   •   •

The white New Left, typified in my mind by SDS, was catalyzed by and could not have existed without the prior rise of a black civil rights movement, exemplified by SNCC. Just as SNCC reached beyond itself and awakened blacks not like themselves; so the SDS activists—sons and daughters of the educated middle class—have had some considerable success in reaching students with other origins and motives and activating them.

In this, they have been helped by several objective conditions. First the fact of affluence for many white college students, a condition which has the paradoxical effect of weakening loyalty to and discipline of narrow capitalist values for some young people. Second, the situation in the universities, where authoritarian control, boring classrooms and curricula, and "impersonality" create discontents which make many students open to the idea of student power. Third, a general disillusionment of youth due to racism and imperialism: what has happened is that the nation has produced a generation of middle class youth raised to expect secure, comfortable and self-fulfilling lives and provided them with a future which seems daily to look increasingly bleak. Fourth, an accurate sense among many of the educated young that their jobs are not going to provide the freedom and autonomy and fulfillment which they have been raised to expect and want. Fifth, the huge size of universities which, like Marx's factories, make large masses of discontented people available to each other for mutual discovery and collective action.

Notice that none of these conditions are accidental or ephemeral. They are necessary consequences of a society which must educate the majority of its youth at high levels while simultaneously harnessing them to bureaucracy and impressing them into military service. They are necessary features of a society whose dominant culture has begun to crack and decay because the operation of the system has made many of its central values irrelevant or superfluous or reactionary. In short, I am arguing that the alienation of educated youth has become a necessary feature of American society and is one of its important "contradictions."

Another way of saying this is that we have finally reached the point where there is a fundamental conflict between those who stand for reason, freedom and humanism and the dominant American culture—a conflict which cannot be absorbed. Earlier generations of the intelligentsia thought they had a chance within this system; the present generation either does not think so or has grave doubts—and this generation is by far the largest in history.

One can imagine that such a situation could be handled by removing reason, freedom and humanism from the curriculum and turning the universities quite thoroughly over to corporatism. This in fact is the situation in graduate training, and, up until Berkeley, seemed to be a quite unopposed trend in undergraduate education.

That the excision of these values is taking place is evidenced by, for example, the prevalence of narrow empiricism in the social sciences; by the publish or perish syndrome; by the rise of research factories under state and corporate sponsorship within the university; by the systematic downgrading of undergraduate education in the major universities; by the very character of mass, packaged education.

As I say, until Berkeley one felt this was definitely the way things were going. After Berkeley, one felt that it was the radical students who stood alone against these trends, with the help of some isolated faculty members, and with some positive result in slowing down the process, but also with the negative result that what was shaping up was the mass repression of the student left, a repression which a great many academics seemed gleefully ready to participate in.

At this point, however, I think it is worth considering that radical faculty need not necessarily be secondary, isolated and essentially impotent in this situation. I believe we do have some leverage, and that the consequences of our organization and action may have a chance of political significance. For what the Vietnam war has made clear—and we have made clearer through our efforts at exposure and agitation—is that to sell the universities and the intellectual disciplines to the state, though this seems beneficial for the tenured professoriat in the socially useful fields and to the university managers—means to put the centers of knowledge in the service of imperialism and militarism. I believe that a large number of our colleagues are not able to stomach this realization. For example, you cannot do anthropology, sociology and related work if these are systematically utilized by U.S. intelligence services. You cannot have a healthy science that is devoted to the production of weaponry—if for no other reason than that research is classified—but also because science in the long run can't be centrally planned in this way. And, as university administrators are now discovering, you cannot run graduate schools when the state insists on drafting your research and teaching assistants.

Underneath these somewhat crass grievances which have come to the fore within respectable academia is a deeper uneasiness. There are deeply troubled feelings about the ethics of social research. There is a widespread re-examination going on in sociology and psychology of the results of narrow empiricism and its failure to work as a set of principles for moving these disciplines forward. There is, among some people in the humanities and among teachers generally, a sense of deprivation and failure, and a fear of becoming totally irrelevant.

There is, in short, a considerable crisis at this moment in the self-definition of the academic. The question for the whole profession is whether to go all the way into the multiversity and the corporate state—or to begin to put up some resistance. I, personally, do not have great hopes for the resistance. Still, I think an experiment on our parts to try to bring it about is worth the effort. There are some conditions which support us. First, the unremitting pressure from below by the students. Second, the arrival on the scene of new faculty who come out of, or at least have been touched by, the radicalism of this generation. Third, the growing awareness of the political power of academics can and is stiffening the spines of some of them. Fourth, I think we can, like the National Liberation Front, count on the continued incompetence of the American ruling elites. We can and should imagine many scenarios of cooptation which "they" might be capable of producing. But I am doubtful that, so long as imperialism remains the essence of their international posture, and militarism the keystone of their political economy, that the American intelligentsia can really be absorbed.

In my opinion, this conference is an effort to help us begin to find what may be an historic role—that is, to turn the universities into a major arena of struggle against imperialism, against militarism, against capitalist culture and ideology, and for the creation of an alternative culture and ideology, and a new class to carry that alternative into the rest of the society.

To do this our immediate tasks are many.

On each campus, we must find each other and begin to create self-conscious groups of radical faculty and graduate students, which can engage in defining local political roles for their members, which can foster mutual criticism of members' teaching and research and political activity, which can serve as sustaining communities for their members, and as catalysts for the far larger group of faculty who can be moved to act on specific issues.

We need also a national community of radical intellectuals and teachers so that the constantly threatening isolation, corruption and emasculation of academic life can be countered by active participation in collective action and real movement.

We need to help each other find ways to make our intellectual work genuinely relevant—relevant on the one hand to the immediate needs of the freedom and peace movements, relevant on the other hand to the long-run task of creating a substantial alternative to the prevailing culture and ideology.

We need finally of course to continue and intensify our commitment to the radical movement as a whole—but perhaps eventually our relation to this movement will take a new form. If we succeed in becoming self-conscious agents of change on the campus, then we will be able to overcome the split in our identities which so many left academics feel—the split between one's role as a political actor and one's vocation. We will be able to come to the movement finally as people who sense our own roles as valuable and potent because we are in struggle at last for our own survival, our own freedom, our own power.

PART TWO

STRUCTURAL PROBLEMS IN AMERICAN SOCIETY

THE DISTRIBUTION
OF POWER

INTRODUCTION

AMERICAN SOCIAL SCIENCE IN-
cludes two schools of thought with regard to the distribution of
power. C. Wright Mills, Floyd Hunter and other students of
the social system have argued that power is skewed—that there
is an elite and then there are the rest of us. Robert Dahl and his
students, on the other hand, take the position that power is dif-
fused and that a number of centers of influence can be found at
the community level.

Contemporary American history suggests that the perspective
of the pluralists is, perhaps, a bit sanguine. The society has under-
gone convulsions as hitherto powerless people—students, blacks,
the welfare poor, etc.—have sought to gain access to the councils
of the powerful.

The selections in this section focus on power. C. Wright Mills's
article "The Structure of Power in American Society" deals at
the macrolevel with the question of who runs America. Irving
Beller's piece suggests that corporate empires, formed through the
merger process, are coming to dominate an ever larger portion of
American economic life. Howard's "Blacks Without Power" suggests that blacks have not benefited greatly from participation in
politics: their rewards have not been commensurate with their
investment, and the formal politic system has not in the past provided blacks with the power necessary to improve their lot.

The last four articles in the section deal with the matter of
ends and means in changing the distribution of power in American
society. Richard Flacks's piece explores the meaning of the con-

cept of "participatory democracy." To what extent such an approach to decision-making prove viable? Flacks, an academic close to the swirling currents of community and student protest, brings insight to the discussion of participatory democracy. Riddell's article focuses on Yugoslavian socialism and suggests ways in which a nation may seek to institutionalize broader participation in making a wider range of decisions.

The last two articles in the section deal with means. Paul Goodman brings his vast gifts as a social commentator to a discussion of civil disobedience. Howard's article focuses on black power and attempts to deal with it analytically. Stripped of emotion and rhetoric, what can black power mean? The piece suggests it can have a pragmatic political meaning and can be translated into a strategy which yields to blacks greater control over their own destiny.

WHERE IT'S AT

THE STRUCTURE OF POWER
IN AMERICAN SOCIETY

C. WRIGHT MILLS

THE POWER TO MAKE DECISIONS OF NATIONAL AND INTERNATIONAL consequence is now so clearly seated in political, military, and economic institutions that other areas of society seem off to the side and, on occasion, readily subordinated to these. The scattered institutions of religion, education and family are increasingly shaped by the big three, in which history-making decisions now regularly occur. Behind this fact there is all the push and drive of a fabulous technology; for these three institutional orders have incorporated this technology and now guide it, even as it shapes and paces their development.

As each has assumed its modern shape, its effect upon the other two have become greater, and the traffic between the three has increased. There is no longer, on the one hand, an economy, and, on the other, a political order, containing a military establishment unimportant to politics and to money-making. There is a political economy numerously linked with military order and decision. This triangle of power is now a structural fact, and it is the key to any understanding of the higher circles in America today. For as each of these domains has coincided with the others, as decisions in each have become broader, the leading men of each

From C. Wright Mills, "The Structure of Power in American Society," *Power, Politics and People: The Collected Essays of C. Wright Mills*, Irving Louis Horowitz (ed.). Copyright © 1963 by the Estate of C. Wright Mills. Appeared in *British Journal of Sociology*, 9: 1:32–38, March 1958. Reprinted by permission of Oxford University Press, Inc., New York, and Routledge & Kegan Paul Ltd., London.

—the high military, the corporation executives, the political directorate—have tended to come together to form the power elite of America.

The political order, once composed of several dozen states with a weak federal-center, has become an executive apparatus which has taken up into itself many powers previously scattered, legislative as well as administrative, and which now reaches into all parts of the social structure. The long-time tendency of business and government to become more closely connected has since World War II reached a new point of explicitness. Neither can now be seen clearly as a distinct world. The growth of executive government does not mean merely the "enlargement of government" as some kind of autonomous bureaucracy: under American conditions, it has meant the ascendancy of the corporation man into political eminence. Already during the New Deal, such men had joined the political directorate; as of World War II they came to dominate it. Long involved with government, now they have moved into quite full direction of the economy of the war effort and of the post-war era.

The economy, once a great scatter of small productive units in somewhat automatic balance, has become internally dominated by a few hundred corporations, administratively and politically interrelated, which together hold the keys to economic decision. This economy is at once a permanent-war economy and a private-corporation economy. The most important relations of the corporation to the state now rest on the coincidence between military and corporate interests, as defined by the military and the corporate rich, and accepted by politicians and public. Within the elite as a whole, this coincidence of military domain and corporate realm strengthens both of them and further subordinates the merely political man. Not the party politician, but the corporation executive, is now more likely to sit with the military to answer the question: what is to be done?

The military order, once a slim establishment in a context of civilian distrust, has become the largest and most expensive feature of government; behind smiling public relations, it has all the grim and clumsy efficiency of a great and sprawling bureaucracy. The high military have gained decisive political and economic relevance. The seemingly permanent military threat places a premium upon them and virtually all political and economic actions are now judged in terms of military definitions of reality: the higher military have ascended to a firm position within the power elite of our time.

In part at least this is a result of an historical fact, pivotal for the years since 1939: the attention of the elite has shifted from domestic problems—centered in the 'thirties around slump—to international problems—centered in the 'forties and 'fifties around war. By long historical usage, the government of the United States has been shaped by domestic clash and balance, it does not have suitable agencies and traditions for the democratic handling of international affairs. In considerable part, it is in this vacuum that the power elite has grown.

(i) To understand the unity of this power elite, we must pay attention to the psychology of its several members in their respective milieux. In so far as the power elite is composed of men of similar origin and education, of similar career and style of life, their unity may be said to rest upon the fact that they are of similar social type, and to lead to the fact of their easy intermingling. This kind of unity reaches its frothier apex in the sharing of that prestige which is to be had in the world of the celebrity. It achieves a more solid culmination in the fact of the interchangeability of positions between the three dominant institutional orders. It is revealed by considerable traffic of personnel within and among these three, as well as by the rise of specialized go-betweens as in the new style high-level lobbying.

(ii) Behind such psychological and social unity are the structure and the mechanics of those institutional hierarchies over which the political directorate, the corporate rich, and the high military now preside. How each of these hierarchies is shaped and what relations it has within the others determine in large part the relations of their rulers. Were these hierarchies scattered and disjointed, then their respective elites might tend to be scattered and disjointed; but if they have many interconnections and points of coinciding interest, then their elites tend to form a coherent kind of grouping. The unity of the elite is not a simple reflection of the unity of institutions, but men and institutions are always related; that is why we must understand the elite today in connection with such institutional trends as the development of a permanent-war establishment, alongside a privately incorporated economy, inside a virtual political vacuum. For the men at the top have been selected and formed by such institutional trends.

(iii) Their unity, however, does not rest solely upon psychological similarity and social intermingling, nor entirely upon the structural blending of commanding positions and common interests. At times it is the unity of a more explicit co-ordination.

To say that these higher circles are increasingly co-ordinated, that this is *one* basis of their unity, and that at times—as during open war—such co-ordination is quite wilful, is not to say that the co-ordination is total or continuous, or even that it is very sure-footed. Much less is it to say that the power elite has emerged as the realization of a plot. Its rise cannot be adequately explained in any psychological terms.

Yet we must remember that institutional trends may be defined as opportunities by those who occupy the command posts. Once such opportunities are recognized, men may avail themselves of them. Certain types of men from each of these three areas, more far-sighted than others, have actively promoted the liaison even before it took its truly modern shape. Now more have come to see that their several interests can more easily be realized if they work together, in informal as well as in formal ways, and accordingly they have done so.

The idea of the power elite is of course an interpretation. It rests upon and it enables us to make sense of major institutional trends, the social similarities and psychological affinities of the men at the top. But the idea is also based upon what has been happening on the middle and lower levels of power, to which I now turn.

There are of course other interpretations of the American system of power. The most usual is that it is a moving balance of many competing interests. The image of balance, at least in America, is derived from the idea of the economic market: in the nineteenth century, the balance was thought to occur between a great scatter of individuals and enterprises; in the twentieth century, it is thought to occur between great interest blocs. In both views, the politician is the key man of power because he is the broker of many conflicting powers.

I believe that the balance and the compromise in American society—the "countervailing powers" and the "veto groups," of parties and associations, of strata and unions—must now be seen as having mainly to do with the middle levels of power. It is these middle levels that the political journalist and the scholar of politics are most likely to understand and to write about—if only because, being mainly middle class themselves, they are closer to them. Moreover these levels provide the noisy content of most "political" news and gossip; the images of these levels are more or less in accord with the folklore of how democracy works; and, if the master-image of balance is accepted, many intellectuals, especially in their current patrioteering, are readily able to satisfy such political optimism as they wish to feel. Accordingly, liberal interpretations of what is happening in the United States are now virtually the only interpretations that are widely distributed.

But to believe that the power system reflects a balancing society is, I think, to confuse the present era with earlier times, and to confuse its top and bottom with its middle levels.

By the top levels, as distinguished from the middle, I intend to refer, first of all, to the scope of the decisions that are made. At the top today, these decisions have to do with all the issues of war and peace. They have also to do with slump and poverty which are now so very much problems of international scope. I intend also to refer to whether or not the groups that struggle politically have a chance to gain the positions from which such top decisions are made, and indeed whether their members do usually hope for such top national command. Most of the competing interests which make up the clang and clash of American politics are strictly concerned with their slice of the existing pie. Labor unions, for example, certainly have no policies of an international sort other than those which given unions adopt for the strict economic protection of their members. Neither do farm organizations. The actions of such middle-level powers may indeed have consequence for top-level policy; certainly at times they hamper these policies. But they are not truly concerned with them, which means of course that their influence tends to be quite irresponsible.

The facts of the middle levels may in part be understood in terms of the rise of the power elite. The expanded and centralized and interlocked hierarchies over which the power elite preside have encroached upon the old balance and relegated it to the middle level. But there are also independent developments of the middle levels. These, it seems to me, are better understood as an affair of entrenched and provincial demands than as a center of national decision. As such, the middle level often seems much more of a stalemate than a moving balance.

(i) The middle level of politics is not a forum in which there are debated the big decisions of national and international life. Such debate is not carried on by nationally responsible parties representing and clarifying alternative policies. There are no such parties in the United States. More and more, fundamental issues never come to any point or decision before the Congress, much less before the electorate in party campaigns. In the case of Formosa, in the spring of 1955 the Congress abdicated all debate concerning events and decisions which surely bordered on war. The same is largely true of the 1957 crisis in the Middle East. Such decisions now regularly by-pass the Congress, and are never clearly focused issues for public decision.

The American political campaign distracts attention from national and international issues, but that is not to say that there are no issues in these campaigns. In each district and state, issues are set up and watched by organized interests of sovereign local importance. The professional politician is of course a party politician, and the two parties are semifeudal organizations: they trade patronage and other favors for votes and for protection. The differences between them, so far as national issues are concerned, are very narrow and very mixed up. Often each seems to be fifty parties, one to each state; and accordingly, the politician as campaigner and as Congressman is not concerned with national party lines, if any are discernible. Often he is not subject to any effective national party discipline. He speaks for the interests of his own constituency, and he is concerned with national issues only in so far as they affect the interests effectively organized there, and hence his chances of re-election. That is why, when he does speak of national matters, the result is so often such an empty rhetoric. Seated in his sovereign locality, the politician is not at the national summit. He is on and of the middle levels of power.

(ii) Politics is not an arena in which free and independent organizations truly connect the lower and middle levels of society with the top levels of decision. Such organizations are not an effective and major part of American life today. As more people are drawn into the political arena, their associations become mass in scale, and the power of the individual becomes dependent upon them; to the extent that they are effective, they have become larger, and to that extent they have become less accessible to the influence of the individual. This is a central fact about associations in any mass society: it is of most consequence for political parties and for trade unions.

In the 'thirties, it often seemed that labor would become an insurgent power independent of corporation and state. Organized labor was then emerging for the first time on an American scale, and the only political sense of direction it needed was the slogan, "organize the unorganized." Now without the mandate of the slump, labor remains without political direction. Instead of economic and political struggles it has become deeply entangled in administrative routines with both corporation and state. One of its major functions, as a vested interest of the new society, is the regulation of such irregular tendencies as may occur among the rank and file.

There is nothing, it seems to me, in the make-up of the current labor leadership to allow us to expect that it can or that it will lead, rather than merely react. In so far as it fights at all it fights over a share of the goods of a single way of life and not over that way of life itself. The typical labor leader in the U.S.A. today is better understood as an adaptive creature of the main business drift than as an independent actor in a truly national context.

(iii) The idea that this society is a balance of powers requires us to assume that the units in balance are of more or less equal power and that they are truly independent of one another. These assumptions have rested, it seems clear, upon the historical importances of a large and independent middle class. In the latter nineteenth century and during the Progressive Era, such a class of farmers and small businessmen fought politically—and lost—their last struggle for a paramount role in national decision. Even then, their aspirations seemed bound to their own imagined past.

This old, independent middle class has of course declined. On the most generous count, it is now 40 percent of the total middle class (at most 20 percent of the total labor force). Moreover, it has become politically as well as economically dependent upon the state, most notably in the case of the subsidized farmer.

The *new* middle class of white-collar employees is certainly not the political pivot of any balancing society. It is in no way polit-ically unified. Its unions, such as they are, often serve merely to incorporate it as hanger-on of the labor interest. For a consider-able period, the old middle class *was* an independent base of power; the new middle class cannot be. Political freedom and economic security *were* anchored in small and independent prop-erties; they are not anchored in the world of the white-collar job. Scattered property holders were economically united by more or less free markets; the jobs of the new middle class are integrated by corporate authority. Economically, the white-collar classes are in the same condition as wage workers; politically, they are in a worse condition, for they are not organized. They are no van-guard of historic change; they are at best a rear-guard of the welfare state.

The agrarian revolt of the 'nineties, the small-business revolt that has been more or less continuous since the 'eighties, the labor revolt of the 'thirties—each of these has failed as an independent movement which could countervail against the powers that be; they have failed as politically autonomous third parties. But they have succeeded, in varying degree, as interests vested in the ex-panded corporation and state; they have succeeded as parochial interests seated in particular districts, in local divisions of the two parties, and in the Congress. What they would become, in short, are well established features of the *middle* levels of balancing power, on which we may now observe all those strata and inter-ests which in the course of American history have been defeated in their bids for top power or which have never made such bids.

Fifty years ago many observers thought of the American state as a mask behind which an invisible government operated. But nowadays, much of what was called the old lobby, visible or in-visible, is part of the quite visible government. The "govern-mentalization of the lobby" has proceeded in both the legislative and the executive domain, as well as between them. The executive bureaucacy becomes not only the center of decision but also the arena within which major conflicts of power are resolved or denied resolution. "Administration" replaces electoral politics; the maneuvering of cliques (which include leading Senators as well as civil servants) replaces the open clash of parties.

The shift of corporation men into the political directorate has accelerated the decline of the politicians in the Congress to the middle levels of power; the formation of the power elite rests in part upon this relegation. It rests also upon the semiorganized stalemate of the interests of sovereign localities, into which the legislative function has so largely fallen; upon the virtually complete absence of a civil service that is a politically neutral but politically relevant, depository of brain-power and executive skill; and it rests upon the increased official secrecy behind which great decisions are made without benefit of public or even of Congressional debate.

THE CONCENTRATION OF CORPORATE POWER

IRVING BELLER

LAST MAY, THE UNITED STATES SUPREME COURT ANNULLED A "marriage." It ordered the dissolution of a merger between the third and sixth largest supermarket chains in Los Angeles. Two weeks later, reversing a lower court decision, it reinstated the Justice Department's challenge of the Pabst-Blatz brewing company merger. Both mergers, the court found, had taken place in industries marked by a steady trend toward economic concentration and both threatened to "substantially lessen competition."

In earlier decisions, federal courts thwarted or dissolved what they regarded as "unholy matrimony" between duPont and General Motors, Bethlehem and Youngstown Steel, Alcoa and Rome Cable, Continental Can and Hazel-Atlas Glass, and others as well.

Yet, in spite of such decisions, an unprecedented wave of mergers continues to sweep the nation. The number recorded by the Federal Trade Commission has climbed spectacularly from a yearly average of 1,162 in the 1955-1959 period to 1,893 in 1965. Since these statistics exclude bank, utility and transportation industry mergers, as well as hundreds of smaller mergers, the actual number in 1965 alone undoubtedly exceeded 2,000.

More recently, W. T. Grimm and Company, a private consulting firm which keeps tab on merger developments, reported

From Irving Beller, "Mergers and the Concentration of Corporate Power," *The American Federationist*, 73: 10:8–15, October 1966. Reprinted by permission of the *AFL-CIO American Federationist*.

a 25 percent jump in the number of corporate mergers between the first-half of 1965 and the first six months of 1966. And hardly a day has passed, even in the period following the latest Supreme Court decisions, without a news story referring to another merger.

Executives known to be interested in mergers "often get half a dozen calls or letters a day from persons peddling companies," reports *Newsweek* (April 25, 1966). "Company hunting is my night-time and weekend sport," says the head of a rapidly growing communications media firm. And *Dun's Review* (May 1966) describes how the president of Hewitt-Robbins "proposed" to Litton Industries, an industrial giant and an experienced hand at mergers, at noon one Thursday, negotiated the terms on Friday and had them approved at a board meeting on the following Saturday morning.

The subject receives few front page headlines. Yet the implications of the frantic merger kick upon which American business has embarked are profound.

The power exercised by America's largest corporations is already enormous. As Professor Andrew Hacker of Columbia University points out: "The decisions made in the names of these huge companies guide and govern, directly and indirectly, all of our lives."

The giants of American industry have tremendous wealth and there are few restrictions on how they spend it. As a result, they have been able to set cultural standards and shape the social and political, as well as the economic, forms of American society to a far greater extent than most Americans realize.

They not only determine the prices we pay and the quality of the products we buy. They have an enormous influence as well, as Professor Hacker observes, over what we buy, the kind of work we do, how and where we do it, the kind of education offered to our children, the "regions of the country which will prosper" and those "which will stagnate," the social goals we set and much more.

If this is true now, what will the future be like if the merger movement continues and an even greater portion of the American economy becomes concentrated in the hands of a small number of extremely powerful enterprises? Will the U.S. indeed become, as the title of an article by Hacker in *The New York Times*

Magazine (July 3, 1966) suggests, "A Country Called Corporate America."

MULTI-INDUSTRY GIANTS

The "urge to merge" is not a new development in American history. Merger waves occurred in 1899, in 1920 and again from 1926 to 1929. However, none of the previous merger booms have been as prolonged as the current wave, now entering its twelfth year and still showing a vigor which belies its age.

The current merger movement involves the giants and semi-giants of American industry—not just the little concerns struggling to keep their heads above water. According to Dr. Willard Mueller, Director of the Bureau of Economics of the Federal Trade Commission, the 200 largest manufacturing companies acquired "more than 2,000 concerns with combined assets of 17.5 billion" during the period from 1950 to 1964. That $17.5 billion exceeded the value of the assets held by all manufacturing corporations between the 1,000 largest and the 2,000 largest in the fourth quarter of 1962. "In other words," said Dr. Mueller, "the acquisition activity of the top 200 was sufficient to more than wipe out the equivalent of the second tier of 1,000 corporations in manufacturing.

Many of the disappearing firms themselves have been large and important. Among those which have vanished as separate entities in recent years are a number whose names had become household words. They include Philco, Sperry, Sylvania, Glenn L. Martin, Squibb and Son, American Viscose, Pure Oil, Frito-Lay, Royal McBee, Briggs Manufacturing, Bell Aircraft and Doehler-Jarvis.

These, however, were only the better-known among the departed. A total of 811 manufacturing and mining firms, each with assets of at least $10 million, disappeared through merger between 1948 and 1965.

Significantly, very few of these large corporations were failing concerns or even losing money in the year prior to being acquired. In fact, says Dr. Mueller, "a substantial percentage were very profitable enterprises." And, he concludes, "had they not been acquired they would most likely have continued as healthy economic enterprises capable of offering effective competition."

The present merger wave also finds more companies invading fields which have little or no relation to their traditional line of business. Horizontal mergers, mergers between firms which have been producing a similar product and selling in the same market, have become less common. Vertical mergers, in which companies link up with a customer or a supplier rather than a direct competitor, have increased somewhat but still account for only a small proportion of all mergers. Instead, conglomerate mergers,

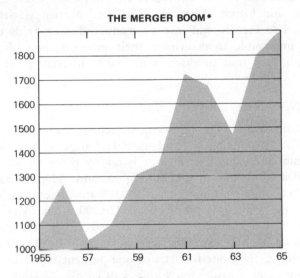

THE MERGER BOOM *

SOURCE: Federal Trade Commission

* Mergers reported in key publications. (Moody's Industrials, Standard Corporation Records, Wall Street Journal, Journal of Commerce, and The New York Times.)

involving mergers between companies operating in different markets and without any previous buyer-seller relationship, have become the great fad.

Some conglomerates are more conglomerate than others. When the large national dairy concerns gobble up smaller dairy firms situated in areas in which the buyers have not previously operated, they are regarded as conglomerate because they have moved into new geographic market areas. When Continental Can merged with Hazel-Atlas Glass, it became a conglomerate by taking on the production of another type of container. In both instances, however, the merged firm was either producing the same product as before the merger or one that was closely related.

But when CBS buys the New York Yankees and Textron, which began as a textile manufacturer, takes over the manufacturing of helicopters, chicken feed, bathroom fixtures, men's shoes, rocket engines, eyeglass frames and hearing aids, conglomeration begins to approach the ultimate. Companies like Textron and Litton Industries, FMC and Martin-Marietta, have expanded so rapidly and into so many different fields that it is almost impossible to determine their principal line of business. Litton, in fact, now produces some 6,000 different products.

USE AND ABUSE OF POWER

This massive merger movement, along with rapid internal growth, is producing a fundamental change in the American economic landscape. The change is taking place on the national scene as a whole and in specific regions and industries as well.

In 1962, there were more than 180,000 manufacturing corporations in the United States. At least 220,000 other firms engaged primarily in manufacturing were owned either by single proprietors or by partners. Of these more than 400,000 separately-owned units, 100—one-fortieth of one percent of all U.S. manufacturing firms—owned more than half of all the land, buildings and equipment in manufacturing. Their share of such assets, according to figures compiled by the staff of the Senate Antitrust and Monopoly Subcommittee, had risen from 45.8 percent in 1947 to 56.9 percent in 1962.

The fact that overall concentration rose at all during this period indicates a fundamental change in the American economy. "I, as an economist, would be concerned even if it had not gone up one percentage point since 1947," Dr. Mueller of the FTC declares. With the economy expanding so rapidly, "one would expect," he says, "that a small absolute number of firms . . . would have shrunk relatively." Yet overall economic concentration neither shrunk nor remained constant. It advanced by 11.1 percentage points, or 24 percent, in a period of 15 years.

If this rate continues, America will be faced with a condition of super-concentration within little more than a decade. By 1977, the 100 largest manufacturing corporations will control more than two-thirds of the nation's net manufacturing assets.

Besides increasing overall concentration, the merger movement has produced fundamental changes within specific industries. Production in a substantial number of sectors is controlled by a few firms. In 1958, the latest year for which figures are available, the four largest companies in 37 major industries accounted for more than 70 percent of their industry's output.

A general increase in such industry concentration ratios may have occurred after 1958 when the merger boom began to pick up additional steam. But, whether it did or not, the character of many industries has changed substantially.

Where the conglomerate giants have replaced independent firms, they have produced a fundamental change in competitive conditions. They may account for no greater share of production than their less powerful predecessors. Yet they have a far greater advantage than their predecessors had over the more specialized firms which continue to operate in the industry into which they have merged.

They can subsidize losses in one market with profits acquired in another market. They can use their huge purchases as leverage to persuade suppliers to buy their own products. And they can refuse to sell one product which may be difficult to obtain unless buyers are willing to accept other products as well. Consequently, when a firm having well over $100 million in sales and producing hundreds of products replaces a company with sales of a few million stemming from a single product, a fundamental change in the character of the single-product market takes place even though sales shares may be no different than before.

Mergers also have resulted in fundamental changes within specific regions. Firms which may not appear large by national standards have acquired significant power in localized markets.

In the Brown and Kinney merger, the record showed that the two firms together accounted for less than 2 percent of U.S. retail shoe sales. Yet, in each of 13 cities throughout the nation, they sold more than 50 percent of women's or children's shoes. And, in the Philadelphia National Bank-Girard Trust merger, the Supreme Court noted that a significant trend toward concentra-

tion in commercial banking had been occurring in the Philadelphia area, with the number of commercial banks declining from
108 in 1947 to 42 in 1963.

This rapid expansion of large corporations may seem like a
great American success story to some. However, it has aroused
a gnawing concern in many others.

The fact is that big firms have enormous power just because
they are big. Money is power and big firms have huge sums of
money at their disposal. The 500 largest industrial corporations—
one-fourth of one percent of all U.S. industrial corporations—
received 72 percent of all industrial profits in 1965. The after-tax
profits of one firm alone, General Motors, exceeded the 1965 tax
revenues of every state in the union except California and New
York. It was greater even than the total revenues of 18 states
combined. Most industry leaders, in fact, make money almost
automatically year in and year out.

As a result, as Professor Corwin Edwards of the University of
Oregon points out:

> A big firm can outbid, outspend and outlose a small firm. It
> can advertise more intensively, do more intensive and extensive
> research, buy up the inventions of others, defend its legal rights
> or alleged rights more thoroughly, bid higher for scarce re-
> sources, acquire the best locations and the best technicians and
> executives. If it overdoes its expenditures, it can absorb losses
> that would bankrupt a small rival.

Such power frequently enables America's industrial giants to
achieve their aims without resorting to grossly illegal and even
criminal actions like price-fixing. In 1960, 29 companies were convicted of a conspiracy to fix prices on the sale of billions of
dollars of electrical equipment. They were fined $1,787,000. And
seven executives were jailed for their part in the conspiracy. Since
1959, 11 firms in the steel industry have pleaded "no contest" to
price-fixing charges.

More commonly, however, executives in industries dominated
by a few powerful firms are able to get around the law by "ad-
ministering" prices. They do so through a system of price leadership under which one of the larger producers in the industry
determines the price and the others follow more or less auto-

matically (the smaller ones in particular feeling they have nothing to gain and much to lose by not "playing the game").

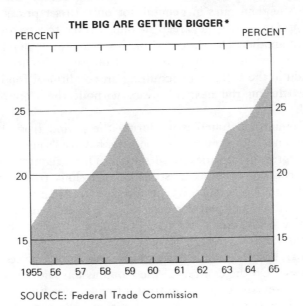

THE BIG ARE GETTING BIGGER*

SOURCE: Federal Trade Commission

*Shares of manufacturing and mining mergers accounted for by companies with assets over $100 million.

After an exhaustive study, the National Commission on Food Marketing described the pricing process and its results in the food industry as follows:

> When a few large firms dominate a field, they frequently forbear from competing actively by price; competition by advertising, sales promotion and other selling efforts almost always increases; and the market power inescapably at the disposal of such firms may be used to impose onerous terms upon suppliers or customers. The breakfast cereal field provides one of the clearest examples in the food industry: Four firms have 85 percent of the business; advertising and sales promotion amount to 19 percent of manufacturers' sales; retail prices of cereals rose more than other retail food prices between 1954 and 1964; profits

are nearly double the average for all food manufacturing; and entry of a new competitor would be extremely difficult.

A specific example of administered pricing reveals the power of larger conglomerates in general not only to set prices but to use the profits which they reap in one market to destroy competitors in another. On March 16 of this year, the Federal Trade Commission forbade the National Tea Company, the fifth largest food chain in the U.S., from acquiring any additional food retailing firms during the next 10 years without the Commission's approval.

The Commission found that, during the period from 1951 to 1956, National had acquired 24 concerns having "some 485 retail grocery stores in 188 cities in 16 states." These acquisitions gave National the power to exact special concessions from suppliers and to charge non-competitive prices in several hundred cities in which it had a significant share of sales. It then used this power to subsidize below-cost operations in 141 cities "where competition is still vigorous enough to limit its pricing power."

National Tea was not undercutting competitors' prices in the latter cities. "On the contrary," the Commission said, "it has . . . a distinct aversion to even normal price competition; its preferred competitive weapons are acquisitions, the receipt of . . . price concessions and promotional allowances from suppliers, and massive store-building and advertising campaigns."

Since National Tea is not a charitable institution, the Commission surmised that it would recover its losses in those 141 cities. And it concluded "that this will be done not by efficiencies and economies in food retailing, but a steady enlargement of its market shares in those cities until it acquires the same kind of pricing power it now enjoys in . . . other cities where it is already the dominant seller."

Merged organizations can ride roughshod over competition by virtue of sheer power in other ways. In 1951, the Consolidated Foods Corporation, a major food wholesaler, acquired Gentry, one of the two largest domestic manufacturers of dehydrated onions and garlic. It then proceeded to induce the food processors who are its own suppliers to buy onion and garlic products from Gentry in return for increased processor sales to Consolidated.

To some, it seemed clear that unless such arm-twisting trade relations were broken up the U. S. economy could end up as a vast cartel system dominated by giant conglomerates. Apparently this fear was shared by others. In 1965, the Supreme Court, concluding that Consolidated's reciprocal buying arrangement was likely to squeeze smaller onion and garlic companies out and to prevent new ones from coming into the market, ordered it to sever its ties with Gentry.

In another key case, the Supreme Court exposed the anti-competitive potential of the vertical type of merger which brings customers and their suppliers under the same management. They found that the du Pont Company's position as a supplier of finishes and fabrics to General Motors had been achieved only after it had purchased a substantial amount of GM stock and one of its directors had become a member of the GM board and a former du Pont sales manager had been appointed as a GM vice president. The Court concluded that "the acquisition had made it difficult, if not impossible, for other companies to sell substantial quantities of automotive finishes or fabrics to General Motors and therefore over the years the acquisition had resulted in a substantial lessening of competitive opportunity of such companies." It therefore ordered du Pont to sell its GM stock holdings.

BENEFITS FOR THE FEW

In spite of occasional court decisions like the du Pont and Consolidated Foods cases, mergers have clearly enhanced corporate power to set prices, bulldoze competition and influence other aspects of American life. In the process, thousands of jobs have been merged out of existence as well—often with little or no provision for cushioning the impact upon those who have been displaced.

Yet not every merger is an unmitigated evil. Some, in fact, have genuine social value.

Conceivably, a merger which rescues a failing firm from extinction may result in greater production, more jobs and even greater competition than might otherwise have been the case.

Mergers, particularly the horizontal and vertical types, may also result in real gains in efficiency. Firms producing the same or related products may be able to use machines and manpower more effectively and more fully when they bring their operations under one management. Buying in larger quantities may provide significant savings in the packaging and handling of materials. An alliance with a supplier may improve the flow of work from one stage of production to another and prevent costly delays. These represent genuine gains in efficiency and they could under some circumstances result in lower prices, higher wages and improved working conditions.

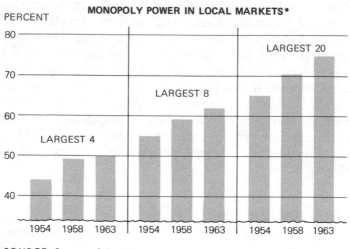

MONOPOLY POWER IN LOCAL MARKETS*

SOURCE: Bureau of Census

* Average share of grocery sales of largest firms in 218 local markets. (Refers to largest firms in each local market, not to largest national firms.)

However, increased size via mergers or internal growth does not invariably result in genuine increases in the efficiency of production or distribution. Numerous studies have shown that medium-sized plants are often at least as efficient and in some cases more efficient than the largest establishments in an industry. They have also shown that the operation of many plants by a single company doesn't necessarily result in significant cost reductions.

This appears to be especially true of the giant conglomerates producing a multitude of totally unrelated products. Horizontal or vertical combinations may in some cases achieve real savings by producing larger quantities of a particular product or by improving the flow of work from one stage to another. But the possibilities for genuine savings by highly diversified conglomerates are minimal. In fact, the effort to coordinate a far-flung industrial empire embracing parking lots, undertaking establishments and countless other unrelated activities may even lead to inefficiency and to added costs.

Nor are the largest firms the ones which invariably produce the greatest technological breakthroughs. One of the most revolutionary technological changes in steelmaking, the basic oxygen process, a process which produces steel six to eight times faster than the openhearth method, was developed by a little Austrian firm less than one-third the size of a single plant of the U.S. Steel Corporation. And the first American firm to use the process was McLouth Steel—a company with less than 1 percent of U.S. ingot capacity.

One of the most important innovations in petroleum refining— catalytic cracking—was developed by Sun Oil, one of the smaller firms in the refining industry. Most of the really significant structural auto changes in recent years have been developed abroad rather than by the giants of the American automobile industry. And it was only after foreign manufacturers and smaller domestic firms had demonstrated that there was a sizable market for them that the largest auto producers began to turn out compact cars in the United States.

The fact is that the incentive to merge is often purely financial. It frequently has little or nothing to do with the introducion of new or improved products or more efficient methods of production.

The one factor which stimulates merger activity more than any other—which produces the kind of feverish search for acquisitions we have been witnessing—is the accumulation of hoards of cash during periods of general business prosperity. With profits and depreciation soaring to alltime highs during the current boom, American corporations have been searching frantically for opportunities to invest their extra funds. And, for a number of reasons, they prefer to buy companies rather than to pay even higher dividends or invest in securities with fixed returns or build additional plants and equipment.

For one, the merger route provides a short-cut to more rapid growth and higher profits; manpower, production facilities and a market for the goods produced by such resources can be acquired overnight in one fell swoop. For another, a merger is a way to enter a new market without increasing the number of competitors.

Even the tightening of credit since the latter part of 1965 has failed to cool the merger boom. "Buying companies is no easy task these days," reports *Dun's Review* (May 1966). This is so, however, not because money is unavailable. It is because, as Dun's says, "in an era of high profits and an embarrassment of cash, the market belongs to the seller, not the buyer."

A soaring stock market offers another inducement, totally unrelated to genuine efficiencies, to the merger-minded corporate executive. In fact, it offers a double inducement:

—An especially rapid increase in the stock price of one firm enables it to pay for another firm with fewer shares of its own stock.

—Such an increase also gives a company a chance to improve its earnings per share by merging with a company whose earnings per share are higher than its own.

The hope that a merger—or even talk of a merger—will in itself cause stock prices to go up offers corporate executives still another purely financial incentive to merge. Many have become substantial stockholders through stock options or other transactions. For them, the rising stock prices resulting from mergers spell rising profits. And such profits have a special attraction because they are subject only to the low capital gains tax rather than the ordinary income tax.

There are other tax "angles" as well. Company A with large losses can be joined with Company B, a profitable firm, and the past losses of A can then be used to reduce the future tax liabilities of B. (This has resulted in some strange combinations, including the merger of a coal producer and an underwear manufacturer.)

Also, when the owners of an acquired company are paid in stock rather than in cash, the law regards the transaction as an exchange of assets. The sellers, therefore, pay no taxes on the gains they realize and this, of course, contributes immeasurably to their eagerness to merge.

The financial benefits for the few which mergers produce are obvious. The improvement in the production of goods and services which they create are not always so obvious. But even if they were, they would not offset the concern aroused by the disappearance of healthy firms with the capacity to compete effectively, the growing concentration of economic power and the frequent abuse of such power.

COPING WITH SUPER-CONCENTRATION

The problem of economic concentration in America is not new. More than 15,000 mergers during the past 11 years, however, have added immeasurably to its urgency. More than ever before, America has become a nation of giant enterprises with enormous power to fix prices, drive small competitors to the wall and deeply influence the behavior and social values of others.

No responsible organization suggests that all mergers should be banned and the tiny enterprises of an earlier era restored. No one really believes that 20th century America can be transformed into a model of 18th century economic theory—a model in which no firm is large enough to exercise any significant power over prices or the volume of production. The American standard of living depends upon modern production methods. And modern production methods frequently require substantial investments in plant, equipment and sales facilities.

However, the fact that relatively largescale operations can yield genuine social benefits does not mean that they automatically will. Presumably, competition would compel firms to produce better products at lower prices. But in industries dominated by a handful of large firms, competition is weak and almost non-existent. Instead of being regulated by the forces of the marketplace, the dominant firms in such industries regulate the marketplace. The conglomerates, in particular, because of their position in so many different markets, are free of the pressures of any single market in which they operate.

Mountains of testimony before congressional committees, administrative agencies and the nation's courts indicate that this enormous power of big business has frequently been abused. But even if there were no evidence of such abuse, the fact that so much power has been lodged in so few private hands should be a matter of deep public concern.

In the past, such concern led to the enactment of laws which have since become landmarks in American history. In 1890, Congress passed the Sherman Anti-Trust Act, making it illegal for a single company to monopolize trade or to conspire with others to fix prices or to divide up markets. Under this Act, the Standard Oil and American Tobacco trusts were broken up and the merger of the Northern Pacific and Great Northern Railroad was blocked.

In spite of such decisions, the Sherman Act had little effect upon the concentration of economic power. As a result, in 1914 Congress made another attempt to check the growth of concentration. It passed the Clayton Act, which prohibited mergers between competitors even before they reached monopoly proportions. "To arrest the creation of monopolies in their incipiency," the Act outlawed mergers which "may substantially lessen competition or tend to create a monopoly."

But the Clayton Act, too, had little effect upon the problem of consolidations. A serious loophole made it virtually useless in coping with the great merger wave of the 1920's.

To close that loophole and to broaden the scope of the Clayton Act, Congress passed the Celler-Kefauver Act of 1950. This amended the 1914 measure so that it clearly applied not only to mergers between competitors but to all mergers "which might substantially lessen competition or tend to create a monopoly"— including the vertical and conglomerate variety.

Still, the verdict of experts remained negative. Some of the cruder abuses, such as agreements to fix prices or divide markets, were either curtailed or driven underground. But the basic problem was still with us. As Professor Joe Bain observed in 1959: "The existing anti-trust laws are considerably better than no such laws at all, but they have fallen significantly short of the task of entirely or largely suppressing monopolistic performance tendencies in the economy."

Faced with the impracticality of wholesale "atomization" on the one hand and the dangers of "giving up" on the other, what can the nation do about the threat of ever-increasing concentration in American industry? Clearly, there are no easy one-shot solutions. There are, however, many measures which may be effective in dealing with parts of the problem. Used selectively and flexibly, with careful attention to the special circumstances of each case, their total contribution could be significant.

In the view of many who have studied the matter carefully, the following measures could be particularly helpful in dealing with the problems arising from mergers:

1. The parties to proposed mergers could be required to notify the government in advance. This would avoid unnecessary litigation and provide an opportunity for making arrangements which would preserve healthy competitive conditions. The American Newspaper Guild, for example, has proposed that the public be given at least 90 days' notice of a contemplated merger. During this period, persons other than competitors would have an opportunity to purchase the property at a fair market value before it could be merged with a competitor.

2. Government agencies which enforce the anti-trust laws could be given the power to temporarily delay, subject to court appeal, mergers which they believe may be in violation of the law. As the National Commission on Food Marketing pointed out in advocating such authority, assets might otherwise "become intermingled before the government can act and, if divestiture is ordered, 'unscrambling' is difficult and expensive."

3. Corporations could be required to disclose sales, expenses and profits for each separate field of operation as well as in total —to tell "not only *how much* money they made but *where* they made it." Although conglomerates with a new kind of corporate structure have grown rapidly, financial reporting requirements have changed very little. For the most part, corporations are required only to divulge data concerning their total activities. As a result, not even the stockholders of Textron know whether Textron is reaping more of its gains from helicopters than men's shoes or fountain pens.

Actually, the Securities and Exchange Commission is now in the process of formulating requirements for information by division and in some cases by product. This should be completed and put into effect without unnecessary delay.

Security analysts favor such a step because knowledge of the industries from which the sales and earnings of a particular firm arise would help in forecasting the future prospects of that firm. Also, it would help the government to determine whether a company was deliberately losing money in a particular market in order to drive out competitors. It would make it more difficult for firms to misleadingly contend, as frequently happens in collective bargaining, that although the company as a whole is making money, the division involved in the bargaining is suffering grievous losses. And it could prevent unwarranted mergers from taking place at all. One investment expert, an officer of the Dreyfus Fund, observes: ". . . Such disclosures may contribute to a much closer examination of new acquisitions, especially in unrelated fields, and may remove some of the incentive to grow for growth's sake without proper regard for the efficiency of existing operations and the stockholders' equity in the company." (Letter to Senator Philip A. Hart, D-Mich., May 26, 1965.)

4. The cloak of secrecy which now surrounds efforts to take over a firm through stock purchases could be lifted. Full disclosure is ordinarily required when one firm seeks to obtain control of another through an exchange of stock. However, legal loopholes make it possible for a corporation or group of individuals to purchase controlling blocks of shares of other firms without the latter's management or stockholders knowing about it.

The Pennzoil Company, for example, spent almost one year secretly buying up at least 275,000 shares of United Gas Corporation before openly indicating its desire to take over that company. One insider observed, according to *Business Week* (February 26, 1966): "We could have made a merger proposal to United but we certainly would have been turned down. That also would have tipped United that we were interested."

To prevent takeovers from occurring in virtual secrecy, Senator Harrison Williams (D-N.J.) has proposed a bill which would require disclosure when more than 5 percent of a company's outstanding shares are acquired by a person or group of persons acting together. The bill would thereby provide safeguards for investors and workers, particularly against what Senator Williams calls "white-collar pirates" whose subsequent mismanagement can endanger jobs as well as stock values.

5. An increase in capital gains tax rates could dampen some of the present ardor for mergers which have little justification in

terms of efficiency. Under present provisions, such gains, including gains from the sale of stock, are subject to lower tax rates
than income from wages, salaries and dividends.

One reason why corporations frequently have more cash than
they know what to do with is that there is less pressure from
stockholders for increases in dividends because of the capital gains
provision. Corporate income which is invested can drive the
price of stocks up. A shareholder can then sell his stocks at a
profit taxable at the lower capital gains rate. On the other hand,
corporate income distributed in the form of dividends is subject
to the higher ordinary tax rates.

An increase in the capital gains tax would encourage stepped-up
dividend payments and compel corporations, to a greater extent
than otherwise, to meet the tests of the money markets for addi-

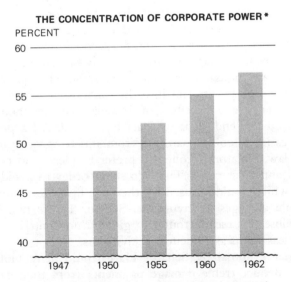

THE CONCENTRATION OF CORPORATE POWER *

PERCENT

SOURCE: Staff of the Senate Antitrust and Monopoly
Subcommittee of the Committee on the Judiciary

* Share of land, buildings, and equipment in manufacturing owned by 100 largest corporations. (All other
firms, including partnerships and single proprietorships
as well as corporations, exceeded 400,000 in 1962.)

tional funds for mergers and other purposes. It would also perhaps reduce some of the enthusiasm for mergers exhibited by executives with huge stock options.

A number of other measures are available to combat monopolistic tendencies in general.

1. Existing legislation could be enforced more aggressively, with increasing attention to the growing number of conglomerate mergers. One of the reasons for the current popularity of conglomerate mergers is the knowledge that it is less likely to be challenged because it results in the substitution of one firm for another rather than in the immediate elimination of a competitor (and, therefore, an increase in concentration) as in the case of a horizontal merger.

However, judgments cannot rest solely on shares of the market controlled by conglomerates. The enforcement agencies must be more vigilant in rooting out anti-competitive practices in such situations. Some experts have even suggested that potential or probable anti-competitive effects be a basis for action. And, in fact, the courts have already upheld such action.

2. Stronger deterrents to anti-trust violations are necessary. Jail sentences where justified are obviously far more effective than fines of a few thousand or even a few hundred thousand dollars for firms whose profits run into the millions.

At the very least, the effect of financial penalties should not be diluted. To this end, Senator Hart has introduced a proposal to make it easier to collect damages from anti-trust violators. Under present law, violators frequently prefer to plead "no contest" in criminal anti-trust cases. They do so in order to avoid a guilty verdict which could be used by their victims as evidence to collect triple damages in civil suits. Senator Hart's bill, however, would close this escape route by giving "no contest" as well as guilty pleas status as evidence in civil suits.

Another proposal by Senator Hart would deny violators the right to deduct treble damage payments from their taxable income as though they were ordinary business expenses. A ruling by the Internal Revenue Service permitting such a deduction resulted in a $200 million reduction of the penalty imposed on the 29 electrical equipment manufacturers convicted of conspiracies to fix prices.

3. Government procurement policies should support rather

than undermine government anti-trust policies. Rising federal purchases can have an impact on the structure of the economy and should be constantly reviewed to ensure that efficiently operated small and medium-size firms are participating in government orders.

4. In industries dominated by a few firms which are difficult to enter because of large investment requirements or other barriers, the government, it has been suggested, should provide special financial assistance to encourage the entry of new firms. Or, as others have suggested, it might even establish a government-owned corporation like the TVA to provide a yardstick by which to judge and improve the performance of other firms in the industry.

5. Determined action along the lines suggested thus far can do much in the longer run to deal with the kind of pricing power which has imposed a heavy burden during the past year upon families with limited incomes and inhibited the government from taking more vigorous steps towards full employment. However, more direct and immediate action is necessary. Such action could take the form of direct congressional investigations of the price-profit-investment policies of dominant firms in important industries. Or it could result in the establishment of a special board which would hold hearings and publish findings and recommendations concerning intended price increases by dominant firms in key industries before such increases actually took effect.

The remedies could be extended. No combination of measures, however, can ever be fully effective without a much greater appreciation of the dimensions of corporate power in the American economy today, the freedom with which that power is currently exercised and the danger of allowing it to continue to reside in the hands of the officials of a few private corporations.

Hopefully, such appreciation will ultimately lead to a new and greater respect for the positive role which a democratically-elected government can and must play in the creation of a better life for all Americans.

BLACKS
WITHOUT POWER

JOHN HOWARD

IN THE SUMMER OF 1966 THE TERM "BLACK POWER" WAS FIRST heard in the land. It came to public attention when used by Stokely Carmichael in the "march against fear" which civil rights leaders took up after James Meredith, its originator, had been shot and wounded on a Mississippi road.

Like many other terms bandied about in political discourse—communism, capitalism, freedom—black power has no clear meaning. Or—perhaps more accurately—it means whatever its user intends it to mean. Whatever the uses of the terms for the street-corner orator, it does suggest to us the utility of attempting to identify those factors which do account for the amount of power blacks have been able to exert politically.

Perhaps the most dramatic challenge to the formal political system in the 1960s came from blacks, the issue being how responsive the system was to their protest. Any assessment of the viability of the system in the face of black demands in the late 1960s has to be based in part on some grasp of how it has responded to black grievances in the past. When blacks have been politically active, to what extent and in what ways has the system rewarded them? That is the question confronted in this article.

The implications of alternative answers to the question are quite important. If analysis indicates that the system has been responsive when blacks have been active in the past, then it might be concluded that more vigorous and widespread participation will bring forth policies that will redress ghetto grievances. On the other hand, if rewards in the past have not been commensurate with investment, then the entire efficacy of working within the framework of the formal system is brought into question.

NEGRO REWARDS FROM POLITICAL PARTICIPATION

Black rewards from political participation through the mid-1960s can be summed up in terms of the following four propositions.

1. At the national level, black have been rewarded largely in the form of offices having only symbolic and ceremonial meaning.

2. Blacks at the local level have been rewarded largely in the form of offices having little power potential, regardless of whether their rewards came from support of a political machine or as a result of competition for black votes.

3. There is no correlation between the number of elective offices blacks hold at the municipal level and the condition of blacks in a city. This suggests that control, rather than mere participation, is necessary if the machinery of government is to be used to divert resources to the ghetto.

4. Black rewards from politics have had a lower power-potential; that is, regardless of their numbers in a community, blacks have not occupied offices which have afforded control over those community resources crucial to black welfare.

Below, each of these propositions is discussed in greater detail.

NEGRO PARTICIPATION AND FEDERAL PATRONAGE

There is not only "colored people's time" and "white people's time," but also colored people's history and white people's history. In terms of white people's history, Woodrow Wilson was a great humanitarian. White people's history characterizes Wilson as a man who wept for the world's oppressed. Colored people's history notes that he turned the screws tighter on Negro Americans by reducing rewards accruing to them from the political system.

From the end of reconstruction in 1876, through 1913, when Wilson was sworn in as President, certain appointive federal jobs were traditionally given to Negroes. Within a short period after

Wilson took office, 29 Negroes in high positions were turned out and their places filled by white appointees.[1] A cry of outrage was heard from Negroes, and a delegation visited the White House to protest both this and an executive order Wilson had signed segregating Negro federal employees in their use of eating and rest-room facilities.[2]

Viewed objectively, only a small number of minor bureaucratic posts were at stake—but these jobs were all that Negroes had at that time. Negro patronage rewards had included such offices as Recorder of Deeds for the District of Columbia, Register of the Treasury, and Marshall of the District of Columbia. In addition, they had received ambassadorial posts to all-Negro nations such as Haiti and Liberia, and minor consular appointments to Central American countries.[3]

These federal appointive offices that Negroes had received were utterly meaningless in terms of actual power. They constituted only symbolic recognition, as a medal does for a serviceman. But just as the Congressional Medal of Honor received by Ira Hayes, the Pima Indian, was not negotiable to obtain water rights for his tribe as they scratched out a living on their parched Southwestern land, the office of Recorder of Deeds for the District of Columbia was worth a cipher in terms of real power to improve the social and economic conditions of Negroes.

The crucial difference between being appointed Minister to Haiti and being appointed to the Supreme Court is that one office does not confer power on its holder, and the other does. Even within the Cabinet there are positions with power and those without it. In the early days of the Kennedy administration, it was rumored that Kennedy was thinking of appointing William Dawson, Congressman from Chicago, the first Negro in the Cabinet by naming him Postmaster-General. The story is that Dawson, appreciative of the power differential between being Postmaster-General and Chairman of the House Committee on Government Operations, chose to remain in the House.

---

[1] G. James Fleming, "The Negro in American Politics: The Past," in John P. Davis (ed.), *The American Negro Reference Book*. Englewood Cliffs, N. J.: Prentice-Hall, Inc., 1965, p. 427.
[2] John Hope Franklin, *From Slavery to Freedom*. New York: Alfred A. Knopf, 1947, p. 446.
[3] Fleming, *op. cit.*, pp. 427–428.

Given the kinds of federal positions which have gone to Negroes, it may be stated as a generalization that at the national level Negroes have until recently been rewarded largely with offices having only symbolic and ceremonial meaning.

Only in the 1960s, with the appointment of Thurgood Marshall to the post of Solicitor General and later to the Supreme Court, and with Robert Weaver's appointment to the Cabinet as Secretary of Housing and Urban Development, has there been any major departure from past practice.

In the area of federal patronage, Negroes have had to work harder to gain less. In the century following the Civil War there were only 30 Negro judicial appointments to United States Courts, 16 of these being to Municipal Court in the District of Columbia; otherwise there were 9 Negroes appointed to District Courts, 3 to United States Customs Courts, and 2 to Circuit Courts of Appeal.[4]

Since the 1960 election, Negro rewards have become more nearly commensurate with investment. The Near East, as well as such European countries as Finland, Norway, and Luxembourg, have been added to the areas where Negro Ministerial appointments may be received. A number of Negroes have also held decision-making posts in the Office of Economic Opportunity.

The key consideration in any federal appointment is not merely whether a Negro receives it, but rather, how much power resides in the office. In that sense, certain executive and judicial posts become key. One might recommend that vegetarians or flying saucer enthusiasts be "honored" with appointments as Minister to Haiti or Recorder of Deeds for the District of Columbia—their appointment would make little difference in the actual affairs of the nation.

NEGRO PARTICIPATION AND LOCAL PATRONAGE

At the local level, Negro rewards for political involvement vary from community to community. Until recently there had been a much larger "payoff" in Chicago and New York, for example, than in Los Angeles. This is partially due to the fact that more

4 *The Negro Handbook*, compiled by the editors of *Ebony*. Chicago: Johnson Publishing Co., 1966, pp. 273–275.

patronage positions are available in Chicago and New York. It seems that Chicago Negroes have been rewarded for faithful support of the Democratic party; thus, they hold a wide range of jobs and sit on a number of committees including the police board, the housing authority, the building and zoning committee, the Committee on Urban Opportunity, the Civil Service Commission board, and the Mayor's Commission for Senior Citizens, to mention just a few. In New York, Negroes receive consideration for office because of the continual strife within the Democratic Party, which makes any block of votes a prize to be sought by rival factions.

It is nevertheless true that Negroes have never been in a position to wield power at the local level, even in these cities. Where a strong party system has existed, as in Chicago, Negroes have never been dominant within it. Where a nonpartisan system has prevailed, they have not managed to get elected to office in sufficient numbers to wield influence.

It may be advanced as a proposition that the kinds of local offices to which Negroes have been appointed, and the kinds of representation they have had, have never been of the sort which would yield to them the power to significantly affect those conditions which plague the race—poor housing, bad schools, etc.

NEGRO POLITICAL REPRESENTATION AND SOCIAL CONDITIONS

Within a democracy it is presumed that the ultimate weapon in the quest for change is the ballot. Henry Lee Moon, in *Balance of Power: The Negro Vote*, took that position:

> . . . the ballot, while no longer conceived of as a magic key, is recognized as the indispensable weapon in a persistent fight for full citizenship, equal opportunity, unrestricted enjoyment of civil rights, freedom of resistance, access to equal and unsegregated educational, health, and recreational facilities.[5]

If politics is a mechanism for group mobility, then it is fair to ask whether, in those cities where Negroes hold a reasonable num-

[5] Henry Lee Moon, *Balance of Power: The Negro Vote*. Garden City, N. Y.: Doubleday and Company, Inc., 1948, p. 11.

ber of offices, we can find evidence of tangible benefit for their
Negro populations. The question might seem unfair, but it must
be asked; otherwise those who recommend politics to the Negro
as a method of social and economic advancement are in the position of doctors who recommend a particular medicine but refuse
to see whether or not it works.

To determine the utility of politics at the municipal level, I
have looked at two sets of cities. In the first set, Negroes hold a
substantial number of city council seats; in the second set they
do not. These cities are then compared in terms of the social and
economic status of Negroes within them.

Negro Representation on City Councils—
Selected Non-Southern Cities (March, 1965)[6]

| | High Representation | | |
	Total City Council	Negro Councilmen	% Negroes on Council	% Popula-tion Negro
Cleveland	33	10	30.3	28.6
St. Louis	29	6	20.7	28.6
Los Angeles	15	3	20.0	13.5
Chicago	50	7	14.0	22.9

| | Low Representation | | |
	Total City Council	Negro Councilmen	% Negroes on Council	% Popula-tion Negro
Detroit	9	0	0.0	28.9
Boston	9	0	0.0	9.1
New York	35	2	5.7	14.0
Cincinnati	9	1	11.1	21.6

In none of the cities do we find a Negro majority on the city
council, but one might expect that Negro city council members

6 This table is adapted from Table IV in James Q. Wilson's "The Negro
in American Politics: The Present," in Davis, op. cit. Wilson's list contained nine cities, I have dropped Philadelphia and divided the remaining
eight into sets of four each.

could exert a broad influence over a wide range of affairs such as the allocation of community resources, municipal hiring practices, and the allocation of contracts. Thus, it is reasonable to ask whether there are any discernible differences between cities where Negroes have high city council representation and those where they have low city council representation.

A comparison of the two sets of cities suggests no differences between them. Three of the four low-representation cities have had riots, as have three of the four high-representation cities. Apparently the presence of Negroes on the city council did not give ghetto Negroes in Cleveland, Chicago, and Los Angeles a sufficiently keen sense of representation "downtown" to deter them from rioting. In fact, it is by no means clear that representation downtown makes much difference in the conditions of life in the ghetto. For all of these cities, the unemployment rate is high and has been for over a decade. In Chicago, Cleveland, Detroit, and Cincinnati the nonwhite unemployment rate has been over 10 percent since 1950. Welfare rights organizations have been in conflict with the authorities both in high-representation Cleveland and low-representation Boston. Police action was the proximate cause of rioting in high-representation Los Angeles and low-representation Detroit. In other words, it is not at all clear that there is any measurable difference in ghetto conditions between the cities in which Negro representation on the city council is roughly proportional to their numbers in the population and those in which they are under-represented.

It is true, but perhaps beside the point, that not all of the issues crucial to Negroes fall within the province of city councils. The fact remains that there are no tangible differences between the two sets of cities. Neither the powers of office nor any spill-overs of influence have resulted in advancement in the high-representation cities.

Those who have been active in the civil rights movement at the community level have quite often heard activists say, "Gee, if we can only get a Negro on the city council," or "If we can only get a Negro on the school board." This kind of aspiration is based on the assumption that a Negro with honesty and integrity will be able to articulate Negro grievances from a platform to which the community will have to listen, that he will be able to introduce programs of benefit to the ghetto community, and further, that he will be able to push through such programs. It is not at all clear that the last of these assumptions, the most crucial one, is correct. Cleveland had three Negroes on its city council as early as the mid-1940's—Charles V. Carr, Harold Gassaway, and Augustus Parker. Even such out-of-the-way places as Canton, Ohio; Charleston, West Virginia; Toledo, Ohio; and Winston-Salem, North Carolina, had Negro city councilmen as early as 1946 without the Negroes' position having been noticeably improved by it.[7]

This is not to say that representation is irrelevant; it only suggests that the whole matter of rewards is much more complicated than one might at first imagine.

To sum up: Negroes have invested politically without receiving impressive rewards. At both the federal and state levels, they have had to be content with patronage offices which lacked power. Only recently has there been some change. At the municipal level, elected office has not been negotiable as a means of improving ghetto conditions. This does not mean that office is meaningless; it suggests, rather, that we have to specify more clearly the relationship between holding office and being effective.

Probably two factors account for the relative meagerness of the rewards Negroes have received from politics. First, given the racist assumptions which underly much popular thinking at least through the early 1960s, there was some conception of the Negroes' "place." Just as the caste system of India was based, in part, on occupational differentiation, so, in the United States there was some feeling that only certain kinds of jobs should be available to Negroes, even "good," prominent, or politically faithful Negroes.

Wilson commented on this in regard to Chicago politics:

> Resistance to Negroes is not, in part, different from the general resistance put up by (for example) the Irish political leadership of the big city to the demands for political recognition expressed by Poles, Italians, or Germans. . . . In the case of the Negro, however, this resistance was intensified by the frequent operation of personal hostility and prejudice.[8]

[7] Florence Murray (ed.), *The Negro Handbook*. New York: The Macmillan Company, 1949, p. 230.
[8] James Q. Wilson, *Negro Politics*. New York: The Free Press, 1960, p. 24.

Second, Negroes have simply not had the numbers to force an improvement in patronage or in legislation affecting ghetto conditions. In a crude, simple sense, the whole thing boils down to the number of votes. Negroes have had the numbers to get onto the city council in many cities, but not the numbers to control council action. Given their peculiar class needs, it is likely that control rather than simple participation in municipal decision-making is necessary to bring forth the kind of legislation and action necessary to correct ghetto ills. Without the ability to shape and direct policy, membership on various municipal bodies seems to yield little more than does lack of membership.

If "black power" has a political meaning, if it is more than simply a slogan of street-corner orators, it means effective control of the machinery of decision-making—first at the community level, then also at the state and national levels.

ALTERNATIVES
AND CHANGE
ON PARTICIPATORY
DEMOCRACY

RICHARD FLACKS

1. THE MOST FREQUENTLY HEARD PHRASE USED FOR DEFINING PAR-
ticipatory democracy is that "men must share in the decisions
which affect their lives." In other words, participatory democrats
take very seriously a vision of man as citizen; and by taking seriously such a vision, they seek to extend the conception of citizenship beyond the conventional political sphere to all institutions.
Other ways of stating the core values are to assert the following:
each man has responsibility for the action of the institutions in
which he is imbedded; all authority ought to be responsible to
those "under" it; each man can and should be a center of power
and initiative in society.

2. The first priority for the achievement of a democracy of
participation is to win full political rights and representation for
all sectors of the population. Democracy, in fact, is an issue for
this generation of radicals largely because their political experience has been shaped by the Negroes' elemental struggle for a
political voice in the U.S. This struggle has not been simply for
the right to vote—though even this right has not yet been guaranteed—but, more broadly, it has been an effort to kin a share of
political power by poor Negroes. It has been the experience of
Negroes in the North, where voting rights have been formally
guaranteed, that Negroes as a group have remained systematically
under-represented in the political process and that, where Negro

From Richard Flacks, "On Participatory Democracy," *Dissent*, November–
December 1966, pp. 701–708. Reprinted by permission of *Dissent*, New York.

representation exists, it operates in behalf of Negro middle-class interests and is highly dependent on the beneficence of white-dominated political machines. The results of this situation are plain to see in every Northern city. Thus the main thrust of radicals in the civil rights movement has to do less with breaking the barriers of legal segregation and formal exclusion than with attempting to build viable grass-roots organizations of poor Negroes, which would actually represent the needs of the poor and remain independent of white and middle-class domination. The ideology of "participatory democracy" has been useful in this effort, since it provides a rationale for avoiding premature "coalition" of grass-roots groups with more powerful white or middle-class organizations, for effectively criticizing "charismatic" styles of leadership which prevent rank-and-file people from learning political skills, for criticizing tendencies toward bureaucratism, demagoguery, and elitism, which are predictable in mass movements. Moreover, "participatory democracy," unlike black nationalist ideology, which also helps to mobilize grass-roots Negroes, offers a possible bridge between Negroes and other groups of poor or voiceless people. Thus we find much of the same rhetoric and organizing technique being used by SNCC workers in Southern communities, SDS organizers among poor whites in Chicago and Cleveland, and farm labor organizers among the multi-national grape workers in California.

Just how is participatory democracy being applied to the organization of economically disadvantaged groups? It has influenced the analysis of the problem of poverty in an affluent society, by stressing political voicelessness and lack of organization as a root cause of deprivation. This analysis leads to an emphasis on grass-roots organization and mobilization of the poor as the main way of ending poverty. Since the people involved lack political skill, organization requires a full-time staff, initially composed of students and ex-students, but soon involving "indigenous" leadership. This staff has the problem of allaying the fear, suspicion, and sense of inadequacy of the community—hence there has been a strong emphasis on building a sense of community between staff and rank-and-file, and of finding techniques which will facilitate self-expression, enable new leadership to emerge, enable people to gain dignity by participation, and the organization to become self-sustaining. Such techniques include: rotation of leadership,

eschewing by staff of opportunities to "speak for" the organization, the use of "consensus" to foster expression by the less-
articulate.

More important than such procedural techniques has been the
attempt to generate institutions which help to bind people to the
organization, to see immediate benefits from participation. Thus,
in Mississippi, alongside the political organization (the Freedom
Democratic party), a variety of related "projects" have grown up
—community centers, freedom schools, a Poor People's Corporation to help finance small business enterprise, cooperatives, and
the like. In Newark, the Newark Community Union has established its own radio station. In California, the Farm Workers
Association established a credit union. In Cleveland, the SDS
Community Project established a traveling street theater. Although these new institutions are sometimes viewed as alternatives to participation in "organized society" (*vide* Staughton
Lynd in *Dissent*—Summer, 1965), in practice, they are a very
important way of sustaining a developing organization. They
enable people to participate in an organization in a continuing
fashion, help develop organizational resources, train people for
leadership, and give people a sense of the possibilities for social
change. But they are in no sense a *substitute* for political activity,
direct action, and the development of a program. These, and not
the development of "parallel institutions," constitute the main
functions of the local political parties, community unions, etc.,
which are developing in many urban slum and rural areas.

The emphasis on participatory democracy has helped these
developing grass-roots organizations formulate and articulate
issues and programs. Although the constituencies of these organizations include the most impoverished sectors of society, it is
remarkable that—particularly in the Northern cities—the main
activity of these organizations has not been focused on economic
issues. They have, rather, been struggling over issues of *control,
self-determination* and *independence:* Shall the poor have a voice
in the allocation of War on Poverty funds? Shall urban renewal
be shaped by the people whose neighborhood is being renewed?
Shall the police be held accountable by the community? Who
is to decide the dispensation of welfare payments? Who makes
the rules in the welfare bureaucracies? Who controls the ghetto?

The outcome of these grass-roots organizing efforts, of course, cannot be predicted. The civil rights movement, in its direct-action phase, began the process of bringing Negroes and the poor into the political arena—and the results, in terms of political align-ments and issues, have already been substantial. The more recent efforts of political organization initiated by the participatory democrats will certainly increase the degree of Negro representa-tion in the political process. These efforts are now being emulated by more established and less insurgent agencies—Martin Luther King's Southern Christian Leadership Conference, for example, in the massive organizing campaign in Chicago, used many of the techniques and rhetorical devices developed by SNCC and SDS.

It seems clear, then, that the poor are being organized and mobilized. But such mobilization can lead in two directions. On the one hand, there is the strong probability that the newly devel-oped constituencies will take their place alongside other ethnic and interest groups, bargaining for benefits within the framework of the Democratic party. An alternative to this path is embodied in the vision of participatory democracy—the development of community-based, self-determining organizations, having the fol-lowing functions:

a. Achieving community control over previously centralized functions, through local election of school and police administra-tors; by forming community-run cooperatives in housing, social services, retail distribution and the like; by establishing community-run foundations and corporations.

b. Maintaining close control over elected representatives; run-ning and electing poor people to public office; ensuring direct participation of the community in framing political platforms and in shaping the behavior of representatives.

c. Acting like a trade union in protecting the poor against exploitative and callous practices of public and private bureauc-racies, landlords, businessmen, etc.

3. The values underlying participatory democracy have, so far, achieved their fullest expression in efforts to organize and mobilize communities of disenfranchised people, but such democ-ratizing trends and potentialities also exist in other sectors of society. The most obvious example is the nationwide effort by university students to change the authority structure in American higher education. For the most part, this activity has been directed at protest against arbitrary restrictions of student political ex-

pression, and against paternalistic regulations limiting students' rights to privacy and self-expression. The most dramatic and widely-known instance of this activity was that of the civil disobedience and student strikes at Berkeley in the fall of 1964. But the Berkeley situation has been repeated in less intense form on scores of campuses across the country. Student reform efforts have increasingly shifted from protest and direct action to demands for a continuing voice in the shaping of university policy. Some students now have demanded representation on administrative committees. Others have looked to the formation of organizations along the trade union model—organizations which would be independent of and could bargain with university administrators, rather than becoming participants in administration. Thus far, the impact of the student protest has been to generate a considerable degree of ferment, of re-examination and experimentation among college faculties and administrators, as well as efforts coercively to repress the protest.

Student protest has spread from the elite, liberal campuses to Catholic schools, and from there to other clerical bodies. The talk at Catholic seminaries now prominently includes "participatory democracy," and "New Left" clergymen have gone so far as to propose the establishment of a trade union for priests. But the University and the Church are not the only institutions witnessing challenges to existing authority structures. In recent years, there has been an enormous growth of unionization among schoolteachers and other white-collar workers, particularly among employees in the welfare bureaucracies. Now one can also observe ferment within the professions: young doctors and young lawyers are developing organizations dedicated to challenging the authority of the highly conservative professional societies, and to bringing an active sense of social responsibility to their professions.

It is not farfetched to predict that the idea of "workers' control" will soon become a highly relevant issue in American life. American industrial unions have largely had to sacrifice the struggle for control in the work place for higher wages and fringe benefits; but at union conventions, control over working conditions is repeatedly urged as a high-priority bargaining demand. The impetus for making such a demand paramount, however, may first come from the ranks of white-collar and professional employees. The authority structure of the modern bureaucratic organization is plainly unsuited for a work force which is highly educated and fully aware of its competence to participate in decision-making. The first impulse of modern managers faced with threats to authority has been to make small concessions ("improve channels of communications"). But the exciting time will come when such insurgency turns from protest over small grievances to a full-fledged realization of the possibilities for first-class citizenship within public bureaucracies and private corporations. The forms of such democratization could include further unionization of the unorganized, worker representation in management, young-turk overthrows of entrenched leaderships in the professions, and, ultimately, demands for elections and recall of managers and administrators, and for employee participation in the shaping of policies and regulations.

4. The most authoritarian sector of public decision-making in the U.S. is in the area of foreign policy. The American Constitution gives enormous power to the President to make foreign policy without substantial built-in checks from Congress. The scope of Presidential power has, of course, been greatly expanded by the technology of modern war; the unchecked power of the government to mobilize support for its policies has been greatly enhanced by the invention of conscription, by the mass media and their centralization, by covert intelligence operations, etc. It is not surprising that foreign policy has been the special province of elites in America and, since World War II, has been carried on within a framework of almost total popular acquiescence.

The simultaneous occurrence of the Vietnam War and the emergence of a New Left in America may generate change in this situation. Due largely to student initiative, we are witnessing more protest during time of war than in any other comparable period in U.S. history. Not only does this protest begin to shatter the foreign policy consensus, but it also shows signs of bringing about more permanent change in the structure of foreign policy decision-making.

First, the teach-ins and similar initiatives mark the emergence of an *independent public* in the foreign policy area—a body of people, satisfied neither with official policy nor with official justifications of policy, determined to formulate alternatives, stimulate debate and criticism, and obtain independent sources of information. This public is to be found largely in universities but now spills over to include much of the intellectual community in the country. Moreover the teach-in as a technique for disseminating information suggests, at least symbolically, a significant breakthrough in the effort to find alternatives to the propaganda media controlled or manipulated by the state.

Second, the emerging foreign policy public has plainly had an at least transitory impact on Congress. The revival of Congressional independence with respect to foreign policy would be a signal advance of democracy in America.

Third, the attempts to find a non-religious moral ground for conscientious objection in time of war has led to a rediscovery of the Allied case at the Nuremberg Trials—a case which argued in essence that individuals were responsible for the actions of institutions taken in their name. This principle, taken seriously, is revolutionary in its implications for individual-state relations; and it converges, interestingly enough, with "participatory democracy." The Nuremberg principle is now being used as a basis for legal defense of draft-refusal and civil disobedience at draft boards; it inspires professors to refuse to grade their students and become thereby accomplices to Selective Service; it inspires intellectuals and artists to acts of public defiance and witness. In fact, it is possible that one positive outcome of the war in Vietnam will have been its impact on the moral sensibility of many members of the intellectual and religious communities—forcing them to rethink their relationship to the state and to the institutions of war.

It is possible, then, that an unforeseen by-product of the highly-developed society is the emergence of potential publics that are (a) competent to evaluate the propaganda of elites and (b) impatient with chauvinistic definitions of loyalty. The organization of such publics in the U.S. may be a significant outcome of the war in Vietnam. These publics do not have the power to change the course of this war, but the spread of their influence may be a factor in transforming the issues and alignments of American politics in the coming period. Moreover, the strength of these publics on the campus is now being reflected in the growing conflict over the role of the universities in national mobilization. The current campaign to prevent university participation in the Selective Service induction process may portend a more profound effort to make universities centers of resistance to encroaching militarization. The outcome of this particular struggle could be important in democratizing the structure of foreign policy decision-making.

5. The development of democratic consciousness in communities, organizations, and foreign policy decision-making will mean little if the national distribution of power remains undisturbed. This means that the social theory of the New Left must be centrally concerned with the development of relevant models for democratic control over public decisions at the national level.

It is clear that implicit in the New Left's vision is the notion that participatory democracy is not possible without some version of public control over the allocation of resources, economic planning, and the operation of large corporations. Such control is, of course, not missing in the United States. The federal government has taken responsibility for national planning to avoid slump, to control wages and prices, and to avoid inflation. Moreover, the postwar period has seen a tremendous increase in public subsidy of the corporate economy—through the defense budget, urban redevelopment, investment in research and education, transportation and communication, etc. In many ways the "two governments"—political and corporate—are merged, and this merger approximates an elitist corporatist model (hence breaking down even the modest pluralism which once characterized the system). The further development of this trend will foreclose any possibility for the achievement of democratic participation.

The demand for more national planning, once the major plank of American socialism, is now decidedly on the agenda of American political and corporate elites. The question for the Left has become how to *democratize* that planning. There are as yet no answers to this, or to the question of how to bring the large corporations under democratic control.

6. Thus the main intellectual problem for the new radicals is to suggest how patterns of decentralized decision-making in city administrations, and democratized authority structures in bureaucracies, can be meshed with a situation of greatly broadened national planning and coordination in the economy.

That no such programs and models now exist is, of course, a consequence of the disintegration of the socialist tradition in America and of the continuing fragmentation of American intellectual life. Unless the New Left consciously accepts the task of restoring that tradition and of establishing a new political community, the democratizing revolts which it now catalyzes are likely to be abortive.

7. These tasks were, less than a generation ago, declared by many American intellectuals to be no longer relevant. Ideology, it was argued, had no place in highly developed societies where problems of resource allocation had become technical matters. But the reverse may be true: the ideological questions—that is, questions about the structure and distribution of power—are *especially* pertinent when societies have the capacity to solve the merely technical problems.

It seems clear that the issue in a highly developed society is not simply economic exploitation; it is the question of the relationship of the individual to institutional and state authority which assumes paramount importance. In America, today, the familiar mechanisms of social control—money, status, patriotic and religious symbols—are losing their force for a population (particularly the new generation) which has learned to be intensely self-conscious and simultaneously worldly; to expect love and self-fulfillment; to quest for freedom and autonomy. All this learning is a consequence of increasingly sophisticated educational opportunities, of increasingly liberated standards in family and interpersonal relations, of affluence itself. Against this learning, the classic patterns of elite rule, bureaucratic authority, managerial manipulation, and class domination will have a difficult time sustaining themselves.

The virtue of "participatory democracy," as a basis for a new politics, is that it enables these new sources of social tension to achieve political expression. Participatory democracy symbolizes the restoration of personal freedom and interpersonal community as central political and social issues. It is not the end of ideology; it is a new beginning.

SOCIAL SELF-GOVERNMENT
IN YUGOSLAV SOCIALISM

DAVID S. RIDDELL

YUGOSLAV SOCIALISM SINCE 1950:
THE THEORY

Since 1950, organizational forms in Yugoslav society have been in continuous change, so much so that it is sometimes difficult to keep up with the latest modification. Among other changes that have taken place, however, are the following—in no absolute order of precedence:

1. The change from bureaucratic centralized regulation of production and distribution to a controlled market regulation of production and distribution.[1]

2. The constant, though hesitant, increase, in the name of political self-government of the amount of political choice and control by citizens, especially at lower levels, instanced most recently in the legislation forcing compulsory replacement of all elected officials after a specified term of office.[2]

3. The re-organization of industry so that legally the supreme

From David S. Riddell, "Social Self-Government: The Background of Theory and Practice in Yugoslav Socialism," *British Journal of Sociology*, 19:47–75, March, 1968. Reprinted by permission of Routledge & Kegan Paul Ltd., London.

[1] A. Waterston, *Planning in Yugoslavia* (Baltimore: Johns Hopkins Press, 1962), pp. 5–19.
[2] Articles 81, 82, 83 of the Constitution. *The Constitution of the Socialist Federal Republic of Yugoslavia* (Belgrade, Secretariat for Information of the Federal Executive Council, 1963). The system has been further amended in a more democratic direction. See "Several Candidates for Each Seat," *Yugoslav Life*, vol. 10, no. 4 (1965), p. 3.

management body in any enterprise is the workers' council, elected by the workers.[3]

4. Legislation constantly increasing the scope of action and control of workers' councils and the amount of finance at their disposal.[4]

5. The devolution, within enterprises, of power from workers' councils to economic units.[5]

6. The spread of the self-management idea to every institution of Yugoslav society—schools, hospitals, universities, social insurance offices, housing districts, etc.[6]

7. The reduction in size of the central organs of bureaucracy,[7] the freeing of the political prisoners,[8] the removal of privilege for party members,[9] the renaming of the party as the League of Communists as an indication that, although it has a leading rôle, its methods are persuasion, not coercion.[10]

[3] F. Singleton and A. Topham, *Workers' Control in Yugoslavia* (London: Fabian Research Series, 1963). In greater detail in *Workers' Management in Yugoslavia* (Geneva: International Labour Office, 1962).

[4] For example, directors of all factories are now appointed by the workers' council of the enterprise, and are subject to re-election every four years: "New Trends in the System of Self-government," *Yugoslav Life*, vol. 9, no. 4 (1964), p. 1.

[5] Discussion of economic or working units within enterprises can be found in M. Drenjamin, "Working Units Within Organizations and Income Distribution," *Socialist Thought and Practice*, no. 17 (1945), pp. 49–70; and in "Workers' Self-management in Economic (working) Units," *Yugoslav Survey*, vol. 4, no. 12 (1963) pp. 1690–3.

[6] See Z. Kovačević, *Communal System in Yugoslavia* (Belgrade, 1958), pp. 25–7, or S. Kavčić, *Self-government in Yugoslavia* (Belgrade, 1961), pp. 30–8 for short accounts of these developments.

[7] There are various estimates of the effects of the new decentralized system on the bureaucracy, but they were clearly drastic. The Federal Civil Service decreased in size from 43,500 in 1948 to 8,000 in 1955. Another source estimates that 58,000 people left offices for production work; and a third that number of trade union officials (full time) was reduced from 4,000 to about 400: Waterston, op. cit., p. 28; J. Fisera, "Enquêtes sur le Cumul des Responsabilités en Yougoslavie," *Archives Internationales de la Sociologie de la Co-operation*, vol. 10 (1961), p. 150; L. Philippart, "La Gestion et l'Organisation des Universités Ouvrières en Yougoslavie," in *Le Régime et les Institutions de la République Populaire Federative de Yougoslavie* (Université Libre de Bruxelles, 1959), p. 34.

[8] Numbers of political prisoners dropped from 52,506 in 1949, to around 200 in 1964—P. Auty, *Yugoslavia* (London: Thames & Hudson, 1965), p. 120.

[9] G. W. Hoffman and F. Neal, *Yugoslavia and the New Communism* (New York: 20th Century Fund, 1962), p. 175.

[10] *Programme of the League of Yugoslav Communists* (Belgrade, 1958), p. 239f.

Although the realization of these laws and trends is, in practice, partial, none of them would support a simplicist explanation of Yugoslav society in terms of a malevolent ruling class, exploiting the masses for its own gain; each makes control by such a class *more* difficult, and in sum they are not compatible with such an explanation. In spite of the fact that it must be accepted that all the more important decisions about the development of the society are still taken centrally by a small group of party leaders, it must also be accepted that there is only one satisfactory interpretation of the trend in the decisions; that it stems from an ideological view of a socialist society as one characterized by the conscious and organized control by the members of society themselves of all the institutions of their society.

In fact, the essence of the theoretical position which is behind this trend has been stated many times by Yugoslav theoreticians, and is given in detail in the well-known 1958 Programme of the League of Yugoslav Communists. Deleon summarizes this position,

> By merely socializing property [the working class] still remains far from achievement of its goals, for being emancipated from the capitalist system does not also mean delivery from the new perils of étatism and bureaucratism . . . From a historical or theoretical viewpoint one cannot speak of a real qualitative change in social development unless government in the name of the people becomes government by the people themselves . . . the withering away of the state is no more than the socialization of its functions and the gradual clarification of a new concept of the social community which, through the network of social organs that it creates for itself, takes into its own hands the power of decision regarding its destiny, its material values and the satisfaction of its common needs . . . The essence of socialism is its mission of creating new social relationships. The extent to which such relationships are effectively created is the surest criterion of a country's evolution towards socialism.[11]

We may present the Yugoslav leaders' conception of the path to Socialism schematically as in Diagram 1.

[11] A. Deleon, "Workers' Management," *Annals of Collective Economy*, vol. 30, nos. 2–3 (1959), p. 148, 9, 150, 8.

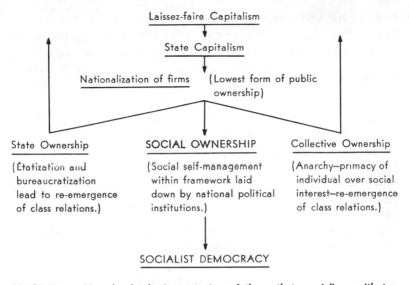

Laissez-faire Capitalism

↓

State Capitalism

↓

Nationalization of firms   (Lowest form of public
                                        ownership)

State Ownership   SOCIAL OWNERSHIP   Collective Ownership

(Étatization and   (Social self-management   (Anarchy—primacy of
bureaucratization   within framework laid   individual over social
lead to re-emergence   down by national political   interest—re-emergence
of class relations.)   institutions.)   of class relations.)

↓

SOCIALIST DEMOCRACY

DIAGRAM I   **Yugoslav leaders' conception of the path to socialism—with two
deviations to be avoided.**

Thus, constant reference is made in theoretical writings to the
dangers of anarchy on the one hand, and to the need to decrease
the amount of state intervention by creating wider areas of group
decision taking on the other.[12]

The drive to implement the conception of socialist democracy
is modified by other, conflicting views of the leadership, which
can be listed as follows:

1. Probably of least importance in internal policy, although it
is very difficult to assess the effect, the international position of
Yugoslavia, particularly in terms of the strings attached to the
many loans at various times from East and West, and the fear
of Yugoslavia's economic isolation in a Europe divided between
trade blocs.[13]

2. There is a desire to maintain, at this top level, power and to

[12] A very good discussion of this problem is by H. Brkić, "La Place des
Conseils Ouvriers dans Notre Système," *Questions Actuelles du Socialisme*,
no. 43 (1957), pp. 69–104.
[13] Hoffman and Neal give details of aid received, and a brief discussion of
its effects, op. cit., p. 384.

some extent, privilege,[14] partly for its own sake, partly because of a feeling that there are divisive elements in the country that might, if not checked by central authority, destroy the whole system.

These latter elements, specific to the Yugoslav situation, have to be taken into consideration. Economic differences between regions were immense, and are still large; determined and continuing efforts to remove them have led to resentment over investment policy and the transfer of funds from rich to poor areas. This economic problem is linked with nationalist rivalries and traditional worries about Serb domination. The policy of allowing freedom of choice to peasants with regard to joining co-operatives has met with traditional peasant suspicion of central government, and memories of the short period of enforced collectivization are still alive (1949–52). Religious strife was connected with terrible atrocities only twenty-five years ago, and is still the cause of much unhappiness on an individual level—parents forbidding marriages, etc. All in all, these problems remain a very serious threat to the stability of any social system in Yugoslavia, and must be taken into consideration.

3. A third factor which holds back the development of the system of socialist democracy in Yugoslavia is a powerful legacy of dogmatic modes of thought which makes itself felt in the work of all the theorists of Yugoslav communism. It is derived from the political socialization of the leadership on the one hand, and reinforced by their social position on the other.

There has been little attempt at reassessment of what might be called the Stalinist demonology among the Yugoslav leadership.[15] More importantly, there is a lack of empirical reference in their work. An analysis of sources in an important theoretical journal indicates that not only is the number of references to other work very small, but the modern work of social scientists, including Yugoslav social scientists, which might be relevant to the func-

---

[14] Tito's penchant for luxurious living is already mentioned by Korbel, and some Yugoslav communists are very critical of it. This is *not* to say that the leadership is corrupt. J. Korbel, *Tito's Communism* (University of Denver Press, 1951).

[15] Kardelj is often cited as one of the most radical of the Yugoslav leaders. But see his attack on Trotsky in *Socialism and War* (p. 28). In spite of disclaimers, the rest of this book is largely an exercise in the interpretation of texts from Marx and Lenin. E. Kardelj, *Socialism and War* (London: Methuen, 1961).

tioning of the Yugoslav system is not referred to at all.[16] The analysis reinforces the author's experience in a seminar at Belgrade university in 1961. The participants found it very hard to convey the idea that they were interested in seeing the organizational forms *at work*.

Since the results of the measures to apply the theory are filtered through a miasma of political jargon, it is very difficult, in reading material put out by the Yugoslav government, to find the *actual* effects of measures, as opposed to what they *ought* to do, and this even applies when one is talking to local officials.[17] This does not just affect outside observers, however. It has had two major effects on the development of the system in the country. In the first place, unparalleled opportunities for experimentation with different forms of organization have been lost. It would have been uniquely possible, for example, to design partially controlled experiments over a longish period, to find which forms of industrial organization most involved workers in responsible decision taking. In addition, and even more importantly, the policy makers, that is, the leaders of the League of Communists, have not been taking into consideration the actual effects of the framework for self-government they have constructed.

In summary, while the Yugoslav leaders have a theoretical aim which directs their policy in general terms, this aim is tempered by caution at real political problems, which in turn are partly responsible for the general wish to retain power at the higher levels of the circle of leadership. This, and the dogmatic legacy in ways of thinking, characterize the policy of "revolution from the top" in Yugoslavia.

[16] *Socialist Thought and Practice* contains translations of the more important articles by leading members of the League of Communists, many of them from the magazine, *Socializam*. 43 articles in this journal from the period 1962–5 were analysed. Only 143 sources were given in text or footnotes. More than half of the references were to socialist classics, and nearly another fifth were to the work of Yugoslav leaders. There were seventeen references to the work of economists and two to that of philosophers, making 13% of the total.
[17] A. Meister, *Socialisme et Autogestion* (Paris: Editions du Seuil, 1964), p. 7.

WHAT ACTUALLY HAPPENS?

There can be no doubt that the mass of the Yugoslav population considers the present system of organization preferable to the pre-1950 situation, and there are signs that as levels of education and sophistication grow, the real possibilities presented by the system are beginning to be used. But there can also be no doubt that the Yugoslav system, as it has evolved since 1950, while in general accord, in its emphasis on decentralization, with the cultural background of the society outlined above, has not arisen directly from the demands of citizens and workers, but has been worked out, legislated and modified from the top.[18] Workers in Yugoslavia are even now for the most part first generation; many still work part time on the land. To master technical skills is a tremendous problem; to express coherently feelings of dissatisfaction over their working lives in organizational terms has been beyond them. Research indicates that neither in the political nor in the industrial order are people able to comprehend and utilize their existing rights, with the result that those who effectively wield control continue to do so, while a very large number of workers and citizens come to regard the whole system with suspicion, thus not trying to explore fully the opportunities open to them. The remainder of this article explores this theme.

(A) POLITICAL INSTITUTIONS

As part of the conception of a socialist society, Yugoslav leaders do not see political institutions in terms of a "bourgeois democracy," in which various party machines compete to bribe the temporary allegiance of otherwise passive and apathetic masses.[19] The renaming of the Communist Party as the League of Communists symbolizes the desire to replace the very party system by one in which citizens themselves will actively participate in political decision-making at all levels, the practice of direct democracy in a range of institutions giving them the experience and interest

[18] "[Self-government] is the creation of lawyers more than of workers, a continuous creation marked by the unceasing promulgation of new rules; and the full and conscious participation in self-government demands knowledge of its legal framework and laws which regulate it"—Meister, Ibid., p. 90.
[19] Cf., M. Popović, "Ideological Trends in the Struggle for Direct Democracy," *Socialist Thought and Practice*, no. 15 (1964), p. 34f.

that will make the problems meaningful to them. However, in the present situation, the social problems mentioned above (p. 00) would form a basis for the development of political parties. The electoral system therefore remains hedged with restrictions. In its latest form, any group of citizens comprising more than 200 people in a constituency can propose a candidate for nomination as a Federal or Republic Deputy. He must then pass the scrutiny of an electoral commission appointed by the existing parliament. After this, he may be accepted as a candidate if a group comprising more than one tenth of the constituency electorate agree to support him (no canvassing is allowed by any candidate). If this is achieved, one third of the sittting deputies in the local Commune council must agree to his candidature. Only then can he stand for election. Candidates for deputy at the local Commune level must pass through the first three steps of this process.[20] This procedure is a slight modification of that outlined in the 1963 Constitution. In the 1965 elections held under this system there were 44,591 candidates for 23,206 seats, so that a contest could have taken place in at most 90.5 percent of the seats.[21] But the higher the level, the fewer the contests. 300 deputies were elected to the Federal Assembly, but only 346 candidates were confirmed: there were 520 more candidates than seats at the Republic level (for 1,139 seats) but 42,526 candidates for 21,967 seats at the Commune level. This represents some improvement over the 1963 elections, but some candidates, especially at the higher levels, withdrew, reducing the number of contests. Such a system can be used to eliminate "undesirable" candidates. On the other hand, the new electoral laws state that if 20 percent of the electorate of a constituency is so minded, a deputy can be re-called. More importantly, a candidate cannot submit himself for re-election to the same position after his four-year term of office. Since candidates can stand for other positions, the provision is not as biting as it might seem at first sight.

The effect of the complexity of the electoral system on the average citizen of Yugoslavia, whose educational level is still low

[20] "Several Candidates for Each Seat," *Yugoslav Life*, op. cit. The system is outlined in some detail in "Electoral System," *Yugoslav Survey*, vol. 4, no. 15 (1963), pp. 2125–42.
[21] "Assembly Elections in 1965," *Yugoslav Survey*, vol. 6, no. 22 (1965), pp. 3174–5. Compare with 1963: "Elections for Assemblies of Socio-political Communities," *Yugoslav Survey*, vol. 4, no. 15 (1963), pp. 2143–52.

—30 percent of commune deputies still had less than four years' schooling in 1963[22]—can only be to discourage him from activity, and to place his reliance on those who have the ability and motivation to try to manipulate the system, i.e., to create just the group of professional politicians it is designed to avoid. Hammond illustrated this in his interesting report of the 1954 election campaign—under a rather simpler system.

> At a voters' meeting in Belgrade attended by the author, a man got up and tried to make a nomination for the nominating committee, but was informed by the Chairman that only groups of 10 could suggest names. After some conversation with people sitting nearby, the man rose again and stated that he now had a group of 10. When asked whom he wished to nominate, he suggested only one nominee, whereupon the Chairman pointed out that he would have to suggest a complete committee. The man . . . thoroughly confused . . . gave up and sat down, amid hisses from the audience.[23]

The multiplication of electoral offices in Yugoslavia has meant that there are a large number of people who serve. Kovčević has estimated that in 1957 there were about one million such offices, including workers' council positions, and that therefore every tenth adult Yugoslav was taking part in some form of self-government.[24] But studies of the personnel of these offices, excluding workers' council members, indicate that there is considerable duplication of office, termed "cumulation of responsibility." Thus, in a study of 703 political office holders in Rijeka, the average number of "socially responsible" positions per office holder was 6.4, with some individuals having as many as 15–20 or more positions. The average activist had been to 11.8 meetings in the last month, again with some having more than one meeting per day! Very many of these people were aware themselves that the qual-

---

[22] Ibid., p. 2149.
[23] T. Hammond, "The Jugoslav Elections: Democracy in Small Doses," *Political Science Quarterly*, vol. 70 (1955), p. 61. A sample survey showed that only 7% of the eligible population attended electors' meetings in Bosnia in 1965—O. Kozomara, *Demokratizacija Društvenopolitičkih Odnosa u Svetlu Skupštinskih Izbora 1965 Godine* (Sarajevo: Centar za Naučnoistrazivački Rad, 1965).
[24] Kovačević, op. cit., p. 28.

ity of the work performed suffered from this duplication.[25] In Smederevo commune, studied in detail by a Franco-Yugoslav research team, 68 percent of office holders held only one function; they held 43 percent of the posts. 6.5 percent of office holders however had more than four functions; they held 21 percent of the posts. As one would expect from its real monopoly of political power, and its assigned "leading role" in Yugoslav society,[26] it is not surprising that League members were over-represented in positions of political responsibility. However, this over-representation does not, at the local level, amount to complete monopoly, and it has been found that there is differentiation within the League. Old communists (pre-1945) tended to be concentrated in the more important positions, and League members as a whole tended to be found more frequently in organizations judged by the researchers to be of more political importance. But, although League membership is positively related to higher administrative occupations and political activity, this is less true of recent League members. Nor do the researches in Smederevo support Djilas' view of a "new class" in other respects. At this level, League members did not differ from other members of the same occupational groups in terms of either pay, housing standards, possession of consumer goods, or frequency of official visits.[27]

The ambivalence of the attitudes of the political leadership towards the Yugoslav population emerges clearly from this account. There is a desire to create the condition of a new, direct, socialist democracy; but there is an extreme caution because of the divisive forces existing in Yugoslav society, and a reference to theoretically conceived but not empirically investigated needs leads to a system of extreme complexity, constantly being modified from the top. The consequences of this are that apathy is hardly diminished by the reforms, and that a small group of activists are overburdened with tasks to the deteriment of performance efficiency.

[25] Fisera, op. cit., pp. 138–154.
[26] E.g., the discussion of the nature of the "leading role" at the 8th Congress of the League—E. Kardelj, et al., "The Leading Role of the League of Communists under Conditions of Social Self-government," Socialist Thought and Practice, no. 16 (1964), pp. 121–166.
[27] A. Meister, "Diffusion et Concentration du Pouvoir dans une Commune Yougoslave," Revue Française des Sciences Politiques, vol. 14, no. 2 (1964), pp. 268–93.

(B) INDUSTRIAL ORGANIZATION

The Yugoslav firm is linked to the socio-political system through the representatives it helps to elect to its chamber of industry of the local Commune.[28] In the early years of workers' self-management, relationships with the local Commune appear often to have been dominated by the latter, but recent legislation has reduced somewhat its power to control the individual firm. Beforehand, the appointment of, and any disagreements with, the director of the factory were controlled by the Commune. This is no longer the case. In the two factories in Belgrade studied by Kolaja, it appeared that the workers' councils adopted an independent attitude towards proposals from the local Commune authorities.[29] More important than its direct relations with political authorities in setting the framework within which the Yugoslav firm operates, are the ways in which it is tied into the planning mechanism.

For the Yugoslav leadership, the lessons that appeared from the administrative period were that fully centralized planning is impossible at a detailed level, since the number of variables to be taken into account is too great, and incompatible with any system of real control by workers, since the latter have no say in what they are going to produce. Nor can consumers effectively exercise any choice beyond what the planners have allowed for.

It thus appears that if self-determination is to be a criterion of Socialism, some form of market organization to allow for it is necessary, at least while goods are in short supply. The Yugoslavs have tried to justify this position in terms of Marxist economics.[30] On the other hand, a free market, even with all firms nationalized, will quickly lead to the success of the more fortunate firms at the expense of the less fortunate, the possible exploitation by some firms of a monopoly position, and a persistence of regional disparity. This the Yugoslav leaders characterize as the deviation to anarchy (Diagram 1). Yugoslav planning involves a position of balance between these extremes, with the aim of expanding as far

[28] There are now four different chambers as well as the directly elected one, representing different areas of social self-government.
[29] J. Kolaja, *Workers' Councils: The Yugoslav Experience* (London: Tavistock, 1965), p. 28.
[30] See M. Todorović, "Some Questions of Our Economic System," *Socialist Thought and Practice*, no. 9 (1963), pp. 17–65.

as possible the area of decision taking open to producers and consumers, while ensuring that socially approved priorities are carried out, that non-profitable areas are subsidized where necessary, and that firms are not in a position to exploit a favourable situation at the expense of the rest of the community.[31] The planning which is indicative in type, and now runs on a five-year system, is based on the estimates by firms of their productive capacity and expansion potential for the next year, together with the proposals of authorities at Commune, Republic, and Federal level as to how they will invest the resources at their disposal. Annual amendments are made.[32] The problem of ensuring that only decisions in line with the general policy of the League of Communists are made, and that resources are available for new investment in backward areas, etc., is solved by the use of two types of influence on the individual firm—economic and social. Economically, the firm is subject to the legally enacted taxation system, which provides funds at each government level.[33] Socially, it is tied into a network of organizations, shown in Diagram 2, which influence the workers' council towards "socially responsible" decisions. A very clear account of the way these organizations operate is given by Waterston.[34] But the system has been bedevilled by planning mistakes, and there has had to be, especially in the sixties, considerable direct intervention to hold down prices. Two sets of economic reforms—of 1962 and 1965—have been introduced in attempts to change the relationships of commodity prices so that this will be less necessary.[35]

Diagram 2 indicates that the individual firm is tied into a national system through complex financial arrangements and by

[31] "The market is not left to the blind action of elementary forces, but consciously controlled by the social plan, which co-ordinates the immediate interests of the enterprise with the interests of the social community"—Anon., "Evolution du Système d'Autogestion Ouvrière," *Questions Actuelles du Socialisme,* no. 41 (1957), p. 120.
[32] "Economic Forecast for the New Year," *Yugoslav Life,* vol. 11, no. 1 (1966), p. 3.
[33] The way the firm is tied into the financial system is clearly shown in the diagram in F. Singleton and A. Topham, "Yugoslav Self-management," *New Left Review,* no. 18 (1963), p. 12.
[34] Waterston, op. cit., pp. 82–5.
[35] A clear and detailed account of the rationale of the later reforms is given in M. Todorović, "Current Tasks in the Development of the Economic System and Social-Economic Relations," *Socialist Thought and Practice,* no. 19 (1965), pp. 13–51.

the pressure of other non-financially based social agencies. The scope of action of the firms workers' management bodies and their relations with the professional managers of the firm is regulated by a complexity of legal enactment, which, like regulations relating to the political system, has constantly been changed.

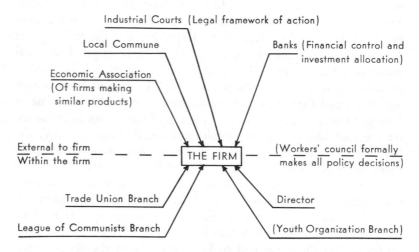

DIAGRAM 2   Organizations linking the Yugoslav firm with the national system of planning and decision taking.

Again, the attempt has been to impose a theoretically correct framework for the development of self-government, without much specific reference to the way the system is working. A large proportion of workers do not have sufficient knowledge of various aspects of the system to be able to operate confidently with it. Thus, in a Smederevo metal working enterprise, 312 workers were asked who takes the decisions in five major areas of factory life—work norms, increases in wages, production plan, bonuses, and distribution of benefits. None answered all five questions correctly, 2 had four correct answers, 67 had three, 69, two, 69, one, and 105 workers did not answer any of the questions correctly.[36] Kolaja found a low level of information about decisions of a workers' council meeting, the day after the meeting.

[36] Meister, "Socialisme . . ." op. cit., p. 91.

Women workers had not read a bulletin posted about the meeting
—one said, "We have children, this is of no interest to us."[37]
Ahtik interviewed 146 workers in a Serbian metal-working enterprise with a schedule designed to investigate the amount of knowledge he considered necessary for efficient participation in workers'
self-management. He did not test unskilled or illiterate workers.
The average score was less than half the possible, with white
collar workers doing considerably better than manual workers.[38]
Ničković investigated the amount of knowledge possessed by 230
workers, as a sample from nine factories in Macedonia. He comments,

> There is a striking fact that a comparatively large number of
> examinees possess no elementary knowledge and lack informa-
> tion on important social, economic and political problems.[39]

But he also states that workers are better informed on problems
of their own enterprise than on wider matters. Radosavljević, in
a survey of ten enterprises in Serbia covering over 1,000 workers,
had a 29 percent "don't know" response in answer to an enquiry
as to whether the workers considered the distribution of income
in the factory to be correct or not.[40] A study in Varaždin, in
Croatia showed that one-third of the workers were "reasonably
well informed about their enterprise."[41] In a survey of over 2,000
workers in eleven factories in Serbia, only one-third knew the
way in which personal incomes were distributed in economic
units, and only one-eighth could understand the actual method

[37] Kolaja, op cit., pp. 58–9.
[38] M. Ahtik, "Ekonomsko Znanje Zaposlenih U Jednom Preduzeću (Economic knowledge of the employed in one enterprise)," *Sociološki Pregled*
(1962), pp. 77–102.
[39] R. Ničković, "Ispitivanje Predznanja Neposrednih Proizvodjaća u Oblasti
Drustveno-Ekonomskog Obrazovanja (Enquiry into the basic knowledge
of direct producers in the field of social economic education)," *Sociologija*,
vol. 3, no. 1 (1961), p. 96.
[40] M. Radosavljević, "Radnici o Nekim Pitanjima Raspodele Čistog Prihoda
i Ličnog Dohodka (Workers on some questions of the distribution of net
profit and personal income)," *Sociologija*, vol. 3, no. 1 (1961), pp. 70–8.
[41] S. Matić, M. Poček and G. Hosanać, *Aktivnost Radnih Ljudi u Samou-
pravljanju Radnom Organizacijom (Activity of working people in the self-
management of work organization)* (Zagreb: Institut za Drustveno Up-
ravljanje, 1962). Cited in B. Ward, "The Nationalized Firm in Yugoslavia,"
American Economic Review, vol. 55, no. 2 (1965), pp. 65–74.

of distribution.[42] This was confirmed by Meister, 53.5 percent of whose sample said they *never* managed to work out what their monthly salary was going to be, the system was too complicated.[43]

Two points should be made in qualification of this picture. First, the ignorance is relative. In interviewing young workers in four factories in Sarajevo, I gained the impression that their knowledge of factory organization was at least as good as that of young workers I had been interviewing in England just before.[44] In Smederevo, one-third of the workers had made suggestions for improvements in production. Secondly, the amount of ignorance varies with the type of worker and the type of factory. It has been shown that women workers, peasant workers, workers in dispersed units know less, and are less involved in the factories than workers with an industrial background.[45] Kolaja's rather negative findings about the efficiency of the self-management system are not unrelated to the fact that in one of the factories he studied, 80 percent of the workers were women, and that in the other, not only were one-third of the workers women, but the factory was in four separate units, dispersed throughout Belgrade. In Sarajevo, in the four factories I visited, the attitude of deference towards the director was strongest in the factory with most women workers, and least strong in that with a long industrial tradition. The office of the director in the former, and his bearing, might have been that of a modern managing director in Britain; in the latter factory, the shirt-sleeved director, in a bare office, met workers continually and informally. Nevertheless, in general the system has become too complicated for most of the workers who have to operate it, so that in practice decision-making tends to revert to managerial staff.

---

[42] V. Hadžistević, H. Kratina and F. Džinić, *Praksa i Tendencije Neposrednog Upravlanja Radnika u Ekonomskim Jedinicama* (*The Practice and tendencies of direct management by workers in economic units*) (Belgrade: Institute of Social Sciences, 1962). Cited in "Workers' Self-management in Economic (working) Units," *Yugoslav Survey*, vol. 4, no. 12 (1963), pp. 1690–1704.

[43] Meister, "Socialisme . . ." op. cit., p. 97.

[44] The author did one month's research in four factories in Sarajevo in central Yugoslavia in Summer 1964 on a Unesco research grant.

[45] See Ničković, op. cit., and V. Ahtik, "Participation Socio-politique des Ouvriers d'Industrie Yougoslave," *Sociologie du Travail*, vol. 5, no. 1 (1963), pp. 1–23. This is an attempt to devise a scale for measuring factors related to participation in social self-government.

Another important way in which the imposition of a "correct" theory impedes the implementation of real workers' self-management in enterprises derives from the conception among the leadership of what it is that leads people to work efficiently. In spite of articles by leading social scientists such as Supek, who are aware of the complexity of this problem, and of the work done with regard to it by such diverse sociologists as Mayo and Friedmann,[46] the official view seems to consist, on the one hand, of vague general assertions about the release of initiative by workers' self-management, and on the other of a specific assertion that the slogan, "From each according to his ability, to each according to his work" is the only basis for stimulating efficient performance in Yugoslav conditions. For instance, in the Report of the Federal Executive Council for 1962, it is stated that, as a result of removing certain restrictions,

> Considerable differences appeared in the position of working organizations in accordance with their business success, and thereby also considerable differences in the level of the personal incomes of workers employed in them. However, these differences, as long as they remained within definite limits, precisely as a result of a more consistent implementation of the principle of distribution according to labour, stimulated the workers' interest in increasing the efficiency of their enterprise's activity, that is in expanding production and raising the productivity of labour.[47]

This attitude has also lead to attempts to introduce piecework as widely as possible, attempts to organize office work and other professional occupations on the same bases—in offices this has led apparently to a multiplication of memos, as one of the only objective ways of measuring output—attempts to introduce payment systems in which the performance of the enterprise, the department and the individual affect the individual's income—this is called "payment by complex output"[48]—and attempts to increase

[46] R. Supek, "L'Humanisation du Travail et l'Autogestion Ouvrière," *Questions Actuelles du Socialisme*, no. 43 (1957), pp. 141–62.
[47] "Socio-economic Relations and Self-government in 1962," *Yugoslav Survey*, vol. 4, no. 13 (1963), p. 1826.
[48] For a description of this payment system see R. Stajner, *Distribution of Income in Enterprises* (Belgrade: Yugoslav Trade Unions, 1961).

differentials. All of these are asserted to stimulate people to greater effort, yet it is abundantly clear that people in clerical and professional occupations dislike the system for themselves, and there is considerable opposition from workers as well.

With regard to differentials, Kolaja reports that the differential of 7 to 1 between the director's income and their own was considered to be "quite excessive" by some workers.[49] In the survey by Hažıstević et al., 29 percent of workers thought that differentials should be reduced, and 24 percent believed that there should be equal pay for all, compared with 22 percent who thought they should be increased. It would have been interesting to know the attitudes to this question of workers in different occupations within the enterprises studied, but the summary does not give this breakdown.[50] With one-fifth of workers giving no reply, Radosavljević found 66 percent thought unskilled workers' wages too low, while 37.5 percent thought wages paid to management officials too high. With regard to piece rates, the same study showed that a clear majority (60.5 percent) of workers preferred time-based payment, although this was 13 percent less than were working on this system.[51]

If to this is added the general dissatisfaction with wage levels which is revealed by all the studies, particularly from lower skill groups—and it is hardly possible to maintain a family without alternative work at the lower income levels[52]—there are substantial grounds for hypothesizing a measure of *alienation* of workers from the very system that is designed to reduce just that. Hadžistević found the following distribution of replies in answer to the question, "Do you submit your proposals and opinions at meetings of collectives of economic units?": 27 percent replied that they did so frequently, 44.5 percent rarely, and 24 percent not at all.[53] Kozomara, a Bosnian sociologist, with wide experience

[49] Kolaja, op. cit., p. 32.
[50] Hadžistević, op. cit.
[51] Radosavljević, op. cit., pp. 74, 76.
[52] President Tito said in 1962, "I am often asked, and I have dreams about it day and night, how people with a family to bring up manage on 15,000 dinars a month, and even less." Cited in Meister, "Socialisme . . ." op. cit., p. 359
[53] Economic units, roughly speaking, correspond to departments of enterprises. As mentioned above, in recent years there had been some devolution of power from the central workers' council to the economic units, with the aim of bringing direct democracy closer to reality in the factories. In a

of research in factories there reports that in spite of the workers' council system, an "us–them" feeling exists between workers and management authorities, paralleling the attitudes which have been so frequently found by sociologists in capitalist countries.[54] When he asked a small group of employees what they thought would strengthen a feeling of ownership of the factory, Kolaja found that unskilled and semi-skilled workers tended to the opinion that increased pay and rewards were the best means; executives thought increased education was of more importance.[55] The latter group, while opposing "payment by results" schemes when applied to themselves, benefit generally from the widespread application of payment according to work done theories as *between* groups, and have a vested interest in supporting them.

Thus, a substantial number of workers do not understand how the system works, except in the broadest outline. They feel they have no control over monetary payments which they disapprove of, and anyway, their main aim must be to try to scrape together as much money as possible to keep their families going. They therefore become alienated from the system as a whole and, as Kolaja points out, such groups have no one to represent their interests, as the trade unions often do not function very effectively at the local level.[56]

A third set of problems of workers' self-management arises from relations between workers, their representatives on the workers' councils, and the managerial staff. In spite of legislation aimed at ensuring proportional representation of manual and non-manual workers,[57] it should be noted that workers' councils seriously underrepresent women workers, young workers, and, most important, semi and unskilled workers. In 1962, women were about 8 percent underrepresented, and skilled and highly skilled work-

---

conversation with me in 1961, the editor of Borba indicated that it was felt that any organization of more than 60–80 workers tended to produce alienation by its very size. Some economic units are much larger than this,

[54] In personal communication. Also confirmed in a recent article: B. Osolnik, "Socialist Public Opinion," *Socialist Thought and Practice*, no. 20 (1965), p. 128. See also J. Goldthorpe and D. Lockwood, "Affluence and the British Class Structure," *Sociological Review*, vol. 11 (1963), pp. 133–63.
[55] Kolaja, op. cit., p. 40. In spite of the small numbers, the difference was statistically significant.
[56] Ibid., pp. 52–5.
[57] "Workers' Management . . ." op. cit., p. 75.

ers about 22.5 percent overrepresented on workers' councils.[58] Second, although there is considerable turnover in workers' councils, there is also considerable continuity. Of those elected in 1962, 28 percent were in their second term of office, 11 percent in their third, and a further 9.3 percent had served more than three times previously, a finding confirmed by the empirical research on individual factories.[59] The workers' council is thus to some extent socially differentiated from the general body of workers of a factory, both in its occupational structure, and in the extent of its experience of management. Radosavljević's study, which compared the attitude of workers' council members with those of ordinary workers over a series of questions, found differences between the two groups on all of them, the workers' council being more oriented towards management/official views.[60] Some observers have explained this exclusively in terms of the overrepresentation of League of Communist members on workers' management bodies,[61] but in the author's view, this is less important as an explanation than the relationships entered into between the workers' council and the director and his full time managerial staff. At the workers' council meetings, members of the latter group present reports giving information and their recommendation as to what decision should be taken. Workers' council members do not have this information beforehand; nor do they have the skills to assimilate it quickly; nor do they have the skills to present criticisms in the form of coherent alternatives.[62]

An analysis of workers' council minutes of the two factories studied by Kolaja indicated a high degree of participation by management in the discussions, and that a large majority of accepted suggestions came from them.[63] His observations of actual meetings indicate that where disagreement between the director

[58] "Workers' Councils and Managing Boards of Economic Organizations, 1950–1962," *Yugoslav Survey*, vol. 4, no. 13 (1963), pp. 1837–8.
[59] Ibid., p. 1838; Meister, "Socialisme . . ." op. cit., p. 102.
[60] Radosavljević, op. cit.
[61] For example, B. Ward, "Workers' Management in Yugoslavia," *Journal of Political Economy*, vol. 65 (1957), pp. 373–86.
[62] The problems raised by Bernstein of the relationships between "public" and "formal" language are as relevant in Yugoslavia as they are here—B. Bernstein, "Social Class and Linguistic Development; a Theory of Social Learning," A. Halsey, J. Floud and C. Anderson (eds.), in *Education, Economy and Society* (Free Press of Glencoe, 1962), pp. 288–314.
[63] Kolaja, op. cit., p. 20.

and workers' council members occurred, the director was easily able to out-argue the latter. Furthermore, discussion of items such as the apportionment of money for flats aroused much more concern than did major problems of finance and policy, which workers clearly did not comprehend.[64] Observations at the workers' council meeting attended by the author at a factory near Sarajevo support this view. This was a factory producing hardboard and plyboard products, with about 1,100 workers, mainly of low skill categories, and a workers' council of 36. It had been set up in 1954, and many of the workers were still part peasant, spending their leisure time cultivating a small plot. At the meeting, three items were discussed:

1. The position of the maintenance department in relation to the distribution of bonuses between departments in the factory.

2. The position of wages in the factory in the light of rises in the cost of living—it was proposed by the director to raise all wages and prices.

3. The allocation of flats to factory workers from funds provided by the factory.

Of these, the second item is clearly the most important from the point of view of the long-term future of the factory. The director made proposals which entailed slight rises in the price of products which, together with greater efficiency in production, would enable 2,400 dinars a month to be added to the wages of the lowest paid, and 1,600 to those of the highest. Thus problems of wages, prices and differentials were involved. The director spoke for about fifteen minutes on the topic, outlining various possible alternatives and his reasons for favouring this one. His proposals were accepted almost without discussion. But on the first and third items there was lively discussion. On the first, some members considered the maintenance department was not entitled to a bonus, since the machines had to stop when being serviced, thus losing productivity. Others countered this view. On the question of flats, "I have several children and relatives to look after—I deserve a flat before anyone else." Others attempted to use some principle of need in general for allocation and sort out priority cases according to them. There was a long discussion as to what to tell those who had been refused flats at this

64 Ibid., p. 45f.

allocation. As in Kolaja's case, in *this* discussion, as opposed to that on price and wage increases, some council members took notes.

Although the problems of wages, prices and differentials were of vital interest to them, workers' council members in this factory found the topic too abstract to be able to grasp. The International Labour Office report on workers' management mentions that in some factories documents and diagrams are cyclostyled to enable workers' council members to comprehend the more difficult problems.[65] In the factory studied by the author, consciousness had not risen to the level of demanding this type of aid.

The factories studied by Kolaja and myself were poor examples of the functioning of workers' management because of the composition of their labour forces. However, they illustrate the problems involved. Because of the superior debating power and information possessed by those at managerial level, workers' councils tend to look to them as a reference group, and to become partially assimilated to their view of factory problems. They find themselves taking decisions which they do not fully understand, based on principles which they, and particularly the other workers in the factory, may not fully accept. This sets them off in their role as worker managers from other workers, a process that is reinforced by the different occupational structure of the workers' council from the rest of the factory and the tendency to re-election. This in its turn reinforces feelings of alienation that have been discussed above. In the survey in Smederevo, half the workers interviewed thought that members of political and social organizations (undefined, but presumably including workers' management bodies) used their positions to get better jobs in the factory and to improve their social/economic situation.[66] There was no evidence as to whether this was actually the case or not, but the perception was real.

There are therefore three sources of retardation in the development of real workers' self-management within the Yugoslav factory:

1. The extreme complexity of the system of factory organization and income distribution for workers with a low educational level.

[65] "Workers' Management . . ." op. cit.
[66] Meister, "Socialisme . . ." op. cit., p. 114.

2. The existence of large-scale dissatisfaction with methods of distribution of income, with income levels, and with differentials.

3. The tendency for members of the workers' council to become assimilated to management perceptions of the problems of the factory in their role as worker-managers.

Clearly, some of the measures, particularly those which have increased the complexity of the system, and above all those which seek to enthrone the principle of remuneration according to work as an absolute, have tended to create an alienation they were designed to combat, with consequent effects on production. As in the political order, however, change is still occurring. There is a tendency for further devolution of authority within enterprises, to the various departments, or "economic units" of which they are composed. In a content analysis of minutes of workers' council meetings over the whole period of workers' self-management Tanić has indicated that, when viewed as part of a *process*, there have been changes away from the personalized towards the generalized approach to problems; the nature of the problems dealt with has itself changed so that the major problems of the enterprises receive a greater amount of discussion.[67] In these terms, it can be argued that advanced workers are slowly "catching up with the system," and the increasing number of strikes which has occurred in the last few years might be considered to indicate that workers' collectives are asserting their real control over dominant directors and workers' councils subservient to them. They have notably been in the more advanced areas of the country.[68]

It is inconceivable that the system should be replaced; weaknesses or not, alienation or not, in general it has become accepted among Yugoslav workers. One young worker in a Sarajevo factory asked me quite seriously at the end of an interview, "Is it true that in England the workers don't manage the factories?"[69]

---

[67] Z. Tanić, "Jedan Vid Istraživanja Radničkog Samoupravljanja Metodom Analize Sadržaja (Analysis of contents as a method of investigating workers' self-management)," *Sociologija*, vol. 3, no. 2 (1961), pp. 101–19.

[68] See Hoffman and Neal, op. cit., p. 398. A Yugoslav comment is B. Kavcić, "O Protestnim Obustavama Rada (About protest stoppages of work)," *Gledišta*, vol. 7, no. 2 (1966), pp. 201–14. 230 strikes were reported in 1964 and 270 in 1965 according to an article in *The Times*, 7 Dec. 1966.

[69] A discussion of the functioning of other forms of self-government in Yugoslavia has been omitted. These exist in the areas of housing, agricul-

CONCLUSION

Some commentators, such as Sturmthal and Kolaja seem to measure the Yugoslav system (in its industrial aspects) against a totally unsociological absolute in which every individual would act perfectly responsibly, in harmony with his own and others' interests. On the discovery that the League of Communists, the managerial group and the director play a large part in the running of the factory, they return with thankfulness to their own system of industrial relations in which, "The management manages and the trade unions perform their functions." Other commentators, on the political system, remain complacent in their prejudices, which are, as McVicker says, "Those of the average scholar who knows no doubts as to the superiority of constitutional democracy as a political system."[70]

Such approaches are unacceptable. The development of Yugoslav society and of its governing party cannot be ignored in any assessment of social self-government in Yugoslavia. Decentralization of effective authority has been a feature of Yugoslav development. The Yugoslav Communist Party reflected this in its own early history, and later through the exigencies of war time activity. The centralized system of authority of 1945–50 was therefore in contradiction with the experience of both the majority of the population, and of party leaders. But the social self-government system whose introduction was occasioned by the break with the Soviet Union in 1948 has been distorted both by the concern of the leadership group with potentially violent sources of social conflict in economic, national and religious divisions, and by their own ideological training in the pre-war period. The result has been the constant, largely arbitrary, multiplication of controls and "improvements," leading to a system of

---

tural co-operatives and a variety of educational and social welfare organizations. Meister, "Socialisme . . ." op. cit., pp. 135–96, does discuss them in the light of the Smederevo research.

[70] Kojala, op. cit.; A. Sturmthal, *Workers' Councils: a Study of Workplace Organization on Both Sides of the Iron Curtain* (Harvard Univ. Press, 1964). It compares workers' councils or their equivalent in France, Germany, Poland and Yugoslavia. There are several inaccuracies in the section on Yugoslavia.

C. McVicker, *Titoism, Pattern for International Communism* (London: Macmillan, 1957), preface.

great complexity, and this in turn has led to incomprehension and suspicion among large sections of the population. It has been shown that self-government in the industrial and political orders suffers when its actual functioning is compared to the claims made for it by some Yugoslav writers:

> Thanks to social self-government in Yugoslavia, a final and true victory has been won by a political system of direct democracy and socialism in which the chief burden of further development is carried by the masses of working people who by their creativeness and everyday experience increasingly influence the further process of socialism, whose aims are, the full progress of working man and of mankind in general.[71]

Nevertheless, a large scale attempt to decentralize the control of social institutions is an unique response on a national basis to problems of organization and development in a modern industrial society, although one based on conceptions that have interested the labour movements of many other countries. The system is still changing, as the current discussion of a complete division between Party and State indicates. For these reasons, the consideration of social self-government in Yugoslavia today has much more than purely local significance. The country provides a laboratory for research on the possibilities of decentralization of control in modern large scale society and its psychological effects. There are virtually no limitations—except those of language—to such research at the present period.

---

[71] L. Tadić, "L'Etat et la Société," *Questions Actuelles du Socialisme*, p. 33.

REFLECTIONS ON CIVIL DISOBEDIENCE

PAUL GOODMAN

I. LAW AND LEGITIMACY

During the early thirties, students got a thorough extra-curricular education in political economy. They experienced the Depression, the labor movement, the New Deal, the subtle infighting of Left sects; and Marxian, Keynesian, managerial and technocratic theories provided adequate terms for discussion. Present-day students are hopelessly ill-informed, and uninterested, in these matters. But they have had other experiences. Sitting-in and being jailed, demonstrating, resisting the draft, defying authority in the schools and on the streets have confronted them with the fundamental problems of political science, the premises of allegiance and legitimacy by which political societies operate at all. For a teacher it is thrilling, if poignant, to see how real these abstractions have become.

But the theoretical framework for discussion has been astonishingly meager. Learning by doing, the young have rediscovered a kind of populism and "participatory democracy"; they have been seduced by theories of mountain guerrilla warfare and putschism, and some of them like to quote Chairman Mao that political power comes from the barrel of a gun. But I have heard little analysis of what Sovereignty and Law really are in modern industrial and urban societies, though it is about these that there is

From Paul Goodman, "Reflections on Civil Disobedience," *Liberation*, 13: 3:11–15, July–August, 1968. Copyright 1968 by *Liberation*. Reprinted by permission of *Liberation* Magazine, New York.

evidently a profound conflict in this period. In the vacuum of historical knowledge and philosophical criticism, the dissenters are too ready to concede (or boast) that they are lawless and civilly disobedient. And the powers that be, police, school administrators, and the Texan President, are able to sound off, and practice, clichés about Law and Order that are certainly not American political science. So it is useful to make some academic remarks about elementary topics. Alas, it is even necessary, to rehearse our case—I am writing in the spring of 1968, and some of us are under indictment.

Administrators talk about Law and Order and Respect for Authority as if these things had an absolute sanction: without them there can be no negotiation, whether the situation is a riot, a strike of municipal employees, a student protest against Dow Chemical, or burning draft cards. The tone is curiously theocratic, as if the government existed by divine right. Law and Order sounds like the doctrine of the authoritarian personality, where the Sovereign has been internalized from childhood and has a nonrational charisma. But although this psychology does exist, by and large the Americans are not conformist in this way. Indeed, they have become increasingly skeptical, or cynical, of their moral rigidity, at the same time as they resort more readily to violent suppression of deviation or infringement.

The "reasons," given in editorials, are that we must have safe streets; in a democracy, there is a due process for changing the laws; violation is contagious and we are tending toward "anarchy." But do safe streets depend on strictly enforcing the law? Every editorial *also* points out that sociologically the means of keeping the peace is to diminish tension, and economically and politically it is to give the disaffected a stake and a say. And in the history of American cities, of course, peace has often been best preserved by bribery, deals under the table, patronage of local bosses, blinking or negligent enforcement. In the complex circumstances of civil disorder, the extralegal is likely to give rough justice, whereas strict enforcement, for instance when the reform-minded *Daily News* makes the police close Eighth Avenue bars, is sure to cause unnecessary suffering.

Even when it is not substantively unjust, Law and Order is a cultural style of those who know the ropes, have access to lawyers, and are not habitually on the verge of animal despair; such a high style, however convenient for society, cannot be taught by tanks and mace. But what is most dismaying is that a well-intentioned group like the Commission on Civil Disorders regards Order and Due Process as a neutral platform to discuss substantive remedies; it cannot see that to an oppressed group just these things are the usual intolerable hang-up of White Power: theft, repression and run-around.

I do not think there is empirical evidence that all violation is contagious. The sociological probability, and what little evidence there is, is the other way: those who break the law for political reasons, articulate or inarticulate, are less likely to commit delinquencies or crimes, since there is less *anomie;* they have a stake and a say if only by being able to act at all. And Jefferson, of course, argued just the opposite of punctilious law: since laws are bound to be defied, he said, it is better to have as few as possible, rather than to try for stricter enforcement.

When a disaffected group indeed has power, nobody takes absolutism seriously. The organized teachers and garbage collectors of New York disregarded the Condon-Wadlin and the Taylor laws against strikes by municipal employees, and got their way—nor did the Republic fall in ruins. Only *The New York Times,* not even Governor Rockefeller or Mayor Lindsay, bothered to mention the threat to Law and Order.

I suppose the climax of divine-right theory in American history has been the law making draft-card burning a felony, punishable by five years in prison or $10,000 fine or both. Since draft-card burning does not help a youth avoid the draft, what is the felony? It is *lèse majesté,* injury to the sacred sovereignty of Law embodied in a piece of paper. Yet Congress enacted this law almost unanimously.

Certainly the disobedient do not *feel* that the law is sacred. If it were, any deliberate infringement—whether by Dr. Spock, a Black Power agitator, a garbage collector or a driver risking a parking ticket—would involve a tragic conflict genre of Corneille: Love *versus* Duty. Among infringers, I see a good deal of calculation of consequences, and on the part of Dr. Spock, Dr. King, etc., an admirable courage and patriotism, but I do not see the signs of inner tragic conflict.

2. THE AUTHORITY OF LAW
IS LIMITED

If we turn, now, to the more tonic American conception that the sanction of law is the social compact of the sovereign people, we see that it is rarely necessary, in the kinds of cases we are concerned with, to speak of "civil disobedience" or "lawlessness." What social promises do people actually consider binding? There are drastic limitations. Let me list half a dozen that are relevant to present problems.

(Of course, few believe in the mythical hypothesis of compact, or in any other single explanation, to account for the real force of law. We must include custom, inertia, prerational community ties, good-natured mutual regard, fear of the police, a residue of infantile awe of the overwhelming, and the energy bound up in belonging to any institution whatever. Yet compact is not a mere fiction. Communities do come to such agreements. Immigrants sometimes choose one system of laws over another; and, nega- tively, there are times when men consciously ask themselves, "What have I bargained for? Do I want to live with these people in this arrangement?")

Since an underlying purpose of the compact is security of life and liberty, it is broken if the sovereign jails you or threatens your life; you have a (natural) duty to try to escape. In our society, this point of Hobbes' is important. There is a formidable number of persons in jail, or certified as insane, or in juvenile reformatories; and there is an increasing number of middle-class youth who have been "radicalized," returned to a state of nature, by incarceration. Likewise, the more brutal the police, the less the allegiance of the citizens.

In large areas of personal and animal life, as in the case of vices harmless to others, high-spirited persons have a definite under- standing that law is irrelevant and should be simply disregarded. Almost all "moral" legislation—on gambling, sex, alcohol, drugs, obscenity—is increasingly likely to be nullified by massive non- publicized disobedience. Not that these areas are "private" or trivial, but one does not make a social contract about them. The medievals more realistically declared that they were subject to canon law, not to the king. For better or worse, we do not have courts of conscience, but it is a human disaster for their functions to be taken over by policemen and night magistrates.

The sovereign cannot intervene in professional prerogatives, as by a law against teaching evolution. Every teacher is duty-bound to defy it. A physician will not inform against a patient, a lawyer a client, a teacher a student, a journalist an informant. At present, there is bound to be a case where a scientist publishes his government-classified or company-owned research, because scientists have an obligation to publish. (By and large, however, for narrow economic reasons, professionals have been playing the dangerous game of giving more and more prerogative in licensing to the state. By deciding who practices, the state will finally determine what is practiced.)

By the Bill of Rights, speech, religion, and political acts like assembly and petition are beyond the reach of the law. As I have argued elsewhere, it is a mistake to interpret these "rights" as a compact; rather, they state areas of anarchy in which people cannot make contracts in a free society, any more than to sell themselves into slavery.

Obviously the compact is broken if the law goes berserk, for example if the government prepares for nuclear war. Therefore we refused the nuclear shelter drills.

The law cannot command what is immoral or dehumanizing, whether cooperation with the Vietnam War or paying rent where conditions are unlivable. In such cases, it is unnecessary to talk about allegiance to a "higher law" or about conflict with the judgments of Nuremberg (though these might be legally convenient in a court), for a man cannot be responsible for what demoralizes and degrades him from being a responsible agent altogether. And note that all these classes of cases have nothing to do with the usual question: "Is every individual supposed to decide what laws he will obey?"—for it is the social contract itself that is irrelevant or self-contradictory.

Finally the bindingness of promises is subject to essential change of circumstances. Due process, electing new representatives to make new laws, is supposed to meet this need and roughly does; but due process is itself part of the social agreement and in times of crises, of course, it is always a live question as to whether it is adequate or whether sovereignty reverts closer to the people, seeking the General Will by other means. The vague concept that sovereignty resides in the People is usually meaningless, but precisely at critical moments it begins to have a vague meaning. American political history consists spectacularly of illegal actions that become legal, belatedly confirmed by the lawmakers. Civil rights trespassers, unions defying injunctions, suffragettes and agrarians being violent, abolitionists aiding runaway slaves, and back to the Boston Tea Party—were these people practicing "civil disobedience" or were they "insurrectionary"? I think neither. Rather, in urgent haste they were exercising their sovereignty, practicing direct democracy, disregarding the apparent law and sure of the emerging law. And by the time many cases went through a long, often deliberately protracted, course of appeals, the lawbreakers were no longer guilty, for their acts were no longer crimes. Hopefully, the current Vietnam protest is following the same schedule. To be sure, this direct political process is not always benign; the Ku Klux Klan also created law by populist means.

Thus, if we stick to a literal social contract, asking what is it that men really mean to promise, the authority of law is limited indeed. It is often justifiable to break a law as unwarranted, and reasonable to test it as unconstitutional or outdated. By this analysis it is almost never necessary, except for cases of individual conscience, to invoke a fancy concept like "civil disobedience," which concedes the warrant of the law but must for extraordinary reasons defy it.

3. THE FUNCTION OF LAW AND ORDER

Clearly, law has more authority than this among the Americans. We are not nearly so rational and libertarian. We do not believe in divine right but we do not have a social contract either. What would be a more realistic theory, more approximate to the gross present facts? I am afraid that it is something like the following:

There is an immense social advantage in having any regular code that everybody abides by without question, even if it is quite unreasonable and sometimes outrageous. This confirms people's expectations and permits them to act out their social roles. If the code is violated, people become so anxious about their roles that they want government to exert brute force to maintain Law and Order—this is part of government's role in the division of labor. Law and Order in this sense does not need moral authority; it is equivalent to saying, "Shape up; don't bother us; we're busy."

The sanction is avoidance of anxiety. This explains the tone of absolutism, without the tradition, religion or moral and ritual imperatives that humanized ancient theocracies. Gripped by anxiety, people can commit enormities of injustice and stupidity just in order to keep things under control. For instance, we enact draconian penalties for drugs, though our reasoned opinion is increasingly permissive. Minority groups that do not or cannot shape up must be squelched and kept out of sight, though everybody now concedes that they have just grievances and that suppression doesn't work anyway. The polls vote for stepping up the Vietnam war just when information, in the press and on television, is that the war is more and more evil and also militarily dubious. Squeamishness and stubbornness can go as far as using nuclear weapons, a massacre on the streets, and concentration camps for dissenters.

Conversely, the strategy of those who protest—the "civil disobedients," the "guerrilla fighters," the "rioters"—ceases to be justice and reconstruction and becomes simply to prevent business as usual. Lively young people, distinguished scholars, and the most talented leaders of the poor spend their time thinking up ways to make trouble. Our ideal aim is certainly to get the politically degenerate Americans back to liberty, law and the business of the commonwealth, but sometimes the purpose gets lost in the shuffle.

4. THE REGIME ITSELF IS ILLEGITIMATE

The rising tide of "civil disobedience" and "lawlessness" is not defiance of law and order; it is a challenge that the regime itself is illegitimate. Maybe it asks a question: Can the modern society we have described be a political society at all? In my opinion, even the rising rate of crime is due mainly to *anomie*, confusion about norms and therefore lack of allegiance, rather than to any increase in criminal types (though that probably also exists under modern urban conditions).

"Civil disobedience" especially is a misnomer. According to this concept the law expresses the social sovereignty that we have ourselves conceded, and therefore we logically accept the penalties if we disobey, though we may have to disobey nevertheless. But in the interesting and massive cases, the warrant of the law is *not* conceded and its penalties are *not* agreed to. Indeed, I doubt that people *en masse* ever disobey what they agree to be roughly fair and just, even if it violates conscience.

Thus, Gandhi's major campaigns were carried on under the slogan Swaraj, self-rule for the Indians; the British Raj who was disobeyed had no legitimate sovereignty at all. It was a war of national liberation. The reasons for the nonviolence, which was what the "civil disobedience" amounted to, were twofold: Materially, Gandhi thought, probably correctly, that such a tactic would be ultimately less destructive of the country and people. (The Vietcong have judged otherwise, probably incorrectly.) Spiritually, Gandhi knew that such a means—of disciplined personal confrontations—would elevate people rather than brutalize them, and ease the transition to a necessary future community with the British.

The campaigns led by Dr. King in the South illustrate the drive against illegitimacy even more clearly. Segregation and denial of civil rights are illegitimate on the face of them; no human being would freely enter into such a degrading contract. Besides, King was able to rely on the contradiction between the illegitimate laws and a larger legitimate tradition of Christianity, the Declaration of Independence and the federal Constitution. Once the blacks made the challenge, the white Southerners could not maintain their inner confusion, and the federal government, though late and gracelessly, has had to confirm the protest.

Now, in resistance to the draft, Dr. Spock and Dr. Coffin declare that they are committing "civil disobedience" and are "willing and ready" to go to jail if convicted. No doubt they have a theory of what they are doing. Most of the co-conspirators, however, including myself, regard the present regime as frighteningly illegitimate, especially in military and imperial affairs; and we are not "willing" to accept the penalties for our actions, though we may have to pay them willy-nilly. The regime is illegitimate because it is dominated by a subsidized military-industrial group that cannot be democratically changed. There is a "hidden government" of C.I.A. and F.B.I. The regime has continually lied and withheld information to deceive the American people; and with a federal budget of $425 millions for public relations, democratic choice becomes almost impossible. Even so, the President deliberately violated the overwhelming electoral mandate of 1964; it transpires that he planned to violate it even while he was running. The regime presents us with *faits accomplis;* the Senate balks with talk but in fact rubber-stamps the *faits accomplis;* it has become an image like the Roman senate in the first century. Many have resigned from the government, but they then do not "come clean" but continue to behave as members of the oligarchy. Disregarding the protests of millions and defying the opinion of mankind, the regime escalates an unjust war, uses horrible means, is destroying a culture and a people. Pursuing this berserk adventure, it neglects our own national welfare. Etc., etc. Then we judge that the government is a usurper and the Republic is in danger. On our present course, we will soon end up like the Romans, or *1984,* or not survive at all.

Naturally, if the government is illegitimate, then at a public trial we ought to win. If the Americans are still a political community, we will—but of course, that is the question.

Let me make another point. The methods of protest we are using are positively good in themselves, as well as for trying to stop the Vietnam war. They characterize the kind of America I want, one with much more direct democracy, decentralized decision-making, a system of checks and balances that works, less streamlined elections. Our system should condone civil disobedience vigilant of authority, crowds on the street and riot when the provocation is grave. I am a Jeffersonian because it seems to me that only a libertarian, populist and pluralist political structure can make citizens at all in the modern world. This brings me back to the main subject of this essay, the social, technological and psychological conditions that underlie the present crisis of sovereignty and law.

5. THE SENSE OF
SOVEREIGNTY LOST

In highly organized countries, each in its own way, most of the major social functions, the economy, technology, education, communications, welfare, warfare and government, form a centrally organized system directed by an oligarchy. I do not think this structure is necessary for industrialization or high technology; it is not even especially efficient, certainly not for many functions. But it has been inevitable because of the present drives to power, reinvestment, armament and national aggrandizement.

The effects on citizenship have been variously compelling. Where the tradition was authoritarian to begin with and the national ideology is centralizing, as in Fascist Germany or Communist Russia, citizens have given allegiance to the industrial sovereign not much differently than to older despotisms, but with less leeway for private life, local custom or religion. In Communist China, where the new ideology is centralizing but the tradition was radically decentralist, there is a turbulence and struggle of allegiances. But in the United States, where both ideology and tradition have been decentralist and democratic, in the new dispensation citizenship and allegiance have simply tended to lapse. Since they can no longer effectually make important decisions about their destiny, Americans lose the sense of sovereignty altogether and retreat to privatism. Politics becomes just another profession, unusually phony, with its own professional personnel.

Our situation is a peculiar one. The Americans do not identify with the ruling oligarchy, which is foreign to their tradition; a major part of it—the military-industrial and the C.I.A. and the F.B.I.—is even a "hidden government." The politicians carefully cajole the people's sensibilities and respect their freedom, so long as these remain private. And we have hit on the following accommodation: in high matters of State, War and Empire, the oligarchy presents *faits accomplis;* in more local matters, people resent being pushed around. Budgets in the billions are not debated; small sums are debated.

The constitution is what I described above: the social compact is acquiescence to the social machine, and citizenship consists in playing appropriate roles as producers, functionaries and consumers. The machine is productive; the roles, to such as have them, are rewarding. And human nature being what it is, there develops a new kind of allegiance, to the rich and streamlined style. This provides the norm of correct behavior for workmen, inspires the supermarkets, and emboldens soldiers at the front.

A typical and very important class is the new professionals. Being essential to tend the engine and steer, they are well paid in salary and prestige. An expensive system of education has been devised to prepare the young for these roles. At the same time, the professionals become mere personnel. There is no place for the autonomy, ethics, and guild spirit that used to characterize them as people and citizens. *Mutatis mutandis*, the same can be said of the working class.

On the other hand, large groups of the population are allowed to drop out as socially useless, for instance, farmers, racial minorities, the incompetent, the old, many of the young. These are then treated as objects of social engineering and are also lost as citizens.

In an unpolitical situation like this, it is hard for good observers to distinguish between riot and riotous protest, or between a juvenile delinquent, a rebel without a cause and an inarticulate guerrilla. On a poll, to say "I don't know," might mean one is judicious, a moron, or a cynic about the question or the options. Student protest may be political or adolescent crisis or alienation. Conversely, there is evidence that good behavior may be dangerous apathy or obsessional neurosis. According to a recent study, a selection by schoolteachers of well-rounded "all-American boys" proves to consist heavily of pre-psychotics.

With this background, we can understand "civil disobedience" and "lawlessness." What happens politically in the United States when the system steers a disastrous course? There is free speech and assembly and a strong tradition of democracy, but the traditional structures of remedy have fallen into desuetude or become phony. Bourgeois reformers, critical professionals, organizations of farmers and workmen, political machines of the poor have mainly been co-opted. Inevitably protest reappears at a more primitive or inchoate level.

The "civil disobedients" are nostalgic patriots without available political means. The new "lawless" are the oppressed without political means. Instead of having a program or a party, the protesters try, as Mario Savio said, to "throw themselves on the gears and the levers to stop the machine." Students think up ways to stop traffic; professionals form groups simply to nullify the law; citizens mount continual demonstrations and jump up and down with signs; the physically oppressed burn down their own neighborhoods. I think few of these people regard themselves as subversive. They know, with varying degrees of consciousness, that they are legitimate, the regime is not.

A promising aspect of it is the revival of populism, sovereignty reverting to the people. One can sense it infallibly during the big rallies, the March on Washington in '63 or the peace rallies in New York and at the Pentagon in April and October '67. Except among a few Leninists, the mood is euphoric, the heady feeling of the sovereign people invincible—for a couple of hours. The draft-card burners are proud. The elders who abet them feel like Americans. The young who invest the Pentagon sing *The Star-Spangled Banner*. The children of Birmingham attacked by dogs look like Christians. Physicians who support Dr. Levy feel Hippocratic, and professors who protest classified research feel academic. On the other hand, the government with the mightiest military power in the history of the world does not alter its course because of so much sweetness and light. The police of the cities are preparing an arsenal of antiriot weapons. Organized workmen beat up peace picketers. We look forward apprehensively to August in Chicago.

But I am oversimplifying. In this romantic picture of the American people rising to confront the usurper, we must notice that Lyndon Johnson, the Pentagon and the majority of Americans are also Americans. And they and the new populists are equally trapped in modern times. Even if we survive our present troubles with safety and honor, can anything like the social contract exist again in contemporary managerial and technological conditions? Perhaps "sovereignty" and "law," in any American sense, are outmoded concepts. . . . This is the furthest I can take these reflections until we see more history.

SOUL POLITICS:
THE POLITICAL MEANING
OF BLACK POWER

JOHN HOWARD

THE WORDS "BLACK POWER" MEAN DIFFERENT THINGS TO DIFFERENT people. To the frightened liberal they provide an excuse for suspending his involvement in the civil rights movement; for tough, angry kids, trapped in the ghetto by race and poverty, they provide an emotional release, a catharsis; for racists they provide a challenge and a stimulus to even more vigorous hate-mongering (George Lincoln Rockwell at the time of his murder was working on a book entitled *White Power*).

If black power is to mean anything to blacks it must be translated into a pragmatic political program. The use of power by an ethnic group to improve its position in American society is certainly not without precedence. As many people have noted, the Irish during the nineteenth century were subject to many of the same kinds of abuses that the Negro encounters in the twentieth century. Political power eventually proved to be the key to Irish mobility. Hugh O'Brien, elected in 1884, was the first Irish mayor of Boston. In his wake the Irish swept to ascendancy in many cities. In a sense, what we are witnessing today in many American cities is the passing of power from one ethnic group to another—from Italians to Negroes in Newark, from the Irish to Negroes in many other cities.

At this juncture politics rather than passion is probably the Negroes' surest road. A speech damning "Whitey" may be emotionally satisfying, but it does not put a dime in any Negro's pocket. What I propose to do here is examine the pragmatic, political meaning of black power by focusing on one city: Oakland, California.

Let me put this discussion within the framework of four broader observations.

1. The chances of Negroes obtaining direct, significant, numerical influence in Congress are nil. Their geographical concentration will limit them to a maximum of 10 to 15 members of the House of Representatives. There are 435 Congressional districts. Blacks cluster in a small number of them. Even if those districts presently having white representation should put a black in office, no more than 15 or so blacks are likely to reach the House. Voting as a bloc, the dozen or more blacks might have some bargaining power, but numerical representation is not likely to be enough to facilitate a more direct exercise of power.

2. Negroes stand their best chance of obtaining power at the municipal level. In many cities (Oakland, Chicago, New York, Philadelphia) Negro school enrollment is close to or over 50 percent of the total; therefore one can anticipate effective Negro political control within the foreseeable future.

3. The powers inherent in municipal government, no matter how the system is structured, are limited. Black-dominated city governments will not necessarily be able to deal more effectively with ghetto problems than white-dominated governments. What they should be able to do is (a) provide impetus and direction in formulating more progressive federal-local programs, i.e., family allowances, a national health insurance plan, etc., (b) introduce marginal changes in the way municipal governments operate, opening a limited number of job opportunities to Negroes, and (c) give the ghetto population some sense that its voice is being heard and its interests represented in the councils of powers.

4. Black power is not nearly as relevant as what can be termed "radical power." Inherent in the "black power" concept is the belief that the objective of blacks is not merely black-dominated government but rather, radically progressive government. It is assumed by black power advocates that blacks are more sensitive to the need for radical programs than are non-blacks. As a means to progressive change, radical power (which ultimately has to be the defining aspect of black power) has meaning for the entire

society. To the extent that black municipal governments would make a thrust for the kinds of programs which democratic socialist countries have had for decades, they would serve the entire population, not just Negroes.

Let us now discuss black power in terms of specifics.

THE PROBLEM OF HAVING TO GOVERN

The problems Oakland faces, and therefore the problems with which a black government would have to deal, are similar to those faced by New York, Cleveland, Newark, and many other American cities. Coming to power in Oakland means coming to control the city council. The council is made up of the Mayor and eight councilmen. The structure of the system dulls the impact of the Negro vote, but the Negro population is increasing so rapidly that a transfer of power seems imminent. Having attained power, however—then what?

Once decisions have to be made, no amount of rhetoric about "blacks controlling their own destiny" will provide an easy way out. Only some understanding of the nature of government, and of the possibilities and limitations of the system within which one operates, will provide the basis for effective action.

A black-dominated government would have to contend with a fairly typical set of big-city problems, including the following:

1. As younger, better-educated whites move to the suburbs, the city is rapidly becoming populated by older whites and young, unskilled blacks.

2. The nonwhite unemployment rate is high. The figures vary from time to time but they all point in the same direction.

3. The school system is an abomination—the high unemployment rate being, in part, a consequence of the fact that the system fails to teach children. The dropout rate is high, and those Negro children who do finish are several years behind national norms for verbal and mathematical skills.

4. The low-income population is growing faster than the supply of decent, low-income housing.

5. The Welfare Department is a particularly punitive one, recipients often having to exchange their dignity and self-respect for the meager financial support they receive.

6. Relations between the ghetto community and the police are characterized by mutual hostility and recriminations.

These are the problems—what does one do?

First, one must ask what kind of power exists at the municipal level. The answer to this varies from city to city. In Oakland, the power of office involves the following:

> . . . the City Council establishes governmental policies, enacts ordinances and passes resolutions by a majority vote; levies taxes; fixes rates of licenses; prescribes fines; forfeitures, and penalties; and adopts City budgets.
> . . . they appoint the City Manager [and] the City Attorney. Upon nomination by the Mayor, the City Council appoints two members of the Board of Administration of the Retirement Fund, and members of the following: Library, Museum, Recreation, and Park Commissioners; Civil Service Board, City Planning Commission, Board of Port Commissioners, the Housing Authority, the Housing Advisory and Appeals Board, Off-Street Parking Commission, Parking Place Commission—Lakeshore Parking Place Commission—Montclair, and the Oakland Economic Development Council.[1]

Finances must be an initial concern of any government—black or white. The City Council has formal control over the city's finances with the ability to tax; however one important consideration places immediate constraints on the scope for action. The city relies heavily upon property taxes to finance required services, approximately 44 percent of its $51,000,000 budget in 1966–67 coming from that source. This is the largest single source of revenue in the budget. An acceleration of changes in the composition of the city's population as a result, for example, of a tax hike to expand certain social services, might erode her financial position. As it is, the city will be pressed to maintain its present level of services. "An analysis of the entire local situation results in the conclusion that the community will have only modest expansion of its traditional revenue sources during the next three to five years."[2]

Given the fact that in the real world we have to think about money, and given the powers that the city council does have, let

[1] City of Oakland: Tentative Budget 1967–1968, p. B-3.
[2] Ibid., p. 2.

me outline some socially desirable and economically feasible programs.

1. There are several possibilities in terms of the city itself becoming an employer. These could be realized through the Civil Service Board. The Board is responsible for ". . . recruitment, classification, the performance rating system, examining, wage and salary recommendations, and the hearing of appeals on personnel matters." There is at least the possibility here of exploring ways and means of throwing out culturally biased tests and hiring Negroes and other nonwhites who can do a job regardless of test performance. The city employs only around 3,300 persons, however, and even allowing for more vigorous recruiting among blacks and some changes in hiring procedures, while at the same time not discriminating against whites, this would still not put much of a dent in the nonwhite employment situation.

2. The city's Industrial Development Commission has had the function of drawing industry to Oakland. A reorganization of certain aspects of city government will change the structure of this group by 1968; nevertheless, certain broad considerations might guide the industrial recruitment effort. The manpower pool in Oakland is youthful and without technical skills. It would be unwise for Oakland to follow the lead of Palo Alto and other communities on the San Francisco Peninsula and become the home of highly technical electronics and engineering firms. Manpower for such employers would be available, but it would be white manpower coming from the suburbs to work in a city filled with masses of unemployed Negroes. The wiser course would lie in attracting businesses not requiring skilled labor. The specter of automation is always raised at this point. The fact is, however, that businessmen do not go to automation because they are fascinated by machinery, but because it is economically desirable. The specter can be evaporated by making it economically more profitable not to automate, this being done through changing tax laws on write-offs and, possibly, through some form of subsidy. Without going into a long discussion, subsidies in the long run should prove wiser than automation with extensive unemployment.

3. The city council has the power to enact ordinances. This power could be effectively used in regard to juveniles. Presently young people in Oakland can be picked up after 10 P.M. for

violation of any of several measures now on the books. In effect, these measures state that any juvenile who is "hanging around" can be stopped by a policeman and if his explanation for being out is not satisfactory to the officer he may be brought "downtown." One of the things that the poor boy is very likely to be doing any night of the week is "hanging around." He has no swimming pool in the backyard, he does not ski or surf, he is not likely to be singing in the church choir. He does what a slum kid does: he "hangs around." The effect of present measures is to punish a teenager because he is poor rather than because he commits a crime. An average of 1,500 juveniles a year have been detained in the early 1960s. These measures are a prime source of tension between ghetto young people and police, the young people feeling that they are being stopped by the police without their having done anything wrong. The city council has power to act in the matter.

Further, a major source of ghetto discontent results from the fact that any person arrested retains an arrest record even if he is released after having been determined innocent of the crime for which he was detained. The arrest record makes it even more difficult for a ghetto dweller to get a job. It is possible, under the laws of the state of California, for a policeman to issue a citation, similar to a traffic ticket, for a nonfelony offense. A suggestion from the council to explore use of this procedure might also ease the tensions between the police and the ghetto.

3. The city has a great deal of authority in the area of housing. Through the exercise of a variety of powers ranging from Code enforcement through more judicious planning, the quality of housing open to the ghetto population could be improved. Current projects, either on the drawing boards or already being carried out, will probably have the effect of exacerbating housing problems for low-income people. The city probably has greater power in terms of housing than in any other sphere crucial to the conditions of ghetto life. Given the nature of federal laws and the kinds of federal assistance available, there is a greater potential for planned, progressive change here than in any other major area.

5. The City Council might explore creating an "Office of Federal Relations." The function of this office, in crude terms, would be to extract from Washington every nickel possible.

Federal funds are available for a wide variety of endeavors and for all kinds of problem populations. Maximum benefit from these funds can be obtained only if the effort to obtain them is carried on in a highly systematic manner. Varying figures are given on the amount of federal monies now expended in Oakland, but no one has suggested that everything which could be gotten has been gotten.

These are some of the possibilities for decision-making by a black-dominated city government. It is clear that no really thoroughgoing structural or economic changes can be brought about with a base of power only in city government. Yet, at the same time, it is not clear that the Negro political potential can go much beyond the control of a certain number of city governments.

Given that this is the case, there are the following implications.

Tom Hayden of Students for a Democratic Society did community organization in Newark from 1963 through 1967. From his life and experience in the ghetto he has written that

> The ghetto . . . needs the power to decide its destiny on such matters as urban renewal and housing, social services, policing, and taxation. Tenants . . . need concrete rights against landlords in public and private housing, or a new system of tenant controlled living conditions. Welfare clients . . . need the power to receive a livable income without administrative abuse, or be able to replace the welfare system with one that meets their needs. Consumers . . . need to control the quality of merchandise and service in the stores where they shop. Citizens need effective control over the behavior of those who police their community. Political structures belonging to the community are needed to bargain for, and maintain control over, funds from government or private sources. In order to build a more decent community while resisting racist power, more than violence is required. People need self-government. We are at a point where democracy—the idea and practice of people controlling their lives—is a revolutionary issue in the United States.[3]

It is not clear that the formal system can be a very effective instrument in implementing that revolutionary idea.

[3] Tom Hayden, "The Occupation of Newark," *The New York Review of Books,* 9, No. 3:24.

Andrew Kopkind has pointed to one possibility whereby the formal system may become more than a vehicle for halfway measures and halting steps.

> Those who are working in the streets need to have a new coalition behind them to absorb the inevitable calls for repression.
> The civil war and the foreign one have contrived . . . to murder liberalism—in its official robes. There are few mourners. The urgent business now is for imaginations freed from the old myths to see what kind of society might be reconstructed that would have no need for imperialism and no cause for revolt.[4]

A new kind of coalition embracing liberal and radical intellectuals, peace advocates, hippies, the Negro poor, and maybe even the white poor might evolve. The poor motivated by a desire for class reform and the intellectuals, inspired by a vision of a more humane society, might be able to unite and use the political system as an instrument for genuine social advancement.

The Negro poor rioting in the cities seem to have at least some intuitive grasp of the nature and causes of their problems. This article has suggested that if they channeled their energies entirely into mainstream politics they would bring about some changes, but none of really substantial dimensions.

Thus, if the political system is to work as an instrument for progress, an enormous number of whites must also develop some awareness of what is wrong with this society and what needs to be done. They too must develop some grasp of what kinds of policies are necessary to make the country a livable place. It can only be hoped that the Negro population in the course of its own political involvement can educate the white population. If that occurs, then progressive and humanistic change may be possible.

[4] Andrew Kopkind, "Soul Power," *The New York Review of Books*, 9, No. 3:6.

THE DISTRIBUTION
OF WEALTH

INTRODUCTION

EVERY SOCIETY FACES THE PROB-
lem of producing and distributing goods. In fact, the field of
economics is designed precisely to study the mechanisms for
accomplishing these tasks—but based upon assumptions of scarcity. Yet, in the United States and other developed Western
nations, a new form of societal abundance has emerged. This is
seen in the surplus production of agricultural goods, the under-
utilization of industrial plant capacity in giant manufacturing
industries such as steel and automobiles, and in the increasing
orientation of the total economy to an affluent population. The
theme of abundance and its challenges has been addressed by
various writers such as Theobald and Myrdal.[1] At the same time
there has been the rediscovery of poverty in the 1960s. A generation after the revelation by Franklin Roosevelt that one-third
of the nation was ill-fed and ill-housed, Michael Harrington and
others wrote about "the other America" and "the invisible
poor."[2] As the total picture is observed, it becomes clear that a
new level of economic production has emerged, largely the result
of technological advances, while the structural arrangements for

[1] Robert Theobald, *The Challenge of Abundance*. New York: New American Library, 1962. Gunnar Myrdal, *Challenge to Affluence*. New York:
Pantheon Books, 1963.
[2] See, Michael Harrington, *The Other America*. New York: Macmillan,
1962. Dwight Macdonald, "The Invisible Poor," published in *The New
Yorker*, reprinted by the Sidney Hillman Foundation, 15 Union Square,
N.Y., N.Y., 1963.

distributing economic goods and services are essentially un-changed.

The student of sociology will recognize the obvious importance of class variables; however, sociologists all too commonly focus upon mobility and fail to give attention to the structural realities of society. The evidence reveals only a very modest change in the concentration of income and wealth in America since the period immediately before the Great Depression. Herman P. Miller, in the essay included in this section, not only indicates the lack of redistribution, but suggests the increasing rigidity of the system which fails to generate change. As for organizational con-centration of wealth, Beller's essay demonstrates that the mergers and acquisitions in the American corporate world have led to a diminution in absolute competition and an increasing amount of economic control in a relatively small number of firms. One is challenged to think about the implications, including those for a theory of power as discussed in the previous section, of statistics such as the following:[3] 1965 gross receipts for the General Motors Corporation were $19 billion, exceeding that of 113 nations in the United Nations; 1.6 percent of the U. S. adult population holds 82.4 percent of publicly-owned stock; in 1964 one-quarter of all corporate profits in the country went to G.M., A.T.&T., Standard Oil of N.J., Texaco, Ford, Gulf Oil, and I.B.M.; from 1951–1961 the top 500 corporations averaged 7 mergers and acquisitions; those 500 top corporations comprise one-quarter of 1 percent of the industrial companies and yet account for 60 percent of sales and 72 percent of all profits.

Recently a number of writers have argued that radical prob-lems compel radical solutions. Some have urged the necessity of revolutionary alternatives—whether in the sense of planning it-self, as Bob Ross ponders, or in terms of the Beatles' song: revolu-tion as a way of changing the world. Most proposals have been based upon traditional notions of the production and distribution of economic goods and services. By these notions, the earned income of an individual is dependent upon society's judgment of the worth of his contribution to the productive process; welfare is merely designed to lubricate the system and minimize eruptions

[3] These statistics come from *The New York Times*, Oct. 31, 1965; from Michael Harrington, *The Accidental Century*. New York: Macmillan, 1965, pp. 81 ff.; and from *Progressive* Magazine, September 1966, p. 9.

and disturbances;[4] the class structure is built upon an interdependent fabric into which all members are woven in their respective parts. But the objective realities in the current period have challenged some of the underlying assumptions. Hence, Theobald argues for the constitutional right to income in a society which is affluent, which produces an abundance, and which can readily provide a decent life-style for all. Economic rewards, then, need not be contingent upon contribution to production, but could come as an inherent parcel of the right to life, liberty, and the pursuit of happiness.

The $30 billion being spent to put an American on the moon by 1970 is sometimes seen in relative terms: (with that money) "We could give every teacher in the United States a 10 percent raise a year for 10 years; endow 200 small colleges with $10 million each; finance the education through graduate school of 50,000 scientists at $4,000 a year apiece; build 10 new medical schools at $200 million each; build and endow complete universities for more than 50 developing countries; create three new Rockefeller Foundations worth $500 million each."[5] This kind of thinking of "first things first"[6] has important implications for a radical sociology, for it serves to engage the thinker into the realm of basic changes, not merely reformist modifications. This type of thinking is politically volatile. It is when we note that more than four million homes in America lack running water and plumbing, that we sense the meaning of the statistic that one air-to-air missile program costs as much as 26,150 new dwelling units at $14,500 each. Senator Robert Taft was known as a political conservative; yet, the federal government housing program he proposed in the late 1940s has yet to be realized.[7] The economic

---

[4] For a discussion of the evolution of welfare and industrialization, see Harold L. Wilensky and Charles N. Lebeaux, *Industrial Society and Social Welfare*. New York: The Free Press, 1965.
[5] Quoted from an article in *The New York Times*, December 1, 1965. Also see Amitai Etzioni, *The Moon Doggle*. New York: Doubleday, 1964.
[6] Note the book by Senator Eugene J. McCarthy, *First Things First: New Priorities for America*. New York: New American Library, 1968. For a broad discussion of the priorities question in America, see *New University Thought*, Winter 1967 issue, "Decisions for America: Priorities and Consequences."
[7] Michael Harrington's "Introduction" in Louis Ferman, Joyce Kornbluh, and Alan Haber (eds.), *Poverty in America*. Ann Arbor: University of Michigan Press, 1965.

resources of the federal government have gone in alternative directions; more than two-thirds of the federal budget goes into the costs of war—past, present, and future.

Is there a place for a radical sociology concerned with the distribution of wealth in society? We have seen a great deal of attention placed upon the formation of class structures, theories purporting to prove the universality of some system of stratification, and a considerable amount of empirical sociological research on class correlates.[8] The selections which follow demonstrate some of the realities in the distribution of wealth in the United States. They offer the reader a perspective, and they provoke two basic and very relevant sociological questions. First, what does the empirical evidence tell us about a theory of social change, and what are its implications for making sociological predictions about the future? Second, if the conventional definition of economics is no longer appropriate, what become the new key problems which stem from abundance and maldistribution? The Ross, Theobald, and Strout pieces direct our thinking along these lines. The selection by Ross raises the broader question of planning, advocacy and change. All together, the material in this section would seem to answer the rhetorical question that opened this paragraph in an overwhelmingly affirmative way. A structural analysis of the distribution of wealth in a society, noting the change or lack of change, does lead to a viewpoint which deals with radical rather than reformist alternatives, both in theory and with programmatic impact.

[8] The sociological literature is replete with studies of social class and class correlates. See, for example, Milton M. Gordon, *Social Class in American Sociology*. New York: McGraw-Hill, 1963. Leonard Reissman, *Class in American Society*. Glencoe: The Free Press, 1959. Thomas E. Lasswell, *Class and Stratum*. New York: Houghton Mifflin, 1965. Joseph Kahl, *The American Class Structure*. New York: Holt, Rinehart & Winston, 1957). Bernard Barber, *Social Stratification*. New York: Harcourt, Brace & World, 1957.

WHERE IT'S AT

WHAT'S HAPPENING TO
OUR SOCIAL REVOLUTION?

HERMAN P. MILLER

A MYTH HAS BEEN CREATED IN THE UNITED STATES THAT INCOMES
are gradually becoming more evenly distributed. This view is
held by prominent economists of both major political parties. It
is also shared by the editors of the influential mass media.

Arthur F. Burns, chief economist for the Eisenhower Administration, stated in 1951 that "the transformation in the distribution of our national income . . . may already be counted as one
of the great social revolutions of history." Paul Samuelson, one of
President Kennedy's leading economic advisers, stated in 1961 that
"the American income pyramid is becoming less unequal." Several major stories on this subject have appeared in *The New York
Times*, and the editors of *Fortune* magazine announced ten years
ago: "Though not a head has been raised aloft on a pikestaff, nor
a railway station seized, the U.S. has been for some time now in
a revolution."   •   •   •

Despite the existence of much poverty in the United States,
there is general agreement that real levels of living are much
higher than they were only ten years ago and that the prospects
for future increases are very good. Since conditions are improving you may wonder why it is important to consider the gap
between the rich and the poor. Isn't it enough that the *amount*
of income received by the poor has gone up substantially? Why

From *Rich Man, Poor Man*, by Herman P. Miller. Copyright © 1964 by
Thomas Y. Crowell Company, New York, publishers, and reprinted with
their permission. Illustrations by William Gorman.

be concerned about their share? Many who have thought about this problem seriously regard the *share* as the critical factor. When Karl Marx, for example, spoke about the inevitability of increasing misery among workers under capitalism he had a very special definition of misery in mind. Sumner Slichter, in summarizing the Marxian position on this point, states: "Marx held that wages depend upon the customary wants of the laboring class. Wages, so determined, might rise in the long run. Hence, Marx conceded that real wages *might* rise, but not the relative share of labor. Even if real wages rose, misery would grow, according to Marx, since workers would be worse off relative to capitalists."

Arnold Toynbee has approached the problem of income shares in still another way. He notes that minimum standards of living have been raised considerably and will continue to be raised in the future, but he observes that this rise has not stopped us from "demanding social justice; and the unequal distribution of the world's goods between a privileged minority and an underprivileged majority has been transformed from an unavoidable evil to an intolerable injustice."

In other words "needs" stem not so much from what we lack as from what our neighbors have. Veblen called this trait our "pecuniary standard of living" and modern economists refer to it as the "relative income hypothesis," but it all comes back to the same thing. Except for those rare souls who have hitched their wagons to thoughts rather than things, there is no end to "needs." So long as there are people who have more, others will "need" more. If this is indeed the basis for human behavior, then obviously the gap between the rich and the poor cannot be ignored, however high the *minimum* levels of living may be raised.

Although the figures show no appreciable change in income shares for nearly twenty years, the problem is complex and there is much that the statistics cannot show. It is conceivable, for example, that a proportional increase in everybody's real income means more to the poor than to the rich. The gap in "living levels" may have closed more than the gap in incomes. Even if exact comparisons are not possible, many believe that by satisfying the most urgent and basic needs of the poor, there has been some "leveling up" in the comforts of life.

Other examples of a similar nature can be cited. The extension of government services benefits low-income families more than those who have higher incomes—by providing better housing, more adequate medical care, and improved educational facilities. The increase in paid vacations has surely brought a more equal distribution of leisure time—a good that is almost as precious as money. Finally, improved working conditions—air conditioning, better light, mechanization of routine work—have undoubtedly reduced the painfulness of earning a living more for manual workers than for those who are in higher paid and more responsible positions.

When allowance is made for all of these factors, and for many others not mentioned, it may well be that some progress has been made during recent years in diminishing the inequality of levels of living. But it is hard to know how much allowance to make and our judgments could be wrong. Most opinions regarding changes in inequality, including those held by professional economists, are based on statistical measures of income rather than on philosophical concepts. With all their limitations, the income figures may well serve as a first approximation of changes in welfare. These figures show that the share of income received by the lower income groups has not changed for twenty years. Let us look at some other evidence that supports this view and then examine the implications of the findings.

The narrowing of income differentials between whites and non-whites (92 percent of whom are Negroes) is sometimes cited as evidence of a trend toward equalization. Several years ago, Professor Joseph Kahl of Washington University stated: "The poorest section of the country, the South, and the poorest group in the country, the Negroes, made the greatest gains of all."

What are the facts? Surely one would expect a change here in view of the major relocation of the Negro population in recent years. Migration and technological change during the past twenty years have altered the role of the nonwhite from a southern farm-hand or sharecropper to an industrial worker. In 1940, about three-fourths of all nonwhites lived in the South and were largely engaged in agriculture. By 1950, the proportion residing in the South had dropped to about two-thirds, and today it is down to a little more than half. Even in the South, nonwhites are now more concentrated in urban areas than ever before.

The change in the occupations of nonwhite males tells the story of their altered economic role even more dramatically.

Twenty years ago, four out of every ten nonwhites who worked were laborers or sharecroppers on southern farms. At present, less than two out of every ten are employed in agriculture, and about five out of ten work as unskilled or semiskilled workers at nonfarm jobs. The change in the occupational status of nonwhites has been accompanied by a marked rise in educational attainment, proportionately far greater than for whites. In 1940, young white males averaged four years more of schooling than nonwhites in the same age group. Today the gap has been narrowed to one and a half years.

The income gap between whites and nonwhites did narrow during World War II. During the last decade, however, it shows some evidence of having widened again (see Table 1 and Fig 1). The census statistics demonstrate this dismaying fact.

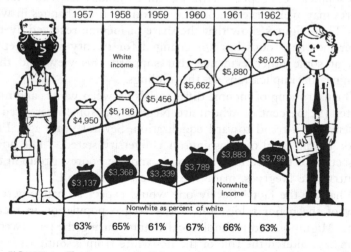

FIGURE 1   **The income gap. White vs. nonwhite workers: 1957 to 1962.**
Source: U.S. Bureau of the Census, Current Population Reports—Consumer Income, Series P-60, annual issues.

In 1947, the median wage or salary income for nonwhite workers was 54 percent of that received by the whites. In 1962, the ratio was almost identical (55 percent). Prior to 1947 there was a substantial reduction in the earnings gap between whites

TABLE 1   The Income Gap: White vs. Nonwhite Male Workers
Aged 14 and Over, in 1939, and 1947 to 1962

	All Persons with Wage or Salary Income:		
Year	White	Nonwhite	Nonwhite as Percent of White
1939	$1,112	$ 460	41%
1947	2,357	1,279	54
1948	2,711	1,615	60
1949	2,735	1,367	50
1950	2,982	1,828	61
1951	3,345	2,060	62
1952	3,507	2,038	58
1953	3,760	2,233	59
1954	3,754	2,131	57
1955	3,986	2,342	59
1956	4,260	2,396	56
1957	4,396	2,436	55
1958	4,596	2,652	58
1959	4,902	2,844	58
1960	5,137	3,075	60
1961	5,287	3,015	57
1962	5,462	3,023	55

	Year-Round Full-Time Workers with Wage or Salary Income:		
Year	White	Nonwhite	Nonwhite as Percent of White
1939	$1,419	$ 639	45
1955	4,458	2,831	64
1956	4,710	2,912	62
1957	4,950	3,137	63
1958	5,186	3,368	65
1959	5,456	3,339	61
1960	5,662	3,789	67
1961	5,880	3,883	66
1962	6,025	3,799	63

SOURCE: U.S. Bureau of the Census, Current Population Reports—Consumer Income, Series P-60, annual issues.

and nonwhites. In view of the stability of the earnings gap during the postwar period, however, the reduction during the war years cannot be viewed as part of a continuing process, but rather as a phenomenon closely related to war-induced shortages of unskilled labor and government regulations such as those of the War Labor Board designed generally to raise the incomes of lower paid workers, and to an economy operating at full tilt.

This conclusion is reinforced by details of the 1960 census which show that in the twenty-six states (including the District of Columbia) which have 100,000 or more Negroes, the ratio of Negro to white income for males increased between 1949 and 1959 in two states (District of Columbia and Florida) and it was unchanged in two others (New Jersey and Oklahoma). In every other state there was a widening of the gap between the incomes of whites and Negroes and in some cases it was fairly substantial.

FIGURE 2   Men's income by occupation in 1939, 1950, and 1961.
Source: U.S. Bureau of the Census, Current Population
Reports—Consumer Income, Series P-60, Nos. 9 and 39.

OCCUPATIONAL DIFFERENTIALS IN EARNINGS ARE NOT NARROWING

One of the most widely and strongly held misconceptions about income concerns the narrowing of the difference in earnings between skilled and unskilled workers. The prevailing view holds that the decrease in the earnings gap between the skilled and the unskilled in the United States is part of a historical process that has been going on since the turn of the century. The Department of Labor reports that in 1907 the median earnings of skilled workers in manufacturing industries was about twice that received by unskilled workers. By the end of World War I, it was only 75 percent greater, and by the end of World War II only 55 percent greater. Thus, during a forty-year period, this income gap was reduced by about 50 percent, an average of about 1 percent per year.

Recent trends in income differentials between skilled and unskilled workers are shown in Fig. 2 and Table 2. These figures

FIGURE 2 (Continued).

represent the median wages and salaries received during the year
in the major occupation groups for men. Women are excluded
because their earnings are highly influenced by the fact that a
large proportion of them work intermittently rather than full
time.

TABLE 2   Men's Income by Occupation: Percent Change

Year	Professional and Managerial Workers	Craftsmen	Semiskilled Factory Workers	Service Workers and Nonfarm Laborers
1939–61	243%	322%	331%	314%
1939–50	96	160	172	180
1950–61	75	62	59	48

SOURCE: U.S. Bureau of the Census, Current Population Reports—Consumer Income, Series P-60, Nos. 9 and 39.

There was not too much variation among occupation groups
in the rate of income growth during the entire twenty-two-year
period. The average income for most of the occupations quad-
rupled. But an examination of the growth rates for two different
periods, 1939–50, and 1950–61, reveals striking differences.

During the decade that included World War II, the lower paid
occupations made the greatest relative gains in average income.
Thus, laborers and service workers (waiters, barbers, janitors, and
the like), two of the lowest paid groups among nonfarm workers,
had increases of about 180 percent. The gains for craftsmen, who
are somewhat higher paid, was 160 percent; professional and managerial workers, the highest paid workers of all, had the lowest
relative gains—96 percent.

During the past decade the picture has been reversed. Laborers
and service workers made the smallest relative gains, 48 percent;
craftsmen had increases of 62 percent, and the professional and
managerial workers had the greatest gains of all, 75 percent. The
narrowing of the income gap between the skilled and the unskilled, the high-paid and the low-paid workers, which was evident up to and including the war years, has stopped during the

past decade and the trend seems to be moving in the opposite direction.

The above figures are national averages in which all industries and regions are combined. They are very useful for identifying major trends, but they can also be very misleading because they average together so many different things. It is important to examine the figures for a particular industry in a particular region to get a better understanding of the underlying trends. The primary and fabricated metals industries have been selected for this purpose. The same analysis was also made for about ten other major American industries and the results are generally the same as those presented below.

About 2,200,000 men were engaged in the production of metals or the fabrication of metal products in 1960. This employment was about equally divided between production and fabrication.

The production of primary metals consists of three major components: blast furnaces and steel mills with about 600,000 men; other primary iron and steel works (mostly foundries) with about 300,000 men; and primary nonferrous metal (mostly aluminum)

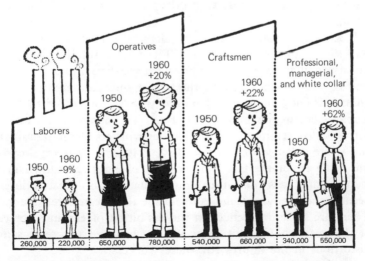

FIGURE 3   **Men employed in the metal industries: 1950 and 1960.** Source: U.S. Census of Population: 1960, Vol. II, Occupation by Industry, Table 2; and U.S. Census of Population: 1950, Vol. II, Table 84.

plants, with about 300,000 men. The iron and steel industry is highly concentrated in the Northeast and North Central states and within these states it can be further pinpointed to the following areas: Pittsburgh-Youngstown, Cleveland-Detroit, and Chicago.

The fabrication industry has a similar geographic distribution. About one-third of the workers are employed in the northeastern states and a somewhat larger proportion are in the North Central region. This industry is divided into several major components, two of which are dominant and account for about nine-tenths of the employment. The largest component manufactures structural metal products—a miscellany ranging from bridge sections to bins, metal doors, windows, etc. It employs 200,000 men. The second major category, called "miscellaneous fabricated metal products," makes everything from dog chains to missiles and employs 700,000 men.

An examination of employment in this industry shows that the total number of workers increased by 24 percent between 1950 and 1960. Professional, managerial, and other white-collar workers increased 62 percent; skilled and semiskilled production workers increased by about 20 percent, but unskilled laborers decreased 9 percent. Thus, despite the general rise in employment and output in this industry, there was a drop in the demand for unskilled labor.

In view of these changes in the demand for labor in this industry, what happened to earnings? The figures for the eight major metal-producing and fabricating states are shown in Table 3. The states are shown in order of the size of their employment in this industry. They accounted for nearly three-fourths of the entire employment in this industry in 1960. The actual dollar earnings for unskilled, semiskilled, and all other workers (largely craftsmen and white-collar workers) for 1939, 1949, and 1959 are shown in the first part of the table; percentage changes are shown in the second part. It is the latter figures that are of greatest interest because they show which groups made the greatest relative gains. There are some differences in the definition of earnings for each of the years shown, but they are not believed to create serious distortions in the figures for these workers.

In all states except Ohio and California, unskilled workers in this industry made greater relative gains than the semiskilled between 1939–49. Similar figures are not available for the higher

TABLE 3 Regional Differences in Income of Men in the Metal Industries in 1939, 1949, and 1959

| State | Amount of Earnings | | | | | | | | Percent Increase, 1939–49 | | Percent Increase, 1949–59 | | |
| | Laborers | | | Operatives | | | Other Workers | | Labor-ers | Opera-tives | Labor-ers | Opera-tives | Other Workers |
	1939	1949	1959	1939	1949	1959	1949	1959					
Pennsylvania	$ 947	$2,414	$3,939	$1,153	$2,767	$4,597	$3,220	$5,624	155%	140%	63%	66%	75%
Ohio	1,006	2,403	4,077	1,091	2,841	4,885	3,367	5,920	139	160	70	72	76
California	1,056	2,411	4,136	1,231	2,814	5,002	3,639	6,866	128	129	72	78	89
Illinois	950	2,506	4,448	1,124	2,931	5,034	3,517	6,321	164	161	77	72	80
New York	918	2,503	3,940	1,060	2,703	4,458	3,318	5,796	173	155	57	65	75
Michigan	962	2,645	4,134	1,150	2,997	4,726	3,691	6,246	175	161	56	58	69
Indiana	1,074	2,526	4,054	1,286	2,918	4,897	3,454	5,792	134	127	60	68	68
Alabama	701	2,032	3,565	887	2,316	4,301	3,073	5,864	190	161	75	86	91

SOURCE: U.S. Census of Population: 1960, Detailed Characteristics, Tables 124 and 130; U.S. Census of Population: 1950, Vol. II, Tables 78 and 86; and U.S. Census of Population: 1940, Vol. III, Table 16.

paid "other" workers for 1939. Thus there was a tendency toward a narrowing of earnings differentials in this industry between 1939–49. But, during the decade 1949–59, the reverse was true. In every state there was a widening of differentials, with the highest paid "other" workers making the greatest relative gains, followed by the semiskilled workers and then the unskilled. In Pennsylvania, for example, laborers had a 63 percent increase in earnings between 1949–59, semiskilled operatives had a 66 percent increase, and professional, managerial, and other white-collar workers had a 75 percent increase. The same general pattern of wage movement was found in each of the other states shown.

There was a time, not too long ago, when economists did not look for changes in income distribution because they did not expect to find any. Indeed, the stability of the income curve was so striking that it was given a name, Pareto's Law, in honor of the economist who conducted some of the earliest statistical inquiries in this field.

Pareto believed that the distribution of income is fixed and that regardless of changes in economic conditions, short of a revolutionary change from a competitive to a collectivist society, the distribution of income is the same in all places and at all times.

Statistical studies in recent years have so thoroughly demolished Pareto's notions that we have now come to look for change where no change exists. The facts show that our "social revolution" ended nearly twenty years ago; yet important segments of the American public, many of them highly placed government officials and prominent educators, think and act as though it were a continuing process. Intelligent public policy demands that things be seen as they are, not as they were.

The stability of income distribution, particularly during the fifties, could be related to the fact that the decade was dominated by a political philosophy committed to stability rather than change. In a different climate income differentials might narrow further. This could be accomplished through legislation designed to raise the levels of living of the poor: expansion of unemployment insurance benefits, federal aid to dependent children of the unemployed, liberalization of social security benefits, increase in the minimum wage and extension of its coverage, federal aid under the Area Redevelopment Act to revitalize the economies of areas with large and persistent unemployment.

In opposition to political factors that seem to favor equalization, there are some very stubborn economic factors that seem to be headed in quite the other direction. For many years now, unskilled workers have been a declining part of the American labor force. This fact has been documented over and over again. Between 1940 and 1950 and again between 1950 and 1960 only one nonfarm occupation group for men—laborers—declined in number at a time when all other groups were increasing. Their income changed erratically. Laborers had the greatest relative income gains during the forties and the smallest relative gains during the fifties. This could mean that unskilled labor was in very short supply during World War II, with millions of young men away in the armed forces and the economy working at full steam. This pressure, with a little help from the government, forced wage rates up more for unskilled workers than for other workers. Since the fifties, on the other hand, there is evidence that the supply of unskilled labor has far exceeded the demand. As a result the unskilled are finding it increasingly difficult to locate jobs and many who are employed live in constant fear of being replaced by machines. Moreover, the overabundance of these workers has prevented their wages from keeping pace with the others; thus the gap between the earnings of skilled and unskilled has widened.

The American economy has been plagued by relatively high unemployment since late 1957. According to the Joint Economic Committee, which has studied this problem in some detail, it is still premature to attribute this unemployment to the technological changes that are rapidly reshaping the economy. However, there can be no doubt that many thousands of unskilled workers in farming, manufacturing, mining, and railroads have been permanently displaced by machines and that this trend will continue. The labor-union leaders who represent these workers certainly tend to view the problem in this light. Even if they do not qualify as impartial observers, they know how these economic developments are interpreted at the grass-roots level. The leader of the Transport Workers Union of America, Michael Quill, is one among many who have spoken out sharply. His words carry a defiant ring that has been virtually absent from the American scene for over twenty years. He stated: "Unless something is done to put people to work despite automation, they may get rough in this country and this country may have a real upheaval, a real turmoil." The increase in racial tension and juvenile delinquency during the past few years may be early manifestations of trouble to come.

Labor-union leaders are not the only ones who have shown a keen awareness of both the bogey and the boon of automation. Many who have given the matter serious thought find it conceivable that, in the absence of remedial action, this nation may soon be faced with an increase in the disparity of incomes. We may then discover that our "social revolution" has not only been marking time for nearly twenty years, but that it is beginning to move backward. Justice William O. Douglas has spoken out eloquently on this subject in the pamphlet *Freedom of the Mind:* "We have a surplus of everything—including unemployed people; and the hundreds of unemployed and unemployable will increase if technology continues to be our master. We have a surplus of food and millions of hungry people at home as well as abroad. When the machine displaces man and does most of the work, who will own the machines and receive the rich dividends? Are we on the threshold of re-entering the world of feudalism which Europe left in the 15th and 16th centuries and which is fastened on much of the Middle East today?"

THE PUBLIC FACILITIES GAP

MARVIN FRIEDMAN

THE GROWTH OF PUBLIC FACILITIES AND PUBLIC SERVICES IN AMERICA
has not measured up to the needs of a steadily growing, increasingly urban population. Despite a stepped-up effort in recent years, there is still a sizable backlog of unmet needs.

With the population continuing to grow—and with more and more people crowding into urbanized areas—these needs also will continue to grow. The nation will require still more in the way of public facilities and public services. And the only way these needs can be met is by substantially increased outlays for these purposes by government—federal, state and local.

In a very real sense, the pressure for expanded public facilities and public services stems from technological progress. This is no longer a nation of farmers as it was at the turn of the century, when approximately 40 percent of the employed manpower was engaged in agriculture. Today, because of improved technology, it takes only about 5 percent of the workforce to produce enough food for the population—and a considerably larger population at that. In 1900, this was a nation of 75 million; now there are nearly 200 million people in the United States.

There has been a steady movement of people off the farms and into the growing industrial and commercial areas. The growing numbers that first crowded into the cities has overflowed into the suburbs—into one suburb after another, stretching the urban area

From Marvin Friedman, "The Public Facilities Gap," *The American Federationist*: 74, 3:6–11, March 1967. Reprinted by permission of the *AFL-CIO American Federationist*.

far beyond the boundaries of the central city and leading to the suburban sprawl.

At the turn of the century, less than one-half of the nation's population lived in such urbanized areas. Now the figure is around 70 percent and still climbing. By 1980, it will be close to 80 percent, but of a much larger population—250 million. And, by the year 2000—when the population is expected to reach 350 million —one estimate places the urbanized portion at 95 percent.

The growth of urban areas—together with the greater aspirations—has led to a growing demand for public facilities and public services: paved streets and highways; bridges and tunnels; storm sewers and sanitary sewers; schools, colleges and libraries; hospitals and clinics; police and fire protection; public utilities; parks, playgrounds and recreation centers; airports; museums and theaters; clean air and clean water; public transportation.

Some of these public services are provided mainly by private businesses for a profit. This is true, for example, in the case of gas and electric utilities. These are usually, but not always, privately-owned operations.

And some are provided by so-called private, nonprofit organizations. Many hospitals fall into this category.

But for most of these services, and for the facilities they require, people depend upon government—mainly state and local government, with a helping hand from the federal government.

A TEN-YEAR PROGRAM

For many years, when the Depression and World War II caused shortages of money, manpower or materials, these public needs went neglected. And programs initiated since the end of the war have hardly reduced the backlog. Of the nation's public schools, for example, 14 percent were built before 1920, while 15 percent of the libraries date from before the turn of the century.

Meanwhile, the needs have continued to grow and they will keep on growing. A reluctance to spend enough money to meet these needs has been the basic problem. But it has not been the only one.

There also has been a lack of information. That is to say, detailed estimates of the full range of needs have been non-existent, especially as regards estimates of future needs. And without such data, long-range planning—the only effective way to meet these needs—is next to impossible.

A major step in closing this gap has recently been taken. Thanks to the efforts of the Joint Economic Committee of Congress, there exists now a pretty solid blueprint—projected to 1975—of state and local public facility needs. It provides the basis upon which to embark on a long-range, planned program to meet those needs —to catch up with the present backlog and meet the future needs as the population grows.

The information contained in the Committee's study, which is titled "State and Local Public Facility Needs and Financing," represents the findings of experts in their respective fields.

And it is comprehensive, covering needs in about 40 different kinds of public facilities: basic community facilities, such as water supply, sewers and waste treatment; transportation facilities, such as roads, turnpikes, tunnels and airports; educational facilities, including all levels of schools as well as college housing; health facilities, such as medical schools, hospitals and clinics; recreation and cultural facilities, including neighborhood centers, arenas and auditoriums; and public buildings, such as jails, fire stations, armories and courthouses.

The study does not deal with housing and urban renewal, important though these items may be. They were regarded as outside the scope of the definition of public facilities. Moreover, the projected cost estimates contained in the study cover only the capital outlays for the facilities—the costs of construction and equipment. They do not include the cost of providing the services —the additional teachers, doctors, policemen and numerous other personnel—after the facilities are built.

Nor is it beyond the realm of possibility that the experts have underestimated state and local public facility needs. "It is conceivable," the introduction to the study says, "that many of the chapter authors preferred to employ conservative judgments . . ."

Even at that, the experts believe that state and local governments will have to step up their public facility capital outlays considerably if they are to meet these needs. In 1965, these expenditures came to $20 billion. By 1975, they will have to total more than $40 billion. And, over the entire 10 years, the experts estimate that state and local governments will be required to spend a grand total of $328 billion to finance public facility needs.

Viewed against a backdrop of needs and capabilities, these projected figures are not as large as they initially appear.

In the first place, these exists a substantial backlog of sorely-needed facilities.

Second, the population, which totalled under 195 million in 1965, is expected to reach 230 million by 1975 and the proportion of the population crowding into urbanized areas will continue to increase. And, finally, by 1975 the total output of the nation's economy, assuming continued high levels of employment, will be in the vicinity of $1,250 billion per year—as against $680 billion in 1965.

Thus state and local expenditures of $40 billion per year for public facilities would not represent a significantly greater rate of spending—in terms of the nation's output—than did the $20 billion in 1965.

Funds for these outlays come essentially from three sources—borrowing, taxes and other current revenues such as user charges, and federal grants-in-aid.

In the recent past, borrowed money has provided about 50 percent of the needed funds. Taxes and other current revenues have accounted for 30 percent and federal grants produced the remaining 20 percent.

On the assumption that high levels of economic activity are maintained, the report of the Committee anticipates that these sources will be adequate to finance the needed increase in outlays. That is to say, with adequate economic growth these outlays can be met in the future in much the same way that they have been in the past and without any greater strain.

In other words, the nation is fully capable of meeting its rapidly-growing needs for additional public facilities.

THE EMPLOYMENT IMPACT

As a matter of fact, a stepped-up, planned program to meet the needs in public facilities—not only state and local, but also federal—will be required in the years ahead to provide jobs for a rapidly-growing workforce. Over the next decade, the labor force will increase by about 1.5 million workers per year and, unless the number of job opportunities keeps pace, unemployment will rise. A logical policy would be to see to it that these two needs—

the growing need for jobs and the pressing need for public facilities—are brought together in a planned program.

The employment impact of these construction activities is substantial. The U.S. Bureau of Labor Statistics has estimated that each million dollars spent in this way creates approximately 100 jobs for the year—about 40 jobs at the construction site and about 60 jobs in industries supplying building materials, equipment and services, including unskilled and semiskilled jobs badly needed in the automated economy.

Moreover, to this must be added the indirect impact—that is, the impact felt as a result of the wages and salaries paid to these workers. As these wages and salaries are spent, retail sales are increased and still more jobs are created—in stores and warehouses and in companies producing consumer goods. This adds another 50 to 100 full-time jobs.

This would mean that $1 billion spent on public facility construction is worth 100,000 jobs directly created on the construction site and in the production and distribution of equipment and materials, plus somewhere between 50,000 to 100,000 more jobs as a result of the increased sales to consumers.

It is obvious from these figures that outlays for these public facilities have a significant employment impact. But the basic reason for these outlays is to provide much-needed public services. And with the growth of the nation and its urban areas, these needs will grow.

It might be well to take a look at a few types of state and local public facilities—and at how much capital outlays will have to be increased, according to the estimates of the Joint Economic Committee's experts, if the needs of the people are to be met.

PUBLIC WATER SUPPLY

Not too many years ago, most Americans took their water from wells or springs. As a matter of fact, not much before the turn of the century, the public water supply system served only about one-third of the population. Today, it serves about 80 percent and it will grow. Increasingly, Americans are getting their water supply by turning on a faucet.

But it costs money to put that water, literally, at the consumer's fingertips.

It first has to be taken from its source and this may necessitate the construction of dams or the creation of reservoirs. Then it must be transported and this means pumping stations and pipe-lines. And it is usually transported first to treatment plans—another expense—because even water of excellent quality very likely needs a disinfectant as a safeguard. And, if it is not of excellent quality, it requires much more extensive treatment to make it safe and palatable.

When the water is ready for consumption, it goes through the distribution system and that system requires pumping and storage facilities and water mains.

In 1965, state and local governments spent just over $1 billion in capital outlays on such public water supply systems. The needs estimated for 1975 will require $2.25 billion. And, from 1966 to 1975, the total amount that will have to be spent by state and local governments for these capital outlays will be roughly $19.5 billion.

STORM SEWERS

If getting water to the urbanized population represents a problem and an expense, so does getting rid of an excess amount. It is estimated that the failure to provide adequately for the runoff—that is, to provide enough storm sewers—costs the nation about $1 billion per year in property loss. The Joint Economic Committee described the problem this way:

"Inadequate disposal of runoff often results in widespread loss of valuable time and frequently causes great inconvenience to urban populations. This is characterized by persons arriving late to places of employment, or perhaps not reporting at all, because of delays in transportation caused by street flooding, or resulting from the need to care for property being endangered by flooding.

"Flooding of basements can result from unsatisfactory or non-existent storm sewer systems. The results may vary, from mere inconvenience and loss of use of basement facilities, upward to very serious threats to health and safety. The extensive use of combined sewers presents a threat of disease to the helpless public in such areas.

"In commercial areas, where food may be served in basement cafeterias and restaurants, such basement flooding admits sewage which could cause disease to spread rapidly to many persons and, if communicable, thence to others over wide geographic areas.

"In industrial and commercial areas, basement flooding from combined sewers frequently causes serious damage to mechanical, electrical and processing equipment, such as power generating equipment, heating and cooling equipment, transformers, mechanical shop equipment and stored equipment, goods and supplies."

And, the report points out, "the present rate of industrial expansion and population growth in urban areas [will very likely mean] an increase in losses due to such property damage."

The cost to state and local governments to meet the nation's needs in storm sewers, in order to cope with the runoff problem, will grow substantially. The needed capital outlays estimated for 1975 will be about $1.8 billion—in contrast to 1965 outlays of approximately $400 million. The total amount required for the 10 years between 1966 and 1975 is estimated at $16 billion.

WASTE DISPOSAL

Inadequate facilities for the disposal of waste are a danger to health and safety. And with the continued growth of the population in urban areas, and with increased industrialization, the need for expanded and improved facilities also grows.

Facilities to dispose of this human and industrial waste include sanitary sewer collection systems as well as waste treatment plants. The waste must be subjected to extensive treatment so its subsequent discharge will not be a health hazard.

According to the report of the Joint Economic Committee, existing combined sewer systems—that is, systems used both for water runoff and for waste—constitute "the single largest problem involving adequate sewage collection facilities which must be resolved. . . ."

In 1965, state and local government capital outlays for sanitary sewers amounted to $385 million and outlays for waste treatment plants amounted to $625 million. To meet the projected needs, these figures will have to rise, respectively, to $1.1 billion and $1.2 billion in 1975. Over the 10-year period, the total outlays required for these two types of facilities are estimated at more than $17.5 billion.

PUBLIC ELEMENTARY AND
SECONDARY SCHOOLS

In the postwar period, there has been a tremendous upsurge in enrollments in public elementary and secondary schools. In contrast to the 25 million pupils who attended public schools in 1947, enrollments in 1965 reached 42 million. The estimate for 1975 is 48 million.

Despite the increase in state and local outlays for additional public elementary and secondary school facilities in recent years —the amounts rose from $111 million in 1946 to about $3.7 billion in 1965—not enough has been spent. Millions of children and youths are still being shortchanged on their education because inadequate and overcrowded classrooms lead inevitably to

The Backlog in Classrooms

The Problem   Number of pupils* adversely affected in 1965

Overcrowded classrooms (over national average
    of 27 pupils per room)

Need heating

Built before World War I

Temporary, makeshift or offsite classrooms

Extensive structural deterioration

Using outdoor privies   EACH SYMBOL = 500,000 PUPILS

*The number of pupils cannot be added together since there is duplication. That is, some of the pupils are in classrooms which suffer from more than one of the problems listed. In other problem areas, 185,000 pupils are in schools without running water and 64,000 are in schools lacking electricity.

Source: "State and Local Public Facility Needs and Financing," Joint Economic Committee of the Congress, December 1966, p. 347.

inferior education. And these are the conditions that presently prevail.

The estimate of the number of classrooms needed depends upon the standards used concerning the number of pupils per room. The U.S. Office of Education, in a chapter written for the Joint Economic Committee study, applied as a standard the present national average of 27 pupils per room. As a result, it estimates that 107,000 classrooms are needed now to handle overcrowding.

This is a highly conservative estimate. Many education experts, including those in the AFL-CIO, believe the present national average itself represents general overcrowding. The AFL-CIO estimate of needs to deal with overcrowded rooms—based on 25 elementary school pupils per room and 20 high school pupils per room—is 286,000 classrooms, considerably in excess of the 107,000 rooms suggested by the Office of Education.

Regardless, however, of which estimate one accepts, it is obvious there is at this time a substantial backlog of classrooms needed simply to deal with overcrowding.

But this is only a small part of the total backlog. According to the Office of Education, there is, in addition, a need for nearly 200,000 classrooms to replace existing facilities that ought to be abandoned because they are unfit. While the exact number of youngsters subjected to schooling under these conditions cannot be determined, it runs in the millions.

All told, the Office of Education places the nation's need for new public elementary and secondary school classrooms at 750,000 over the next 10 years. Of this number, 300,000 would be required to cope with the present backlog and 350,000 to take care of increased enrollment. The remaining 100,000 will be needed to replace facilities which will become outmoded.

In order to meet these needs, state and local outlays for public elementary and secondary classroom construction will have to rise to $5.3 billion by 1975. In 1965, the outlays came to $3.7 billion. Over the entire 10-year period, the amount which will be required totals $42 billion.

Included in these figures are outlays for area vocational schools. Over the 10 years between 1965 and 1975, capital expenditures for these facilities will absorb over $6 billion of the $42 billion total.

In recent years, there has been a growing recognition of the need to modernize vocational education. The quality of the training has left much to be desired and, as a consequence, too many youngsters have been turned out inadequately prepared for the modern job market.

Area schools are essential to this effort to improve vocational training because, for many occupations, facilities for small numbers of students cannot be economically provided. The cost involved for adequately-equipped shops and laboratories—if students are to be trained for some of the better jobs in a highly-automated economy—makes it necessary to develop more of such facilities on an area basis.

HIGHER EDUCATION

In part reflecting greater aspirations as a people, an ever-growing number of young people are attending college. And, while a substantial number seek their higher education in private schools, the large majority depend upon publicly-supported institutions.

In 1955, publicly-supported institutions of higher education—four-year colleges and junior colleges—had approximately 1.5 million students enrolled. By 1965, this figure had risen to more than 3.5 million. And in the years ahead it is expected to increase still further, by about 5 percent per year.

If this growing demand for higher education opportunities is to be met, state and local governments will have to spend $13.9 billion for academic facilities during the 1966–75 decade. And, in addition, another $6.1 million will be required in order to provide housing and related facilities for the students. As a result, outlays for academic and housing facilities will have to climb from approximately $1.2 billion in 1965 to nearly $2.5 billion in 1975.

HEALTH FACILITIES

According to the projected needs, state and local capital outlays for health facilities will have to reach $1.7 billion in 1975. In 1965, these outlays amounted to $500 million.

The growing needs in this field reflect both the growth of the population and the growth of aspirations. An ever-growing number of people are intent upon receiving the best possible health care and existing facilities in many instances are either inadequate or overburdened.

Although most of the hospitals in the country are not governmentally operated, a substantial number—approximately 25 percent of the total—are operated by state and local governments. Over the decade of 1966–75, total capital outlays by states and localities to provide the additional facilities that will be required will come to nearly $4 billion.

The health needs of the people also will compel state and local governments to step up outlays for many other health-related facilities, such as clinics, mental health centers, medical research facilities and medical schools.

The total capital outlays by state and local governments for all types of health facilities in order to meet the growing needs of the people will have to reach over $13 billion during 1966–75.

TRANSPORTATION

As a people on wheels, Americans depend heavily on highways, roads and streets—to move commerce, to get to work, to take care of chores and to enjoy leisure hours. And since people are so dependent on a big and growing network of highways and streets, it is not at all surprising that these types of facility should represent a fairly substantial expenditure by state and local governments.

In 1965, $7.9 billion was spent by state and local governments for road construction. In order to meet estimated needs for 1975, the annual expenditure should be over $15 billion, or not quite double the rate of spending in 1965. And over the 10-year period of 1966 to 1975, the total outlays—if expected needs are to be met—will have to be more than $121 billion.

The nation's transportation needs, however, do not end with highways, roads and streets. They include bridges and tunnels and parking facilities, as well as airports and marine port facilities. During the 10 years of 1966–75, state and local capital outlays to meet these needs are estimated to total nearly $12 billion.

Moreover, several million Americans, especially those living in the urbanized areas, depend daily on mass transit facilities. The fact that a declining number of people rely on such public service—while a growing number have turned to the automobile—does not mean that mass transit is any less of a problem. Service is generally inadequate and fares constantly rise and, as a result, more and more people turn to the automobile. As the number of riders shrink, the fares go up again, and service may be reduced. This forces still more commuters to turn to the automobile.

One end result of all this is substantially increased automobile traffic and frequent traffic jams—and the demand for still more roads and highways which, of course, means more spending.

Congress finally recognized the transportation plight of the urban-area dweller in adopting the 1964 Urban Mass Transportation Act. As a result, federal grants are now available to aid state and local governments in connection with capital outlays for mass transit facilities.

In 1965, state and local governments spent $242 million in capital expenditures for urban mass transit facilities. In order to meet the needs estimated for 1975, spending for these purposes will have to climb to nearly $1 billion in that year. The total cost projected for the entire 10-year period is about $5 billion.

THE NEED FOR
LONG-RANGE PLANNING

These are but a few examples of growing public facility needs and the estimates of experts as to how much they will cost. And, as the urbanization process continues and as the population grows, these needs also will continue to grow. And they will grow also because man's aspirations—spurred on by scientific and technological advances—will continue to rise.

President Johnson in 1965 called the city and its suburbs "a community for the enrichment of the life of man." But it can be this only if it serves his wants—only if it helps to make his life more pleasant. And, in the crowded, urbanized areas—indeed, also in the less crowded areas—this cannot be done without adequate attention to needed public services. And these require public facilities.

The fact that the nation has the capability—the money, manpower and materials—in no way guarantees that these needs will be met. There is still the problem of commitment and planning. That is, government at all levels still must make the decision to meet the needs and this can be done effectively only if there is adequate long-range planning.

The study of the Joint Economic Committee has provided numbers in the aggregate. What is sorely needed at this point are the details—state by state, community by community. The federal government should lose no time in urging these other governmental units to come up with the specific projects, based on their anticipated needs over the next decade.

The federal government can then plan ahead in terms of its grant-in-aid programs. During the current year, federal grants to help state and local governments with capital outlays for public facilities approximate $4.9 billion. In the years ahead, this figure will obviously have to increase considerably in view of the expected growth in public facility needs.

The development of such an inventory and a long-range planned program has been long advocated by the AFL-CIO. In its policy resolution on "Public Investment to Meet America's Needs," the 1965 AFL-CIO convention declared:

"A vast and planned national effort, under federal leadership, is needed to apply as much of our resources as possible to meet these [public] needs within a reasonable period of years. Such effort should be based on a national inventory of needs in the various categories. . . .

"The AFL-CIO urges the federal government to develop, coordinate and maintain a national inventory of needs . . . based on present backlogs and future population growth. Each state and metropolitan area should be encouraged to develop an inventory of needs within its geographical jurisdiction, in addition to the development of a coordinated national inventory, prepared by the federal government.

"Such comprehensive inventory of needs should provide the foundation for nationwide programs in each category—based on federal financial and technical assistance to the state and local governments, including federal grants-in-aid and guaranteed loans, as well as direct federal efforts. Target dates should be established for achieving specified objectives and the pace should be speeded up or slowed down, depending upon changes in defense requirements and the availability of manpower and productive capacity.

"We urge the federal government, the states and metropolitan

Public Facility Needs: Projected Capital Outlays of State and Local Public Agencies

(Dollars in Millions)

	1965 Actual	1975 Estimated to Meet Needs	Percent Increase in Annual Outlays 1975 vs 1965	1966-75 Estimated 10-Year Total
BASIC COMMUNITY FACILITIES				
Regional and river basin water supply systems	$2	$30	1,400%	$170
Public water supply systems	1,040	2,250	116	19,440
Rural-agriculture water supply systems	*	140	*	1,100
Sanitary sewer collection systems	385	1,090	183	7,750
Storm sewer systems	417	1,820	336	16,000
Water waste treatment plants	625	1,240	98	9,830
Solid wastes collection and disposal facilities	130	270	108	2,170
Electric power	766	1,350	76	12,250
Gas distribution systems	44	70	59	550
Subtotal, basic community facilities	**$3,409**	**$8,260**	**142%**	**$69,260**
TRANSPORTATION FACILITIES				
Highways, roads, and streets	7,782	15,330	97	121,650
Toll bridges, tunnels, and turnpikes	388	500	29	4,000
Offstreet parking facilities	102	300	194	2,400
Urban mass transit facilities	242	960	297	7,600
Airport facilities	261	530	103	4,980
Marine port facilities	159	50	(−)69	430
Subtotal, transportation	**$8,934**	**$17,670**	**98%**	**$141,069**
EDUCATION FACILITIES				
Public elementary and secondary schools	3,650	4,480	23	35,500
Area vocational school facilities	**	790	*	6,300
Academic facilities for higher education	915	1,750	91	13,870
College housing and related service facilities	301	720	139	6,080
Educational television	5	30	500	230
Subtotal, educational facilities	**$4,871**	**$7,770**	**60%**	**$61,980**

* Not available.
** Included in Public Elementary and Secondary Schools.

SOURCE: "State and Local Public Facility Needs and Financing"; Joint Economic Committee of the Congress; December 1966, Vol. I, Pages 24-25.

(Dollars in Millions)

	1965 Actual	1975 Esti- mated to Meet Needs	Percent Increase in Annual Outlays 1975 vs 1965	1966-75 Esti- mated 10-Year Total
HEALTH FACILITIES				
Hospitals	⎫	480	*	3,930
Clinics and other outpatient facilities	⎪	100	*	810
Long-term care facilities	⎬ 494	130	*	1,060
Community mental health centers	⎭	220	*	1,470
Facilities for the mentally retarded	34	130	282	1,070
Health research facilities	*	240	*	1,920
Medical and other health schools	*	360	*	2,880
Subtotal, health facilities	**$528**	**$1,660**	**214%**	**$13,140**
RECREATIONAL AND CULTURAL FACILITIES				
State and Federal outdoor recreation facilities	313	530	69	4,400
Urban local outdoor recreation facilities	360	2,200	511	17,600
Arenas, auditoriums, exhibition halls	600	910	52	7,200
Theaters and community art centers	*	460	*	3,620
Museums	14	40	186	270
Public libraries	103	240	133	1,910
Subtotal, recreation and cultural	**$1,390**	**$4,380**	**215%**	**$35,000**
OTHER PUBLIC BUILDINGS				
Residential group care facilities for children	*	70	*	560
Armories	1	15	1,400	150
Jails and prisons	*	120	*	920
Fire stations	191	170	(−)11	1,370
Public office and court buildings	218	400	84	3,250
Other	214	*	*	*
Subtotal, other public buildings	**$410**	**$775**	**89%**	**$6,250**

government authorities to develop such inventories of needs in housing, community facilities and public services as soon as possible and to move ahead rapidly, with sufficient funds and resources, to meet the requirements of a rapidly growing, urban population."

Each year the needs increase. There is more and more pressure for additional facilities to catch up with the backlog and to provide for growth. These needs can be met effectively only by a planned national effort, with vigorous federal leadership and financial aid.

THE ANNOTATED
GREAT SOCIETY
DICTIONARY

EDWARD S. HERMAN

This short work was inspired by Ambrose Bierce's Devil's Dictionary, along with a Great Society environment strongly conductive to a Biercian view of the world. That great cynic would have had a field day in our age of the welfare-warfare state, the credibility gap and the manipulated consensus, of over-kill and the doomsday machine.

In the absence of the master I have put together a collection of definitions, more or less in the Biercian style. They differ from those in the original in the substitution of learned footnotes and a touch of the didactic for Bierce's purer cynicism and original verse—a sorry exchange, but inescapable for an academician anxious to bring home the fact that Double-Speak is reality, and that the meaning and interpretation of an evolving Great Society language cannot be unjoined from the actions of the state which determine them.

• • •

ACHESON, Dean, n. An influential statesman noted for his advocacy of negotiations at some future date from a position of strength still to be attained.[1] (See, "Negotiations.")

From Edward S. Herman, "The Annotated Great Society Dictionary," *Viet-Report*, 3, 3:27–30, June–July, 1967. Reprinted by permission of *Viet-Report*, New York.

[1] "We are ready to negotiate, but not at the expense of rousing false hopes which would be dashed by new failures. . . . The only way to deal with the Soviet Union, we have found from hard experience, is to create situations of strength" (Speeches of Dean Acheson reprinted in the *Dept. of State Bull*, March 20 and March 27, 1950).

AGGRESSION, n. Providing aid and comfort to the side that we oppose.[2]

ALLIANCE FOR PROGRESS, n. A program for the export of soft soap to Latin America. Its Spanish translation, "La Alianza Para El Progreso," means "The Alliance stops progress."[3]

ANTI-COMMUNISM, n. The accelerator in the souped-up American model of "containment" (q.v.). Without any particular goal, this hot-rod tends to end up against a telephone pole.

ATTACK, SNEAK, n., adj. A successful enemy foray, especially late at night,[4] for which we are unprepared. Syn.—underhanded, cowardly, dirty. (See, "Terrorism.")

ATTACK, CONVENTIONAL, n., adj. Dropping bombs on unprotected enemy villages from 20,000 feet.[5] Syn.—provoked, retaliatory, in measured response. (See, "Retaliation.")

BACKLASH, n. The surfacing of some large, partially submerged lumps in the melting pot, upon a brief but vigorous stirring of the ladle.

---

[2] In June 1966, Senator Mike Mansfield stated (and a spokesman for the Department of Defense subsequently confirmed) that at the time of the escalation of the war to North Vietnam in February 1965 there were about 400 North Vietnamese troops in South Vietnam. At that time there were over 23,000 uniformed Americans in South Vietnam (*Washington Daily News*, June 23, 1966).

[3] "The inability to score a success even in the public relations aspect of the Alliance was especially noteworthy because with the ignorance which had marked the U.S. economic policy determinations, this was alone the field where a measure of success might have been expected. As Senator Case . . . has noted when asked whether he thought the Johnson Administration had lost ground in its appeal to the great mass of the Latin American people . . . 'I don't think the Kennedy Administration achieved very much. I think its heart was in the right place but I don't think we got very far frankly. It was more a public relations matter.' Yet, even the public relations effort failed" (Simon G. Hanson, "The Alliance For Progress: The Fourth Year," *Inter-American Economic Affairs*, Autumn, 1966, p. 8).

[4] Speaking of the Vietcong attack at Pleiku, in early February 1965, Secretary McNamara stated that "The fact is that the attack was carried out in the dead of night; it was a sneak attack" (*N.Y.T.*, 2/8/65).

[5] "I is fortunate that young pilots can get their first taste of combat under the direction of a forward air controller over a flat country in bright sunshine where nobody is shooting back with high-powered ack-ack. He learns how it feels to drop bombs on human beings and watch huts go up in a boil of orange flame when his aluminum napalm tanks tumble into them. He gets hardened to pressing the firing button and cutting people down like little cloth dummies as they spring frantically under them" (Frank Harvey, in *Flying Magazine*, Nov. 1966).

BATISTA, FULGENCIO, n. Once manager of a former American owned vacation resort.

"BAY OF TONKIN PRINCIPLE," A military action against the Communist Enemy (for whatever reason) which will raise a President's ranking in public opinion polls.[6] This effect is transitory, however, and increased doses are required for successive poll-raising effects.

BRAUN, WERNER VON, n. Formerly, Professor of Explosives, University of Heidelberg; a lecturer on democracy and the Free World.

CALCULATED RISK, adj., n. An incalculable risk.

CHINA, n. A non-existent country with 700 million inhabitants.

COMMITMENT, n. Among the multitude of promises made and obligations incurred in the past, the one consistent with the line of action now planned. Sometimes a purely hypothetical obligation, self-imposed to lend moral sanction to actions decided upon today; in this case it is referred to as a "solemn commitment."[7] Syn.—Preference.

COMMUNISM, n. The totalitarianism of the countries outside of the Free World. (See, "Junta.")

CONSENSUS, n. The position taken by the government; quickly established by means of Public Information (q.v.) dispensed by a Responsible Press. (See, "Responsible.")

CONTAINMENT, n. The exclusion of lesser powers from areas in which we intend to maintain hegemony. Syn.—Expansion.

CREDIBILITY, n. The public's capacity for absorbing official lies; subject to the law of diminishing returns.[8]

---

[6] The Harris poll, taken shortly after the Bay of Tonkin incidents, indicated that "The Vietnam action has brought President Johnson up from 45 percent of the vote in the South to an even 50-50" (*Phila. Inquirer,* 8/14/64).
[7] "Our present commitment to oppose force and terror by the National Liberation Front in South Vietnam is as solemn an engagement as any modern nation has made" (Herman Kahn, *Look Magazine,* 8/9/66). Mr. Kahn does not indicate when or where this commitment was entered into; nor does he discuss its possible conflict with other unmentioned but more explicit agreements, such as the U.N. Charter and the Geneva Accords.
[8] On December 19, 1965, Ambassador Arthur J. Goldberg stated that "We have had a great problem here maintaining our credibility with our own people" (*N.Y.T.,* 12/20/65). This was followed almost immediately by a "peace offensive," described by one reporter as a "virtually public campaign of propaganda and psychological warfare to win support for the U.S. position and respect for its intentions" (Max Frankel, *N.Y.T.,* 1/5/66).

DEFENSE DAPARTMENT, n. A huge, blind machine seeking "defensible frontiers." These are now understood to extend at least as far as the moon.

The Defense Department was known in earlier times as the "War Department." After c. 1945 this body did not wage war; instead, it carried out police actions and flexible responses to aggression (q.v.). The change in nomenclature followed the change in function.

DOVE, n. One who favors the last escalation but is opposed to the next.

DRAFT, n. A system of forcible recruitment of military labor, which compels the underprivileged to serve their country at less than market wage rates.

ELECTION, FREE, n., adj. A ceremonial common among higher barbarian societies which creates among the underlying population an illusion of choice and power. This mysterious effect is obtained without the use of hashish or any other drug, merely by the impact of verbal incantations.

ELECTION, "DEMONSTRATION," n. A circus performed in a client state to reassure the populace of the intervening country that their intrusion is well received. The outcome is guaranteed in writing by the authorities of the client and dominant powers.[9]

ENEMY STRUCTURE, adj., n. A thatched hut that we destroy.[10]

ESCALATION, n. A moving stairway leading to Kingdom Come.

FREE, adj. Non-Communist. Syn.—Good.

GENOCIDE, n. The end product of arrogance, dehumanization, and superior force. (See, "Gook.")

GOLDWATERISM, n. Political recklessness, particularly in foreign affairs; named after the defeated Republican candidate for President in the election of 1964, who advocated escalation of the war in Vietnam.

GOOK, n. A small, stubborn, yellow aborigine of Southeast Asia;

[9] "Three months ago an influential American in Saigon confided that there wasn't any danger of 'losing' the promised national election in South Vietnam, adding: 'No hostile government will get in. We'll see to that'" (C. L. Sulzberger, *N.Y.T.*, 7/29/66).

[10] "The (U.S.) planes were credited by military spokesmen with having destroyed or damaged 473 'enemy structures'. . . . According to some American advisors to Vietnamese military units, 'enemy structures' . . . include civilian houses. Once destroyed, they are listed as 'enemy structures'" (Charles Mohr, *N.Y.T.*, 8/9/66).

lacking modern technology this inferior breed faces extinction. (See, "Genocide.")

GREAT SOCIETY, n. The biggest bull in the china shop. Unfortunately for the shop, as well as the china, this bull goes berserk at the sight of the color red.

HITLER, ADOLF, n. A premature anti-Communist.

HUMPHREY, HUBERT HORATIO, n. Deputy Sheriff of Johnson County. "His not to reason why; his but to cheer and lie" ("Charge of the Great Society Brigade," stanza 12).

INDEPENDENT, n. Aligned with us. (See, "Satellite.")

JUNTA, n. The principal form of government of the Free World.[11]

LAND REFORM, adj., n. Generally, redistributing the land of inactive and absentee landlords to those working the soil; in South Vietnam, taking land formerly redistributed to the peasantry and giving it back to the landlords.[12]

---

[11] On departing from South Vietnam, ex-Ambassador Lodge presented the American philosophy of the military junta (and the case for retaining General Ky at the helm):

> Certainly the biggest nation-building entity is the military. Also, it has the reservoir of administrative talent . . . I grant you, ideally speaking it is better for the military not to get into those things, and it's better for the community not to have the military do them. But in a country at this stage of development (i.e. South Vietnam) they must do it. . . . So, I believe the military must be a participant in the Government here in the future" (*N.Y.T.*, 4/26/67).

[12] "Usually it is the tenants who are most eager for land reform and landlords who are reluctant. In the southern half of Vietnam, however, the landlords are accepting the Government's land reform more readily than the tenants" (*N.Y.T.*, 4/5/55).

No land had in fact been distributed since Diem's "Reform" validated the landlords' seizure of land redistributed to peasants by the Vietminh. Nine years later, a *Wall Street Journal* report stated: "Lang Anh Province just Southwest of Saigon is a potentially rich area. . . . But prosperity hasn't touched most of the 300,000 inhabitants. Many live on small plots of rented land and pay 50-75% of their crops to the landlords" (*W.S.J.*, 6/15/64).

Two years later: "In the secure areas, tenant farmers—that means 70% of the farmers in the Delta—still are forced to pay up to 50% and more of their rice crops to absentee landlords who have absolutely no obligation in return" (*U.S. News & World Report*, 12/5/66).

The truth today is even more devastating: "Absentee landlords are still riding with pacifying troops, not merely to grab their lands but to extort back rents for the time they fled the Vietcong" (Fred Emery, Saigon correspondent of the *London Times*, 3/10/67).

Land reform is virtually non-existent in South Vietnam—except that which enriches the old landlords. Why? As Richard Critchfield notes, it is because "most of the military officers, civil servants, and community leaders come from the land-owning gentry" (Washington *Evening Star*, 1/24-27/66).

LIBERAL, n. A responsible critic and reformer. (See, "Responsible.")

LIE, n. An official pronouncement.

MC NAMARA, ROBERT, n. A computer in search of a program.[13]

NAPALM, n. A fire bomb which, when dropped on villages, burns to death the enemy and spares innocent bystanders. A weapon with the remarkable property of creating two enemies where one existed before.

NATION-BUILDING, n. Nation-busting. (See, "Junta.")

NATIONALISM, n. Kickapoo war juice. Large quantities are essential to provide the stamina needed for protracted conflict. (See, "Stamina.")

NEGOTIATIONS, n. The process of accepting the surrender of the ill-gotten gains of the enemy. Negotiation in its archaic meaning referred to the process of arriving at a settlement by mutual concessions. This is now recognized to be appeasement. Syn.— Victory.

PACIFICATION, n. Subjugation. Sometimes referred to as "winning the hearts and minds of the people," pacification takes three principal forms: bribery, coercion, and extermination.[14]

PATRIOTISM, n. Judging the merits of disputes on the basis of one's place of birth and residence.[15]

PEACE, n. A temporary lull in armed hostilities to which every politician is sincerely devoted, if deemed consistent with his political advancement.

PROPAGANDA, n. Their lies. (See, "Public Information.")

PUBLIC INFORMATION, n. Our lies. (See, "Propaganda.")

PUSH-BUTTON, n. A mechanism which permits us to achieve re-

[13] Mr. McNamara has moved from the Edsel to the Bay of Pigs to Vietnam, in each case mobilizing with great efficiency the massive forces required for the ensuing fiasco.

[14] "Soon the Government will have no need to win the hearts and minds of Bensuc. There will be no Bensuc." (*N.Y.T.*, 1/11/67).

"Four villages—Bensuc, Rachhap, Bungcong, and Rachkeim—have in fact already ceased to exist. As they left, many of the women saw their homes put to the torch or bulldozed flat. 'I was very poor in my village, but I didn't mind that. I wanted to stay. Last week the fish-shaped planes flew over our fields. My husband didn't know what they were. He stood up and they shot him down and killed him. I wish I had stayed and got killed too" (*N.Y.T.*, 1/15/67).

[15] This is clearly a more objective and scientific definition than that of Dr. Samuel Johnson ("the last refuge of a scoundrel") or Ambrose Bierce ("the first refuge of a scoundrel").

sults without knowledge of the processes involved. (See, "War, Push-Button.")

RESPONSIBLE, adj. Pertaining to the form but not the substance, as "responsible criticism." Also, starting from the premise that those wielding power seek admirable ends which are justified by secret and superior knowledge.

RETALIATION, n. Killing civilians wholesale. (See, "Terrorism.")

REVOLUTION, COMMUNIST, n., adj. The destruction of democracy, freedom, law, order, and the rights and prerogatives of private property, by an unpatriotic clique that is beyond reason or purchase.

REVOLUTION, MILITARY, n., adj. A temporary suspension of representative government by the armed forces, necessitated by imminent Communist subversion. The number of Communist conspirators in these cases is usually firmly established by intelligence reports as increasing on successive days by a factor of three. Free elections are generally scheduled to be resumed by the forces of law and order in from six to eighteen months.

RUSK, DEAN, n. A clock cuckoo that pops out every hour, pecks viciously at a dead field mouse, and pronounces solemnly, "You must leave your neighborhood alone." On Sundays and Holidays the cuckoo appears alone, and states with great sincerity that "We must do unto others as we would have others do unto us."

SATELLITE, n. Aligned with them. (See, "Independent.")

SELF-DETERMINATION, n. The right of a people to select a government acceptable to us.[16]

SINCERITY, n. The last refuge of an apologist for a scoundrel.

STAMINA, n. The capacity to inflict and absorb injury without permitting the intervention of either narrow self-interest or sentimental humanity.

TERRORISM, n. Killing civilians retail. (See, "Retaliation.")

[16] Mr. Lodge stated before a Congressional Committee in the summer of 1965 that the U.S. would not withdraw from South Vietnam even if the government of that country asked us to. This was shortly thereafter amplified by an anonymous "high official" in Washington, who explained that Mr. Lodge meant that we would not leave if asked to do so by a left-wing or even neutralist government that, in the U.S. view, did not reflect the true feelings of the South Vietnamese people or military leaders (*N.Y.T.*, 8/13/65).

VIETCONG, n. A Vietnamese peasant, especially one that we have killed.[17] (See, "Enemy Structure.")

WAR, LIMITED, n., adj. A localized military venture where combat experience can be gained, new weapons tested, surplus military inventories disposed of, and freedom and independence defended, all simultaneously, at a calculated risk (q.v.)

WAR, OF NATIONAL LIBERATION, n. A civil upheaval provoked by gross misgovernment.[18] When inconvenient to a great power, intervention on behalf of the rejected government is carried out on the ground that aid given the rebels by outsiders makes the case one of "aggression." (See, "Aggression.")

WAR ON POVERTY, n. Riot control.

WAR, PUSH-BUTTON, n., adj. A clean war in which damage is inflicted from a distance, on the basis of moral principles, without any unpleasantness disturbing the eyes, ears, nostrils, or hearts of the pushers of buttons. Highly conducive to stamina in doing what must be done to save face, etc.

[17] "When asked by Robert Guillain what proportion of the reported 700 'Vietcong' killed in Operation Masher were civilians, a U.S. military officer replied: 'In a Vietcong area like that one, civilians and military are all the same" (*Le Monde*, Feb. 24–March 2, 1966).

[18] "Behind a facade of photographs, flags and slogans there is a grim structure of decrees, political prisons, concentration camps, milder 're-education centers,' secret police. . . . The whole machinery of security has been used to discourage active opposition of any kind from any source" (*Life Magazine*, describing the Diem government of South Vietnam, 5/13/57).

ALTERNATIVES
AND CHANGE

IS PLANNING
A REVOLUTION?

BOB ROSS

IF NOT TOO LONG AGO MOST AMERICANS AND THEIR LEADERS DID NOT
realize the enormity of their homefront problems, then the fiery
glow of cities by night has enlightened them. Reactions have
been characteristically mixed, but nowhere apathetic—an indication that public intervention in domestic crises will be far more
deliberate and widespread than it ever was during the years of
the Vietnam buildup.

For blacks and major sectors of young people and professionals,
the ghetto explosions have triggered a breakthrough to a new
political awareness of the necessity for genuine resistance movements. Other Americans have substituted alarm at the problem
posed by "riots" in place of concern for the problems which
precipitated them in the first place. Like the British in India,
lower middle and working class white America reasons that it
is better that the law be certain than that it be just. And these
groups are being joined by articulate liberals whose notions of
justice and equality are traditionally dependent upon the preservation of the existing social order.

There are others in Democratic or liberal administrative circles
whose only tradition for reform has been the New Deal and the
incremental perspective that succeeded it. For them radical
changes were expunged as programmatic alternatives when socialism was thought-reformed out of American life. Trapped

From Bob Ross, "Is Planning a Revolution?" *Viet-Report*, Special Urban
Issue, 3, 8–9:8–11, 61. Summer 1968. Reprinted by permission of *Viet-Report*,
New York.

between what they see as the "crazies" on both sides, most are anxious to do good if that is what "fire insurance" and bipartisan foreign policy require—and it appears that it is. It is the efforts of these groups which are beginning to dominate the agencies of social change within America's racially torn, economically blighted cities, just as they once dominated the attempted reconstruction of a collapsed economy in the Thirties. The first task of this paper will be to anticipate and evaluate the impact of their programs on urban America through a study of their defining operational techniques.

THE IDEOLOGY OF PLANNING: WHAT "EFFICIENCY" MEANS

Planning is the more or less efficient and foresightful devising of means to reach specified goals. Aside from military preparations, we have not had much of it in American government. But now wherever one turns a new kind of planning is proposed for solving slum housing, unemployment, consumer exploitation, and the myriad conditions of ghetto oppression.

In the thick undergrowth of the social policy bureaucracies— Departments of Health, Education, and Welfare (HEW), Housing and Urban Development (HUD), Labor, Office of Economic Opportunity (OEO), the Ford Foundation, Rockefeller Fund, departments of urban renewal, city planning, and planning firms —lies a series of responses to the urban crises which, in turn, fascinate, repel and amuse. They all claim to increase the efficiency of social programs but not one challenges the system which creates the crises.

No one does or should expect reformers to be revolutionaries or expect capitalist politicians to assert socialist principles; but even on their terms, can the various attempts to uplift the blacks, clean-up the slums, and re-do the educational system really work? Moreover, at what cost and with what consequences? How efficient *are* the new technocrats?

In recent years systems analysis, cost-benefit analysis (CBA) and planned program budgeting systems (PPBS) have become the new and revered tools of the technocratic planner. Developed by the high technology defense complex, today government, business and municipal leadership look to these tools to locate structural faults and inefficient funding investments in the service bureaucracies.

After a year of listening to government people talk about systems analysis to a group of social work professors and sociology graduate students, this writer concluded that for all the heat there was little light. For hardware systems, or economic models, in which each component of a process can be quantified and controlled, systems analysis had a particular procedural function. As it moves deeper into social and behavioral problem-solving, the variables defy quantification, except arbitrarily. How does one specify a model of a family maintenance system or labor market recruitment system? Systems analysis in social problems is merely an attempt to be rational and complete in visualizing what causes and what might change a given phenomenon. But herein lies the rub. The most creative applications of systems analysis still ignore the ordinary political processes for social change—legislation, lobbying, and social movements—and end up being as utopian as any New Left program for decentralization.

Cost-benefit analysis (CBA), a more modest method, can facilitate certain decision-making processes, but it too fails where it counts the most: in its long-range effects on the social life of individuals and groups.

CBA assigns a cost to each element of a program; it then attempts to assign a monetary value to benefits accruing from the program. For example, a study done in a California county on vocational rehabilitation for welfare recipients was "costed out" by including staff time, use of plant, supplies, etc. Two of the several benefits accruing from the project were measured by the savings in welfare payments to ultimately employed recipients and by the taxes the former recipients would pay on earned-income. The ratio of monetary cost to monetary benefit was found to be 1:37: a finding which, nevertheless, will neither convince nor have meaning for a cost-conscious Congress when it is asked to fund such a program.

What is not measured in CBA studies is far more important to the creation of a society beneficial to all than those limited instances when ability to compare costs and benefits help to decide the monetary worth of a program investment. Can we measure in monetary or any quantifiable terms how much or how little it hurts a mother to work or to stay at home with her fatherless children? In assessing the cost of compulsory assignment to the ghetto of experienced teachers, can we also measure the extent and effect of black children's resentment to having another white person in authority over them? Repeatedly, these important but immeasurable social and political values are the unmentioned ones in CBA studies.

Within the complex of OEO-HEW, the use of monetary measurement of cost and the search for higher benefit to cost ratio, possess systematic biases in the short run which are oppressive in the long run. Specifically, what we should fear from the dominance of CBA is its perpetuation of a permanent underclass. For example, in the rehabilitation project discussed above, the potential participants were screened to insure the highest possible ratio of benefits. Only the most rehabilitatable were chosen, which insured fewer dropouts from the program and more employed participants. The efficiency of picking those who least need a service has a contagious logic. You help those who can use help, the argument goes. But the cumulative effect over time and through many such programs is that the search for efficient use of resources will always leave a bottom of the barrel, a "hopeless" section of the population. Once so designated, they remain hopelessly outside the web of service and justice, hopelessly neglected and, in fact, hopelessly unknown. (The last Census missed a substantial number of unemployed inner city young men.)

The third planning method, PPBS, attempts to use cost-benefit reasoning in the budgeting processes of an administrative agency. This is the system which former Defense Secretary McNamara brought to the Pentagon, and which, by virtue of an Executive Order, will become the standard system in social policy government agencies. Many students of this process have concluded that PPBS is more than a way of justifying decisions to skeptical publics. By proposing an objective way to measure whether one program or another is more efficient in reaching a goal and by positing the goal and finding the cheapest way to attain it, PPBS is an impressive instrument of power in the hands of central budgeting analysts. In fact, it is *the* centralizing mechanism within agencies and a weapon in the fight for power between agencies. It allows an agent of an administrative leader, by virtue of his claim to a sound basis of judgment, to stop one idea, encourage another, and have final say over many.

That a basis for judgment is needed in social policy programs is not denied. Social service workers and the public programs they have for years defended have never developed persuasive empirical justification for any given service program. Even minimum support programs—Aid to Dependent Children, for example— have not successfully accomplished any of its many aims. This is also true of nongovernment social policy planners. In comparison to government planning efforts, they have no particular methodology to integrate social and physical policy. They criticize the bricks and mortar approach but have not come up with an alternative approach. In the face of the government's Model Cities Program, for example (today's most celebrated catch-all program for the inner city), critics appear mute.

Model Cities contains three objectives: (1) to integrate physical and social planning; (2) to provide for citizen participation; and (3) to accomplish physical renewal without displacing poor people. Reasonable, perhaps laudable goals. Yet there is no reason to believe that Model Cities will accomplish a single one of them.

Take the first. In addition to the traditional contest of power between city planners and social policy advocates, there seems to be no systematic link between the two types of development. Do the advocates of the physical/social integration also advocate the development of a different kind of economic base for black communities? No, they promise employment of blacks on prospective construction, although no city mayor has yet begun to do battle with the building trade unions to win even this goal. Occasionally there are sounds about reviving or creating black capitalism for the black community. But is the need really for black grocers, furniture stores, etc.? In an age in which the marginal small businessman is as predatory, or more so, than the big retailing chain, this is an odd benefit to bestow on the exploited black consumer. Or does anyone seriously envision a black IBM rising from the ashes of Watts?

Without a theory of what keeps black people down, of how the whole system works, talk of integrating different types of planning has no content, no concrete meaning.

The second objective, citizen participation, could be important if for no other reason that that it would generate conflict which would be socially educative and a catalyst to organizing in the black community. But participation is not authority. No budgetary power is proposed for the Model Cities Advisory Councils (the name used in Chicago); no actual policy on the use of city resources will be decided by indigenous representatives. At present there is not much hope that *any* decisions at all will be made by "citizens." Fighting in the War on Poverty was also educative: it taught us that the majority of city administrators will struggle, manipulate, dodge, and finally win the battle to keep these power instruments in hands that are friendly and representative of themselves.

Even if honest efforts were made to keep the citizen participation boards in the hands of residents who reflected the diversity of the black communities, and even if "advice" were taken seriously in the absence of power and authority, the idea would still be skewed in the wrong direction. If any community is to decide its fate, it needs a number of things which poor communities often lack; among these is access to technical skills in order to compete with and compel attention from government agencies. Moreover, for citizen participation to be representative and significant the apparatus which organizes it must be as broad and determined as that which induces response to other major political events. Neither of these is part of Model Cities plans. For example, to make the technical prerequisites to participation available would entail the release of funds to the citizens' group so it could hire its own planning firm. To legitimize the granting of this money might require obtaining a percentage of the community's signatures on a petition declaring support for the essential ideas of the group soliciting. And for the participation to be intense every plan would have an alternate; groups given monies for planning would each produce at least one, and the choice between plans might be made at the polls, or town meetings, etc. But this entails a true devolution from white to black power, a democratization of planning which is unlikely to be considered by the Daleys, Yortys or, for that matter, the Stokes of the American cityscape.

There is evidence that Model Cities' third objective represents a sincere effort to avoid massive dislocation. But consider the following situation. A house has an average of 10 six-person families. The 10 families live in 10 units which total, say, 40 rooms. The house will be bought, rehabilitated and then rented by the local housing authority. Part of the rehabilitation goal is to bring the building up to code standards for overcrowding (average 1.01 persons per room). After rehabilitation perhaps only 8 units will be left; in any case, if the code standards are to be maintained, all those families cannot go back. Therefore, dislocation.

There is no substitute for simply increasing the supply of housing for the poor.

SHAPING A CORPORATE CONSTITUENCY

Most modern politicians recognize the limits of all these techniques and programs. Thus many have turned to private business to meliorate the urban crisis. Senator Charles Percy started a Presidential boomlet for himself with a rather ordinary proposal to have government underwrite mortgages for ghetto dwellers of moderate income. The late Robert F. Kennedy raced through Indiana claiming that government can't do everything, that the welfare system was obsolete, that the greatest untapped resource for urban redevelopment was the dynamic of private enterprise. And the Urban Coalition plans to rescue the cities with an alliance comprised of the traditional sources of activist liberalism with the addition of enlightened Corporate Enterprise.

Corporate planners have already taken certain tentative steps. In late 1966 President Johnson moved to generate jobs for the hard-core unemployed through the Concentrated Employment Project (CEP). And ever since it became apparent that the basic development and deployment of missile capability had been managed, science-based aerospace and high technology companies have been taking on urban research and development contracts. In San Diego, Ford engineers are designing a long-range transportation plan; in New Jersey, Litton Industries has taken over a Job Corps camp. All over the country hip young men with a smattering of knowledge about computerized teaching are working on vocational and remedial literacy training.

There are two conditions under which business will welcome or foster both extensions of government subsidies and direct utilization of private enterprise in the realm of social welfare. The first is when domestic crises threaten the foundations of the business system itself, as they did in the dual political and economic crisis of the Great Depression. The second is when business (or the leading sectors of the most advanced industries) believe that certain government policies will lead to secure or attractive profit potentials for themselves—as with the railroad land grants, the land grant colleges, the designation of private insurance companies as carriers of medicare insurance, and the federal insurance of mortgage loans. Each of these conditions obtains today; coupled with the proven incapacity of government welfare programs to meet the needs of the urban poor, they herald a growing investment of corporate planning in the ghettos.

To date, corporate programs have been easy to dismiss as token responses, flashy PR gestures, or simply as irrelevant applications of technology to social conflicts. All this they may be, but the thrust behind them does represent an institutional ideology which stands as a far more compelling feature of the postwar political landscape than the welfare statism of Democratic/liberal circles.

After World War II many articulate spokesmen and analysts from within the business community began to extrapolate the accumulated benefits of the Progressive regulatory period and the New Deal-Fair Deal period, while also taking note of the increased scope of corporate enterprise after vigorous government subsidization for capital expansion during and following the War. Radical thinkers claimed to perceive in this discussion the genesis of a new ideological commitment, which they called corporatism. (In the early Sixties the founders of Students for a Democratic Society argued that "corporatism"—or corporate liberalism—was a distinct ideological formation which represented the gravest threat to those who believed that America needed to *ventilate* not subdue conflict and ideology in the coming years.)

For themselves, the corporate ideologues had mustered an apparently fail-safe social vision. Harmony of interest and the obsolescence of class keynoted the views of theorists like A. A. Berle and the people William B. White addressed in *Is Anybody Listening?* (an earlier and more pointed version of *The Organization Man*). That social stability could be guaranteed by the unique ability of the professional manager was central to this literature. The ability to coordinate facts, human attributes and financial possibilities within workable programs, and to motivate people to fulfill them: these were the qualities which brought the manager to the foremost role in the solution of society's problems. Another feature of the work of these laureates was their clarity about the need for collective identity at a time when the intellectual remnants of reform and liberalism were adrift with hocus-pocus theories of alienation and mass society. The corporatists assumed and/or argued that the corporate entity was a fitting and inevitable base to which the roots of identity could be tied. Industrial civilization could be integrated through love, not of Big Brother, but of The Firm. Finally, not without controversy, the image of the corporation with a soul gained ground. Business could and should assume social responsibility for the survival of a civilization which, after all, business had largely engineered.

Much of this was elaborated when the permanent war economy needed to be rationalized, when institutional public relations was coming of age. Fearful memories of the possibilities of depression radicalism lingered to remind business statesmen that they had to have something more than Hobbesian self-interest to legitimize their privileges in the polity. Berle (in the *Twentieth Century Capitalist Revolution*) noted this, and argued that the chief problem of the future would be the legitimation of the sovereign powers now held, but unjustified, by the corporation.

What is so very interesting about the present spate of corporate rhetoric on the "Urban Crisis" is the consistency with which business has sustained—but also crucially modified—these themes.

The important modification is the new perception exemplified by business leadership as well as by political liberals such as Percy and the authors of the Kerner Commission Report, that the welfare system and, more broadly, the welfare state in its American variant is a failure: it holds no promise of completing its task of creating an egalitarian, uniformly affluent society. There is no articulate sector of the polity that maintains confidence in the New Deal bag of tricks. That is the real reason why corporatism is a relevant discussion and why socialism would be if there were a political base for it. There is no longer an articulate constituency which defines its hopes and aspirations as merely more of the same—more unemployment compensation, social security, etc., etc. Confronted with the nature of black destitution in the ghettos, the integrative social mechanisms which brought immigrant groups and dissident labor into the American mainstream have proved to be irrelevant or impotent, and at worst, explicitly repressive.

The technocrats of systems and cost benefit analyses are beginning to understand this. They seek to harness industry because they have experienced (or anticipate) failure through government welfarism. Their new rhetoric stresses coordination of all efforts, public and private alike. Knowing that the old security planning failed and the new salvage planning is shallow, they look to the efficient corporate managerial planner as a last hope.

But the move from welfare statism to corporatism surely holds no more promise of success. The evidence for this is, literally, the record of our whole civilization. Business can't and won't move into housing or vocational education or preventive medicine unless it can make a good or sure profit. To ensure profit means once again that high risk sectors—in this case, social reconstruction—must be "baited" with government guarantees (tax incentives, cost-plus contracts, and the like). It means that the most intolerable social ills—more often than not, directly traceable to the anti-social priorities of the profit motive itself—will now be sought *for a price*. It means that over and above immobile or inept municipal governments a far more cynical and politically alien system of power will hold sway. But equally persuasive is the simple fact that modern industry, presently organized, has little or nothing to offer the angry poor.

Consider, for example, the problem of "hard core" unemployment. It is becoming increasingly clear that the location, recruitment, "motivation," training and hiring of these young men is next to impossible by any means yet in use. There is no reason to believe that private industry will find people the census missed or train people the militants miss. These members of the underclass will become "employable" when the society seems to be theirs, working in their interests, run by their folk.

The scope of this article does not allow for a developed alternative to the strategies of enlightened businessmen or the new technocrats. A mere suggestion must suffice. If one looks at the experience of China, Cuba, Algeria, one sees that the problems which confronted the revolutionary governments were often similar in content to those facing the American inner city. They faced demoralized populations beset with varying degrees of self-defeating pathologies (drug addiction, prostitution, gambling, unemployment, etc.), and people who had never been governable or "treatable" by the regimes of the past. Chiang could never organize the masses, despite the fact that he attempted to duplicate Leninist organization. It has been reserved for the victories of revolutionaries to introduce the "subjective" tonic. Under a Mao, a Castro or even a Ben Bella, morale could rise rapidly throughout a population. People could and did organize themselves for work and transformation. All being poor they made do with improvised (social and material) instruments and trained themselves quickly for difficult tasks. The difference between a social program and a revolution, as far as poor people are concerned, is the subjective consciousness that in revolution the situation is one which is the people's to define and lead.

Is planning a revolution? One hears the word repeatedly among social policy planners. No meeting on the inner city or on any aspects of welfare is without the incantation to a revolutionary new scheme of service-delivery, or a revolution in development techniques, or a revolutionary proposal for housing. I don't know what the American Revolution will look like. But another system of coordination, or another invitation to private investment—that it is not.

THE GUARANTEED INCOME PROPOSAL

ROBERT THEOBALD

WHAT PRACTICAL STEPS NEED TO BE TAKEN IN ORDER TO REAP THE benefits of the scientific and technological revolution rather than its destructive growths? It is the attempt to keep the economy growing fast enough to provide jobs for all that harnesses man to the juggernaut of scientific and technological change and that keeps us living within "a whirling-dervish economy dependent on compulsive consumption." *This book proposes the establishment of new principles specifically designed to break the link between jobs and income. Implementation of these principles must necessarily be carried out by the government as the sole body concerned with every member of society and with the adequate functioning of the total socioeconomic system.* W. H. Ferry has enlarged on the necessity for "due-income" principles: "Abundance may compel social justice as conscience never has. The liberated margin (those unable to find work) will have to get 'what is its due.' This means developing a basis of distribution of income which is not tied to work as a measure. For decisions about "dueness' will have to be made without economic criteria; at least without the criterion of what members of the liberated margin are worth in the employment market, for there is no such market for them."

In order to ensure that government concern with the total socioeconomic system would not outweigh its responsibility to every member of society, a due-income from government should

From *Free Men and Free Markets* by Robert Theobold. © 1963 by Robert Theobold. Used by permission of Clarkson N. Potter, Inc., New York.

be given as an *absolute constitutional* right; for unless this is guaranteed, the government would have the possibility of developing the most extreme form of tyranny imaginable. During the process of implementation of the due-income principles, the number of people obtaining the totality of their living expenses from the government would increase rapidly; if the right to these incomes could be withdrawn under *any* circumstances, government would have the power to deprive the individual not only of the pursuit of happiness but also of liberty and even, in effect, of life itself. This *absolute right* to a due-income would be essentially a new principle in jurisprudence. Most present constitutional rights can be curtailed when the over-all good of society is held to require this; however, the right of an individual to a due-income could not, in itself, endanger the state.

It is clear that any attempt to break the strangle hold of the job-income link will have to be made with the interests of both the individual and society kept firmly in mind. There is now a growing awareness that in recent years the interest of the individual has been subordinated to the drives of the economy, and that this subordination is withdrawing the values of freedom and human dignity from the lives of a significant proportion of the American population. In an . . . article in *The New Yorker*, Dwight MacDonald outlines the case for a recognition of the necessity to provide for the individual:

> . . . a second line of government policy [is] required; namely, direct intervention to help the poor.
>
> We have had this since the New Deal, but it has always been grudging and miserly, and we have never accepted the principle that every citizen should be provided, at state expense, with a reasonable minimum standard of living regardless of any other considerations.
>
> It should not depend on earnings, as does Social Security, which continues the inequalities and inequities and so tends to keep the poor forever poor. Nor should it exclude millions of our poorest citizens because they lack the political pressure to force their way into the Welfare State.
>
> The governmental obligation to provide, out of taxes, such a minimum living standard for all who need it should be taken as much for granted as free public schools have always been in our history.

The need is clear: the principle of an *economic floor* under each individual must be established. This principle would apply equally to every member of society and carry with it no connotation of personal inadequacy or implication that an undeserved income was being received from an overgenerous government. On the contrary, the implication would clearly be one of responsibility by the total society for ensuring that no member of the society lived in a manner incompatible with the standards acceptable to his fellow men merely because he lacked purchasing power. In this respect his position as a member of society would be secure; such a principle should therefore be called *Basic Economic Security*.

Basic Economic Security can be best regarded as an extension of the present Social Security system to a world in which conventional job availability will steadily decline.

We will need to adopt the concept of an absolute constitutional right to an income. This would guarantee to every citizen of the United States, and to every person who has resided within the United States for a period of five consecutive years, the right to an income from the federal government sufficient to enable him to live with dignity. No government agency, judicial body, or other organization whatsoever should have the power to suspend or limit any payments assured by these guarantees.

We can first examine how entitlements to BES might be established. One of the fundamental principles of the present United States tax system is the "exemption" of part of an individual's income from taxation. At its inception, this exemption ensured that taxes would not be paid on that portion of income required to provide a reasonable standard of living. However, the government lost sight of this original aim when increasing the tax load to pay for World War II, and the value of the exemption has been *further* reduced since the end of World War II by the effects of inflation. The original aim of the federal tax exemption should be restored and exemptions should be raised immediately to a level which would guarantee an untaxed income adequate for minimum subsistence. Those whose incomes from earnings or from capital did not reach this level would then be entitled to receive federal government payments sufficient to raise their incomes to this level and ensure their Basic Economic Security.

At what levels should these BES entitlements be set initially?

Two factors must be taken into account in making this decision: first, the necessity of providing an income adequate for minimum subsistence for everybody; and second, the necessity to prevent the overburdening of the administrative operation at the beginning of the scheme. The full economic implications of any particular level of BES entitlements would probably have to be worked through on computers, but it might be expected that a level of $1000 a year for every adult and $600 for every child would in fact be feasible levels to use as a starting point for calculations.

So long as entitlements are only adequate to allow minimum subsistence, it seems appropriate that the exemption pattern should be *very* simple and probably this split between adults and children would be sufficient. When incomes were raised to a level adequate to allow human dignity, the question of introducing a declining level of exemptions for families with more than two or three children would have to be seriously considered. Indeed, there would have to be detailed examination, at this time, of the degree of complexity that would be desirable in the pattern of exemptions; for the monetary cost of supporting a six-year-old child is very different from that of a fourteen-year-old, while the cost of living varies widely from place to place. On the other hand, the amount of government verification necessary would increase if the pattern of exemptions were made more complex.

In spite of the evidence on disparity of incomes presented in this volume, a considerable number of readers may still deny the need for any proposal which would provide such low income guarantees. It should shock these people to learn that in 1960, 16.4 percent of all unattached *individuals*, or about 1,800,000 Americans, received less than $1000 per year; almost all these people would benefit from BES entitlements. Although it is not possible to determine with equal certainty how many *families* would benefit, almost all the 7.3 percent of families receiving incomes below $2000 would benefit, as would many of the 15.8 percent of families receiving between $2000 and $3999. The total number of people in all these families amounts to 34,000,000. It therefore seems reasonable to estimate that *twenty million* Americans, or one person in nine, would be covered immediately by the initial level of BES.

It may be asked why a higher level of exemptions should not

be set even at the outset of the scheme. The difficulty is not in terms of the financial burden; this would not of course be of any great magnitude in terms of the productive capacity of the United States and the effect on the budget. However, an immediate higher level for the exemption would probably not be wise, for it is essential that the operation of the scheme be efficient, and this goal might not be achieved if the initial number of beneficiaries were too high. An overload and consequent breakdown would be disastrous for confidence in the feasibility of the plan. However, a rapid rise in entitlements should be achieved, for the $2000 suggested for a retired couple is about $1000 below the Bureau of Labor Statistics estimate of a "modest but adequate" budget in cities, and the $3200 allowed for a man, his wife, and two children is little more than half the sum required for a similar "modest but adequate" budget.

One of the difficulties in determining an appropriate level for initial BES entitlements stems from the fact that certain additional free services urgently need to be introduced. Sufficient evidence now exists to show that one of the major causes of poverty among the old is excessive medical bills, and that it is precisely those who have been poor all their lives who are most likely to suffer from chronic ill health. A full-scale medical-care bill is required to ensure that nobody's savings are wiped out because of an unavoidable illness for which they are not responsible and which they cannot avoid. Health is a community responsibility. Similarly, education must be treated as a community responsibility. This has, of course, always been recognized in the United States, and free education has been provided as the essential basis for upward mobility in the population, as the method of giving everybody an opportunity to make use of his talent. However, the policies necessary to fulfill this valid and accepted principle have not been re-examined in the light of the new conditions of the middle of the twentieth century, when a university education is often essential if people are fully to realize their potential.

Basic Economic Security would be very simple to operate compared to the present mosaic of measures—Social Security, unemployment compensation, welfare, "stamp plans," subsidies to housing—which have been introduced at various times in the past to meet the same goal. Payments under BES would progressively take the place of these schemes. Recalculations of BES entitlement, based on the individual's total income record for the year, would be made annually; the entitlement payments would be made weekly. Although this simplicity of operation is attractive, it nevertheless appears necessary to add one complication, which is probably required both to secure equity in the early states of the scheme and also to encourage acceptance. Although soon after the introduction of the plan, many recipients of BES would come to depend on BES payments for their total income, others would continue to receive private income from their market-supported work or would have some interest payments on their savings. (We will use "private income" to cover both income received from a conventional market-supported job and income received from interest on savings throughout this discussion.) In calculating BES payments, the amount of this private income should not simply be deducted from the BES entitlement so that those with private income and those without receive the same total income. Instead, those with private income should be entitled to additional payments in the form of a premium, thus raising the level of their total entitlement. The size of the premium could only be determined after extensive study—a figure of 10 percent is here adopted for purpose of discussion. Thus any family (or individual) with some private income of their own would not only receive payments to make up the difference between their private income and their regular entitlement under BES, but also a premium of 10 percent of the value of their private income.

To take an example, let us examine the case of a man with a wife and two children. The family's exemptions of $1000 for each adult and $600 for each child add up to a BES entitlement of $3200. If the family received no private income of their own, their total income would simply be the $3200 from BES. However, if they received private income amounting to $2000 during the year they would have a total income of $3400—$2000 of private income, $1200 of make-up payments to reach the BES entitlement of $3200, plus $200 accruing to them as a 10 percent premium on their private income of $2000.

PAYING FOR THE RIGHT TO LIFE

RICHARD LEE STROUT

THE FIRST YEAR CANADA INSTITUTED FAMILY ALLOWANCES (1946) sales of children's shoes leaped from 762,000 to 1,180,000 pairs a month. The last time Dr. Gallup asked Canadians how they liked the program, 90 percent called it a "good thing"—a fantastic majority. Sixty-two nations have family allowances. Every industrial nation has them but one—the United States. Almost certainly we are going to adopt them shortly; here's why.

Family allowances are directed principally at helping children. About half of all people living in poverty in the US are children. America wants to aid them but hasn't been quite clear how to do it. We discovered poverty in the 60's, went promptly into action but we've been trying to do so much so fast that mistakes have occurred. There's a "maddening insistence of the federal government in giving help to the poor," says Daniel Moynihan, "through a bewildering array of agencies, programs, services and such, the benefits of which trickle down so slowly and—when they arrive —seem so small."

The case for family allowances is quite simple. Joe Puzzluski and Sam Jacobstein work in the same shop; each gets $5000 a year. They do identical work. The first has no children, the second three. Is this distribution of wages fair? If you think about it and answer "Yes," you must ask yourself if you would justify placing an economic handicap on parenthood or, for that matter, on the family as a social institution? It is not an easy question.

From Richard Lee Strout, "Paying for the Right to Life," *The New Republic*, November 23, 1968, pp. 15–16. Reprinted by permission of *The New Republic*, © 1968, Harrison-Blaine of New Jersey, Inc.

But it's a real problem, not just theory. Statistics show a striking correlation between big families and poor families at the low income level. Whether they have children because they are poor, or are poor because they have children is hard to say. What matters is the children. Millions of American children are getting a raw deal.

Since we discovered poverty we have also learned that our wealth is distributed quite unevenly. The lowest fifth gets only about five percent of total income; the upper five percent gets about one-fifth of income.

Well, so what? Even five percent of America's cornucopia is a lot of goodies! America's poor are India's rich. True, but consider some of the consequences:

▶ At least 10 nations have lower infant mortality than the US.

▶ Two out of three disadvantaged US youngsters (five to 14) have never seen a dentist.

▶ More than 60 percent of poor children with disabling handicaps get no medical treatment.

And so on.

The country has known these things vaguely for a long time. But every now and then poverty and neglect send in a due bill. When this happens at a time of national stress the experience is rather scary. Take the draft:

▶ If all young men turning 18 in a given year were to be examined for induction into the armed services, it is revealed, one-third would be disqualified.

▶ About half of those would be rejected on medical grounds. The others couldn't pass the mental test (fifth grade).

▶ The majority of failures, according to the President's Task Force on Manpower Conservation, ("One-third of a Nation"— 1964) would be the victims of inadequate educational and health services. That's what we're doing to our children.

For present purposes the best book ever written on family allowances has . . . been offered by James G. Vadakin, University of Miami, with a foreword by Daniel Moynihan. It is published by Basic Books, 222 pages, $6.50. Vadakin wrote an earlier book in 1958; now he thinks Congress is finally going to act. I do, too. The book is simple, straightforward and low-keyed. It is written for people who are worried about urban riots, who are unhappy about the War on Poverty, and who have heard something about family allowances, guaranteed incomes and negative income tax without quite understanding them.

Family allowances, Vadakin explains, are a system whereby all families with children, regardless of income, receive payments simply by virtue of their membership in society. It is like the bread and butter put on your table at a restaurant whether you order soup or steak.

[A] proposal . . . backed in Congress by Rep. John Coyners, Jr., (D) Michigan, and others, would pay $10 per month for every child of every American family under the age of 18, so long as the child went to school. Checks would go to mothers. Mrs. Nelson Rockefeller and the squaw living in a Navajo hogan would each get $10 a month per child. But the rich, of course, would immediately pay most of it back in higher income taxes. For 1968, it is estimated, the program would have cost $8.6 billion annually, from which sum $1.3 billion would be recovered by income tax. Net annual cost—$7.3 billion.

Wild? Canada has been living under this system for 20 years and loves it. With modifications and variations it is used all over the world. America is the one extraordinary exception. On this and the failure to license firearms the US is unique.

Why include the rich? Primarily for simplicity of operation. The cost of administration in Canada is surprisingly low. For each $100 paid in benefits the administration cost is about 69 cents —one-seventh of one percent. When the US adopts the plan it will be administratively cheap, too, because it won't be Washington that controls it, nor the states, nor the welfare worker snooping on a man-in-the-house; it will be the child's mother. It is the ulimate in welfare decentralization.

The plan, in short, is founded on a simple matter of faith, that you can trust parents to do what's right for their kids. It strengthens family bonds instead of tearing them apart as present Aid to Families with Dependent Children sometimes does.

The first question always asked is: Has it increased the birth rate? The answer, No. Quebec, predominantly Catholic, showed a birth rate decline, 1957–61. There are a lot of other similar statistics Vadakin offers. The question is natural but rather silly, too. Are parents really going to have a baby to get $120 a year? France has tried baby bonuses but the birth rate remains low. Both Fascist Italy and Nazi Germany tried subsidies; in Italy the birth rate declined; in Germany in the 1930's the rate rose slightly but probably for various causes. The system doesn't seem to have changed the birth rate much anywhere in the 62 nations using it.

But it's a "subsidy," critics say. Yes it is. There are US subsidies now for merchant ships, airlines, locks and canals, interstate roads, cotton, rice and corn and even tobacco; there's the depletion allowance for oil. There is a whole gleaming Christmas Tree of subsidies as the late Sen. Richard Neuberger said, for every element in it except the most precious of all, the children.

Some economists say the negative income tax would be more efficient than family allowances. The negative income tax is aimed directly at those below the arbitrary poverty line, $3000 or so for a family of four. They would be getting direct cash checks back from the government while the rest of us were paying in checks.

There are two comments about this. First, it isn't just the no-income families who desperately need help; the blue-collar and working-class earner ($5000–$8000, say) needs help, too; he is largely ignored by the recent spate of welfare programs. He is aggrieved; he feels left out, he begins to hate the no-income group. It is class consciousness in reverse. . . .

The second comment is, yes, the negative income tax might be more efficient in lifting the burden of a single disadvantaged group, the very poor. But is it politically feasible? Can you imagine Congress actually voting for it? The lobby for the very poor in America is very small. In crass political terms, to get something done you probably have to broaden your base of support. Vadakin analyzes various NIT plans and some of them get passing marks. He and Moynihan, however, back family allowances because the system works. Should the best be the enemy of the good, he asks?

Family allowances would benefit all children whether or not their parents were employed. They would redistribute income not only between rich and poor people but between rich and poor regions.

The $600 income tax dependency allowance already commits us, of course, to aiding children. But a $600 income-tax dependency allowance is no good for a widow with six children and no income. She pays a sales tax every time she buys something—at a six percent rate in Wallace's Alabama. If only she paid income tax she could deduct $3600 from it. Some $20 billion of available

exemptions and deductions go unused each year, sociologist Robert
J. Lampman estimates.

There is a final question about the plan, often unuttered: Can
we trust the parents? If you can't you might as well quit; but
there is a more pragmatic answer than that. Other nations trust
them and they stack up pretty well. In Canada they were worried
about it, too. The check goes to mothers; would it be spent for
liquor, dope, high living? Well, it isn't.

Repeated studies show the vast majority of Canadian families
use the payments properly. The government reminds people of
the program through radio, TV, booklets and the like, and if
complaints come in they are investigated. Few cases are bona fide.
The money goes quietly for food, shoes, medicine, who knows—
piano lessons. The plan is self-administrative.

That's the story. Family allowances aren't a panacea. They
won't eliminate poverty (but they will help). Primarily they will
help children. Every other advanced country has the system. Isn't
it strange, when you come to think of it, that the US is all alone?

THE DISTRIBUTION OF EDUCATIONAL OPPORTUNITIES

INTRODUCTION

THE PUBLIC SCHOOL SYSTEM HAS traditionally had the function of transmitting values and imparting skills. In an earlier day it was seen as a huge factory which at one end took in the bewildered children of recent immigrants and at the other end turned out processed Americans. Presumably the system was to perform similar functions for blacks from the South, and for Puerto Ricans and Mexicans, the modern analog of the immigrant masses who flooded the schools in the early days of the century. Increasingly, however, the public school system has come under attack from social scientists and political activists. Some persons have argued that the system no longer performs its historic function, others that this function is not worthy of being performed in the first place. In this section we have gathered a number of pieces which speak to these points.

Patricia Cayo Sexton has indicated in *Education and Income* that there are systematic differences between slum and nonslum schools, especially with regard to the quality of the physical plant. Slum schools are inferior to nonslum schools along a number of dimensions. The excerpt from Sexton's book focuses on the differences between schools attended by the children of the poor and those attended by children from more affluent families.

Jonathan Kozol taught in an elementary school in Boston, Massachusetts. The book *Death at an Early Age* recounts his experiences. What happens in the kind of school Sexton wrote about? What are the day-to-day experiences of black children in a slum school? Who lives, who dies, and who are their judges and executioners? Kozol charges the administrators and teachers in the Boston public school system with killing the hearts and minds of black children. An excerpt from the book reflects the basis of his charge.

Herbert Kohl's piece is a review of Robert Rosenthal and Lenore Jacobson's *Pygmalion in the Classroom.* The Rosenthal and Jacobson research focused on the relationship between teacher expectations and pupil performance. They concluded that teachers' expectations play a key role in children's performances. If their teachers regard them as stupid to begin with, they tend to perform poorly; if their teachers treat them as if they do have a potential for learning, they do learn.

These first three articles deal with a complex of factors which account for failure of slum children in school: slum children often go to poorer schools and are taught by teachers who have no faith in them.

What then is to be done?

A variety of approaches have been advocated by various radicals and reformers. Chris Trée and Joseph Featherstone suggest that there may be no solution within the framework of the existing public school system. Both suggest that new and different kinds of schools may be needed to respond effectively to the failure of the traditional school system.

Richard Zamoff's short, satirical article deals with the concept of "cultural deprivation"—but applied to teachers rather than to slum children. Whether one is "culturally deprived" or not depends upon who is defining the dimensions of culture.

Taken together, the last three pieces in the section explore some unusual but not implausible approaches to dealing with the current failures of the school system.

WHERE IT'S AT

SOCIAL CLASS AND THE
QUALITY OF EDUCATION

PATRICIA CAYO SEXTON

THERE ARE NOT AS MANY ESRPS (SUBSTITUTES WHO ARE USUALLY unqualified teachers) in Big City high schools as in elementary schools. The highest proportion of these unqualified teachers is 9.8 percent (in the lowest-income school); in the elementary schools the highest proportion was found to be 24 percent. As

Income Group		Percentage of ESRPs to Total Teaching Time
1	($5000—)	9.8%
2		6.3
3		8.0
4		6.6
5		6.4
6	($6000—)	3.8
7		2.5
8		1.4
9	($7000—)	3.3
10		1.9
11		1.5
12		2.0
13	($8000—)	1.5
14		1.4
15		1.8
16		0
17	($9000—)	2.9

From Patricia Cayo Sexton, *Education and Income.* Copyright © 1961 by Patricia Cayo Sexton. All rights reserved. Reprinted by permission of The Viking Press, Inc., New York.

in the early grades, the number of ESRPs in the high schools is closely related to income levels, with a few interesting variations.

Almost one out of every ten teachers in the lowest-income high school is an emergency substitute working on a regular assignment.

School 17 has an unexpectedly high percentage of ESRPs as compared with other high-income schools. Whether true or not it is at least *claimed* by many teachers that students in school 17 are "hard to handle"; because of this the school may have trouble holding qualified teachers and may have to accept ESRPs instead.

In the major income groups the percentage of ESRP teaching time to total teaching time is:

Income Group	Percentage of ESRPs to Total Teaching Time
I ($5000—)	7.4%
II ($6000—)	2.6
III ($7000—)	2.2
IV ($8000—)	1.5
V ($9000—)	2.9
A (below $7000)	5.6
B (above $7000)	2.0

Thus the percentage of ESRPs in the lower-income half is almost three times greater than the percentage in the upper-income half.

CLASS SIZE

Class size is only a fraction larger in the lower-income half than in the upper half, with an average size in group A of 33.6 and in group B of 33.3. The distribution among major income groups is:

Income Group	Class Size
I ($5000—)	33.2
II ($6000—)	34.3
III ($7000—)	33.6
IV ($8000—)	32.6
V ($9000—)	34.8

The largest class size, by a small fraction of 1 percent, is found in group V, which is contrary to what might have been expected.

CONTINUOUS CLASS PROGRAMS
AND OVERCROWDING

A student with a continuous class progam is one whose high school is so crowded and whose program is so compact that he must go to classes without any breaks except a lunch period. These continuous programs have been under hot attack in Big City recently, and a clamor has risen to relieve congestion in certain schools so that students can have more free periods.

Certainly continuous programs do not provide the best possible educational situation, since they do not allow time for relaxation and study between classes. Students with continuous programs, however, are not disadvantaged *educationally;* they take as many classes as they can handle, and they are as free as other students to take classes of their own choice. Frequently students *prefer* continuous programs because of the shortened school day.

The protests, it would therefore appear, may be somewhat out of proportion to the size of the problem, especially since there is so little public clamor for correction of other school problems—delinquency, failure, dreary curriculums, unqualified teachers, school buildings unfit for use, totally inadequate health and psychological services, etc. Nor has there been much clamor about overcrowding at the elementary school level, perhaps because crowding at this level is more common in lower-income areas, while high-school crowding is found mostly in upper-income areas. In elementary schools overcrowding is dealt with by transporting students to other schools; the high-school problem could also be handled this way except that upper-income students might object to being sent to the less crowded lower-income schools. Table 1 shows that overcrowding and continuous class programs are more common in upper-income areas.

Thus more than half the schools in the upper-income half have continuous class programs; in the lower-income half only one school out of eight has a continuous program. In this aspect of school life, lower-income groups appear to be receiving better school service than upper-income groups.

TABLE I   **Continuous Class Programs**

Income Group	Number of Schools in Each Income Group	Number of Schools with Continuous Programs
I ($5000—)	5	0
II ($6000—)	3	1
III ($7000—)	4	1
IV ($8000—)	4	3
V ($9000—)	1	1
A (below $7000)	8	1
B (above $7000)	9	5

SCHOOL BUILDINGS

High-school buildings in the lower-income half are more than twice as old as buildings in the upper-income half. Except for the reversed positions of groups III and IV, the age of school buildings tends to decrease as income increases. Schools in group I are more than four times as old as in group V.

Income Group	Average Age of Buildings
I ($5000—)	45.0
II ($6000—)	38.0
III ($7000—)	18.5
IV ($8000—)	24.5
V ($9000—)	10.0
A (below $7000)	42.5
B (above $7000)	20.2

Most high schools in Big City are cramped for outdoor recreational space, some more than others. The most serious shortage of outdoor space is found in the lower-income areas, where homes and neighborhoods tend to be overcrowded, parks and recreation areas in short supply, and delinquency rates unusually high. Unexpectedly, group III has the most adequate acreage.

The first table on page 245 indicates the percentage of acreage increase needed to provide proper outdoor space for the pupils and staff housed in the school buildings.

Schools in the lower-income half need almost twice as great an acreage increase as schools in the upper-income half, and schools in group I need an 86-percent acreage increase.

The almost total inadequacy of outdoor school space in group I, in addition to the shortage of park and recreation space, raises the serious question: Where do students in these lowest-income schools find space for healthy outdoor recreation? They live in crowded homes with little yard space; there are almost no vacant lots in their downtown neighborhoods, and they cannot play in the streets because of heavy traffic. They seldom go to parks outside their neighborhoods, and they almost never go camping or hiking. Where do they play?

Income Group	Percentage of Acreage Increase Needed*
I ($5000—)	86%
II ($6000—)	66
III ($7000—)	35
IV ($8000—)	43
V ($9000—)	47
A (above $7000)	78
B (below $7000)	40

* Schools with acreage used by adjacent elementary and junior highs were not included here.

Facilities in the highest-income high school are much better than in the lowest-income school, as Table 2 shows.

By major income groups the average number of "Lacking or sub-standard" facilities per school is as follows.

Income Group	Lacking or Sub-Standard Facilities
I ($5000—)	23
II ($6000—)	19
III ($7000—)	14
IV ($8000—)	17
V ($9000—)	11

Except for the reversals of groups III and IV, facilities tend to improve as income increases.

TABLE 2 Lacking or Sub-Standard Facilities*

	School 1 (Lowest Income)	School 17 (Highest Income)
Counselors' offices	o	x
Auditorium workroom	o	x
Choral music room	S	x
Orchestral music room	S	x
Music practice room	o	x
Electrical shop	o	x
Shop lecture room	o	x
Arts and crafts	o	x
Home living	o	x
Library workroom	o	x
Orthopedic room	o	x
Clinic	o	x
Retailing	o	x
ROTC classroom	o	x
Student publication room	o	x
Age of building	44	10

Key

o = lacking
S = sub-standard
x = facility present and in good condition

* Those facilities which were found to be lacking or sub-standard in **both** schools are not included in this list; only the differences are included.

. . . [The citizen's] committee visited all schools in the city, studied all aspects of the school plant, and gave separate ratings to every building detail examined. The ten major categories of the study were: adequacy, suitability, safety, healthfulness, accessibility, flexibility, efficiency, economy, expansibility, and appearance. The highest possible score in each of these ten categories was 100. A "perfect" score in all ten categories would therefore be 1000. Total building scores of each high school are shown in Table 3.

TABLE 3 Total Building Scores (perfect score: 1000)*

1. ($5000—)	575—
2.	706
3.	501—
4.	641—
5.	761
6. ($6000—)	661—
7.	+888
8.	606—
9. ($7000—)	+816
10.	+948
11.	788
12.	+841
13. ($8000—)	792
14.	717
15.	+833
16.	+879
17. ($9000—)	+893

* A plus indicates a rating of over 800; a minus of under 700.

Thus five high schools in the lower-income half (below $7000) received scores of less than 700, and only one school had a rating of over 800.

In the upper-income half, there were no schools scoring below 700, and there were six (out of nine) scoring over 800.

Scores of the major income groups were as follows.

Income Group	Building Score
I ($5000—)	637
II ($6000—)	718
III ($7000—)	848
IV ($8000—)	805
V ($9000—)	893
A (below $7000)	667
B (above $7000)	834

Again, except for the reversed positions of groups III and IV, the quality of school buildings and facilities tends to improve as income increases.

A very substantial difference in the scores of groups A and B will be noticed, a difference amounting to 167 points.

Among the *individual* schools the difference between the lowest- and the highest-income schools is 318 points!

Table 4 gives these scores some concrete meaning by pointing out specific factors contributing to the superiority of upper-income high schools. The comparison is made between the lowest and the highest major income groups (groups I and V).

In all items listed, building scores are higher, often much higher, in the upper-income group.

According to a citizens' committee report, "schools serving the wealthy areas of the city frequently receive gifts of equipment either from parent organizations or from individual citizens." Such facilities include radios, television sets, tape recorders, records, phonographs, mimeographs and office machines, etc. Since these facilities have never been inventoried, it is suggested that a tabulation be made of them with a view to equalization.

Many of these facilities are essential to school operation and should be provided for by the school budget rather than by voluntary contributions or "special" funds. To illustrate, the author recently spent some time in two Big City high schools, one the lowest-income school and the other among the highest. In the lowest-income high school there was only one ditto machine available for teacher use, and no mimeograph machine or other office equipment. The ditto machine was rarely used, since teachers were required to buy their own paper and ditto stencils, costly items when a teacher has some 175 students who need materials. In addition, since no office staff was provided, it was necessary for teachers to type their own stencils and run off their own ditto copies. Needless to say, this was seldom done.

In the upper-income school an unlimited quantity of paper and stencils was available to teachers, without charge. The funds for these supplies had been raised through special student-parent activities. Office services were also available, saving teachers the trying and time-consuming job of typing and duplicating their own material (a job which teachers without typing and office skills could not perform at all). Yet duplicated materials, prepared by

TABLE 4 Breakdown of Building Scores (numbers in parentheses indicate the "perfect" score)

	Scores	
	Group I	Group V
Adequacy		
Play areas (5)	1.2	5.0
Size of classrooms (10)	6.6	8.0
Equipment classrooms (5)	4.4	5.0
Enough chalk boards (2)	1.4	3.0
Suitability		
Art (5)	3.6	5.0
Music (5)	2.4	5.0
Business (5)	3.8	5.0
Library (5)	4.4	5.0
Assembly (2)	1.2	2.0
Hot lunches (3)	2.0	3.0
Homemaking (5)	4.2	5.0
Shop work (5)	2.8	5.0
Audio-visual equipment (5)	3.6	5.0
Outdoor site suitably equipped and developed (5)	.6	3.0
Safety		
Stairway safe (5)	3.8	5.0
Fire control facilities (5)	4.0	5.0
Hazards walks & drives (5)	2.8	5.0
Equipment hazards (5)	0	5.0
Separate play areas (5)	1.0	5.0
Healthfulness		
Proper lighting (15)	10.4	15.0
Seats proper size (10)	6.4	10.0
Heating & ventilation satisfactory (10)	7.6	10.0
Toilet facilities adequate (10)	6.6	10.0
Flexibility		
Multiple use of rooms (10)	4.2	10.0
Furniture movable (10)	2.6	8.0

the teacher (tests, assignments, bibliographies, charts, tables, text supplements, etc.) are essential to high-quality education, and should be provided for by the schools and not by special funds.

Such inequalities in basic educational tools are commonplace in the schools of Big City.

WHICH INCOME GROUP
IS WORST OFF?

In most aspects of school life, the lowest major income group (group I) appears to be much worse off than any of the other groups. However, group II (the second-lowest income group) appears to be worse off in the following ways.

In the elementary schools, class size was largest in group II (30.9 as compared with 29.7 in group I).

There were more unqualified teachers (19.1 percent as compared with 13.9 percent in group I).

The average age of buildings was somewhat higher (46 years as compared with 45 years in group I). Total building scores in group II, however, were slightly higher than in group I (578.3 as compared with 573.5).

Only the lowest-income families can qualify for admission as tenants in Big City's public housing developments, on the sites of which new school buildings have been erected. Because children living in these developments go to the newly constructed schools on the site, they have available to them facilities often equal to those provided in the highest-income areas. Children of the lowest-income group who do not live at these sites, however, are housed in the city's oldest and most inadequate buildings.

Parent membership in elementary-school groups was slightly higher in group II (12.3 per 100 students, as compared with 10.1 in group I), although some of the very lowest levels of parent participation were found in group II—in the $6000 income range.

In high school, summer-school enrollment was lowest in group II. On the other hand, in high school, there were more unqualified teachers and school buildings were older and considerably more inadequate in group I, the lowest-income group.

It appears, therefore, that in some important respects, particularly in the elementary schools, group II is somewhat worse off than group I. It should not be assumed, then, that the very lowest income groups are *always* at the bottom of the educational ladder.

In almost all aspects of school life, the greatest differences have been between schools under $7000 income and those over $7000. The great divide separating these two groups is apparent in the number of "gifted" children chosen, the number of parents active in school affairs, school buildings and facilities, the percent of unqualified teachers, etc.

Thus the line of greatest separation seems to coincide almost exactly with the average family income level—which in Big City is $6900 a year.

DEATH AT AN
EARLY AGE

JONATHAN KOZOL

PERHAPS A READER WOULD LIKE TO KNOW WHAT IT IS LIKE TO GO
into a new classroom in the same way that I did and to see before
you suddenly, and in terms you cannot avoid recognizing, the
dreadful consequences of a year's wastage of real lives.

You walk into a narrow and old wood-smelling classroom and
you see before you thirty-five curious, cautious and untrusting
children, aged eight to thirteen, of whom about two-thirds are
Negro. Three of the children are designated to you as special
students. Thirty percent of the class is reading at the Second
Grade level in a year and in a month in which they should be
reading at the height of Fourth Grade performance or at the
beginning of the Fifth. Seven children out of the class are up
to par. Ten substitutes or teacher changes. Or twelve changes.
Or eight. Or eleven. Nobody seems to know how many teachers
they have had. Seven of their lifetime records are missing: symp-
tomatic and emblematic at once of the chaos that has been with
them all year long. Many more lives than just seven have already
been wasted but the seven missing records become an embittering
symbol of the lives behind them which, equally, have been lost
or mislaid. (You have to spend the first three nights staying up
until dawn trying to reconstruct these records out of notes and
scraps.) On the first math test you give, the class average comes
out to 36. The children tell you with embarrassment that it has
been like that since fall.

From Jonathan Kozol, *Death at an Early Age*. Boston: Houghton Mifflin
Company, 1967, pp. 185–191. Reprinted by permission of Houghton Mifflin
Company.

You check around the classroom. Of forty desks, five have tops with no hinges. You lift a desk-top to fetch a paper and you find that the top has fallen off. There are three windows. One cannot be opened. A sign on it written in the messy scribble of a hurried teacher or some custodial person warns you: DO NOT UNLOCK THIS WINDOW IT IS BROKEN. The general look of the room is as of a bleak-light photograph of a mental hospital. Above the one poor blackboard, gray rather than really black, and hard to write on, hangs from one tack, lopsided, a motto attributed to Benjamin Franklin: *"Well begun is half done."* Everything, or almost everything like that, seems a mockery of itself.

Into this grim scenario, drawing on your own pleasures and memories, you do what you can to bring some kind of life. You bring in some cheerful and colorful paintings by Joan Miro and Paul Klee. While the paintings by Miro do not arouse much interest, the ones by Klee become an instantaneous success. One picture in particular, a watercolor titled "Bird Garden," catches the fascination of the entire class. You slip it out of the book and tack it up on the wall beside the doorway and it creates a traffic jam every time the children have to file in or file out. You discuss with your students some of the reasons why Klee may have painted the way he did and you talk about the things that can be accomplished in a painting which could not be accomplished in a photograph. None of this seems to be above the children's heads. Despite this, you are advised flatly by the Art Teacher that your naïveté has gotten the best of you and that the children cannot possibly appreciate this. Klee is too difficult. Children will not enjoy it. You are unable to escape the idea that the Art Teacher means herself instead.

For poetry, in place of the recommended memory gems, going back again into your own college days, you make up your mind to introduce a poem of William Butler Yeats. It is about a lake isle called Innisfree, about birds that have the funny name of "linnets" and about a "bee-loud glade." The children do not all go crazy about it but a number of them seem to like it as much as you do and you tell them how once, three years before, you were living in England and you helped a man in the country to make his home from wattles and clay. The children become intrigued. They pay good attention and many of them grow more curious about the poem than they appeared at first. Here again, however, you are advised by older teachers that you are making a mistake: Yeats is too difficult for children. They can't enjoy it, won't appreciate it, wouldn't like it. You are aiming way above their heads . . . Another idea comes to mind and you decide to try out an easy and rather well-known and not very complicated poem by Robert Frost. The poem is called "Stopping By Woods on a Snowy Evening." This time, your supervisor happens to drop in from the School Department. He looks over the mimeograph, agrees with you that it's a nice poem, then points out to you—tolerantly, but strictly—that you have made another mistake. "Stopping By Woods" is scheduled for Sixth Grade. It is not "a Fourth Grade poem," and it is not to be read or looked at during the Fourth Grade. Bewildered as you are by what appears to be a kind of idiocy, you still feel reproved and criticized and muted and set back and you feel that you have been caught in the commission of a serious mistake.

On a series of other occasions, the situation is repeated. The children are offered something new and something lively. They respond to it energetically and they are attentive and their attention does not waver. For the first time in a long while perhaps here is actually some real excitement and some growing and some thinking going on within that one small room. In each case, however, you are advised sooner or later that you are making a mistake. Your mistake, in fact, is to have impinged upon the standardized condescension on which the entire administration of the school is based. To hand Paul Klee's pictures to the children of this classroom, and particularly in a twenty-dollar volume, constitutes a threat to this school system. It is not different from sending a little girl from the Negro ghetto into an art class near Harvard Yard. Transcending the field of familiarity of the administration, you are endangering its authority and casting a blow at its self-confidence. The way the threat is handled is by a continual and standardized under-rating of the children: They can't do it, couldn't do it, wouldn't like it, don't deserve it . . . In such a manner, many children are tragically and unjustifiably held back from a great many of the good things that they might come to like or admire and are pinned down instead to books the teacher knows and to easy tastes that she can handle. This includes, above all, of course, the kind of material that is contained in the Course of Study.

Try to imagine, for a child, how great the gap between the outside world and the world conveyed within this kind of school must seem: A little girl, maybe Negro, comes in from a street that is lined with car-carcasses. Old purple Hudsons and one-wheel-missing Cadillacs represent her horizon and mark the edges of her dreams. In the kitchen of her house roaches creep and large rats crawl. On the way to school a wino totters. Some teen-age white boys slow down their car to insult her, and speed on. At school, she stands frozen for fifteen minutes in a yard of cracked cement that overlooks a hillside on which trash has been unloaded and at the bottom of which the New York, New Haven and Hartford Railroad rumbles past. In the basement, she sits upon broken or splintery seats in filthy toilets and she is yelled at in the halls. Upstairs, when something has been stolen, she is told that she is the one who stole it and is called a liar and forced abjectly to apologize before a teacher who has not the slightest idea in the world of who the culprit truly was. The same teacher, behind the child's back, ponders audibly with imagined compassion: "What can you do with this kind of material? How can you begin to teach this kind of child?"

Gradually going crazy, the child is sent after two years of misery to a pupil adjustment counselor who arranges for her to have some tests and considers the entire situation and discusses it with the teacher and finally files a long report. She is, some months later, put onto a waiting-list some place for once-a-week therapy but another year passes before she has gotten anywhere near to the front of a long line. By now she is four-teen, has lost whatever innocence she still had in the back seat of the old Cadillac and, within two additional years, she will be ready and eager for dropping out of school.

Once at school, when she was eight or nine, she drew a picture of a rich-looking lady in an evening gown with a handsome man bowing before her but she was told by an insensate and wild-eyed teacher that what she had done was junk and garbage and the picture was torn up and thrown away before her eyes. The rock and roll music that she hears on the Negro station is considered "primitive" by her teachers but she prefers its insistent rhythms to the dreary monotony of school. Once, in Fourth Grade, she got excited at school about some writing she had never heard about before. A handsome green book, brand new, was held up before her and then put into her hands. Out of this book her teacher read a poem. The poem was about a Negro—a woman who was a maid in the house of a white person—and she liked it. It remained in her memory. Somehow without meaning to, she found that she had done the impossible for her: she had memorized that poem. Perhaps, horribly, in the heart of her, already she was aware that it was telling about her future: fifty dollars a week to scrub floors and bathe little white babies in the suburbs after an hour's street-car ride. The poem made her want to cry. The white lady, the lady for whom the maid was working, told the maid she loved her. But the maid in the poem wasn't going to tell any lies in return. She knew she didn't feel any love for the white lady and she told the lady so. The poem was shocking to her, but it seemed bitter, strong and true. Another poem in the same green book was about a little boy on a merry-go-round. She laughed with the class at the question he asked about a Jim Crow section on a merry-go-round, but she also was old enough to know that it was not a funny poem really and it made her, valuably, sad. She wanted to know how she could get hold of that poem, and maybe that whole book. The poems were moving to her . . .

This was a child in my class. Details are changed somewhat but it is essentially one child. The girl was one of the three unplaced special students in that Fourth Grade room. She was not an easy girl to teach and it was hard even too keep her at her seat on many mornings, but I do not remember that there was any difficulty at all in gaining and holding onto her attention on the day that I brought in that green book of Langston Hughes.

Of all of the poems of Langston Hughes that I read to my Fourth Graders, the one that the children like most was a poem that has the title "Ballad of the Landlord." The poem is printed along with some other material in the back part of this book. This poem may not satisfy the taste of every critic, and I am not making any claims to immortality for a poem just because I happen to like it a great deal. But the reason this poem did have so much value and meaning for me and, I believe, for many of my students, is that it not only seems moving in an obvious and immediate human way but that it *finds* its emotion in something ordinary. It is a poem which really does allow both heroism and pathos to poor people, sees strength in awkwardness and attributes to a poor person standing on the stoop of his slum house every bit as much significance as William Wordsworth saw in daffodils, waterfalls and clouds. At the request of the children later on I mimeographed that poem and, although nobody in the classroom was asked to do this, several of the children took it home and memorized it on their own. I did not assign it for memory, because I do not think that memorizing a poem has any special value. Some of the children just came in and asked if they could recite it. Before long, almost every child in the room had asked to have a turn.

All of the poems that you read to Negro children obviously are not going to be by or about Negro people. Nor would anyone expect that all poems which are read to a class of poor children ought to be grim or gloomy or heart-breaking or sad. But when, among the works of many different authors, you do have the will to read children a poem by a man so highly renowned as Langston Hughes, then I think it is important not to try to pick a poem that is innocuous, being like any other poet's kind of poem, but I think you ought to choose a poem that is genuinely representative and then try to make it real to the children in front of you in the way that I tried. I also think it ought to be taken seriously by a teacher when a group of young children come in to him one morning and announce that they have liked something so much that they have memorized it voluntarily. It surprised me and impressed me when that happened. It was all I needed to know to confirm for me the value of reading that poem and the value of reading many other poems to children which will build upon, and not attempt to break down, the most important observations and very deepest foundations of their lives.

GREAT EXPECTATIONS

HERBERT KOHL

MOST EDUCATIONAL RESEARCH FOCUSES UPON THE SUCCESS AND FAIL-
ure of students or on the economic "effectiveness" of school systems. But there seems to be a tacit agreement between teachers
and researchers (usually psychologists and sociologists) not to
raise questions concerning the teachers themselves. It is difficult
for researchers to enter a school to study teacher behavior, and
they rarely do so. Yet two researchers, Robert Rosenthal, a psychologist, and Lenore Jacobson, a school administrator, have violated the non-aggression pact between teachers and researchers
and studied the manipulation of teacher behavior in the classroom.
Pygmalion in the Classroom is a report on the effect of a teacher's
expectations upon the performance of his pupils. The study is
ingenious and the results obtained highly significant.

Rosenthal and Jacobson are concerned with self-fulfilling
prophecies—i.e., those predictions of future events that become
central factors in bringing about predicted effects.[1] As they say,
"the central proposition of this book is that one person's prophecy
of another's intellectual performance can come to determine that
other's intellectual performance." They got the faculty of a
school in South San Francisco to cooperate with them by pre-

From Herbert Kohl, "Great Expectations," *New York Review of Books,*
September 12, 1968, pp. 30–31. Reprinted with permission from *The New
York Review of Books,* Copyright © 1968 The New York Review.

[1] An example of a self-fulfilling prophecy is a favorable medical prognosis
in a case of a cancer which caused the patient to move from despair to
hope and became a crucial part of his cure.

tending that they were conducting a scientific study of the performance of certain students in the school who were "late bloomers." An official document describing the project was presented to the teachers:

STUDY OF REFLECTED ACQUISITION
(Harvard—National Science Foundation)

All children show hills, plateaus, and valleys in their scholastic progress. The study being conducted at Harvard with the support of the National Science Foundation is interested in those children who show an unusual forward spurt of academic and intellectual functioning. When these spurts occur in children who have not been functioning too well academically, the result is familiarly referred to as "late blooming."

As a part of our study we are further validating a test which predicts the likelihood that a child will show an inflection point or "spurt" within the near future. This test which will be administered in your school will allow us to predict which youngsters are most likely to show an academic spurt. The top 20 percent (approximately) of the scorers on this test will probably be found at various levels of academic functioning.

The development of the test for predicting inflections or "spurts" is not yet such that *every* one of the top 20 percent will show the spurt or "blooming" effect. But the top 20 percent of the children *will* show a more significant inflection or spurt in their learning within the next year or less than will the remaining 80 percent of the children.

Because of the experimental nature of the tests, basic principles of test construction do not permit us to discuss the test or test scores either with the parents or the children themselves.

Upon completion of this study, participating districts will be advised of the results.

There is no "inflected acquisition," of course, nor is there a "test of late blooming." Students were given an ordinary test of intelligence and achievement, but one unfamiliar to the teachers; "late bloomers" were selected at random from the student body. The teachers were then told that some of their pupils had turned out to be "late bloomers," and that they were ready to "bloom." The researchers then sat back and waited to see how the students performed.

There is one aspect of Rosenthal and Jacobson's work which they themselves didn't explore: the effect of Rosenthal's Harvard credential's and the false credentials of the test upon the teachers' expectations. The teachers were fooled into believing that the test of "inflected acquisition" was actually measuring something. Presumably they were persuaded by the weight of authority (Harvard, The National Science Foundation, etc.) that a simple paper and pencil test could tell them more about crucial characteristics of their pupils than they were able to perceive in their daily contacts with the children. The timidity with which the teachers seemed to accept the premises of the "test of inflected acquisition," and the ease with which their expectations were manipulated by the researchers show how obedient and trusting they were, and all too willing to accept external authority. It may also indicate why teachers, themselves obedient, expect their pupils to be as blindly responsive to authority as they are.

The main proposition of *Pygmalion in the Classroom* was supported by the results of the experiment—the "late bloomers" bloomed. The reading scores of students designated as late bloomers grew at a significantly greater rate than that of the non-blooming pupils they had been matched against. These changes were particularly dramatic in the lower grades and for pupils in the "middle tracks."

> Girls bloomed more in the reasoning sphere of intellectual functioning, and boys bloomed more in the verbal sphere of intellectual functioning when some kind of unspecified blooming was expected of them. Furthermore, these gains were more likely to occur to a dramatic degree in the lower grades. That susceptibility to the unintended influence of the prophesying teacher should be greater in the lower grades comes as no special surprise. All lines of evidence tend to suggest that it is younger children who are the more susceptible to various forms of influence processes.

There are two particularly interesting cases of late blooming. Jose, a Mexican-American boy, had an IQ of 61 before he was labeled a "late bloomer." A year later he had gained 45 IQ points, testing at 106. Thus he moved in a year from being classed as mentally retarded to above average. Another Mexican-American child, Maria, moved from 88 to 128—i.e., from "slow learner" to "gifted child," according to the school's classification. These two results alone are staggering, yet many similar, though less dramatic, advances occurred when the teachers' expectations of the children changed.

The implications of these results will upset many school people, yet these are hard facts. Can failure in ghetto schools be attributed to teachers' expectations and not to the students' environment or ability? Can one even carry Rosenthal's results a bit further and speculate, for example, on whether discipline problems in ghetto schools arise because teachers expect them to? Do students lack "motivation" because teachers don't expect them to be motivated? The results described in *Pygmalion in the Classroom* reach beyond the ghetto. They condemn the tracking system prevalent in elementary and secondary schools throughout the country. Often in the first, or at least second, grade, children are grouped according to "ability." The determination of ability is made by the teachers or by whatever "objective" tests of school achievement they administer. Some schools have higher, middle, and lower tracks. Others draw the line finer and often seven IQ points or four months' difference in reading achievement scores become the criterion for class placement. Teachers are keenly aware of how their class stands in the general school hierarchy. Almost without exception the grouping according to track is self-perpetuating; and the students usually remain in the same track throughout their school career.[2]

Tracking also becomes a self-fulfilling prophecy. Both the teacher and the student are aware that upper-track classes are supposed to perform well and lower-track ones aren't. They expect things to work out that way and usually see to it in many unspoken ways that they do. This is as true in white middle-class suburban schools as in those of the urban ghettos. Not long ago I visited a C-stream class in a suburban high school. The students were demoralized and the teacher bored. He felt that nothing could be done with the students, and they agreed. One of the students asked me what I was doing visiting his class since the students were dumb and couldn't possibly interest a visitor. This boy of fifteen considered himself dumb because he was told that

[2] The little movement that does take place in the tracking system seems to be downward as "behavior" and "discipline" problems are weeded out of the top tracks and consigned to the bottom.

in school; it seemed to me a devastating commentary on the destructiveness of the schools.

But the tracking system is also a disservice to the so-called bright students who come to believe that brightness consists of the ability to perform well on tests. It frequently alienates them from their true abilities. It also cuts them off from children in the lower tracks, making the notion of the public school as a community a mockery; though it certainly succeeds in reflecting a society which pretends to be democratic and yet limits participation in the democracy to those who succeed and conform to the people in power.

The implications of the study described in *Pygmalion in the Classroom* also extend beyond education. For Rosenthal and Jacobson's research methods also involved the manipulation of teachers, whose cooperation was enlisted in bad faith. The researchers assumed god-like roles; they were the only people in the school who knew what the "experiment" was all about and who were not themselves the subjects. They presumed their involvement was neutral and that their work was simply an attempt to uncover "objective" (though statistical) knowledge. Yet can a social science "experiment" involving the manipulation of human beings be neutral? Moreover, what is the moral and human cost of acquiring knowledge through deceit and bad faith? This study does not reveal what the teachers who have been studied feel, nor whether they have learned something about themselves that could have some effect.

The results of Rosenthal's work are, of course, gratifying. They confirm what many critics of the schools have been saying. Yet an approach which is itself so totalitarian makes one question the value of acquiring knowledge by treating people as objects of an experiment. Surely there must be a more direct way of confronting teachers with their attitudes, and studying them in a more direct way. We do not need more people in the schools who cannot be trusted, even if they happen to be social scientists.

ALTERNATIVES
AND CHANGE
STOREFRONT
SCHOOLS

CHRIS TREE

LAST OCTOBER A FEW DROPOUTS AND STUDENTS FROM BENJAMIN
Franklin High School in East Harlem began coming to classes in
an empty store near the school. Unaccredited, supported partly
by federal funds channeled through the Board of Education and
partly by funds raised by the New York Urban League, this
storefront is cutting a pattern for schools half in, half outside the
public system.

Its purpose is to lift the percentage of Ben Franklin students
who enter college from two to 50 percent. Directors of the experiment predict that this will happen within two years; in the
meantime they hope to secure financing for similar storefronts
near every high school in the city.

The combined public and private financing of the Ben Franklin
storefront, and its ambitious plans for replication, are a new
venture for the Urban League. But the program of which this
venture is a part was born a few years ago. The idea was to find
ways of offering high school dropout and academic flunkouts a
realistic alternative to the choice between formal classrooms and
unskilled labor, and that the alternative could be provided on the
emptied premises of a bankrupt shopkeeper. During the past two
years over three hundred students have been coached in over a
dozen such schools. Ninety-two young men and women, once
dropouts, are now studying at colleges from Berkeley to Fordham,

From Chris Tree, "Storefront Schools," *The Urban Review*, 2: 4:16–18, 28–
29. Reprinted by permission of *The Urban Review*, a publication of the
Center for Urban Education, New York.

and over one hundred and fifty more are preparing for college in private schools. This, and many less statistical results, are the record which has so impressed a few private corporations and Mr. Sviridoff. It warrants a closer look.

The storefront program in fact has always been less a program than a constant search for the right set of steps from street to college. This search might be said to have begun over ten years ago when a young social worker called Harv Oostdyk began his "streetwork" on the Lower East Side. His job required him to know young gang leaders, to watch boys get jailed for selling dope, for burglary, sometimes for nothing at all. He watched them come out of prison and managed to get some into night school and, eventually, a few into a private school, Newark Prep.

But Oostdyk felt that many more such youngsters wanted and could go to college. Four years ago he persuaded Dr. Eugene Callender, then pastor of the Presbyterian Church of the Master on Morningside Avenue (one of Harlem's largest congregations) to start a tutorial center for high school dropouts in the church basement. He recruited some co-workers and soon had a few dropout students. Eventually a half-dozen of these entered the eleventh and twelfth grades of Newark Prep. Some were successful, but some failed. It was difficult for young men in their late teens and early twenties to settle into school routine. To prepare them to do so, an "Academy of Transition" was begun in a brownstone next to the church. It was called "academy," Oostdyk explains, because "school" meant frustration and "academy" sounded tonier, while "transition," he says, suggests movement, "a step." But soon another step appeared to be needed to modulate the change from the streets to the Academy—and so the "street academy."

Shortly thereafter the first street academy was opened on 114th Street (the center of Harlem's swift traffic in narcotics) and the second on 135th Street. In June 1966, when Dr. Callender was chosen executive director of the New York Urban League, the Street Academy Program, under Oostdyk's direction, became a part of the League's Education and Youth Incentives Program.

There are now over thirty Urban League storefronts for dropouts in all boroughs of the city. Some of these are Youth Business (job-training) centers. Some of them are "preacademies" in which boys prepare for the increasingly rigorous street academies. One, the People's Program, is to assist young men on narcotics. Only six storefronts, in fact, are formal and structured enough to be called street academies. Two of these, with a total enrollment of 30, are on the Lower East Side (most students in the Catherine Street school are Italian; at the "Blue Elephant" school on Division Street, they are Chinese). The four others (aside from the Ben Franklin storefront) are in central Harlem: one is for girls, the rest are for boys. Each has its own style, set by the head of the academy, the project director, who lays down the rules and sets up the curriculum. The latter is built on basic math and reading skills, but may often include courses such as African history. Each academy has three teachers who have BA's and often additional degrees. Each academy also has one to three streetworkers (of whom there are 50 in the entire storefront program) who recruit and constantly encourage students. Graduates of schools like Princeton and Union Theological, recognizing that local residents are often better qualified to reach and guide local boys, willingly work under project directors, few of whom have more than a community college degree. But staff roles often blur: project directors teach and sometimes recruit students themselves, teachers visit homes, and a streetworker can be an "area director," responsible for several storefront operations. As a matter of fact, "streetworker" is the most prestigious, though poorest paying position in the program ($6,000 per year). All staff members are available after five o'clock, and some keep apartments for students without homes.

The number of students in each academy varies from under ten to over twenty. In the past, roughly half of the students have graduated to the Academy of Transition after anywhere from a month to a year. Then, after a term or two, nine-tenths of the Transition students have moved on to prep school. In contrast, students from Ben Franklin will be pointed back toward public high school, then local colleges. Until recently, life in the Academy of Transition was more formal and study more intensive than in the street academies. Now, however, all the street academies are raising their academic requirements; most students may soon pass on directly to prep school (some already have) or even to college, with the help of a program like City University's SEEK. Nevertheless, there are still 40 students in the Academy of Transition this year, and the Newark Prep students come back there each afternoon for basketball and tutoring. (They ride back and forth in a yellow school bus—at first this made them feel sheepish but the bus is now a neighborhood status symbol.) Last year, 15 former dropouts graduated from Newark Prep. One, the class valedictorian, is now at Fordham on a full scholarship.

Last year the number of students passing through the street academies and the Academy of Transition grew too large for the one prep school in Newark. A few weeks before the Benjamin Franklin storefront opened, classes at a fully accredited prep school began in an armory on 142nd Street near the East River. Its board of directors includes Dr. Charles Silverman, an editor of *Fortune* and director of the Carnegie Foundation's Institute to Service Education, and Cyril Tyson, a deputy administrator of the Human Resources Administration. The school, Harlem Prep, offers French or Spanish, and some advanced math and science among other subjects. Most students have come up the standard program steps, but some are from League centers in the Bronx and Brooklyn and a few simply applied and were accepted. Admittance criteria include a ninth-grade reading level and the recommendation of a streetworker. When the school opened, there were 100 applicants, of whom 52 (47 boys and five girls with an average age of 18) were accepted. Soon the school will move to a supermarket on 136th Street, converted with the help of the Educational Facilities Laboratory.

The creation of Harlem Prep is an example of the exploratory way in which the entire street academy program works. Each academy has evolved its own methods of what educators call, in their special sense, "motivation to achieve." To understand this process requires a close look at the manner in which academy staff understand and attempt to meet the needs of a specific neighborhood like Harlem.

HOW IT WORKS

It is difficult to generalize about what has happened in the more than a dozen academies that have opened and closed in Harlem during the past two years. This winter a representative of a large corporation, visiting the academy on 119th Street, heard a young man call from the back of the room: "Do me a favor, read it again in African, Owino." To the delight of the visitor and a dozen Negro students in their late teens, Owino, a tall teacher from Kenya, began to translate into Swahili the outline of a history lesson he had put on the board. The lesson was on "The Era of Firearms and Slave Trade," and point number two under "The Decline of African Political Interests" was "Conflict of Interests." It sounded like *Kutukuku* and brought a whoop of approval. It was 2:30; the history class had run overtime. Beginning his own lesson, Lynn Gray, the next teacher, stepped to the center of the room and suggested that anyone seriously interested in Swahili form a seminar with Owino. Then he asked, "Where does the word Harlem come from? How long have people lived here? How long have black people lived here?"

Twenty or so blocks away on Amsterdam Avenue, the visitor might have seen the outside of another storefront, coated black. It displayed a sign in one window: "The Body." The single room inside was painted red. Two tables in the back were pushed together to form a working space for the five students around it. One of them, Robert, should have been in high school, but he had not made it there that day. "I like it here," he said. "I want to study, to go to college, but at school the teachers aren't interested . . . here they don't fly at you . . . if you want help you get it." From across the table Hubert explained that he had been in a "600" school last year. A friend told him about the academy and he had been attending for a month. School was pulling him "in the wrong direction," he said. Hubert said he liked science, discovering and creating. He wanted more education, "so I can get the better things in life."

By the time a youth reaches a street academy, he has had enough practical experience to form definite ideas about the meaning of college, of money, of any program—ideas which differ from those of the staff—even though most of them are only in their twenties. In fact, staff members define "motivating" as changing their students' aspirations for themselves to conform with their own goals for them. They see this process of change as the core of the program.

The most obvious difference of outlook is over the possibility and meaning of college. College, for the staff, is the goal the kids should have. But it is one thing to expect dropouts to go to college and another to get them to have the same expectations. To most Harlem youths, college is a fantasy, and they have heard plenty of "sweet talk" before. There is more than a grain of truth to one observer's remark that the program "sounds good, but it doesn't mean anything. These kids have closed minds. They are cynical, disillusioned, strictly on the make. You can't kid them any more."

Most street academy recruits *are* at first skeptical about the whole program. They are more impressed with the fact that the academies offer them $38.63 per week (after taxes).[1] At first the boys are suspicious of the white streetworkers and teachers because they know that these people are accustomed to "the better things in life." They steal their watches and badger them for cash. They know that downtown these graduates of top universities could be making twice as much money.

Even Negro workers must weather initial heckling. Ronald Rasdall, director last year of the 114th Street academy, says: "At first the kids give you all kinds of games—ask for money, then favors." A student corroborates: "When I first met Ron, like all the rest I took advantage of him, but then I stopped and thought . . . he gave me all the breaks I needed in the program." Negro staff report that students are more puzzled about them than about white workers, about why they too prefer working in the program to making big or easy money. They explain that for most of the youngsters success must be tangible and immediate. They point out that the $55 Italian knit sweaters, the $299 suits from A. J. Lester, the Eldorado cars and the pretty girls are the status symbols in Harlem—which most often belong to dope pushers, to numbers men, to pimps. All streetworkers see their jobs, first alone, then in conjunction with the teacher and project director, as the task of convincing a future leader that there is another way of "making it." The fact that most of the streetworkers who came to Harlem two years ago from the Middle

---

[1] Practically speaking, this stipend from the Neighborhood Youth Corps (currently funded by OEO) allows young men to be students; it may help to support parents, children, or morale. To receive the money, however, they must do something more than simply attend the academy. They can write, type, or sell *The Academy News* of their specific storefront or the newspaper *Forty Acres and a Mule* which represents all the academies. They can tutor slower students, make toys for sale or "back to school" posters for the community, or plan a discotheque. Some directors now also require their students to invest portions of their pay in individual and joint savings accounts to gain experience in saving and spending as a group.

and Far West have remained attests that satisfactions offset struggles in their job.

But changing attitudes is constant and inconclusive work. One day a student may be enthusiastic and the next he has vanished. It is because Urban League staff expect this pattern, because the streetworker's job begins where that of the staff of other programs end, in constantly searching out and encouraging young men who have walked out on them, that they are confident of helping dropouts throughout the city. It is recognized, for example, that a student's difficulty with institutional schooling does not end with college admission; and, because the League is a nationwide organization with contacts near most campuses, it can attempt to provide friends for youths who may never before have been beyond the city.

"VERY INFORMAL, VERY UNSTRUCTURED"

The academies have discovered the value of discipline along with that of support. Last year Rasdall found that the leaks and holes in his decrepit academy were unimportant—that "the big worry is working your show academically." He discovered that to do this it was necessary to establish "law and order." He did. A poster in his storefront reads:

> No hat wearing at any time
> No smoking
> No eating and drinking
> Leave friends outside the academy
> No leaving the academy until class is dismissed
> No using of profanity
> Lateness will not be tolerated
> No unnecessary noise during class

As soon as he had put it up he began getting a much better response.

This may seem surprising in a class whose students will not be remembered in their old public schools as models of deportment. But most project directors in Harlem agree with Rasdall that "too many guys are lazy—they blame whitey for their hang-ups."

Rasdall maintains: "You have to develop discipline because these guys have not been exposed to it. . . ."

This year in Rasdall's new academy on 140th Street (a former liquor store) his dozen students are working hard from 9:00 to 5:00. They have old books, dishes and drapes from the Cornell Club (whose treasurer is on their board of directors) and two new rules: "no dungarees, no sneakers." Rules vary, however, from academy to academy. At the 119th Street storefront the 16 students may smoke, eat, and wear hats during class but to graduate they must fulfill ten criteria:

1. an individual research project
2. an interview with adults in the neighborhood
3. a writing project (each student keeps a daily journal)
4. a work project (his job)
5. 10th grade level reading
6. 10th grade math ability
7. near perfect attendance and fulfillment of a daily chore (sweeping, mopping, etc.)
8. knowledge of a general outline of world history
9. three books read
10. physical requirement (totally undefined)

The rules for Miller's academy in which the students are all Five Percenters, a group of young Muslims, might read:

> Instill the importance of a clear way of thinking.
> If you have problems, then what are you going to do about them?
> No matter how many negative people say it can't be done, you find the positive one—prove it—and it can be beautiful.
>   and
> If you have unity, you can't go wrong.

"KUTUKUKU"

There is unity in each storefront; each in fact is known by its project director's name. It is "Herb's" or "Ron's" more than an "Urban League Street Academy." But no one pretends there is perfect unity among the street academy staff. One director describes what any observer can plainly see: "As a group, we're in so many different bags. There are the Christian seminarians, the

Black Nationalists, the Black Muslims, the Five Percenters." Mixing these strong elements into any kind of a system is difficult; indeed the question is whether it is possible at all.

Yet this is perhaps the most intriguing aspect of the street academies. A century ago Catholics could form their own school system because they were united in one religious faith. The demands of street academies may require the same degree of zeal. But the men who can give it in this case have different ideologies and different methods of achieving the goal which they all share.

Oostdyk and his first recruits to the program were members of a nationwide organization called "Young Life," which works mainly with suburban high school students who do not belong to a specific religious denomination, trying to interest them in broadly Christian values. As the storefront program grew, more and more Negroes joined the staff. With them came a special, potentially divisive faith which centers on being "Black."

More a fashion than an ideology, Black Power expresses a probably ephemeral but certainly important mood in young Negroes today. It is particularly appealing to much of Harlem's youth because, at their stage in life as well as in the history of Negroes in America, they are searching for a sense of identity and pride. Whether or not they will be able to find it in being "Black" is an open question. In any case, it is felt that to motivate dropouts to study reading, writing and arithmetic, in 1968, in Harlem, one director may teach Arabic and another, African history.

In theory each project director in the Harlem street academies, as elsewhere, is free to set the curriculum and tone of his academy. The League appears, however, to set limits to this freedom. One director, James Johnson, a Negro graduate of a fine New England university, advocates Black Power to the extent that he feels it necessary to "equip black students to deal with white ideas" and that "only a black man can give another black man a sense of identity." He represents an extreme in the spectrum of ideologies within the street academy program. The fact that in November his academy (the Body) was converted into a discotheque and its students moved to the 140th Street academy, where Johnson now teaches, suggests that his view was too extreme for the committee headed by Oostdyk, who is ultimately responsible for recruiting new staff and channelling money.

NEW DIRECTIONS

To attract cautious financial backers, the leadership believes, the right tone must be maintained in the present academies. This is a critical moment for the storefront program. The academy at Ben Franklin is a new departure for the Urban League, a pilot project for an ambitious program to bring the storefront idea into the public high schools.

In terms of the proportion of students who go to college, Benjamin Franklin is one of the less successful city's high schools. The academy there is aimed at the 80 percent of the school's students who are neither in college-bound courses nor in the special federally funded ninth grade cluster program. From 9:00 until 3:00 regular classes are held in the storefront for dropouts (currently 42 percent of the students over 17) and for students on the verge of suspension. The latter have been recommended by the Ben Franklin staff to join the storefront classes for a month or so. At the same time, a few streetworkers are observing classes inside the school, suggesting to some students that they enter the school's own academic, college-bound courses. After 3:00, they can be tutored at the storefront. The academy is envisioned as a place where students can eventually come to relax; it will have a library and perhaps a building of apartments for students with no other homes. It is staffed by two teachers and ten streetworkers (called "student advisors" by the Board of Education, which is sponsoring them). The program is receiving enough federal Title I and Title II (of the ESEA) money to cover books and operating expenses, but it is seeking more extensive private funding for expansion and better facilities.

If this is a critical moment for storefront schools, it is also, in another sense, a good moment. Certainly the public educational system is loosening up. Advocates of decentralization say that New York and other big-city public schools are not better than they are because they have a captive clientele which has nowhere else to go. New York City's upper-middle class students go to private schools, its lower-middle class, to parochial schools. Yet, while the style and staff of the public schools remain white middle class, over half their students are now Negro and Puerto Rican. In any case, some degree of decentralization is inevitable, and it may, for better or worse, lead to the establishment of competing subsystems within the system.

Last year the Ford Foundation put $700,000 worth of faith in the street academies. This year the program is taking on over a dozen times the number of students in its old-style storefronts (getting 50 percent of the students at Benjamin Franklin into college involves 1,300 young men and women). It is clear that the working methods used in the Harlem proving grounds of the academies cannot be mass-produced. But it is also clear that the street academies have thrived while other programs have limped and fallen around them. In fact, they are cropping up across the country in cities from Seattle to Miami.

It may well be that street academies will prosper precisely because the creation of each new one depends on testing the old, because, rather than being centrally prefabricated, they will continue to be built on the resources and skills of individual staff members in meeting the needs of individual students. Of course there is a risk in any greatly expanded program that its initiative and freedom will be dissipated.

Yet, whatever the future course of the street academies, their history may already contain some important lessons. Today, in theory, the public schools are dedicated to the social aim of "equal opportunity" for all. But in the present shuffle in New York between slower and brighter classes on each grade, students from poor families are often lost; they graduate with a general high school diploma which does not require passing State Regents tests. Over half the high school students from Harlem drop out; and of those who remain in school, three-fourths receive general diplomas. Employers know what a "general" credential means; they may even know that over two-thirds of the youths who possess or have worked toward it in Harlem read no better than the average sixth grader.

"Equal opportunity" is also the goal of the street academies. But they use different means to achieve it. For example, public school administrators complain that students do not react to traditional curricula. Yet in the street academies, dropouts work diligently at basic and conventional subjects, spurred by special studies which may satisfy their specific interests. Administrators complain that "disruptive pupils" disturb their classes, while in street academies students who might have been regarded as disruptive submit to, even learn under, greater constraints than exist in any public school. Again, even the staunchest professional advocates of heterogeneously grouped classes claim that mixing students of different abilities cannot work past the eighth grade. On the other hand, in street academies, students along a spectrum of six reading levels learn together and teach each other. Administrators, echoing many social scientists, further claim that ability level is set at an early age. But the street academy students, all over 16 years old, have performed much better on standard tests than when the same tests were taken in school; some IQ's have jumped in the course of the program. Still another difference: administrators begin by setting up programs, by mobilizing teachers, while the street academies focus on the students first, then let a program build. Finally, public school guidance counselors prescribe job training and vocational courses for slow and disruptive students, while the street academies have shown that many of these young people want to go to college and *can* go to college.

NOTES ON
COMMUNITY SCHOOLS

JOSEPH FEATHERSTONE

THE NEW SCHOOL FOR CHILDREN OCCUPIES A CHEERFUL, CLUTTERED
building across the street from a public school that looks a lot
like the prison ship in *Great Expectations*. It has 90 children,
kindergarten through the fifth grade. The Community School
has, at the moment, settled its 49 children—kindergarten through
second grade—in a cramped maze of small rooms in the basement
of St. Ann's Episcopal Church. Both are Boston's examples of a
new kind of school—independent private schools set up by
parents in the ghetto. Both began last year and are showing a
tenacious ability to endure in the face of very steep odds. Each
is a different variation on a theme, community schooling, and
each is thus a separate, uncompleted essay in definition of elusive
words like "community" and "participation."

They have common roots, for at the outset there was only one
group of Roxbury people interested in starting an independent
school. Mostly black, but with some whites, it formed in a mood
of desperation after Louise Day Hicks' sweep of the 1965 school
board election—a mood which Kevin White's recent mayoral
victory over Mrs. Hicks has done little to dispel. Some were
associated in one way or another with the tutorial program run
out of St. Ann's. Most were parents who had come to distrust and
fear the public schools, and although they differed on many
points, they were united in wanting a school that could be de-

From Joseph Featherstone, "Notes on Community Schools," *The New
Republic*, December 9, 1967, pp. 16–17. Reprinted by permission of *The
New Republic*, © 1967, Harrison-Blaine of New Jersey, Inc.

pended upon not to cripple their kids; that was the minimum. Some wanted the feeling of being able to shape at least part of their children's future, and a few had a specific interest in seeing their children placed in informal classes, where they could work at their own level and in their own time.

The division into two groups came about for a number of reasons; in part it reflected a faint division along class and neighborhood lines. What became the Community School group contains more of what are wryly called the certifiable poor—people whose income falls below official poverty levels—most of them clustered in the framehouse apartments around St. Ann's. What became the New School group has more people whose incomes are middling, more whites, and more people from the general Roxbury area. The Community School operates without tuition; the New School charges $250 a year, granting scholarships to its needy children.

One point of contention between the groups was the degree to which a good school in the ghetto needed outside help. Obviously outside money was needed; but to what extent could a school go it alone? A number of the New School people wanted a crack school for their children, and they were eager, or at least willing, to enlist the support of schools of education in the Boston area and educational experts of one kind or another, as well as the energies of various prominent Roxbury figures. This bent was reinforced by the principal, Mrs. Bernice Miller, a former Chicago school principal who believed that the New School would have to go beyond its own circle to draw on a wide base of support if it was to survive and flourish as a model enterprise. The Community School people, on the other hand, were interested in having a good school, but they wanted the school to be *theirs;* they were suspicious of the amount of outside involvement in the New School. They were also wary of administrators, and they decided to call their principal simply the head teacher. (This year the head teacher is Mrs. Doreen Wilkinson, a lovely Haitian lady with a good deal of sympathy for the parents' outlook.) Both schools have tried to set up a network of Friends of the School for raising money in fairly small sums around Boston and in the suburbs. So far they seem to have made this precarious kind of financing work, but as each plans to add on a grade each year, budgets will grow and fund-raising will become chancier.

There is no rivalry between the two schools; they are simply different. The New School has come to identify with Roxbury as a whole. Its wider base of support and its ability to appeal to many different interests have made it a community venture in a broad, almost political sense—the sense that Roxbury Negroes use when, prematurely and not always accurately, they speak of themselves as a black community. It has become one of the symbols of Roxbury's aspirations, and draws on the support of people sympathetic to those aspirations—liberal educators, people in the suburbs, and other private schools like Shady Hill. Classes are informal, the atmosphere is hectic and warm. (Kids come and sit on a visitor's lap.) A tendency toward faddishness and the kind of chaos you see in the rare self-consciously experimental suburban school exists, but so far it has been checked by the extraordinary quality of the two former Boston schoolteachers who took the first and second grades last year and have remained on this year.

The Community School has defined its community in a different way: it consists of the parents, most of whom live right around St. Ann's. (The school has a loan to renovate part of a nearby house, which in time it will move to.) There are a few outsiders on its board, but the school is very much a neighborhood affair. Classes are also quite informal and warm, although maneuvering in tiny basement rooms puts a strain on teachers and children. (There are three teachers and two assistant teachers, ladies from the neighborhood—at the New School parents work in the office and in a variety of other ways, but they don't teach.)

It would be hard to argue, in the language of the social scientists that dominates our educational discourse, that these two schools amount to models, or even hypotheses, and what they prove is still being worked out, assuming that a wild tangle of variables, such as a school, can ever be said to have proved anything. They testify to a fierce desire on the part of a lot of ordinary people to develop workable alternatives to the public schools. They show that parents in the inner city will approve of informal classes quite unlike anything they went through when they were in school. (One lady, however, said she liked the informal classes, because they were like sessions in the one-room schoolhouse she attended as a girl in rural Alabama.) They illustrate a curious species, community schools, that seem to be spreading, despite the absence of any workable means of financing them. They may represent a Children's Crusade. Or they may, after all, be telling everybody a lesson about educational reform: don't wait to work out theories of what community participation means, and certainly don't wait for guarantees about money. Begin a school, do good work on a small, manageable scale, and perhaps reality will catch up to you. If there are enough such enterprises, learned men will do studies concluding that they reflect some kind of real need, and other learned men will be set to devising ways that their existence can be made to square with common sense, public finance, and all that. In the meantime, they exist, they teach live children; that's miracle enough to stagger the experts.

THE ATTITUDINALLY
DISADVANTAGED TEACHER

RICHARD B. ZAMOFF

STUDIES OF SCHOOL DESEGREGATION HAVE REVEALED A SIZABLE PER-
centage of teachers who can charitably be labelled "attitudinally
disadvantaged." That large numbers of teachers hold negative
attitudes toward Negro children is not surprising to social researchers. It probably comes as no surprise to members of local
school establishments either, despite the "amazement" such reve-
lations have produced. A superintendent of schools who has even
a minimal knowledge of his system might wonder *why* many of
his teachers believe that a larger percentage of Negro than white
pupils are incapable of learning basic reading and arithmetic
skills. However, he should be anything but amazed at this finding.

The primary consequence of uncovering such attitudes has
been remarkably similar in many communities. There have been
vague assertions that these teachers must no longer be allowed
to enter the public school system—assertions combined with appropriate expressions of astonishment that they ever succeeded in
infiltrating in the first place. But accompanying these predictable
reactions has been the pronouncement that special preparation in
the form of in-service training must be initiated before desegregation occurs. I assume that this "sensitization" of teachers is intended to equip them with what is necessary to confront Negro
students—lest the teachers be overcome by the integrated setting.
Of course, this "sensitization" is to be accomplished in the cus-

From Richard Zamoff, "The Attitudinally Disadvantaged Teacher," *The
Urban Review*, 1: 5:4, December 1966. Reprinted by permission of *The
Urban Review*, a publication of the Center for Urban Education, New
York.

tomary 15 weeks and naturally, teachers will be paid handsomely for learning how to react to the "newcomers."

I would be more concerned with equipping Negro students with what is necessary to confront biased teachers. And in this article I would like to propose in-service training for Negro pupils about to enter classes, which will be taught by "attitudinally disadvantaged" teachers. The outline of such courses awaits further research. In the meantime, the following brief attitude instrument will help us explore the feelings of Negro pupils toward some of the teachers who will "serve" them when schools become desegregated. I suggest we investigate this carefully and ask Negro students to give their reactions to the following ten statements.[1]

1. Because the attitudinally disadvantaged teacher is unused to intellectual stimulation, she should be exposed to it in very small doses.

2. It is unrealistic for the student of the attitudinally disadvantaged teacher to set too high sights for his teacher's achievement.

3. Even the most creative Negro student can expect to attain only very limited success with an attitudinally disadvantaged teacher.

4. If a Negro student succeeds in motivating only one out of five of his attitudinally disadvantaged teachers, he is doing very well.

5. One of the frustrations of working with attitudinally disadvantaged teachers is that they do not really appreciate your efforts.

6. The attitudinally disadvantaged teacher's capacity for learning is pretty well set by the time she begins to teach.

7. An attitudinally disadvantaged teacher's use of "hip" expressions should be corrected at once by her students.

8. The Negro student should avoid references to the attitudinally disadvantaged teacher's home and community because these are likely to be painful and unpleasant subjects for the teacher.

[1] Any similarity between these statements and those appearing on other instruments is purely intentional. See, for example, *Center for Urban Education: Summer Institutes for Teachers of the Disadvantaged Child*, July, 1966.

9. A Negro student cannot be expected to mitigate intellectual damage suffered by an attitudinally disadvantaged teacher before she begins to teach.

10. As long as the parents of attitudinally disadvantaged teachers remain apathetic and unconcerned, Negro students can expect to accomplish very little with these teachers.

Undoubtedly this brief instrument will uncover negative attitudes on the part of Negro students. Perhaps administrators will be shocked and unhappy with my new approach. But perhaps they will be moved to introduce "sensitivity" courses for Negro students to prepare them for desegregation. The prospects are limitless. Attitude instruments could then be given to Puerto Rican, white, American Indian, Chinese, and other students. Attitudes could be explored toward teachers, students, and even toward teaching materials. Sensitivity courses could be introduced for all concerned. Mathematicians would be elated at the possible combinations and permutations of these efforts, and school superintendents would rejoice at the number of articles they could write about these innovative experiences. I hope we might at least end up with students and teachers preparing for desegregation together. This would save money which, if I can be bold enough to suggest, could be used to prepare teachers to teach and students to learn. This, I understand, is what education is all about.

THE DISTRIBUTION
OF WORK
OPPORTUNITIES

INTRODUCTION

ALL SOCIETIES REQUIRE A LABOR
force of persons who are assigned work tasks, generally seen as
productive labor of some kind. It is assumed that work is economically productive and an activity for which one is remunera-
ted or rewarded. Work roles are a primary way of identifying
and classifying people, particularly in complex and technologically advanced societies. It is assumed that all able-bodied adult
males, at least, will work. This value is internalized by the child
as he learns that work is religiously sanctioned—the Protestant
Ethnic. Work is critical in determining one's status in society;
work is the determinant of one's economic position, class level,
and life-style. In fact, the United Nations Bill of Rights attests
to the right of all to work. And the Congress of the United States
passed an Employment Act in 1946 which stipulated that the
federal government had a responsibility to work toward economic
growth and full employment.

Yet, as discussed in an earlier section (p. 175 ff.), the economic
structure in cybernated societies will alter the premises of scarcity, and will affect the nature of work, the type of labor force,
and the role of work in people's lives. At the present time there
is little serious effort to reconceptualize work and career patterns;
however, the structural defects of the market economy have somewhat shifted the blame for unemployment from the individual to
the society. When one-quarter of Americans were unemployed
and the Depression affected most of the population, the context
gave rise to the New Deal and its social and labor legislation. In
the contemporary scene, where the nation is affluent and all of

its institutions are geared toward the middle mass of growing prosperity, the context for those in the locked-out underclass is different. The half-million coal miners after World War II did not disappear—their jobs did. The Southern Negro farmer workers did not vanish, they were moved off the land and into urban ghettos. The superfluous people of today are, in fact, not relevant for the productive process in the automating economy. Attempting to make blacks white is not an answer, as David Wellman points out. Yet, the economic situation for black people, one-half of whom live in poverty, is critical. Sidney M. Peck reinforces the classical sociological studies which demonstrate the existence of a caste-like occupational structure in the United States.[1] Other recent works have pointed out that automation and an inadequately growing economy will lead in the direction of Marx's predicted army of the unemployed, especially if the society loses the artificial props of a war-time economy.[2]

Given the nature of a changed economy, an altered labor force, and a revolutionary change in technological capabilities, it is striking that the attitudes toward work have varied so little. But in the context of mostly conventional wisdom, to use Galbraith's term, some thinking is being altered. Earlier we saw Robert Theobald's proposal for a guaranteed income—a constitutional right independent of the person's productive contribution—not based upon what work the person does, or that he be working, in the traditional sense, at all. Arthur Pearl offers another creative alternative. He notes the reliance upon set patterns of careers, whereby increasing evidence is placed upon acquired educational credentials prior to beginning work. He suggests an alternative pattern which, he argues, accounts for the changing labor force and technology, and which he feels will deal with the immediate problems of unemployed and poor people. W. H. Ferry reminds us of the interlocking nature of the revolutionary changes in human relations, international relations, and technology.

Sociologists in the past few years have been fascinated by the concept of alienation. It is clear that this concept is closely asso-

[1] See the study by S. Clair Drake and Horace Cayton, *Black Metropolis*. New York: Harcourt, Brace & World, 1945.
[2] A provoking analysis is offered by Ben Seligman, *Most Notorious Victory*. New York: Free Press, 1966.

ciated with the social changes in the past few years. As blacks have become more militant, and as large numbers of people are economically deprived and politically disenfranchised, the notions of class consciousness and racial awareness have become practically and theoretically relevant. Writers such as Erich Fromm move from an examination of Marx's theory of estrangement from labor, self, and society in capitalist economics to an analysis of the dehumanizing nature of work and technology, and they ponder how to cope with such realities.[3] The debates do not significantly question whether work is of central interest in the lives of industrial workers and professionals; rather, as seen in the Mills essay, the discussion centers on the relationship between work and nonwork, and on the central sociological question about social integration into society.[4] The student of sociology needs to ask not about the decline in the average workweek over the past century, and not about the changes in social and labor legislation which affect the economics of work; but his question should deal more fundamentally with the broader structural matters. Is alienation from work the product of a capitalist economic order, or is there an inherent barrier imposed by industrialism per se?[5] Is there a psychological property of man which prompts a form of work commitment, or might we redesign a cybernated society to allow for greater creativity through activities not related to economic production?[6] Is there an emerging black proletariat which will not demand an equal amount of work involvement and work estrangement, but will insist upon a broader societal reorganization?[7] These questions touch at the heart of the matter of the changing distribution of work opportunities, and they generate a far-reaching complex of queries.

[3] Erich Fromm, *Marx's Concept of Man*. New York: F. Ungar, 1961. Erich Fromm, *The Revolution of Hope: Toward a Humanized Technology*. Harper & Row, 1968.
[4] This has been a central question in sociology. See Emile Durkheim, *On the Division of Labor in Society*. New York: The Free Press, 1947.
[5] This question is addressed by William A. Faunce, *Problems of an Industrial Society*. New York: McGraw-Hill, 1968.
[6] Erich Fromm, "The Psychological Aspects of the Guaranteed Income," in Robert Theobald (ed.), *The Guaranteed Income*. Garden City, N.Y.: Doubleday & Company, 1966.
[7] See John Leggett, *Class, Race and Labor*. New York: Oxford University Press, 1968. James Boggs, *The American Revolution: Notes from a Negro Worker's Notebook*. New York: Monthly Review Press, 1963.

WHERE IT'S AT

THE CONDITIONS
OF MODERN WORK

C. WRIGHT MILLS

I. THREE TRENDS

The managerial demiurge has come to contain three trends which increasingly give it meaning and shape. As it spreads (I), its higher functions, as well as those lower in the hierarchy, are rationalized; as this occurs (II), the enterprise and the bureau become fetishes, and (III), the forms of power that are wielded, all up and down the line, shift from explicit authority to manipulation.

I. The rationalization of the corporate structure, even at the top, may not be lodged in the head of a single living man, but buried in an accounting system served by dozens of managers, clerks, and specialists, no one of whom knows what it is all about or what it may mean. The man who started the enterprise, if there ever was such a man, may long be gone. Franz Kafka has written of ". . . a peculiar characteristic of our administrative apparatus. Along with its precision it's extremely sensitive as well . . . suddenly in a flash the decision comes in some unforeseen place, that moreover, can't be found any longer later on, a decision that settles the matter, if in most cases justly, yet all the same, arbitrarily. It's as if the administrative apparatus were unable any longer to bear the tension, the year-long irritation caused by the same affair—probably trivial in itself—and had hit

From C. Wright Mills, *White Collar: The American Middle Classes*, pp. 106–111, 224–238. Copyright 1951 by Oxford University Press, Inc. Reprinted by permission of Oxford University Press, New York.

upon the decision by itself, without the assistance of the officials. Of course, a miracle didn't happen and certainly it was some clerk who hit upon the solution or the unwritten decision, but in any case it couldn't be discovered by us at least, by us here, or even by the Head Bureau, which clerk had decided in this case and on what grounds . . . we will never learn it; besides by this time it would scarcely interest anybody."

It seems increasingly that all managers are "middle" managers, who are not organized in such a manner as to allow them to assume collective responsibility. They form, as Edmund Wilson has observed of "capitalistic society in America," "a vast system for passing the buck."

In trade, the department manager, floorman, and salesperson replace the merchant; in industry, the plant engineers and staffs of foremen replace the manufacturing proprietor; and in practically all brackets of the economy, middle managers become the routinized general staff without final responsibility and decision. Social and technical divisions of labor among executives cut the nerve of independent initiative. As decisions are split and shared and as the whole function of management expands, the filing case and its attendants come between the decision maker and his means of execution.

An "inventory control" is set up for the management cadre and, as the U.S. Naval Institute has it, there is a "detailed man-by-man analysis of all the people in a company who hold supervisory jobs"; classifying each man as "promotable, satisfactory, unsatisfactory" on the basis of interviews "with him, his superior, and his subordinates and perhaps some scientific testing"; working out a concrete time-schedule "for each promotable man" and another "for getting rid of the deadwood." Since top managers cannot serve the market properly and at the same time manage their "giant bureaucracy," they rationalize the top, divide themselves into Boards, Commissions, Authorities, Committees, Departments; the organization expert thus becomes a key person in the managerial cadre, as it shifts from the open occupational market to managed selection and control. This administrative official, a sort of manager of managers, as well as of other personnel, is in turn rationalized and acquires a staff of industrial psychologists and researchers into human relations, whose domain includes personal traits and mannerisms, as well as technical skills.

These officials and technicians embody the true meaning of the "personal equation" in the mass life of modern organization: the rationalization of all its higher functions.

II. In the managerial demiurge, the capitalist spirit itself has been bureaucratized and the enterprise fetishized. "There is," Henry Ford said, "something sacred about a big business." "The object of the businessman's work," Walter Rathenau wrote in 1908, "of his worries, his pride and his aspirations is just his enterprise . . . the enterprise seems to take on form and substance, and to be ever with him, having, as it were, by virtue of his bookkeeping, his organization, and his branches, an independent economic existence. The businessman is wholly devoted to making his business a flourishing, healthy, living organism." This is the inner, fetish-like meaning of his activity.

The giant enterprise, Werner Sombart has shown, impersonally takes unto itself those sober virtues that in earlier phases of capitalism were personally cultivated by the entrepreneur. Thrift, frugality, honesty have ceased to be necessary to the managerial entrepreneur. Once these virtues were in the sphere wherein personal will-power was exercised; now they have become part of the mechanism of business; they "have been transferred to the business concern." They were "characteristics of human beings"; now they are "objective principles of business methods." When "the industrious tradesman went through his day's work in conscious self-mastery" it was necessary "to implant a solid foundation of duties" in the consciousness of men. But now "the businessman works at high pressure because the stress of economic activities carries him along in spite of himself." When the private and business "housekeeping" of the entrepreneur were identical, frugality was needed, but now the housekeeping is rigidly separated, and the frugal enterprise makes possible the lavish corporate manager, if he wants to be lavish. And so, "the conduct of the entrepreneur as a man may differ widely from his conduct as a tradesman." The name of the firm is all that matters, and this name does not rest upon the personal quality of the entrepreneurial flair of its head; it rests upon business routine and the careful administration of appropriate publicity.

No matter what the motives of individual owners and managers, clerks, and workers, may be, the Enterprise itself comes in time to seem autonomous, with a motive of its own: to manipulate the world in order to make a profit. But this motive is embodied in the rationalized enterprise, which is out for the secure and steady return rather than the deal with chance.

Just as the working man no longer owns the machine but is controlled by it, so the middle-class man no longer owns the enterprise but is controlled by it. The vices as well as the virtues of the old entrepreneur have been "transferred to the business concern." The aggressive business types, seen by Herman Melville as greedy, crooked creatures on the edges of an expanding nineteenth-century society are replaced in twentieth-century society by white-collar managers and clerks who may be neither greedy nor aggressive as persons, but who man the machines that often operate in a "greedy and aggressive" manner. The men are cogs in a business machinery that has routinized greed and made aggression an impersonal principle of organization.

The bureaucratic enterprise itself sets the pace of decision and obedience for the business and governmental officialdom and the world of clerks and bookkeepers, even as the motions of the worker are geared to the jump of the machine and the command of the foreman. Since the aims of each of its activities must be related to master purposes within it, the purposes of the enterprise in time become men's motives, and vice versa. The manner of their action, held within rules, is the manner of the enterprise. Since their authority inheres not in their persons, but in its offices, their authority belongs to the enterprise. Their status, and hence their relations to others in the hierarchy, inhere in the titles on their doors: the enterprise with its Board of Directors is the source of all honor and authority. Their safety from those above and their authority over those below derive from its rules and regulations. In due course, their very self-images, what they do and what they are, are derived from the enterprise. They know some of its secrets, although not all of them, and their career proceeds according to its rule and within its graded channels. Only within those rules are they supposed, impersonally, to compete with others.

III. Coercion, the ultimate type of power, involves the use of physical force by the power-holder; those who cannot be otherwise influenced are handled physically or in some way used against their will. Authority involves the more or less voluntary obedience of the less powerful; the problem of authority is to find out who obeys whom, when, and for what reasons. Manipulation is a secret or impersonal exercise of power; the one who is influenced is not explicitly told what to do but is nevertheless subject to the will of another.

In modern society, coercion, monopolized by the democratic state, is rarely needed in any continuous way. But those who hold power have often come to exercise it in hidden ways: they have moved and they are moving from authority to manipulation. Not only the great bureaucratic structures of modern society, themselves means of manipulation as well as authority, but also the means of mass communication are involved in the shift. The managerial demiurge extends to opinion and emotion and even to the mood and atmosphere of given acts.

Under the system of explicit authority, in the round, solid nineteenth century, the victim knew he was being victimized, the misery and discontent of the powerless were explicit. In the amorphous twentieth-century world, where manipulation replaces authority, the victim does not recognize his status. The formal aim, implemented by the latest psychological equipment, is to have men internalize what the managerial cadres would have them do, without their knowing their own motives, but nevertheless having them. Many whips are inside men, who do not know how they got there, or indeed that they are there. In the movement from authority to manipulation, power shifts from the visible to the invisible, from the known to the anonymous. And with rising material standards, exploitation becomes less material and more psychological.

No longer can the problem of power be set forth as the simple one of changing the processes of coercion into those of consent. The engineering of consent to authority has moved into the realm of manipulation where the powerful are anonymous. Impersonal manipulation is more insidious than coercion precisely because it is hidden; one cannot locate the enemy and declare war upon him. Targets for aggression are unavailable, and certainty is taken from men.

In a world dominated by a vast system of abstractions, managers may become cold with principle and do what local and immediate masters of men could never do. Their social insulation results in deadened feelings in the face of the impoverishment of life in the lower orders and its stultification in the upper circles. We do not mean merely that there are managers of bureaucacies and of communication agencies who scheme (although, in fact, there are, and their explicit ideology is one of manipulation); but more, we mean that the social control of the system is such that irresponsibility is organized into it.

Organized irresponsibility, in this impersonal sense, is a leading characteristic of modern industrial societies everywhere. On every hand the individual is confronted with seemingly remote organizations; he feels dwarfed and helpless before the managerial cadres and their manipulated and manipulative minions.

That the power of property has been bureaucratized in the corporation does not diminish that power; indeed, bureaucracy increases the use and the protection of property power. The state purportedly contains a balance of power, but one must examine the recruitment of its leading personnel, and above all the actual effects of its policies on various classes, in order to understand the source of the power it wields.

Bureaucracies not only rest upon classes, they organize the power struggle of classes. Within the business firm, personnel administration regulates the terms of employment, just as would the labor union, should a union exist: these bureaucracies fight over who works at what and for how much. Their fight is increasingly picked up by governmental bureaus. More generally, government manages whole class levels by taxation, price, and wage control, administrating who gets what, when, and how. Rather than the traditional inheritance of son from father, or the free liberal choice of occupation on an open market, educational institutions and vocational guidance experts would train and fit individuals of various abilities and class levels into the levels of the pre-existing hierarchies. Within the firm, again, and as part of the bureaucratic management of mass democracy, the graded hierarchy fragments class situations, just as minute gradations replace more homogeneous masses at the base of the pyramids. The traditional and often patriarchal ties of the old enterprise are replaced by rational and planned linkages in the new, and the rational systems hide their power so that no one sees their sources of authority or understands their calculations. For the bureaucracy, Marx wrote in 1842, the world is an object to be manipulated.

•   •   •   •

2. THE CONDITIONS OF
   MODERN WORK

As practice, craftsmanship has largely been trivialized into "hobbies," part of leisure not of work; or if work—a marketable activity—it is the work of scattered mechanics in handicraft trades, and of professionals who manage to remain free. As ethic, craftsmanship is confined to minuscule groups of privileged professionals and intellectuals.

The entire shift from the rural world of the small entrepreneur to the urban society of the dependent employee has instituted the property conditions of alienation from product and processes of work. Of course, dependent occupations vary in the extent of initiative they allow and invite, and many self-employed enterprisers are neither as independent nor as enterprising as commonly supposed. Nevertheless, in almost any job, the employee sells a degree of his independence; his working life is within the domain of others; the level of his skills that are used and the areas in which he may exercise independent decisions are subject to management by others. Probably at least ten or twelve million people worked during the 'thirties at tasks below the skill level of which they were easily capable; and, as school attendance increases and more jobs are routinized, the number of people who must work below their capacities will increase.

There is considerable truth in the statement that those who find free expression of self in their work are those who securely own the property with which they work, or those whose work-freedom does not entail the ownership of property. "Those who have no money work sloppily under the name of sabotage," writes Charles Péguy, "and those who have money work sloppily, a counter and different sloppiness, under the name of luxury. And thus culture no longer has any medium through which it might infiltrate. There no longer exists that marvelous unity true of all ancient societies, where he who produced and he who bought equally loved and knew culture."

The objective alienation of man from the product and the process of work is entailed by the legal framework of modern capitalism and the modern division of labor. The worker does not own the product or the tools of his production. In the labor contract he sells his time, energy, and skill into the power of others. To understand self-alienation we need not accept the metaphysical view that man's self is most crucially expressed in work-activity. In all work involving the personality market, as we have seen, one's personality and personal traits become part of the means of production. In this sense a person instrumentalizes and externalizes intimate features of his person and disposition. In certain white-collar areas, the rise of personality markets has carried self and social alienation to explicit extremes.

Thoreau, who spoke for the small entrepreneur, objected, in the middle of the nineteenth century, "to the division of labor since it divided the worker, not merely the work, reduced him from a man to an operative, and enriched the few at the expense of the many." "It destroyed," wrote F. O. Matthiessen, "the potential balance of his [Thoreau's] agrarian world, one of the main ideals of which was the union of labor and culture."

The detailed division of labor means, of course, that the individual does not carry through the whole process of work to its final product; but it also means that under many modern conditions the process itself is invisible to him. The product as the goal of his work is legally and psychologically detached from him, and this detachment cuts the nerve of meaning which work might otherwise gain from its technical processes. Even on the professional levels of white-collar work, not to speak of wage-work and the lower white-collar tasks, the chance to develop and use individual rationality is often destroyed by the centralization of decision and the formal rationality that bureaucracy entails. The expropriation which modern work organization has carried through thus goes far beyond the expropriation of ownership; rationality itself has been expropriated from work and any total view and understanding of its process. No longer free to plan his work, much less to modify the plan to which he is subordinated, the individual is to a great extent managed and manipulated in this work.

The world market, of which Marx spoke as the alien power over men, has in many areas been replaced by the bureaucratized enterprise. Not the market as such but centralized administrative decisions determine when men work and how fast. Yet the more and the harder men work, the more they build up that which dominates their work as an alien force, the commodity; so also, the more and the harder the white-collar man works, the more he builds up the enterprise outside himself, which is, as we have seen, duly made a fetish and thus indirectly justified. The enterprise is not the institutional shadow of great men, as perhaps it seemed under the old captain of industry; nor is it the instrument through which men realize themselves in work, as in small-scale production. The enterprise is an impersonal and alien Name, and the more that is placed in it, the less is placed in man.

As tool becomes machine, man is estranged from the intellectual potentialities and aspects of work; and each individual is routinized in the name of increased and cheaper per unit productivity. The whole unit and meaning of time is modified; man's "life-time," wrote Marx, is transformed into "working-time." In tying down individuals to particular tasks and jobs, the division of labor "lays the foundation of that all-engrossing system of specializing and sorting men, that development in a man of one single faculty at the expense of all other faculties, which caused A. Ferguson, the master of Adam Smith, to exclaim: 'We make a nation of Helots, and have no free citizens.'"

The introduction of office machinery and sales devices has been mechanizing the office and the salesroom, the two big locales of white-collar work. Since the 'twenties it has increased the division of white-collar labor, recomposed personnel, and lowered skill levels. Routine operations in minutely subdivided organizations have replaced the bustling interest of work in well-known groups. Even on managerial and professional levels, the growth of rational bureaucracies has made work more like factory production. The managerial demiurge is constantly furthering all these trends: mechanization, more minute division of labor, the use of less skilled and less expensive workers.

In its early stages, a new division of labor may specialize men in such a way as to increase their levels of skill; but later, especially when whole operations are split and mechanized, such division develops certain faculties at the expense of others and narrows all of them. And as it comes more fully under mechanization and centralized management, it levels men off again as automatons. Then there are a few specialists and a mass of automatons; both integrated by the authority which makes them interdependent and keeps each in his own routine. Thus, in the division of labor, the open development and free exercise of skills are managed and closed.

The alienating conditions of modern work now include the salaried employees as well as the wage-workers. There are few, if any, features of wage-work (except heavy toil—which is decreasingly a factor in wage-work) that do not also characterize at least some white-collar work. For here, too, the human traits of the individual, from his physique to his psychic disposition, become units in the functionally rational calculation of managers. None of the features of work as craftsmanship is prevalent in office and salesroom, and, in addition, some features of white-collar work, such as the personality market, go well beyond the alienating conditions of wage-work.

Yet, as Henri De Man has pointed out, we cannot assume that the employee makes comparisons between the ideal of work as craftsmanship and his own working experience. We cannot compare the idealized portrait of the craftsman with that of the auto worker and on that basis impute any psychological state to the auto worker. We cannot fruitfully compare the psychological condition of the old merchant's assistant with the modern saleslady, or the old-fashioned bookkeeper with the IBM machine attendant. For the historical destruction of craftsmanship and of the old office does not enter the consciousness of the modern wage-worker or white-collar employee; much less is their absence felt by him as a crisis, as it might have been if, in the course of the last generation, his father or mother had been in the craft condition—but, statistically speaking, they have not been. It is slow historical fact, long gone by in any dramatic consequence and not of psychological relevance to the present generation. Only the psychological imagination of the historian makes it possible to write of such comparisons as if they were of psychological import. The craft life would be immediately available as a fact of their consciousness only if in the lifetime of the modern employees they had experienced a shift from the one condition to the other, which they have not; or if they had grasped it as an ideal meaning of work, which they have not.

But if the work white-collar people do is not connected with its resultant product, and if there is no intrinsic connection between work and the rest of their life, then they must accept their work as meaningless in itself, perform it with more or less disgruntlement, and seek meanings elsewhere. Of their work, as of all of our lives, it can truly be said, in Henri Bergson's words, that: "The greater part of our time we live outside ourselves, hardly perceiving anything of ourselves but our own ghost, a colourless shadow. . . . Hence we live for the external world rather than for ourselves; we speak rather than think; we are acted rather than act ourselves. To act freely is to recover possession of oneself. . . ."

If white-collar people are not free to control their working actions they, in time, habitually submit to the orders of others and, in so far as they try to act freely, do so in other spheres. If they do not learn from their work or develop themselves in doing it, in time, they cease trying to do so, often having no interest in self-development even in other areas. If there is a split between their work and play, and their work and culture, they admit that split as a common-sense fact of existence. If their way of earning a living does not infuse their mode of living, they try to build their real life outside their work. Work becomes a sacrifice of time, necessary to building a life outside of it.

3. FRAMES OF ACCEPTANCE

Underneath virtually all experience of work today, there is a fatalistic feeling that work *per se* is unpleasant. One type of work, or one particular job, is contrasted with another type, experienced or imagined, within the present world of work; judgments are rarely made about the world of work as presently organized as against some other way of organizing it; so also, satisfaction from work is felt in comparison with the satisfactions of other jobs.

We do not know what proportions of the U.S. white-collar strata are "satisfied" by their work and, more important, we do not know what being satisfied means to them. But it is possible to speculate fruitfully about such questions.

We do have the results of some questions, necessarily crude, regarding feelings about present jobs. As in almost every other area, when sponge questions are asked of a national cross-section, white-collar people, meaning here clerical and sales employees, are in the middle zones. They stand close to the national average (64 percent asserting they find their work interesting and enjoyable "all the time"), while more of the professionals and executives claim interest and enjoyment (85 percent), and fewer of the factory workers (41 percent) do so.

Within the white-collar hierarchy, job satisfaction seems to follow the hierarchical levels; in one study, for example, 86 percent of the professionals, 74 percent of the managerial, 42 percent of the commercial employees, stated general satisfaction. This is also true of wage-worker levels of skill: 56 percent of the skilled, but 48 percent of the semi-skilled, are satisfied.

Such figures tell us very little, since we do not know what the questions mean to the people who answer them, or whether they mean the same thing to different strata. However, work satisfaction is related to income and, if we had measures, we might find that it is also related to status as well as to power. What such questions probably measure are invidious judgments of the individual's standing with reference to other individuals. And the aspects of work, the terms of such comparisons, must be made clear.

Under modern conditions, the direct technical processes of work have been declining in meaning for the mass of employees, but other features of work—income, power, status—have come to the fore. Apart from the technical operations and the skills involved, work is a source of income; the amount, level, and security of pay, and what one's income history has been are part of work's meaning. Work is also a means of gaining status, at the place of work, and in the general community. Different types of work and different occupational levels carry differential status values. These again are part of the meaning of the job. And also work carries various sorts of power, over materials and tools and machines, but, more crucially now, over other people.

  I. *Income:* The economic motives for work are now its only firm rationale. Work now has no other legitimating symbols, although certainly other gratifications and discontents are associated with it. The division of labor and the routinization of many job areas are reducing work to a commodity, of which money has become the only common denominator. To the worker who cannot receive technical gratifications from his work, its market value is all there is to it. The only significant occupational movement in the United States, the trade unions, have the pure and simple ideology of alienated work: more and more money for less and less work. There are, of course, other demands, but they can be only "fixed up" to lessen the cry for more money. The sharp focus upon money is part and parcel of the lack of intrinsic meaning that work has come to have.

Underlying the modern approach to work there seems to be some vague feeling that "one should earn one's own living," a kind of Protestant undertow, attenuated into a secular convention. "When work goes," as H. A. Overstreet, a job psychologist writing of the slump, puts it, "we know that the tragedy is more than economic. It is psychological. It strikes at the center of our personality. It takes from us something that rightly belongs to every self-respecting human being." But income security—the fear of unemployment or under-employment—is more important. An undertow of anxiety about sickness, accident, or old age must support eagerness for work, and gratification may be based on the compulsion to relieve anxiety by working hard. Widespread unemployment, or fear of it, may even make an employee happily thankful for any job, contented to be at any kind of work when all around there are many workless, worried people. If satisfaction rests on relative status, there is here an invidious element that increases it. It is across this ground tone of convention and fear, built around work as a source of income, that other motives to work and other factors of satisfaction are available.

II. *Status:* Income and income security lead to other things, among them, status. With the decline of technical gratification, the employee often tries to center such meaning as he finds in work on other features of the job. Satisfaction in work often rests upon status satisfactions from work associations. As a social role played in relation to other people, work may become a source of self-esteem, on the job, among co-workers, superiors, subordinates, and customers, if any; and off the job, among friends, family, and community at large. The fact of doing one kind of job rather than another and doing one's job with skill and dispatch may be a source of self-esteem. For the man or woman lonely in the city, the mere fact of meeting people at the place of work may be a positive thing. Even anonymous work contacts in large enterprises may be highly esteemed by those who feel too closely bound by family and neighborhood. There is a gratification from working downtown in the city, uptown in the smaller urban center; there is the glamour of being attached to certain firms.

It is the status conferred on the exercise of given skills and on given income levels that is often the prime source of gratification or humiliation. The psychological effect of a detailed division of labor depends upon whether or not the worker has been downgraded, and upon whether or not his associates have also been downgraded. Pride in skill is relative to the skills he has exercised in the past and to the skills others exercise, and thus to the evaluation of his skills by other people whose opinions count. In like manner, the amount of money he receives may be seen by the employee and by others as the best gauge of his worth.

This may be all the more true when relations are increasingly "objectified" and do not require intimate knowledge. For then there may be anxiety to keep secret the amount of money earned, and even to suggest to others that one earns more. "Who earns the most?" asks Erich Engelhard. "That is the important question, that is the gauge of all differentiations and the yardstick of the moneyed classes. We do not wish to show how we work, for in most cases others will soon have learned our tricks. This explains all the bragging. 'The work I have to do!' exclaims one employee when he has only three letters to write. . . This boastfulness can be explained by a drive which impels certain people to evaluate their occupations very low in comparison with their intellectual aspirations but very high compared with the occupations of others."

III. *Power:* Power over the technical aspects of work has been stripped from the individual, first, by the development of the market, which determines how and when he works, and second, by the bureaucratization of the work sphere, which subjects work operations to discipline. By virtue of these two alien forces the individual has lost power over the technical operations of his own work life.

But the exercise of power over other people has been elaborated. In so far as modern organizations of work are large scale, they are hierarchies of power, into which various occupations are fitted. The fact that one takes orders as well as gives them does not necessarily decrease the positive gratification achieved through the exercise of power on the job.

Status and power, as features of work gratification, are often blended; self-esteem may be based on the social power exercised in the course of work; victory over the will of another may greatly expand one's self-estimation. But the very opposite may also be true: in an almost masochistic way, people may be gratified by subordination on the job. We have already seen how office women in lower positions of authority are liable to identify with men in higher authority, transferring from prior family connections or projecting to future family relations.

All four aspects of occupation—skill, power, income, and status —must be taken into account to understand the meaning of work and the sources of its gratification. Any one of them may become the foremost aspect of the job, and in various combinations each is usually in the consciousness of the employee. To achieve and to exercise the power and status that higher income entails may be the very definition of satisfaction in work, and this satisfaction may have nothing whatsoever to do with the craft experience as the inherent need and full development of human activity.

4. THE MORALE OF THE
CHEERFUL ROBOTS

The institutions in which modern work is organized have come about by drift—many little schemes adding up to unexpected results—and by plan—efforts paying off as expected. The alienation of the individual from the product and the process of his work came about, in the first instance, as a result of the drift of modern capitalism. Then, Frederick Taylor, and other scientific managers, raised the division of labor to the level of planful management. By centralizing plans, as well as introducing further divisions of skill, they further routinized work; by consciously building upon the drift, in factory and in office, they have carried further certain of its efficient features.

Twenty years ago, H. Dubreuil, a foreign observer of U.S. industry, could write that Taylor's "insufficiency" shows up when he comes to approach "the inner forces contained in the worker's soul. . ." That is no longer true. The new (social) scientific management begins precisely where Taylor left off or was incomplete; students of "human relations in industry" have studied not lighting and clean toilets, but social cliques and good morale.

For in so far as human factors are involved in efficient and untroubled production, the managerial demiurge must bring them under control. So, in factory and in office, the world to be managed increasingly includes the social setting, the human affairs, and the personality of man as a worker.

Management effort to create job enthusiasm reflects the unhappy unwillingness of employees to work spontaneously at their routinized tasks; it indicates recognition of the lack of spontaneous will to work for the ulterior ends available; it also indicates that it is more difficult to have happy employees when the chances to climb the skill and social hierarchies are slim. These are underlying reasons why the Protesant ethic, a work compulsion, is replaced by the conscious efforts of Personnel Departments to create morale. But the present-day concern with employee morale and work enthusiasm has other sources than the meaningless character of much modern work. It is also a response to several decisive shifts in American society, particularly in its higher business circles: the enormous scale and complexity of modern business, its obviously vast and concentrated power; the rise of successfully competing centers of loyalty—the unions —over the past dozen years, with their inevitable focus upon power relations on the job; the enlargement of the liberal administrative state at the hands of politically successful New and Fair Deals; and the hostile atmosphere surrounding business during the big slump.

These developments have caused a shift in the outlook of certain sections of the business world, which in *The New Men of Power* I have called the shift from practical to sophisticated conservatism. The need to develop new justifications, and the fact that increased power has not yet been publicly justified, give rise to a groping for more telling symbols of justification among the more sophisticated business spokesmen, who have felt themselves to be a small island in a politically hostile sea of propertyless employees. Studies of "human relations in industry" are an ideological part of this groping. The managers are interested in such studies because of the hope of lowering production costs, of easing tensions inside their plants, of finding new symbols to justify the concentrated power they exercise in modern society.

To secure and increase the will to work, a new ethic that endows work with more than an economic incentive is needed.

During war, managers have appealed to nationalism; they have appealed in the name of the firm or branch of the office or factory, seeking to tap the animistic identifications of worker with work-place and tools in an effort to strengthen his identification with the company. They have repeatedly written that "job enthusiasm is good business," that "job enthusiasm is a hallmark of the American Way." But they have not yet found a really sound ideology.

What they are after is "something in the employee" outwardly manifested in a "mail must go through" attitude, "the 'we' attitude," "spontaneous discipline," "employees smiling and cheerful." They want, for example, to point out to banking employees "their importance to banking and banking's importance to the general economy." In conferences of management associations (1947) one hears: "There is one thing more that is wonderful about the human body. Make the chemical in the vial a little different and you have a person who is loyal. He likes you, and when mishaps come he takes a lot from you and the company, because you have been so good to him; you have changed the structure of his blood. You have to put into his work and environment the things that change the chemical that stimulates the action, so that he is loyal and productive. . . Somebody working under us won't know why, but . . . when they are asked where they work and why, they say 'I work with this company. I like it there and my boss is really one to work with.'"

The over-all formula of advice that the new ideology of "human relations in business" contains runs to this effect: to make the worker happy, efficient, and co-operative, you must make the managers intelligent, rational, knowledgeable. It is the perspective of a managerial elite, disguised in the pseudo-objective language of engineers. It is advice to the personnel manager to relax his authoritative manner and widen his manipulative grip over the employees by understanding them better and countering their informal solidarities against management and exploiting these solidarities for smoother and less troublesome managerial efficiency.

Current managerial attempts to create job enthusiasm, to paraphrase Marx's comment on Proudhon, are attempts to conquer work alienation within the bounds of work alienation. In the meantime, whatever satisfaction alienated men gain from work occurs within the framework of alienation; whatever satisfaction they gain from life occurs outside the boundaries of work; work and life are sharply split.

5. THE BIG SPLIT

Only in the last half century has leisure been widely available to the weary masses of the big city. Before then, there was leisure only for those few who were socially trained to use and enjoy it; the rest of the populace was left on lower and bleaker levels of sensibility, taste, and feeling. Then as the sphere of leisure was won for more and more of the people, the techniques of mass production were applied to amusement as they had been to the sphere of work. The most ostensible feature of American social life today, and one of the most frenzied, is its mass leisure activities. The most important characteristic of all these activities is that they astonish, excite, and distract but they do not enlarge reason or feeling, or allow spontaneous dispositions to unfold creatively.

What is psychologically important in this shift of mass leisure is that the old middle-class work ethic—the gospel of work—has been replaced in the society of employees by a leisure ethic, and this replacement has involved a sharp, almost absolute split between work and leisure. Now work itself is judged in terms of leisure values. The sphere of leisure provides the standards of which work is judged; it lends to work such meanings as work has.

Alienation in work means that the most alert hours of one's life are sacrificed to the making of money with which to "live." Alienation means boredom and the frustration of potentially creative effort, of the productive sides of personality. It means that while men must seek all values that matter to them outside of work, they must be serious during work: they may not laugh or sing or even talk, they must follow the rules and not violate the fetish of "the enterprise." In short, they must be serious and steady about something that does not mean anything to them, and moreover during the best hours of their day, the best hours of their life. Leisure time thus comes to mean an unserious freedom from the authoritarian seriousness of the job.

The split of work from leisure and the greater importance of leisure in the striving consciousness of modern man runs through the whole fabric of twentieth-century America, affect the meaningful experiences of work, and set popular goals and day-dreams. Over the last forty years, Leo Lowenthal has shown, as the "idols of work" have declined, the "idols of leisure" have arisen. Now the selection of heroes for popular biography appearing in mass magazines has shifted from business, professional, and political figures—successful in the sphere of production—to those successful in entertainment, leisure, and consumption. The movie star and the baseball player have replaced the industrial magnate and the political man. Today, the displayed characteristics of popular idols "can all be integrated around the concept of the consumer." And the faculties of reflection, imagination, dream, and desire, so far as they exist, do not now move in the sphere of concrete, practical work experience.

Work is split from the rest of life, especially from the spheres of conscious enjoyment; nevertheless, most men and many women must work. So work is an unsatisfactory means to ulterior ends lying somewhere in the sphere of leisure. The necessity to work and the alienation from it make up its grind, and the more grind there is, the more need to find relief in the jumpy or dreamy models available in modern leisure. Leisure contains all good things and all goals dreamed of and actively pursued. The dreariest part of life, R. H. Tawney remarks, is where and when you work, the gayest where and when you consume.

Each day men sell little pieces of themselves in order to try to buy them back each night and week end with the coin of "fun." With amusement, with love, with movies, with vicarious intimacy, they pull themselves into some sort of whole again, and now they are different men. Thus, the cycle of work and leisure gives rise to two quite different images of self: the everyday image, based upon work, and the holiday image, based upon leisure. The holiday image is often heavily tinged with aspired-to and dreamed-of features and is, of course, fed by mass-media personalities and happenings. "The rhythm of the week end, with its birth, its planned gaieties, and its announced end," Scott Fitzgerald wrote, "followed the rhythm of life and was a substitute for it." The week end, having nothing in common with the working week, lifts men and women out of the gray level tone of everyday work life, and forms a standard with which the working life is contrasted.

As the work sphere declines in meaning and gives no inner

direction and rhythm to life, so have community and kinship circles declined as ways of "fixing man into society." In the old craft model, work sphere and family coincided; before the Industrial Revolution, the home and the workshop were one. Today, this is so only in certain smaller-bourgeois families, and there it is often seen by the young as repression. One result of the division of labor is to take the breadwinner out of the home, segregating work life and home life. This has often meant that work becomes the means for the maintenance of the home, and the home the means for refitting the worker to go back to work. But with the decline of the home as the center of psychological life and the lowering of the hours of work, the sphere of leisure and amusement takes over the home's functions.

No longer is the framework within which a man lives fixed by traditional institutions. Mass communications replace tradition as a framework of life. Being thus afloat, the metropolitan man finds a new anchorage in the spectator sports, the idols of the mass media, and other machineries of amusement.

So the leisure sphere—and the machinery of amusement in terms of which it is now organized—becomes the center of character-forming influences, of identification models: it is what one man has in common with another, it is a continuous interest. The machinery of amusement, Henry Durant remarks, focuses attention and desires upon "those aspects of our life which are divorced from work and on people who are significant, not in terms of what they have achieved, but in terms of having money and time to spend."

The amusement of hollow people rests on their own hollowness and does not fill it up; it does not calm or relax them, as old middle-class frolics and jollification may have done; it does not re-create their spontaneity in work, as in the craftsman model. Their leisure diverts them from the restless grind of their work by the absorbing grind of passive enjoyment of glamour and thrills. To modern man leisure is the way to spend money, work is the way to make it. When the two compete, leisure wins hands down.

THE **WRONG** WAY
TO FIND JOBS
FOR NEGROES

DAVID WELLMAN

IN THE SUMMER OF 1966 I STUDIED A FEDERAL GOVERNMENT PRO-
gram designed to help lower-class youths find jobs. The program
was known as TIDE. It was run by the California Department of
Employment, and classes were held five days a week in the Youth
Opportunities Center of West Oakland.

The TIDE program was anything but a success. "I guess these
kids just don't want jobs," one of the teacher-counselors told me.
"The clothes they wear are loud. They don't talk decent English.
They're boisterous. And they constantly fool around. They refuse to take the program seriously."

"But isn't there a job shortage in Oakland?" I asked. "Does it
really *matter* how the kids act?"

"There's plenty of jobs. They're just not interested."

The students were 25 young men and 25 young women selected
by poverty-program workers in the Bay Area. Their ages ranged
from 16 to 22, and most were Negroes. The government paid
them $5 a day to participate. Men and women usually met sepa-
rately. I sat in on the men's classes.

The young men who took part in TIDE had a distinctive style.
They were "cool." Their hair was "processed." All sported sunglasses—very lightly tinted, with small frames. They called them
"pimp's glasses." Their clothes, while usually inexpensive, were
loud and ingeniously altered to express style and individuality.

From David Wellman, "The *Wrong* Way to Find Jobs for Negroes,"
Trans-action, 5: 5:9–18. Copyright © 1968 by *Trans*-action Magazine, St.
Louis, Missouri. Reprinted by permission of *Trans*-action and the author.

They spoke in a "hip" vernacular. Their vocabularies were small but very expressive. These young men, as part of the "cool world" of the ghetto, represent a distinctively black working-class culture.

To most liberals these young men are "culturally deprived" or "social dropouts." Most had flunked or been kicked out of school. Few had any intention of getting a high-school degree. They seemed uninterested in "making it." They had long and serious arrest and prison records. They were skeptical and critical of both the TIDE program and white society in general.

The TIDE workers were liberals. They assumed that if the young men would only act a little less "cool" and learn to smooth over some of their encounters with white authorities, they too could become full-fledged, working members of society. The aim of TIDE was not to train them for jobs, but to train them how to *apply* for jobs—how to take tests, how to make a good impression during a job interview, how to speak well, how to fill out an application form properly. They would play games, like dominoes, to ease the pain associated with numbers and arithmetic; they would conduct mock interviews, take mock tests, meet with management representatives, and tour places where jobs might be available. They were told to consider the TIDE program itself as a job—to be at the Youth Opportunities Center office on time, dressed as if they were at work. If they were late or made trouble, they would be docked. But if they took the program seriously and did well, they were told, they stood a pretty good chance of getting a job at the end of four weeks. The unexpressed aim of TIDE, then, was to prepare Negro youngsters for white society. The government would serve as an employment agency for white, private enterprise.

The program aimed to change the youngsters by making them more acceptable to employers. Their grammar and pronunciation were constantly corrected. They were indirectly told that, in order to get a job, their appearance would have to be altered: For example, "Don't you think you could shine your shoes?" Promptness, a virtue few of the youngsters possessed, was lauded. The penalty for tardiness was being put on a clean-up committee, or being docked.

For the TIDE workers, the program was a four-week exercise in futility. They felt they weren't asking very much of the youngsters—just that they learn to make a good impression on white society. And yet the young men were uncooperative. The only conclusion the TIDE workers could arrive at was: "They just don't want jobs."

Yet most of the youngsters took *actual* job possibilities very seriously. Every day they would pump the Youth Opportunities Center staff about job openings. When told there was a job at such-and-such a factory and that a particular test was required, the young men studied hard and applied for the job in earnest. The TIDE program *itself*, however, seemed to be viewed as only distantly related to getting a job. The youngsters wanted jobs, but to them their inability to take tests and fill out forms was *not* the problem. Instead, they talked about the shortage of jobs available to people without skills.

Their desire for work was not the problem. The real problem was what the program demanded of the young men. It asked that they change their manner of speech and dress, that they ignore their lack of skills and society's lack of jobs, and that they act as if their arrest records were of no consequence in obtaining a job. It asked, most important, that they pretend *they*, and not society, bore the responsibility for their being unemployed. TIDE didn't demand much of the men. Only that they become white.

PUTTING ON THE PROGRAM

What took place during the four-week program was a daily struggle between white, middle-class ideals of conduct and behavior and the mores and folkways of the black community. The men handled TIDE the way the black community in America has always treated white threats to Negro self-respect. They used subtle forms of subversion and deception. Historians and sociologists have pointed to slave subversion, to the content and ritual of Negro spirituals, and to the blues as forms of covert black resistance to white mores.

Today, "putting someone on," "putting the hype on someone," or "running a game on a cat" seem to be important devices used by Negroes to maintain their integrity. "Putting someone on," which is used as much with black people as with whites, allows a person to maintain his integrity in a hostile or threatening situation. To put someone on is to publicly lead him to believe that you are going along with what he has to offer or say, while privately rejecting the offer and subtly subverting it. The tactic fails if the other person recognizes what is happening. For one aim of putting someone on is to take pride in feeling that you have put something over on him, often at his expense. (Putting someone on differs from "putting someone down," which means active defiance and public confrontation.)

TIDE was evidently interpreted by the men as a threat to their self-respect, and this was the way they responded to it. Sometimes TIDE was put on. Sometimes it was put down. It was taken seriously only when it met the men's own needs.

There was almost no open hostility toward those in charge of TIDE, but two things quickly led me to believe that if the men accepted the program, they did so only on their own terms.

First, all of them appeared to have a "tuning-out" mechanism. They just didn't hear certain things. One young man was a constant joker and talked incessantly, even if someone else was speaking or if the group was supposed to be working. When told to knock it off, he never heard the command. Yet when he was interested in a program, he could hear perfectly.

Tuning-out was often a collective phenomenon. For instance, there was a radio in the room where the youngsters worked, and they would play it during lunch and coffee breaks. When the instructor would enter and tell them to begin work, they would continue listening and dancing to the music as if there were no one else in the room. When *they* were finished listening, the radio went off and the session began. The youngsters were going along with the program—in a way. They weren't challenging it. But they were undermining its effectiveness.

A second way in which the young men undermined the program was by playing dumb. Much of the program consisted of teaching the youngsters how to fill out employment applications. They were given lengthy lectures on the importance of neatness and lettering. After having filled out such forms a number of times, however, some students suddenly didn't know their mother's name, the school they last attended, or their telephone number.

This "stupidity" was sometimes duplicated during the mock job interviews. Five or more of the students would interview their fellow trainees for an imaginary job. These interviewers usually took their job seriously. But after it became apparent that the interview was a game, many of the interviewees suddenly became incredibly incompetent. They didn't have social-security numbers, they couldn't remember their last job, they didn't know what school they went to, they didn't know if they really wanted the job—to the absolute frustration of interviewers and instructors alike. Interestingly enough, when an instructor told them one morning that *this* time those who did well on the interview would actually be sent out on a real job interview with a real firm, the stupid and incompetent were suddenly transformed into model job applicants.

The same thing happened when the youngsters were given job-preference tests, intelligence tests, aptitude tests, and tests for driver's licenses. The first few times the youngsters took these tests, most worked hard to master them. But after they had gotten the knack, and still found themselves without jobs and taking the same tests, their response changed. Some of them no longer knew how to do the test. Others found it necessary to cheat by looking over someone's shoulder. Still others flunked tests they had passed the day before. Yet when they were informed of actual job possibilities at the naval ship yard or with the post office, they insisted on giving and taking the tests themselves. In one instance, some of them read up on which tests were relevant for a particular job, then practiced that test for a couple of hours by themselves.

Tuning-out and playing stupid were only two of the many ways the TIDE program was "put-on." Still another way: Insisting on work "breaks." The young men "employed" by TIDE were well-acquainted with this ritual, and demanded that it be included as part of their job. Since they had been given a voice in deciding the content of the program, they insisted that breaks become part of their daily routine. And no matter what the activity, or who was addressing them, the young men religiously adhered to the breaks.

The program started at 9:30 A.M. The youngsters decided that their first break would be for coffee at 10:30. This break was to last until 11. And while work was never allowed to proceed a minute past 10:30, it was usually 11:15 or so before the young men actually got back to work. Lunch began exactly at 12. Theoretically, work resumed at 1. This usually meant 1:15, since they had to listen to "one more song" on the radio. The next break was to last from 2:30 to 3. However, because they were finished at 3:30 and because it took another 10 minutes to get them back to work, the fellows could often talk their way out of the remaining half-hour. Considering they were being paid $5 a day for five hours' work, of which almost half were regularly devoted to breaks, they didn't have a bad hustle.

TRIPS AND GAMES

Games were another part of the TIDE program subverted by the put-on. Early in the program an instructor told the students that it might be helpful if they mastered arithmetic and language by playing games—dominoes, Scrabble, and various card games. The students considered this a fine idea. But what their instructor had intended for a pastime during the breaks, involving at most an hour a day, they rapidly turned into a major part of the instruction. They set aside 45 minutes in the morning and 45 minutes in the afternoon for games. But they participated in these games during their breaks as well, so that the games soon became a stumbling block to getting sessions back in order after breaks. When the instructor would say, "Okay, let's get back to work," the men would sometimes reply, "But we're already working on our math—we're playing dominoes, and you said that would help us with our math."

To familiarize the students with the kinds of jobs potentially available, the TIDE instructors took them on excursions to various work situations. These excursions were another opportunity for a put-on. It hardly seemed to matter what kind of company they visited so long as the visit took all day. On a trip to the Oakland Supply Naval Station, the men spent most of their times putting the make on a cute young WAVE who was their guide. One thing this tour did produce, however, was a great deal of discussion about the war in Vietnam. Almost none of the men wanted to serve in the armed forces. Through the bus windows some of them would yell at passing sailors: "Vietnam, baby!" or "Have a good time in Vietnam, man!"

The men would agree to half-day trips only if there was no alternative, or if the company would give away samples. Although they knew that the Coca-Cola Company was not hiring, they wanted to go anyway, for the free Cokes. They also wanted to go to many candy and cookie factories. Yet they turned down a trip to a local steel mill that they knew was hiring. TIDE, after all, was not designed to get them an interview—its purpose was to show them what sorts of jobs might be available. Given the circumstances, they reasoned, why not see what was *enjoyable* as well?

When the men were not putting-on the TIDE program and staff, they might be putting them down. When someone is put-down, he knows it. The tactic's success *depends* on his knowing it, whereas a put-on is successful only when its victim is unaware of it.

THE INTERVIEW TECHNIQUE

Among the fiercest put-downs I witnessed were those aimed at jobs the students were learning to apply for. These jobs were usually for unskilled labor: post-office, assembly-line, warehouse, and longshore workers, truck drivers, chauffeurs, janitors, bus boys, and so on.

The reaction of most of the students was best expressed by a question I heard one young man ask an instructor: "How about some tests for I.B.M.?" The room broke into an uproar of hysterical laughter. The instructor's response was typically bureaucratic, yet disarming: "Say, that's a good suggestion. Why don't you put it in the suggestion box?" The students didn't seem able to cope with that retort, so things got back to normal.

Actual employers, usually those representing companies that hired people only for unskilled labor, came to TIDE to demonstrate to the men what a good interview would be like. They did *not* come to interview men for real jobs. It was sort of a helpful-hints-for-success-interviews session. Usually one of the more socially mobile youths was chosen to play the role of job applicant. The entire interview situation was played through. Some employers even went so far as to have the "applicant" go outside and knock on the door to begin the interview. The students thought this was both odd and funny, and one said to the employer: "Man, you've already *seen* the cat. How come you making him walk out and then walk back in?"

With a look of incredulity, the employer replied: "But that's how you get a job. You have to sell yourself from the moment you walk in that door."

The employer put on a real act, beginning the interview with the usual small talk.

"I see from your application that you played football in high school."

"Yeah."

"Did you like it?"

"Yeah."

"Football really makes men and teaches you teamwork."

"Yeah."

At this point, the men got impatient: "Man, the cat's here to get a job, not talk about football!"

A wisecracker chimed in: "Maybe he's interviewing for a job with the Oakland Raiders."

Usually the employer got the point. He would then ask about the "applicant's" job experience, draft status, school record, interests, skills, and so on. The young man being interviewed usually took the questions seriously and answered frankly. But after a while, the rest of the group would tire of the game and (unrecognized, from the floor) begin to ask about the specifics of a real job:

"Say man, how much does this job pay?"

"What kind of experience do you need?"

"What if you got a record?"

It didn't take long to completely rattle an interviewer. The instructor might intervene and tell the students that the gentleman was here to help them, but this would stifle revolt for only a short while. During one interview, several of the fellows began loudly playing dominoes. That got the response they were looking for.

"Look!" shouted the employer. "If you're not interested in learning how to sell yourself, why don't you just leave the room so that others who are interested can benefit from this?"

"Oh no!" responded the ringleaders. "We work here. If you don't dig us, then *you* leave!"

Not much later, he did.

Sometimes during these mock interviews, the very nature of the work being considered was put-down. During one mock interview for a truck-driving job, some of the men asked the employer about openings for salesmen. Others asked him about executive positions. At one point the employer himself was asked point-blank how much he was paid, and what his experience was. They had turned the tables and were enjoying the opportunity to interview the interviewer. Regardless of a potential employer's status, the young men treated him as they would their peers. On one tour of a factory, the students were escorted by the vice-president in charge of hiring. To the TIDE participants, he was just another guide. After he had informed the students of the large number of unskilled positions available, they asked him if he would hire some of them, on the spot. He replied that this was just a tour and that he was in no position to hire anyone immediately. One youth looked at him and said: "Then you're just wasting our time, aren't you?"

Although shaken, the executive persisted. Throughout his talk, however, he innocently referred to his audience as "boys," which obviously bothered the students. Finally one of the more articulate men spoke up firmly: "We are young *men*, not boys!"

The vice-president blushed and apologized. He made a brave attempt to avoid repeating the phrase. But habit was victorious, and the word slipped in again and again. Each time he said "you boys" he was corrected, loudly, and with increasing hostility.

The students treated State Assemblyman Byron Rumford, a Negro, the same way. The meeting with Rumford was an opportunity for them to speak with an elected official about the job situation in the state. The meeting was also meant to air differences and to propose solutions. At the time, in fact, the men were quite angry about their rate of pay at TIDE. An instructor had suggested that they take the matter up with Rumford.

The meeting was attended by both the young men and women in the TIDE program. The young women were very well-dressed and well-groomed. Their clothes were not expensive, but were well cared for and in "good taste." Their hair was done in high-fashion styles. They looked, in short, like aspiring career women. The young men wore their usual dungarees or tight trousers, brightly colored shirts and sweaters, pointed shoes, and sunglasses.

The women sat quietly and listened politely. The men spoke loudly whenever they felt like it, and constantly talked among themselves.

Rumford, instead of speaking about the job situation in the Bay Area, chose to talk about his own career. It was a Negro Horatio Alger story. The moral was that if you work hard, you too can put yourself through college, become a successful druggist, then run for public office.

The moment Rumford finished speaking and asked for questions, one of the men jumped up and asked, "Hey man, how do we get a raise?" A male chorus of "Yeah!" followed. Before Rumford could complete a garbled answer (something like, "Well, I don't really know much about the procedures of a federally sponsored program"), the battle of the sexes had been joined. The women scolded the men for their "disrespectful behavior" toward an elected official. One said: "Here he is trying to help us and you-all acting a fool. You talking and laughing and carrying on while he talking, and then when he finishes you want to know about a raise. Damn!"

"Shit," was a male response. "You don't know what you talking about. We got a *right* to ask the cat about a raise. We elected him."

"We supposed to be talking about jobs," said another. "And we're talking about *our* job. If y'all like the pay, that's your business. We want more!"

The debate was heated. Neither group paid any attention to Rumford, who wisely slipped out of the room.

BATTLE OF SEXES—
OR CLASS CONFLICT?

During the exchanges it became clear to me that the differences in clothing and style between the sexes reflected their different orientations toward the dominant society and its values. In the minds of the young women, respect and respectability seemed paramount. At one point, a young woman said to the men, "You acting just like a bunch of *niggers*." She seemed to identify herself as a Negro, not as a "nigger." For the men, on the other hand, becoming a Negro (as opposed to a "nigger") meant giving up much that they considered positive. As one young man said in answer to the above, "You just ain't got no soul, bitch."

The women's identification with the values of white society became even clearer when the debate moved from what constituted respect and respectability to a direct attack on a personal level: "Do you all expect to get a job looking the way you do?" "Shit, I wouldn't wear clothes like that if I was on welfare."

The direction of the female attack corresponded closely with the basic assumptions of the TIDE program: People are without jobs because of themselves. This barrage hit the young men pretty hard. Their response was typical of any outraged male whose manhood has been threatened. In fact, when one young woman gibed, "You ain't no kinda man," some of the fellows had to be physically restrained from hitting her.

One of the men explained that "maybe the reason cats dress the way they do is because they can't afford anything else. Did you ever think of that?"

The woman's response was one I had not heard since the third or fourth grade: "Well, it doesn't matter what you wear as long as it's clean, pressed, and tucked-in. But hell, you guys don't even shine your shoes."

The battle of the sexes in the black community seems to be almost a class conflict. Many observers have noted that the black woman succeeds more readily in school than the black man. Women are also favored by parents, especially mothers. Moreover, the black woman has been for some time the most stable force and the major breadwinner of the Negro family. All these things put Negro women in harmony with the major values attached to work and success in our society. Black men, however, have been estranged from society, and a culture has developed around this estrangement—a male Negro culture often antagonistic to the dominant white society. The black woman stands in much the same relation to black men as white society does.

Even including Rumford, no group of officials was put down quite so hard as the Oakland police. Police brutality was constantly on the youngsters' minds. A day didn't pass without at least one being absent because he was in jail or one coming in with a story about mistreatment by the police. A meeting was arranged with a sergeant from the Community Relations Bureau of the Oakland police. The students seemed excited about meeting the officer on their own turf and with the protection provided by the program.

In anticipation of his arrival, the fellows rearranged the room, placing all the separate tables together. Then they sat down in a group at one end of the table, waiting for the officer.

PUTTING DOWN THE POLICE

Sergeant McCormack was an older man. And while obviously a cop, he could also pass for a middle-aged businessman or a young grandfather.

"Hi boys," he said as he sat down. His first mistake. He began with the five-minute speech he must give to every community group. The talk was factual, uninteresting, and noncontroversial: how the department is run, what the qualifications for policemen are, and how difficult it is for police to do their work and still please everyone. His talk was greeted with complete silence.

"I understand you have some questions," McCormack finally said.

"What about police brutality?" asked one man.

"What is your definition of police brutality?" the sergeant countered.

"How long you been a cop?" someone shouted.

"Over 20 years."

"And you got the nerve to come on sounding like you don't know what we talking about. Don't be jiving us. Shit, if you've been a cop *that* long, you *got* to know what we talking about."

"Righteous on that, brother!" someone chimed in.

"Well, I've been around a while, all right, but I've never seen any brutality. But what about it?"

"What *about* it?" There was a tone of disbelief mixed with anger in the young man's voice. "Shit man, we want to know why you cats always kicking other cats' asses."

The officer tried to draw a distinction between necessary and unnecessary police violence. The fellows weren't buying that. They claimed the police systematically beat the hell out of them for no reason. The officer asked for examples and the fellows obliged with long, involved, and detailed personal experiences with the Oakland Police Department. The sergeant listened patiently, periodically interrupting to check details and inconsistencies. He tried to offer a police interpretation of the incident. But the fellows were simply not in a mood to listen. In desperation the sergeant finally said, "Don't you want to hear *our* side of the story?"

"Hell no, motherfucker, we *see* your side of the story every night on 14th Street."

One young man stood up, his back to the officer, and addressed his contemporaries: "We *tired* of talking! We want some action! There's a new generation now. We ain't like the old folks who took all this shit off the cops." He turned to the sergeant and said, "You take that back to your goddamn Chief Preston and tell him."

McCormack had a silly smile on his face.

Another youngster jumped up and hollered, "You all ain't going to be smiling when we put dynamite in your police station!"

The officer said simply, "You guys don't want to talk."

"You see," someone yelled, "the cat's trying to be slick, trying to run a game on us. First he comes in here all nice-talking, all that shit about how they run the police and the police is to protect us. And then when we tell him how they treat us he wants to say we don't want to talk. Shit! We want to talk, he don't want to listen."

From this point on, they ran over him mercilessly. I, with all my biases against the police, could not help feeling compassion for the sergeant. If the police are an authority figure in the black community, then this episode must be viewed as a revolt against authority—*all* authority. There was nothing about the man's life, both private and public, that wasn't attacked.

"How much money you get paid?"

"About $12,000 a year."

"For being a cop? Wow!"

"What do you do?"

"I work in the Community Relations Department."

"Naw, stupid, what *kind* of work?"

"I answer the telephone, speak to groups, and try to see if the police treat the citizens wrong."

"Shit, we could do that and we don't even have a high-school education. Is that all you do? And get that much money for it?"

"Where do you live?"

"I'll bet he lives up in the hills."

"I live in the east side of Oakland. And I want you to know that my next-door neighbor is a colored man. I've got nothing against colored people."

"You got any kids?"

"Yeah, two boys and a girl."

"Shit, bet they all went to college and got good jobs. Any of your kids been in trouble?"

"No, not really."

"What do they do?"

"My oldest boy is a fighter pilot in Vietnam."

"What the hell is he doing over there? That's pretty stupid."

"Yeah man, what are we fighting in Vietnam for? Is that your way of getting rid of us?"

"Well, the government says we have to be there and it's the duty of every citizen to do what his country tells him to do."

"We don't want to hear all that old bullshit, man."

"Hey, how come you wear such funny clothes? You even look like a goddam cop."

"Yeah baby, and he smells like one too!"

The barrage continued for almost half an hour. The instructor finally called a halt: "Sergeant McCormack has to get back, fellows. Is there anything specific that you'd like to ask him?"

"Yeah. How come Chief Preston ain't here? He's always talking to other people all over the country about how good the Oakland cops are and how there ain't going to be no riot here. Why don't he come and tell us that? We want to talk with the chief."

The next day, Deputy Chief Gain came—accompanied by the captain of the Youth Division, the lieutenant of that division, and a Negro sergeant. It was a formidable display of police authority. The youngsters were noticeably taken aback.

Chief Gain is a no-nonsense, businesslike cop. He takes no static from anyone, vigorously defends what he thinks is correct, and makes no apologies for what he considers incorrect. He is an honest man in the sense that he makes no attempt to cover up or smooth over unpleasant things. He immediately got down to business: "All right now, I understand you guys have some beefs with the department. What's the story?"

The fellows started right in talking about the ways they had been mistreated by the police. The chief began asking specific questions: where it happened, when it happened, what the officer looked like, and so on. He never denied the existence of brutality. That almost seemed to be assumed. He did want details, however. He always asked whether the youth had filed a complaint with the department. The response was always No. He then lectured them about the need to file such complaints if the situation was to be changed.

He explained the situation as he saw it: "Look fellows, we run a police force of 654 men. Most of them are good men, but there's bound to be a few rotten apples in the basket. I know that there's a couple of men who mistreat people, but it's only a few and we're trying our best to change that."

"Shit, I know of a case where a cop killed a cat and now he's back on the beat."

"Now wait a minute—"

"No more waiting a minute!" someone interrupted. "You had two cops got caught taking bribes. One was black and the other Caucasian. The black cat was kicked off the force and the white cat is back on."

"Yeah, and what about that cat who killed somebody off-duty, what about him?"

"Hold on," Gain said firmly. "Let's take these things one at a time." He didn't get very far before he was back to the "few rotten apples" argument.

"If its only a few cops, how come it happens all the time?"

The deputy chief told them that he thought it was the same few cops who were causing all the problems. "Unless you file complaints each time you feel you've been mistreated, we can't do anything about it. So it's up to you as much as it is up to us."

For the first time in weeks, I intruded into the discussion. I pointed out to Gain that he was asking citizens to police their own police force. He had argued that in most situations the department had a good deal of control over its own men—the same argument the police had used against a civilian-review board. Now he was saying the opposite: that it was up to the citizens. This seemed to break the impasse, and the students howled with delight.

"What happens if a cop beats my ass and I file a complaint?" demanded one. "Whose word does the judge take?"

"The judge takes the evidence and evaluates it objectively and comes to a decision."

"Yeah, but it's usually two cops against one of us, and if both testify against me, what happens? Do you think the judge is going to listen to me?"

"Bring some witnesses."

"That ain't going to do anything."

"That's your problem. If you don't like the legal system in this country, work to change it."

"Okay man," one fellow said to Gain, "You pretty smart. If I smack my buddy here upside the head and he files a complaint, what you gonna do?"

"Arrest you."

"Cool. Now let's say one of your ugly cops smacks *me* upside the head and I file a complaint—what you gonna do?"

"Investigate the complaint, and if there's anything to it, why we'll take action—probably suspend him."

"Why do *we* get arrested and *you* investigated?"

The deputy chief's response was that most private companies with internal difficulties don't want to be investigated by outside agencies. The fellows retorted: "Police are *not* a private business. You're supposed to work for the people!"

"And shit, you cats get to carry guns. No businessman carries guns. It's a different scene, man."

"How come you got all kinds of squad cars in this neighborhood every night? And have two and three cops in each of them?"

"The crime rate is high in this area," replied Gain, "and we get a lot of calls and complaints about it."

"Yeah, and you smart enough to know that when you come around here, you better be wearing helmets and carrying shotguns. If you that clever, you got to be smart enough to handle your own goddamn cops."

At this point the fellows all jumped on the deputy chief the same way they had jumped on the sergeant the day before:

"Why don't you just let us run our own damn community?"

"Yeah. There should be people on the force who've been in jail because they the only people who know what it means to be busted. People in West Oakland should be police because they know their community; you don't."

"Why do we get all the speeding tickets?"

"How come we got to fight in Vietnam?"

"Why the judges so hard on us? They don't treat white cats— I mean dudes—the way they do us."

The chief began assembling his papers and stood up. "You guys aren't interested in talking. You want to yell. When you want to talk, come down to my office and if I'm free we'll talk."

But the fellows had the last word. While he was leaving they peppered him with gibes about how *they* were tired of talking; promised to dynamite his office; and called the police chief a coward for not coming down to speak with them.

When the deputy chief had gone, the instructor asked the fellows why they insisted on ganging up on people like the police. The answer provides a lot of insight into the young men's actions toward the police, businessmen, and public officials:

"These people just trying to run a game on us. If we give them time to think about answers, they gonna put us in a trick. We've *got* to gang up on them because they gang up on us. Did you dig the way that cat brought three other cats with him? Besides, how else could we put him down?"

A SUBTLE FORM OF RACISM

In effect, the young men had inverted the meaning and aims of the TIDE program. It was supposed to be an opportunity for them to plan careers and prepare themselves for their life's work. The immediate goal was to help them get started by showing them how to get a job. The youngsters had a different view. The program was a way to play some games and take some outings—an interesting diversion from the boredom and frustration of ghetto life in the summer. In some respects it was also a means of confronting, on equal terms, high-status people normally unavailable to them—and of venting on them their anger and hostility. But primarily they saw it as a $5-a-day job.

The program simply did not meet the needs of these young men. In fact, it was not really meant to. The Great Society was trying to "run a game on" black youth. TIDE asked them to stop being what they are. It tried to lead them into white middle-class America by showing that America was interested in getting them jobs. But America does not provide many jobs—let alone attractive jobs—for those with police records, with few skills, with black skins. The youths knew that; TIDE workers knew that, too. They did not train youths for work, but tried to make them believe that if they knew *how* to get a job, they could. The young men saw through the sham.

Ironically, the view that Negro youths, rather than society, are responsible for the employment problem is very similar to the familiar line of white racism. Negroes will not work because they are lazy and shiftless, the old Southern bigot would say. The Northern liberal today would put it a little differently: Negroes cannot get jobs because of their psychological and cultural impediments; what they need is cultural improvement, a proper attitude, the ability to sell themselves. Both views suggest that inequities in the job and opportunity structure of America are minor compared to the deficiencies of Negroes themselves. In the end, Northern liberals and Southern racists agree: The problem is mainly with Negroes, not with our society. This fallacy underlies much of the war on poverty's approach and is indicative of the subtle forms racism is taking in America today.

THE ECONOMIC
SITUATION OF
NEGRO LABOR

SIDNEY M. PECK

SOME FIFTY YEARS AGO SCOTT NEARING, THEN PROFESSOR OF POLITI-
cal economy at the Wharton School of Finance, wrote a classic
work on the monetary rewards for services rendered and from
property owned in the United States.[1] He titled his book *Income*
and proceeded to differentiate sources of income derived from the
ownership of land and capital on the one hand and the rendering
of services (productive labor) on the other. In an exhaustive
analysis of income and employment statistics, Nearing pointed to
the great disparity in the accumulation of wealth between the
owners of property (land and capital) and the laboring mass
(producers of wealth), and predicted that "with the passing years,
the producers of wealth will file a protest of ever-increasing
volume against an economic system which automatically gives to
those who already have."[2]

Concerned about the concentration of wealth among the few
while the many lived in poverty, Nearing argued that minimum
wage standards paid to the laboring man merely kept "body and
soul together" but did not maintain the health and efficiency of
the family.[3] He argued that workers should receive a fair wage

From Sidney M. Peck, "The Economic Situation of Negro Labor," *The
Negro and the American Labor Movement*, Julius Jacobson (ed.), pp. 210–
231. Copyright © 1968 by Julius Jacobson. Reprinted by permission of
Doubleday & Company, Inc., New York.

[1] Scott Nearing, *Income* (1915).
[2] Ibid., 200.
[3] Ibid., 175.

standard rather than a scale based on bare subsistence. A fair wage standard for a man and wife and three youngsters living in the industrial cities of the Northeast in 1915 was between $750 and $1000 a year.[4] Today the question is whether a family can keep body and soul together on $3000 a year—or $4000.

Scott Nearing is still writing his pungent analyses in political economy,[5] and the problem of "rich man, poor man" still troubles the public mind.[6] For in 1963 nearly 36 per cent of the American people lived in poverty or deprivation, at family income levels below $3000 and $4000 respectively.[7]

A whole new literature about the poor has emerged since the late John Kennedy raised the specter of mass impoverishment during the preliminaries to the 1960 presidential campaign. With the publication of Michael Harrington's *The Other America* (1963), the question of poverty in the midst of affluence became firmly rooted in the soil of politics. Studies on income distribution, collected essays on poverty, journalistic polemics, and academic monographs apparently found their mark in the State of the Union message which President Lyndon B. Johnson delivered to Congress on January 8, 1964. "This administration," he said, "today, here and now, declares unconditional war on poverty in America,"[8] and the following March 16 he sent Congress a Message on Poverty pointing to "the great unfinished work of our society." "To finish that work," wrote President Johnson, "I have called for a national war on poverty. Our objective: total victory."[9] He urged that one billion dollars be set aside for the task. Some considered this a small sum indeed, compared to the

[4] Ibid., 176.
[5] See his regular editorial column "World Events" in the *Monthly Review*, an independent Socialist journal of opinion.
[6] Cf. Herman Miller, *Rich Man, Poor Man* (1964).
[7] Leon H. Keyserling, *Progress on Poverty*, Conference on Economic Progress (1964), 23.
[8] *The New York Times* (Jan. 9, 1964). Recent collected works on the poverty question include:
    Arthur B. Shostak and William Gomberg, eds., *New Perspectives on Poverty* (1965).
    Robert E. Will and Harold G. Vatter, eds., *Poverty in Affluence* (1965).
    Louis A. Ferman, Joyce L. Kornbluh, and Alan Haber, eds., *Poverty in America* (1965).
[9] From the "Message on Poverty" (March 16, 1964), reproduced in Will and Vatter, eds., op. cit., 16.

continued appropriation of billions of dollars for the military budget.

It would be naïve to suggest that the governing Administration has finally bowed to the wishes of reformers and Socialists indignant over the extent of poverty in this nation of concentrated wealth. The fact is that the thirty-four million persons who live in poverty and the thirty-two million more subject to income deprivation constitute the raw social dynamite for politically explosive events. And the struggle for civil rights among Negroes driven to frustration could provide the necessary ideological spark. The Administration was obviously aware that the civil rights movement, North and South, had turned increasingly to the mass base of poor Negroes in the urban ghettos and rural hinterlands. And out of this class of poor Negroes arose new leaders, young, militant, and potentially revolutionary.

If the revolution to destroy color segregation also ignited the struggle to eliminate social poverty, then the Establishment would surely be endangered. It is difficult enough to assert military presence against the "have not" revolutions in Asia, Africa, and Latin America without having to contend with potentially revolutionary "have nots" at home. The current strategy of established power is to increase the supply of butter at home while exporting the supply of guns abroad. The "war on poverty" and the "war in Vietnam" are strategic politico-military responses to latent and manifest challenges of "have not" revolutions. These are wars being fought by the Establishment to channel and contain the thrust for social change so as to preserve the industrial-military complex intact. What is the likelihood that the governing powers will be able to lead the revolution of the poor to victory at home while mounting a military war to put down the revolutionary poor in Vietnam? It is the thesis of this essay that the prerequisites for total victory in the war against poverty necessitate a transformation of the national power structure and the concurrent disengagement of military power abroad. The economic situation of Negro labor in the United States will be considered as the historic case in point.

Following emancipation the great majority of the Negro people turned to the land as small-crop farmers, but the image of a Southern Populist countryside economically based on "forty acres and a mule" did not long prevail. With the restoration of Southern plantocracy to power after a decade of black reconstructionism, Negro farm ownership came under the immediate domination of the planter class.[10] Under a system of farm tenancy and sharecropping, Negroes became rural peons subordinated to the landed power of Southern segregation. In the countryside of the South, Negro laborers were the backbone of the cotton-belt economy as sharecroppers, tenants, or marginal farmers. While the Southern Negro has been close to the soil for most of his history in the United States, he has rarely been able to make a go of it. Lacking capital, credit, and machinery, Negro farmers in the South were easily displaced. Between 1920 and 1960 nearly 700,000 Negro farm operators disappeared from the Southern land, and in the thirty years since the great depression nearly a half million Negro sharecroppers have been eliminated.[11]

Nowhere has the agricultural revolution had more consequences than in the Southern farming states. In the decade 1950–1960 Southern agricultural employment dropped a full 50 percent. Between 1940 and 1959 the national drop in the number of farms was 39 percent; in the South the decline was 45 percent. Negro farms have been the hardest hit, dropping 60 percent. Total farm employment dropped 41 percent in the nation between 1950 and 1960, but southern agricultural employment was cut exactly in half. Fully 1.6 million Southern workers were forced out of farming, out of a nationwide total of 2.8 million lost jobs.[12] The most dramatic change in the occupational and residential situation of the Negro people has been "the disappearance of the southern Negro farmer."[13] Only 15 percent of Negro labor still farm for a livelihood and they are unable to cope with the advances of agricultural technology. Most of the remaining Negro farm operatives are tenant farmers and sharecroppers.[14]

The great demographic shift of Negro people from the Southern countryside to the urban centers of the North took place

[10] Cf. C. Vann Woodward, *The Strange Career of Jim Crow* (1957).
[11] See Robin Williams, "Social Change and Social Conflict: Race Relations in the United States, 1944–64" (unpublished paper, 1964), 4.
[12] Michael Munk, "Revolution on the Farm," *Monthly Review* XIV (1963), 547.
[13] Williams, op. cit., 4.
[14] Tom Kahn, *The Economics of Equality*, League for Industrial Democracy (1964), 26.

during the war years of the forties. The need for industrial labor to supply the military juggernaut continued through the Korean war. The interesting fact is that the total population growth of the ten largest central cities during the period 1930–1940 was equivalent to the growth of the Negro population in those cities. During the two decades between 1940 and 1960, more than three million Negroes who had been displaced from the soil relocated in the ten largest central cities of the nation.[15] Nearly two thirds of the Negro population of the North came to live in the great slums of the urban centers. As a consequence of metropolitan residential segregation, an apartheid ecology has emerged.[61]

The vast majority of ghettoized Negroes are wage workers. They constitute the core of what David Danzig has called the new working class.[17] They are essentially a class of factory operative and service workers, fast becoming obsolete. The very same technological processes that have largely emptied our farmlands of people, and impoverished the bulk of small rural landholders who remain, now wreak havoc on the ghettoized workers in the industrial centers.

Because of the rapid introduction of labor-displacing equipment in the mass-production industries, a large segment of Negro workers has become part of a new class of minimal labor value. The economic marks of unemployment, underemployment, and unemployability characterize them as unwanted workers in the great urban centers.

Most Negroes (over 70 percent of the Negro labor force in 1962) are employed in the blue-collar and service occupations.[18] In blue-collar work, more than four out of five nonwhite workers occupy semiskilled or unskilled jobs. In service work, Negroes are most likely to be employed in low-paying domestic and un-

[15] L. Schnore and H. Sharp, "The Changing Color of Our Big Cities," *Trans*-action (1963), 12–14. "It is no exaggeration to call the growth of non-white populations in our major cities one of the truly outstanding social trends of the twentieth century." Ibid., 14.
[16] M. Grodzins, "The Metropolitan Area as a Racial Problem" in *American Race Relations Today*, Earl Raab, (1962), 98.
[17] David Danzig, "The Meaning of Negro Strategy," ed. *Commentary*, Feb. 1964, 46.
[18] M. A. Kessler, "Economic Status of Nonwhite Workers, 1955–62," *Special Labor Force Report* no. 33, U. S. Department of Labor, Bureau of Labor Statics (1963), 3.

skilled service jobs. These are the very jobs which are becoming increasingly marginal to the economy, for it is precisely in these occupational categories that the demand for routine labor will cease as automatic equipment is introduced. And yet Negro entrance into blue-collar and service work continues to increase even though the proportion of jobs in these areas continues to decline. The cybernation of routine industrial and service labor is proceeding at a fantastic pace. Industrialist John Snyder has estimated that 40,000 jobs are being displaced each week. While the work force has decreased in the goods-producing industries, productivity has continued to increase at a growing pace. In addition to the traditional heavy industries, cybernation has also caused large-scale labor displacement in chemical and food-processing areas, in the painting trades, clerical operations, and the burgeoning service industries. Given this continued pattern of job displacement, the AFL-CIO has suggested that the economy must have at least 75,000 new and additional jobs each week for the next ten years in order to have full employment. Yet less than 5 percent, or about 200,000 new jobs, were provided by private industry during the years 1957–1963.[19]

While it is difficult to come by reliable unemployment figures, a reasonable estimate is that over eight million people who would like to have jobs are not working. In an interesting breakdown of data for 1962, the Labor Department found that actually 18.2 percent of the labor force had been unemployed for a significant period of time during that year. Long-term unemployment continued to be reflected in the 1964 labor-force statistics, which showed that more than one third of the unemployed were out of work for ten weeks or more. In round numbers, at least four million persons had been out of work for nearly four months of the year.[20] The economist Leon Keyserling has observed that "close to two thirds of the poverty in the United States is directly connected with a deficient overall economic performance, of which excessive unemployment is the most important single manifestation."[21]

[19] H. Rowen, *The Free Enterprisers* (1964), 264.
[20] Ben Seligman, "Automation and the Union," *Dissent*, Winter 1965, 50–51.
[21] Leon H. Keyserling, "Poverty and the Economy," *Nation*, June 7, 1965, 616; see also Robert H. Ferguson, "Unemployment: Its Scope, Measurement, and Effect on Poverty," New York State School of Industrial and Labor Relations, May 1965.

Early in 1965, experts from the United States, Canada, and a half dozen other nations met in Washington (Organization for Economic Cooperation and Development) and reached these major conclusions:

1. Maximum economic growth alone will not relieve current economic employment levels.

2. Between automation and population expansion . . . the potential job force is growing so fast that present policies won't cut back the current percent unemployment ratio—and it will probably continue to climb.[22]

The expectation is that fifteen million persons will be unemployed at the end of this decade.

It is also projected that 50 percent of this future army of unemployed will be under twenty-five years of age, over half will be black labor, and two thirds will be blue-collar workers. Of course, these three categories overlap with one another. The point is that the 1960s have witnessed the emergence of a new laboring class, largely "colored," economically exploited, and outside of the union movement and the main economy. Joseph Zeisel has noted that "The major increase in this squeeze-out from the labor force among nonwhites seems to have occurred after 1958, a year of recession from which there has been only imperfect recovery in many respects."[23]

As S. M. Miller has suggested, it is important to recognize that labor in the U.S. may be moving into a dual economy. In the main economy, fairly stable employment with regular income rises guaranteeing higher living standards may continue to be available for those who remain in it. But in the marginal economy centered upon low-level service trades and occupations, employment is unstable, wages are low, and the standard of living is depressed. Miller has commented that "In this kind of [colonial] situation of a successful white economy and a meager bush economy there are wide disparities . . . for the gains in the main economy do not rapidly trickle down to those in the 'other America.' "[24]

[22] Quoted in Peter Irons, "The Cybernation Revolution," *Progressive*, Feb. 1965, 20.
[23] Joseph Zeisel, "A Profile of Unemployment," in *Men Without Work*, S. Lebergott, ed., (1963), 124.
[24] S. M. Miller, "Poverty, Race, and Politics," in *The New Sociology*, I. Horowitz, ed., (1964), 298–99.

It is estimated that the real unemployment rate among Negroes is about 20 percent. While Negroes constitute 11 percent of the labor force, they compose 22 percent of the unemployed. The color line is also apparent when it is known that proportionately *twice* as many Negro adults as whites are unemployed *whatever the occupation, educational level, sex, or age*. Also proportionately, three times as many Negro teen-agers are unemployed as whites in the same age group, and the same holds true for the twenty-four to forty-four age categories. While the unemployment rate of Negro teen-agers is about 30 percent, it is also true that in some cities today 70 percent of Negro youths between the ages of sixteen and twenty-one who are out of school are also out of work. In some of the more depressed urban areas Negro unemployment rates climb to 50 percent. The pointed statistic is that one out of every nine Negro males is out of work, and in Chicago the proportion of unemployed Negro males is even higher.[25] S. M. Willhelm and E. H. Powell have written that:

> With the onset of automation the Negro is moving out of his historical state of oppression into uselessness. Increasingly, he is not so much economically exploited as he is irrelevant. And the Negro's economic anxiety is an anxiety that will spread to others in our society as automation proceeds.
>
> The tremendous historical change for the Negro is taking place in these terms: he is not needed. He is not so much oppressed as unwanted; not so much unwanted as unnecessary; not so much abused as ignored. The dominant whites no longer need to exploit him. If he disappeared tomorrow he would hardly be missed. As automation proceeds it is easier and easier to disregard him. . . .
>
> The historical transition for the Negro . . . is a movement out of the southern cotton fields, into the northern factories and then to the automated urbanity of "nobodiness."[26]

All of this is immediate and automatic. To paraphrase Harrington, it is done without the intervention of a single racist, yet it is a profound part of racism in the United States.[27]

[25] Harold Baron, "Negro Unemployment," *New University Thought*, Oct., 1963, 44-45.
[26] S. M. Willhelm and E. H. Powell, "Who Needs the Negro?" *Transaction*, Oct. 1964, 3.
[27] M. Harrington, *The Other America* (1963), 71, 79.

Since 1954, Negroes have usually constituted between 20 and 30 percent of all long-term unemployment covering between fifteen and twenty-seven weeks or more. In 1962 *over 46 percent* of the nearly five million workers who were unemployed for a minimum *period of fifteen weeks* were Negroes.[28] In short, the cybernation revolution has resulted in "structural" unemployment for the American work force; that is, the permanent destruction of jobs rather than cyclical layoffs. When this happens, the blow falls disproportionately upon the Negro worker. As the last significant ethnic group to enter the factory, Negroes have low seniority (in a union shop) and they will be laid off first. As one of the least-skilled groups in the work force, they will have the hardest time getting other jobs. The "older" Negro (over forty) may well be condemned to unemployability for the rest of his life. The young Negro worker has twice as difficult a time becoming employed as his white counterpart.

In an exhaustive review of the literature, O. R. Gursslin and J. L. Roach have examined the extent to which federal programs of job retraining fail to reach into this large category of unwanted Negro labor. In addition to the central fact that there are more job seekers than jobs, they have cited several social-psychological factors related to ghettoized living which inhibit the process of retraining for the demands of an automated economy. Finally, they have concluded that it would be quite unlikely for "any appreciable number of lower-status Negroes to reach the point of working in automation-type jobs."[29]

Not only has Negro unemployment increased but the unemployment gap between Negro and white also continues to grow. Thus, in 1940 the unemployment rates were 13 percent for whites and 14.5 percent for nonwhites. Twelve years later the gap had increased tenfold, for in 1962 the corresponding figures were 4.9 percent (whites) and 11 percent (nonwhites). The figures for 1964 stood at 5.9 percent and 12.4 percent respectively. These statistics demonstrate quite conclusively that semiskilled and unskilled Negro labor have become increasingly obsolete. The long-term unemployment of black labor is the direct consequence of the rapid introduction of industrial cybernation in the major

[28] Rowen, op. cit., 268–69.
[29] O. R. Gursslin and J. L. Roach, "Some Issues in Training the Unemployed," *Social Problems,* Summer 1964, 95.

goods-producing and service industries. The impoverished economic situation of the Negro may be generally attributed to his status as a marginal worker on the land, in the factory, and at the service counter. Professor Kenneth Clark has summed up the situation for Harlem Negroes in this way:

> Many of the jobs now held by Negroes in the unskilled oc- occupations are deadend jobs, due to disappear during the next decade. Decreases, or no expansions, are expected in industries in which more than 43 percent of the labor force in Harlem is now employed. . . . As the pressure of unemployed white workers in the few expanding areas of unskilled jobs grows, the ability of ghetto residents to hold on to such jobs becomes doubtful. And by 1970, there will be 40 percent more Negro teen-agers (16–21) in Harlem than there were in 1960.[30]

The most dramatic expression of this displacement of human labor from land and factory is the massive institutionalization of Negro poverty. Unemployment and poverty go hand in hand when one reflects on the fact that two thirds of all Negro families have annual incomes below the $3000 poverty level; that one fourth of all Negro families do not receive more than $2000 yearly; that 41 percent of all unattached Negro males had incomes under $1000 a year. More than 40 percent of all Negroes in rural areas have less than $1000 a year income. The income gap between Negro and white is readily apparent when it is realized that only one out of eight families in the United States as a whole falls below the $2000 income level. This gap has been steadily increasing in the recent past and is expressed in the fact that the incidence of poverty among Negroes increased to nearly two and a half times the white rate during the period from 1950 to 1962. Professor Robin Williams has commented that "in the midst of continuous reminders of rising affluence, Negroes have not increased their income levels relative to whites for over a decade."[31] Thus, in 1963 more than 43 percent of all nonwhite families in the U.S. lived in poverty, compared to less than 16 percent of all white families. In 1954, for instance, the average male Negro worker earner $1623 less than the average white worker. By 1960 this differenec increased to $2062. In that same

[30] Kenneth B. Clark, *Dark Ghetto* (1965), 36.
[31] Williams, op. cit., 19.

year 75 percent of all Negroes earned less than the white average of $5981. Hence, the income pattern for Negro families in the U.S. has hardly changed since the early fifties. Herman Miller has stated that "In the last decade . . . there has been no change in income differential between [Negroes and whites]. The median pay of the Negro worker has remained stuck at about 55 percent of the white."[32]

In Professor Williams's words, "the color of one's skin influences what share of the nation's wealth one receives."[33] David Danzig had recorded that "between 1952 and 1962, the average Negro income dropped from 57 percent to 53 percent of the average white income, and the future looks even darker than the present."[34] A recent survey conducted by the Labor Department showed that the annual income differential between Negro and white for the year 1960–1961 amounted to $2320. Siegel's intensive statistical analysis of the color-income differential concluded that in its "net regional, educational, and occupation effects, the cost of being a Negro is roughly a thousand dollars." And further, "about two fifths of the difference in average earnings of whites and nonwhites is what it costs to be black."[35] His research demonstrated that irrespective of regional, occupational, and educational similarities of Negroes and whites, the income differences between black and white are clearly revealed as a thousand-dollar billing for blackness. When it is recalled that two out of three Negro households earn less than $4000 a year, then the financial expense of being Negro is tragic indeed. Residential segregation, long-term unemployment, low incomes, all add to costs that defy translation into mere dollar-and-cents terms. The great mass of impoverished Negroes in the urban ghettos have become human beings unwanted at any cost. As Willhelm and Powell have emphasized:

> Basically millions of Negroes are unwanted . . . so we discard them by establishing new forms of "Indian reservations" called "Negro ghettos." We even make them somewhat economically self-sufficient through an "Indian hand-out." One out of every

32 Quoted in Kahn, op. cit., 17.
33 Williams, op. cit.
34 Danzig, op. cit., 45.
35 Paul Siegel, "On the Cost of Being Negro," unpublished paper, National Opinion Research Center (1964), 15–17.

four Negroes in Chicago . . . receives some form of public welfare assistance. . . .

Is it an exaggeration to suggest that the deteriorated city has now become the junk heap upon which the economically worthless are thrown? [36]

In Harlem the median income is $3480 as compared to $5103 for all New York City residents. Professor Clark has warned:

> The total economy is threatened by the decay of the heart of American cities, long the creative centers of industry, transportation, communication, education, and by the dangers of Negro unemployment, and Negro concentration in low status menial service jobs. No longer can the potential consuming power of one tenth of the American people be ignored, and the power of consumption be artificially limited by the low wages of Negroes and the heavy load of Negro welfare dependency, a product of broken families caused in turn in large part by male unemployment. [37]

In Greater Cleveland, for instance, the situation of Negro labor is dramatic proof of an apartheid economy which links color to poverty. Data from the 1960 census show that while Negroes constituted 15 percent of the total population they accounted for 32 percent of the families with an income under $3000. [38] While the median income for the total population was $6943, it came to $4763 for nonwhites. Negroes made up 33 percent of the unemployed men in the county although they accounted for only 14 percent of the male labor force. The unemployment rate for Negro men was 12.6 percent compared to 4.2 percent for white men.

During the period 1952–1963 the number of blue-collar jobs in Greater Cleveland decreased by eighty thousand at the same time that eighteen thousand more Negro males were entering Cleveland's labor force. The consequence of this displacement is that while the Negro population increased to 16.3 percent of the county total, they accounted for approximately:

[36] Willhelm and Powell, op. cit., 3.
[37] Clark, op. cit., 47.
[38] These data have been compiled in an excellent report by L. E. Schaller and C. W. Rawlings, *Race and Poverty*, Office of Race and Religion (May 1964).

84.5 percent of all families receiving Aid to Dependent Children;
75.3 percent of all families receiving City Relief;
64.3 percent of all families receiving County Relief;
58.8 percent of all persons receiving Aid to the Disabled;
54.6 percent of all persons receiving Aid for the Blind.

In Chicago Negro families pay 28 percent higher rent per month than whites and receive more defective housing in return. In Philadelphia nearly half of the housing used by Negroes is listed as "dilapidated" or "deteriorated" as compared to only 15 percent of white houses. And in Cleveland the Urban League has rendered the conservative estimate that the "color tax" paid by Negroes for rental units in 1960 was approximately three and a quarter million dollars.[39] In concrete terms this means that "every Negro family renting a house must pay at least one dollar more per month for a sound unit and fifteen dollars more for a deteriorating or dilapidated unit than would be normally paid in an open market."[40] Urban renewal adds to this financial burden, as it forces many Negro families to relocate in high-rental substandard housing units. The evidence is that "Negroes dispossessed by urban renewal pay 10 percent higher rent after the relocation than before."[41]

In addition to higher costs in housing, impoverished Negroes generally pay more for consumer goods as well. David Caplovitz has demonstrated in detail how the credit system in the black ghetto allows local merchants to exploit poor Negroes in the consumer market.[42] The high rate of illiteracy coupled with the role of the child shopper in single-parent Negro families suggests the possibilities for merchant manipulation of the Negro poor. If the "poor pay more" in general for consumer items, the poor Negro, in particular, is confronted with a "color tax" in the purchase of goods and services.

The real income of Negro labor bound to the apartheid ecology of job, school, and residence is measured in the cost of being a Negro as producer and consumer. Paid $1000 less than whites for labor services rendered irrespective of occupational, age, sex,

---

[39] *The Negro in Cleveland, 1950–1963*, Research Department, Cleveland Urban League (1964), 18.
[40] Ibid.
[41] Batchelder, op. cit., 6.
[42] David Caplovitz, *The Poor Pay More* (1963), 12–20.

and educational categories, Negroes also pay more as consumers in the marketplace. And, at the same time, most low-income Negro families must support a larger number of children than whites. Developments in urban renewal, higher education, industrial technology and ecology, and wage standards "injure the Negro poor by reducing their supply of housing, increasing their distance from natural education rooms, creating manufacturing jobs where Negroes are excluded, and sending uneducated Negroes from farms to cities where the number of unskilled jobs is falling as the social minimum wage rises above the marginal revenue product of these Negro unskilled."[43]

It is apparent that the circle of impoverishment that Scott Nearing located a half century ago in an income structure which favors property-owning income over service income is now centered on marginal Negro labor. Little wonder that a leading prophet of the "triple revolution," W. H. Ferry, has observed that:

> We had better make up our minds to basic repairs of our ramshackle economic scheme, which has been held together since the Depression by war and threat of war and is now buffeted, as never before, by the technological typhoon. If others won't make up their minds to this task, the Negroes will make it up for them. As I look around for the historical force that will bring today's chaotic elements into a revolutionary point, the unemployed Negro sails inexorably into view. The un-integrated Negro is the symbol of our democratic failure and the unemployed Negro is the most conspicuous evidence we have of the breakdown of the economic machinery. I do not believe there is any chance that the private self-adjusting economy can provide today's unemployed Negro with a job, the traditional means to dignity and self-respect. Tax-cut and war on poverty not withstanding, most Negroes now without work are not likely to be taken up into the private economy again.[44]

If Ferry is correct in his observation that the established system cannot provide the unemployed Negro with a job, then what is

[43] Batchelder, op. cit., 13–14.
[44] W. H. Ferry, "Further Reflections on the Triple Revolution," Center for the Study of Democratic Institutions reprint (Spring 1965), 11.

the Negro to do? How can unwanted black labor re-enter the main economy? In the absence of organizational power, where is the displaced Negro worker to turn? To whom can he speak and how should he phrase his demands? If the unemployed Negro has sailed into view as a new historical force, then what is the direction of the winds of change which have blown him on to the scene? Or is the current situation best described as the drift of castaways having no port in view?

One could suggest that the sudden, explosive resistance of individual black workers against acts of political injustice, police brutality, and the like are the expressions of anger vented against an oppressive system by those who have been reduced to powerless despair. But the venting of anger in individual acts against the symbols of oppression is anarchic and desperate conduct. It is action without objectives or goals in view. Yet the basis for a concerted class-consciousness is there. As Willhelm and Powell have stated, ". . . the Negro knows what is happening to him. He knows that the main problem is unemployment and that he is being removed from economic participation in white society. . . . He is aware of the attempt to wall him off, out of sight and out of mind. And he also knows that he cannot let this happen to him."[45] In his study of unemployed Negro workers in the Detroit area, J. C. Leggett concluded that "Employment insecurity continues to be a source of working-class consciousness in the industrial community. The unemployed prove to be more militant than the employed, while a disproportionately large number of Negro workers take militant positions in class matters."[46]

The obvious political problem is for unemployed Negroes to determine what are militant positions to take in matters which affect the class as a whole. In Cleveland, as elsewhere, it is apparent that current trends in industrial technology jeopardize the livelihood of all semiskilled and unskilled workers. Unemployment is not restricted to Negro labor nor is the condition of income impoverishment reserved for black workers. The pocket of poverty in Cleveland's near Westside reflects the increasing number of white workers drawn into the circle of impoverishment. As Charles Rawlings has noted, "Cleveland's near Westside white

[45] Willhelm and Powell, op. cit., 4.
[46] J. C. Leggett, "Economic Insecurity and Working-Class Consciousness," *American Sociological Review*, April 1964, 234.

residents and the Eastside low-income Negroes have more in common than their racial prejudices reveal."[47] Or as Gabriel Kolko has written:

> . . . It should not be thought that income inequality is primarily a racial problem, for the overwhelming majority of the low-paid are white. Their economic position is due to factors that are far more difficult to cope with than racial discrimination. The vested interests in income inequality, and the economic fabric that support that inequality, are very much stronger than any opposition to better job opportunities for Negroes.[48]

The vicious circle of income impoverishment that engulfs between thirty and fifty million Americans is structured in an economic order dominated by corporate power. It is not enough to demand a legitimate share for the black of skin when whites are suffering in poverty as well. It is not enough to plead for integrated education when the education of the urban poor of all colors is totally inadequate. It is not enough to break down the residential barriers of color when insensitive programs of urban renewal have wrought havoc among all the urban poor. Every knowledgeable commentator on the current American scene knows full well that the solutions to the problems posed by the existence of possibly fifty million American poor must involve major structural changes in the American political economy.

Herbert Gans has presented a series of proposals for the governing administration to adopt in coping with the twin conditions of poverty and unemployment in an automating society.[49] Bayard Rustin[50] and Tom Kahn[51] have pressed hard for a massive public-works program which would rebuild our central cities anew. If carried to their logical conclusion, these are proposals that necessitate fundamental decisions about the allocation of valued resources in the effort to provide a dignified livelihood for all of the American people.

Shall the American economy build one B-70 bomber or five

[47] Shaller and Rawlings, op. cit., 27.
[48] Gabriel Kolko, *Wealth and Power in America* (1962) 93–94.
[49] Herbert Gans, "Some Proposals for Government Policy in an Automating Society," in Shostak and Gomberg, op. cit., 142–57.
[50] *The New York Times*, April 27, 1964, 1.
[51] Kahn, op. cit., 52–55.

hundred new school classrooms? Shall the government order one new air-to-air missile or construct 26,150 dwelling units at $14,500 each? Shall the administration requisition one Polaris nuclear submarine or twenty-three hospitals of 160 beds each?[52] These are decisions of economic policy that rest upon the structure of national power which dispossessed black and white labor must eventually confront. In the absence of any significant power confrontation, millions of dollars will continue to be spent in the current pork-barrel effort to rehabilitate the great metropolitan slums. These projects, funded by an overlapping involvement of federal agencies and private foundations, are part and parcel of the grand scheme of welfarism which Charles Silberman has so cogently described.[53] The whole effort is illustrative of the great waste of productive energy characteristic of corporate reformism in modern times. While millions of dollars are expended to "cool off" the victims of impoverishment, billions are spent to safeguard "national interests" abroad. The questions, of course, are what shall be the national interests at home and abroad? And who will determine how the national interests are best implemented?

The Establishment hopes to lead the "war on poverty" by funding projects of community action in which the poor are "directly involved" in the local decision-making structure. Thus, the poor are encouraged to participate actively at all levels of organization in those community programs designed to eliminate local poverty. Borrowing a page from Saul Alinsky, this approach gives the poor the opportunity to *confront* the local power structure directly through organizational representation. When two B-52 Hustler bombers crashed on return from a saturation bombing mission in Vietnam, eighteen million dollars went to the bottom of the sea. This loss amounted to several million dollars more than all of the federal money now allocated to fight the war on poverty in the Greater Cleveland community with its Eastside-Westside pockets of poor blacks and whites. How do the spokesmen for the poor confront the local power structure on this matter? The fact is that the war on poverty program has served to fragment the political concerns of the impoverished into

52 These comparative costs were brought together by Martin Oppenheimer, "Disarmament and the War on Poverty," American Friends Service Publication (1964), 7.
53 Charles Silberman, *Crisis in Black and White* (1964), 308–55.

local issues of petty consequence which oftentimes lead to further divisions between black and white, as well as between employed workers and the unemployed.

What is apparent to many is the need for an organizational way to unite the automated jobless and the ill-paid marginal labor with harried industrial workers into "new working-class" unions which, in turn, might well provide the political leverage for substantial social change. It is the structure of national power that the poor and their political allies need to confront. The transformation of the national power structure and the concurrent disengagement of military power abroad are requisite to decisions of political economy which aim to reallocate valued resources in order to eliminate mass impoverishment in our society. It is fallacious to conceive that established power in the corporate economy will lead the poor to a total victory in the "war against poverty" without keeping the *poor in their established place*. The economic situation of Negro labor today is a particular case in point.

A full eleven decades have passed since free Northern labor abruptly shifted gears in support of the anti-slavery movement, as the slave system sought to extend to free soil. In an age of nuclear power, automation, and cybernation the white working class is confronted with a decision of similar import. The role of labor as a vehicle for meaningful social change apparently depends on this issue. It depends on the degree to which white workers, and their leaders, will identify with the interests and welfare of the segregated working class living in the great urban ghettos. For it is also the case that white workers have been hit by plant closedowns, technological displacement, and seasonal unemployment. They live under the constant shadow of automation. The facts are that 76 percent of the long-term unemployed and 74 percent of the *very long-term* unemployed are white. The total consequence is that trade unionism in the U.S. is losing its basic membership as a result of the new technology. That is why union leaders today have the difficult task of carrying out the ideology and logic of "business unionism"—that is to say, of protecting those not yet fired against the pressures of those not yet hired. Under this policy the contracts negotiated by union officials usually lead to either the outright dismissal of a substantial share of the work force in order to protect the job situation of those who remain, or the protection of job rights for those currently employed while the reservoir of jobs in the economy dries up through natural attrition.[54] Both approaches ensure the fact that new employees will not be hired.

It is apparent that these approaches are mere holding actions that do not begin to deal with the larger consequences of automation and unemployment. Furthermore, these holding actions of official leadership are subject to intense criticism by rank-and-file dissidents. Opposition groups have formed in several international unions over issues of production speed-up and impending labor displacement.[55] In some industries the introduction of measured day-rate pay has set off political disturbances of electoral significance in the union. While the measured day rate eliminates incentive pay, it retains the labor incentive because the worker must now fill a production standard in order to receive full pay for the day. The rate and flow of production, of course, are determined by the company in line with its market situation. The result is a union-sanctioned policy of management speed-up which ordinary workers are unable to block through the grievance procedure. Not only have some union leaders guaranteed higher productivity rates in exchange for job protection through the acceptance of the measured day rate, other union officials have advocated wage reductions in order to prevent threatened plant closure for alleged economic reasons. Oftentimes voluntary wage cuts on the part of the labor force are successful in persuading company officials to postpone or delay decisions to terminate plant operations. But again, this tactic proves to be a mere holding action which fails to succeed in the long run.[56]

There is increasing recognition in the labor movement that collective bargaining with a given company or industry cannot hope to contend with the larger effects of increased productivity and the new technology. As Seligman has phrased it, "No one has yet come up with the idea of 'bargaining' for those outside the gates."[57]

[54] For a presentation of labor responses, see E. M. Kassalow, "Labor Relations and Employment Aspects After Ten Years," in Morris Phillipson, ed., *Automation* (1962), 316–33.

[55] See the interesting account of the rank-and-file dispute with the leadership of unionist Harry Bridges in Stanley Weir, "The ILWU: A Case Study in Bureaucracy," *New Politics*, Winter 1964, 23–28.

[56] Cf. James Matles (interview), "Against the Mainstream," *Studies on the Left*, Winter 1964, 43–54.

[57] Seligman, op. cit., 44.

The structures of craft and industrial unionism have not as yet adapted to the changed social conditions in the productive sphere. *Once a terminal plant situation develops for particular workers, the union also terminates collective responsibility for the conditions of unemployment.* The archaic pattern of union organization, which excludes the jobless from the bargaining unit, has unwittingly brought into being a new marginal working class. In their discerning manner, R. Bendix and S. M. Lipset once referred to this splintering of the working class as "a major element in the preservation of the stability of the American social structure."[58] The implication of their view is that for workers to unite around agreed-upon class interests would obviously be dysfunctional for the established system of power.

In reviewing the history of trade union growth in the United States, B. Cochran concluded that stages of union expansion were directly related to the struggles of workers in periods of social crisis. His thesis was that in every one of the five major periods of union growth a heavy undertone of radical struggle moved organized labor to specific concerns for social change. Writing in the late fifties, he was moved to predict that American labor in midpassage will once more respond to the developing economic and military crisis with a new stage of determined union militancy.[59] His prediction may hold if the fragmented struggles in the shop are joined with the sometimes anarchic struggles of unwanted workers in the Negro ghettos.

The significant question is whether the potential for class concern becomes expressed in meaningful organization among the jobless, and between the unions and the unemployed. The initiative for organizational involvement will probably arise from the most radical sources of alienated Negro labor. The rumble of social disturbance from below may not take to manipulative channeling by the established powers. While metropolitan police generally serve to block anarchic acts from leading to uncontrolled mass rioting, disenchantment and outmoded approaches to poverty and unemployment in a setting of advanced technology could become expressed in forms of political mobilization resistant to

[58] S. M. Lipset and R. Bendix, *Social Mobility in Industrial Society* (1959), 106.
[59] Bert Cochran, "American Labor in Midpassage," in B. Cochran, ed., *American Labor in Midpassage* (1959), 39.

external control. The potential for such mobilization of effort undoubtedly exists and its implications for social power are apparent. The central political problem would be to find ways and means of establishing organizational links with dissident elements in the workshop who have recently been successful in challenging established union policy regarding industrial speed-up and job dsplacement. Wildcat strikes in the shop may have relationship to wildcat strikes in the street if the objectives of each are bound to the common need for a decent income and a dignified life. Miller has written that "Members of the new working class will increasingly not look to others to produce change for them but will demand and act themselves for change and improvement in their conditions."[60]

But this insight is predicated on the belief that dispossessed workers will act as a class around common power interests. When the impact of structural unemployment goes beyond the bounds of color, it is a dangerous game to play with ideas of quota employment and preferential hiring. It is one thing to press militantly for the abolition of racist job barriers maintained by companies and unions alike. It is quite another matter to ask for the assignment of rigid job quotas as a civil rights demand.

Danzig has made a salient point in his comment that the "inadequacy of the trade-union movement today forces the Negro group into acting to mitigate its own economic plight. Thus the sectarian character of the Negro's economic and political demands can be understood as a consequence of the absence of any political movement in the United States that speaks for the new American proletariat in general."[61] If it is indeed the case that there exists a lack of political leadership from the established trade unions, then it is doubly important for civil rights groups to move into the political void and provide the kind of leadership that will inspire the impoverished of whatever color.

The civil rights revolution, if it be so, is torn between the sectarian nationalists impatiently demanding a "legitimate share" for their striving black bourgeoisie and the integrationists who seek white allies in the common quest for liberal social reform. More than anything else, the freedom movement needs a proletarian

---

[60] S. M. Miller, op. cit., 305.
[61] D. Danzig, op. cit., 46.

perspective that responds to the needs of the working class as a whole. "Black and white—unite and fight" may be an old slogan but it is needed today more than ever to heal the wounds of divisiveness which tend to separate working people into hostile camps. Some thirty years ago the American left worked to create a unity of effort between black and white in the industrial workshops and communities of our land. While they were not altogether successful, the fact is that in the industrial workshops of today many white workers are led by Negroes, and in many plants there is an overwhelming white vote for Negro leadership.

Although it is apparent that individual white workers may hold prejudices toward Negroes that are linked to the prevailing attitudes of the community, it does not follow that at any given moment they will act in accord with these prejudices, or that they cannot act in opposition to them. It is one thing to suggest and document that white workers are racist, bigoted, and prejudiced.[62] Nevertheless, it is quite possible for white workers of varied ethnicity to engage in common alliances with civil rights groups, student groups, peace groups, or radical groups when their interests as workers are at stake. There are potential allies in the white working class which the Negro rights movement has not even begun to tap, mainly because localized rights leadership has very little perspective and hardly any approach at all. The great potential in the labor movement is on the level of rank-and-file involvement. And the rank and file will respond if the issues are openly and honestly communicated to them. In another context I wrote that "the absence of intellect and organization which can appeal to the spontaneous concerns of class-conscious underdogs in the industrial workshops is the most serious void in American politics."[63] That void has yet to be filled, and as a result marginal black and white labor pay more every day in every way. Is it more a hope than prediction to suggest once again that "there is every indication that, with the passing years, the [marginal] producers of wealth will file a protest of ever-increasing volume against an economic system which automatically gives to those who already have"? Possibly not.

In sum, structural developments in the productive sphere have

---

[62] Cf. Sidney M. Peck, *The Rank-and-File Leader* (1963), 166–72.
[63] Ibid., 350.

led to changed conditions of industry. These changed conditions, in turn, cause ordinary workers of whatever color to become aware of those technologic forces in society that control their destiny in the labor market. It also throws into sharp relief those archaic union structures which fail to adapt to the new social environment of cybernation technology. Worker dissatisfaction in the shop over conditions of industrial speed-up through measured day-rate schemes has led to open disenchantment with union leadership. Anarchic disturbances and radical politics have come to characterize the behavior of many unwanted workers now ghettoized in the metropolitan center. Class-conscious organizational links between these splintered working-class segments become more probable as the dynamic within the system becomes more obvious in its social and economic effects.

ALTERNATIVES AND CHANGE

NEW CAREERS FOR THE POOR

ARTHUR PEARL

THE BASIC THESIS OF THIS ARTICLE IS THAT A HEALTHY PEOPLE NEED opportunity. They need to have command over their lives and that all choices that affect man's life begin with opportunities to earn a living. Persons who have access to positions which pay well have a considerable measure of freedom over their lives. If they have the means they can live where they want to live. They have control over the education offered to their children even to the extent of purchasing a private education if they so desire. They have control over leisure time, and they have political power. They are in the most desirable of bargaining positions. It is the employer who searches them out, not the reverse condition, which is the lot of poor people.

Two slogans get to the heart of the New Career position. One is, service *from* rather than service *to* the poor, and the other is, job first and education later. New Careers offers a form of social engineering, defining first what needs to be done and a population which needs something to do and then organizing the functions of work to meet the characteristics of the work-seeking population. There are a number of basic principles that affect the New Career program: (1) there must be enough work for all people seeking work, (2) there must be sufficient guarantee of job permanence to which people can commit themselves to that activity without that gnawing anxiety that comes with transient employment, (3) the entering position must pay sufficiently well to enable people to move out of poverty, e.g., they must be able to exercise control over where they live, the education of their children, and factors of this kind, (4) there must be opportunities for horizontal mobility; that is, increments for years of worthy service, and opportunities for limited promotion without a marked commitment to advanced education; (5) there must be opportunities for vertical mobility which would require a flexibility in the training and educational establishment to allow the person to go as far as his talents and his motivation can carry him; and (6) there must be transfer and cross-over which allow the person the flexibility to move to related occupations or to other geographical regions.[1]

Education can serve as a model for the projection of New Careers. At the present time the organization of the teaching function is absurd. Not only is the universe of potential teachers much too restricted, but also the teacher role incorporates a wide range of different activities ranging from the most menial to the most complicated. Highly trained persons are engaged in unchallenging tasks. Certainly much that a teacher does does not require a college education. Some of the things the teacher does requires little more than bare literacy. Such things as supervising hallways, taking roll, operating audio-visual equipment, and other non-teaching functions are a waste of a professional's time. Even many of the so-called "teaching" activities are minimally challenging. Helping students with homework or reading to a class, or even explaining a scientific principle can be effectively managed by relatively untrained personnel if they are supervised by more highly trained staff. It has been demonstrated that even very young, apparently intellectually impaired ten-year-olds, can be enormously helpful in aiding younger children in their school work. There are many other more complicated tasks which teachers perform which do demand a measure of experience, knowledge and skill, but not the four years plus of college that is currently a requisite for certification. Education in particular could benefit from a hier-

[1] The New Career idea is expanded in Pearl, Arthur, and Riessman, Frank, *New Careers for the Poor.* New York: Copyright © 1965 by The Free Press, a division of The Macmillan Company. Reprinted with permission of The Macmillan Company.

archy of roles—a series of landings to allow for a wider range of persons to function in the field. This could be organized as follows:

1) Teacher Aide

Prerequisite: six weeks on-the-job training or equivalent.

Duties: clerical functions, supervisor of hallways, homework help, laboratory aide, library aide, showroom attendant, audio-visual operator. Junior member of teaching team.

Post Service Training: Training on the job for which college credits are received (especially classroom management and teaching practice). Supportive theory and content courses in evenings and summer.

Promotional Opportunities: Eligibility for teacher assistant if complete prerequisite or Aide II—more responsibilities in above described duties.

Salary: Aide I $3500 to $5150
      Aide II $4200 to $5850

2) Teaching Assistant

Prerequisite: Two years of appropriate college work or two years of service as Aide and 36 units of college work in growth and development and specific course content.

Duties: Assisting teacher or teacher associate in the classroom, conducting small groups, supervising teacher aide. Intermediate member of teaching team.

Post Service Training: Continuation of program described for aide, additional college work (education theory and further sophistication in content areas).

Promotional Opportunities: Eligibility for teaching associate if complete prerequisites or Assistant II; more responsibilities in above described duties.

Salary: Assistant I $4500 to $6150
      Assistant II $5200 to $6850

3) Teaching Associate

   Prerequisites: Five years of appropriate college work; three years of service as assistant and 36 units of college work in supervision and content specialization.

   Duties: Classroom instruction, senior member of teaching team, supervisor of aide and assistant.

   Post Service Training: Continuation of program described for aide and assistant, additional college work (education theory, further sophistication in content areas—consultation and supervision).

   Promotional Opportunities: Eligibility for teacher on complete prerequisites

   Salary: $7,000 to $10,500

4) Teacher

   Prerequisite: M.A. in Education, three years of service as associate and 48 units of college work in consultation, supervision and content speciailzation.

   Duties: Teaching of aide, assistant and associate teachers; consultation to lower echelon staff; supervision and specialist in content areas (guest lecturer on teaching team) and administration.

   Post Service Training: Continuation of program with goal of further development leading to doctoral degree.

   Promotional Opportunities: Opportunity to advance to local, state or national structures, transfer to university setting.

   Salary: $9000 to $15,000

The establishment of a series of landings, while providing handsome salaries for top echelon personnel would actually allow for more people to teach without necessarily increasing the expense to the taxpayer. The following chart indicates how this could be accomplished.[2]

---

[2] Other models for incorporation of New Career personnel in education are inserted in Pearl and Riessman, *op. cit.*

CHART I   Comparison of Cost of Two Systems of Educational Programming

Role	System I Certified Teacher Only			System 2 Echelon of Staff of Aide, Assistant, Associate and Teacher		
	No.	Rate	Salary	No.	Rate	Salary
Teacher	100	$8,000	$800,000	10	$10,000	$100,000
Associate				40	$8,000*	320,000
Assistant				40	$6,000*	240,000
Aide				35	$4,000*	140,000
TOTAL	100		$800,000	125		$800,000

* Assuming some of the staff in these categories had earned wage increments for years of service.

Thus it would be possible to actually add 25% more staff, increase the salary of the professional by more than 20% and not increase the cost to the taxpayer![3]

If the New Career thesis is tuly to have utility, the following must be realized:

1) Only activities worth doing should be contemplated. No teacher aide should be engaged in activities not necessary for the education task, e.g., teacher aides should not be employed in those repressive roles which create antagonism between student and staff and thereby distort the education process.
2) Only activities which are beyond the capacities of the client should be delegated to the New Careerist, e.g., teacher aides should not collect milk money from eight year olds; an eight year old can collect milk money, and the teacher aide could be better utilized with the eight year olds in learning activity.
3) The entry position should be so designed that even the least skilled can be considered for the job.

THE "MODEL CITY"

Implicit and crucial to a "New Career" development in a model city is change in the nature of service. The essential inhumanity

[3] Pearl, Arthur, "New Careers: One Solution to Poverty," *Social Policies for America in the Seventies: Nine Divergent Views*, Robert Theobald (ed.), New York: Doubleday, 1968.

of alleged human services in the city will not be altered if the only change is reassigning activities to non-professional personnel. At the present time there are things done in human service which should not be done at all. Much of current human service hinders rather than helps and all of the necessary functions of the city must be transformed into enabling rather than restrictive activities. The key to a successful model city is relevant, quality service. The following is suggested change in selected service domains:

WELFARE

The goal of a legitimate welfare service is to enable disadvantaged populations to cope. Poverty-stricken populations are burdened by a host of disabling conditions. And probably the most defeating is the "locked out" condition that leaves them without appropriate skills and information to negotiate the system. The essential function of a welfare system is to provide the necessary information and to generate, in a relatively non-threatening environment, the requisite coping behavior to facilitate entrance into the complicated social structures of a modern urban society. The welfare function should be just that—sensitivity to the welfare of residents. The major thrust must be to offer an increasing range of alternatives to the recipient.

In the staffing of the agency the entry positions (aide) should be assigned to making contact with persons in need and disseminating information about available resources. The intermediate roles (assistant and associate) are higher level tacticians who offer consultation to the aides, supervise their training and provide specialist service to clients with particular problems and needs. The professonal is the strategist. He evaluates whether the service is attaining the specified goals. He plans for program changes consistent with new developments in the field and the changing urban condition.

EMPLOYMENT

At the present time the employment agencies could be accurately described as unemployment services. And the consequence of such distortion is denigration of the client. Employment service must be primarily job and career development. The emphasis must be on rearranging job specifications to meet the attributes of the population. The entry workers' duties are to make contact with the job-seeking population and facilitate their contact with the prospective employer. The functions of those in intermediate positions should be to supervise and consult with the lower echelon personnel, to negotiate with employers to organize the work activities to meet the qualifications of the applicant, and, to generate training programs to enhance the skill level of the job seeker. The professional, in addition to evaluating the aforementioned activities and supervising continuous staff development, must plan for impending changes in the deployment of manpower.

URBAN DEVELOPMENT

The urban development agency must transform its essentially inanimate and often oppressive activities of rent collection, code enforcement, surveying, business management and resident relocation into personal assistance. The extent to which the above functions can become community responsibilities, i.e., are taken over by the residents who assist rather than control and who help rather than restrict, is seen as the program becomes growth producing.

The staff of the development agency takes on, in place of the more traditional direct service, community organizational activities. The entry aide becomes a contact man and information gatherer. The intermediate personnel are group leaders, specialists and consultants. And, similar to other agencies, the professional evaluates current efforts and maps out future strategies.

POLICE

The police present a unique problem for the urban community. It is no exaggeration to assert that police have triggered many of the violent outbursts in the ghetto. It is not difficult to understand why. The police are viewed by the impoverished ghetto resident as an occupying army to protect the property and interests of the overlord. Police are not perceived as servants to the community. Most community relation efforts of police departments fail because the efforts are perceived as superficial flim-flam designed to deceive the residents. Only when police service become of, by, and for the people will the situation change. Police service must become primarily concerned with the protection of person and property of the ghetto resident. The police must be scrupulously concerned for laws of evidence. Proscriptive laws that have an ethnic or economic status coloration, e.g., drug abuse, must be re-examined for possible unequal protection of the law implications. It is more appropriate in matters concerning drug or alcohol abuse that health officers rather than the police have jurisdiction. The emphasis here should be upon helping the afflicted instead of apprehending the law violator.

The entry police worker should be drawn from the community and be representative of the various resident groups. His service demands should not place him in an untenable position with community residents. His role must be unambiguous and non-alienating. He must be perceived as an advocate of the people. It is extremely important that there be well articulated channels of upward mobility with intermediate positions of supervision and specialization and eligibility for the highest ranking administrative posts.

HEALTH

The health services in a model city must depart radically from traditional services. Health services through the years have been packaged to repair the sick or the disabled. The focus has been on tertiary prevention and has been most effective with acute communicable diseases. The urban complex still has a considerable problem with communicable disease but this is a minor consideration for modern urban existences. The chronic disorders are the critical problems and these must be attacked at the primary prevention level. Respiratory, heart, and cancer disorders coupled with alcoholism, emotional disorder and drug abuse are among the major health problems of a modern society. The most vulnerable populations are the very young and very old.

The health services which will both serve those in need and have maximum impact on the major influences on morbidity and mortality are those which affect the way of life of the inhabitants. Health service must reach into each home and must influence diet, recreation and pace of living. It helps not one iota to attach a label of danger on a pack of cigarettes and have more people smoke cigarettes (at an ever younger age) each year. Health services must influence the day to day behaviors of the residents and this can only happen when the service is taken from the hospital and the doctor's office and brought to the streets where people live.

The entry worker must be a health educator capable of communicating effectively to residents. He must also be a case finder and a repository of information about available service. The intermediate worker is supervisor and a specialist. He has the knowledge to (under supervision of more highly trained personnel) to treat ailments and to lead group discussion. The professional is either the specialist or the evaluator and planner.

EDUCATION

Every aspect of education must undergo metamorphosis in the city of the future and particularly education must be changed for the urban poor. At the present time education is both an indignity and an irrelevancy. If any population needs an education it is the urban poor and yet it is this group that is maximally disengaged from education. The tragic truth is that recent efforts to improve the situation have only worsened it. Most educational programs for the urban poor end up insulting the intelligence of the student (this because there is an assumption of ignorance, stupidity and apathy in the student population). The programs only further segregate the already overly segregated. The program offers little if anything concretely meaningful to the student. The school becomes perverted into an unending struggle for dominance between youth and adults and that totally unnecessary struggle distorts every aspect of the education process.[4]

A good school depends upon optimum utilization of manpower. The entry and intermediate worker can generate a spirit of trust and support of the school in the community only if they are drawn representatively from the community. The urban elementary school can become more alive to the boy if more males are recruited into teaching assignments.

[4] For more detail on necessary changes in the urban communities see Arthur Pearl, "Educational Change: Why—How—For Whom?" from unedited speeches of Dr. Arthur Pearl. Distributed by the Human Rights Commission of San Francisco, 1254 Market Street, San Francisco, California, 1966. (Mimeo)

Also see Fantini and Weinstein, *Toward A Contact Curriculum*, Anti-Defamation League, 315 Lexington Avenue, New York.

Arthur Pearl, "A Critical Look at Teacher Evaluation." Paper for the National Institute for Advanced Study in Teaching Disadvantaged Youth, November, 1966. (Mimeo)

Higher education typifies all that is inappropriate in the city. Unlike the dodo bird which it resembles in grace and vitality, the urban university hasn't even the decency to acknowledge its death. And contrary to Mark Twain's assertion—any reports of its *life* are highly exaggerated. In no way does the urban university meet the needs of the city. It neither spawns the scholars capable of conceptualizing solutions to the city problems nor does it accommodate the impoverished city dweller's quest for a credential which is the primary path out of the world of poverty. Instead of true scholarship the university ruminates antiquated theory and quietly, ever so quickly, criticizes the modern day Philistine. More concerned with grants than deeds, the university projects, in areas of greatest need, show a dearth of imagination, a shocking lack of reflection and evaluation. And rather than making a place for the urban dweller, rather than reorganizing curriculum to meet needs and to reward prior experiences, the university apparently revels in its repudiation of the poor. Rather than scheduling for the convenience of the working student, the urban college imitates the prestigious university and places success through the matriculation of a graduate program beyond the reach of almost all urban dwellers. Remember it was not always thus. The ghetto residents of not so long ago were able to go to part-time social work and medicine schools. Two years in a normal school qualified the student to teach. Anyone could enter. The costs of education, if there were any at all, were minimal. In the quest of an illusive quality of higher standards of excellence, all of these virtues were lost and a meaningless ritual was substituted in its place. Urban universities must at least capture the best of the past and must adjust to the demands of the present. Every student must be accommodated! Admission requirements based on examinations which reflect social or economic bias must be eliminated. The freshman year must not be a year for screening out the undesirables but rather must be a year where prior deficiencies are corrected. The dreary English Composition class must be replaced with more utilitarian approaches to language skill. There must be more imaginative use of media. Rather than discouraging the working student, the academic program must be integrated into work situations and English, history, math, etc., introduced into the life setting of the student. The New Career idea should be a the heart of every urban university and for those students not in a career sequence where education is brought to him, other education programs must be developed to accommodate the working student. It is imperative that urban universities be around the clock operations with library facilities open to the student 24 hours a day and supportive assistance available on call.

FURTHER REFLECTIONS
ON THE TRIPLE
REVOLUTION

W. H. FERRY

ON MARCH 23 OF LAST YEAR THE TRIPLE REVOLUTION APPEARED ON
the front pages of most of the nation's newspapers. On March 24
what was to become a tidal bore of criticism and comment began
to rise. By the end of the month most members of the Ad Hoc
Committee had been asked to give lectures, write books, supply
copies, appear on television programs, and often to stand trial for
treason to the American Way of Life.

The waves of comment crested some time ago but not before
The Triple Revolution had made its way into the vernacular of
political debate, and not before members of the Ad Hoc Committee had learned a good many valuable things. My intention here
is to discuss the shortcomings of The Triple Revolution as disclosed by editorial writers, statesmen, gentlemen of the cloth,
economists, and other moral guides. My comments cover hundreds of letters as well as some 500 editorials and newspaper and
magazine columns. The provocations of The Triple Revolution
were so strong as to lure some of our critics into spicy language
and patriotic howls, and it is with a sigh that I turn away from
the temptation to put on display some of this thunder and light-
ning.

I wish to make plain to you, as it was *not* plain to many, that
our committee did not invent the phenomena we sought to diag-
nose. We did not discover these developments, either. The kind of
society we perceive in the making is not of our manufacture, nor,

From W. H. Ferry, "Further Reflections on the Triple Revolution," *Fellowship*, 31: 1:13–17, January 1965. Reprinted by permission of *Fellowship*
Magazine, Nyack, N.Y.

as you will see, are the various prescriptions that we were driven to by the logic of our analysis.

Not all of the editorials and divers observations were messages of wrath. It is from those critics who tried to understand what the Ad Hoc Committee was saying that we learned most, and mainly by them that the shortcomings soon to be discussed were made plain.

Before proceeding, however, it is doubtless advisable to outline what we had to say, even though many . . . readers have doubtless read the memorandum.

The Triple Revolution refers to three concurrent developments: the cybernation, race, and weaponry revolutions. Important relations between these three phenomena are asserted by the Ad Hoc Committee, but these connections are only sparsely argued. The bulk of the memorandum concerns the cybernation revolution, which is said to have broken the link between jobs and income. An ever-widening pool of men and women is being exiled from the economy by the new technology. This development becomes a primary challenge to political thought, which has up to this point regarded full employment, in the customary usage of the term, as a chief object of public policy.

Cybernation, denoting the coupling of computers and automatic machines, means the end of full employment by inexorably doing away with jobs at every level of the employment pyramid. Cybernation signifies the opening of the era of abundance. Since economics is the science of the allocation of scarcities, cybernation as the main agent of plenty calls for the reformation of economic theory. Political ideas and institutions will be radically affected.

A REAL ECONOMIC
CRISIS LOOMS

The Triple Revolution declares that neither statesmen nor scholars have been willing to assess the tendencies of the new technology at anything near their full weight, and that consequently we are approaching an economic crisis all unbuttoned and defenseless.

The Ad Hoc Committee advocated that a guaranteed annual income be paid to the head of every household and single wage-earner as a matter of right. This recommendation was made as an example of the kind of radical departure from contemporary practice that will be necessitated as cybernation hits harder and wider. A guaranteed income is proposed not as the sole requirement of the era of abundance but as an indispensable one.

The Committee did not believe that this suggestion would be taken up and acted upon at once by Congress. To bridge the transition between, so to speak, the oncoming of abundance and official appreciation of that fact, the Committee advocated widely expanded public works. Its intention in doing so was not primarily to furnish jobs, for the public sector of the economy is virtually as cybernation-prone as the private sector, but to remind both politicians and the electorate of their novel opportunities for collective action in a historical phase of abundance.

There is a good deal more to The Triple Revolution, including advocacy of federal planning, regulation of technological development, and bolstering of democratic theory.

I turn now to the shortcomings of the Committee's memorandum. In this brief category I shall not present explanations for apparent omissions and oversights, though I would be glad to provide them later. In justice to those who composed the memorandum, it must be mentioned that most of the shortcomings I shall list were discussed but not included because we were preparing a paper, not a book. To turn to the shortcomings:

The Triple Revolution is misnamed. It purports to take up three significant developments but in fact deals at length with only one —cybernation.

THREE REVOLUTIONS
ARE OMITTED

We did not mention other and more widely-heralded revolutions, mainly the revolution in people—the notorious population explosion. The Committee was scolded also for omitting the psychic revolution, i.e., aimlessness and alienation as the apparent destiny of Western Man. We were reviled for not having mentioned the Communist revolution, said by the revilers to be at the root of all American difficulties even unto crabgrass. A good many saw in Betty Friedan's The Feminine Mystique the beginnings of a sort of revolutionary female populism, and told us so.

Although the redefintion of work was said by the Committee

to be of the greatest importance, it did little redefining itself. This shortcoming led in turn to the impression among many if not most readers that we were in effect advocating the indolent society, a cushioned technological epiphany in which cashing government income checks, beer-drinking, television watching, and general lolly-gagging would be the main activities of the majority of people. Equally unfortunately, we left the impression that we were not disturbed about such unwholesome side effects and social costs.

The Triple Revolution gave no estimate of the possible money costs of its guaranteed income proposal. Among less friendly critics, this omission provoked calculations more astronomical than financial in their dimensions.

The suggestion that the condition of our economic machine both permitted and required an income to all guaranteed by the government drew more notice than any other feature of the memorandum. Those who did not trouble to get hold of the document itself (a group, melancholy to report, estimated at about 99 percent of those reacting most vigorously to it) assumed that we considered this proposal an all-purpose medication, with healing properties for delinquency and drop-outs, broken-down cities, and the farm problem.

The Triple Revolution made too little distinction between the conditions of the impoverished and those of the unemployed and underemployed. As Adam Walinsky cogently argued in *The New Republic*, the middle class can be trusted to resist the income-for-all proposal because it threatens a movement upward into its ranks, and we ignored such sociological musings in the memorandum.

Then there was the question of the memorandum's prose, which many found tepid and others declared was hot with rebellion. The Triple Revolution was denounced for its length, turning out to be both too long and too short. The organizers of the Ad Hoc Committee were charged with elitism and gross thoughtlessness by a good many people who would gladly have signed the document but inadvertently were not invited to do so.

THIS IS NOT UTOPIA

Finally, the Committee managed to convey the notion that it was suggesting a brand-new radical utopia, fabricated out of

modern technology and terrible economic philosophies imported
from you know where. On this point we were quite unfair
to ourselves and our readers. We should have anticipated and
dealt with anti-utopianism. We should have emphasized the
antiquity of most of the ideas. For in fact one of the basic notions
in TR, as I shall refer to it from now on, runs back to Aristotle,
and others have been present in utopian thought for centuries.
And, it might be added, present also in kakotopian works like
Orwell's *1984* and Huxley's *Brave New World*. TR is not a blueprint of the delectable community but a sort of tachometer reading for society, warning of the necessities and the consequences of
the velocities at which the new technology is travelling. We
might have cited the late Senator Robert Alonzo Taft and Prof.
Milton Friedman in support of the minimum income scheme,
though it would not have been accurate to label them as Utopians.

Some 40 years ago Lewis Mumford classified Utopias. There
are two kinds, he said, one the Utopia of retreat or escape from
the world, the other looking to its reconstruction. Strains of both
utopias were discovered in TR and strenuously deplored by
critics who found the nation in perfectly good shape and in need
of only such improvement as might result from balancing the
budget and the restoration of states' rights.

Cries of heresy resonated from every point along the Right-
Left spectrum. The Committee was reproved, in accents sharp
and sorrowful, by Henry Hazlitt, Raymond Moley, Leon Keyserling, Billy Graham, Secretary of Labor Wirtz, Ralph Borsodi,
Victor Perlo in the *Worker*, and a good many members of Congress. There is evidence, inconclusive though it may be, that
something approximating 95 percent of the economists of the
country disagree with our conclusions, a finding that comforted
at least one member of the Ad Hoc Committee.

Yet the response was far from uniformly hostile and morose.
For many, TR provided a convincing explanation of the anxieties
of a contemporary economy that finds it necessary simultaneously
to proclaim wild prosperity and widespread poverty. Bringing
concealed or unconscious trepidations into the open is a useful
public act. The memorandum reminded millions of Americans
that they are only eight years into a period for which history
offers little instruction and no precedent, for cybernation came

into being only in 1956. Radical problems demand radical solutions; this is the shorthand of The Triple Revolution.

For others The Triple Revolution presented a welcome connection among the jangling parts of an apparently disconnected society. The memorandum thus proposed a kind of constructive agenda, one supplying the dim beginnings of a national purpose to replace the lamentable anti-Communism that has been the mainspring of domestic and foreign policy for so many sterile years.

As I remarked a moment ago, the Ad Hoc Committee did not aspire to describe the society of the future but only certain relentless tendencies in the community today. Just how relentless these tendencies are, and how imminent the need for fundamental change, are of course the crucial issues. I confess that the evidence seems mixed. The statistics about unemployment and underemployment can be read to come to many differing conclusions about their scope and points of impact. I confess that I am also deeply impressed by the almost universal anguish aroused by the proposal for a guaranteed income. This anguish I at first interpreted as the normal abhorrence of an unusual idea, but I now see it as genuine fear of demoralization of the community.

Which is only to say that the widespread perturbation is understandable, and that I must also—I do not speak here for any other members of the Committee—acknowledge the possibility that our surmises are wide of the mark. However, with all present testimony now in the record I must still take my stand with the poet,

> and his spirit leaps within him to be gone before him, then
> Underneath the light he looks at, in among the throngs of men:
> Men, my brothers, men the workers, ever reaping something
> new:
> That which they have done but earnest of the things that they
> shall do.
>
> TENNYSON: Locksley Hall

SPIRITUAL MEANING IN A THERMONUCLEAR ERA

By this time you will have noticed that I have not got to the spiritual connotations of The Triple Revolution. It is about this stage of my remarks that the idea should come in, but I am not easy about it. Every day I feel less capable of grasping the spiritual outlook. I have been bewildered by the fact, sometimes referred to by those among this readership that the nation's spiritual leaders have in the main endorsed the genocidal policies of the thermonuclear era. I cannot distinguish in this regard between Christian and un-Christian nations. I have listened often and carefully to the explanations of our spiritual mentors, but always come away more confused than ever. If there is a difference between worldliness and other-worldliness in these men, I am not bright enough to discern it.

Living in California does not help either. Big in everything, California is very big in radio preachers, to whom I tune in every time I get the chance. My private poll discloses that roughly half of this ministry preaches salvation from communism. Most of the other half wants to relieve my gout, backache, or ulcer. Such an exposure leaves one stunted in spiritual outlook, and I ask that you bear these limitations in mind in the very few comments I have to make under this heading.

One of the few points on which the Committee and its critics agree is that most of the jobs in the future will be in service. We are agreed that blue collars are shrinking in the technical wash. We agree that the production end will not take up the share of the working force from now on, that it has in the past, and that we should pin our hope, such as it may be, on the service trades for more jobs and opportunity. I am going to by-pass all the things you already know about this development, which is well under way.

SERVICE A NEW BUT POSSIBLE MOTIVATION

The significant point is that service means taking care of one another, while production means taking care of a machine. That service today mostly describes activities prompted into being by the industrial society and the yearning for a profit, activities often trivial and wasteful and sometimes vicious, is negligible next to the possibilities. Here resides one of the immense spiritual connotations of The Triple Revolution, in the possibility that the idea of service—the care of one's fellow man as a good in itself—may become habitual. It seems to me that it will be a great human gain to remove people from the impersonality of the factory assembly line and office and allow them to work with one another. Who can predict where experience in serving one another may lead? It might even lead away from the present American creed of every man for himself and into what my associate, Robert Hutchins, calls "a deep sense of our own unimportance and a deep conviction of the importance of others."

A second spiritual implication arises from the great gains in leisure that the memorandum foresees. In a workless or semi-workless society, men will have to confront themselves in a new way, and ask the old questions about where they came from and whither they are bound. This, I am sure, will be an agonizing experience. It is, in fact, precisely what people have on their minds when they ask, "But what will we do?"

Yet I think we must assume that we will get through this agonizing period; and that we shall be better as a result, better for standing on more secure spiritual ground. There cannot after all be much doubt that the ground we stand on now is spiritually depressed. There perhaps has been an excuse for industrial man's systematic non-confrontation of himself. He's been busy. "Getting and spending," Wordsworth said, "we lay waste our powers." Matters of spirit, which is what I suppose is what spiritual means, have been delegated to priests and philosophers, and dozed through on Sunday morning. One might hope for a spiritual rejuvenation when there are no alibis for failure to meditate and take counsel of one's self. E. M. Forster says: "It is in what we value, not in what we have, that the test of us resides." Which is to say only that it is quite conceivable that American values can stand improvement, and that there is a good chance the new society heralded by TR will find its way to higher ground.

These half-lit and badly-stated notions are about all I feel capable of venturing on the spiritual implications of the memorandum. It may be added that considerable spiritual yardage will be gained when we all—and now I am talking about people like me, not people like you—when we all find it natural and easy to talk in terms of service, of justice and injustice, and of the general good, terms that now are of low standing in the American glossary.

THE TRIPLE REVOLUTION
IS STILL NEWS

The remainder of this paper will be devoted to consideration of the chief indictments drawn against TR. We must be grateful on the whole for the vast if often erroneous attention paid to our arguments, for it justifies Mumford's remark that "Nowhere may be an imaginary country, but News from Nowhere (Utopia) is real news."

Let me summarize and comment on the main points against the contentions of The Triple Revolution:

There is the argument from history. This argument says that cybernation is only another step in the toolmaking process. We are, this argument declares, just going through a rough spot in technological development that will soon be smoothed out. Soon we can expect a technical breakthrough to mop up the unemployed. The jobs furnished at different stages by the automobile, radio, household appliance and television industries, illustrate why we can depend on history to clear up the temporary headache we are suffering. Those who do not work—the heirs and heiresses, the *rentiers* and the impoverished and the shiftless—all such people are unavoidable sports in any culture. This historical argument is very attractive to those who think that the thermonuclear bomb is just like the hand-grenade, only bigger.

Then there is the argument from economics. According to this argument, work is the only way of distributing wealth. Work is the only proper claim to goods. Work is the energy that keeps the economic flywheel in motion. Work paid for in salaries and wages equals demand; demand then calls forth production. It is not economically feasible to distribute wealth in any other way. This view is founded on the idiotic presumption that the purpose of life is the production and consumption of material goods, and that all activities and ideas, public and private, must therefore meet some test of the marketplace. This attitude is naturally much favored by economists, bankers, and businessmen who tend to confuse obsolete economic slogans with the Ten Commandments.

Again, there is the argument from human nature and ethics. This argument says that men have worked by the sweat of their brow and always will. To work is man's nature and he knows no other. Freed from toil conventionally connected with the production of goods and services, men would not know what to do with themselves. Idle hands breed mischief. The social structure of industrial society depends on a hierarchy of work. Work tells us what to think of one another. Puritanism teaches that what feels bad and oppressive, like most drudgery, is good for one, and what feels good, like the non-necessity for drudgery, is bad. This is the view cherished by those who are unable to conceive that men at leisure can be well and happily occupied, by those who cannot imagine that the word "work" can properly be applied to manifold activities that have nothing whatever to do with production or profit.

I conclude my remarks with a few general observations:

THE GROUND WELL PLOUGHED

As noted earlier, The Triple Revolution cuts no new furrows. Aristotle foresaw a takeover by machines 2000 years ago. The possibility of a workless or nearly workless society emerging from technology is part of our literature. H. G. Wells told his readers about it 50 years ago. Forty years ago, C. H. Douglas wrote "We can produce at this moment goods and services at a rate very considerably greater than the possible rate of consumption, and this production and delivery of goods can, under favorable circumstances, be achieved by the employment of not more than 25 percent of the available labor working, let us say, seven hours a day." Olaf Stapledon and Stuart Chase, in very different ways, told us the same story 30 years ago. Jacques Ellul in *The Technological Society*[1], just published, says, "By the end of the nineteenth century people saw in their grasp the moment in which everything would be at the disposal of everyone, in which man, replaced by the machines, would have only pleasures and play." In a neglected report of December, 1963, the Research Institute of America anticipated the Committee when it remarked:

> "The moment of truth on automation is coming—a lot sooner than most people realize. The shattering fact is that the U.S. is still almost totally unprepared for the approaching crisis."[2]

[1] A. A. Knopf, 1964—p. 191.
[2] Report of RIA, December 27, 1963.

My second observation is that we are held in bondage by ideas, not by the economic facts of the matter. No one contests the almost limitless potential capacity of technological society to turn out wealth, in the form of goods and services. Nor does anyone doubt the wish and the need of people to consume these goods and services. It is the ancient coinage known as the conventional wisdom that stands in the way of putting together the technological capability for the production of wealth with the need for a decent distribution of it—the conventional wisdom about money, about the inseparabilty of work and income, about capitalism, socialism, man's natural avarice, man's inability to do anything constructive with his time except work, and a host of other durable totems.

Technology can indefinitely expand the production of goods, using fewer and fewer hands as it does so. But technology *cannot* produce the atmosphere in which the radical political and social ideas needed for its full utility can flourish. All of the sciences are burgeoning with fresh approaches to old matters except, alas, the political economic science. Here is the last pre-Copernican stronghold among the natural and social sciences, heavily patrolled by economic astrologers and other magistrates of the status quo. The most notable aspect of our world of novelty and rapid change is the unwillingness of economists and political scientists to perceive it, and their hostility toward those who do. We chiefly suffer from a failure to sense the implications of our technical accomplishment.

ONE PERCENT IS CYBERNATED

My third observation is that we are only at the beginning of the cybernating process. Yet the ability of cybernation to supplant men is already breathtaking. We haven't seen anything yet. Only about one percent of the machine-tool operations open to cybernation have yet been cybernated. The modern computerized bank can already add the weekly paycheck to your balance, debit payments on your automobile, television set, groceries, and last year's vacation, credit your dealers, and post the results more accurately than a platoon of clerks—all this, we are told, in less than a tenth of a second. A respected executive of a research and development corporation recently said that he "shuddered to think" of the convulsions in society that will result from the work in progress he daily observed in laboratories and research centers. John Diebold, a management consultant learned in the ways of computers, declares that businessmen haven't begun to know how to make the best use of them.[3] Adlai Stevenson recently remarked,

> The image of the automation engineer may not excite the imagination as does the image of the astronaut, but the fate of mankind in the foreseeable future will depend more on what we do manipulating machines here on earth than on how we do hurtling them through the heavens.[4]

My final observation is that we had better make up our minds to basic repairs of our ramshackle economic scheme, which has been held together since the Depression by war and threat of war and is now being buffeted as never before by the technological typhoon. If others won't make up their minds to this task, the Negroes will make it up for them. As I look around for the historical force that will bring today's chaotic elements into a revolutionary point, the unemployed Negro sails inexorably into view. The *un-integrated* Negro is the symbol of our democratic failure and the *unemployed* Negro is the most conspicuous evidence we have of the breakdown of the economic machinery. I do not believe there is any chance that the private self-adjusting economy can provide today's unemployed Negro with a job, the traditional means to dignity and self-respect. Tax cut and war on poverty notwithstanding, most Negroes now without work are not likely to be taken up into the private economy again. This likelihood is strongly emphasized in the short section of the Ad Hoc Committee's memorandum dealing with the race revolution.

THE NEGRO NEEDS AN UNGRUDGED INCOME

What is required is a theory of economics and politics that will at a minimum furnish the unemployed Negro with an *income*, and an income not on the grudging terms of the welfare agency

---

[3] Harvard Business Review, October 1964.
[4] Address, New School for Social Research.

but on terms of dignity and self-respect—that is to say, as a right. This will not perform the job of cultural transformation that is the principal meaning of cybernation. But ending the debasing dependence on doles is a necessary step in the process. It would mark the beginning of contemporary understanding that economic organization, like war, can never be the same again.

By now we sadly realize that it is ingenuous to expect progress in our economic organization and cultural and political life commensurate with the achievements of the machines we so adroitly hitch together. Some will think that depraved is too strong a word for the current situation, and they may be right; yet the emergence of material poverty and evidences of moral poverty, North and South, from Birmingham to Chicago to Dallas to the Cow Palace indicate that we Americans are in a more brutalized condition than we have been willing to admit. At any rate, there is no doubt about wholesale apathy, hatred, boredom, anomie, and other psychic ailments in the community.

There is, perhaps, a certain inevitability about such a spiritually barren result when one considers the technological achievements on which the United States has lavished most attention and cash. One is the dark alchemy of thermonuclear and biological warfare. Whether we are willing to admit it or not, these alchemies show that our policy is genocide, if need be. Another achievement is Telstar. It was only a few days after its launching that we understood that we had nothing worth while saying via this remarkable medium of communication, so it was not hard for the military to establish first claim on it. Third is cybernation itself. In offices and on factory floors men see their jobs being performed by cybernated equipment far better than they can perform them. The first of these achievements reminds us of the end of civilization under certain circumstances. The second reminds us of the purposelessness of our culture and the perverse harnessing of great accomplishment to lethal ends. The third reminds us that the welfare of machines has priority over the welfare of men. The computer scientists have a useful word, GIGO, that summarizes the possibilities of the new technology. GIGO means garbage in, garbage out: that is to say, if you put bad programs into a computer you get bad results. If we give bad or even indifferent instructions to our technology, we cannot expect anything but bad results.

A WORLD FOUNDED ON A
FALSE DOCTRINE OF MAN

This is the world before us, beset by novelty on every hand, already deeply perturbing to the individual personality, changing by the hour, promising mainly the unexpected, and founded on a false doctrine of man.

I think that man's only chance of escaping the iron maiden he is fashioning for himself is through a self-conscious and sedulous attack on the enclosing walls. Mumford remarks that "we seem to be paying for an excess of physical power by our spiritual impotence, and for an excess of automatism by our inability to control the process once it is started." The central issue is whether we can bring our technical achievements under political control, in the interests of compassion and rationality, and put them to the service of man rather than the other way around. This control has never yet been achieved, nor even tried. Technical advance has seemed a self-evident good, and encouraged to go according to its own imperatives. The results are all around us, from the slums and dirty air of Megalopolis to the thermonuclear and neutron bombs. The issue is whether we can re-construct our political and social ideas with something like the speed at which we pursue far more frivolous objects, like supersonic jets and the silent automatic toothbrush.

The Triple Revolution aimed to startle readers into an appreciation of the increasing dominance of technology in respect to war, prejudice, and economic machinery. In retrospect I fear it barely merits passing marks. On its central and fateful implication, that our virtuosity in megadeath weaponry is carrying us into calamity, The Triple Revolution produced only a twitter of comment. The memorandum asserted cybernation was daily compounding the difficulties in coping with the race situation; but this too was drowned almost at once in clamor about discrimination against white workers, the uneducability of Negroes, and similar claptrap. Even the central emphasis on the evitable effects of cybernation on employment and the entire structure of political economic theory was diminished into a temporal and trivial contention about "paying people to do no work." We sought to delineate the closing of one era and the opening of another, full of promise and novelty and hazard. It is a majestic theme; but if we did not elicit a majestic response, the fault must be just as much ours as that of our critics.

All the evidence is that we are entering the technological epoch before we have begun to understand or heal the wounds, psychic and economic, of the industrial epoch just closing. Jacques Maritain said, "Spirit never manages to keep pace with the rapidity of the development of matter." In view of the radical alterations in every circumstance of the common life, the need for a radically new theory and practice of political science seems to me inescapable.

I do not say that the formulation of such a new science is easy, considering the barricades of musty slogans that will continue to be thrown up against it. I say that it is the nation's most important intellectual and political task, surpassing in urgency any of the other issues on which we are expending our treasure and thought.

TOWARD A HUMANIZED TECHNOLOGY

ERICH FROMM

A SPECTER IS STALKING IN OUR MIDST WHOM ONLY A FEW SEE WITH clarity. It is not the old ghost of communism or fascism. It is a new specter: a completely mechanized society, devoted to maximal material output and consumption, directed by computers; and in this social process, man himself is being transformed into a part of the total machine, well fed and entertained, yet passive, unalive, and with little feeling. With the victory of the new society, individualism and privacy will have disappeared; feelings toward others will be engineered by psychological conditioning and other devices, or drugs which also serve a new kind of introspective experience. As Zbigniew Brzezinski put it, "In the technetronic society the trend would seem to be towards the aggregation of the individual support of millions of uncoordinated citizens easily within the reach of magnetic and attractive personalities effectively exploiting the latest communication techniques to manipulate emotions and control reason."[1] This new form of society has been predicted in the form of fiction in Orwell's *1984* and Aldous Huxley's *Brave New World*.

Perhaps its most ominous aspect at present is that we seem to lose control over our own system. We execute the decisions which our computer calculations make for us. We as human

[1] "The Technetronic Society," *Encounter*, Vol. XXX, No. 1 (January, 1968), p. 19.

beings have no aims except producing and consuming more and more. We will nothing, nor do we not-will anything. We are threatened with extinction by nuclear weapons and with inner deadness by the passiveness which our exclusion from responsible decision making engenders.

How did it happen? How did man, at the very height of his victory over nature, become the prisoner of his own creation and in serious danger of destroying himself?

In the search of scientific truth, man came across knowledge that he could use for the domination of nature. He had tremendous success. But in the one-sided emphasis on technique and material consumption, man lost touch with himself, with life. Having lost religious faith and the humanistic values bound up with it, he concentrated on technical and material values and lost the capacity for deep emotional experiences, for the joy and sadness that accompany them. The machine he built became so powerful that it developed its own program, which now determines man's own thinking.

At the moment, one of the gravest symptoms of our system is the fact that our economy rests upon arms production (plus maintenance of the whole defense establishment) and on the principle of maximal consumption. We have a well-functioning economic system under the condition that we are producing goods which threaten us with physical destruction, that we transform the individual into a total passive consumer and thus deaden him, and that we have created a bureaucracy which makes the individual feel impotent.

Are we confronted with a tragic, insolvable dilemma? *Must we produce sick people in order to have a healthy economy, or can we use our material resources, our inventions, our computers to serve the ends of man? Must individuals be passive and dependent in order to have strong and well-functioning organizations?*

• • •

There is a growing polarization occurring in the United States and in the whole world: There are those who are attracted to force, "law and order," bureaucratic methods, and eventually to non-life, and those with a deep longing for life, for new attitudes rather than for ready-made schemes and blueprints. This new front is a movement which combines the wish for profound changes in our economic and social practice with changes in our psychic and spiritual approach to life. In its most general form, its aim is the activation of the individual, the restoration of man's control over the social system, the humanization of technology. It is a movement in the name of life, and it has such a broad and common base because the threat to life is today a threat not to one class, to one nation, but a threat to all.

• • •

Man, lacking the instinctual equipment of the animal, is not as well equipped for flight or for attack as animals are. He does not "know" infallibly, as the salmon knows where to return to the river in order to spawn its young and as many birds know where to go south in the winter and where to return in the summer. His decisions are *not made for him* by instinct. *He* has to make *them*. He is faced with alternatives and there is a risk of failure in every decision he makes. The price that man pays for consciousness is insecurity. He can stand his insecurity by being aware and accepting the human condition, and by the hope that he will not fail even though he has no guarantee for success. He has no certainty; the only certain prediction he can make is: "I shall die."

Man is born as a freak of nature, being within nature and yet transcending it. He has to find principles of action and decision making which replace the principles of instinct. He has to have a frame of orientation which permits him to organize a consistent picture of the world as a condition for consistent actions. He has to fight not only against the dangers of dying, starving, and being hurt, but also against another danger which is specifically human: that of becoming insane. In other words, he has to protect himself not only against the danger of losing his life but also against the danger of losing his mind. The human being, born under the conditions described here, would indeed go mad if he did not find a frame of reference which permitted him to feel at home in the world in some form and to escape the experience of utter helplessness, disorientation, and uprootedness. There are many ways in which man can find a solution to the task of staying alive and of remaining sane. Some are better than others and some are worse. By "better" is meant a way conducive to greater strength, clarity, joy, independence; and by "worse" the very opposite. But more important than finding the *better* solution is finding some solution which is viable.

. . .

In spite of the fact that there is a tragic disproportion between intellect and emotion at the present moment in industrial society, there is no denying the fact that the history of man is a history of growing awareness. This awareness refers to the facts of nature outside of himself as well as to his own nature. While man still wears blinders, in many respects his critical reason has discovered a great deal about the nature of the universe and the nature of man. He is still very much at the beginning of this process of discovery, and the crucial question is whether the destructive power which his present knowledge has given him will permit him to go on extending this knowledge to an extent which is unimaginable today, or whether he will destroy himself before he can build an ever-fuller picture of reality on the present foundations.

If this development is to take place, one condition is necessary: that the social contradictions and irrationalities which throughout most of man's history have forced upon him a "false consciousness"—in order to justify domination and submission respectively—disappear or at least are reduced to such a degree that the apology for the existent social order does not paralyze man's capacity for critical thought. Of course, this is not a matter of what is first and what is second. Awareness of existing reality and of alternatives for its improvement helps to change reality, and every improvement in reality helps the clarification of thought. Today, when scientific reasoning has reached a peak, the transformation of society, burdened by the inertia of previous circumstances, into a sane society could permit the average man to use his reason with the same objectivity to which we are accustomed from the scientists. This is a matter not primarily of superior intelligence but of the disappearance of irrationality from social life—an irrationality which necessarily leads to confusion of the mind.

. . .

STEPS TO THE HUMANIZATION OF TECHNOLOGICAL SOCIETY

If we are now to consider the possibility of humanizing the industrial society as it has developed in the second Industrial

Revolution, we must begin by considering those institutions and methods which for economic as well as psychological reasons cannot be done away with without the total disruption of our society. These elements are: (1) The large-scale centralized enterprise as it has developed in the last decades in government, business, universities, hospitals, etc. This process of centralization is still continuing, and soon almost all major purposeful activities will be carried on by large systems. (2) Large-scale planning within each system, which results from the centralization. (3) Cybernation, that is cybernetics and automation, as the major theoretical and practical principle of control, with the computer as the most important element in automation.

But not only these three elements are here to stay. There is another element which appears in all social systems: the system Man. As I pointed out earlier, this does not mean that human nature is not malleable; it means that it allows only a limited number of potential structures, and confronts us with certain ascertainable alternatives. The most important alternative as far as the technological society is concerned is the following: if man is passive, bored, unfeeling, and one-sidedly cerebral, he develops pathological symptoms like anxiety, depression, depersonalization, indifference to life, and violence. Indeed, as Robert H. Davis wrote in a penetrating paper, ". . . the long-range implications of a cybernated world for mental health are disturbing."[2] It is important to stress this point, since most planners deal with the human factor as one which could adapt itself to any condition without causing any disturbances.

The possibilities which confront us are few and ascertainable. One possibility is that we continue in the direction we have taken. This would lead to such disturbances of the total system that either thermonuclear war or severe human pathology would be the outcome. The second possibility is the attempt to change that direction by force or violent revolution. This would lead to the breakdown of the whole system and violence and brutal dictatorship as a result. The third possibility is the humanization of the system, in such a way that it serves the purpose of man's well-being and growth, or in other words, his life process. In

[2] "The Advance of Cybernation: 1965–1985," in *The Guaranteed Income*, ed. by Robert Theobald (New York: Doubleday Anchor Books, 1967).

this case, the central elements of the second Industrial Revolution will be kept intact. The question is, Can this be done and what steps need to be taken to achieve it?

*   *   *

Given these general aims, what is the procedure of humanistic planning? *Computers should become a functional part in a life-oriental social system and not a cancer which begins to play havoc and eventually kills the system.* Machines or computers must become means for ends which are determined by man's reason and will. The values which determine the selection of facts and which influence the programming of the computer must be gained on the basis of the knowledge of human nature, its various possible manifestations, its optimal forms of development, and the real needs conducive to this development. That is to say, man, not technique, must become the ultimate source of values; optimal human development and not maximal production the criterion for all planning.[3]

*   *   *

WHAT IS THE NATURE OF "HUMANISTIC MANAGEMENT" AND ITS METHODS?

The basic principle of the humanistic management method is that, in spite of the bigness of the enterprises, centralized planning, and cybernation, the individual participant asserts himself toward the managers, circumstances, and machines, and ceases to be a powerless particle which has no active part in the process. Only by such affirmation of his will can the energies of the individual be liberated and his mental balance be restored.

The same principle of humanistic management can also be

[3] Hasan Ozbekhan has formulated the problem very succinctly: "What we have failed to do in all this is to ascribe operational meaning to the so-called desirables that motivate us, to question their intrinsic worth, to assess the long-range consequences of our aspirations and actions, to wonder whether the outcome we seem to be expecting does in fact correspond to that *quality of life* we say we are striving for—and whether our current actions will lead us there. In other words, in this writer's conception of planning we are in the deeper sense failing to plan." (Cf. the article by Hasan Ozbekhan, "The Triumph of Technology: 'Can' Implies 'Ought'," System Development Corporation. I also gratefully acknowledge the suggestions I received by subsequent personal communication from Mr. Ozbekhan; furthermore, from Martin K. Starr and Raymond G. Brown.)

expressed in this way: While in alienated bureaucracy all power flows from above downward, in humanistic management there is a two-way street; the "subjects"[4] of the decision made above respond according to their own will and concerns; their response not only reaches the top decision makers but forces them to respond in turn. The "subjects" of decision making have a right to challenge the decision makers. Such a challenge would first of all require a rule that if a sufficient number of "subjects" demanded that the corresponding bureaucracy (on whatever level) answer questions, explain its procedures, the decision makers would respond to the demand.

. . .

If the bureaucratic mode were changed from an alienated to a humanistic one, it would necessarily lead to a change in the type of manager who is successful. The defensive type of personality who clings to his bureaucratic image and who is afraid of being vulnerable and of confronting persons directly and openly would be at a disadvantage. On the other hand, the imaginative, nonfrightened, responsive person would be successful if the method of management were changed. These considerations show how erroneous it is to speak of certain methods of management which cannot be changed because the managers "would not be willing or capable of changing them." What is left out here is the fact that new methods would constitute a selective principle for managers. This does not mean that most present managers would be replaced by the new type of manager. No doubt there are many who under the present system cannot utilize their responsive capacities and who will be able to do so once the system gives them a chance.

Among the objections to the idea of active participation of the individual in the enterprises in which he works, perhaps the most popular one is the statement that, in view of increasing cybernation, the working time of the individual will be so short and the time devoted to leisure so long that the activation of the individual will no longer need to take place in his work situation, but will be sufficiently accomplished during his leisure time. This idea, I believe, is based on an erroneous concept of human ex-

[4] In the following, I shall call those subject to control by bureaucracy "subjects."

istence and of work. Man, even under the most favorable technological conditions, has to take the responsibility of producing food, clothing, housing, and all other material necessities. This means he has to work. Even if most physical labor is taken over by the machines, man has still to take part in the process of the exchange between himself and nature; only if man were a disembodied being or an angel with no physical needs, would work completely disappear. Man, being in need of assimilating nature, of organizing and directing the process of material production, of distribution, of social organization, of responses to natural catastrophes, can never sit back and let things take care of themselves. Work in a technological society may not be a "curse" any more, but that paradisiacal state in which man does not have to take care of his material needs is a technological fantasy. Or will the solution be, as Brzezinski[4] predicts, that only the elite will have the privilege of working while the majority is busy with consumption? Indeed, that could be a solution to the problem, but it would reduce the majority to the status of slaves, in the paradoxical sense that they would become irresponsible and useless parasites, while the free man alone would have the right to live a full life, which includes work. *If man is passive in the process of production and organization, he will also be passive during his leisure time.* If he abdicates responsibility and participation in the process of sustaining life, he will acquire the passive role in all other spheres of life and be dependent on those who take care of him. We already see this happening today. Man has more leisure time than before, but most people show this passiveness in the leisure which is forced upon them by the method of alienated bureaucratism. Leisure time is mostly of the spectator or consumption type; rarely is it an expression of activeness.

• • •

Our society, like many of the past, has accepted the principle "he who does not work should not eat." (Russian Communism has elevated this old principle into a "socialist" precept, phrasing it slightly differently.) The problem is not whether a man fulfills his social responsibility by contributing to the common good. In fact, in those cultures which have explicitly or

[4] Zbigniew Brzezinski, "The Technetronic Society," *Encounter*, Vol. xxx, No. 1, (January, 1968).

implicitly accepted this norm, the rich, who did not have to work, were exempted from this principle, and the definition of a gentleman was a man who did not have to work in order to live in style. The problem is that any human being has an inalienable right to live regardless of whether or not he performs a social duty. Work and all other social obligations should be made sufficiently attractive to urge man to desire to accept his share of social responsibility, but he should not be forced to do so by the threat of starvation. If the latter principle is applied, society has no need to make work attractive and to fit its system to human needs. It is true that in many societies of the past the disproportion between the size of the population and the available techniques of production did not permit the freedom to dispense with the principle of what is, in fact, forced labor.

In the affluent industrial society there is no such problem, and yet even the members of the middle and upper classes are forced to follow norms laid down by the industrial system for fear of losing their jobs. Our industrial system does not give them as much leeway as it could. If they lose a job because they lack "the right spirit"—which means they are too independent, voice unpopular opinions, marry the "wrong" woman—they will have great difficulties in finding another job of equal rank, and getting a job of inferior rank implies that they and their families feel their personality has been degraded; they lose the new "friends" they had gained in the process of rising; they fear the scorn of their wives and the loss of respect from their children.

The point I want to make is to uphold the principle that a person has an inalienable right to live—a right to which no conditions are attached and which implies the right to receive the basic commodities necessary for life, the right to education and to medical care; he has a right to be treated at least as well as the owner of a dog, or a cat treats his pet, which does not have to "prove" anything in order to be fed. Provided this principle were accepted, if a man, woman, or adolescent could be sure that whatever he did his material existence would not be in jeopardy, the realm of human freedom would be immensely enhanced. Acceptance of this principle would also enable a person to change his occupation or profession by using one or more years in preparing himself for a new and, to him, more adequate activity. It happens that most people make a decision about their career at an age when they do not have the experience and judgment to know what activity is the most congenial to them. Perhaps in their mid-thirties they wake up to the fact that it is too late to start that activity which they now know would have been the right choice. In addition, no woman would be forced to remain unhappily married because she did not have what it takes even to prepare herself for a job at which she could make a living. No employee would be forced to accept conditions which to him are degrading or distasteful if he knew he would not starve during the time he looks for a job more to his liking. This problem is by no means solved by unemployment or welfare dole. As many have recognized, the bureaucratic methods employed here are humiliating to such a degree that many people are afraid of being forced into the dole-receiving sector of the population, and this fear is sufficient to deprive them of the freedom not to accept certain working conditions.

THE NATURE OF THE WELFARE SYSTEM

INTRODUCTION

IN THIS SECTION WE HAVE BROUGHT together a number of articles dealing with the welfare system. Welfare is defined in two ways: Richard Elman's piece, "The Welfare Bureaucracy," deals with public assistance and welfare recipients. Bob Ross's article, "Notes on the Welfare State," deals with a wide range of public policies intended to sustain the population at some level of adequacy.

There are two themes in the first section: (1) the welfare system is not adequate to meet the needs of those who cannot find a place in the job market, and (2) the welfare state has not provided a set of mechanisms adequate to insure the livelihood of those who are not on public assistance. Elman brings to the discussion of public assistance first-hand experience with New York City's welfare department. The "welfare chiseler" has entered the gallery of American villains, probably only slightly behind communists. It seems to be popularly assumed that large numbers of people choose to live in ease and comfort on public assistance rather than go out and find work. Elman deals with what welfare recipients actually receive.

Ross and Mayer deal, in different ways, with the shortcomings of the welfare state. While such mechanisms as social security, unemployment insurance and the like are necessary and have saved substantial numbers of Americans from poverty, they have not penetrated to significant elements in the population.

Those for whom the system has not been beneficial find themselves forced to deal at a disadvantage with others (see Conot's piece) or to surrender their status as adults in order to obtain public assistance (see Elman's article).

In the last four articles, attention is given both to certain concrete strategies for altering welfare systems and to the values and perspectives which sustain social mechanisms for alleviating dire need on the part of population. John R. Seeley and Richard M. Titmuss address themselves to the latter, Merlin Miller and Cloward and Pivan to the former.

It was not always possible to maintain symmetry in organizing the readings. The Conot and Miller pieces are meant to be symmetrical, though, as are the Ross and Titmuss articles and the Mayer and the Cloward and Pivan pieces.

An address to the issues of welfare (in both senses of the word) is particularly crucial for a radical sociology. These phenomena pose a number of significant sociological questions:

► To what extent is welfare a moral rather than an economic category? In other words, can it be plausibly argued that the oil depletion allowance, the soil bank program, and a whole host of other mechanisms for the transfer of public funds into private hands constitute welfare programs? Can it be that the crucial difference between the soil bank program and Aid to Families with Dependent Children is that the recipients of the latter are low in status while the recipients of the former are high in status? In short, then, might it be the case that if a low-status person receives public funds under certain kinds of arrangements it is called welfare, while if a high-status person receives such funds it is called a subsidy, or some other less negative term?

► What is the relationship between broad social values and the possible efficacy of radical strategies for changing public policy? For example, Cloward and Pivan argue for disruptive tactics as a mechanism for bankrupting the welfare system in order to create the conditions under which a new and more adequate system can be created. However, if the present system is sustained, in part, by a given value complex in the larger society, then interesting and significant questions arise about the conditions under which values change. If, on the one hand, values are seen as responsive to changes in the environment, then the Cloward and Pivan approach is defensible. If, on the other hand, values are seen as relatively resistant to change, then their approach becomes dangerous—as by efforts welfare recipients and low-income people to disrupt the system might be interpreted by the public as an effort by the morally inadequate to increase even more the amount of their ill-gotten gains.

These readings are intended to raise questions as to the nature of radical sociology, and questions on the substantive issues themselves. It is our hope that the readings in this section serve these twin functions.

WHERE IT'S AT

THE WELFARE BUREAUCRACY

RICHARD M. ELMAN

WITH THE EXCEPTION OF SOCIAL WORKERS AND OFFICIAL ANTIPOVERTY
propagandists, far too many people in a city like New York seem
to believe that Welfare clients drive around in Cadillacs when
the total annual sum allotted to a family of four on Public Assistance may just about equal the cost of a small Ford.

When the public reads how the national Welfare budget increases by $1 billion every three years, they are usually not
willing to distinguish the soaring administrative costs of such a
program from what eventually goes into the pocket of the consumer.[1] When taxpayers' groups clamor for residency laws to
keep new applicants from coming to New York and consuming
tax dollars, they do not usually point out that the federal share
of assistance has risen from less than 15 percent in 1940 to as
much as 75 percent of every Welfare-expended dollar, in some
categories through various federal incentive programs and systems of matching funds. The cost of programs for dependent
children goes up, but the cost of Home Relief programs drops
absolutely when compared with the whopping $112 million dis-
bursed by the State of New York in 1940. Naturally, the $5.5

From Richard M. Elman, *The Poorhouse State*, pp. 53–64. Copyright ©
1966 by Richard M. Elman. Reprinted by permission of Pantheon Books,
a division of Random House, Inc., New York, and the author's representative, Gunther Stuhlman.

[1] According to the National Association of Social Workers there were
85,000 Welfare caseworkers in America in 1960. If each was paid $5,000 a
year, that alone would account for nearly half a billion dollars annually in
Welfare costs.

billion annually consumed by Welfare families purchases clothing, food, home furnishings, and other important employment
and wealth-producing items, yet the expenditure is constantly
viewed as a drain on the economy. And if ignorance about Welfare economics allows the irate local taxpayer to conclude that
he is bearing a disproportionate share of the cost of supporting
vice and ignorance, only ignorance about what such a family
may actually receive allows him to think that it may be living
well enough to merit his censure.

A typical Welfare budget is designed to deprive. It standardizes
bare subsistence in a country in which luxuries have become
necessities. The budget attempts to meet the family's needs economically, expeditiously, and efficiently, but it carefully defines
these needs and expects the needy individual to abide by such
definitions. In New York the system is known as budget deficit,
which means that the family's supposed resources are subtracted
from its supposed requirements, and the difference is supplied. In
other states, even more deprivating budget "ceilings" have been
established, which often penalize large families by not varying by
one penny whether the family includes three or six children. In
Arizona, for example, the maximum grant for any family is $220
a month, although some Mexican-American families have as many
as a dozen dependents.

New York State budgets are more liberal because they are
so highly individualized. Each person in the family has his own
budget. Constantly under the revision of the Department's home
economists, who base their allotments on a 50-50 weighting of
current market prices in New York City as opposed to the rest
of the State, the budget for a city person will also determine the
necessary but varied caloric intakes of each member of every
family unit according to his age, sex, and occupational status.
Food budgets increase as children reach their maximum growth
periods of adolescence and then dip as they grow into adulthood.
Adult males receive less than their children do with this arrangement, but there is so little fat on any budget that nobody in the
family is likely to get much of an edge on anybody else. The
Welfare budget will so conform to the frugal standards for adequacy imposed by the State Department of Social Welfare that
it will clamor to be violated, either by buying on credit or by
misrepresenting the facts to the caseworker. Such a budget can-

not begin to supply the resources needed to support middle-class standards. Consequently people on Public Assistance are constantly vying among themselves to see who can do better with the Welfare. Often they are given no option but to duplicate middle-class acquisitiveness on their somewhat pettier scales. Some may even invent disabilities because they will be rewarded with more money on the budget.

A modest budget for four people based on 1962 prices in the City of New York was prepared in 1963 by the Community Council of New York. If that family consisted of a husband and wife, a boy of thirteen and a girl of eight, the Council believed that it would need to spend $36.26 a week on food, exclusive of the working father's lunches away from home. Since 1962 food prices have significantly increased. Eggs have risen from forty-five cents to approximately sixty cents a dozen, milk has increased two to three cents a quart and bread by approximately the same amount, and the price of fresh pork has nearly doubled. If the same family were living on a Welfare budget at present, it would be expected to make do on $25.62 weekly for food, approximately $11 a week less than the Community Council thought was necessary for modest eating in 1962 but still $7.00 more than one nation-wide "economy standard" diet presently recommended for public assistance families by the U.S. Department of Health, Education, and Welfare.[2]

To feed itself on $25.62 weekly a family will have to be sparing with fresh milk or butter; fresh eggs, fruits, and vegetables will also have to be considered luxuries. The average American is said to consume 160 pounds of meat annually, but this family would eat beans to supply its major protein dosages. They would learn to substitute peanut butter for chicken (as one manual that I read recommended) and government surplus cornstarch for potatoes. Rice and the various cereals would be consumed in large quantities. They would—if truly frugal—reboil their coffee grounds and mix their stale bread with government-surplus molasses to make pudding.

[2] In 1916 the City's Board of Child Welfare allotted such families an average of $25.09 a month. Given the enormous increases in the cost of living since 1916, when $16 a week was considered a good salary, it is anybody's guess whether the citizen of the Poorhouse State is much better off now as compared with then.

There are probably as few such thrifty families among our present-day Welfare population as there are among Americans in general. Practically speaking, Welfare families are enticed by the same advertisements as the non-Welfare population. They do not know so much about home economics as the people who devise their budgets; and they often receive less than the stipulated budgetary entitlements. They generally have second-rate kitchen equipment and tiny larders, so they prefer to eat canned meals, TV dinners, and lots of sweet things for taste. When they over-spend on a meal, they have no resources to fall back on; they either run up a bill at the grocery store or do without.[3]

The 1963 Community Council budget included $14.70 a week for reading materials, recreation, tobacco, stationery supplies, gifts, insurance, and telephone service. On Welfare, every two weeks the thirteen-year-old boy and the eight-year-old girl members of the family would be given a total of $1.25 for their expenses "incidental to education" (paper, pencils, reading materials), but no members of such a family would be allowed money for tobacco, entertainment, telephone service, transportation (except, reluctantly, on Welfare business), gifts, toys, or even a daily newspaper. If the person wanted to have any of these items, they would have to be purchased out of the food budget or his sole clothing budget of $3.90 weekly, the allotments for personal care ($1.40)[4] or household expenses ($1.20), or the family would have

---

[3] Welfare checks are paid out on the 1st and 16th of the month in the city of New York. In many Welfare neighborhoods the mails are tardy, and checks arrive routinely late to the budgeted family. This situation was further aggravated, until recently, by Welfare's practice of mailing the checks so they will arrive no earlier than the following Monday wherever either the 1st or 16th of the month falls after a weekend, so that the clients will not have the money to spend in bars over the weekend.

[4] Based on 1965 standards established by the homemakers of the New York City Department of Welfare, here is a list of items to be acquired with regular semimonthly grants for personal care and their proposed duration of use:

Women and Girls

1. Toilet soap	(12 bars per year)
2. Tooth brush	(2 per year)
3. Dentifrice	(2 four-oz. cans per year)
4. Cleansing tissue	(100 per year)
5. Nail file	(1 for 4 years)
6. Face powder	(2–3 oz. per year for employed woman)
	(1–3 oz. per year for unemployed woman)

to find ways of getting the extra income and face the risk of being penalized for the withholding of such income if they were caught.

The family living on the Community Council budget could expect to pay $82.00 a month for a four-room apartment, including kitchen and bath. It would have at its disposal the usual mechanical aids to facilitate housekeeping, i.e., access to a washing machine, a refrigerator, a vacuum cleaner, and an electric iron. When the Department of Welfare consents to pay $82.00 a month for rent, it is generally for the larger family. That family would have difficulty finding an apartment of value equal to the one described above, and the client would be required to pay his rent semimonthly. Although it is illegal to discriminate in renting to persons because of race, color, sex, or religious beliefs, there is no law in the State of New York prohibiting a landlord from discriminating against persons who are on Public Assistance.

The typical Welfare family is likely to reside in an old-law tenement or a tiny railroad flat with a bathtub in the kitchen in a neighborhood such as 80th Street. Once housed, it receives money to purchase cooking equipment, beds, blankets, tables, chest of drawers, and chairs, if it can prove need, but it is assumed that the semimonthly allotment covers need, so each separate request has to be adjudicated individually. By special permission of departmental home economists the family can acquire a refrigerator if equipment on the premises is faulty, but a vacuum cleaner is considered a luxury. If convincing medical reasons are presented, the family may be allowed to purchase a semiautomatic washing machine with a "hand wringer." If hospitalization removes the mother from the household, the children, eligible for the services of a Welfare housekeeper, are usually sent to the shelters. A portion of the family's living space is sometimes rented

7. Lipstick	(2 per year for employed woman)
	(1 per year for unemployed woman)
8. Deodorant	(2 per year for employed woman)
	(1 per year for unemployed woman)
9. Comb	(1 every 2 years)
10. Bobby pins	(48 pins per year)
11. Haircuts	(1 per year 16+; 2 per year 7+)
12. Permanent wave refill	(3 per year for employed woman)
	(1 per year for unemployed woman)
13. Sanitary belt	(1 for 2 years)
14. Sanitary pads	(144 per year)
15. Shoe polish	(1 can per year)

to a relative—an "uncle" or a "friend"—without Welfare's knowledge and permission. Sleeping arrangements in such a home are deemed adequate if no more than two persons of the same sex share the same bed.

"We give people money for underclothing, and we find that they are using it to buy liquor," a Department employee complained to me one day. The same employee confessed on another occasion that he could understand "culturally" why it might be permissible for an old Italian couple to "take wine with their meals," but, though he thought most Welfare families should be teetotalers, he was particularly offended by the fact that his carefully-budgeted grants were being used by Negro and Puerto Rican women to purchase beer. Since there are no Welfare grants for beer, wine, or liquor, the only way a family can acquire such things is by dipping into the money for food, the new bed, or the new winter coat. A good deal of the petty cheating that goes on among Welfare recipients is merely an effort to obtain some of the comforts that have become more or less standard expectations—necessities?—in working-class America. Condemned to his meager half-world of preadded family budgets and special nonrecurring grants, the Welfare deadbeat learns to conspire against his wife's budget, his child's budget, or even his own budget. And when a family "makes it" on Welfare, it has learned to be as ruggedly individualistic, as resourceful, and as aggressive in its demands on the system as those earlier generations who crossed the wilderness or amassed large fortunes by hard work and thrift; but it is also learning to conceal, to lie if necessary, and to hide behind the protective coloring of the defective, which may be the only continuing grounds for eligibility. Such a family would make it its business to apply for every special grant, every tiny extra benefit, and it would probably be described by Welfare workers in an unflattering way; but if the family did not lie, conspire, and manipulate, it might never even receive its t, for not only do the economic penalties we impose on t pervade every aspect of his daily life, defining his hbors, his accommodations, and even his furnish- commonly do not take the trouble to instruct tails of that entitlement.

that you or I decide that we need a new itchen floor. We can select the linoleum, buy it outright, charge it, buy it on time, or—if we are especially thrifty—save enough money each week to eventually purchase the linoleum. The Welfare deadbeat does not even know that he can have linoleum, so, lacking any of the above options, he applies to his investigator, bearing in mind, of course, that—as one New York City Welfare manual points out—it is the investigator's "responsibility to establish that need exists" and that "mere statements to that effect are of little value." After listening to his client's "unsubstantiated assertion" of need, the investigator may decide that his client does not need the linoleum to cover his otherwise serviceable strip of concrete flooring, or he may feel that the old strip of linoleum can be cleaned another time, or, after inspecting the old linoleum to make certain another time that it has served out its "maximum durability," the investigator may consult with the home economist and decide to grant the recipient an amount sufficient to purchase a second-hand strip of linoleum or a very cheap new strip of linoleum. The recipient might be obliged to submit estimates from as many as three different storekeepers before he makes his purchase, and he might be charged a nonrefundable fee for these estimates. Whatever the estimated costs, the family may now have to use a portion of their linoleum grant to pay a bill at the grocery store, and the linoleum they may finally be able to buy with the difference, perhaps on another expensive credit arrangement, may be so shoddy that it will wear out before the payments are completed. Then the applicant will have to petition once more for linoleum, but it may take a while before his investigator will be willing to find the time to undertake another investigation of need (home visit), and when he does, the applicant's Welfare dossier may be used to show that he was improvident in the purchase of his initial strip of linoleum. The second grant for linoleum may, consequently, be smaller than was the first, and again it probably will have to be used to pay off creditors. Grateful for whatever linoleum he gets, never very troublesome about the linoleum he cannot have, the person who wants linoleum will probably not know enough to demand that his investigator pay him a visit. There may be reasons why he does not want him to visit. Probably he will never know (because he has never been told) what type of linoleum he is entitled to. At his local Welfare center he is exhorted with gaudy posters from the Department of Health, Education, and

Welfare about proper eating habits, but he will not be posterized to ask his investigator for enough money to buy a standard brand of linoleum.[5]

Nowhere that the recipient is likely to go during his dependency will there be signs advising him about his linoleum rights in such terms as those in which Social Security recipients are constantly advised that under such-and-such an Old Age and Survivors Insurance Program the claimant can now receive so many additional dollars in income. The War on Poverty has recently announced Operation Medicare Alert, an attempt to recruit all those over sixty-five to the Medicare Program, but no such effort has ever been made to recruit people to the public assistance lists. Persons on public assistance seemingly have no vested right to their benefits. Whatever rights they do have are, as a matter of policy, kept deeply guarded secrets by the functionaries. Thus, whenever there is a raise in the level of public assistance grants from HEW, little effort is made to pass the news on to the potential consumers. When New York State, for example, made it possible for unemployed fathers to receive AFDC funds under the provisions of a 1962 amendment to the Social Security Act, there was much self-congratulation among the professional social welfare fraternity, but nobody bothered to publicize the news among the unemployed fathers. One man thrown off Home Relief put the matter this way: "They don't want to know about us. We have to go looking for them."

And because it is this way, it is even more so in the administration of the individual semimonthly grants for income maintenance, which are to nurture and fulfill that dependency. When members of a four-person family received $24.15 weekly for food, they were not informed that they were strictly entitled to this $24.15. They knew with even less certainty that they could be allowed up to $150 a year in special grants for clothing before their case would be reviewed by a Case Consultation Unit. If they had a less knowledgeable or less charitable investigator, they might be given $23.67 a week for food and $50 per year for their clothing

[5] That nobody takes the trouble to tell the poor that they can collect public assistance can perhaps be gauged from this figure from the 1962 Annual Report of the Department of Welfare: An average of 59,000 persons in 12,600 family units in New York City received surplus foods but were not in receipt of public assistance.

(or, more commonly, $5); and they wouldn't, typically, be in a position to argue with authority about what they were getting. There would be no published lists or schedules in public places notifying the father that as an unemployed man over twenty-one he could expect $6.25 weekly for his food and $7.35 for food for his thirteen-year-old son. In some Welfare Centers there are still rules against seeing such schedules. In others, if the client knows enough to ask, he may be given an explanation, but he will not be encouraged to ask, never advised, solicited, or otherwise stimulated to inquire. Even if his worker bears the client no malice, he may be such a newcomer to the system that he himself does not know that certain deserving sick people can receive money for special diets, or that young people are to receive so much for their cod liver oil, or that some slum families are to have their utilities allowances supplemented in order to keep their lights burning at night to discourage rats.

Despite the tiny increases, Welfare still has access to a body of information by which it makes decisions concerning its clients' standards of living, standardizing their needs even to the number of haircuts and razor blades they are to be allowed; but the needy petitioner cannot browse through such a "black book" at his local Welfare center during the many hours he must sit awaiting service. With every new action taken to minister to his need, his humiliation is made the more severe as his dependency is further stressed. If he objects to such a procedure, the benefit can be withheld. Presumably, that is why it took Antonio Ortiz nearly four months to receive winter clothing grants for his three children so that it was spring when the money finally arrived.

THE POSITION
AND PROGRESS
OF BLACK AMERICA

THOMAS MAYER

THE BLACK COMMUNITY IN AMERICA IS TODAY IN A STATE OF IN-
tense ferment. This contention is both a truism and an understate-
ment. To comprehend the meaning of the contemporary "Black
Movement" it is imperative to have accurate information about
the present position of black America and the path by which this
position was reached. We present below some of the relevant
information as well as a small sample of the social science research
which has sought to illuminate its meaning.

THE BLACK POPULATION
AND ITS DISTRIBUTION

In the early days of the American Republic, blacks constituted
about one-fifth of the total population. The foreign slave trade
was halted in 1808 while white immigration continued. Hence
the proportion of blacks in the population declined more or less
continuously until 1930. Since this date the proportion of blacks
has risen steadily (see item one of Table 1). If the 1960 rates of
population increase were sustained, blacks would require slightly
more than thirty years to double their population size, while

Appeared originally in *The Bulletin of the Ann Arbor, Michigan, Citizens
for New Politics*, 1: 5:1–7, 1967, reprinted by *The Radical Education
Project*, Box 625, Ann Arbor, Michigan, 1968. Reprinted by permission of
the author.

whites would need in excess of fifty years (see item two of Table 1).

The life expectancy of blacks in America has always been shorter than that of whites, although in recent years the gap has narrowed somewhat (see item seven of Table 1). This in conjunction with higher black fertility rates explains why the median age of whites in 1960 was about 6.8 years greater than the average age of nonwhites (see item three of Table 1). According to the 1960 census, 45.6 percent of blacks were under twenty, while only 39.5 percent of whites fell in this age range.

During the twentieth century an immense migration of blacks occurred from rural Southern regions to urban areas in both the North and South (see items four and five of Table 1). California, Illinois, Michigan, New York, Ohio, and Pennsylvania absorbed about 70 percent of the black net in-migration between the years 1910 and 1960. Today the black population is more highly urbanized than the white population. Furthermore, the proportion of blacks dwelling in the central cities of the 24 largest US metropolitan areas more than doubles the comparable proportion for whites (see item six of Table 1).

RESIDENTIAL SEGREGATION

The authoritative study by Karl and Alma Taeuber on residential segregation in the United States presents convincing evidence that this phenomenon actually increased between 1940 and 1960. There appears to have been a slight decline in residential segregation—particularly in Northern and Western regions— between 1950 and 1960, but not enough to counter the more substantial rise which occurred from 1940 to 1950.

The Northern and Western regions of the United States seem to be making some very slow progress towards residential desegregation while the trend in the South is in the opposite direction. Perhaps the most surprising aspect of the Taeuber and Taeuber data is the homogeneity it reveals in the extent of regional residential segregation. Although this homogeneity has decreased since 1940, it was still substantial in 1960.

TABLE I Some Relevant Demographic Statistics

	1790	1840	1860	1880	1900	1910	1920	1930	1940	1950	1960	1966	1967
Black population:													
Number (in millions)	.76	2.9	4.4	6.6	8.8	9.8	10.5	11.9	12.9	15.0	18.9		21.9
Percent of total population	19.3%	16.8%	14.1%	13.1%	11.6%	10.7%	9.9%	9.7%	9.8%	10.0%	10.6%		11.1%
Live births per thousand:													
White							26.9	20.6	18.6	23.0	22.7	17.4	
Nonwhite							35.0	27.5	26.7	33.3	32.1	26.1	
Median age:													
White		17.9							29.5	30.8	30.3		
Nonwhite		17.3							25.2	26.1	23.5		
Percent of black population living in major geographic regions:													
North									22%	28%	34%	37%	
South									77%	68%	60%	55%	
West									1%	4%	6%	8%	
Black population as a percent of regional population:													
North									4%	5%	7%	8%	
South									24%	22%	21%	20%	
West									1%	3%	4%	5%	

	1	2	3	4	5	6
Percent living in urban areas:						
White	48%			64.3%		69.5%
Nonwhite	27%			61.7%		72.4%
Percent living in central city of metropolitan areas:						
White				34%	30%	27%
Black				43%	51%	56%
Life expectancy at birth: White						
Male	54.4	59.7	62.1	66.5	67.4	67.6
Female	55.6	63.5	66.6	72.2	74.1	74.7
Life expectancy at birth Nonwhite						
Male	45.5	47.3	51.5	59.1	61.1	60.7
Female	45.2	49.2	54.9	62.9	66.3	67.4

SOURCE: Statistical Abstract of the United States, Sept. 1968. Bureau of the Census, U.S. Dept. of Commerce, pp. 1-86; and Talcott Parsons and Kenneth B. Clark (eds.), The Negro American (Boston: Beacon Press, 1965), pp. 71-101, 102-133.

TABLE 2   Average Values of Segregation Indexes[1] for Regions
and Subregions in 1940, 1950, 1960

Region and Subregion	Cities	1940	1950	1960	Changes 1940–50	1950–60
Total all regions	109	85.2	87.3	86.1	2.1	−1.2
Northeast	25	83.2	83.6	78.9	0.4	−4.7
New England	7	81.9	81.9	75.8	0.0	−6.1
Middle Atlantic	18	83.7	83.7	80.0	0.6	−4.3
North Central	29	88.4	89.9	88.4	1.5	−1.5
East North Central	20	88.3	90.0	88.4	1.7	−1.6
West North Central	9	88.6	89.8	88.3	1.2	−1.5
West	10	82.7	82.9	76.4	0.2	−6.5
South	45	84.9	88.5	90.7	3.6	2.2
South Atlantic	22	86.9	88.7	90.6	1.8	1.9
East South Central	9	84.8	88.1	91.4	3.3	3.3
West South Central	14	81.7	88.5	90.5	6.8	2.0

SOURCE: Karl E. Taeuber and Alma F. Taeuber, Negroes in Cities (Chicago: Aldine Publishing Co., 1965), p. 44, Table 5.

[1] The index of segregation used here is called the **index of dissimilarity.** It gives the smallest percentage of blacks who would have to change residence to make the white and black residential distribution identical.

SOME GENERAL INDICATORS OF RACISM IN AMERICAN LIFE

The significance of color permeates virtually every aspect of American society. A short review cannot do justice to the numerous statistics which demonstrate the omnipresent impact of racism. Table 3 presents time series data on fifteen "social indicators" with respect to which whites and nonwhites can be compared. On all but one of these indicators—suicide rate—nonwhites, occupy a severely disadvantaged position relative to whites. In some cases the gap appears to be narrowing, though usually at a very slow pace. In other cases this is not so.

An economist, Rashi Fein, has suggested that ratios such as those used in Table 3 tend to underestimate the gap between whites and nonwhites, since improvement occurs more readily (and often in larger pieces) when starting from a low base, but subsequently becomes more difficult to achieve. He suggests instead a time lag statistic which for a specific variable and a specific date gives the number of years earlier that the white population

TABLE 3 White-Nonwhite Comparisons on Fifteen "Social Indicators" for 3-Year Intervals from 1948 to 1965

		1948–50	1951–53	1954–56	1957–59	1960–62	1963–65
School enrollment, percent males aged 14–17	N	70.7	75.5	83.1	86.2	88.8	92.4
	W	84.5	87.2	89.6	91.7	92.9	94.6*
	N/W	.84	.87	.93	.94	.96	.98
Percent high school graduates, male labor force	N	NA	15.1**	NA	21.7**	27.3**	32.3*
	W	NA	42.1**	NA	49.4**	53.5**	56.8*
	N/W		.36		.44	.51	.57
Percent of male workers with year-round full-time jobs	N	50.2**	53.0	55.6*	51.3	51.8	55.2*
	W	66.8**	69.9	58.8*	66.0	65.3	67.2*
	N/W	.75	.76	.81	.78	.79	.82
Percent of employed persons in white-collar jobs	N	9.6*	9.7**	12.2*	14.0*	16.4	18.6
	W	39.7**	39.8**	42.2*	45.6*	46.8	47.2
	N/W	.24	.24	.29	.31	.35	.39
Median income of families (in dollars)	N	1762	2277	2529	2797	3251	3758
	W	3329	4122	4646	5370	6018	6859
	N/W	.53	.55	.54	.52	.54	.55
Infant deaths per 1000 live births	N	46.1	45.5	42.6	44.4	41.8	41.3*
	W	28.5	25.4	23.6	23.4	22.5	21.9*
	N/W	1.62	1.79	1.81	1.90	1.86	1.89
Deaths from tuberculosis per 100,000 population	N	71.5	42.2	21.9	16.2	12.3	10.4*
	W	21.0	13.0	7.7	6.0	4.6	3.8*
	N/W	3.40	3.25	2.84	2.70	2.67	2.74
Homicides per 100,000 population	N	29.1	26.1	23.6	22.0	21.5	22.4*
	W	2.8	2.5	2.3	2.4	2.6	2.7*
	N/W	10.4	10.4	10.3	9.2	8.3	8.3

TABLE 3 (continued)

		1948–50	1951–53	1954–56	1957–59	1960–62	1963–65
Suicides per 100,000 population	N	4.2	3.9	3.9	4.3	4.6	4.8*
	W	12.2	10.9	10.9	11.1	11.4	11.8*
	N/W	.34	.36	.36	.39	.40	.41
Percent married women with husband absent	N	NA	16.0	19.6	20.3	19.8	21.0
	W	NA	4.6*	5.0	4.2	.3	4.4
	N/W		3.48	3.92	4.83	4.60	4.77
Incomplete families per 100 families	N	12.1	10.1*	10.4	9.2	7.4	6.4
	W	6.1	4.4*	4.2	3.4	2.8	2.4
	N/W	1.98	2.30	2.48	2.71	2.64	2.67
Births per 1000 women aged 15–44	N	135	144	156	162	152	143*
	W	103	110	114	116	111	102*
	N/W	1.31	1.31	1.37	1.40	1.37	1.40
Percent of live births illegitimate	N	17.1	18.6	20.2	21.2	22.3	24.0*
	W	1.8	1.6	1.9	2.1	2.5	3.2*
	N/W	9.5	11.6	10.6	10.1	8.9	7.5
Percent of aged population receiving old-age and survivor insurance benefits	N	9.3	18.3	28.4	41.0	53.0	65.0
	W	17.3	30.0	43.8	59.4	69.6	77.0
	N/W	.54	.61	.65	.69	.76	.84
Prisoners executed under civil authority, annual number	N	65	42	40	31	25	5
	W	42	41	34	23	23	9
	N/W	1.55	1.02	1.18	1.35	1.09	.56

SOURCE: Duncan, Otis Dudley. "Discrimination Against Negroes," The Annals of the American Academy of Political and Social Science, Philadelphia, Vol. 371 (May 1967), p. 91.

W = white; N = nonwhite; N/W = ratio of nonwhite to white; NA = data not available.
* Indicates data based on **two** rather than three years; ** Indicates data based on **one** rather than three years.

attained the level on this variable attained at the given date by the nonwhite population. Some of Fein's data are given in Table 4. Item seven of Table 1 suggests that the gap between the life expectancy of whites and blacks is eroding. The statistic used by Fein, however, suggests this gap to be larger in 1960 than it was in 1940.

TABLE 4   Time Gap Between Blacks and Whites on Ten Social Indicators[1]

	1930	1940	1950	1960
Life expectancy		27	28	28
Hospital births			11('52)	16('62)
Infant mortality	15	17	11	20
Maternal mortality		26('41)	8	11
School years completed				20+
Percentage of persons 25 or older completing college				20+
Percentage of persons 20–24 with some college				35+('63)
Percentage white collar workers				63
Income				17('64)
Persons per dwelling room				20+

SOURCE: Rashi Fein, "An Economic and Social Profile of the American Negro," in Talcott Parsons and Kenneth B. Clark (eds.), The Negro American (Boston: Beacon Press, 1965), pp. 102–133.

[1] Figures indicate the number of years prior to the date given when whites first achieved the level at which Negroes stood at the given date with respect to the listed social indicator. Dates in parentheses indicate dates to which the figures pertain when these deviate from the date listed at the column head. A plus indicates "more than."

INCOME

The difference between white and nonwhite average income has increased steadily since 1939 at least. The ratio of nonwhite to white income has remained relatively stable since 1947, indicating that the relative income position of nonwhites has not changed since that time. World War II and the social transformation associated with it apparently produced a major redistribution of income between white and nonwhite, but liberal programs and legislation did not perpetuate this process into the post-war period.

TABLE 5   **The Income Gap: White vs. Nonwhite Male Workers aged 14 and over, in 1939, and 1947–1962**

Year	Average Income			N/W ratio
	White	Nonwhite	Diff.	
1939	$1112	$ 460	$ 652	.41
1947	2357	1279	1078	.54
1948	2711	1615	1096	.60
1949	2735	1367	1368	.50
1950	2982	1828	1154	.61
1951	3345	2060	1285	.62
1952	3507	2038	1469	.58
1953	3760	2233	1527	.59
1954	3754	2131	1623	.57
1955	3986	2342	1644	.59
1956	4260	2396	1864	.56
1957	4396	2436	1960	.55
1958	4596	2652	1944	.58
1959	4902	2844	2058	.58
1960	5137	3075	2062	.60
1961	5287	3015	2272	.57
1962	5462	3023	2439	.55

SOURCE: U.S. Bureau of the Census, Current Population Reports—Consumer Income, Series P-60, annual issues.

Differences between white and nonwhite incomes do not result entirely from differences between white and nonwhite occupational structures (i.e., from the fact that whites monopolize high paying white collar jobs while nonwhites are disproportionately represented in low paying manual occupations). As Table 6 demonstrates, white-nonwhite income differentials occur even within the same occupation.

Nor does the evidence reveal education as the royal road to income equality. In fact, the relative income deprivation of nonwhites increases with education, as can be seen from Table 7. Low education apparently acts as a barrier to the career aspirations of both whites and nonwhites. This prevents poorly educated whites from utilizing the full advantages available under the discriminatory occupational system. College educated whites suffer from no such handicaps. Willingly or unwillingly they reap the full income benefits of unequal opportunity.

TABLE 6   Median Income for Total Population and for Nonwhite, by Occupation in 1959

Occupation	Median Income		
	Nonwhite	Total	Ratio
Bakers	$3354	$4633	.72
Carpenters	2320	4271	.54
Welders and flame cutters	4454	5116	.87
Elevator operators	3122	3487	.90
Automobile mechanics	3173	4372	.73
Tinsmiths, coppersmiths, and sheet metal workers	4710	5542	.85

SOURCE: Rashi Fein, "An Economic and Social Profile of the American Negro," in Parsons & Clark, op. cit.

This line of thought has been extended by Paul M. Siegel, who has calculated the amount of the difference between white and nonwhite incomes at each educational level which can be attributed to differences in the regional and occupational distributions of whites and nonwhites, and the amount which must be attributed to other (presumably sheerly discriminatory) factors. Siegel's main results are given in Table 8. The last column of this table reveals that the income differences attributable to discriminatory factors increase with education. Even the percentage of the income difference attributable to discriminatory factors tends to increase with education. Thus highly educated nonwhites suffer the brunt of income discrimination more intensely than those with less education.

TABLE 7   Nonwhite Estimated Lifetime Income as a Percentge of White Estimated Lifetime Income at Three Educational Levels

Educational Level	
Elementary school graduates	64%
High school graduates	60%
College graduates	50%

SOURCE: "Statement of Herman P. Miller, Special Assistant, Office of the Director, Bureau of the Census," Hearings Before the Committee on Labor and Public Welfare on Bills Relating to Equal Employment Opportunity, U.S. Senate, 88th Congress, 1st Session, July and August 1963.

TABLE 8   **Decomposition of Mean Differences between White and Nonwhite Earnings in 1959 for United States Males Aged 25–64**

Years of School Completed	Mean Income			Decomposition of Difference	
	White	Non-White	Differ-ence	Reg'l, etc.[1]	Discrim'tion[2]
Elementary: 0–7 years	$3,983	$2,562	$1,421	$ 725 (51%)	$ 696 (49%)
Elementary: 8 years	4,837	3,318	1,519	601 (40%)	918 (60%)
High School: 1–3 years	5,555	3,522	2,033	757 (37%)	1276 (73%)
High School: 4 years	6,250	4,021	2,229	823 (37%)	1406 (73%)
College: 1–3 years	7,554	4,355	3,199	1441 (45%)	1758 (54%)
College: 4 or more years	10,238	5,671	4,567	767 (17%)	3800 (83%)

SOURCE: Paul M. Siegel, "On the Cost of Being Negro," Sociological Inquiry, Vol. 35, No. 1, Winter 1965, p. 53, Table 2.

[1] Figures given in this column indicate the part and percentage of the difference between white and nonwhite income (for each education group) which **can** be explained by the differences between the occupational and regional distributions of whites and nonwhites.

[2] Figures given in this column indicate the part and percentage of the difference between white and nonwhite income (for each education group) which **cannot** be explained by the differences between the occupational and regional distributions of whites and nonwhites and presumably result from sheer discrimination.

Using these methods, Siegel has attempted to determine the average "cost" of being nonwhite. In 1959 the difference between white and nonwhite earnings for males 25 to 64 was $2,852. Differences in the regional, occupational, and educational distributions of whites and nonwhites accounted for 61.5 percent of this difference, or $1,755. The remaining 38.5 percent, or $1,097, would have existed even if whites and nonwhites had had identical regional, occupational, and educational distributions. Siegel calls this quantity the average "cost" of being nonwhite in 1959.

UNEMPLOYMENT

Since 1950 official nonwhite unemployment rates have almost always been more than twice as great as official white unemployment rates. Unemployment for both whites and nonwhites is heavily concentrated in the younger age brackets. Unemployment among 14–19 year old nonwhites has exceeded 20 percent in every year since 1958, while it has hovered around 15 percent for nonwhites in the 20–24 age bracket. Interestingly, the ratio of non-white to white unemployment is somewhat lower in these age brackets than in others which experience less unemployment. Thus age cohorts who suffer less unemployment experience more inequality, while age cohorts for whom inequality is less pronounced endure more unemployment. (See Table 9.)

The official unemployment rates given in Table 9 seriously underestimate the actual unemployment levels. They include only those persons actively looking for work who do not have even a part-time job. A recent Department of Labor report on subemployment uses an index which in addition to persons counted in conventional unemployment statistics includes (1) those who have dropped out of the labor market in despair; (2) those who are working part-time but want full-time employment; (3) heads of households under 65 but earning less than $60 a week; (4) persons under 65 who are not heads of households and earn less than $56 a week in full-time jobs; and (5) a conservatively estimated portion of males living in the slums who do not appear in either employment or unemployment counts. The ten cities surveyed revealed an average subemployment rate of 35 percent. Presumably the black subemployment rate would be even higher.

THE BLACK FAMILY

Daniel Moynihan and several other commentators have noted the effect of racism on black family structure. The financial, occupational, and educational disadvantages under which the black male must operate makes it difficult for him to fill the role of family head. This militates for a matriarchal family structure and severely curtails the longevity of the family unit. The family is the crucial socializing agency in American society. It provides material and emotional support for the child and motivates him to acquire the educational and occupational skills necessary for social advancement. The instability of the black family—itself induced by racist discrimination—helps perpetuate the disadvantaged position of American blacks. Items ten and eleven of Table 3 furnishes evidence in support of this argument.

At any moment about 36 percent of black children are living in homes with one or both parents missing, and less than one-third of all black youth reach eighteen having lived all their lives with

TABLE 9 Unemployment Rates by Color and Age in Selected Years

Age	1950	1953	1957	1958	1959	1960	1961	1962	1963	1964
Total										
N	8.9	4.4	8.4	13.7	11.5	10.7	12.9	11.0	10.6	9.1
W	4.5	2.2	3.7	6.1	4.6	4.8	5.7	4.6	4.7	4.2
N/W	1.98	2.00	2.27	2.25	2.50	2.23	2.26	2.39	2.26	2.17
14–19										
N	13.2	7.1	17.5	24.3	22.8	22.0	24.7	20.7	25.4	23.3
W	10.5	6.3	10.5	14.0	12.5	12.9	14.1	12.3	14.2	13.4
N/W	1.26	1.12	1.67	1.74	1.82	1.71	1.75	1.68	1.79	1.74
20–24										
N	12.4	7.1	12.7	19.5	16.3	13.1	15.3	14.6	15.5	12.6
W	7.3	3.7	7.1	11.7	7.5	8.3	10.0	8.0	7.8	7.4
N/W	1.70	1.92	1.79	1.67	2.17	1.58	1.53	1.83	1.99	1.70
25–34										
N	9.4	3.7	8.5	14.7	12.3	10.7	12.9	10.5	9.5	7.7
W	3.7	1.6	2.7	5.6	3.8	4.1	4.9	3.8	3.9	3.0
N/W	2.54	2.31	3.15	2.63	3.24	2.61	2.63	2.76	2.44	2.57
35–44										
N	7.3	3.1	6.4	11.4	8.9	8.2	10.7	8.6	8.0	6.2
W	3.0	1.5	2.5	4.4	3.2	3.3	4.0	3.1	2.9	2.5
N/W	2.43	2.07	2.56	2.59	2.78	2.48	2.68	2.77	2.76	2.48
45–54										
N	7.0	4.3	6.2	10.3	7.9	8.5	10.2	8.3	7.1	5.9
W	3.5	1.7	3.0	4.8	3.7	3.6	4.4	3.5	3.3	2.9
N/W	2.00	2.53	2.07	2.15	2.14	2.36	2.32	2.37	2.15	2.36
55–64										
N	7.4	3.2	5.5	10.1	8.7	9.5	10.5	9.6	7.4	8.1
W	4.5	2.2	3.4	5.2	4.2	4.1	5.3	4.1	4.0	3.5
N/W	1.64	1.45	1.62	1.94	2.07	2.32	1.98	2.34	1.85	2.31
65+										
N	7.0	2.6	5.9	9.0	8.4	6.3	9.4	11.9	1.1	8.3
W	4.4	2.1	3.2	5.0	4.5	4.0	5.2	4.1	4.1	3.6
N/W	1.59	1.24	1.84	1.80	1.87	1.58	1.81	2.90	2.46	2.31

W = white; N = nonwhite; N/W = ratio of nonwhite to white.

SOURCE: Manpower Report of the President, March 1965, Table A-3, p. 206.

both parents. The most recent figures indicate that one-fourth of all nonwhite births are illegitimate (see Table 3). In fact, most black children are at some time supported by the Aid to Families with Dependent Children program.

CONCLUDING REMARKS

The data presented above illuminate a few aspects of the unique problems faced by black Americans. They indicate as clearly as anything can the racism which infects every aspect of American life. They also document the near total failure of liberal solutions to the problem of discrimination. There is little reason to believe that education, job programs, and increased welfare expenditures within the context of contemporary American socio-economic structure will make even a dent in the situation of American blacks. Racism is deeply embedded in American society. It was present in the colonial seed from which this society grew and it poisoned the milk which nurtured the young Republic. Color has for centuries been a major American emblum of status, and whites have appropriated for themselves all leading positions in virtually all institutions of American life. Blacks, on the other hand, monopolize the cellar of American society, despised by poor whites who view them as a status threat and patronized by liberals fearful lest the fury of black discontent explode their comfortable accommodation with racist society.

Persons of radical persuasion must not, however, content themselves with belaboring liberals. Indeed, this would imply adoption of liberal technique. Although the task is staggering, the outlook is not hopeless. Any strategy, to have the slightest chance of ending American racism, must be radical in the fullest sense of the word: universal in scope, daring in conception, and drastic in intent. We must study the strategy of liberalism and learn from the failure of its programs. Then with greater wisdom and resolution we must join the insurgent black masses in their historic struggle against the appalling heritage of four racist centuries.

THE SLUM MERCHANT

ROBERT CONOT

ON STORE WINDOWS EVERYWHERE HASTILY LETTERED NOTICES WERE blossoming: NEGRO OWNED, SPERE THE SOLE FOLK, WE ARE BLOOD, BLOOD BROTHER—*We shall overcome.* Many had the x x x indicating Muslim sympathies. Orientals were inscribing COLORED OWNER, and some Caucasians, figuring that they had nothing to lose, scrawled BLOOD on their shops. One white liquor store owner boarded up his place, dumped glass and debris in front, scorched and smudged the outside, and then hoped for the best. The ruse worked. Figuring that the loot was already gone, rioters passed the building by.

Some merchants who had good reputations were spared, sometimes because of the action of the rioters, more often because people in the community protected the stores. One of these was the ABC Market at 52nd and Main, whose owner employed a Negro manager and contributed to scholarship programs. Another was the drug store at 103rd and Beach Streets, right in the midst of the heaviest destruction in Watts, where Amos "Big Train" Lincoln, Cassius Clay's sparring partner, sat cradling a shotgun in his lap. Across the street the Food Giant Market was still standing, not because it was beloved, but because Carl Margolis and his men refused to abandon it.

In his five-and-ten-cent store Nathan Finckel had been without sleep for more than 24 hours, and, at 62, he did not know how much longer he could last. Finckel, a German Jew, had arrived in the United States in 1937, and it had taken him eight years to have enough money to open the small store. He did not make a great deal of money, and he had been robbed more than once, but he had gained the respect of the more stable element of the community. Friday at noon Bill Black, a six-foot-five 250-pound Negro had come, carrying a machete, and sat down in the doorway.

"Mr. Finckel," he had said, "they going to burn this town down. But we gonna see that they don't do nothing to you."

For years the business practices of many of the merchants had terrified Finckel. They would brag about how they could get away with adding 10¢ or 15¢ to a customer's check, about how they could play their little switching games, substituting a piece of inferior merchandise for one of higher quality marked at the same price, about how they could get away with almost anything because the Negroes were so ignorant.

"Look, look! You see how you do it, Nathan!" an acquaintance had, helpfully, tried to show him. "You add a little here, and you subtract there, and then you add some more, and they don't know what it all comes to. You see, this is what I mean. . . ." He had pulled out a bill of sale for a television set:

$285.00	base price
$ 14.95	90-day warranty
$299.95	selling price
$ 12.00	tax
$311.95	total
$ 31.95	down
$280.00	balance
$ 88.42	carrying charges (24 months)
$368.42	grand total

"That grand total is a really fine gimmick—my own thinking!" he had said. "You subtract the down payment, so that doesn't figure in at all—otherwise it comes to over $400, and that would be no good, no good—they wouldn't buy. And then, the 90-day warranty, that's pure gold. The carrying charges, well, if you want to know the truth, after you take the down payment away, they're between 25 and 30 percent a year. But you've got to do it, Nathan! It's the only way to come out. These people, there aren't

half of them that are going to pay for two years, so you've got
to figure—one year! One year, and you make a profit. I have this
woman, and she comes to me and she still owes me $100, and she
tells me they have cut her check, and she cannot afford to pay
$20 a month. So I tell her, 'Okay, you're a good woman, I trust
you. Just pay me the interest. Five dollars a month.' So she has
paid me now $5 a month for two years, and she still owes me
$100. I can't complain!"

SOCIAL WELFARE AND
THE ART OF GIVING

RICHARD M. TITMUSS

THE HISTORY OF SOCIAL WELFARE IN WESTERN COUNTRIES AS AN
organized system of "giving" shows that over the past century
it has played a variety of roles in the processes of change. One
of the most important but least acknowledged in the historical
literature has been its educational role. In Britain and other countries exposed to the early stages of industrialization, it was a major
force in sustaining the social conscience. To give aid without regard to economic criteria and to differences in race, color, religion,
and class brought it into direct conflict with the values of the
market place. To act as an agent of redistributive social justice
meant opposing discrimination; the concept of economic man had
to be confronted with noneconomic criteria; the natural dignity
and uniqueness of everyman had continually to be publicly re-
stated, fought for, and demonstrated.

While time and circumstances have changed for the mass of the
people in the West, the fundamental need for social welfare as an
instrument of social justice and community education remains.
This is one of the underlying themes of this essay; a second and
less explicit one is that only a society which is firmly dedicated
to the principle of greater equality and the diffusion of humanistic
values will have sufficient moral conviction to make available the
resources necessary to help close the gap between the "have" and

From Richard M. Titmuss, "Social Welfare And The Art of Giving,"
Socialist Humanism, Erich Fromm (ed.). New York: Doubleday and Company, Inc., 1965. Reprinted by permission of Doubleday and Company, Inc.,
and the author.

the "have-not" nations of the world. The ideas which move men and which they hold about their own societies must influence them in their attitudes toward the need for change in other societies.

It is of course possible to preach reform for others but not for one's own social group. The history of colonialism and race relations in the East and the West is littered with sad examples of hypocrisy. But, considered in collective terms, such attitudes today require a high degree of calculated cynicism. In effect, they can mean that the rich nations advocate social reform for the poor nations in order to prevent the spread of communism or some other hostile ideology or to further the defense and economic interests of the rich. According to Professor Seymour Martin Lipset (writing of underdeveloped countries): "only parties which promise to improve the situation of the masses through widespread reform . . . can hope to compete with the Communists."[1] A philosophy of the status quo at home can cynically purvey the notion of social welfare as a reforming agent among the poorer nations of the world simply to protect an already established "good" society in the West. Fortunately, the development of social welfare values and policies among the poorer nations does not wholly depend on the influence or attitudes of the rich nations.

Nevertheless, however determined and able the "have-not" nations are to shape their own internal policies, there will still remain a major dilemma of "giving" on an international scale. The income gap between the rich and poor nations is continually widening and, more serious still, there is evidence that this widening is now proceeding at an accelerating rate. Professor Gunnar Myrdal has recently drawn the conclusion that "without a radical change in policies in both groups of countries, the world is headed for an economic and political cataclysm."[2] How societies give collectively, and their motives for giving are questions as fundamental to the health of social welfare systems at home and abroad as the question of what they give.

[1] Seymour Martin Lipset, *Political Man: The Social Bases of Politics* (New York: Doubleday & Company, Inc., 1960), p. 416.
[2] Gunnar Myrdal, *The Urgent Need for Scientific Breakthroughs if Great Misery Shall Not be the Destiny of Underdeveloped Countries*, paper presented to the Conference on Global Impacts of Applied Microbiology, Stockholm, August 2, 1963.

II

We come then to the question of the present and future role of social welfare in the West—particularly in Britain and the United States. If there is any substance in the foregoing view, then this question is of more than national interest: how we conduct our own domestic affairs will influence the quality of our relationships with our poorer neighbors.

"Modern social welfare," it has been said in the United States, "has really to be thought of as help given to the stranger, not to the person who by reason of personal bond commands it without asking."[3] It has, therefore, to be formally organized, to be administered by strangers, and to be paid for collectively by strangers.

Social welfare or the social services, operating through agencies, institutions, and programs outside the private market, are becoming more difficult to define in any society with precision. As societies become more complex and specialized, so do systems of social welfare. Functionally, they reflect, and respond to, the larger social structure and its division of labor. This process makes it much harder today to identify the causal agents of change— the microbes of social disorganization and the viruses of impoverishment—and to make them responsible for the costs of "disservices." Who should bear the social costs of the thalidomide babies, of urban blight, of smoke pollution, of the obsolescence of skills, of automation, of the impact of synthetic coffee, which will dispense with the need for coffee beans, on the peasants of Brazil? The private benefits are to some extent measurable and attributable, but the private losses are not. Neoclassical economics and the private market cannot make these allocations; they are not organized to estimate social disruption and are unable to provide adequately for the public needs created by social and economic change.

Our growing inability to identify and connect cause and effect in the world of social and technological change is thus one reason for the historical emergence of social welfare institutions in the West. Altruism by strangers for strangers was and is an attempt to fill a moral void created by applied science. The services and

---

[3] H. L. Wilensky and C. N. Lebeaux, *Industrial Society and Social Welfare* (New York: Russell Sage Foundation, 1958), p. 141.

programs developed in the West to give aid to the stranger victims of industrialism and change have inevitably and necessarily
become more specialized and complex. In this paper we shall only
be able to speak of them in general terms.

III

The social services, as they are named in Britain, are largely
the product of the twentieth century—a delayed response to the
industrialism of the nineteenth century. The term is generally and
loosely interpreted today to cover such public (or publicly supported) services as medical care, education, housing, income maintenance in old age and during periods of unemployment, sickness,
disability and so forth, child allowances, and a variety of specific
services for particular groups of people with special needs, e.g.,
neglected children, unmarried mothers, the blind, mental defec-
tives, young delinquents, discharged prisoners, and other categories. All these services came apologetically into existence to
provide for certain basic needs which the individual, the family,
and the private market in capitalist societies were unable or unwilling to meet. In the United States and other Western countries,
the terms "social welfare" or "social policy programs" are used as
alternative generic labels to embrace a similar variety of collectively organized services which may differ widely in scope and
structure, methods of administration and finance, and in the fundamental objectives underlying them.

The concept of "The Welfare State," which entered the arena
of political thought in the 1940s, is generally accepted as a wider
definition of the role of the State in the field of social and economic policy, embracing more than the provision of social services. Most writers on the subject, whether on the right or left
politically, take it to mean a more positive and purposeful commitment by government to concern itself with the general welfare
of the whole community and with the social costs of change. In
his book *Beyond the Welfare State*, Gunnar Myrdal concluded
that "In the last half-century, the State, in all the rich countries
in the Western world, has become a democratic 'Welfare State',
with fairly explicit commitments to the broad goals of economic
development, full employment, equality of opportunity for the
young, social security, and protected minimum standards as re-

gards not only income, but nutrition, housing, health and education, for people of all regions and social groups."[4]

In this view, it can be argued that "Welfare Statism," either as an established fact or as a political objective, is a common phenomenon of large-scale, industrialized societies. The renaissance of private enterprise during the past two decades in North America and Europe, the Keynesian revolution and the adoption of techniques of economic management, rising standards of living and the achievements of political parties and trade unions on behalf of the underprivileged—have led all these culturally different societies along the same road to "Welfare Statism"—a road unforeseen by Marx. Whether they know it or not, and whether they like it or not, Democrats and Republicans, Conservatives, Socialists, and Liberals in North America and Europe have become "welfare-statists." The Germans and the Swedes may have more "advanced" pension systems, the British a more comprehensive health service, the French more extensive family allowances, and the Americans may spend more on public education but, when all these national differences are acknowledged, the generalized welfare commitment is nevertheless viewed as the dominant political fact of modern Western societies. Governments of the liberal right and the liberal left may come and go; the commitment to welfare, economic growth, and full employment will remain with minor rather than major changes in scope and objectives.

IV

In historical and comparative terms, these are sweeping conclusions and leave many questions of values and facts unexamined. To what extent are they based on the real facts of income and wealth distribution, property, power, and class? Has the "Welfare State" abolished poverty, social deprivation, and exploitation? Has man a greater sense of social control and participation in the work and life of his community? What will be the human consequences of further social and technological changes? Will the future resemble the immediate past, or are these views a simple projection of a transient phase in the development of large-scale and predominantly competitive societies?

[4] Gunnar Myrdal (Yale University Press, 1960), p. 45.

In recent years a growing number of political commentators, economists, and sociologists on both sides of the Atlantic, in proclaiming the end of political ideology in the West, have either ignored such questions or have tended to imply that they are no longer of primary importance for our societies. Their reasons for doing so are explicit or implicit in their general thesis. Professor Lipset in his book *Political Man* (1960) spoke for many when he said (in summarizing the discussions of a world congress of intellectuals in 1955) that "the ideological issues dividing left and right [have] been reduced to a little more or a little less government ownership and economic planning"; and there was general agreement that it really makes little difference "which political party controls the domestic policies of individual nations." With minor differences, parties of both the right and the left will attempt to alleviate those social injustices that still remain, and will continue to seek improvements in social welfare, education, medical care, and other sectors of the economy for the general well-being. All will share, rich and poor, in the benefits of growth. By a natural process of market levitation all classes and groups will stand expectantly on the political right as the escalator of growth moves them up. Automatism thus substitutes for the social protest.

To quote Lipset again (though writers in a similar vein in England, France, and Germany could equally be cited): ". . . the fundamental political problems of the industrial revolution have been solved: the workers have achieved industrial and political citizenship, the conservatives have accepted the welfare state, and the democratic left has recognised that an increase in overall state power carries with it more dangers to freedom than solutions for economic problems. This very triumph of the democratic social revolution in the West ends domestic politics for those intellectuals who must have ideologies or utopias to motive them to political action"[5]

As a generalization, it is conceivable that this statement may serve as a summing-up for the 1950s in the history books of the next century. But from the perspective of 1960 it is, to say the least, a dubious proposition. However, we would not wish this

---

[5] Lipset, op. cit., pp. 404–6. For other references to this thesis see Lipset and also Daniel Bell, *The End of Ideology: On the Exhaustion of Political Ideas in the Fifties* (Glencoe, Illinois: Free Press, 1960).

essay to take the form of a critique of any one particular writer. To do so would carry with it the obligation to discuss in detail an individual interpretation of recent trends and the many qualifications attached to them. We shall, therefore, treat these statements as an expression not of the views of Professor Lipset but of a collective *Weltanschauung*, and one that seems to be growing in influence in the West, to judge by the number of its adherents.

Though we make no attempt to examine the thesis at length, we shall speculate about some of its basic assumptions so far as they relate to the future role of a humanist social policy in Britain and the U.S.A.

First, it is unhistorical. Implicit in the thesis is the assumption that the "industrial revolution" was a once-and-for-all affair. Thus, it ignores the evidence concerning the trend toward monopolistic concentrations of economic power, the role of the corporation as private government with taxing powers, the problems of social disorganization and cultural deprivation, and the growing impact of automation and new techniques of production and distribution in economically advanced societies. If the first phase of the so-called revolution was to force all men to work, the phase we are now entering may be to force many men not to work. Without a major shift in values, only an impoverishment in social living can result from this new wave of industrialism.

Second, it states that the workers have achieved "industrial citizenship." The only comment we feel able to make on this is to say that it is a misuse of language to imply that membership of a trade union is synonymous with "industrial citizenship." Conceptions of what constitutes "citizenship" for the worker must be related to what we now know about man's potential and his basic social and psychological needs; they cannot be compared with conditions of industrial slavery in the nineteenth century.

Third, the thesis implies that the problem of the distribution of income and wealth has either been solved or is now of insignificant proportions in Western society. In any event, such disparities as do exist are justified on grounds of individual differences and the need for economic incentives, and are considered to present no threat to democratic values.

In the 1950s, 1 percent of the British population owned 42 percent of all personal net capital and 5 percent owned 67.5 percent.[6] Even these proportions are underestimates for the figures exclude pension funds and trusts (which have grown enormously in recent years), and they do not take account of the increasing tendency for large owners of property to distribute their wealth among their families, to spread it over time, to send it abroad, and to transform it in other ways.

This degree of concentration in the holding of wealth is nearly twice as great as it was in the United States in 1954, and far higher than in the halcyon days of ruthless American capitalism in the early 1920s. Since 1949, wealth inequality has been growing in the United States, the rate of increase being more than twice as fast as the rate of decline between 1922 and 1949. Measured in terms of the increase in the percentage of wealth held by the top 1 percent, the growth of inequality during 1949–1956 (the latest available data) was more striking than at any time during at least the past forty years. Not unexpectedly, the distribution of income also appears to be becoming more unequal in recent years, affecting in particular the one fifth to one quarter of the United States population living below the currently defined "poverty line."[7] These are not all Negroes; 80 percent of the American poor are white, and only one fifth receive welfare aid. Economic growth in the richest society in the world has not been accompanied by any automatic, built-in equalizer. Crime for the young unemployed acts as a substitute within the prevailing system of values —the modern form of acquisitive social mobility for the lower classes.

There is no evidence to suggest that Britain has not been following in the same path since the end of the 1940s. It is even possible that inequality in the ownership of wealth (particularly in terms of family holdings) has increased more rapidly in Britain than in the United States since 1949. The British system of taxation is almost unique in the Western world in its generous treatment of wealth-holders in respect of settlements, trusts, gifts, and other arrangements for redistributing and rearranging income and wealth. This is reflected in the remarkable fact that, in the mid-

[6] See my Introduction to the third edition of R. H. Tawney's *Equality*.
[7] R. J. Lampman, *The Share of the Top Wealth-Holders in National Wealth 1922–56*, 1962; M. Harrington, *The Other America: Poverty in the United States*, 1962; Conference on Economic Progress, *Poverty and Deprivation in the United States*, 1961, known as the Keyserling Report.

1950s, it was in the young adult age group that the tendency for wealth to be concentrated in a few hands was most marked.

Such evidence as this is ignored by those who proclaim the end of political ideology. Similar trends are probably in operation in De Gaulle's France and Erhard's Germany.[8] Over a quarter of a century of political upheaval, global war, "welfare statism," managed economies, and economic growth have made little impression on the holdings of great fortunes in at least two of the largest industrial nations: the United States and Britain. The institution of concentrated wealth appears to be as tenacious of life as Tawney's intelligent tadpoles. Wealth still bestows political and economic power, more power than income, though it is probably exercised differently and with more respect for public opinion than in the nineteenth century.

Changes in the distribution of incomes appear to be following a similar pattern in Britain as in the United States. Toward the end of the 1940s a wartime movement toward more equality (before and after tax) in both Britain and the United States was reversed. The poorest tenth of the British population were relatively worse off compared with the higher standards of the rest of the nation in 1963 than they were in 1948.[9]

How can these great disparities in the private ownership of wealth and in the exercise of economic power be viewed as consistent with the thesis that we have reached the end of the political dialogue? No political utopia since Plato has ever envisaged such degrees of economic inequality as permanent and desirable states for man. Socialists protest at such disparities not because they want to foster envy; they do so because, as Tawney argued, these disparities are fundamentally immoral. History suggests that human nature is not strong enough to maintain itself in true community where great disparities of income and wealth preside.

Fourth and finally, there is in this thesis an assumption that the establishment of social welfare necessarily and inevitably contributes to the spread of humanism and the resolution of social injustice. The reverse can be true. Welfare, as an institutional

---

[8] According to Mr. Christopher Johnson, "The statistics which are available show what is evident to anyone living in France; that the rich are getting richer while the poor are barely maintaining their standard of living." (*New Society*, February 21, 1963, p. 15).

[9] T. Lynes, "Poverty in the Welfare State," *Aspect*, No. 7, August 1963.

means, can serve different masters. A multitude of sins may be committed in its appealing name. Welfare can be used simply as an instrument of economic growth which, by benefiting a minority, indirectly promotes greater inequality. Education is an example. We may educate the young to compete more efficiently as economic men in the private market one with another, or we may educate them because we desire to make them more capable of freedom and more capable of fulfilling their personal differences irrespective of income, class, religion, and race.

Welfare may be used to serve military and racial ends—as in Hitler's Germany. More medical care was provided by state and voluntary agencies not because of a belief in everyman's uniqueness, but because of a hatred of men.

Welfare may be used to narrow allegiances and not to diffuse them—as in employers' fringe benefit systems. Individual gain and political quietism, fostered by the new feudalism of the corporation, may substitute for the sense of common humanity nourished by systems of nondiscriminatory mutual aid.

What matters then, what indeed is fundamental to the health of welfare, the objective toward which its face is set? To universalize humanistic ethics and the social rights of citizenship, or to divide, discriminate, and compete?

V

In reality, of course, the issues are never as clear-cut as this. The historical evolution of social security measures in Britain since the end of the nineteenth century shows how complex and various were the forces at work. Fear of social revolution, the need for a law-abiding labor force, the struggle for power between political parties and pressure groups, a demand to remove some of the social costs of change—for example, industrial accidents—from the back of the worker, and the social conscience of the rich—all played a part.

But the major impulse came from below—from the workingman's ethic of solidarity and mutual aid. It found expression and grew spontaneously from working-class traditions and institutions to counter the adversities of industrialism. By means of a great network of friendly societies, medical clubs, chapel societies, brotherhoods, cooperatives, trade unions, and savings clubs, schemes of mutual insurance were developed as a method of pre-payment for services the members could claim when they were in need—in sickness, disablement, unemployment, old age, widow-hood, and death. The "good" risks and the "bad" risks, the young and the old, shared one another's lot. They constituted micro-scopic welfare states, each struggling to demonstrate that man could still exercise some control over the forces of technology. By the end of the century some 24,000 different friendly societies were in existence, with a total membership representing about half the adult male population of the country. Aptly and sig-nificantly named, during a century of unbridled competition, they were *the* humanistic institution for the artisan and his family, far outdistancing in active membership all trade unions, political parties, and religious bodies.

We can now see this great movement as the amateur's com-passionate answer to the challenge of the economic and psycho-logical insecurities of industrialism and individualism. It expressed also the ordinary man's revulsion from a class-conscious, dis-criminating charity and a ruthless, discriminating poor law. The poor law was hated because it spelled humiliation; it was an as-sault on the individual's sense of self-respect in an age when "re-spectability"—the quality of meriting the respect of others—governed the mores of society.

The values and objectives which underlay in the past the search for security in an increasingly insecure world are still relevant to an understanding of the role of social welfare in Britain today. The ways in which they shaped its origins and early development still permeate the principles on which the systems of medical care and social security operate today—comprehensive in scope, universal in membership. That they have not yet solved the prob-lems of poverty and neglect, and still provide little place for citizen participation, is another story, and one that remains as a formidable challenge for socialism. But we cannot retrace our footsteps to the intimate "friendly societies" of yesterday; we must find imaginative ways and new institutional means of com-bining humanity in administration with redistributive social jus-tice in the future development of welfare policies.

VI

These are two of the central unresolved issues for humanists: the problem of bigness and the problem of inequality. They affect every aspect of social policy; education from the primary school to the university and into adult life; social security in unemployment, sickness, and old age; the care of the physically and mentally ill; housing and urban planning; leisure and recreation.

The demand for these services will grow in the future as living standards rise among some sections of the population and fall, relatively or absolutely, among others. The consequences of automation and its technological cousins on the one hand, and more dependent needs in childhood and old age on the other, will call for a much greater investment in people and social service than in consumption goods. Science and technology are today beginning to accomplish as thorough a revolution in social and economic theory as they are in the theory of war and international relations. The conventional doctrine that machines make work is losing its validity; machines are now replacing workers. It is already clear from American experience that these victims of technological displacement are no longer "resting between engagements" (which is the theory of unemployment insurance): they are *permanently* out of work; permanently liberated from work. By the end of 1962 nearly one third of all young Negroes between the ages of 16 and 21 who were out of school were also out of work. Relatively speaking, they were also more handicapped educationally than unemployed young Negroes twenty years earlier. Between 1939 and 1958 the disadvantage of not having a college diploma grew in the U.S.A.[10]

In an age of abundance of things, the production of consumption goods will become a subsidiary question for the West. The primary question will be just distribution; in particular, the distribution of services according to needs in place of the principle of productivity and performance in a market economy which today powerfully influences access to education and other social services.

In the past we have distributed resources on the basis of success and failure in economic competition; in the future we must de-

[10] H. P. Miller, "Money Value of an Education," *Occupational Outlook Quarterly*, September 1961, p. 4.

cide whether it is morally right to do so in an economy of abundance. To distribute services on the basis of needs will help us to discover equality in our neighbors. "Awareness of equality," wrote Daniel Jenkins, "always arises in personal relationships and nearly always confronts us as a challenge, for it means placing a greater value upon our neighbor than we had previously been disposed to do. We are all ready to love ourselves. The discovery of equality might be defined as the discovery that we have indeed to love our neighbors as ourselves."[11]

And so we have to ask, "What are we to do with our wealth?" This is a more relevant social question to ask today than those that seek to find more effective ways of punishing criminals, enforcing the law against deviants, preventing abuse of public assistance, forcing men to search for work, compelling them to save for old age when they cannot feed their children adequately, shifting them out of subsidized housing, inventing cheap technological substitutes for education, and charging them more for access to medical care.

Yet these aims reflect the values which are often applied today in the administration of social services. According to one writer, Professor Mencher, "The present United States welfare [public assistance] program is in keeping with the philosophy of 1830"— the philosophy of less eligible citizens enshrined in the English Poor Law Act of 1834.[12] Social workers, teachers, doctors, and social administrators find their functions imprisoned by the "virtues" of hard work and profit; virtues that are rooted in the economics of scarcity. Their role is to police these virtues as, in a more ruthless context, medical certification of fitness for work became one of the central directives under the Stalinist regime. They have no relevance to the economics of abundance.

And, as Gerard Piel has emphasized, any "hard work that a machine can do is better done today by a machine; 'hard' these days means mostly boring and repetitive work, whether in the factory or the office. But the instinct for workmanship, the need to feel needed, the will to achieve, are deeply felt in every human heart. They are not universally fulfilled by the kind of employment most people find. Full employment in the kind of employ-

[11] D. Jenkins, *Equality and Excellence*, 1961, p. 21.
[12] S. Mencher, "Perspectives on Recent Welfare Legislation," *Social Work*, Vol. 8, No. 3, 1963, p. 62.

ment that is commonly available, whether blue-collar or white-collar, has been plainly outmoded by technology. The liberation of people from tasks unworthy of human capacity should free that capacity for a host of activities now neglected in our civilisation: teaching and learning, fundamental scientific investigation, the performing arts and the graphic arts, letters, the crafts, politics, and social service. Characteristically these activities involve the interaction of people with people rather than with things. They are admittedly not productive activities; nor are they profitable in the strict sense."[13]

Science and technology in alliance with other structural and demographic changes under way in our societies will call for a major shift in values; for new incentives and new forms of reward unrelated to the productivity principle; for new criteria applied to the distribution of resources which are not tied to individual "success" as a measure; for new forms of socially approved "dependencies." They will make the conventional criteria of capitalism largely irrelevant.

Many years ago Keynes foresaw that the time would come when these changes would be needed: ". . . we shall be able to rid ourselves of many of the pseudo-moral principles which have hag-ridden us for 200 years, by which we have exalted some of the most distasteful of human qualities into the position of the highest virtues . . . All kinds of social customs and economic practices affecting the distribution of wealth and of economic rewards and penalties, which we now maintain at all costs, we shall then be freed to discard."

We shall need different rules domestically to live by; more examples of altruism to look up to. Indeed, our societies in Britain and the United States are already in need of them. In no other way in the long run will it be possible for us to prevent the deprived and the unable from becoming more deprived and unable; more cast down in a pool of apathy, frustration, crime, rootlessness, and tawdry poverty.

In all this, what we call the social services will have a central role to play. If this role is defined at all it will have to be defined by socialists in the language of equality. Here it is that ethics will have to be reunited to politics. The answers will not come and, indeed, logically cannot come from those who now proclaim "the end of political ideology"; those who would elevate the principle of pecuniary gain and extend it to social service by equating education and medical care with refrigerators and mink coats; and those who advocate that more and more people should "contract out" of universal social services and create for themselves new areas of privilege and discrimination. They, today, are the utilitarian doctrinaires; prisoners of the economics of scarcity; oblivious to the social consequences of the march of science and technology; and blind to the need for a sense of moral purpose in their own societies as the motive power in the art of giving to our international neighbors.

ALTERNATIVES AND CHANGE

PROGRESS FROM POVERTY?

JOHN R. SEELEY

NO PROGRESS WILL BE MADE IN REFERENCE TO THE PROBLEM OF poverty—or any other problem—without an appropriate perception of what the problem is.

Poverty is a lack of power to command events.

Hence, existentially, we are all poor, poor almost beyond enduring. Part of that poverty may be irremediable. We may never be able to prevent or offset the cooling of the sun; we may never fully conquer death; we may never, perhaps, learn even to avoid self-defeat, self-stultification or self-destruction. Hence we may always be poor in some sense.

But this is not the poverty that is pointed to in the scriptural statement "The poor you have always with you." Those poor are the *differentially* poor: those who have less command over events than others.

To have command over events requires schemes, skills and command of means. Means, in this context, are persons and things. Perhaps—probably—command over persons is decisive. Command over things is largely a means to command, coerce, control or cajole others—and, circularly, a product of doing so. Schemes and skills can be hired, provided control over persons is assured. In a fully developed scheme of command (developed fully, that is, as far as the technology permits) the slaves provide the means of their own enslavement: the food to be given or withheld, the

From John R. Seeley, "Progress From Poverty?" *Liberation*, 11:5:9–14, August, 1966. Copyright 1966 by *Liberation*. Reprinted by permission of *Liberation* Magazine, New York.

whips to their own backs, even the "internal controls" to stabilize the system and polish it with politeness. Finally, their own hands —under command—wield these self-fashioned weapons against themselves and their own.

Poverty, differential poverty, has the structure of slavery. There is the primary insult, with all that it entails, of lack of command over events, so that the children of the poor die when (under a mere redistribution of means) they need not. There is the secondary insult of involvement in a productive process that gives the non-poor the means to increase, maintain, or very slowly diminish the existing relative poverty, i.e., to maintain command. There is the third and final insult that causes the poor to become willing poor—"happy slaves"—who support the system of poverty, whether or not any particular one tries to struggle out of it.

We need to distinguish sharply between three very different schemes for "improvement" in the existing state of affairs. One, the one on which we pride ourselves most, is the rendering of the system "open." We say we have "an open society," or a fairly open one that we aim to make more so. We point to the fact of "mobility." The progressive equalization of opportunity, the career open to talent. These are undoubted goods—relative, at least, to closed societies with similar advantage—disadvantage distributions. Perfected, the scheme resembles one in which it is possible (or easy) for slaves to become slave-owners.

In sharp contrast, are schemes directed to the diminution or extirpation of slavery.

And still different, of course, are schemes designed to give "comforts" to the slaves.

None of these schemes is wholly to be despised. Given a slave-system, and given its perpetuation with reference to particular persons or categories—"once a slave, always a slave"—it is better that there be mitigating comforts, bibles and mouth-organs, than not. Or, given a slave-system, it is better it be open than closed. But if the necessity for a slave-system is *not* given, then not only are these measures not good *enough*, they are not even good, since they militate against the abolition of slavery itself.

The need for a slave-system—whether mediated by whips or money—is not wholly a matter of wish. Or at least not a matter of wish regarding slavery itself. It depends on the real world at a given time or place and on other, seemingly unrelated, wishes.

If what men wish—or those who make public policy wish—in a given situation and state of the arts, *entails* that most men must mostly do what they do not want (and cannot reasonably be persuaded to want) to do—then the wishes must be foregone or the men must be enslaved. (Again whether the means are "economic" or "politic," though important, is, relatively, mere detail.) We cannot, for instance, conquer the world (or police it, likely) without a slave-society; and we may not be able to sate our limitless hunger for security or gadgets without it either. Even such esoteric desires as the wish to "conquer space" or land men on moons may entail such slavery.

Political democracy by itself is not a sufficient hedge against such enslavement. We may not wish to remember that Hitler *was* elected. But even failing such extreme examples, and assuming that the makers of public policy do reflect and act upon the wishes of the majority of their constituents, the tasks men so elect to impose on themselves, may well—indeed, commonly do—commit them to a perpetual program of doing what they must then be made to do, i.e., to a "voluntary" program of servitude. If force, naked, is not to enforce such a program, patently poverty must.

Political democracy, even conjoined with national affluence, could act to diminish or dissolve that kind of slavery only if the majority of voters were sufficiently educated with reference to means to see the connections between their choices, and sufficiently enlightened with respect to ends to know (and vote for) their true desires. But poverty itself—the problem!—entails above all insufficient knowledge and freedom for the informed votes necessary to poverty's abolition or sizeable reduction.

"Poverty in the midst of affluence" is thus no puzzle—let alone a paradox. Even in the face of affluence, and even given political democracy, it is entailed, necessitated by the choices the poor in their poverty make—or are caused to make.

Indeed—and perhaps here is the real paradox—if the poor can be persuaded to hunger after gadgets, and to measure their progress from poverty by a census of such gadgets, and if they can then be persuaded to value the armaments that protect them against those who have still less—then they can be made accomplices in the systems of poverty, internal and external, that yield such dividends. The system of external poverty, then—the existence and

JOHN R. SEELEY   433

perpetuation of relatively poor or "underdeveloped" nations, rein-forces and necessitates the system of internal poverty, which sup-plies the motive to produce the defense of the "developed" sys-tem. Absolutely, planes of living can move up, internally and externally—as they have—without any real attack on poverty and its problems, which is relative. To starve where there is no food for anyone is a malign fate to be suffered or accepted. To hunger where some are overfed, and there would otherwise be enough for all, is a human insult, an enslavement if suffered unwillingly, a self-enslavement if accepted. And even when the "base" shifts from starvation to poor medical care and poor housing and poor schooling, or from these to what is relatively poor later, the in-sult and the resultant psychological and social damage are the same or similar. Again, the shift in the base is not to be despised or deplored—it *is* better that no man be corporeally starved. But if we develop secondary hungers—such that, for instance a man needs a corporeal cleanliness to retain self-respect and being thought "decent" by others—and if then the means to satisfy such hungers are withheld from some, then for nearly all pur-poses these "starve" no less, suffer no less cruel pangs, reap no less really the rewards of poverty.

Any serious attack on poverty, then, is an attack on the *dis-crepancies* among men in their power to command events, and, principally, one another. A successful attempt, for instance, to increase everybody's real income by, say, one half, is at most a prologue to such an attack, and, most often, a way of avoiding it. For the operative problem of poverty—psychologically and socially—is like the problem of minority status in its form and consequences. It would help the Negro-white problem very little if we were twice as nice to each other: the problem, that which is intolerable, personally poisoning and socially destructive, is the *difference*.

Clearly, the personal poisoning and social destruction have been borne—and are perhaps to be borne—where higher values are at stake. For the other side of the coin is that, like beating, humilia-tion or death, people will do a great deal to avoid them. And if pyramids are to be built, there may be no other way. The more humane we become in the direction of demanding mass effort (or its effects) and the more skilled we become in directing those efforts to ends ever more remote from the immediate wishes and needs of living men, the more we need poverty as the only effective spur to secure men in such obedience and bind them in such bondage.

Rather clearly, that is what we have hitherto done. And our "prosperity" has hence rested upon and rests now upon our poverty. Not without poverty could we have had our industrial revolution. Not without radically differential pay-off (combined with the linking of advantageous pay-off), to self-respect, could we have kept men at work—or, at least, at such work. Certainly no other scheme would have yielded such "happy slaves."

But by an ironic, unforeseen and unforeseeable twist of history the scheme has yielded a successor-scheme: industrialization has given birth to automation.

Whatever else automation means, it means the multiplication of power, at least over material things, into another order of magnitude, without an attendant increase in the burden of human labor to be borne. The problem in sight—under specific conditions— is no longer governed by the necessity to keep men at work, intrinsically meaningless work, like horses in harness. That particular ground for the perpetuation of poverty is, under the specific conditions, removed.

These specific conditions are essentially two: First, that equal and simultaneous attention be directed toward the external poverty system, so that what we gain does not get dissipated upon armaments to preserve what we (materially) have. And second, that we do not open up or expand essentially limitless schemes—like conquering the universe or the world or achieving absolute security—that consume the increase and indeed make it necessary to perpetuate the coercion that is needed to keep men at arduous and demeaning tasks. (It should be noted that these specific conditions point away at a 180° angle from our current course which "keeps the economy going" by flinging the output at the moon and "the enemy.")

But assuming the conditions can be assured, another temptation will open up that has something to do with a problem and with the preference of men (not only the ostensible beneficiaries) for systems of slavery, anyway.

The new problem will be that once we no longer have, at least in recognizable form, the "problem of production," we shall still have the problem of order, public and private, and we may well have it in a form acute beyond anyone's imagining. One side of the problem—difficult, but still easier than the next—is that work itself, with its routines, formal and informal, has filled so much of the temporal space of life, that a great deal of order, private and public, has been provided just by its presence and pervasiveness. The second, the more difficult side, lies in the deeper "meaning" of work, at least in our "ascetic" cultures. Work is now virtually the only positively sanctioned outlet for those vast aggressions which in so pleasure-denying a culture run so deep and press so hard for release. It is difficult to imagine vividly enough what will be the situation once those outlets for aggression—now mediated by assaults on objects or labor-management conflict (in the case of blue-collar workers) and by piracy, conspiracy, fraud and cheating which are the essence (or payoff) of a great deal of white collar enterprise—are removed.

Men so situated may be glad of almost any "direction," and those less afraid of themselves than of others may, as at present, be only too glad to direct them. And if the coercion is to be disguised, to appear "internalized," we may have to preserve—or re-institute—differential poverty, so that the coercion may have the air, as now, of "voluntary" striving, the so-called "struggle to get ahead."

Any release from "the grip of poverty"—i.e., from the system by which we actively or passively engineer ourselves into the donkey-stick-carrot penal servitude that we have—will have to solve the problem of restraining aggression or channeling it so that it does not disrupt the psyche or the society or both—or we shall have to find methods that do not generate the same quanta of aggression. Restraint on this scale requires a police state or the threats of severe poverty or both. Channels, even though machines can readily cut canals and level mountains, are hard to come by. It looks as though the only way to abolish differential poverty, *especially* in the face of such general affluence as now faces us, is to reduce characterological aggression.

So the problem of poverty is bound up with the problem of character change which is bound up with the problem of child-raising.

But the problem of child-raising does not exist in a vacuum. Children are raised in the way they are—ignorance and fashion apart—because of the way their parents were raised, modified to a considerable extent by those same parents' perception or vision of the future society into which the children are to "get." But since those parents, rich or poor, were nearly all raised in a world of poverty (where the question is to be "up" or "down" on the competitive ladder, slaveholder or slave or a little of both) and since they have not even been brought to imagine a free (poverty-free) world, what else can they do but raise their children in poverty for poverty? By raising them "in poverty" I mean that the children learn under conditions of *conditional* non-deprivation; they are rewarded for doing—not being—and for doing only what is contrary to nature. And by raising them "for poverty," I mean so structuring them that they cannot be comfortable under unlike circumstances, e.g., in the presence of free goods. Even when they are "retired," i.e., finally given a respite, a breather before death, they die before they have had the breather. They "cannot stand prosperity," or, more exactly, they are so poor they cannot bear escape from the goad of poverty. People— nearly all people—have the "minority problem" built into them in their minority: self-distrust, except under constraint and confinement (the boss or the balance-sheet indifferently); self-hate and identification with the aggressor; anxiety about those who "pass," or escape the system; false pride in the miserable status occupied.

IS THERE A WAY OUT?

Perhaps so, but it is very difficult. Just as punishment generates a need that cannot be slighted with impunity (to punish and be punished), so poverty, a variant of punishment, generates a need to continue in a poverty-system (as rich man or poor), and, more radically, an inability to imagine any better workable system. The spurred horse comes to need the spur on his flank, if he continues to be a horse, on his heel if he becomes a jockey. Horse and jockey are more alike than anatomy indicates or zoology suggests.

Such self-sustaining systems of cripplement are hard to break into. A deprived child cannot accept a gift; he can seize a proffered object, but his deprivation does not permit him to receive it in its intended meaning; the giver appears as the bearer of ulterior designs or a sucker or both. To such a child the very threat of a gift may endanger his security-system so strongly that he wards it off with more energy than he would a blow. The prospect of a workless world, or a world in which worth no longer depends on work, or in which plenty might descend, like the rain, on the working and workless, seems to generate, as a prospect, nothing but anxiety in the hearts of rich and poor alike.

For the deprived person, the first step out of the vicious circle of seeking to be depriver or deprived, is the establishment of belief that another and better order is possible. The belief must be (a) that there *is* enough for all, and (b) that what is to be desired is enough for oneself, and not competitive more-ness or less-ness. And the belief can only be established by repeated experiences of non-deprivation and non-depriving, accompanied by affection-warmed reeducation, persuasion into faith and trust in that better game.

What is true here for a person is not directly but analogically true for the social problem of poverty. There must be belief that another state of affairs is possible—and better—before it will be possible to perform those acts (especially in a political democracy) that will lead to that better state. If what is wanted is the breaking of bondage—not merely the moving into a cozier bondage—then the faith in and longing for an unbondaged state must go before and accompany the breaking of the bonds. The fear that unbound we would be dangerous to ourselves or others, the belief that unspurred, unbitted, unbridled we would be worthless or pointless or worse, the fear of freedom for others or ourselves —these fears must precede and go along with the progressive and rapid abandonment of the prison-system that the current poverty-riches system permanently provides.

Unfortunately, as things stand at present, the pace in the two systems of events is not even loosely co-ordinated. The progress that will render us all soon workless (or nearly all nearly so) goes on apace. The radical re-education that would make such a potential state supportable—that would make thinkable the removal of poverty as spur and bit—is not well begun, perhaps hardly begun at all. Indeed, even at this instant, in virtually every last corner, cranny and reach of the educational system, every last resource and effort is employed in bending as many as can be bent into the internalization of the poverty-system. (Indeed, the "educational system" with its credit-hours, degrees and grades, simulates and incorporates the poverty-system, using such symbols for counters—in place of the symbols such as money, carpeted offices and parking places or club memberships of the "real world outside the academic environment.") And the process that the educational system stamps and puts its seal upon is, of course, begun at the womb's mouth and well launched before ever the child is thrust through the school door.

The job we confront—most especially given the time in which we have to do it—staggers the imagination and appalls the heart. For what is needed is a new national character (and, eventually, world character)—*and* a way of getting from here to there, i.e., of having the impoverished prepare to be the affluent. Incidentally, but not trivially, it means dealing with widespread, perhaps nearly endemic, masochism: the desire to be poor (or poorly) with all its attendant benefits by way of treasured resentments and grievances, and the agenda these bespeak, and the point, or seeming point, thus lent to life. Such investments—especially when they are institutionally dovetailed, as they now are, with opposite needs in the same or other person—are not lightly, or by simple act of will, renounced.

But how are we thus to lift ourselves by our own bootstraps, as it seems?

If the "we" were a uniform and structureless we, the task would be, as the phrase suggests, impossible. Even an illiterate nation, so-called, is not uniformly illiterate, and each-one-teach-one programs have therefore been successful, while simultaneously the most literate have not ceased to become more so.

The problem of poverty is structurally similar while much more far-reaching and profound. It is a pity that the fine phrase "The War on Poverty" has become attached to what can only be seen, with the greatest generosity, as some preliminary stirrings and skirmishes. For a *war* on poverty is what is required, if "war" calls up the right images of life-and-death issues, utter determination, limitless commitment, and the risk—if not the certainty—that all institutions and practices may be made over in the course of it. What the conquest of poverty requires is a national (and world) reorganization for that purpose, the necessary means and resources made available, and the needed time to wage so far-reaching and long-lasting a war taken and set aside from the other tasks of history on which we might otherwise wish to embark.

Given the fundamental set and determination, I think that the
task is not impossible. But let us make sure one last time that we
know what the fundamental set is, what we are looking toward.
We are looking toward a world in which everybody will be
"rich," objectively and subjectively. By "rich subjectively" we
mean that the goods of life can be accepted and enjoyed. And
since we have specified "everybody," successful sibling rivalry
cannot be a condition (let alone, as now, a principal ingredient
as well) of enjoyment. Indeed, the opposite must be the case:
enjoyment by others must be a condition of one's own (as in a
good, and sufficiently common, suckling situation, or in a good,
but sufficiently uncommon, sexual one). The whole present basis
of the social order that induces guilt, and then mines for life the
golden yield of it, must be overset. The associated hyper-aggres-
sion that served so well to motivate and sustain the "attack upon
the world" will find no further use. And with it must go its
linked instrument for self-attack—the kind of "conscience" we
have known which has been hitherto not the warden of life (ours
and others) but the driver to death, the father of the ulcer and
mother of the coronary. We are, in a phrase, thinking of turning
our backs on an anal and phallic world, to bring into being a
reign of genitality.

In one sense the situation contains the seeds of its own solution.
(But seeds must be recognized for what they are and nurtured
for what they can become.) The seeds lie in the imminence of
unemployment and boredom for everybody unless we find ways
to turn our energies to the cultivation of men—viewed in all their
severalty, and viewed as a society. But one cannot cultivate men
—if one correctly appreciates what is involved in cultivation—
without becoming oneself both more cultivated and more capable
of more cultivation—of self and others. So the process is potentially benign and self-sustaining. But only potentially, for, as I
indicated in hedging, "*if* one correctly appreciates what is involved in cultivation."

We have a suggestive model in good parenting—when it occurs.
The relation is a relation-in-depth, mediated at every level from
unconscious-to-unconscious, through touch, to speech or even the
force-of-example. It is a nearly total, certainly non-segmental relation. It is not only not—in the words of the trade—a "zero-sum
game," but it is a game in which losses to one are sharply felt

losses to the other; and gains likewise. It is a relation that transcends and embraces the parties to it, so that they may love not merely themselves and each other, but that which joins them, their love itself. (Here the true unity is the true Trinity: Father, Son and Holy Spirit, each implicit in everyone.) It is a process of mutual evocation in which the more and better the parent assumes his role and nature, the more and better the child assumes his, thus providing the next succeeding better conditions (and rewards) for the parent . . . and so on indefinitely. It is a condition that provides— again at every level from the "acquisition of skills" to the structuring of the unconscious—for its own succession, such that the best (virtually only) way to provide better parents and parenting next, is to have better parenting (and children) now.

In extending the essence of parenting to the whole society, in rendering it immanent and transcendent—which is what is required for a poverty-free society—we must preserve what we want without carrying over the implications of profound and long-lasting inequality that normally inheres in the parent-child definition, and something of an air of patronage (in its worst sense) that attends it. It may be that if everyone is parenting someone no problem need arise, and children, real children, are always there as potential residuary legatees of anyone's need to bestow love lest he be shamed before the love he receives. As in so many vital processes, it seems that we cannot have a very clear idea of "steps" until we committedly engage in and are borne along by our past commitments; even as at every stage, new vistas open sufficient to illuminate what is the next succeeding necessary step.

In the realm of child-rearing, this requires "only" the speeding-up of a process now imminent, I believe, and requiring primarily for its acceleration the endowment of all parents with generous material means and a recognition of the unrestricted world within which their children and their children's children will "have to" exist. Let me not trivialize this task: it is an immense task in principle, to discover new ways and new institutions to support parents in their fear-laden steps to the authentication, legitimization and suitable expression of their generous impulses.

But if the task is difficult enough with regard to family, it is of overwhelming difficulty when we turn to the institutions of formal education. (For what is required here is not an acceleration, and perhaps mild directional correction, but a turn of 180°.)

What, in rough outline, educational institutions now do is to take the child—warm, living flesh-and-spirit in the kindergarten and nursery school—and turn him into sinew, skeleton, scar-tissue at the high-school, college or grad school exit. He comes full of life, and leaves full of schemes. He comes open, and leaves closed. He comes in sensitive self-awareness and goes clad in clanking armor. He comes singing, skipping and dancing and leaves carrying himself, presenting himself, "using himself," posing and posturing. He comes to give and receive; he leaves to trade at the door of life. Not out of some inherent necessity of "growing up" —indeed this is growing down—but out of the very structure and content of education designed to that end. And rightly so. For what we have "needed" hitherto were not human beings but skilled ants, and the institutions appropriate to their production— our schools and colleges—have been and are mostly anthills.

Look at any high school today—close up. Then try to think of a process not patently punitive which would secure a different effect—better calculated to produce empty meaning, value, sense, sensibility out of life—to produce pseudo-robots ("free" enough to manage, but not free enough to ask "what for?"), to institute triviality as normative, to lead straight to the life of "kicks" as the only appropriate response, to "cool out"—for life—the life that still presents itself not wholly chilled by the grade school lock-up! And college and university are not visibly worse or better. The educators speak of "educating the whole child," but unless he checks pretty nearly everything that makes him a child and a human being at the door, they panic. Let him show at the right time the pervasive smoldering sexuality and love that holds the whole promise of the future, and they clip his hair and legislate the tightness of his trousers. Let him show even the faint and stippled shadow of the aggressiveness he needs to hold out against his own castration, and they involve the already castrated on the "student council" in complicity in making "student rules" that elevate politeness and smoothness into arbiters against life. Let the "kids"—even at the age of Berkeley students—take seriously for a moment the pretensions of their own society, let them act for a moment to demand that we act as we *say*, and the whole state quakes, and firearms must be carried onto the campus in the hands of men to confront children—who ask them to be men!

This is a falling away from a high calling, by design and in essence, not by accidental defect. The "whole child" may not come to school at all; he is too frightening. What we will accept is a little *simulacrum*, a *homunculus*, a cheerful little idiot to be homogenized—except for what David Riesman calls "marginal differentiation"—like a Skinner pigeon. Indeed, more truly a "pigeon" in the underworld sense, since he is needed as a party to his own undoing. What the school wants and worships is "cooperation"—and that means collaboration in the task of self-constraint, self-constriction and self-evisceration. (Not that the school is to be "blamed"; it is immeasurably better than, but also necessarily "preparatory for," the institutions that lie ahead, and need such fodder.)

What is wanting in the school is not a matter of defective educational theory—in the sense that we do not know how to do better—though what the school "takes up" out of such theory as there is, is clearly distorted and defective. But the child who goes to school is not suddenly and thereby another child, even when his capacity to grow up has been enhanced by the vast powers of visual-symbolic communication. He is not suddenly a thought-processing machine, with a sad necessity to be relieved occasionally to go to the bathroom, whisper to his neighbor or be paraded down the *down* staircase. He is a living, sentient, and, unless distracted, vitally engaged little human being, *naturally* organizing the world around him, objectively and subjectively, in terms of his (growing) concerns. Good education takes him *in toto* and links his expansion and reviews, not artificially but naturally, to the concerns he has now. The difference between liberation and enslavement, education and training, parenting and manipulating, lies in the nature of the linkage effected. There is little to add to Dewey—except Freud. And little to add to that, as far as theory is concerned, except the new economics and the new psychologies they carry with them.

But how is education in fact to be reformed, root and branch? It is hard to say. Patently, many things must be done at the same time. It must be endowed, very heavily endowed, on a different scale of magnitude altogether. It must, "worthy" or not, be loved and respected, in order that it may become lovable and respectable. It must be given, on the highest authority, a new and highly different mandate: to "humanize" its children, or help them humanize themselves, not mechanize or "program" them. It must be encouraged to let the children do the "work" (as they would, if we did not prevent them) for one another; four-fifths of the energy and "skill" needed is already there among them. Finally, teachers themselves—and, even more, "educators" and educational administrators—must themselves be helped to be less frightened of themselves and their charges, so that they act less like beleaguered burghers and more like (literally) kindergartners. Perhaps then they would welcome what they now hysterically resist, the implication of the to-be-educated in the government and control of the process wherein he is becoming educated.

It will be a long, slow, hard process and blood, sweat, toil and tears will not be enough. We may be in some way too poor to be able to dispense with poverty. But perhaps we only need to realize how rich we are—in order to become truly rich.

NOTES ON THE WELFARE STATE

BOB ROSS

WHAT EVER HAPPENED TO THE CENTURY OF THE COMMON MAN?
There is an American welfare state; but there is not much
"welfare" in America for the poor people it was to have served.
Automation is accused of *creating* a human slag heap of useless
people; but the welfare state has already done that. To the extent
that welfare programs do reach the people who need them, their
very "professionalization" combined with the realities of American
politics and class divisions in the corporate era, has created and
maintained a dependency, while suffocating political initiatives.

As distinct from the immigrant poor, restlessly pushing up and
out of their ethnic ghettoes, today's low-income Americans have
before them the grim prospect of passing their condition on to
their young. Already a third generation of welfare children is
growing to child-bearing age.[1] A number of secular trends combine to make poverty more grim and hopeless today than previously.

Along with the trend in the occupational structure from blue-
to white-collar work there has been an absolute decline in the
number of factory jobs available to the unskilled or mis-educated.

From Bob Ross, "Notes on the Welfare State," *Liberation*, March 1966, pp.
12–17, 32. Copyright 1966 by *Liberation*. Reprinted by permission of *Liberation* Magazine, New York.

[1] See *Poverty in the United States*, Report of the Comm. on Education and
Labor, U.S. House of Representatives, 88th Congress, 2nd session, p. 78.
Combine this with our knowledge of the 13 and 14 year old girls who are
pregnant now, and we can see a fourth generation being born.

From 1956 to 1962, manufacturing lost one million jobs (7½ percent). The number of jobs open to "operatives" or non-farm and non-mine laborers is expected to decline an additional 6.2 percent by 1970. The increasing labor surplus will damage even further the ability of unskilled workers in already underpaid service jobs to command adequate income.

In the meantime, however, affluence for the rest of the population means higher levels of living, opening wider the gap between the cultures of rich and poor. Between 1949 and 1959, median family income rose from about $4000 to more than $5600. It is true that America employs a rising definition of the level of living called poverty. Nevertheless, it is clear that at least a fifth, and perhaps a quarter or more, of the nation is excluded from general prosperity, and condemned to the "slag heap."

The Department of Labor has created a model of the "modest but adequate" budget. Though "below the average enjoyed by American families," it is considered above "maintenance." It includes, for example, $160 for clothing for a family of four for one year in Washington, D.C. (which is the city closest to the average) and allows $102 for rent for each month; the budget is not designed for gracious living. The 1959 average, in 1960 dollars, was $6,142 for a family of four. By now, the figure for Washington, D.C. is approximately 6% higher—the amount of increase between 1959 and 1963 in the Consumer Price Index.

With this budget as his basis, Leon Keyserling, an economist for the liberal Conference on Economic Progress and former chairman of the Council of Economic Advisers under President Truman, chooses to call "poverty" incomes of less than $4000 a year for families and $2000 a year for unattached individuals. On this basis, Keyserling estimates that thirty-eight million were poor in 1959. Government sources, however, and the President's Council of Economic Advisers use $3000 a year for families, and $1500 for individuals, as their criteria. This defined the lowest income fifth in 1963: about 35 million people. Current discussion accepts the lower figures. (Calculations based on Keyserling's standard are not available for the last couple of years.) But whatever the results of the numbers game, for too many people there is no Santa Claus.

For some time it has been acceptable at cocktail parties and the like (including State of the Union messages and university lectures) to finish discussion by saying that all other things that need doing depend on "education" of low income and minority-group people—the culturally deprived. In the right way and the right place and time that *may* be true. But education of poor people today, it seems, helps guarantee their degradation.

In Big City (Detroit) schools, Patricia Sexton found the quality of facilities of elementary and high schools within the same municipality paralleled the income of the areas they served. Besides finding that I.Q. and scholastic achievement were positively associated with income, Sexton found other things about the school system which might be the basis of that finding.
An illustrative list follows:

1. Nearly all of the children of low-income families (below $3000) did not have the optional health examination upon admission to the first grade; only 7 percent of the highest income group ($9000) did *not* have such an examination.

2. Emergency substitute teachers in a Regular Position—that is, teachers without full qualifications—were teaching in disproportionately large numbers in low-income-area schools.

3. School buildings for low-income areas were older than those in high-income areas, and had fewer facilities; what they had were of lower quality.

4. Free milk was *not* available in 42 percent of the low-income schools, but it was not available in only 22 percent of the higher income schools.

The meaning of poor facilities for poor children is clarified by a detailed study of the effects of the Harlem school system upon its children. Eighty-nine and nine-tenths percent of Harlem's elementary school children are Negroes as are 95.7 percent of its junior high school and 91 percent of its public high school population. At least half of the families in Harlem earn less than $4000 per year.

In its report, Harlem Youth Opportunities Unlimited (Haryou) says: "The basic story of academic achievement in central Harlem is one of inefficiency, inferiority, and massive deterioration." It is the deterioration which is most striking if one is looking for the institutional generation of poverty.

Between their third and sixth grades Harlem's school children lose their relative academic ability:

1. Relative reading comprehension drops: at third grade 30.9 percent are below grade level; in the sixth, 80.9 percent.

2. Relative word knowledge drops: the third grade sees 38.9 percent below grade level; the sixth, 77.5 percent.

3. By the end of the sixth grade more than half of the children are below grade level in computation, and two-thirds are behind in "problems and concepts."

4. Most striking is the fact that median I.Q. descends from 90 to 86.3 between third and sixth grades.

Compared to the rest of New York City and the U.S., Harlem is losing its intelligence by going to school.

TABLE I

	Median IQ		
Grades	3rd	6th	8th
Central Harlem	90.6	86.3	87.7
N.Y.C.	98.6	99.8	100.0
National	100.0	100.0	100.0

SOURCE: Haryou Report, page 193.

The current discussions of educational reform are latent with even more insidious possibilities. The emphasis on "skill-training" and vocational education in present contexts puts liberal thinkers dangerously close to proposing class-determined educational horizons. James N. Conant's proposal (in *Slums and Suburbs*) that "prospective dropouts" be given a heavy dose of "vocational" courses is an influential statement of this view. Intensive and remedial methods of teaching language and mathematical skills are fading from fashion among urban reformers. By consigning young people in poor areas to expectation of a "good job," defined as becoming a "mechanic" or "bricklayer," they reveal a vision of an educational system that varies its expectation for children according to where they are brought up. The danger is: pursuing this goal of "equipping" young people with minimum skills may also ensure merely those skills as *maximum* possible achievements. This is an example of the way in which present thinking about what to do for the poor can become a terribly dangerous kind of enterprise when the poor are not part of the planning process.

It is the aspiration for upward mobility through education, which the welfarists hoped would provide the engine for the structure they had created. But Horatio Alger has refused to step off Andrew Carnegie's bookshelf and become real.

Mobility has had a certain magic for American social analysts. It has been felt that critics could either be vindicated or silenced by being shown that mobility was very high or very low. Because American social thought has defined questions of justice very largely in terms of opportunity, and not of distribution, mobility is not the same kind of key to the question of poverty as it is supposed to be for other issues. That many people leave the lowest occupational slots does not mean that these slots are eliminated.

Poverty is about what a man has or doesn't; mobility is about how many people in society are changing (favorably in this instance) their occupation. If we look more closely at mobility studies, though, it is possible to get some idea of the economic level from, and to which, people are moving. Though relatively high percentages of workers are upwardly mobile, in the period from 1957-1963 the rate of reduction in the number of families below $3000 annual income was a little less than one percent a year.

A breakdown of a recent study of mobility, for manual workers, will indicate some of the conditions of movement. In 1957, unskilled workers—who had a median income below poverty for families—had inherited their jobs from their fathers only 15 percent of the time. But 81.9 percent of manual laborers are sons of manual workers. Downward mobility accounted for over 38 percent of semiskilled workers—more than a third of which is from skilled workers. "Being poor" is part of the actuality or fear of most sons of manual workers.

Assuming that high aspiration is necessary for mobility, and mobility necessary for the reduction of poverty, many thinkers argue that aspiration has to be "inserted" into the learning process in the schools. But young people are smarter than that. Low-income children distinguish between aspirations and plans. Accordingly, they aspire high and plan low, in distinct contrast to their richer schoolmates' confidence in their ability to become what they'd like to be. (See Richard Stephenson, "Mobility Orientation and Stratification of 1000 Ninth Graders," *American Sociological Review*, V.22, pp. 204–212.) What this means is that low aspiration (usually confounded with plans in most studies) need not be seen as a pathology; but rather high aspiration may be seen as a quality of mind that working class and poor youngsters regard as unrealistic. The problem then becomes, not to give them aspiration, but, in fact, to change society so that these dreams are not crushed.

To this task, the Welfare State is inadequate.

WHAT WELFARE?

Despite the skepticism about the role of the schools in the welfare state, there are still the financial-support programs to be proud of: "income-maintenance," as it is called.

The most well-known of these programs is A.D.C.—Aid to Families with Dependent Children. (It is also the most attacked and the most Negro—40 percent.) In most states families in A.D.C. are getting less than those states' own minimum budgets would require. In Michigan the minimum budget requirement for a mother and two children is $191 a month (this is $2292 a year—way under the federal government's poverty mark); but families on A.D.C. of a mother and two children receive $140 a month. More than half of a group of A.D.C. mothers in Detroit claimed their children were underfed; many were behind on rent, which in most cities is jacked up to the level which the welfare agency will pay; then the vilest rooms get very substantial rents, because the places where welfare clients can go are often limited. In this way slumlords literally feast off welfare; but among the clients, the children are underclothed. Some women set the children to cashing in pop bottles; others talk bitterly of prostitution as a way out. As Charles Lebeaux, the author of the Detroit study, put it, their poverty is "killing them and isolating them from the community of human life."

In 1963, four million people participated in the A.D.C. program. Many more millions, though, are recipients of various types of Social Security benefits. The act which created this system is one of the joys and proud achievements of the New Dealers and their descendents. The table below indicts that pride for the weak thing it is:

TABLE 2

Average weekly benefits under Social Security, June 1963	
$17.50	Retired worker
15.33	Aged widow
20.86	Disabled worker
29.72	Aged couple
44.25	Widowed mother with two children

The "budgets of despair" about which Lebeaux and others have written are only one aspect of the general despair of the welfare-state's clients. Put in a dependent situation which the rest of the society considers near-sinful in itself, the welfare-state client is treated like . . . a sinful dependent. Tyrannical procedures and bureaucratic despotism are not merely trends for so many of these people. . . They are the reality of every grinding day.

In Alameda County, California, for example, county police, using powers all counties use to some extent in the administration of A.D.C., descended upon hundreds of homes in night raids, to make sure that A.D.C. recipients were not entertaining men visitors. The New York City welfare department drops all pretense, calling its case-workers "welfare investigators." Yet, according to a Chicago welfare administrator, the A.D.C. requirement that no man be present in the home actually encourages desertion of the father.

Recipients of the more "respectable" programs, like unemployment compensation, find that, in the words of a North Side Chicago man, "they act like it was *their* money. But *I* paid it all these years, and it's mine, isn't it?" Complaints about abusive behavior by agency staffs are only part of the problem; the rest is structurally lodged in the way the law is written in most states. Delays which permit company-retainered lawyers to hold up checks through harassing "challenges" (while a man might be thrown out of his place for back rent), petty despotism such as regulations insisting that people report in person every week, and totally inadequate amounts of money ("comp" pays an average of under $37 a week for a fully insured worker) make this particular program a symbol of much that is wrong with our welfare system.

Perhaps the most degrading of the institutional practices which poor people face is the means test. A universal practice, it is particularly vicious in some places, even requiring, for example, that parents sell their homes to the county in order to support a child's relief checks. Many states require that welfare recipients pauperize themselves before they can be eligible for assistance. Thus, the relief system feeds on itself.

The institutionalization of poverty—the production of dependency—proceeds through situations which sometimes seem paradoxical. For example, in Cleveland's Near West Side, there is a lovely, low-rise public housing project. Physically, it seems a nice place to live. But to live there your family income must be very low, and if it grows, you must move within one month. The results are that people are encouraged to stay at an existing job and wage level so that they may remain in their living accommodations; and, when the more ambitious leave, models for the others are removed. This thrust is perfectly exemplified in the census data for a Chicago area: it has 47 percent of its families below the $3000 a year income bracket; it has 16 percent unemployment (1960); 40 percent of its people are supported by public assistance; and 21 percent of its children are born illegitimate; yet it has only 1.6 percent substandard housing, near the city's best. This is an area with a large project.

Public housing is often an outright evil. Federal requirements are so budget-conscious, anxious that public housing won't compete with private developers (others say so that the poor will know they're poor), that the housing is often bare, shoddy, inadequate upon occupation. No doors between rooms, or for closets, bare cement floors, hospital-like hallways, elevators that won't work, fifty stories high-rise (for efficient utilization of plant) and usually located within Negro ghettoes to avoid "spread." Public housing has become well-heated slum production.

On top of all this is the omnipresent, seemingly omnipotent administrative staff. Empowered to search apartments for overcrowding and to inspect cleanliness, encouraging informer networks amongst tenants, the management of the welfare state's housing is the embodiment of that set of institutions, and is hated.

In many ways the class struggle has deserted the industrial arena, and is being enacted with the cities as the prize. In Chicago's liberal Hyde Park the issue (for the first urban renewal project) was clear: to keep the area around a great university "compatible" with its "educational" goals the community had to purge much of its low-income inhabitants. That these were Negroes attests to the proposition that the Negro movement is now learning, that racism, Liberal-Northern style, is class discrimination.

Cramped ever more tightly, the burgeoning Negro population has been advancing the borders of its ghettos. Often because of inferior education, and because Negroes are the object of unbridled exploitation by slum-lords and housing officials, by salesmen and collection agencies, Negro expansion has meant slum spread to the rest of the city's people.

The public housing act of 1949, which enabled cities to build low-income housing at the federal government's expense, has not, by and large, helped. Sites on vacant land are rarely selected—because of white politicians' fear of upsetting the racial composition of their wards; and slum clearance often destroys more housing units (albeit inferior ones) that it creates. Thus, pressure for expansion persists.

In response to threatened Negro and other low-income expansion and encroachment upon "good" (middle-class) neighborhoods, in 1954, the federal machinery for urban renewal was created.

Urban renewal is a complex series of operations—this is one of the things that make citizen involvement in its planning, or opposition to its plans, so pathetically weak. A neighborhood-renewal plan works its way through myriad boards, councils and commissions, to approval. Even then, the private developers (Webb and Knapp of New York are the best known) have a good deal of discretion in how they are going to spend their money.

Urban renewal has become the most important physical, social, and political process which the welfare state planners use to preserve their urban areas. But too often, rescuing an inner-city area from blight means eliminating low-income people's housing, and stabilization of racial composition means eliminating low-income Negroes. Urban renewal becomes Negro removal.

The essence of the process is this: using federal monies and municipal powers for condemnation, clearance of land, and land purchase, community interests invite and persuade developers, banks and investment houses to rebuild. With this kind of public subsidy behind them, the plans are notorious for the way Negro and low-income people are displaced, and have their interests ignored. Even the nominal attempt at "citizen participation" usually functions merely to "inform" and "persuade" people of the choices already made by the planners.

With interest in a community defined as business or property-owning, it is no surprise that poor and minority groups get left out of the city's considerations. But when urban renewal is *the major federal program for dealing with urban problems*, to the extent that welfare is considered a governmental responsibility for problem-solving at general expense, urban renewal is state welfare for private developers and a public made up of "solid citizens" and local business interests. For the poor and nonwhite, it is just another invitation: "Here's your hat, what's your hurry?"

At the same time, as urban renewal raises high-rise salutes to affluence, talk is rife of cities becoming "black" unless some program to keep the white middle class is devised. Washington, D.C. is 58 percent Negro, and Newark, N.J. is a majority Negro town. One quarter of Chicago's 3.2 million are Negro. The suburbs grow, the inner city loses in population. "Crisis" grips both thought and rhetoric as the educational system finds race and class impossibly complicated problems, and as the city ties itself into ever tighter knots.

Whether or not urban renewal "stabilizes" the white population in the city in the long run, if urban renewal is the only solution that the white, middle-class liberals who created the institutions and the culture of the cities' politics can come up with, their "political will" is bankrupt. Calling the militants irresponsible, yet unable politically to devise a program that ungluts the glut they created, the urban liberals look to Washington for help. This usually means bull-dozers or delinquency-control projects. It's rare to find a "community leader" who recognizes that blight could be fought by minimum wages or adequate welfare or democratic control of cities.

WHOSE ECONOMY?

Dependency and powerlessness are a structural part of American society. They involve more than the calamities of weak or disadvantaged minorities. If most poor people were unable to participate in the labor force, then perhaps an incremental and quantitative approach to welfare institutions would begin an attack on poverty. This would imply setting our sights on raising welfare and social security payments through a long, gradual legislative process. Realizing that the people who needed help were in fact unable to be "full" participants in economic life, we would concern ourselves with overcoming familiar hurdles, and not *basically* changing the structure of existing economic and political institutions. Our demand would simply be "*more.*"

The operating political theory which corresponds with this view deals with the out-dated laissez-faire ("individualist") ideology of Congressional opponents to expanding welfare. It seeks, once again, to thwart the coalition of Republicans and Southerners and their attachments to an image of rural America. The strategic implication of this view is the need to correct urban under-representation in Congress. Thus, by understanding the barriers to, and reforms necessary for, more adequate income for the recipients of "transfer" payments, this view attempts an "explanation" of poverty. However, this theory, and the assumption on which it is based, just won't work.

Six and one-half million out of 9.3 million families with income less than $3000 in 1962 had one or more members on a payroll or operating their own farms or business. Only 2 million worked 50-52 weeks, but 5.7 million heads of families living in poverty worked full or part time in 1962.

As George Meany has said, "More than half the poverty problem is directly connected with unemployment, low wages, and involuntary part-time work." He backed this up by pointing out "Nearly one million Americans are now working for fifty cents an hour or less; about twelve million Americans are now working for $1.50 or less." The federal minimum wage of $1.25 an hour guarantees only $2500 per year to a fully employed worker, and sixteen million workers are not even protected by that legislation.

Low wages and relatively high unemployment accompany each other. This is especially the case when the statutory and minimum wage is not an adequate one. The relationship between labor surplus and low wage is especially evident in unorganized small businesses and in the service sector generally, where either the operation is near the margin, or union organization has been unsuccessful.

Despite a "booming" war economy, and the longest "peace-time" recovery ever, four percent of the work force is still officially counted as unemployed. These figures can underestimate; the Conference on Economic Progress estimates that if involuntary part-time work, and unemployment that doesn't show in the surveys, were calculated, true unemployment would be about three percent higher than government sources use.

With unemployment stable at high rates (over four percent; Western Europe ranges from .5 percent in West Germany to 3.2 percent in Italy) wages have fallen behind productivity gains, and corporate profits are higher than ever before. Increase in productivity outstripped the increase in manufacturing wages by at least 10 percent between 1956–1962, and cash flow to corporations outstripped personal income by 23 percent in 1953–1963.

Automation, which could be the means of generally shared abundance, introduced by extraordinarily powerful corporations, within highly organized oligopoly and monopoly markets, means great gains for these corporations but insecurity for those whose low skill or vulnerable jobs puts them in its path.

Given such a framework, the meaning of "welfare" changes drastically. When one-half of one percent of the population owns more than 25 percent of all wealth, and one percent of adults holds 76 percent of all corporate shares then the question: Who does the economy work for? must be back of our concern for welfare. Anything Big Government does must be judged in terms of equality and democracy—without embarrassment for the naive sound these words have.

The top 100 corporations own 58 percent of all corporate assets; that means for example, that a tax-cut program which favors corporations so they can "modernize" will encourage the competitive advantage of the giants who can use that money to automate. Similarly the tax-cut for upper incomes heightens the already tremendous income inequality which is so important in producing poverty (see Table 3).

The granting of licenses for the private development of atomic energy means that the corporations with the huge capital necessary will gain an even more dominant grip on the economy of tomorrow.

So, when the War on Poverty proposes to spend 150 million dollars on job training, a good bit of which will permit private industry to train workers at government expense, the important question, which should determine an attitude to that program, is who benefits in the long run?

The people's money gets spent by the millions—as was the case in the development of the communications satellite; but only a handful will make a profit from that.

It is important to understand that without conscious exploitation (although that exists, for example in slum real estate), it is the "normal" functioning of American capitalism which maintains and creates inequalities.

Dividing the population into income fifths shows that wealth is distributed in 1960 just as unequally as in 1947, and only barely more equally than in 1929. And the position of the lowest tenth of the population has descended since 1929, and is still descending.

TABLE 3

Percentage of Total Income Received by Highest and Lowest Fifths of All Consumer Units				
	1929	1947	1953	1960
Highest	54.4%	46.0%	44.7%	45.7%
Lowest	3.0%	5.0%	4.9%	4.5%

As outdated as the doctrine of increasing misery might be, these figures argue that for the poor relative deprivation is real and growing.

Now, the trade union movement has traditionally been considered the defender of the economic position of the underprivileged. The figures on poverty argue that the success of the labor movement has certainly been limited, but there is a more important problem involved. Labor can only bargain for its members and their industries; the poor, on the whole, are not in the unions. And the political muscle of the trade union movement just is not what it is mythologized into being. Moreover, industrial unions—those whose social base most nearly borders on the poor—are losing that base as production-line jobs are eliminated. The automobile industry, for example, in 1963 produced 4.3 million more cars than in 1947, with 54,000 fewer workers.

Big labor as an important power element in American society has become a political myth; as a power resource for the poor it is as yet absent.

Who then is to assert the interests and needs of poor people? The U.A.W.-inspired coalition against poverty will be non-partisan and apolitical, and will exclude poor people. Will it be the technicians in social problems? Is there any record of "virtual" representation (the thing against which the American colonies revolted) really working in the interests of those supposedly represented?

In fact, this means that the moon shoots will take precedence over rat shoots; for the people who have an "interest" involved in the pro-space coalition (for example) are those claiming to abolish poverty. In the longest of all possible runs, the question of Whose economy? will be answered by the solution to the problem, Who's got the political "clout" to serve his ends?

American capitalism has established a series of institutions and regulatory agencies within its midst which are supposed to protect society at large from the natural, cyclical effects of unregulated markets, and certain weaker groups from the negative effects of those so regulated. It is not properly seen as a "managed" economy from the point of view of the actual extent of governmental planning power; nor is it seen properly as a "welfare state" from the point of view of the extent of poverty and the lack of any sort of welfare it bears for so many of its people.

What America is, as Mills put it, is a "political capitalism" which puts the fruit of government's huge resources up for grabs, by the highest bidder or strongest contestant. This does not mean corruption (though there is that); it does mean that the way we define the business of government turns out to be helping business —even when other groups suffer.

Certain industries, for example commercial maritime shipping, railroads, and aerospace, have found themselves in untenable market situations. High capital requirements, poor profit prospects in certain aspects of their operations, or exclusive dependence on public contracts for their existence, produced those situations. Without losing their prerogatives to claim handsome profits on capital returns, however, these industries have had recourse to political arenas and have obtained either direct governmental subsidies, as with the first two, or, in the latter case, guaranteed profits through "cost-plus" contracts. They have been able to defend politically what they could not defend economically.

On the other side, in the face of automation, unskilled and semi-skilled workers have been unable, to date, to muster that kind of power to bolster a weakening economic position.

Is there not something instructive about the difference between cost-plus contracts and the satellite give-away on one hand, and miserable education and starvation welfare budgets administered tyranically on the other? Is not urban renewal the real story of the contemporary welfare state, and not any "war on poverty?" What does welfare mean to the residents of Chicago's Oakland community area (98 percent are Negro; 45 percent are in poverty, and 47 percent live in substandard housing)? More than sixty million dollars was spent by public agencies to halt "deterioration" in the middle-class environs of the University of Chicago—what is happening to the Oaklands of America?

The liberal founders of public housing hoped that better houses would make better people. But aside from their physical inadequacies, public housing projects embody a political theory to the people who live in them; to them it means that they are somehow set off, and not as good as the others. They are left out of the planning and the power-wielding, both when sites are selected and when projects are administered. In essence, this is the way clients of the welfare state are treated generally—when they are poor. When they are middle-class rich, however, their welfare, in the form of boodle, is well and liberally served.

The principle should be stated plainly, understandably: people should have the right of participation in the decisions which affect their lives, and institutions should encourage that right. Powerlessness describes only part of, but then compounds and multiplies, the problems and plight of the poor. Yet, at every turn, even in education, dependency is taught and forced upon these men and women.

Like all benevolences, the welfare institutions today mark the concepts of what others thought were good for people, not what they built and won themselves. That so many people are left out of these programs is terrible, inhumane; that so many are miserable within them is obscene.

The experience of the liberal coalition which built the institutions we now have teaches us this: the poor cannot rely on others to speak for them. The Negro movement has learned this and taught it for a race; it must be learned and taught for a class.

The first need, then, is not more this and more that; rather, it is different ways of doing this or that. And *that* requires a political movement which speaks in terms of the intransigence of *its* needs, not the needs it thinks are "realistically acceptable"—the slogan of the post-war "effective" liberals. The time of the white man's and philanthropist's burden is over.

With justice, though, *little sense can be made of a demand for "power" unless it is placed concretely in the context of what is currently being done with power.* The use of figures on the distribution of wealth was not gratuitous. Despite the moderates' "consensus" that poverty can be abolished without conflict between rich and poor, is it reasonable to think that poor people would tolerate such inequality, if they could do anything about it? No, it is not. But the old struggle for the economic surplus is now in the political arena.

If government, through the monies it spends and programs it supports, is the largest consumer in the society, then the impact of political power for poor people becomes more than merely a social-psychological therapy. The purposes for which just under one hundred billion dollars is spent is variable to a great extent. Money spent in urban renewal and the profitable defense and aerospace boondoggles, the fruits of publicly supported technological innovation, could be used not to line pockets and to perpetuate inequality, but to build a better, more equitable society. The impact of new political power would be to change the business of government.

Self-government means that a people sets its own priorities for allocation. The priorities of America today subordinate poor people to middle-class and Big Business culture. On one hand, the culture is undemocratic; on the other, it provides boodle for the already affluent; and in between are the crumbs, fearfully picked up by the poor.

Traditionally, the Left has seen The People as a Sleeping Giant, always about to awake. Today, the poor are a minority; whether they have the interests which are distinct from the workers generally is a matter of controversy. (This writer opts for the notion of solidarity rather than cleavage.) But the point is this: nowadays, the people who say that thirty years ago they fought for the Wagner Act (etc.) now argue moderation, order, responsibility, and "effectiveness," and find the advocates of a movement of poor people either extremist or romantic. Filled with phrases like "iron law of oligarchy," and theories of the professionalization of dissent, these people forget that outside of an increasingly isolated West, the world's poor people *are* an awakening giant who demand power and justice.

History guarantees little; it offers opportunity. When we ask "whose welfare" will be served, we ask,

"Who will struggle?"

ORGANIZING
THE CONSUMER
COOPERATIVE

MERLIN MILLER

IF IN EVERY COMMUNITY WHERE COOPERATIVES ARE ORGANIZED among the poor there could be efficient legal services for the poor consumer, the problems of these cooperatives would be very much less. Unfortunately, most lawyers are as unfamiliar with the problems of cooperatives as most cooperative organizers and educators are with the problems of the poor. What the cooperative organizer can suggest to the lawyer can be condensed into four topics: First, what is a cooperative? Second, the problems of the poor in organizing cooperatives; Third, the legal problems; and Fourth, steps in organizing a cooperative.

WHAT IS A COOPERATIVE?

First, what is a cooperative? To a New Yorker a cooperative is a high-rise apartment building owned by the tenants. To a grain farmer from Kansas a cooperative is a tall grain elevator with the word CO-OP in bold letters across the top. They're both right and they're both wrong. "Cooperative" is used commonly—and loosely—to describe a business enterprise operated on a cooperative basis. Still more loosely it is used to describe the business buildings and facilities of such an enterprise. But, in its essence, a cooperative is the group of people who have banded together to

This article was originally prepared for presentation at the Ohio State Legal Services Association 1967 Consumer Conference, and is reprinted by permission of the Ohio State Legal Services Association from *Course on Law and Poverty: The Consumer*, pp. 392–399 (1968).

carry on a business enterprise for the benefit of all of them, which acting as individuals they could not do, or could not do as well. The cooperative, then, is the organized group of people who have provided their own self-help, user-owned, group business enterprise. Every word of this functional definition is important; *self-help, user-owned, group business enterprise.*

VARIETIES OF COOPERATIVES
AVAILABLE TO THE POOR

All kinds of business enterprises can be organized on a cooperative basis. The variety of cooperatives being organized now in the South, for example, as an aftermath of the civil rights developments there, is extremely limited if compared with the varieties to be found around the world. There are cooperatives of shoemakers and garment makers in India or Mexico or Honduras. There are cooperatives of the blind and the handicapped, producing handicrafts and electronic components in Poland. There is a cooperative in Burma capturing and taming wildlife. There are fishermen's cooperatives on every ocean and sea and almost every coast around the world. This infinite variety of economic activity which can be undertaken by people who want to help themselves is a challenge to their legal advisors, a challenge to use imagination and to discover new things that can be done cooperatively.

The term consumer cooperative tends to restrict our imagination. We think in terms of the foodstore, the supermarket. In the urban poverty programs there are a good many things that are being done on a cooperative basis. Organizing a big supermarket that requires an investment of hundreds of thousands of dollars may be done as part of a large housing project. But small groups of poor people can organize buying clubs. They can go a step further and offer a "food fair," a sort of "exposition," a very small supermarket for one day. They can organize to get their drugs and medicines at substantial savings. They can organize to provide a business counseling service, showing members of the group how they can buy certain appliances, for example, at much reduced prices through buying at specific recommended places of business. This leads naturally to a sort of "bargaining association," and agreements with reputable businesses that want to aid the poor and are quite willing to aid them if the transactions are cash, avoiding the credit and collection problems which increase the cost of doing business so sharply. In short, a cooperative discount house for the poor. So all of these can be done and many other things, through multi-service buying centers or business advisory centers.

There are other services which can be provided at a saving. Insurance is one of these—the saving comes largely through group premiums. Burial service is another important service which can be obtained cooperatively at a lower cost, although it's pretty hard to get the extremely poor who are thinking about tomorrow's meals and paying for a radio, TV or washing machine to think ahead to that inevitable day when they or their families will be faced with the heavy expense of a funeral service. And then there's credit, the most universal need next to food and housing. The answer is the credit union, the cooperative savings and loan association. This is the most fundamental of all cooperative organizations, the one that provides the most basic services to its members: encouraging thrift and savings, providing credit when needed, and developing financial independence and human dignity.

THE PROBLEMS OF THE POOR IN ORGANIZING COOPERATIVES

When considering the bewildering variety of possible cooperative enterprises, it is wise to go back to the definition of a cooperative: a business enterprise organized by a group of people on a self-help and user-owned basis. Look at each separate part of that definition and it becomes clear that those who organize cooperatives among the poor face difficulties that most businesses never face.

SELF-HELP

In the first place, *self-help* for the poor. There is some truth in the oft-repeated generalizations that the poor are poor by and large because they are uneducated, even illiterate, apathetic or unambitious. In some quarters there is also an element of fear— fear of the loss of a job or fear of being evicted from a home. And finally there is a long dependence upon various forms of welfare and relief. No one of these handicaps applies to all of the poor; there are some among the poor who have none of these handicaps. But generally the poor do have handicaps in getting together for self-help. That means there has to be a well planned program, involving gradually increasing information and education—in the action sense of that word—and self-reliance, before any group of the poor is going to be able to organize on a self-help basis. They are the people least qualified to pull themselves up by their own boot straps, but that is essentially what a cooperative is—a group pulling themselves and each other up by their boot straps. If the enterprise is run by somebody else for the poor, then it may be welfare or charity but, certainly, it is not a cooperative.

USER-OWNERSHIP

In the second place, *user-ownership*—that the people who use the business own it. By definition, the poor lack capital. Nevertheless, user-ownership is impossible without the investment by the prospective members of some risk capital—and the would-be cooperator must understand this. No lawyer—nor any other counselor—should let anyone he advises join a cooperative under the assumption that he's going to get something for nothing. He is not going to get, but he is going to give. He's going to give his patronage, and pay for what he gets in food or appliances or medical services or whatever it is that he is acquiring through this cooperative. He is also going to have to make an investment—a capital investment. The poor today are going to have to do the same thing that the poor have always done when organizing cooperatives; they are going to have to put in a little money of their own. They are going to have to leave money in the business as they use it if it is to be a successful cooperative. This is true, even though the various agencies aiding may put in considerably more capital than the cooperators themselves initially. But still, the prospective cooperative member is going to have to gamble a little of his limited money. He must make the plunge of "going into business" if he is going to be a true cooperator. These two elements, investment and patronage, are necessary for a cooperative to succeed. The other side of the coin is that, in order to get off the ground, many kinds of cooperatives of the poor will need, in addition to the members' pennies or dollars, proportionately large amounts of capital investments from outside sources.

GROUP ENTERPRISE

Third, a *group enterprise*. Now confidence and trust in each other are the very foundation for the ordinary business transactions in western society. If no man could trust another's word, his checks, his telephoned orders, his price quotations, where would our vaunted corporate business structure and our affluent society be? Confidence and trust in each other is even more significant in the democratic corporate structure of the cooperative —especially among the poor, who have so little to lose, and to whom that little means so much.

The poor weavers of Rochdale, who started the worldwide cooperative movement, saved their money, some of them only a penny a week, for a whole year and trusted those meager savings to one person who was their treasurer—a year before they could go into any business and expend any of their savings for even their first small stock of goods. The Raifeissen Credit Societies, organized among the poor farmers of Germany about the same time as the Rochdale pioneers, organized on a basis of unlimited liability. They saved their money in a society which could loan the money to any of their members who needed it. But if he didn't pay back, all the members of the society were liable— unlimited liability. That is the foundation of trust upon which cooperatives started in a day when they had no government aid. The poor in our cities have been conditioned to be wary, to be suspicious, to distrust the stranger, to distrust the businessman from outside the community who has a place of business in their immediate vicinity. These suspicions can be overcome only by dynamic, trustworthy leadership; patient, continuous education; and small steps, one at a time, in cooperative action.

AIDED SELF-HELP COOPERATIVE

There is a fourth factor in the definition of a cooperative organized among the poor under the provisions of the Economic Opportunity Act. It is not only a self-help, user-owned, group business enterprise. It is an *aided* self-help cooperative. There are many kinds of assistance available under the Economic Opportunity Act. There can be grants for developing an organizational base for cooperative programs. There can be grants for the conduct and administration of cooperative programs in their initial stages. There can be payment for advice and assistance of specialists, technicians and consultants for various cooperative programs. There can be grants for training personnel needed in cooperative programs. There can be loans to cooperatives for furnishing essential services. This last is particularly true in the rural areas through the Farmers Home Administration. All these and other aids available are described in the book, *Moving Ahead with Cooperatives*, a manual prepared by the Cooperative League of the USA at the express request of and in cooperation with the Office of Economic Opportunity.

The very terms *aided* and *self-help* seem to be contradictory. They are not, they do go together. We have learned, I think all of us, that there is no such thing as a truly self-made man. We all get assistance from others in the development of our own characters, our own business enterprises, and our own careers, our own professional skills. So do cooperatives, even the most prosperous middle-class cooperatives.

The Hyde Park Cooperative Society in Chicago, which now does about $6,000,000 worth of business a year and has the biggest food store within the confines of the City of Chicago, began as a little buying club meeting, doing business in one room of a private house. Individuals gave their time without pay to carry on the business in those depression years. Also, most of the new prosperous farmers' cooperatives in the Middle West had in their initial stages persons and organizations giving time and energy without pay.

Today, it is even more true that most cooperatives among the poor will have to be aided self-help cooperatives. The trick is to get the aid at all, to get it at the right time, and to get enough to get the business going. At the same time, the help must not be too much. It must not be enough to kill the cooperators' own sense of self-achievement.

LEGAL STRUCTURE OF COOPERATIVES

Turning to the legal organizational structure of cooperatives, it is possible for a small cooperative to operate for a time without being incorporated. But it is wise for a group getting started to have a lawyer point out that this involves certain hazards. As long as a buying club is unincorporated, every person joining or placing an order to be delivered at a later date kisses his money goodbye when he prepays that order. If the treasurer runs off before the next meeting he hasn't much recourse. But this experience with the unincorporated cooperative buying club or association does have the advantage of impressing upon all the members that they are dependent on each other, not upon Uncle Sam and not upon the lawyer. They must make it on their own and they must trust each other. Just to get that far with a cooperative group may be a matter of character building that will mean the difference between the members of that group staying in the disadvantaged class and being on their own.

But the time comes for most cooperatives when the business must be incorporated or abandoned. When this time comes, it is important to know the essential distinctive differences between a cooperative and an ordinary business corporation. There are four of these distinctive features which every member of a cooperative should understand.

First, the cooperative is organized under non-profit corporate laws. The application charter should specifically state that the cooperative is organized not for profit.

The second feature is the implementation in a business enterprise of the not for profit restriction: the dividend, if any, paid on the shares of stock or the investment shall be strictly limited. In practice this means that the return on the investment in a cooperative is limited to an amount equivalent to a modest rate interest, or nothing at all on the investment.

If a cooperative is successful it does "make money" in the bookkeeping sense—it does have "profit." But there is a sharp distinction between "profit" in the bookkeeping sense and "profits" in the sense of the word used in defining a corporation as "nonprofit." That term, as used in defining both eleemosynary corporations and cooperatives, means that no one (organizers of, officers in, contributors to, nor members of the organization) shall share in any moneys received from either its philanthropic or its business operations. The non-profit definition as applied to a cooperative requires that the money that is made on the transactions shall not be distributed to the members as investors at a rate that is any higher than they could have gotten as interest if they had made a loan to the cooperative. That is the basic ethical principle.

It is not legally stated quite that way in most laws but it is exceedingly important. This limitation on distribution of earnings or savings makes it possible for the cooperative earnings or savings to be returned to the members as *users* in proportion to their use of the business.

This, then, is the third and most distinctive feature of the cooperative—the patronage refund principle. This principle does not require that the members take their earnings out of the business. If they desire to devote their savings to social or community uses, such as a playground, they are perfectly free to do that under most cooperative laws. But if they do vote to "take their earnings out," it must be distributed in proportion to the volume of business done with the cooperative.

Finally, the fourth distinctive feature is the principle of democratic control. This requirement is often stated as "one member, one vote." This requirement is stated in all consumer cooperative laws. It is the direct antithesis of the ordinary or profit corporate business practice which gives each stockholder as many votes as he has shares. In cooperatives it is men not money that controls.

There are, of course, many other detailed requirements for incorporation under specific cooperative laws. Moreover, the laws vary from state to state. Some states have no laws for consumer cooperatives at all. Ohio, for example, has a detailed Cooperative Marketing Act for farmers' cooperatives, Ohio Revised Code, Chapter 1729, Sections 1729.01 to 1729.27, but only one section on consumers' cooperatives, Section 1729.28. In most states, it is advisable that cooperatives for low income persons be incorporated under the District of Columbia Cooperative Association Act passed June 19, 1940, D.C. Code Sections 29-801 et seq.

The steps in organizing a cooperative are set out in detail in the manual, *Moving Ahead with Cooperatives*. It was prepared jointly by the Cooperative League of the USA and the Office of Economic Opportunity. It is written in simple language with the poor in mind, but it contains all the essential information found in more sophisticated publications.

A second source of information is a 32-page booklet entitled *A Model Consumer Action Program for Low Income Neighborhoods*, by Harry S. Shaden, Jr. This booklet was prepared expressly for neighborhood urban groups in the city of Chicago.

A third manual entitled, *Moving Ahead with Group Action*,

details the step-by-step organization of a consumer buying club. In simple language and with numerous line drawings, it discusses the work members of buying clubs will have to perform for themselves, e.g., pooling their orders; ordering from the wholesaler, packaging, pricing and handling the cash; and keeping the financial records. This manual also sets forth sample business forms and simple by-laws. In short, it is a complete guide to a simple but well-managed self-help consumer cooperative. This manual, like the other two mentioned above, can be obtained from the Cooperative League of the USA, 59 East Van Buren Street, Chicago, Illinois 60605.

THE LAWYER'S ROLE

The problem of organizing a consumer cooperative for the poor is not a problem of educating the poor until they are ready to start cooperative action and then incorporating. The most successful organizing procedure is to provide a little education, then a little action; another step in education, the corresponding action, and so on, with action and education reinforcing each other until the group has acquired sufficient experience to go into a larger business enterprise and has some capital to invest in that business. Then it is time to incorporate.

The lawyer has two functions in this educational process: first, to see that the group does not incorporate too soon before its members understand thoroughly what they are doing; and second, to see that they do not put off incorporation too long, and so unnecessarily jeopardize the capital—and the enthusiasm—they are accumulating.

The attorney for the organizing group can perform another valuable service during this organizational period. He can give some sound business advice under the guise of legal counsel. This includes, in part, the following:

1. He can point out the legal responsibility of the officers of the buying club to get the money in advance or when goods are delivered for their own protection and to prevent that most frequent cause of cooperative failure—uncontrolled credit.

2. Also, he can stress the legal and sound business necessity of recording every member transaction from the start. The alloca-

tion of patronage savings is impossible without such records. Unexpected liability for income tax may be incurred without records of all transactions between the cooperative and the individual member. It is not only the members of the cooperative who need this advice. The community action people who are going to finance the initial organizational expenses of a cooperative venture must stress that any cooperative which gets assistance from the taxpayers' money has to keep good records. Nothing creates more suspicion, doubt, and finally, hostility, than the failure to keep records that show where every penny of every member and every dollar of the government's investment has gone. That means, in practice, a monthly operating statement and balance sheet.

3. The attorney should see that the adopted by-laws require bonding of all employees responsible for handling funds. If possible, he should check to see that the proper bonds are promptly obtained.

4. Finally, the attorney who by this time has established himself as the friend and protector of the cooperative can give this sound advice: "Get a good manager and pay him what he's worth." This advice may need to be given to the OEO officials as much as the poor themselves. If this means going outside of the immediate community, hiring somebody who isn't within the "poverty guidelines," insist on it as good business and sound legal advice. Some OEO officials may not be happy about such counsel, but the fact remains that the co-op manager and co-op board, or OEO officials who share in hiring him, are trustees handling other people's money. They must have someone who has had experience and whose reliability is beyond question.

The foregoing bits of advice may be beyond the strictly legal requirements of the law. But they are quite in keeping with the purposes of legal aid. For, in a very real sense, the cooperative's attorneys, like the cooperative's organizers, are also trustees— trustees of the spirit of a people attempting to lift themselves out of poverty.

DISRUPTING CITY SERVICES TO CHANGE NATIONAL PRIORITIES

FRANCES PIVAN
RICHARD CLOWARD

WE OFTEN SAY THAT THE NATION'S POOR, ESPECIALLY THE BLACK poor, are carrying the main burdens of the war in Vietnam. Yet little is being done to make the poor an effective force in shifting national priorities from war to domestic programs. Mass demonstrations such as the Poor People's Campaign, which rely on "moral confrontation," are at best a limited form of pressure, and then only when conditions are ripe for new political accommodations. So far, the Administration has shown itself to be capable of absorbing countless demonstrations staged in the capitol itself.

The Administration is most vulnerable, we think, in the cities, especially if tactics more politically disruptive than demonstrations are employed. It is in the cities that the national Democratic Party has its base, and it is there that most of the black poor now live. Whatever happens in the cities reverberates on national Democratic leaders. Indeed, the growing demand from a wide variety of groups that the Administration give priority to trouble in the cities is becoming a major encumbrance on war policies. Trouble has been brewing over a number of years as masses of black poor have been forced off the land and into the cities, where they aggravate municipal fiscal problems because of the public services they need, and aggravate the white working class by competing for scarce housing and jobs. Riots have further escalated tensions within urban Democratic constituencies, push-

From Frances Pivan and Richard Cloward, "Disrupting City Services to Change National Priorities," *Viet-Report*, 3:8–9:27–31, Summer 1968. Reprinted by permission of *Viet-Report*, New York.

ing municipalities nearer bankruptcy and worsening black-white electoral cleavages. Except for the war, massive federal grants-in-aid for welfare, health, housing, education, and employment could be used to ease this divisiveness between groups in the Democratic coalition, but that money now goes to the military establishment. If strategies can be found which substantially worsen tensions in the cities, the Administration might be forced to alter these priorities.

Disruptive strategies to produce this result are available. The cities are peculiarly vulnerable to disruption at this time, for city agencies serve older Democratic constituents at the expense of blacks who are a vast new electoral force in the cities. The key to disrupting services—and to exposing this anachronism—is to mobilize the poor either to withhold payments to a system from which they do not receive fair services because the system defers to other groups, or to mobilize people to claim benefits which have been withheld, again out of deference to other groups. First, we propose massive rent stoppages to bankrupt slum landlords and to force municipal takeover of slum buildings. Second, we will describe current efforts to organize actual and potential welfare recipients to claim hundreds of millions of dollars which are withheld from them, usually illegally. These strategies could force city governments into fiscal crisis, exacerbating already evident political strains in the cities, and escalating pressure on the Administration to bail out its urban political apparatus with massive subsidies for the poor.

DISRUPTING THE SLUM
HOUSING SYSTEM

The slum is the underbelly of the real-estate market: tenants who cannot compete for housing elsewhere are preyed on by entrepreneurs who lack the capital or competence to compete for profit elsewhere. More prosperous and stable real-estate investors put their capital in the regular market, where money can be made in less demeaning ways, leaving the slum to be exploited by men who seek to gain on speculative exchanges or who, restrained by rent-control laws from levying large increases, shore up their declining profits by skimping on repairs and services. The result is inflated prices and deteriorated buildings—a situation that can be remedied only by public subsidies and public action.

But there is little political pressure for housing subsidies for the poor—only for affluent groups. And although deteriorated housing is illegal, public agencies make no effort to enforce housing codes, for a crackdown would produce massive dislocation of landlords and tenants. Repairs are extremely expensive, and building income is limited by the poverty of the captive tenant market. Slum landlords often do not have the funds to rehabilitate their buildings—not, at least, without substantial increases in rents. Just a modest step-up in enforcement activity under a new administration in New York City recently resulted in a rapid upsurge in the number of foreclosures, tax delinquencies and vacate orders. If slumlords were pushed out, government would have to house the minority poor. So the enforcement agencies use their powers gingerly and selectively, usually paying heed only when tenants have the tenacity or the "pull" to compel enforcement. In other words, slum profits depend on collusion between city agencies and landlords: in return for nonenforcement of the codes, the slumlord takes the blame for the slum and enables the city to evade the political ire of the ghetto.

To disrupt these collusive arrangements, the funds that fuel the slum system must be cut off. Tenants should be told to keep the rent money, and to spend it rather than put it aside for later payment to the landlord.

Some liberal jurisdictions have laws which authorize tenants in buildings with code violations to hold their rents in escrow accounts while they pursue an elaborate set of procedures culminating in a court action. But legalistic rent strikes have been a failure. Low-income tenants cannot secure redress in housing agencies and courts. At worst, the agencies and courts are corrupt instruments of real estate interests; at best, they are hamstrung by elaborate statutes and regulations written to safeguard private property. Even if this were not so, the sheer volume of tasks involved in pursuing a court case is overwhelming: canvassing buildings for violations; filling out complaint forms, arranging appointments for housing inspectors; checking to make sure that the inspectors file reports and that violations have been recorded; arranging for lawyers; chauffering tenants to trials—not once, but repeatedly as landlords successfully obtain adjournments. In short, everything we know about the failure of past legalistic rent strikes points to the futility of attempts to solve a widespread problem by making use of cumbersome procedures for individual legal redress.

PHASE I: ENDING EVICTIONS

The great obstacle to mounting a disruptive rent strike is the danger that tenants may be evicted. Fear of eviction will make tenants reluctant to withhold rent in the first place, and evictions later can break the morale of a rent-strike movement, causing its collapse. Thus the first phase of organizing should concentrate on resisting evictions. During this first phase, the momentum for a strike movement can also be built.

During a campaign to "Stop All Evictions!" in a particular neighborhood, resistance squads could be organized and tactics for dealing with marshals and police could be tested without exposing tenants to risk. In the meantime, organizers could talk up the idea of a rent strike. The key problem in this phase is to develop a neighborhood communications system for reporting evictions. One way is to leaflet a neighborhood, asking tenants threatened by eviction to call a central telephone number so that organizers can be dispatched to watch the apartment. Another way is to have organizers hang around on the block, telling people to let them know the moment the marshal appears in the vicinity.

There are several tactics for resisting evictions. For example: organizers can mass both in front of the building and within the threatened apartment to block the marshal. They can sit on the furniture, return the furniture to the apartment as quickly as it is carried out, or neighborhood people could be deployed along the hallways and stairways through which the furniture must pass. To overcome even such simple tactics, a marshal must call for the police, who then must contemplate mass arrests in order to carry out a routine eviction. (So far, when these tactics have been tried, the police have been very reluctant to do the landlord's job.)

If resistance works, many more neighborhood people may be emboldened to join in. And when more people join, organizers can capitalize on the public's fear of riots. City officials are now extremely sensitive to the temper of ghettoes and exert themselves to avoid the minor incidents which have often set off conflagrations. Mayors have emergency power to halt evictions by executive order, and under the threat of riot would be likely to do so. Even tough-talking Mayor Daley of Chicago ordered all evictions halted during July and August of last year.

PHASE II: RENT REVOLT

Aside from reasonable assurances that they will not be evicted, tenants need an incentive to strike. The rent money is such an incentive, but only if the tenant can pocket it or spend it. Tenants who in past rent strikes were called upon to place their rent in escrow derived some satisfaction in just keeping the rent from the landlord, but the satisfaction would be far greater if that money could also be spent on family needs, particularly since rent absorbs so large a percentage of the typical slum family's income —sometimes more than half. At least as important, only the massive denial of rent will bankrupt the slum system; if the money is left to accumulate in escrow accounts, it will eventually be returned to landlords by the courts (or by tenants themselves, frightened by either the reality or the rumor that court cases are being lost).

The spread of rent-strike action must be controlled. If those withholding rent are dispersed over too wide an area, the logistics of resisting evictions may become overwhelming. It is probably preferable for organizers to work intensively on a few blocks at first, concentrating their energies to ensure complete coverage of eviction threats. As the area of strike action expands, organizers will need to make sure that a viable communication system exists, and that there are neighborhood cadres capable of resisting evictions. In addition, reserve forces—perhaps sympathetic student groups—should be available for quick mobilization to protect a particular block if public officials decide to try to break the strike by a dramatic show of force. (If some money is available, leaders of the strike may want to rent several vacant apartments, holding them in reserve in the event that a few evictions do in fact occur.)

PHASE III: DEALING WITH RESPONSES TO THE RENT REVOLT

The response of landlords and municipal housing agencies to a successful rent revolt will vary depending on local conditions.

Where landlords have little equity in their buildings, many may simply abandon them. In other situations, landlords may try to wait out the strikers, exerting counter-pressure by turning off utilities and discontinuing services. But there is nothing a landlord can turn off that tenants can't turn back on. And if marshals can be successfully resisted, so can utility men threatening to turn off gas and electricity.

When landlords terminate services or abandon the buildings, tenants may want to take over the task of providing minimum services. If they have the organizational capability to do so, they can then settle down to rent-free living until politicians decide to institute programs for refurbishing housing or subsidizing the construction of new housing.

But if a neighborhood does not or cannot take over the servicing of buildings, the consequences might turn into a political advantage for the strikers. Under such circumstances, dangerous conditions would quickly develop: hazards to health, threats of fire, the spread of disorder and suffering. Political leaders can ill afford to ignore these conditions in dense urban communities, where disease and fire can readily spread beyond the boundaries of the slum and ghetto.

Warm-weather months afford many tactical advantages. Lack of heat, the most serious inconvenience to tenants, is not a problem, and even the fear of eviction loses some of its force: hot pavements are not so fearsome as ice-covered ones. More important, people are much more likely to be on the streets in warm weather, making it easier to assemble crowds at the sites of attempted evictions. And until now, at least, the potential for riots and mass violence has been greatest in the summer, so that official repression of strikes is not so likely then.

Municipal political leaders, it should be stressed, possess the powers to act in emergencies. They can take over buildings, institute emergency repairs, and otherwise divert public funds from programs for other groups to cope with a crisis in the slum and ghetto. The question is, what will it take to force these actions. The answer, we suggest, is nothing short of a major crisis in the slum system.

DISRUPTING THE PUBLIC
WELFARE SYSTEM

The growing national movement of welfare recipients is already revealing the fiscal punch of tactics which upset the longstanding practices by which local welfare systems withhold lawful benefits from the poor. In New York City, for example, organizing drives to claim benefits have forced the welfare rolls up by 50 percent in less than two years and doubled costs (to $1.3 billion). And this has been accomplished by a movement which has no support at all from civil rights or peace groups, and scarcely any funds or organizers of its own.

Americans regard every dollar spent for public relief to the unemployed and the unemployable as a sign that something is wrong. Many in the middle class are convinced that poverty should be dealt with by "rehabilitating" the poor rather than by redistributing income; the working class is preoccupied with taxes and hostile toward those below them; and many black leaders seem embarrassed to fight for "handouts," even for those who should not or cannot work, or for those who cannot get a decent job at a decent wage. It is in deference to these widespread sentiments that administrators of public-welfare agencies design policies and procedures to keep their budgets low, an objective achieved by keeping the poor ignorant of their eligibility, by erecting a tangle of bureaucratic barriers against those who do apply, by arbitrarily and illegally rejecting many applicants, and by refusing to allot the full benefits provided by law to those who do get on the rolls. The result is that only half of those who are eligible actually get on the rolls, and most of these are cheated out of full allowances.

PHASE I: BREAKING THE
SECRECY BARRIER

Welfare organizing across the nation has usually begun with efforts to inform people of their rights.

(1) Organizers obtain the official manual of welfare regulations. Welfare administrators ordinarily will not release this manual, but a sympathetic welfare worker can usually be found who will steal a copy. Otherwise, recipients can hold a sit-in or, since manuals are public documents, initiate litigation to obtain copies.

(2) A simplified handbook for the use of clients and organizers is prepared on the basis of the manual.

(3) Thousands of copies are distributed in ghetto neighborhoods, through churches, stores and other outlets.

The handbook is especially useful if it is written to alert organizers and clients to the ways in which the system withholds benefits from people—e.g., giving illegal grounds for rejecting applicants, describing typical forms of underbudgeting, telling people about the availability of special grants for heavy clothing which are ordinarily kept secret. Overcoming the secrecy barrier is a crucial step in organizing: people cannot fight what they do not understand.

PHASE II: DEVELOPING CADRES OF RECIPIENTS

The national welfare movement has been built largely by indigenous leaders (usually mothers on the Aid to Dependent Children rolls). Once information gets around regarding the extent to which recipients are being cheated out of various benefits, groups form quickly. In the early stages, these groups usually focus on settling the individual grievances of their members. Since negotiations with welfare officials over the intricacies of individual cases consume enormous amounts of time and energy, groups which continue to concentrate on settling individual grievances do not tend to grow. Other tactics, noted in the next phase, are necessary to produce mass action. But grievance work has had the useful consequence of developing cadres of recipients who are confident of their knowledge about the system and of their ability to stand up to it. These cadres, in turn, have often become the spearhead of efforts to mount mass campaigns against the system.

PHASE III: MASS CLAIMS FOR BENEFITS

Large-scale campaigns are based on identifying a benefit to which many people are entitled but which few receive. Most welfare regulations, for example, allow grants for special purposes, but people are rarely told about them and generally don't get them. Staging a "mass benefit campaign" is much simpler than adjusting individual grievances and has far greater impact. Once the particular benefit is identified as the focus of the campaign (such as demands for school clothing), a check-list is mimeographed and distributed widely through the ghetto, together with an announcement of a demonstration. When several hundred people assemble to demand a common benefit, welfare departments usually release the grants, particularly in cities with large ghettoes, where public officials fear violence. In New York City, for example, campaigns staged by welfare groups around special grants for household items, clothing, and emergencies have released some 50 million dollars in extra allowances over the past year.

One of the most useful tactics learned from these campaigns is to make the waiting rooms in the welfare center the locus of organizing activity. In the big cities these waiting rooms are constantly jammed with people, many of whom will respond to on-the-spot offers of aid in getting on the rolls or in obtaining special allowances. In a number of places organizers are beginning to go into the centers with leaflets about welfare rights, with checklist forms for special grants, and with simplified eligibility forms which people can fill out before being called to the interviewing cubicle for an initial interview. If organizers are barred from waiting rooms by the police, they set up tables on the sidewalks outside to distribute literature and talk with people moving in and out of the centers.

Similar issues could be raised by mobilizing unemployed and underpaid black men who are kept off the rolls despite jurisdictions which allow some to obtain benefits under a "home relief" or "general relief" category, and others whose wages are less than they would receive on welfare to receive supplementary payments.

Some groups are contemplating mass advertising to inform people of their possible eligibility for welfare, or to inform those who are already on the rolls of the special allowances they are probably not receiving. The actions being considered include:

(1) taking ads in newspapers or making spot announcements on radio stations that reach the ghetto;

(2) placing posters in supermarkets and other stores in slum neighborhoods;

(3) enlisting ghetto clergymen to preach on welfare rights;

(4) mass leafletting of neighborhoods.

Advertising techniques should be especially effective in reaching the millions of poverty-stricken people who are still not on the rolls, sometimes for reasons of pride, but more often because of ignorance produced by secrecy about eligibility barriers.

In summary, strategies to bankrupt the cities have a double thrust. First, rising municipal costs mean that the poor are getting money, whether it's the rent money they keep or the higher welfare payments they receive. The promise of money is a powerful incentive in mobilizing mass action; the continued flow of money is a powerful force in sustaining it. Protest and demonstration tactics, by contrast, depend on the much less certain and usually less compelling appeal of ideology or momentary drama.

Second, the more money the poor get, the greater the leverage on the national Administration. Urban political leaders, already on the brink of fiscal disaster because they are squeezed between the services needed by an enlarging ghetto constituency and the indignation of their white taxpaying constituents, are becoming insistent lobbyists for increased federal subsidies. It will not be easy for a national Administration that depends on the cities to ignore these claims, or to ignore the worsening divisions in their urban constituency which these strategies can generate.

BUREAUCRACY, THE GARRISON SOCIETY, AND THE FUTURE

INTRODUCTION

IN THE TWENTIETH CENTURY, where the empirical evidence calls for a new form of international community living,[1] we see instead a heightened nationalism. It is not the mere legacy of the nineteenth century; it is rather a more articulated form of bureaucracy and state organization. The colonialism of the previous era has developed into international policies of containment and new forms of imperialism.[2] The consequences of this process are of deep sociological concern.

First, there is nationalism among the new and newly independent states of the world, which will be approached in Part Three. Second, the costs and consequences of the post-World War II period known as the Cold War,[3] are important for individual nations, for the groupings of countries associated in so-called security pacts, and in their impact on the total world scene. The empirical evidence shows that during the 1960s—UNESCO's Development Decade, in fact—the gap between the rich and the poor nations increased, largely due to a lack of investment by the rich in the poorer countries. Specifically, the developed nations

---

[1] See Kenneth Boulding, *The Meaning of the Twentieth Century*. New York: Harper & Row, 1964.

[2] For discussion on this theme, see David Horowitz (ed.), *Containment and Revolution*. Boston: Beacon Press, 1967.

[3] D. F. Fleming, "The Costs and Consequences of the Cold War," *Annals of the American Academy of Political and Social Science*, Vol. 366 (July, 1966): 127–138. Also see D. F. Fleming, "Can Pax Americana Succeed?" *Annals of the American Academy of Political and Social Science*, Vol. 360 (July 1965): 127–138.

spend on armaments much more than the equivalent of the total wealth of all of the poor nations in the world.

As to the consequences for American society, the data are extensive. Seymour Melman documents the extent to which the United States is weakening its economic base and deteriorating the quality of future life through malinvestment in defense and military expenditures. Vernon K. Dibble extends the classic Lasswellian discussion of Japan's role in Manchuria in the early 1930s, and describes the United States today as a "Garrison Society." Kenneth E. Boulding argues that the conscription system is the extension of a state whose legitimacy must be called into question.

A generation ago Robert Merton conceptualized the idea of the "bureaucratic personality."[4] He was identifying the characteristics of increasing numbers of persons who were employed in the typical bureaucratic structures of our society. However, the meaning of the concept has been clarified and dramatized in the so-called "Eichmann phenomenon": the individual who can be a major cog in a machinery designed to exterminate people and yet maintain his innocence since he "only obeyed orders." This phenomenon illustrates the fullest implication of bureaucratization—and calls for sociological concern.

In a society which spends two-thirds of its federal budget on the costs of war, it is logical to observe the economy's inability to deal with other societal needs. The "Great Society" offers massive evidence of the fallacy of "both butter and guns" as a political, economic and social policy.[5] The initial social programs of the early and mid-1960s are already known in history for their irrelevance and failure. Congress passes acts without any financing due to the military expenditures already committed. While antipersonnel weapons are utilized in Southeast Asia, antipersonnel social policies are executed in Watts, Hough, Harlem, Appalachia and elsewhere in the United States.

Alternatives have been proposed. In fact, as Deutsch points out, the realities compel a sociology of alternatives. Richard Shaull outlines one direction. Senator Fulbright pinpoints some of the

[4] Robert Merton, *Social Theory and Social Structure*. New York: The Free Press, 1957, Chapter 6.
[5] For a review of the "Great Society" and some cogent critiques, see Marvin E. Gettlemen and David Mermelstein (eds.), *The Great Society Reader: The Failure of American Liberalism*. New York: Random House, 1967.

particular programmatic implications of current policies and the immediate alternatives available. The discussion in this section perhaps overlaps some of the previous material, and yet quite logically follows the early discussion as we work toward a conclusion in our search for a radical sociology.

WHERE IT'S AT

OVERKILL: THE DRAIN
ON AMERICA

SEYMOUR MELMAN

A HUMAN BEING OR A COMMUNITY CAN BE DESTROYED ONLY ONCE. This is a limit of military power, and no conceivable technological break-through is going to change that. But the defense budgets and military policies of the United States embody a denial of these propositions, in the form of the weapons and the forces in being and in preparation.

In 1965 more than 7,000 nuclear warheads are carried by the 1,400 intercontinental missiles and the 2,000 long-range-bombing aircraft of U.S. armed forces. Each of these 7,000 warheads is capable of destroying a city. The warheads range in size from less than 1 million tons of TNT-equivalent to explosives whose power is equivalent to that of 20 million tons of TNT, and more. The 3,400 strategic aircraft and missiles of the U.S. armed forces can carry about 19 billion tons of TNT-equivalent, or about 6 tons for each human being on earth.

Apart from these there are more than 25,000 "tactical" nuclear warheads whose average explosive force is 100,000 tons of TNT-equivalent, or 5 times the power of the bomb that destroyed Hiroshima in World War II. These tactical warheads are encased in short-range missiles, artillery shells, and bombs, or fashioned into various sorts of nuclear demolition kits. The tens of thousands of nuclear warheads that Secretary of Defense McNamara declared that the military had during 1963 are carried by an array of short-range aircraft, and in missiles of every description: ground-to-ground, ground-to-air, air-to-air, and air-to-ground. This stockpile of strategic and tactical nuclear weapons is being increased constantly.

How much military power is represented by this stockpile? The bomb that destroyed the city of Hiroshima and took the lives of about 100,000 people in August, 1945, had the power of 20,000 tons of TNT-equivalent. A standard boxcar on American railroads can carry about 20 tons of TNT. In other words, the bomb used to destroy Hiroshima had explosive power equivalent to the TNT that could be carried in 10 freight trains, each made up of 100 freight cars, each car carrying 20 tons of TNT. By similar reckoning, a warhead of 1 megaton—that is, 1 million tons of TNT-equivalent—has the explosive power equivalent to the TNT carried by 500 freight trains each of them with 100 carloads of TNT.

We can try to visualize the present power of the U.S. strategic nuclear stockpile in another way. Suppose a Hiroshima-size bomb had been exploded every day of every year for the last 1,965 years, or since the birth of Christ. The combined force of all of these explosions would be just over 14,000 megatons; this is only 70% of the destructive capability now encased in the U.S. long-range bombers and missiles alone.

Nuclear military power involves a factor of concentration of destructive capability that has no precedent in human experience. In wars fought with bullets, the idea of overkill has been held to mean having more bullets than enemy soldiers. There were, in fact, more bullets than soldiers in World War II. But it was technically impossible to deliver the firepower of billions of bullets and shells and bombs at once place and at one time. Now this is possible, owing to the concentration of energy-release by nuclear weapons. One large missile or bomber-load of warheads produces an energy-release greater than the cumulation of explosives used from 1939 to 1945 on several continents. A single 10-megaton warhead load means an explosion equivalent to 10,000,000 tons or 20,000,000,000 pounds of TNT. As the photographs of Hiroshima show, the fast release of two tenths of one percent of this much explosive force at that place, at one time, produced, not damage or partial destruction, but atomization of 100,000 people, scorched earth, and durable damage to the genes of many survivors. The present warheads are immensely more powerful than the one used at Hiroshima. That is the meaning of overkill.

The Department of Defense of the United States employs 3.7 million people, of whom 2,680,000 are in the uniformed forces. These forces include 16 elaborately equipped Army divisions, 1,987 ships of the Navy, of which 620 are warships, 28,000 air-crafts of all types, and 30,000 to 40,000 missiles of all varieties and sizes armed with nuclear warheads. Stockpiles of raw mate-rial for potential military use are valued at $8.5 billion. The armed services use 340,000 buildings. The total property value of the installations and equipment exceeds $171 billion.

These numbers are so large as to defy visualization. I will there-fore elaborate one aspect of U.S. military power: the strategic delivery forces. The intercontinental aircraft and missiles of the United States probably account for about one third of the military spending during the last years. Here is an estimate of the principal

	Number of Vehicles	Yield in Millions of Tons of TNT-Equivalent per Vehicle (Megatons)	Total Yield in Millions of Tons of TNT-Equivalent (Megatons)
B-52 Bombers	630	20	12,600
B-47 Bombers	225	10	2,250
B-50 Bombers	80	20	1,600
Atlas Missiles	60	3	180
Titan II Missiles	54	10	540
Minuteman Missiles	800	1	800
Skyhawk A-4D Navy Aircraft	1,000	1	1,000
Skywarrior A-3D Navy Aircraft	150	1	150
Polaris Submarines (29 with 16 missiles each)	464	1	464
	3,463		19,584 (Megatons)

U.S. strategic nuclear-weapons system operational in 1965. Bear in mind that this enumeration includes only the delivery vehicles with intercontinental range; it does not include the largest number of aircraft and missiles—which have less than intercontinental range.

This tabulation brings up to 1965 an estimate of the U.S. nuclear forces that was originally prepared for the report "A Strategy for American Security," which several colleagues and I published in 1963.[1]

All told then, U.S. armed forces in 1965 included 3,400 strategic delivery vehicles with the destructive capability that totaled 19,000 million tons of TNT-equivalent. Just what this means in terms of military power is almost beyond comprehension. A 1-megaton warhead (1 million tons of TNT-equivalent) is capable of destroying most cities by its blast, radiation, and fire effect, which can extend across an area 24 miles in diameter. Therefore, the 3,400

	Vehicles	Total Warhead Power in Megatons (Million Tons TNT-Equivalent)
10% of 225 B-47 bombers	22	220
10% of 630 B-52 bombers	63	1,260
10% of 80 B-58 bombers	8	160
10% of 1150 Navy Aircraft	115	115
25% of 54 Titan missiles	13	130
25% of 60 Atlas missiles	15	45
25% of 464 Polaris missiles	116	116
25% of 800 Minuteman missiles	200	200
Total	552 Vehicles	2,246 Megatons

U.S. strategic delivery vehicles must be considered in relation to the 140 cities with populations of 100,000 or more in the Soviet Union, or the 370 cities of this size in the entire Sino-Soviet bloc.

There is no way of giving reliable numerical statements of the military power contained in these strategic weapons. No one has

[1] Seymour Melman (ed.), "A Strategy for American Security," Lee Service, 48 East 21 Street, New York, New York (50¢).

This sort of tabulation represents a system that is being constantly altered; some vehicles are being retired—like the B-47 bombers that numbered 600 in 1963 and the Atlas and Titan I missiles that were ordered dismantled by June 30, 1965; others are being added—like the Minuteman and Polaris; and altogether new types of strategic vehicles are being produced—like the 1700 TFX (F-111) planes, each able to carry the equivalent of 10 megatons between continents.

ever seen a nuclear war and therefore no one is able to say what size of error is involved in a particular estimate of nuclear military power. Nevertheless some reckoning can be made. Let us assume, for example, that for some combination of reasons 90 percent of the U.S. forces' strategic aircraft are destroyed and 75 percent of the intercontinental missiles are lost. Here is an estimate of the residual strategic delivery capability.

The 552 vehicles that remain after the assumption of massive attrition are still almost 4 times the number of Soviet cities with populations of 100,000 or more.

It is also possible to estimate the size of this destructive power by taking into account the demonstrated capability of a nuclear device of 20,000 tons of TNT-equivalent, the bomb that killed 100,000 people at Hiroshima.[2] Let us refer to 100,000 people

[2] In order to estimate the destructive capability of U.S. strategic forces I assumed that 20,000 tons of TNT-equivalent in the Hiroshima bombing destroyed 100,000 people. Since no one has ever observed a nuclear war, all forecasts concerning the effect of the use of nuclear weapons on a large scale involve estimations for circumstances where the error of estimate cannot be known. Gauging the number of fatalities at Hiroshima involves this problem.

The U.S. Atomic Energy Commission (*The Effects of Nuclear Weapons*, 1962, p. 550) says that casualties at Hiroshima included 68,000 killed. The U.S. strategic Bombing Survey reporting on *The Effects of Atomic Bombs on Hiroshima and Nagaski* (1946, p. 15), stated:

. . . the exact number of dead and injured will never be known because of the confusion after the explosion. Persons unaccounted for might have been burned beyond recognition in the falling buildings, disposed of in one of the mass cremations of the first week of recovery, or driven out of the city to die or recover without any record remaining. No sure count of even the pre-raid population existed. Because of the decline in activity in the two port cities, with constant threat of incendiary raids, and formal evacuation programs of the Government, an unknown number of inhabitants had either drifted away from the cities or been removed according to plan. In this uncertain situation, estimates of casualties have generally ranged between 100,000 and 180,000 for Hiroshima . . . the Survey believes the dead at Hiroshima to have been between 70,000 and 80,000.

A Japanese study on *Atomic Bomb Injuries* (Nobuo Kusano, Ed. 1953, p. 60) accounted for 92,000 dead and missing by February 2, 1946, and further stated:

. . . these figures do not include the deaths among the army in the city. According to information published later by Hiroshima City the number of dead, including those in the military employees and Army, and the injured who died in the meantime, is estimated at 210,000 to 240,000. Another estimate put the number of dead as 270,000.

The effect of a warhead like that used on Hiroshima is influenced by

killed by 20,000 tons of TNT as one "Hiroshima unit"; the megatonage deliverable by U.S. strategic forces can be calculated in terms of "Hiroshima units." In these terms, the 140 Soviet population centers of 100,000 or more comprise approximately 500 "Hiroshima units."

On the assumption of 90 percent attrition of aircraft and 75 percent attrition of strategic missiles, the resulting overkill factor would be about 220 times on the main population-industrial centers of the USSR. If the assumption of attrition were relaxed to 50 percent, then the overkill rate on Soviet industrial-population centers would be more than 1,000 times.

As noted above, all such calculations embody unknown errors of estimate, and there is no way of verifying such numbers. In the event of a nuclear war it is doubtful that the survivors, if any, would be either competent to master or would be interested in such arithmetic. What is important is this: In the realm of overkill, there is no difference between an overkill of 1, or 2, or 220, or 1,000. The United States has been spending billions of dollars to overkill—that is, to do an impossible thing.

· · ·

What has been the cost of overkill to American society?

The pile-up of meaningless military capability is a form of expensive busy-work. Its cost is not only the budgeted money for these purposes, but also the shoddy education system, the poor housing, the neglected medical-care needs, the polluted streams —in short, the whole array of depletion at home and abroad due to the productive activity foregone because of the concentration of talent and capital and materials in the military sphere.

The 1964 defense budget of $56.7 billion included the budgets of the Department of Defense, the Atomic Energy Commission, and the military-assistance program overseas. With the sparse data available to the public on the Department of Defense budget, I have attempted to estimate the portion of the budget that consists of additions to the overkill stockpile. The essential idea is

---

many factors—for example, population density, which is much higher in large modern cities. Deaths traceable to the Hiroshima bombing are still occurring and are not counted. Since estimates of deaths at Hiroshima range from 68,000 to 270,000, I regard the figure of 100,000 fatalities at Hiroshima as one reasonable yardstick for estimating the destructive power of nuclear weapons.

this: Removing the sums that add to overkill should leave a remainder sufficient to operate and maintain the military establishment as it exists. Such a maintenance-of-present-forces budget was calculated. It totaled $34.2 billion, or $22 billion less than the Administration budget in 1964. Here is the comparison between these two budgets, using the titles that appear in the budget of the United States Government:

Major Military Functions	Administration Budget (1964) (Millions of $)	Maintenance-of Present-Forces Budget (Millions of $)
Military personnel		
Present programs	$13,235	$13,235
Pay increase	900	900
Operation and Maintenance	11,792	11,792
Procurement	16,725	5,725
Research, Development, Test	7,262	262
Military construction	1,232	—
Family housing	734	734
Civil defense	300	—
Military assistance	1,480	480
Atomic Energy Commission	2,893	1,093
Defense-related Activities		
Strategic materials stockpile	28	—
Selective Service	38	38
Emergency preparedness	82	—
Totals	$56,702	$34,260

I want to indicate immediately that the limited information available from published sources does not enable anyone outside of the Defense establishment to do a detailed analysis of the cost of overkill in the 1964 budget. The best I could do with more detailed categories than those I show above was to estimate a range of possible budget reductions totaling $16.45 to $25.65 billion. I presented these suggested reductions to the Committees on Armed Services of the House of Representatives and the Senate with the proposal that they be used as guides in the sort of detailed examination for which these Committees are responsible.

In the maintenance-of-present-forces budget, the Personnel and Operations and Maintenance proposals of the Administration are left intact, while Procurement is slated for a cut of $11 billion. The rate of spending for long-range missile production, research, testing, and development was running close to $7 billion a year. (This does not include aircraft and other types of delivery vehicles such as Polaris submarines and other naval vessels.)

Major reduction is recommended for the Research, Development, and Test item on the grounds that there is no conceivable technological break-through that could end the nuclear stalemate. Furthermore, it is no longer reasonable to expect that improvement in a military system as a whole could result from a sum of detailed improvements such as a better rifle, a better engine, missiles that would land a calculated 50 yards closer to their targets. Fifty yards does not count for much when the warhead atomizes everything within one mile of its center.

Research and Development also includes more than $1 billion for military astronautics and related equipment. This is apart from the $5 billion budget of the National Aeronautics and Space Administration. The military item is for spending by the Air Force, mostly in an effort to find some role for the military in space where, apart from designing and launching observation satellites, no one has been able to define a meaningful role. Putting nuclear bombs in orbit is an incredibly dangerous exercise and, in any case, delivering warheads is done more cheaply and more reliably from one place on earth to another, rather than launching them from outer space. But the Air Force, accounting for about half of the military budget, is a political power to be reckoned with; it has been able to command substantial sums to be used in an effort to discover new military goals for itself, even while its classic function as an operator of military aircraft has decreased in importance because of the development of missile technology.

It seems reasonable to curtail new military construction on the grounds that by 1963 the Defense Department already had 341,000 buildings within the United States alone. The civil-defense item is cut out on the ground that the civil-defense concept is technically faulty and politically dangerous. [See data and analysis in S. Melman, *No Place to Hide,* Grove Press: New York, N.Y., 1962.] Military assistance deserves major reduction or combination with other activities.

The Atomic Energy Commission budget is slated for major reduction on the grounds that the operation of its weapons-producing factories at Hanford, Washington, Paducah, Kentucky, Oak Ridge, Tennessee, and elsewhere, cost $1.8 billion a year. In 1963, it was disclosed that the AEC already had in stock surplus fissionable material valued at about $1 billion. Further operation of these factories for the military is the most obvious sort of waste.

The sum of these calculations is a sharp reduction in a military budget designed to be responsive to the simple provision of not adding further to overkill. This is not in any sense a disarmament budget insofar as it does not reduce, but rather maintains, existing military power.

It is difficult to comprehend the magnitude of possible expenditures for military purposes were we to follow the escalating recommendations of the various armed services. Some officers have pressed for a $15 billion program for the development and construction of antimissile weapons systems, despite the fact that such systems would be doomed to ineffectiveness for technical reasons. No conceivable defensive system could overcome the offensive advantage that is inherent in the number and power of nuclear weapons, in relation to population-industrial centers. Such a program, however, would require the construction of a major shelter system to try to protect the population from the radioactive fallout caused by the antimissile warheads bursting overhead. A large-scale shelter system for the United States would cost about $300 billion and would not work. All told, the recommendations of the military enthusiasts could easily lead to an annual military budget of $175 billion. . . .

The prospect of more elaborate and more costly military technologies has, predictably, excited those people who try to forecast the future of particular industries. In 1963 the U.S. Department of Labor, for example, forecast growth in the electronic industry from 1961 to 1970. Out of an estimated $306 million of increased annual sales during that period, 61 percent is supposed to be due to growth in the military and space markets. Large-scale spending for defense purposes over a long period has generated intense economic dependency in the important military-industrial areas. In Los Angeles, for example, 42.6 percent of all manufacturing employment during 1961 was tied directly or indirectly to orders from the Department of Defense and the National Aeronautics and Space Administration.

Perhaps we can get a more meaningful view of the cost of defense and overkill if we think of their price in terms of dwelling, schools, and medical-care items. Here are some illustrations:

One TFX airplane, $5,000,000.

= 13 elementary schools, or
570 dwelling units in low rent public housing projects, or
278 hospital beds.

One Polaris Submarine with 16 missiles, $122,600,000.

= 331 elementary schools, or
6,811 hospital beds, or
13,723 dwelling units in low rent public housing.

Military Space Program (Military Astronautics and Related Equipment) 1965 estimate, $1,283,714,000.

= 71,317 hospital beds, or
3,469 elementary schools, or
143,688 dwelling units in low rent public housing.

Civil Defense Budget for Fiscal Year 1965, $358,000,000.

= 40,071 dweling units in low rent public housing projects, or
967 elementary schools, or
249 secondary schools, or
19,900 hospital beds, or
32,545 nursing home beds, or
795 miles of highway in rural areas, or
223 miles of highway in urban areas.

Atomic Energy Commission, Nuclear Weapons Program 1965, $1,800,000,000.

= 4,864 elementary schools, or
201,477 dwelling units in low rent public housing projects, or
100,000 hospital beds.

Based upon:

elementary school $370,000
secondary school $1,433,000
1 mile rural road $450,000
1 mile city road $1,600,000
1 hospital "bed" $18,000
1 nursing-home "bed" $11,000
1 low-rent apartment $8,934

THE
GARRISON SOCIETY

VERNON K. DIBBLE

THE UNITED STATES TODAY IS A GARRISON SOCIETY. A GARRISON SOCIETY is one in which it makes no sense to ask whether or not civilians control the military. It is a society in which the institutions and the men who hold military, economic, and political power have become so dependent upon one another; in which their goals and interests are so complementary; and in which the traditional boundaries between military and civilian spheres have broken down to such an extent, that the very conception of civilian versus military control has no meaning.[1]

In militia societies, too, it makes no sense to talk of civilian control of the military. For in militia societies—England before the English Civil War, for example—there are few or no full-time soldiers, and no independent military establishment, for civilians to control.[2]

From Vernon K. Dibble, "The Garrison Society," *New University Thought*, 5:1–2:106–115, Winter 1967. Reprinted by permission of *New University Thought*, Detroit.

[1] The term "garrison society" is, of course, a variation of Harold Laswell's term, "garrison state." But the two terms do not refer to the same phenomena. In Laswell's words, "The simplest version of the garrison-state hypothesis is that the arena of world politics is moving toward the domination of specialists in violence." As seen in greater detail below, the term "garrison society" refers instead to a coalescence, in various ways, of "specialists" in "The Garrison State Hypothesis Today," in Samuel P. Huntington, ed., *Changing Patterns of Military Politics*, The Free Press of Glencoe: New York, 1952, 51–70.

[2] For more details about this example, see the section entitled "Lords Lieutenant And Their Deputies" in Vernon K. Dibble, "The Organization of

In a civilian society—the United States before World War II —there are full-time soldiers and an independent military establishment. Professional soldiers live, in large measure, within their own, somewhat isolated world. Many of their values—obedience to hierarchical superiors, discipline, physical courage, military honor—are at odds with, or are at least different from, the values of the rest of the society.[3] But they remain subordinate to civil authority.

In an old-fashioned militarist society—Bismarck's Germany, in some respects—the military establishment was not subordinate to civil authority. For example, military budgets in Imperial Germany did not require the approval of the *Reichstag*. Distinctly military values and styles, of which the duels in German fraternities are the best known example, spill over into civilian society.

But these old-fashioned distinctions between civilian or militarist societies, or between civilian versus military control, have no meaning in the United States today. For example, when hundreds of civilian institutions are closely involved with the military, civilian censorship of the public utterances of officers does not prevent them from having their say in public debate, or in public indoctrination. In August, 1914, President Wilson wrote to the Secretary of War as follows:[4]

> My dear Secretary, I write to suggest that you request and advise all officers of the service, whether active or retired, to refrain from public comment of any kind upon the military and

---

Traditional Authority: English County Government, 1558–1640," in James G. March, ed., *Handbook of Organizations*, Rand McNally: Chicago, 1965, 879–909. See also the relevant chapters in Thomas G. Barnes, *Somerset, 1625–1640: A County's Government During The Personal Rule*," Harvard University Press: Cambridge, 1961.

[3] Samuel P. Huntington, in *The Soldier and the State*, notes a number of ways in which "the military ethic" is in conflict with the liberal ideology that has been dominant in American political history. For example, "The heart of liberalism is individualism. It emphasizes the reason and moral dignity of the individual, and opposes political, economic, and social restraints upon individual liberty. In contrast, the military ethic holds that man is evil, weak, and irrational and that he must be subordinated to the group. The military man claims that the natural relation among men is conflict." Quoted in Allen Guttman, "Political Ideals And The Military Ethic," *The American Scholar*, 34:2, Spring, 1965, p. 22.

[4] Quoted in Jack Raymond, *Power At The Pentagon*, Harper and Row: New York, 1964, p. 178.

political situation on the other side of the water . . . It seems to me highly unwise and improper that officers of the Army and Navy of the United States should make any public utterances to which any color of political or military criticism can be given where other nations are involved.

That policy still holds. The White House or civilian secretaries censor the speeches of officers, or forbid their presentation altogether. But in a garrison society the silencing of men in uniform is irrelevant. For handmaidens of the military, out of uniform, abound in politics, in scholarship, in the mass media, and in business.

It makes little difference whether the men who make speeches are generals; or retired generals working for armaments firms; or professors whose research is paid for by the Pentagon, or by the CIA; or journalists whose bread and butter depend upon good relations with Pentagon sources; or Congressmen whose re-election may be jeopardized if the bases in their districts are shut down; or researchers in institutes and think shops that survive on military contracts; or corporate executives whose firms manufacture missiles or napalm.

Whoever makes the speeches, and whatever their disagreements with one another—missiles or manned bombers, bomb Hanoi or hold up in enclaves, get tough with Russia or try peaceful coexistence—we will hear no challenge to the basic assumptions of American foreign and domestic policy. We will hear no challenge to the false view that freedom versus communism is what our cold wars and our hot wars are all about.

The point, then, is not simply the size and power of the American military establishment. To be sure, its size and power are basic features of the garrison society. The Pentagon is the headquarters of the largest corporation in the world. As Bert Cochran describes it:[5]

> The sprawling bureaucracy housed in this enormous fortress . . . controls an empire that elicits the respectful attention of any of the heads of our leading corporations. The Cordiner Report of several years ago set a valuation of $160 billion on the property owned by the Defense Department, "by any yardstick of

[5] Bert Cochran, *The War System*, Macmillan: New York, 1965, pp. 138–139.

measurement, the world's largest organization." This wealth includes weapons arsenals, air bases, naval stations, army reservations, in all, more than thirty-two million acres of land in the United States, and another two and a half million acres abroad. The total is larger than the combined area of Rhode Island, Connecticut, Massachusetts, Maryland, Vermont, and New Hampshire.

. . . The assets of the military are three times the combined assets of United States Steel, American Telephone and Telegraph, Metropolitan Life Insurance, General Motors, and Standard Oil Company of New Jersey. Its paid personnel is three times as large as that of these corporations. Of a grand total of five million federal employees, more than three and one half million are working for the Defense Department: two and a half million in the armed forces, one million civilian workers. The civilian payroll alone is $11 billion a year, equal to one and a half times the combined payrolls of the iron and steel industry and of all other basic metal producers, and equal to twice the payroll of the automobile industry. The annual military budget is larger than the annual net income of all the corporations in the country.

But these figures alone do not define the garrison society. The garrison society consists, rather, of (1) a large and powerful military that penetrates deeply into civilian life; of (2) the great importance of civilians in military affairs, the increasing resemblance between military officers and civilian executives in politics and business, and the greater contact and cooperation between officers and civilians in politics, in science, and in business; such that (3) the traditional boundaries between civilian and military society break down; and (4) the military are blended into an alliance with government and with large corporations, whose goals include (a) counter revolution and American hegemony abroad and (b) a large dose of centralized, executive control of the economy and of politics at home.

PENETRATION INTO CIVILIAN LIFE

You cannot administer a military outfit as big as the Pentagon's without penetrating deeply into civilian society. And even if you could, the largest corporation in the world, like all large corporations, seeks to expand, and to reach out for monopoly control over its environment. It sets up or takes over subsidiary corporations like the non-profit think shops. It diversifies its products. These products now include not only weapons, strategic theories, and military skills. They also include ideological indoctrination, social research, and, in Secretary McNamara's proposal to "salvage" the rejects of the draft, social work, pedagogical theory, an implicit denunciation of the failures of the welfare state, an attack upon the teaching profession, a veiled attack upon the humanities,[6] and "advanced educational and medical techniques." If our schools have failed, the Department of Defense will rescue us.[7] ". . . the imperatives of national security in our technological age make the Defense Department the world's largest educator of highly skilled men. Those same imperatives require that it also be the world's most efficient educator."

The military penetrates into education, into research and scholarship, into labor unions, into the political decisions of Senators and Congressmen, and, most crucially, into business and the economy. In education, the use of class standing as a basis for student deferments requires every college instructor in the country to confront his students as an agent of the state. He helps to decide which of his students shall live and which shall die. The selective service system has intruded into the internal government of colleges and universities, has appropriated the ordinary relations between students and teachers for its own administrative convenience, and has transformed these relations into instruments of the garrison society.[8]

The military's penetration into research and scholarship is even

[6] I take it that the Secretary's statement that "One of the department's key concepts is that traditional classroom training is often largely irrelevant to actual on-the-job performance requirements" and his reference to "pruning from existing courses all non-essential information" are veiled attacks on the humanities.

[7] The quotation which follows, the quotation in the previous sentence, and the quotation in Note 3 are from the excerpts from Secretary McNamara's address to the Veterans of Foreign Wars, *New York Times*, August 24, 1966, p. 18.

[8] The administration of a number of colleges (including Wayne State, Haverford, Cornell, and a few others) have indicated that their colleges will either submit no class standings to draft boards or will otherwise refuse to go along (for example, by refusing to compute class standings separately for male and female students). The faculties of a few other colleges, including Columbia College, have voted in favor of this position.

more direct. "There was a period after the war," writes Louis J. Halle, "when various departments of the Government tried to marry themselves to the universities." That marriage did not work well in the case of the State Department. But it "worked in the case of the Pentagon and the faculties of science and technology, a wartime precedent having already been established at Oak Ridge and Los Alamos."[9]

Since that time, the military has continued to purchase some of the best minds in the country. Professor Melman has described some of the consequences of that fact for civilian Research and Development, for the internal structure of American universities, and for the financially neglected fields outside the natural sciences.[10] The military provides large percentages of the annual budget of many major universities.[11] And it, along with the CIA, have transformed scholars and researchers into intelligence analysts, military technicians, and apologists. Michigan State University's fronting for the CIA in Vietnam, and the University of Pennsylvania's secret research for the Pentagon are extreme, but not unique instances. For example, at last count thirty-eight universities and institutes affiliated with universities were conducting research on chemical and biological warfare for the Department of Defense.[12]

Government money for research has consequences, in turn, for education. A professor who has research money from outside his university acquires an economic base that tends to free him from collegial and departmental control. Whether he operates alone with his assistants or in a research institute with colleagues, he is under less pressure to be concerned with all the varied tasks of a university, including the task of teaching students. He is more free, if so inclined, to regard his university as a home base for his operations elsewhere. One result, even among some teachers in undergraduate colleges, is professorial disdain for teaching and for

9 Louis J. Halle, "On Teaching International Relations," *Virginia Quarterly Review*, 40:1, Winter, 1964, p. 13.
10 Seymour Melman, *Our Depleted Society*, Dell Publishing Co.: New York, 1965, Chapter 4, entitled "Cold War Science and Technology."
11 *Ibid.*, Appendix C, "Index of 500 Largest Military Prime Contractors For Experimental, Development, Test and Research Work." See also Raymond, *op. cit.*, Chapter VIII, "Research and the Federal Government" and Cochran, *op. cit.*, pp. 155–161.
12 This figure is from Carol Brightman, "The 'Weed Killers'—A Final Word," *Viet Report*, 2:7, 1966, 3–5. Miss Brightman relies on "a Pentagon spokesman" as reported in the *Washington Post*.

education, as opposed to the specialized training of selected students. From the students' point of view, some of the best of them are suspicious of all scholars and of all scholarship, because they see the confusion of scholarship with military intelligence or apologetics.

In many labor unions, members and dues depend upon war plants. I doubt (as Isaac Deutscher recently expressed it) that most American workers are happy about working for death instead of for life. But a man needs a job. And a union needs members. Hence, unions help munitions firms to secure or retain military contracts, or lobby to prevent the closing down of shipyards and airplane plants. And some labor leaders are among the most chauvinistic heralds of the American counter-revolution abroad.

The no-strike pledge during World War II is to the unions' relations with the government as Oak Ridge and Los Alamos are to the post-war marriage between the Pentagon and departments or institutes of science and technology. That is, the organizational mobilization of American society that the second World War brought about has continued ever since. For the managers of unions, business firms, research institutes, and governmental agencies find advantages—less militant unions, access to power, money for research, or whatever—in continuing cooperation with one another. These advantages are quite independent of their original military significance. Hence, the organizational coordination of World War II goes on, but, of course, with a new definition of the enemy.

Thus, during the Korean War the Research Director of the Textile Workers Union wrote:[13]

> The present emergency found American trade-unions prepared to unite with other groups on a common program of national mobilization. They were keyed to an all-out extended battle against Communist totalitarianism, for they knew its dangers and the threat it represented to the people's well-being.

One decade later the Executive Council of the AFL-CIO declared, "The nation's defense requirements obviously have top

[13] Solomon Barkin, "American Trade-Unions In The Present Emergency," *Monthly Labor Review*, the Bureau of Labor Statistics, 73:4, October, 1951, 409.

priority."[14] And in 1963, Secretary McNamara awarded the AFL-CIO a well-deserved citation for, among other things, military propaganda. The Secretary praised the union for "utilizing extensive communications media to promote greater understanding among its millions of members and the public of the vital objectives of defense programs."[15]

In Congress, we read, many silent Senators are "concerned" about Vietnam. But only three voted against the latest Vietnam appropriation. Dozens of Congressmen signed a statement of "concern" about escalation, and proceeded to vote in favor of the appropriation. In contrast, the draft was reinstated in 1948 by a vote of 70 to 10 in the Senate and 259 to 136 in the House.[16] For (except when they want to appropriate more money than the Pentagon requests) a mere Senator or Congressman does not tangle with the largest corporation in the world, whether his state or district wants to keep the bases and war plants it already has, or feels neglected and wants to acquire some. Its economic importance stifles debate. And with most labor unions, or their leaders, committed to the garrison system, one potential source of pressure on Congressmen to behave differently is eliminated.

The acquiescence of Congress and of the labor movement has repercussions, in turn, on education. Many of the most intelligent and most serious college students today spend more time on political activity than on their studies. For as they see it, and they see it correctly, America faces desperate problems that almost no one in public life is willing to face. If a dozen silent Senators who are "concerned" about Vietnam would only speak up, political activists on college campuses would feel free to spend more time on chemistry formulae and the Greek dative.

In the economy, some ten to twenty percent—depending on what you include and how you measure it—of the national product depends on the military. And some ten to twenty percent of the labor force work at jobs that also depend upon the military. About 25,000 private industrial plants operate under systems of

[14] *Proceedings of the AFL-CIO Fourth Constitutional Convention,* 1961, Vol. II, p. 70.
[15] *Proceedings of the AFL-CIO Fifth Constitutional Convention,* 1963, Vol. I, p. 355.
[16] *The New York Times,* June 11, 1948 and June 23, 1948.

ctement...

military security, over four million employees were required to obtain security clearance during a period of ten years, and, to be on the safe side, some firms have extended military security to all of their operations, including those which have nothing to do with military work.[17]

To be sure, many, perhaps most American firms do not benefit directly from the garrison society. If twenty percent depend upon it, eighty percent pay taxes to make it possible. Nor would all munitions firms, even, be hurt seriously by sudden disarmament. And some firms, in banking and in men's clothing for example, have been hurt by the war in Vietnam. But we cannot look to businessmen who are left out of the profits of the garrison society, or to firms that are hurt by the war, to lead the way toward "dismantling the cold war institutional machine."[18] For to do so would be a basic challenge to their aerospace colleagues; to the existing system of political power; in some cases to the unions that operate in their plants; and to the entire ideology of anti-communism from which they, too, derive strength and comfort in these trying times. Terminating the war in Vietnam tomorrow would be in the economic interest of many American firms. But adherence to the reigning ideology, and class solidarity with other businessmen more directly involved in the garrison society, seem thus far to be stronger than immediate economic interests. In short, as concerns the military and the American economy, a little penetration goes a long, long way.

[17] The information on military security in business is from Raymond, *op. cit.*, pp. 154–156. On the extent to which the economy depends upon military spending, Harry Magdoff, using the estimates of the U.S. Arms Control And Disarmament Agency in its volume, *Economic Impacts of Disarmament* (Washington, D. C., 1962), writes as follows: "The more than $55 billion spent annually on what the government agencies classify as 'national defense' has a chain-reaction effect on the rest of the economy, just as other forms of investment and spending have a 'multiplier' effect. It is estimated that for every $1 spent on 'national defense' another $1 to $1.40 of economic product is stimulated. A crude, but conservative, calculation shows that in addition to the approximately 7.4 million people engaged in some phase of 'national defense,' another 6 to 9 million are employed due to the economic stimulus of defense spending." Harry Magdoff, "Problems of United States Capitalism," in R. Miliband and J. Savile, eds., *The Socialist Register: 1965*, Monthly Review Press: New York, 1965, p. 63. See also Cochran, *op. cit.*, pp. 140–141.
[18] This phrase is the title of Chapter 12 of Melman, *op. cit.*

THE BOUNDARIES
BREAK DOWN

But, as noted in the second element in our definition of the garrison society, the penetration of the military into civilian society is only part of the story. While civilian life has become increasingly militarised, civilians have become more important in military affairs, military men have more contact with civilians, and military men come to resemble civilians more than ever before. The office of the Secretary of Defense is no longer that of a coordinator. The Secretary and his civilian aides are makers of military policy. The number and the influence of civilian military theorists, in and out of the Department of Defense, moved General Thomas D. White, former Air Force Chief of Staff, to remark, "in common with other military men I am profoundly apprehensive of the pipe-smoking, trees-full-of-owls type of so-called defense intellectuals who have been brought into this nation's capitol."[19] And no longer do armaments firms simply manufacture what the military orders. They have their own staffs to devise their own weapons systems, which they try to sell to Congress and to the Pentagon.

But the military, too, is developing its own generation of military intellectuals and technological specialists. Advanced technology and a complex, sprawling organization (no longer limited to a simple command structure plus some staff positions) make brains and managerial talent more important than old-fashioned heroism in the upper reaches of military hierarchies. And, of course, constant dealings with corporate executives, plus the prospect of a career in business after retirement from the service, reinforce tendencies within the services themselves toward making the work of military leaders increasingly similar to the work of corporate executives.[20] More generally, as Allen Guttman suggests, the end of *laissez faire* liberalism in this country—the transformation, in Guttman's words, "from an imperfect liberal democracy to an imperfect social democracy"—means that "the

[19] Quoted in Raymond, *op. cit.*, p. 289. More generally, see Raymond's Chapter 16, "The 'McNamara Monarchy'."
[20] See Morris Janowitz, *The Professional Soldier: A Social And Political Portrait*, The Free Press: Glencoe, Illinois, 1960. Especially Section II, "Organizational Realities: Heroic and Managerial" and Chapter 20, "The Future of the Military Profession."

American soldier can for the first time in our history square the
dictates of his professional ethic with the accepted values and
institutions of our society."[21]

In short, the traditional social and cultural boundaries between
civilian and military society have broken down. The military,
civilian government, and large corporations do not form a single,
monolithic ruling group. There are conflicts within, and between,
each party to the alliance. But on all essentials—American world
power, the Cold War and anti-communism, and the shape of our
domestic economy and social structure—they are as one.

The historical origins of the garrison society are reflected in
this coalescence of military and civilian executives, and in this
fading away of traditional boundaries. The garrison society did
not come about because a military clique imposed itself on the
rest of America. It was built—base by base, contract by contract,
and professor by professor—through the cooperation of military
leaders, politicians, and corporate executives that began during the
second World War. Universities, labor leaders, intellectuals, and
the mass media followed along.

One of the earliest prophets of the garrison society was Charles
E. Wilson, former president of General Electric. In January, 1944,
in an address before the Army Ordnance Association, Wilson proposed an alliance of the military, the executive branch of the
Federal government, and large corporations in "a permanent war
economy." He proposed that every large corporation have on its
roster a colonel in the reserves for liaison with the military, and
he spelled out the role of the Federal executive, of Congress, and
of business as follows:[22]

> First of all such a [preparedness] program must be the
> responsibility of the Federal government. It must be initiated
> and administered by the executive branch—by the President
> as Commander-in-Chief and by the War and Navy Depart-

21 Guttman, *op. cit.*, p. 237. See note #3, above for further explanation of
this point.
22 Quoted in Fred J. Cook, *The Warfare State*, Macmillan: New York,
1962, pp. 76–77. Mr. Cook, in turn quotes from an article by John M.
Swomley in *The Progressive*, January 1959. I was unfortunately not able to
locate the full text of Mr. Wilson's speech in any of the usual sources
such as *Vital Speeches* or *The New York Times*. Note that this man is
Wilson of G.E., not Wilson of General Motors.

ments. Of equal importance is the fact that this must be, once
and for all, a continuing program and not the creature of an
emergency. In fact one of its objects will be to eliminate emergencies so far as possible. The role of Congress will be limited
to voting the needed funds . . .

Industry's role in this program is to respond and cooperate
. . . in the execution of the part allotted to it; industry must
not be hampered by political witch hunts, or thrown to the
fanatical isolationist figure tagged with a "merchant of death"
label.

The cooperation that Wilson proposed, and that in fact came
about, does not create a monolithic ruling group. But it does create a system in which each party has a great stake in the other
party's interests and success. That is one of the system's strong
points. If one party to the alliance were imposing itself on the
other two, the whole system would be weaker than it is. The
economy is dependent in an important degree on the military. But
it is equally true that the military are dependent on big business.
If armaments firms acted like old-fashioned entrepreneurs, keeping their capital mobile and seeking out the most profitable
markets, they might go in for pea canning plants in Sicily instead
of missiles. The military and the government depend upon their
continued preference for government-sponsored, low-risk capitalism.

Another source of the alliance's strength is the fact that most
participants—politicians, generals, corporate executives, and professors—really believe in what they are doing. They are, by their
lights, patriotic servants of the public weal. And the combination
of power, profits, and sincerity is more powerful than power and
profits alone.

INTERNATIONAL POWER AND
DOMESTIC CONTROLS

This powerful combination, of motives and of institutions, has
profound consequences for American society. The world-wide
goals of the garrison society—preventing social revolution and
preserving both capitalism and American world power abroad—
have repercussions on domestic politics and on the domestic political economy. The preservation of the American imperial system

requires economic stability and steady, manageable, predictable economic growth at home. Management and predictability are crucial.

Suppose the United States had a free market economy, subject to uncontrolled fluctuations. Think of the international consequences.[23] A big depression, a great and sudden decline in profits and in employment, would mean a great decline in Federal revenues. There would also be increased political pressure to use these declining revenues for more domestic relief of one kind or another. Foreign aid programs might be threatened. American purchases abroad, public and private, would be curtailed. American multinational corporations might import more of their undistributed profits from abroad and engage in less foreign investment, especially if low prices in capital goods made the depression a good time to invest here. And imports of the products of other nations, including unstable and potentially revolutionary nations, would go down. Previously friendly governments and businessmen in foreign countries would have to look elsewhere for friends. And, what is more crucial, what would happen to our counter-revolution in Colombia if we could not buy Colombian coffee?

On the other hand, a boom that is too big or too sudden is no good either. For one thing, booms tend to produce their opposite. But apart from that fact, too great an increase in dividends and in corporate investment creates inflationary pressure and invites social conflict in the form of wage demands and perhaps crippling strikes. Inflation means that foreign nations have less purchasing power in the United States and would take their business elsewhere, while production at high capacity forces American business to purchase more from abroad than they otherwise would. Both developments place further strain on the balance of payments, which might require, at some later point, either great cuts in foreign purchases, or a great cut in the foreign military bases of the United States.

In short, some of the international repercussions of a big boom are identical to those of a big depression. Both must be avoided if the American imperial system is to remain intact.

Avoiding both the big boom and the big depression requires an

[23] I am grateful to Mr. William Martin for his suggestions about the links between the current international and domestic economic policies of the Kennedy-Johnson administration.

increasingly guided economy—guidelines, dumping surplus commodities on the market to prevent an increase in price, the confrontation between President Kennedy and the steel industry, using the White House instead of old-fashioned bargaining sessions to settle strikes, and using tax policy to make investment and consumption go up or down as the moment requires. These policies, in turn, have further consequences for the society.

For example, labor leaders come under pressure to suppress any signs of an active internal life, and of mass rank-and-file involvement in labor unions. Such things are unmanageable. They have unpredictable consequences. To cite a second example, we cannot permanently abolish unemployment—the classic test of the success of the welfare state—because we must worry about attendant inflationary pressure. That fact, in turn, makes any genuine integration of the mass of Negroes into American society most unlikely, so long as the garrison system lasts.

There are, to be sure, strains in the system. The airline machinists did not go along. The guidelines are breaking down. And there is probably an inherent contradiction between the requirements of the system and the interests of each single firm or industry. Guidelines are most advantageous to you if your firm or your union is the only one that does not go along with them.

But suppose, for the moment, that the economic management that is inherent in the garrison society works well enough for the foreseeable future. What, then, are the lessons of Vietnam? The obvious lesson is that future garrison governments, in time of peace, must always manage to keep unemployment relatively high and production well below capacity. For reasons that Professor Terence McCarthy has expounded that extra slack is needed in order to fight our next colonial war without overheating the economy. That is how you incorporate Keynesian economics and the historic achievements of the New Deal and of American liberalism into the garrison society.

THE IMPACT OF THE DRAFT
ON THE LEGITIMACY OF
THE NATIONAL STATE

KENNETH E. BOULDING

THE RISE AND FALL
OF LEGITIMACY

One of the most neglected aspects of the dynamics of society is the study of dynamic processes which underlie the rise and fall of legitimacy. This neglect reflects, in the United States at least, not merely a deficiency in social sciences and social thought; it reflects a grave deficiency in what might be called the popular image of the social system. We all tend to take legitimacy for granted. Thus, the economist hardly ever inquires into the legitimacy of exchange, even though this is the institution on which his science is built. The political scientist rarely inquires into the legitimacy of political institutions or of the institutions of organized threat, such as the police and the armed forces. Consequently we are much given to discussions of economic development as if this were a mechanical or quasi-automatic process without regard to the conditions of legitimacy of various activities and institutions. Similarly, in our discussions of the strategy of threat we rarely take account of the legitimacy of the institutions which either make the threats or provide their credibility. To put the matter simply, we tend to regard both wealth and power as self-justifying and this could well be a disastrous error.

The truth is that the dynamic of legitimacy, mysterious as it may seem, in fact governs to a remarkable extent all the other

From Kenneth E. Boulding, "The Impact of the Draft on the Legitimacy of the National State," pp. 191–196, *The Draft: A Handbook of Facts and Alternatives*, Sol Tax (ed.), Chicago: The University of Chicago Press, 1967.

processes of social life. Without legitimacy no permanent relation can be established, and if we lose legitimacy we lose everything. A naked threat, such as that of the bandit or the armed robber, may establish a temporary relationship. The victim hands over his money or even his person at the sword's point or the pistol's mouth. If we want to establish a permanent relationship, however, such as that of landlord demanding rent or a government demanding taxes, the threat must be legitimized. The power both of the landlord and of the government depend in the last analysis upon the consent of the rentpayer or the taxpayer and this consent implies that the whole procedure has been legitimated and is accepted by everyone concerned as right and proper. Legitimacy may be defined as general acceptance by all those concerned in a certain institution, role, or pattern of behavior that it constitutes part of the regular moral or social order within which they live. Thus legitimacy is a wider concept than the formal concept of law, even though the law is a great legitimator. At times, however, law itself may become illegitimate and when it does so its capacity to organize society is destroyed.

Legitimacy has at least two dimensions which might be described as intensity and extent. Its intensity refers to the degree of identification or acceptance in the mind of a particular individual, and it may be measured roughly by the extent of sacrifice which he is prepared to make for an institution rather than deny it or abandon it. The extent of legitimacy refers to the proportion of the relevant population which regards the institution in question as legitimate. An overall measure of the legitimacy of any particular institution might be achieved by multiplying its intensity by its extent, but such a measure might easily obscure certain important characteristics of the system. A case in which an institution was regarded with intense allegiance by a small proportion of the people concerned would be very different from one in which there was a mild allegiance from all the people; the former, indeed, would probably be less stable than the latter. In considering any particular case, therefore, it is always important that we consider both dimensions.

The creation, maintenance, and destruction of legitimacy of different institutions presents many difficult problems. Legitimacy is frequently created by the exercise of power, either economic power in the form of wealth or political power in the form of threat capability. Legitimacy, furthermore, frequently increases with age so that old wealth and old power are more legitimate than new. The nouveau riche may be looked upon askance but their grandchildren easily become aristocrats. The conqueror likewise is illegitimate at first, but if his conquest is successful and his empire lasts, it eventually acquires legitimacy. All these relationships, however, seem to be non-linear, and reverse themselves beyond a certain point. Thus, the display of wealth tends to become obscene and damages the legitimacy of the wealthy. In order to retain legitimacy they often have to diminish their wealth by giving it away, establishing foundations, or at least by abstaining from ostentatious consumption. Similarly, political power often seems to lose its legitimacy when it is apparently at its very height. It is at the greatest extent and power of a regime, nation, or empire that it often suddenly collapses through sheer loss of belief in it. Even age does not always guarantee legitimacy. After a certain point an ancient person or institution simply becomes senile or old-fashioned and its legitimacy abruptly collapses.

There have been enough examples of collapse of legitimacy of apparently large, prosperous and invincible institutions to suggest that we have here a general, though not necessarily a universal, principle at work. It is perhaps an example of another much-neglected proposition, that nothing fails like success because we do not learn anything from it. Thus in Europe the institution of the absolute monarchy seemed to be most secure and invincible at the time of Louis XIV, yet only a few decades later it was in ruins. Similarly, in the early years of the twentieth century the concept of empire seemed invincible and unshakably legitimate, yet in another few decades it was discredited, illegitimate, and the empires themselves collapsed or had to be transformed.

It looks indeed as if there is some critical moment at which an institution must be transformed if it is to retain its legitimacy of either its wealth or its power in some degree. Thus, after the eighteenth century the only way in which the institution of the monarchy could retain its legitimacy was to abandon its power and become constitutional. By abandoning his political power, that is, his threat of capability, the monarch was able to become a symbol of the legitimacy of the state and hence was able to preserve his role in the society. Where the monarch did not make this transition, as for instance in France, Germany, and Russia, the incumbent frequently lost his head, the whole institution was destroyed, and the role simply abandoned. Similarly, in the twentieth century, if any semblance of empire was to be maintained, the political power had to be abandoned and the empire transformed into a commonwealth or community based on sentiment rather than on threat. Even the church in the twentieth century has largely had to abandon the fear of hell, that is, its spiritual threat system, as the prime motivation in attracting support. In most countries, furthermore, it has likewise had to abandon the support of the state and the secular arm, that is, the secular threat system, in an attempt to enforce conformity. Here again we see an example of the abandonment of power in the interests of retaining legitimacy.

THE NATIONAL STATE

At the present time by far the most wealthy, powerful, and legitimate type of institution is the national state. In the socialist countries the national state monopolizes virtually all the wealth and the threat capability of the society. Even in the capitalist world the national state usually commands about 25 percent of the total economy and is a larger economic unit than any private corporation, society, or church. Thus the United States government alone wields economic power roughly equal to half the national income of the Soviet Union, which is the largest socialist state. Within the United States government the United States Department of Defense has a total budget larger than the national income of the People's Republic of China and can well claim to be second largest centrally planned economy in the world. It is true that the great corporations wield an economic power roughly equal to that of the smaller socialist states; there are, indeed, only about 11 countries with a gross national product larger than General Motors. Nevertheless, when it comes to legitimacy the national state is supreme. All other loyalties are expected to bow before it. A man may deny his parents, his wife and his friends, his God, or his profession and get away with it, but he cannot deny his country unless he finds another one. In our world a man without a country is regarded with pity and scorn. We are expected to make greater sacrifices for our country than we make for anything else. We are urged, "Ask not what your country can do for you, ask what you can do for your country," whereas nobody ever suggests that we should "Ask not what General Motors can do for you, ask what you can do for General Motors."

An institution of such monumental wealth, power and legitimacy would seem to be invincible. The record of history suggests clearly, however, that it is precisely at this moment of apparent invincibility that an institution is in gravest danger. It may seem as absurd today to suggest that the national state might lose its legitimacy as it would have been to suggest the same thing of the monarchy in the days of *le Grand Monarque*. Nevertheless both monarchy and empire have lost their legitimacy and that at the moment of their greatest power and extent. If history teaches us anything, therefore, it should teach us at this moment to look at the national state with a quizzical eye. It may be an institution precisely filling the conditions which give rise to a sudden collapse of legitimacy, which will force the institution itself to transform itself by abandoning its power or will create conditions in which the institution cannot survive.

These conditions can be stated roughly as follows: An institution which demands sacrifices can frequently create legitimacy for itself because of a strong tendency in human beings to justify to themselves sacrifices which they have made. We cannot admit that sacrifices have been made in vain, for this would be too great a threat to our image of ourselves and our identity. As the institution for which sacrifices are made gains legitimacy, however, it can demand more sacrifices, which further increases legitimacy. At some point, however, the sacrifices suddenly seem to be too much. The terms of trade between its devotees and the institution become too adverse, and quite suddenly the legitimacy of the whole operation is questioned, and ancient sacrifices are written off and the institution collapses. Thus men sacrificed enormously for the monarchy, and the king was able to say for centuries, "Ask not what I can do for you, ask only what you can do for me," until the point when suddenly people began to ask, "What can the king do for me?" and the answer was "Nothing." At that moment the monarchy either died or had to be transformed.

We may be in a similar moment in the case of the national state.

The real terms of trade between an individual and his country have been deteriorating markedly in the past decades. In the eighteenth century the national state made relatively few demands on its citizens, and provided some of them at least with fair security and satisfactory identity. As the nation has gathered legitimacy however from the bloodshed and treasure expended for it, it has become more and more demanding. It now demands ten to twenty percent of our income, at least two years of our life—and it may demand the life itself—and it risks the destruction of our whole physical environment. As the cost rises, it eventually becomes not unreasonable to ask for what. If the payoffs are in fact low, the moment has arrived when the whole legitimacy of the institution may be threatened.

We must here distinguish the internal from the external payoffs of the national state. Internally the payoffs may still be quite high, though it is perhaps still a question whether governments today, like the medical profession a hundred years ago, really do more good than harm. In the external relations, however, there can be no doubt that the system of national states is enormously burdensome and costly. It is not only that the world-war industry is now about 140 billion dollars, which is about equal to the total income of the poorest half of the human race, it is that this enormous expenditure gives us no real security in the long run and it sets up a world in which there is a positive probability of almost total disaster. It is perfectly reasonable indeed to ask ourselves this question: After a nuclear war, if there is anybody left, are they going to set up again the institutions which produced the disaster? The answer would clearly seem to be "No," in which case we may say that as the present system contains a positive probability of nuclear war it is in fact bankrupt and should be changed *before* the nuclear war rather than afterward. It can be argued very cogently indeed that modern technology has made the national state obsolete as an instrument of unilateral national defense, just as gunpowder made the feudal baron obsolete, the development of the skills of organization and public administration made the monarchy obsolete, and economic development made empire obsolete. An institution, no matter how currently powerful and legitimate, which loses its function will also lose its legitimacy, and the national state in its external relations seems precisely in this position today. Either it must be transformed in the direction of abandoning its power and threat capability or it will be destroyed, like the absolute monarchy and the absolute church before it.

THE IMPACT OF THE DRAFT

What then is the role of the draft in this complex dynamic process? The draft may well be regarded as a symbol of a slow decline in the legitimacy of the national state (or of what perhaps we should call more exactly the warfare state, to distinguish it from the welfare state which may succeed it), that slow decline which may presage the approach of collapse. In the rise and decline of legitimacy, as we have seen, we find first a period in which sacrifices arc made, voluntarily and gladly, in the interests of the legitimate institution, and, indeed, reinforce the legitimacy of the institution. As the institution becomes more and more pressing in its demands, however, voluntary sacrifices become replaced with forced sacrifices. The tithe becomes a tax, religious enthusiasm degenerates into compulsory chapel, and voluntary enlistment in the threat system of the state becomes a compulsory draft. The legitimacy of the draft, therefore, is in a sense a subtraction from the legitimacy of the state. It represents the threat system of the state turned in on its own citizens, however much the threat may be disguised by a fine language about service and "every young man fulfilling his obligation." The language of duty is not the language of love and it is a symptom of approaching delegitimation. A marriage in which all the talk is of obligations rather than of love is on its way to the divorce court. The church in which all worship is obligatory is on its way to abandonment or reformation, and the state in which service has become a duty is in no better case. The draft therefore, which undoubtedly increases the threat capability of the national state, is a profound symptom of its decay and insofar as it demands a forced sacrifice it may hasten that decay and may hasten the day when people come to see that to ask "what can your country do for you" is a very sensible question.

The draft, furthermore, inevitably creates strong inequities. It discriminates against the poor, or at least against the moderately poor; the very poor, because of their poor educational equipment, may escape it just as the rich tend to escape it, and the main burden therefore falls on the lower end of the middle-income groups. As these groups also in our society bear the brunt of taxation—for a great deal of what is passed as "liberal" legislation in fact taxes the poor in order to subsidize the rich—an unjust distribution of sacrifice is created. Up to now it is true this strain has not been very apparent. It cannot indeed be expressed directly because of the enormous legitimacy of the national state, hence it tends to be expressed indirectly in alienation, crime, internal violence, race and group hatreds and also in an intensified xenophobia. This is the old familiar problem of displacement. We dare not vent our anger at frustrations upon their cause and we therefore have to find a legitimated outlet in the foreigner, or the communist, or whoever the enemy happens to be at the moment. What is worse, the frustrated adult frequently displaces his anger on his children who in turn perpetuate the whole miserable business of hatred and lovelessness.

Like compulsory chapel or church attendance, which is its closest equivalent, the draft has a further disadvantage in that while it may at best produce a grudging and hostile acquiescence in the methods of the society, it frequently closes the mind to any alternative or to any reorganization of information. The psychological strains which are produced by compulsory service of any kind naturally result in displaced aggressions rather than in any reform of the system which created them. Consequently the draft by the kind of indoctrination and hidden frustation which it produces may be an important factor in preventing that reevaluation of the national policy and the national image which is so essential in the modern world if the national state itself is to survive. The draft therefore is likely to be an enemy of the survival of the very state in the interests of which it is supposedly involved. It produces not a true love of country based on a realistic appraisal of the present situation of human society but rather a hatred of the other which leads to political mental ill health, and an image of the world which may be as insulated from the messages which come through from reality as is the mind of a paranoid.

Perhaps the best thing that can be said in defense of the draft is that the alternative, namely, raising a voluntary armed force by offering sufficient financial inducements, or by persuasion and advertising, would involve even more the whipping up of hatred of the foreigner and the reinforcement of paranoid political attitudes. The draft by its very absurdities and inequities at least to some extent helps to make the whole operation faintly ridiculous, as we see it in comic strips like Beetle Bailey or in movies such as *Dr. Strangelove,* and hence makes the operation of national defense commonplace rather than charismatic. The draft certainly represents the institutionalization of the charisma of the national state, to use an idea from Max Weber, and this may be something on the credit side. Even this merit, however, is dubious. Insofar as the draft leads to widespread commonplace acceptance of mass murder and atrocities, and an attitude of mind which is blind to any but romantically violent solutions of conflict, its influence is wholly negative. Certainly the political wisdom of the American Legion is no advertisement for the political virtues of having passed through the Armed Forces.

It seems clear therefore that those of us who have a genuine affection for the institution of the national state and for our own country in particular should constantly attack the legitimacy of the draft, and the legitimacy of the whole system of unilateral national defense which supports it, in the interest of preserving the legitimacy of the national state itself. The draft, it is true, is merely a symbol or a symptom of a much deeper disease, the disease of unilateral national defense, and it is this concept which should be the prime focus of our attack. Nevertheless, cleaning up a symptom sometimes helps to cure the disease, otherwise the sales of aspirin would be much less, and a little aspirin of dissent applied to the headache of the draft might be an important step in the direction of the larger objective. Those of us, therefore, who are realistically concerned about the survival of our country should probably not waste too much time complaining about the inequities and absurdities of the draft or attempt the hopeless task of rectifying it when the plain fact is that the draft can only begin to approach "justice" in time of major war, and a peacetime draft has to be absurd and unjust by its very nature. The axe should be applied to the root of the tree, not to its branches. An attempt to pretty up the draft and make it more acceptable may actually prevent that radical reevaluation of the whole system of unilateral national defense which is now in order. We are very close to the moment when the only way to preserve the legitimacy of the national state will be to abandon most of its power. The draft is only a subplot in this much greater drama.

ALTERNATIVES
AND CHANGE

THE SEARCH FOR
A NEW STYLE OF LIFE

RICHARD SHAULL

ONE OF THE MAIN FOCUSES OF CONCERN IN OUR MODERN WORLD IS the search for a new style of human existence. The ideal of the "bourgeois man" has lost much of its power, and the peoples of Asia, Africa, and Latin America have discovered the inauthenticity of a pattern of life imported from and imposed by the West. Existentialism has developed its own models for the new humanity, and the Russians speak constantly of "the new Soviet man." The appearance of beatnik or rebel in many different cultures testifies to the seriousness of the problem. There is a growing awareness that the context in which human life is shaped has changed, and that only if a new style of life soon develops will modern man be able to find meaning in his existence and act responsibly.

The new revolutionary is in an advanced position in this search, because of his sensitivity to what is going on around him and his responsible involvement where the decisive issues about the future of man are being raised. I realize that this cannot be empirically demonstrated; it has more of the character of an affirmation of faith. Many of those who are most active in these movements are quite confused, and are often unable to articulate even what is most central in their own experience. Any attempt to outline the main elements in this new revolutionary posture will probably not offer an adequate description of any one particular group. However, my experience in very diverse revolutionary situations

indicates that a specific style is emerging, the main lines of which
are clear:

1. Much attention has been given to the process of seculariza-
tion as it has developed in the Western world in recent centuries,
and that has now reached a climax, expressed by the intensity of
concern on the part of modern man with existence within history.
The new revolutionary has a heightened awareness of this; at the
same time, his actual participation in the revolutionary struggle
intensifies his concern for man and what happens to him within a
concrete historical process. The change that has occurred in the
attitudes of SNCC (Student Nonviolent Coordinating Committee)
workers in Mississippi is paralleled by the experience of Catholic
and Protestant students in Latin America. Their involvement in
revolutionary movements quickly exposed the irrelevance of the
traditional metaphysical world-view, and forced them to recognize that the old, abstract concepts no longer meant anything to
them. If these absolutes have vanished, then the future is open;
man has the freedom and responsibility to determine his own
destiny. Nation and community provide the context for human
fulfillment; and their transformation, in the light of certain pre-
determined goals, is the important thing.

In this situation, it is only natural that many people whose
former attitude was one of cool detachment now have a new
sense of involvement. Here the experience of the revolutionary
is accentuated by the atmosphere accompanying recent developments in technology. As Marshall McLuhan points out in his book
on *Understanding Media: The Extensions of Man:*

> In an electric age, when our central nervous system is tech-
> nologically extended to involve us in the whole of mankind and
> to incorporate the whole of mankind in us, we necessarily
> participate, in depth, in the consequences of our every action.
> It is no longer possible to adopt the aloof and dissociated role
> of the literate Westerner.[1]

To live responsibly means to take a stand, to put one's life on
the line; to act even though one cannot be entirely sure of the
results of one's action, or guarantee its success.

Along this road of participation, the nature of the intellectual

[1] New York: McGraw-Hill, 1965, p. 4.

effort is redefined. Creative thought about a problem cannot come solely from abstract rational analysis of it. It is only from within the situation, in which the concrete stuff of reality is constantly changing, that we can work out our perspective or engage in serious reflection. The search for truth is a question of finding some patterns of meaning in the richness and variety of elements making up concrete reality. If the experience of former generations and the wider human perspectives are to mean anything, it is not enough to present them in books or university courses; the attempt must also be made to relate them to the present moment. Only thus can academic work be an exciting adventure rather than a meaningless burden.

Decisions must be made from within the situation, and help in decision-making can only come from those who are in some way identified with it. When someone who does not share this involvement takes it upon himself to warn of dangers and to offer advice, he should not be surprised if no one pays attention to him. If he is not willing to pay the price of the struggle, why should anyone take him seriously? Moreover, if he is not free to enter into the situation, and understand the ethical dilemmas as they are raised *there*, in all probability his insights will be of little assistance.

One of the interesting developments here, and for some the most disturbing, is the revolt against authority-structures and the repudiation of anything that smacks of paternalism. This should not surprise us; it is the almost inevitable result of the process we have described. As a metaphysical world-view loses its hold upon us, all patterns of authority that depend upon it are undercut. In a dynamic situation moving toward the future, the past may offer resources for our orientation, but it cannot impose its solutions upon us. When young people or the underprivileged begin to take initiatives to change their society, they are on the road to the discovery of authentic selfhood, and to the type of maturity that will repudiate all traditional paternalistic relationships.

This concentration on historical existence is the source of the strong humanistic emphasis in the new revolutionary movements. Young people of the upper and middle classes have become aware of the tremendous amount of suffering and injustice in the world and of the dehumanizing situation in which so many people are caught. To know the Negro as a human being is to know the dehumanizing conditions under which he lives. To establish contact with the peasants in Latin America is to be shocked by their subhuman existence. To take seriously the new developments in the technological revolution means to see the new possibilities and threats to human life that are latent in it. Thus, a deep moral passion is a major element in the revolutionary posture. Action is urgently needed and it cannot be delayed indefinitely by questions of prudential calculation. To be realistic cannot mean to limit oneself to what now seems politically possible, but to undertake the impossible in an attitude of daring and of trust.

We have no way of knowing whether this humanism will continue to play a central role in these movements in the years ahead. Nor do we know whether our culture can provide the resources needed to sustain such action. But one of the reasons why the new revolutionary movements are so important for our society is that they do incarnate this concern. Although they do not yet have the support of large numbers, they have succeeded in many instances in winning those young people who are most sensitive to the human situation, and who are prepared to do something about it. Thus they provide the context not only for the development of a new style of life, but also for the formation of a dynamic leadership, so badly needed at the present time.

2. Many of those who have taken their participation in historical existence seriously and are concerned about man and his future have been shocked to find that the order under which they live is almost intolerable. Among the colonial peoples of the world as well as the dispossessed in our own country, this has meant a keen awareness of their own exclusion from the enjoyment of the benefits and experiences that our society considers most important. The promise of material well-being is one thing; the way the economic order operates is another. The myths about a democratic society are appealing; the hard realities of political power are something different.

For many belonging to the privileged classes in the more advanced countries, this dissatisfaction has another dimension: the feeling that society, and especially the older generation, has failed to provide the possibility of a rich and meaningful life, yet cannot face the fact of its emptiness. A poignant sign of this malaise is a brief passage from a recent Russian novel, quoted in *The New York Times Magazine*:

"Your life, Victor, was devised by papa and mamma when you were still in the cradle. A star in school, a star in college, graduate student, junior scientific worker, master of arts, senior scientific worker, doctor of philosophy, member of the academy, and then . . . a dead man, respected by all. Never once in your life have you made a truly important decision, never once taken a risk. To hell with it! It's better to be a tramp and fail than to be a boy all your life, carrying out the decisions of others."[2]

What is striking about this statement is that it parallels so closely what many of the leaders of the new student left in our own country are saying.[3] They express the same rebellion against being treated as children indefinitely, the same feeling that the world in which they live "is a complete mess, a world which in their eyes preceding generations have botched up"; the same protest against a society which, possessing such extraordinary potential, "is simply no longer exciting." As Mario Savio put it, we in America are part of an automated, sterilized order, in which all the rules of the game "have been made up, which one cannot really amend" and the " 'futures' and 'careers' for which American students now prepare are for the most part intellectual and moral wastelands."[4]

This deep dissatisfaction with the *status quo* is hardly enough, in itself, to produce revolution. At the most, it could create a new sense of urgency about social change and a desire to move more quickly toward solutions. What makes the present situation so revolutionary among the younger generation is their discovery that when they begin to work for change at any specific point, they are confronted by a total system—a complex of attitudes, institutions, relations, and power alignments—which blocks fundamental changes in society.

Catholic students in Latin America respond to the incredible poverty of the masses by initiating social service programs in the slums or literacy projects in the rural areas. They soon awaken

[2] Quoted by Deming Brown, "The Man from S.M.O.G.," March 20, 1966, p. 88.
[3] See, for example, *Thoughts of the Young Radicals,* a collection of recent articles from the *New Republic*. Also Mitchell Cohen and Dennis Hale, eds., *The New Student Left* (Boston: Beacon Press, 1966).
[4] "An End to History," in Seymour Martin Lipset and Sheldon S. Wolin, eds., *The Berkeley Student Revolt* (New York: Doubleday, 1965), p. 219.

to the fact that all such efforts are ineffective palliatives; only by getting to the roots of the problem can any significant change come about. This leads them to recognize that they confront a feudal-colonial system, and that only a fundamental change in the nature and direction of that system will make it possible to meet these problems. Negro youth in the South take part in a few demonstrations. As they do so, they see that they are up against a whole way of life that must be changed if the Negro is to occupy a new place in society. The poor in our Northern slums who are encouraged to take initiatives in solving their problems understand that they will find no solution for them until basic changes occur in the economic order. And those who try to do something about our official policy toward the poor nations of the world, cannot long ignore the fact that capital *and* labor, the military *and* the State Department are in many ways working together to preserve the present situation, and that it is this order that must be changed in the interests of peace and justice. In other words, participation in movements for social change leads many young people to take a revolutionary position *vis-à-vis* the whole established order. As one Berkeley student stated, their experience exposed "not merely a vast and inept bureaucracy, but a coherent ruling-class structure."

If those in positions of power in our society were prepared to understand this phenomenon, admit the elements of truth in it, and struggle honestly with it, then our situation might not be so explosive. But all too often what stands out is the way all this is hidden by ideologies and myths that make it impossible for us to see what is happening, although facile rationalizations are provided to justify the preservation of the *status quo*. Certain basic presuppositions, it is assumed, should not be challenged, and when any significant group of students dare to do so, they are considered to constitute a threat that must be neutralized as quickly as possible. How else can we explain the facility with which some of our more liberal political leaders spoke of communist influence among those who protested against the acceleration of the war in Vietnam? So long as this situation continues to exist, participation in the struggle toward a better society will in itself constitute a process of radicalization for those so involved, and young social idealists will rapidly be transformed into revolutionaries.

Under these circumstances we should not be surprised if the

new revolutionaries conclude that the established order is incapable of bringing about the changes now demanded, and no longer trust in the traditional means of working for social transformation. In many places, the former dispersion and balance of power, which kept certain structures open, is no longer evident. They see the close identity of interest of the large corporations, labor, and government in the United States, which goes under the name of "consensus politics." In many of the developing nations, the political power traditionally concentrated in the hands of a very small minority—to the almost complete exclusion of other classes—now seems to be even stronger with the support of Western economic and political alignments. And, what is even more frightening, as Carl Oglesby has indicated, is the possibility of a *Pax Russo-Americana*, which would attempt to preserve more or less the present relationships between the rich and poor nations at the moment when fundamental changes are desperately needed.

Within the present order, those new forces which could make the greatest contribution toward social change find that they have been effectively excluded from the exercise of political power: the students in the university, the new leadership in the developing nations, the poor in the "inner cities." New developments in technology in our society have produced a situation in which the average citizen or worker is increasingly excluded from significant participation in the decision-making process within those institutions that determine his destiny. At the same time, technology provides extraordinary resources which can be and are being used to preserve the present system.

Intense awareness of this situation can only have drastic consequences in the orientation of young people and of the dispossessed in our own country and elsewhere in the world. It leads, on their part, to an almost complete breakdown of confidence in the institutions of the society to which they belong. As Mario Savio put it, university students question whether they can be committed to the society into which they were born. Negro young people are no longer interested in imitating whites; the colonial peoples are not attracted to the Western way of life; and the poor in the cities do not want to become middle-class. From a revolutionary perspective, institutions which were once the object of unquestioning loyalty, no longer occupy that position. Those that are open and flexible enough to adjust rapidly to new conditions, may offer an opportunity to work for their renewal from within. To work in the same way for the transformation of those that are more rigid, may simply not be worth the effort. If we want to serve the cause which they represent, then we may be called to make a concerted effort to subvert them from within, or to challenge them from without. Only thus can we hope for their survival and renewal. Otherwise, we can serve the future best by allowing them to die.

3. Many young people who have been led to this conclusion now adopt an attitude of defeat or rebellion; they try to find some way to escape from an impossible world, or at least to steer clear of the adult community. For the revolutionary, however, this situation is the occasion for the gradual shaping of a new vision of a new social order. In this sense, he is the authentic expression, in our time, of that which has been most central in the Western revolutionary tradition. As Hannah Arendt describes it in her book *On Revolution*,[5] this tradition represents the coincidence of the idea of freedom and the experience of a *new beginning*. It is an attempt to liberate man and to build a new order— the *novus ordo saeculorum*—by means of daring human initiative. The most surprising thing is that this has occurred at the very moment when all utopias have been exposed and all visions of a new order debunked. Our dominant myths are those of estrangement, not of hope—*1984, Brave New World,* and so forth; and many of our most outstanding intellectuals reflect a mood of cynicism and despair, or place great emphasis upon realistic calculation of the possible as the only basis for action.

This concern for a new order cannot be understood if it is seen as a return to a former type of superficial optimism and liberalism. The new revolutionary is very much aware of the failings of human nature and of the power of evil in society. He cannot avoid seeing them. But he also is confronted by the fact that modern technology has given man the resources he needs to create the type of society he wants. And the breakdown of all the old authority structures forces upon us the freedom to determine the shape of the future. The question is whether or not we have the will to act in such a way that we can build a new society.

In this context, what is called for is creativity, imagination, plus

5 New York: Viking Press, 1963.

the constant willingness to risk all. Utopia becomes an explosive force in the present, and the only way to act intelligently and responsibly is to repudiate narrow rational calculations about what things can and cannot be done. To allow politics to be determined by what appears to be possible means to limit our possibilities and render the political struggle petty and uninteresting. In the Port Huron Statement of the Students for a Democratic Society, the consequences of this ineffectual posture are recognized and repudiated: "It has been said that our liberal and socialist predecessors were plagued by vision without program; while our generation is plagued by program without vision."

This revolutionary vision of a new society may still be somewhat blurred. Certainly it is conditioned by the specific character of each revolutionary struggle. And yet, the diagram of a new society is gradually taking shape, one in which certain specific elements can already be distinguished.

One of these is the growing conviction that society can and must assume responsibility for ordering its economic life, by determining the goals of economic development and the means by which these can best be reached. It is now clear that the economic realm is not a mysterious order of nature which we must allow to go its own way; it is simply one of those structures that a community can use for the ends it determines. With the resources now at our disposal, the material poverty that still exists is an evil we need no longer tolerate. The wastefulness of the free-enterprise system—even with the restrictions now placed upon it—and its orientation toward production for profit rather than attention to the most basic needs of man and society, represent luxuries we cannot allow much longer without disastrous consequences. Thus, the construction of a new order involves a certain degree of socialism, not in terms of the adoption of the Marxist philosophy, but in the most basic sense of the concept itself: *control of the economic order by society itself*. Rather than wasting any more time on the hackneyed, sterile debate between capitalism and socialism, we must meet today's challenge to create new models for the ordering of economic life by society, and engage in the type of experimentation that will blaze the way toward the future.

A second element in the revolutionary vision of the new society is indicated by the emphasis upon participation of all groups and classes in the life of community and nation, and especially in the process of decision-making by which their future will be determined. Hannah Arendt sees this as the major emphasis which has emerged spontaneously in the revolutions of the West. In her analysis of Jefferson's revolutionary outlook, she points out that it was his conviction "that no one could be called happy without his share in public happiness, that no one could be called free without his experience in public freedom, and that no one could be called either happy or free without participating, and having a share, in public power."[6] The recognition of this fact is almost universal today. Classes, groups, and races that have been marginalized in the past, are now coming to see that they are part of a history in which something has been and is now happening. As they awaken to this reality, they gradually understand that they can have a meaningful life only as they become *participants* in this history, and that their situation can be altered only if they take part in the struggle to change it.

In the developing countries as well as in those more advanced, the limitations of many of our so-called democratic institutions have been exposed. The new democratic society must be one in which young people and students, the dispossessed as well as the ordinary citizen, can have a share in the use of public power within the institutions in which they live their lives: the political structures of local communities and nation, *and* the factory or office in which they work. Many people may be quite happy without this opportunity, and no organization will be able to offer a perfect balance between the demands of order and efficiency and such participation. But our present structures are woefully inadequate, and human imagination and creativity can go a long way toward opening up new possibilities for participation in these spheres.

Third, the new revolutionary is gradually coming to understand that a basic change must occur in the relationship between the rich nations and the poor nations. He can see that almost all our attitudes and approaches are vitiated by paternalism, and that the programs of assistance we have so far developed do not go far enough. Our attempts to work out an adjustment between our national self-interest (as now understood) and the interest of the developing nations are highly ideological, and shot through and

[6] *Ibid.*, pp. 258–259.

through with myths and illusions. On these foundations, international peace and stability will be impossible; and the situation of the poor people of the world will become more desperate each year.

New problems call for new solutions. Our economic resources are such that we can encourage and support new models for development in the less advanced nations, and experiment with new patterns of relationships—economic and political—with them. In the younger nations, leaders are emerging who have been trained in the technology of the West and are free to work for authentic solutions for their national problems. But they are not inclined to accept the peripheral position to which their countries were condemned during the colonial period. They are committed to working for a new international order. They are now being joined in this struggle by a number of people from the West who realize what the nature of our economic and political relationships with the colonial peoples have been. Modern technology has made a new international order possible and necessary, and created a situation of unrest, hope, and interdependence which can be met only as such as an order takes shape.

Ultimately, the revolutionary is searching for a *new form of personal existence*, for himself and for others. The realm of history has become the center of his concern; with this comes an intensification of human self-awareness. Technology and bureaucracy constitute a tremendous threat to man; they also create conditions never before imagined for freedom, human relatedness, and self-realization. It is within our power to meet the basic material needs of everyone; at the same time, full personal existence involves much more than the satisfaction of these needs. This leads to the paradox that the revolutionary who is committed to the struggle to better the economic condition of the poor can also repudiate the materialism of bourgeois society. It is not surprising that both capitalism and communism have lost their attraction. A new generation calls for a vision of personal existence that reaches beyond both these systems.

All this does not mean that anyone has a clear blueprint for the future. But one thing is clear: To build a new society requires a "new beginning." We must develop new ideas and perspectives on life and society by the cultivation of the creative imagination. So often the social thinking of many of us is sterile because we allow ourselves to be boxed in by a logic of our own making. We remain bound by presuppositions that are no longer valid, and are slow at finding alternatives for obsolete institutional patterns. The new revolutionary rightly senses that our historical experience has not exhausted all the possibilities that exist for the ordering of society. He shatters our complacency and challenges us to forge new models and respond to the impact of the future.

New thoughts about society must be accompanied by new politics; a new game calls for new rules. We may not know just what these rules should be, but for the civil rights worker in Mississippi or for those trying to bring about fundamental changes in urban society, it is all too clear that the old rules no longer suffice. To the liberal as well as the conservative, this conclusion comes as a shock. It creates a situation in which many who are working for the same objectives as the revolutionary find it difficult to communicate with him, and almost impossible to participate with him in the same struggle. Those who live by the old rules quickly forget that their way of acting was once an offense to the generation that preceded them. They cannot understand that the profound changes in recent decades may require an even sharper break with earlier ways of doing things.

Because of the nature of his vision and commitment, the revolutionary finds himself caught in an almost unbearable tension. He has been captivated by a vision of a different society; he is also aware that the *status quo* stands in sharp contradiction to it and represents an integrated order with great power. Only a fundamental change in this structure can open the way to even an approximation of the revolutionary's goals, but there is no obvious way by which such change can be brought about.

In the long run, a satisfactory solution of this problem depends upon a basic transformation in the structure of our institutions. Only as they are oriented more toward the future than toward the past, and have built into them the machinery for constant self-renewal, can we hope to have a stable and more human society. The revolutionary struggles of today may be an important factor in bringing about such a change if this generation of revolutionaries has the courage, wisdom, and persistence demanded of it.

Whatever the personal resources required for this effort, it is not likely to succeed unless the revolutionary has a clearly defined strategy by which he can expect to bring about significant changes. Here too he faces a serious dilemma. A previous generation of reformers worked for the renewal of society by serving the given structures according to the established rules. The new revolutionary is convinced that this will not produce results fast enough. But the logical alternative to this strategy seems even less promising. To move out of the Establishment and attack it head-on will also accomplish very little. To attempt to develop new institutions to replace those now existing in each major area of society—a new church or university system, a new labor movement, new political parties—would be an impossible task. Even if such an undertaking were to succeed, there is no guarantee that it would produce institutions any less rigid or more open to the future than those that now exist. Little wonder that so many young people assume an attitude of rebellion; while others who were most radical during their early years give up the struggle, and concentrate on their personal life and careers.

Modern revolutionary experience has developed another strategy, the importance of which we have been slow to apprehend, due partly to its origin and associations. In the face of the massive military power of an established order, *guerrilla warfare* has, under some circumstances, proved effective. But the strategy of guerrilla warfare need not be restricted to its military expression. At this stage in the development of a technological society, *its political equivalent* may offer a valuable instrument for bringing about changes in our major institutions.

The focus here is on the formation of small groups and movements which, whether based inside or outside an institution, force it to accelerate its own renewal. By means of many limited attacks at various points, a small group of people may be able to liberate large institutions for more effective service. This can be accomplished by a variety of techniques: the concentration of effort on limited objectives for a short period; flexibility and freedom of operation, which make it possible to advance to new fronts whenever blocked; the maintenance of initiative and the element of surprise; and the attempt to bring about those relatively small changes that will set a much wider process in motion. Institutions which, as a whole, are unable to act in new ways, can support movements which do have the freedom to do so. One small team, with a certain amount of autonomy and freedom, can transform a large organization; while the renewal of one institution in the center of society can affect others related to it.

Many examples of the effectiveness of this approach could be mentioned. The Freedom Democratic Party may be able to bring about changes in the political order in Mississippi that would be almost impossible within the Democratic Party. One of the reasons for the surprising success of some aspect of the civil rights movement is that it tends to erupt at times and places where least expected, and to move on to new frontiers whenever it is stopped at any one particular point. The participation of the poor and dispossessed in projects of urban renewal may have unforeseen consequences in city life and politics.

Revolutionary movements in this country have developed, almost spontaneously, a variety of guerrilla tactics that have proved more or less effective. What is needed is more systematic reflection on the significance of these developments, and a clearer understanding of the best ways to take advantage of the potential here available for social change. Greater attention should be given, within this framework, to the question of the relationship of those working for radical change to the institutions of the established order. Service in the framework of a particular institution does not necessarily demand complete subservience to it; nor is there any virtue in maintaining one's independence. The question is rather how, in each particular situation, to contribute to the renewal of the institution being served. In some cases, this can best be achieved from within; in others, by working from outside it. At the present time, the essential thing is for those who have adopted a revolutionary position to preserve a certain degree of group identity. Thus they may be able to run the risks of being "in" but not "of" the structures, and live as "exiles" within the society to which they belong.

Those who are accustomed to a more traditional pattern of institutional loyalty will probably look upon the strategy we have just suggested with deep suspicion. But for those committed to revolution, it may be the one ground for hope that powerful interdependent institutions of a technological society can be changed. In fact, we may eventually discover that in this way a dynamic process can be set in motion that will bring about more fundamental transformations than have occurred as a result of previous forms of revolution.

. . . What we have tried to indicate here is that in our world today, a significant number of people are deliberately choosing *a revolutionay style of life,* and that it represents a type of thought and action that stands in sharp contrast to our former ways of reform. For many, this is a disastrous development that threatens our whole social fabric. But it will not go away, and we have no choice but to try to understand it and deal with it.

For many others, the choice of revolution is the only road to authentic and responsible existence. Those who take this step face a quite different task. They confront difficult human problems and must discover how to act responsibly in relation to them. Their own concerns and attitudes, as well as the specific situation in which they live, have been shaped by a particular cultural and spiritual heritage. Today, however, the forms in which that heritage is expressed are so identified with the old order that the revolutionary finds little or no meaning in it. What is even more serious, those institutions that could perform this mediating task —family, school, church, *et al.*—have by and large failed to do so. In some instances they seem to exist in order to preserve the old forms. Where this is not the case, they often reflect the same uncertainty and confusion the younger generation knows so well.

If we are to understand ourselves and live responsibly in this new era, the question of the relationship between the revolutionary posture and our Western cultural heritage and history, must receive our attention. Is this spirit of revolt a foreign growth, which now appears as a virulent cancer threatening to destroy us? Or does it represent the natural flowering of certain ideals and hopes that are at the heart of that tradition?

ALTERNATIVES, SOCIAL CHANGE, AND THE FUTURE

STEVEN E. DEUTSCH

WHILE SOCIAL CHANGE IS SEEN AS AN IMPORTANT PART OF SOCIOLOGY, both conceptually and as an area of inquiry, there really is no clearly identified "sociology of alternatives" or "sociology of the future." It is the intent of the following discussion to examine the necessity for sociological thinking along these lines both in terms of intelligent social theory, and in terms of any sociology which is to emerge as radical. What I propose to discuss is not so much the ideology of social theory, but (1) the existence of some voids in our sociological thinking, and (2) the need for theoretician and layman alike to pursue certain modes of thinking.

ON THINKING ABOUT
THE FUTURE

Basically, I think Arthur Waskow is correct in commenting: "one of the major tasks of liberal and radical thought in America today is to imagine the future in order that the future may be created."[1] Robert Heilbroner calls upon this same principle as an intellectual framework in his book *The Future As History*.[2] That a historian and an economist should come to these conclusions is not surprising; that sociologists should in large measure fail to do so is disturbing. The emergence of the social sciences in the latter part of the last century was due to the shift from backward-

[1] Arthur I. Waskow, "Looking Forward: 1999," *New University Thought*, Spring 1968, p. 34.
[2] Robert Heilbroner, *The Future As History*. New York: Harper & Row, 1960.

looking to forward-looking views of models of society. Sociology was born to examine contemporary and future society and to lend an intellectual framework for shaping the future. Yet, this futuristic orientation is generally absent in empirical sociology.

Waskow argues that ". . . one of the most powerful ways of achieving social change is to imagine in vivid detail a desirable and achievable future, and then build a part of that future in the present."[3] This framework is not common to sociologists, as Winthrop has recently pointed out in an article which cites very few members of the sociological profession.[4] It is clear that on strictly intellectual grounds a sociological foundation for thinking about the future is important. Coupled with a position of social advocacy and planning, it is all the more remarkable that future models and planning are not a central concern among sociologists. Or is it really so surprising?

As was pointed out in an earlier essay, there are a variety of ways of defining radical sociology.[5] But there really is not any one such thing—it is, rather, represented by a perspective. That perspective is not dominant in the field of sociology; it is, therefore, by necessity antiestablishment. Gouldner is fundamentally correct in identifying most sociologists as liberals and hence bolstering the establishment.[6] For a time it was considered radical to attack the functionalists and adopt the "conflict theory" perspective. Yet, as has been pointed out by Lockwood, such a position is intellectually inadequate for developing a social change theory concerned with societal integration, and it also fails to build a future model into its framework.[7] Two points are now suggested. First, few perspectives in sociology are radical, and hence the field neglects the study of the future that Waskow urges. Second, in fact, most sociology is establishment-oriented and hence explicity avoids the future-planning perspective.

[3] Waskow, *op. cit.*, p. 34.
[4] Henry Winthrop, "The Sociologist and the Study of the Future," *The American Sociologist*, 3 (May 1968):136–145.
[5] See, Howard, "Notes On The Radical Perspective in Sociology," p. 1 of this book. Also see Steven E. Deutsch, "The Radical Perspective in Sociology," *Sociological Inquiry* (forthcoming).
[6] Alvin W. Gouldner, "The Sociologist As Partisan: Sociology and the Welfare State," *The American Sociologist*, 3 (May 1968):103–116.
[7] David Lockwood, "Social Integration and System Integration," in G. K. Zollschan and Walter Hirsch (eds.), *Explorations in Social Change*. Boston: Houghton-Mifflin, 1964.

One must look outside of sociology for a serious discussion of the future. Michael Harrington, in his book *The Accidental Century*,[8] argues that men in the past had no vision of the future, that the present is the result of his limited viewpoint, and that the contemporary realities must be met with an eye to future planning. In some ways this is Kenneth Boulding's point as well: the meaning of the twentieth century must be seen in terms of current realities and the absolute necessity for planning into the future.[9] Both of these writers are presenting once again what I see as an inherently sociological perspective, and yet they are not in the mainstream of sociological writing (and neither of them is, in fact, a sociologist). However, there *is* a retinue of thinkers about the future. Some are in various government and foundation commissions, some are RAND-type systems analysts such as Herman Kahn who thinks about the unthinkable and writes about the future.[10] Most such thinking is predicated upon particular traditional assumptions and much is mission-oriented—for example, the studies of the future being done by the behavioral systems planners in the private corporations, particularly those which are involved in government contracts.[11] Thus, future-oriented thinking is not always radical. Can one simultaneously evoke a plea for the importance of sociological thinking about the future, and also note with some implicit alarm that most of the future thinkers and planners are traditionalists whose work is open to question? I believe the answer is affirmative. There is the need for sociologists to think intelligently about the future, to cast models in terms of current planning possibilities, and to initiate their implementation. At the same time I believe that the RAND-type thinking is inadequate, that it is antithetical even to enlightened progessivism, and much less amenable to radicalism. The question of alternatives will help in our thinking about the need for appropriate future perspectives by sociologists.

[8] Michael Harrington, *The Accidental Century*. New York: Macmillan, 1965.
[9] Kenneth Boulding, *The Meaning of the Twentieth Century*. New York: Harper & Row, 1964.
[10] See, for example, Herman Kahn, *Thinking About the Unthinkable*. New York: Horizon Press, 1962. Herman Kahn and Anthony J. Wicher, *The Year 2000*. New York: Macmillan, 1967.
[11] On this broader question see Bob Ross, "Is Planning a Revolution?" *Viet-Report*, Summer 1968, pp. 8–11, 61. (See article in this book, p. 217.)

ON THE MEANING AND
NECESSITY OF ALTERNATIVES

Even the most deterministic theory can allow for some discretionary power, or what might lead to alternatives, though generally within a narrow range. Yet, in the social sciences, most forms of deterministic theory—from geographical determinism, to racial determinism, to rigid pseudo-Freudian theories—have been rejected. We have been operating on a theoretical base which leads in a particular direction, but which potentially allows other formulations and conclusions. The fact that man possesses noninstinctive behavior lets us understand something of learning, adapting, and altering values and behaviors. As Erich Fromm points out, man alone has the possibility of insanity—and, of course, the alternative.[12] We know that man does possess, by definition, a wide range of potential cultures and that alternatives are a priori one of the realities of man's existence.

Having drawn the conclusion above, we still must notice that most social theory rejects alternatives beyond a narrow range. American sociologists are not cultural relativists, and their alleged theories of human behavior are indeed based upon empirical observations of a very small proportion of mankind. But it is not merely a matter of being culture-bound; for we are very much value-bound as well. Most Americans are "freaked-out" by hippie styles, hippie affect, and most important—the real threat—hippie values. While most writing on social change in American society deals with a very moderate range, there are still statements such as the title of Fred Davis's article, "Why All of Us May Be Hippies Someday."[13] Yet, my point is that sociologists have been restrictive in their conceptualizations—which is an intellectual paradox, since it is in the social sciences that we find the evidence for the likelihood for social-cultural-economic-political alternatives.

In a nuclear age, where the capabilities of human extinction are a daily reality, where the overkill quest continues literally and

[12] Erich Fromm, *The Revolution of Hope: Toward a Humanized Technology.* New York: Harper & Row, 1968, Chapter Four. (See article in this book, p. 374.)
[13] Fred Davis, "Why All of Us May Be Hippies Someday," *Trans*-action, December 1967, pp. 10–18.

figuratively to starve the poor and deprived, we come finally to normative imperatives: there *must* be alternatives! But at a less dramatic level, the fact is that in the cumulative knowledge of sociology, we have an abundance of evidence of various kinds which purports to show what alternatives readily exist and how they can become effective with humans. There are alternative theories of learning in the classroom; alternative environments to deter delinquent boys; alternative therapeutic and treatment milieus for working with deviants; alternative patterns of industrial relations; alternative patterns to urban planning; alternative modes of accommodation of all sorts. These, though, all lie within a relatively narrow range. Some proposals are truly more radical. The guaranteed income concept is illustrative. The "new careers for the poor" suggestion is another. These offer alternatives and proposals based on conceptualizations of the future—something lacking in most social change theory.

Another form of dramatic reorientation is that type of alternative theory which challenges the very assumptions underlying the "garrison society" concept—that is, alternatives based on future models of society in which there is a fundamental realignment of priorities, a change in value commitment, and a shift in power. The writings on alternative priorities generally touch on this question, but they are limited in their affront on the basic structures of society: elitism, militarism, and totalitarianism. In an article theorizing about his own conceptualization of the garrison society, Dibble offers an alternative model based upon some dramatic assumptions, such as the literal interpretation of the U. S. Constitution with regard to the tripartite separation of federal governmental powers.[14] Basically, the institutional power arrangement in our society is the prime factor. As the shift from business-economic dominance has moved towards a sharing with the governmental and military institutions,[15] a situation has arisen which offers two very different models of the future. The first is predicated upon a future society with an all-powerful military-industrial-welfare federal state which subordinates other societal institutions into very minor roles. The alternative is the virtual elimination of

[14] Vernon K. Dibble, "Some Alternative Ways to Organize Political Power," *New University Thought*, Spring 1967, pp. 116–133.
[15] On this theme, see C. Wright Mills, *The Power Elite*. New York: Oxford University Press, 1957.

the military institutions, with the welfare-education and state institutions most powerful, while aesthetics, labor, recreation, and the family are institutions of well-developed secondary importance.[16] Put simply, the dominance of the military establishment in the United States today overshadows all other institutions; the alternative directions of the future hinge directly on what happens to what Swomley calls "the military establishment."[17]

WHAT KIND OF ALTERNATIVES?

The discussion thus far has attempted to document the inadequacies of most sociological thinking in terms of culture- and time-boundedness. Specifically, I have suggested that the futuristic models which are essential for radical thinking and a relevant sociology have generally been absent, and that where such thinking has been done at all, it is overwhelmingly done by advocates of conservatism or establishmentarian liberalism. Yet, I have argued that the structural realities of the United States compel alternatives. The evolving garrison, the unstable international relations picture with nuclear proliferation and various forms of international hegemony and imperialism, the explosive domestic picture in America's inner cities—these all necessitate alternatives for the future.

The question, then, becomes one of the kinds of viable alternatives. In all fairness to the history of social theory, we must note that a variety of societal forms have been envisioned—from the positivistic state run by sociological priests as proposed by August Comte, to the Marxian projections of the postcapitalist state. But in the current scene, most theories are projections of mainstream thinking: namely, the relatively uncritical acceptance of contemporary social-political-economic forms, with modest reformist revisions to increase stability, efficacy, and societal harmony. Alternatives which are at considerable variance are sometimes, in my judgment, correctly criticized. For example, with Jack Newfield I too utter, "one cheer for the hippies," for I support the hippie challenge to hypocrisy and the life-affirming stress on individual

---

[16] Delbert Miller and William H. Form, *Industrial Sociology*. New York: Harper & Row, 1964, Chapter 19, "The Future of Industrial Society."
[17] John Swomley, *The Military Establishment*. Boston: Beacon Press, 1964.

creativity.[18] Nevertheless, as Newfield concludes: ". . . Dylan, pot and bright colors are the *hippies'* liberation. The poor, the voteless, the manipulated, the spiritually undernourished—they are oppressed by injustice that is crystallized in institutions. Only a radical political movement can liberate *them*. I want to save the squares too."[19]

The kind of alternatives which are compatible with cogent sociological thinking and a radical perspective will stress a humanistic ethos which will liberate the spirit of the free individual, and which will also structurally alter the social-economic-political institutions to guarantee the absence of oppression, the potential for full expression, and the very possibility of continued human existence with an appreciable qualitative betterment in the conditions of life for the masses of people.

The hints for such alternatives come to us from a variety of sources. The Yugoslav experiment suggests that the structural arrangements which maximize citizen participation in all phases of life do indeed generate democratic political environments.[20] Participatory democracy can be seen as a theoretical viewpoint,[21] or as a substantive basis of social organization.[22] The proposals for the guaranteed annual income[23] and the new careers for the poor[24] all indicate directions toward viable alternatives. They are all predicated on the rejection of our contemporary international and domestic policy norms: nothing succeeds like failure! We can no longer endure complacent advocacy of irrelevance and irresponsibility. For some this requires experimentation with alter-

[18] Jack Newfield, "One Cheer for the Hippies," *The Nation*, June 26, 1967, pp. 309–310.
[19] *Ibid.*, p. 310.
[20] Sidney Lens, "Yugoslavia's New Communism," *Progressive*, December 1968, pp. 33–37.
[21] Richard Flacks, "On the Uses of Participatory Democracy," *Dissent*, November–December 1966, pp. 701–708. (See article in this book, p. 121.)
[22] David S. Riddell, "Social Self-Government: The Background of Theory and Practice in Yugoslav Socialism," *British Journal of Sociology*, 19 (March 1968), pp. 47–75. (See article in this book, p. 130.) Also see Erich Fromm (ed.), *Socialist Humanism*. Garden City, New York: Doubleday, 1965.
[23] Robert Theobald, *Free Men and Free Markets*. New York: Clarkson Potter, 1963.
[24] Arthur Pearl, "New Careers for the Poor: One Solution to the Problems of Poverty," in Robert Theobald (ed.), *Social Policies for the 1970's*. Garden City, New York: Doubleday, 1968. (See article in this book, p. 348.)

native school systems and learning environments.[25] For others this compels acts of civil disobedience and advocacy.[26] And for still others, the alternatives mean the fundamental realignment of spiritual and social values.[27] Among the varying proposed forms of thinking about the future are some which call for a re-raking of priorities or a shift in the emphasis among a menu of choices already given;[28] others question the very assumptions underlying the inclusion of some items in the cafeteria which is offered.[29]

CONCLUSION

The basic point is that the meaning of the present century is that for the first time in his history, a capability is within man's grasp.[30] Man has the technological skills to adapt incredible energy from his environment, to translate this energy into operable forms of production mechanisms, to harness it in concert with computers, and thus to free himself from the burdensome tasks which have dominated his history. Furthermore, this provides the possibility of altered interpersonal, intergroup, and international relations. Yet, as Boulding points out, there still exist the severe traps represented by war, the population explosion, and international poverty.[31] The current period in man's history is blessed by unique capacity for solving human dilemmas and providing abundance, security, and free expression of man's full needs; at the same time,

[25] See for example, Robert Rosenthal and Lenore Jacobson, *Pygmalion in the Classroom: Teacher Expectation and Pupils' Intellectual Development.* New York: Holt, Rinehart & Winston, 1968. John Holt, "Education for the Future," in Robert Theobald (ed.), *Social Policies for the 1970's, op. cit.*

[26] Paul Goodman, "Reflections on Civil Disobedience," *Liberation*, July–August, 1968, pp. 11–15. (See article in this book, p. 154.)

[27] Erich Fromm, *The Revolution of Hope: Toward a Humanized Technology.* New York: Harper & Row, 1968. (See article in this book, p. 374.) Carl Ogelsby and Richard Shaull, *Containment and Change.* New York: Macmillan, 1967, Part Two, "Revolution: Heritage and Contemporary Option." (See article by Schaull in this book, p. 518.)

[28] See J. William Fulbright, "For a New Order of Priorities At Home and Abroad," *Playboy*, July 1968, pp. 110–112, 116, 152–157 (p. 542 in this book). Also see the special issue of *New University Thought* (Spring 1967) on the theme, "Decisions for America: Priorities and Consequences." Finally there is the short book by Eugene J. McCarthy, *First Things First: New Priorities for America.* New York: New American Library, 1968.

[29] For example, see Waskow, *op. cit.;* Pearl, *op. cit.;* Goodman, *op. cit.*

[30] This theme is borrowed from Boulding, *op. cit.*

[31] *Ibid.*

this period of history is damned or at least threatened with extinction of the species. As Robert Theobald points out quite brilliantly, this is truly a unique period for man.[32] Some old assumptions must be declared invalid—such as the idea of war as an instrument of solving disputes. Other assumptions are nearly as suspect for their irrelevance—such as the concept of the nation-state, a critical concept of the past century, but a questionable one for the next century. Other assumptions are challenged on the basis of a morality altered by reality: poverty is not the necessary state of large masses of mankind.

What is so very striking in this brief discussion is the sparseness of sociologists, to whom one would logically turn for insights into the problem or for models for consideration. This essay is designed not only to make the points concerning the necessity for futuristic thinking and alternatives, but also to expose the failure of traditional sociology to accept these intellectual and practical challenges. Part of the task of a radical sociology is to meet such tasks with vitality and enthusiasm.

[32] For an excellent provocative discussion of this total series of questions, see Robert Theobald, *An Alternative Future for America*. Chicago: Swallow Press, 1968.

FOR A NEW ORDER
OF PRIORITIES
AT HOME AND ABROAD

J. WILLIAM FULBRIGHT

AS THE PRESIDENTIAL CAMPAIGN PROGRESSES AND THE POSSIBILITY
arises of major changes in foreign and domestic policies, it seems
appropriate to review some of the major events of the past year
or so and their effects on the American people. I think we will all
agree that it has not been a happy time for the Executive, for Congress or for our country. The divisions among us are deep and
the problems that beset us seem intractable. The center of our
troubles is the war in Vietnam—a war that has isolated the United
States from its friends abroad, disrupted our domestic affairs and
divided the American people as no other issue of the twentieth
century has divided them. (There has arisen, as of this writing,
hope that peace negotiations will soon begin in Paris. At this early
stage it is difficult—and perhaps unwise—to comment on their
prospects, except to express the wish that they will, indeed, occur
and will bring the war to an early end.)

• • •

The St. Louis Cardinals are a superior baseball team, but in the
1967 World Series, most Americans outside of the St. Louis area
itself rooted for the Boston Red Sox. Why was that? Was it because the Red Sox were better sports, or better players, or better
looking? Certainly not; the Cardinals matched their rivals on all
these counts and in the end they showed themselves to be the

stronger team. Why, then, couldn't they match the Red Sox in popular affection? Because they had committed one of the worst crimes in Christendom—the crime of being top dog. Top dogs are not very popular, as a rule, just because there are so few of them. The underdogs are a vast majority in the world, and when, now and then, one of their multitude soars to the top in a sport or in politics or in some other highly visible pursuit, millions of other underdogs take heart, catching as by electric impulse the magic message: That could be *me* up there, at bat or on the pitcher's mound or in the high councils of power.

Our heritage reinforces our instincts; most of us have been raised on David and Goliath; and by the time we reach adulthood, we have been thoroughly indoctrinated—one might even say brainwashed—in the belief that every time a little guy knocks down a big guy, it is reason for rejoicing. Few people stop to think about the merits of the case, about the possibility that the top dog may have reached the heights by diligent and honest labor or that his cause may be virtuous and true or—unthinkable thought—that the little guy might just possibly be venal, self-seeking, or otherwise unworthy.

That is what the Cardinals were up against. Like the Yankees before them, they had committed the crime of succeeding too well. They were Goliath; the Red Sox were David. They were the wicked stepmother; the Red Sox were Cinderella. The Cardinals were King John, the wicked queen and General Cornwallis; the Red Sox were Robin Hood, Snow White and George Washington. Their success was won by skill and courage and luck against overwhelming odds. They won in the only way that millions of underdogs could ever imagine themselves winning; and when in the end they lost, as had been probable right from the start, it seemed, nonetheless, as though something impossible had happened. Goliath had beaten David; the prince had eluded Cinderella; and a million hearts were broken.

The United States is not the St. Louis Cardinals; the Viet Cong are not the Red Sox; and the war, God knows, is not a game. But there is something pertinent in the metaphor.

America is top dog in the world and, although we may be convinced that we are *good* top dogs, most people around the world are convinced that there is no such thing. Because we are rich, we are perceived as voracious; because we are successful, we are perceived as arrogant; because we are strong, we are perceived as overbearing. These perceptions may be distorted and exaggerated, but they are not entirely false. Power does breed arrogance and it has bred enough in us to give some substance to the natural prejudices against us. Much to our puzzlement, people all over the world seem to discount our good intentions and to seize upon our hypocrisies, failures and transgressions. They do this not because we are Americans but because we are top dogs and they fear our power. They are frightened by some of the ways in which we have used our power; they are frightened by the ways in which we might use it; and most of all, I suspect, they are frightened by the knowledge of their own inability to withstand our power, should it ever be turned upon them. They are, so to speak, tenants in the world at our sufferance, and no amount of good will on our part can ever wholly dispel the anxiety bred by the feeling of helplessness.

What do these feelings about American power have to do with the war in Vietnam? They go far, I think, to explain why our war policy commands so little support in the world. Anxiety about America's great power predisposes people, even against their better judgment, to take satisfaction in our frustrations and our setbacks. The French, for example, who well understand the importance to themselves of America's weight in the world balance of power, nevertheless seem to derive some satisfaction from seeing more than half a million Americans fought to a stalemate —or worse—by a ragtag army of Asian guerrillas. Seeing the Americans cut down to size like that is balm for the wounds of Dien Bien Phu, salve for the pride that was lost in the days of the Marshall Plan, when France survived on American generosity. If our military failures in Vietnam have this effect on the French, as I believe they do, think what they must mean to the real underdogs of the world, to the hundreds of millions of Asians, Africans and Latin Americans who can easily identify themselves with the Viet Cong guerrillas but could never see themselves in the role of the lordly Americans. There may even be people in our own country who feel some sneaking respect for a resourceful enemy, an enemy who, in a curious and purely emotional way, may even remind them of the ragtag American revolutionaries who humbled the mighty British Empire almost 200 years ago.

Such attitudes, it will be argued, are irrational and unfair; and so, in large measure, they are. People, it will be said, should be rational and should act on their interests, not their emotions; and so, indeed, they should. But they don't. I might be able to think up some good reasons why elephants should fly, but it would not be rewarding; elephants cannot fly and there is nothing to be done about it. So it is with men; they ought to be cool and rational and detached, but they are not. We are, to be sure, endowed with a certain capacity for reason, but it is not nearly great enough to dispel the human legacy of instinct and emotion. The most we can hope to do with our fragile tool of reason is to identify, restrain and make allowance for the feelings and instincts that shape so much of our lives.

That brings me to one of the most important of the many flaws in our war policy in Vietnam—its failure to take account of people's feelings and instincts, especially those pertaining to top dogs and underdogs. American policy asks people to believe things that they are deeply reluctant to believe. It asks them to believe that the world's most powerful nation is not only strong but motivated by deeply benevolent and altruistic instincts, unrelated even to national interests. Even if that were true—and on occasion it probably has been true—nobody would believe it, because nobody would *want* to believe it.

This is an extremely serious problem for the United States, because the success of its stated policy in Vietnam ultimately depends less on winning for its own sake than on persuading the world that American aims are what American policy makers say they are. That is the case because the war, as often explained by the Secretary of State and by others in the Administration, is said to be an *exemplary* war, one that will prove to the Communists, especially China, that wars of liberation cannot succeed, and prove to the rest of the world that America will not fail to honor its commitments, to whomever made and for whatever purpose. It is a war—so say our policy makers—to inspire confidence in the United States and to prove certain points; and once these points are proved, it is said, we will withdraw, within six months of a peace settlement, said President Johnson at Manila.

These being our stated aims, the success of our policy depends in great part upon whether people believe that our objectives are what we say they are. You cannot make an object lesson out of a war if people do not believe that is what you are trying to do; you cannot prove a point if people do not believe that you mean what you say.

Setting aside for a moment the question of whether American purposes are really what American policy makers say they are, it is apparent that much or most of the world believes that they are not. I do not think that very many people, least of all the Viet Cong and the North Vietnamese, believe that we plan to withdraw from Vietnam as soon as arrangements for self-determination are made, arrangements that could result in the establishment of a Communist government. I do not think that very many people, least of all the Asians, Africans and Latin Americans for whose benefit the example is supposedly being set, really believe that, with virtually no help from the presumed beneficiaries, America has sacrificed over 21,700 lives and spent 100 billion dollars—thus far—simply to set their minds at rest about America's determination to come to their assistance should they ever be threatened with Communist attack or insurrection. Insofar as they do not believe us, our war policy is a failure, neither setting the intended example nor proving the stated point.

Prejudice is not the only basis of world-wide skepticism about American intentions. The war, after all, is not going well and, even if our sincerity were granted, our success could not be. Far from proving that wars of national liberation cannot succeed, all that we have proved so far is that, even with an army of more than half a million men and expenditures of 30 billion dollars a year, we are unable to suppress this particular war of national liberation. Far from demonstrating America's willingness and ability to save beleaguered governments from Communist insurgencies, all that we are demonstrating in Vietnam is America's willingness and ability to use its B-52s, its napalm and all the other ingenious weapons of "counterinsurgency" to turn a small country into a charnel house. Far from inspiring confidence in and support for the United States, the war has so isolated us that, despite all our alliances and the tens of billions we have spent on foreign aid, we cannot, according to the Administration, get 9 out of 15 votes to put the Vietnam issue on the agenda of the United Nations Security Council. Far from demonstrating America's readiness to discharge all of its prodigal commitments around the world, the extravagance and cost of Vietnam are more likely to suggest to the world that the American people will be hesitant, indeed, before permitting their Government to plunge into another such costly adventure.

There are already signs of such a reaction. In the days before the recent war in the Middle East, for example, strong and virtually unanimous sentiment was expressed in the Senate against any unilateral American military involvement in that part of the world. If America ever does withdraw into the neoisolationism of which our policy makers are so fearful, it will not be because of the influence of those of us who advocate *selectivity* in foreign commitments; it will be in reaction to the heedless interventionism of Vietnam.

Yet another reason why some of our stated purposes are disbelieved is the simple fact of their implausibility and inconsistency. It is implausible to contend that we are defending a valiant democracy when everyone knows that the Saigon generals can inspire neither the loyalty of their people nor the fighting spirit of their sizable army. It is implausible to contend that an act of international aggression has taken place when it is clear that the war began as a civil war within one half of a divided country abetted by the other half and did not become an international war until the United States intervened. It is implausible to argue, as the distinguished Minority Leader, Senator Dirksen, has argued, that, but for the war in Vietnam, the West Coast of the United States would be exposed to attack, when the United States Navy and Air Force are virtually unchallenged over the entire Pacific Ocean.

Finally, it is implausible and inconsistent, on the one hand, to maintain that the United States seeks only to assure self-determination for the South Vietnamese people and will withdraw within six months of a peace settlement and, on the other hand, to assert that our real purpose is to protect a billion Asians from the power of a billion Chinese armed with nuclear weapons. If the latter is the American purpose, if the real enemy is not the Vietnamese guerrilla army but "Asian communism with its headquarters in Peking," then we are likely to have to remain in Vietnam indefinitely, all the more so because most of the presumed beneficiaries of our intervention, including the three greatest nations among them—India, Japan and Indonesia—show not the slightest inclination to take over even a small part of the military burden.

So implausible and so inconsistent are the statements about one principle or another that is supposed to be being vindicated in Vietnam that one comes to feel that what our policy makers have really been trying to vindicate is their own judgment in having led us into this war in the first place. Even former ambassador Edwin O. Reischauer, an Asian expert and a temperate man who, until recently, supported the Administration's policy because he saw little prospect of a negotiated peace, nonetheless expressed in a magazine article fundamental disagreement with the Administration's rationale for the war. "It seems highly probable," wrote Reischauer, "that Ho's Communist-dominated regime, if it had been allowed by us to take over all Vietnam at the end of the war, would have moved to a position with relation to China not unlike that of Tito's Yugoslavia toward the Soviet Union. . . . Wars sometimes seem justified by their end results, but this justification hardly applies to the Vietnam war. Even the most extravagantly optimistic outcome would still leave far greater losses than gains." It is doubtful, he added, "that even a favorable outcome to the war would do much to deter Communist subversion in other less developed countries. Instead of being discouraged by our ultimate victory in Vietnam, would-be revolutionaries might be encouraged by the obvious pain of the war to the United States and the clear reluctance of the American people to get involved in further wars of this type. . . . I have no doubt that if those who determined American policy toward Vietnam had foreseen even dimly the costs and futilities of the war, they would have made different choices at several times in the past and thus avoided the present situation, with only trifling costs, if any, to American interests."

Despite the Tet offensive, General Creighton Abrams and other Administration spokesmen continue to make statements about military success. It is, of course, possible that this time they may be right, that Ho Chi Minh will surrender or die or the Viet Cong will collapse or just fade into the jungle. But even in that highly unlikely event, it should not be supposed that the American commitment would be at an end; we would still be the sole military and economic support of a weak Saigon regime, at a cost of perhaps 10 or 15 billion dollars a year. This, of course, would assume —as we cannot safely assume—that the Chinese and the Russians would do nothing to prevent the collapse of the Viet Cong or of North Vietnam. But even if these most optimistic prospects should be realized, grateful for peace though we would be, we would still have little to be proud of and a great deal to regret. We would still have fought an immoral and unnecessary war; we would still have passed up opportunities that, if taken when they arose, would have spared us and spared the Vietnamese the present ordeal, and done so, as Ambassador Reischauer says, "with only trifling costs, if any, to American interests."

For all these reasons, much of the world and an increasing number of our own people are deeply skeptical about the American purpose in Vietnam. Underlying the skepticism is deep disappointment, a feeling that America has betrayed its own promise —the promise of Roosevelt and the United Nations and of Wilson and the League of Nations, but, most of all, the promise of the American Revolution, of free men building a society that would be an example for the world. Now the world sees that heritage being betrayed; it sees a nation that seemed to represent something new and hopeful reverting instead to the vanity of past empires, each of which struggled for supremacy, each of which won and held it for a while, each of which finally faded or fell into historical oblivion.

We are, in this respect, a disappointment to the world: but, far more important than that, we are a disappointment to ourselves. It is here at home that the traditional values were formed, here at home that the American promise was born, and it is here at home—in our schools and churches, in our cities and on our farms, in the hearts and minds of our people and their chosen leaders—that the American promise will finally be betrayed or resurrected.

•   •   •

While young dissenters plead for resurrection of the American promise, their elders continue to subvert it. As if it were something to be very proud of, it was announced not long ago that the war in Vietnam had created a million new jobs in the United States. Our country is becoming conditioned to permanent conflict. More and more, our economy, our Government and our universities are adapting themselves to the requirements of continuing war—total war, limited war and cold war. The struggle against militarism into which we were drawn 27 years ago has become permanent, and for the sake of conducting it, we are making ourselves into a militarized society.

I do not think the military-industrial complex is the conspiratorial invention of a band of "merchants of death." One almost wishes that it were, because conspiracies can be exposed and dealt with. But the components of the new American militarism are too diverse, independent and complex for it to be the product of a centrally directed conspiracy. It is, rather, the inevitable result of the creation of a huge, permanent military establishment, whose needs have given rise to a vast private defense industry tied to the Armed Forces by a natural bond of common interest. As the largest producers of goods and services in the United States, the industries and businesses that fill military orders will in the coming fiscal year pour some 45 billion dollars into over 5000 cities and towns where over 8,000,000 Americans, counting members of the Armed Forces, comprising ten percent of the labor force, will earn their living from defense spending. Together, all these industries and employees, drawing their income from the 76-billion-dollar defense budget, form a giant concentration of socialism in our otherwise free-enterprise economy.

Unplanned though it was, this complex has become a major political force. It is the result rather than the cause of American military involvements around the world; but, composed as it is of a vast number of citizens—not tycoons or merchants of death but ordinary good American citizens—whose livelihood depends on defense production, the military-industrial complex has become an indirect force for the perpetuation of our global military commitments. This is not because anyone favors war but because every one of us has a natural and proper desire to preserve the sources of his livelihood. For the defense worker, this means preserving or obtaining some local factory or installation and obtaining new defense orders; for the politician, it means preserving the good will of his constituents by helping them get what they want. Every time a new program, such as Mr. McNamara's five-billion-dollar "thin" anti-ballistic-missile system, is introduced, a new constituency is created—a constituency that will strive mightily to protect the new program and, in the case of the ABM, turn the thin system into a "thick" one. The constituency-building process is further advanced by the perspicacity of defense officials and contractors in locating installations and plants in the districts of key Members of Congress.

In this natural way, generals, industrialists, businessmen, workers and politicians have joined together in a military-industrial complex—a complex that, for all the inadvertency of its creation and the innocent intentions of its participants, has nonetheless become a powerful new force for the perpetuation of foreign military commitments, for the introduction and expansion of expensive weapons systems and, as a result, for the militarization of large segments of our national life. Most interest groups are counterbalanced by other interest groups, but the defense complex is so much larger than any other that there is no effective counterweight to it except concern as to its impact on the part of some of our citizens and a few of our leaders.

The universities might have formed an effective counterweight to the military-industrial complex by strengthening their emphasis on the traditional values of our democracy; but many of our leading universities have instead joined the monolith, adding greatly to its power and influence. Disappointing though it is, the adherence of the professors is not greatly surprising. No less than businessmen, workers and politicians, professors enjoy money and influence. Having traditionally been deprived of both, they have welcomed the contracts and consultantships offered by the military establishment. The great majority of American professors are still teaching students and engaging in scholarly research; but some of the most famous of our academicians have set such activities aside in order to serve their Government, especially those parts of the Government that are primarily concerned with war.

The bonds between the Government and the universities are no more the result of a conspiracy than are those between Government and business. They are an arrangement of convenience, providing the Government with politically usable knowledge and the universities with badly needed funds. Most of these funds go to large institutions that need them less than some smaller and less well known ones; but they do, on the whole, make a contribution to higher learning, a contribution that, however, is purchased at a high price.

That price is the surrender of independence, the neglect of teaching and the distortion of scholarship. A university that has become accustomed to the inflow of Government-contract funds is likely to emphasize activities that will attract those funds. These, unfortunately, do not include teaching undergraduates and the kind of scholarship that, though it may contribute to the sum of human knowledge and to man's understanding of himself, is not salable to the Defense Department or to the CIA. As Clark Kerr, former president of the University of California, expressed it in *The Uses of the University:*

> The real problem is not one of Federal control but of Federal influence. A Federal agency offers a project. A university need not accept but, as a practical matter, it usually does. . . . Out of this reality have followed many of the consequences of Federal aid for the universities; and they have been substantial. That they are subtle, slowly cumulative and gentlemanly makes them all the more potent.

From what one hears, the process of acquiring Government contracts is not always passive and gentlemanly. "One of the dismal sights in American higher education," writes Robert M. Rosenzweig, associate dean of the Stanford University graduate division,

> is that of administrators scrambling for contracts for work that does not emerge from the research or teaching interests of their faculty. The result of this unseemly enterprise is bound to be a faculty coerced or seduced into secondary lines of interest, or a frantic effort to secure nonfaculty personnel to meet the contractual obligations. Among the most puzzling aspects of such arrangements is the fact that Government agencies have permitted and even encouraged them. Not only are they harmful to the universities—which is not, of course, the Government's prime concern—but they ensure that the Government will not get what it is presumably buying; namely, the intellectual and technical resources of the academic community. It is simply a bad bargain all the way around.

Commenting on these tendencies, a special report on Government, the universities and international affairs, prepared for the United States Advisory Commission on International Educational and Cultural Affairs, points out that "the eagerness of university administrations to undertake stylized, Government-financed projects has caused a decline in self-generated commitments to scholarly pursuits, has produced baneful effects on the academic mission of our universities and has, in addition, brought forward some bitter complaints from the disappointed clients. . . ."

Among the baneful effects of the Government-university contract system, the most damaging and corrupting are the neglect of the university's most important purpose, which is the education of its students, and the taking into the Government camp of scholars, especially those in the social sciences, who ought to be acting as responsible and independent critics of their Government's policies. The corrupting process is a subtle one: No one needs to censor, threaten or give orders to contract scholars; without a word of warning or advice being uttered, it is simply understood that lucrative contracts are awarded not to those who question their Government's policies but to those who provide the Government with the tools and techniques it desires. The effect, in the words of the report to the Advisory Commission on International Education, is "to suggest the possibility to a world—never adverse to prejudice—that academic honesty is no less marketable than a box of detergent on the grocery shelf."

The formation of a military-industrial complex, for all its baneful consequences, is the result of great numbers of people engaging in more or less normal commercial activities. The adherence of the universities, though no more the result of a plan or conspiracy, nonetheless involves something else; the neglect and, if carried far enough, the betrayal of the university's fundamental reason for existence, which is the advancement of man's search for truth and happiness. It is for this purpose, and this purpose alone, that universities receive—and should receive—the community's support in the form of grants, loans and tax exemptions. When the university turns away from its central purpose and makes itself an appendage to the Government, concerning itself with techniques rather than purposes, with expedients rather than ideals, dispensing conventional orthodoxy rather than new ideas, it is not only failing to meet its responsibilities to its students; it is betraying a public trust.

This betrayal is most keenly felt by the students, partly because it is they who are being denied the services of those who ought to be their teachers, they to whom knowledge is being dispensed wholesale in cavernous lecture halls, they who must wait weeks for brief audiences with eminences whose time is taken up by travel and research connected with Government contracts. For all these reasons, the students feel themselves betrayed, but it is doubtful that any of these is the basic cause of the angry rebellions that have broken out on so many campuses.

It seems more likely that the basic cause of the great trouble in our universities is the students' discovery of corruption in the one place, besides perhaps the churches, that might have been supposed to be immune from the corruptions of our age. Having seen their country's traditional values degraded in the effort to attribute moral purpose to an immoral war, having seen their country's leaders caught in inconsistencies that are politely referred to as a "credibility gap," they now see their universities— the last citadels of moral and intellectual integrity—lending themselves to ulterior and expedient ends and betraying their own fundamental purpose, which, in James Bryce's words, is to "reflect the spirit of the times without yielding to it."

* * *

Students are not the only angry people in America nor the only people with cause for anger. There is also the anger of the American poor, black and white, rural and urban. These are the dispossessed children of the affluent society, the 30,000,000 Americans whose hopes were briefly raised by the proclamation of a "war on poverty," only to be sacrificed to the supervening requirements of the war on Asian communism or, more exactly, to the Executive preoccupation and the Congressional parsimony induced by that war.

In our preoccupation with foreign wars and crises, we have scarcely noticed the revolution wrought by undirected change here at home. Since World War II, our population has grown by more than 59,000,000; a mass migration from country to city has crowded over 70 percent of our population onto scarcely more than one percent of our land; vast numbers of rural Negroes from the South have filled the slums of Northern cities while affluent white families have fled to shapeless new suburbs, leaving the cities physically deteriorating and financially destitute and creating a new and socially destructive form of racial isolation combined with degrading poverty. Poverty, which is a tragedy in a poor country, blights our affluent society with something more than tragedy; being unnecessary, it is deeply immoral as well.

Distinct though it is in cause and character, the Negro rebellion is also part of the broader crisis of American poverty, and it is unlikely that social justice for Negroes can be won except as part of a broad program of education, housing and employment for all of our poor, for all of the great "under class," of whom Negroes comprise no more than one fourth or one third. It is essential that the problem of poverty be dealt with as a whole, not only because the material needs of the white and colored poor are the same—better schools, better homes and better job opportunities—but because alleviating poverty in general is also the best way to alleviate racial hostility. It is not the affluent and educated who primarily account for the "backlash" but the poorer white people, who perceive in the Negro rights movement a threat to their jobs and homes and—probably more important—a threat to their own meager sense of social status.

There is nothing edifying about poverty. It is morally as well as physically degrading. It does not make men brothers. It sets them against one another in competition for jobs and homes and status. It leaves its mark on a man and its mark is not pretty. Poverty constricts and distorts, condemning its victims to an endless, anxious struggle for physical necessities. That struggle, in turn, robs a man of his distinctly human capacities—the capacity to think and create, the capacity to seek and savor the meaning of things, the capacity to feel sympathy and friendliness for his fellow man.

If we are to overcome poverty and its evil byproducts, we shall have to deal with them as human rather than as racial or regional problems. For practical as well as moral reasons, we shall have to have compassion for those who are a little above the bottom as well as for those who are at the bottom. We shall have to have some understanding of the white tenant farmer as well as the Negro farm laborer, of the urban white immigrant workingman as well as the Negro slum dweller. It would even benefit us to acquire some understanding—not approval, just understanding—of each other's group and regional prejudices. If the racial crisis of recent years has proved anything, it is that none of us, Northerner or Southerner, has much to be proud of, that our failures have been national failures, that our problems are problems of a whole society, and so as well must be their solutions.

All these problems—of poverty and race, jobs and schools—have come to focus in the great cities, which, physically, mentally and aesthetically, are rapidly becoming unfit for human habitation. As now taking shape, the cities and suburbs are the product of technology run rampant, without effective political direction, without regard to social and long-term economic cost. They have been given their appearance by private developers, builders and entrepreneurs, seeking, as they will, their own short-term profit. Lakes and rivers are polluted and the air is filled with the fumes of the millions of cars that choke the roads. Recreation facilities and places of green and quiet are pitifully inadequate and there is no escape from crowds and noise, both of which are damaging to mental health. At the heart of the problem is the absence of sufficient funds and political authority strong enough to control the anarchy of private interest and to act for the benefit of the community. Despite the efforts of some dedicated mayors and students of urban problems, the tide of deterioration is not being withstood and the cities are sliding deeper into disorganization and demoralization.

The larger cities have grown beyond human scale and organizing capacity. No matter what is done to rehabilitate New York and Chicago, they will never be places of green and quiet and serenity, nor is there much chance that these can even be made tolerably accessible to the millions who spend their lives enclosed in concrete and steel. Ugly and inhuman though they are, the great urban complexes remain, nonetheless, a magnet for Negroes from the South and whites from Appalachia. Crowding the fetid slums and taxing public services, they come in search of jobs and opportunity, only to find that the jobs that are available require skills that they lack and have little prospect of acquiring.

One wonders whether this urban migration is irreversible, whether it may not be possible to create economic opportunities in the small towns and cities, where there are space and land and fresh air, where building costs are moderate and people can still live in some harmony with natural surroundings. The technology of modern agriculture may inevitably continue to reduce farm employment, but we have scarcely begun to consider the possibilities of industrial decentralization—of subsidies, tax incentives and other means—to make it possible for people to earn a living in the still-human environments of small-town America.

A decent life in a small town is not only very much better than slum life in a big city; it is probably cheaper, too. The Secretary of Agriculture has suggested that it would be better to subsidize a rural family with $1000 a year for 20 years than to house them in a cramped urban "dwelling unfit" at a cost of $20,000. In New York or Chicago, $2500 a year of welfare money will sustain a family in destitution; in the beautiful Ozark country of Arkansas, it is enough for a decent life.

Aggravating the material ills is the impersonalization of life in a crowded urban America. Increasingly, we find wherever we go —in shops and banks and the places where we work—that our names and addresses no longer identify us; the IBM machines require numbers: zip codes, account numbers and order numbers. Our *relevant* identity in a computerized economy is statistical rather than personal. Business machines provide standard information and standard services and there are no *people* to provide particular information or services for our particular needs. The governing concept, invented, I believe, in the Pentagon, is "cost effectiveness," which refers not to the relationship of cost to human need or satisfaction but to the relationship of cost to the computerized system. Technology has ceased to be an instrument of human ends; it has become an end in itself, unregulated by political or philosophical purpose. The toll that all this takes on the human mind can only be guessed at, but it must surely be enormous, because human needs are different from the needs of the system to which they are being subordinated. Someday the human requirements may be computerized, too, but they have not, thank God, been computerized yet.

The cost of rehabilitating America will be enormous beyond anything we have even been willing to think about. When Mayor Lindsay said that aside from Federal, state and city funds, it would cost an additional 50 billion dollars over ten years to make New York a fit place to live in, his statement was dismissed as fanciful, although 50 billion dollars is less than we spend in two years in Vietnam. The Swedish sociologist Gunnar Myrdal has ventured the guess that it will cost trillions of dollars to rehabilitate our slums and their inhabitants. "[The] common idea that America is an immensely rich and affluent country," he says, "is very much an exaggeration. American affluence is heavily mortgaged. America carries a tremendous burden of debt to its poor people. That this debt must be paid is not only a wish of the do-gooders. Not paying it implies the risk for the social order and for democracy as we have known it."

Before we can even begin to think of what needs to be done

and how to do it, we have got to re-evaluate our national priorities. We have got to weigh the costs and benefits of going to the moon against the costs and benefits of rehabilitating our cities. We have got to weigh the costs and benefits of the supersonic transport, which will propel a few business executives across the Atlantic in two or three hours, against the costs and benefits of slum clearance and school construction, which would create opportunity for millions of our deprived under class. We have got to weigh the benefits and consider the awesome disparity of the 935.4 billion dollars we have spent on military power since World War II against the 114.9 billion dollars we have spent, out of our regular national budget, on education, health, welfare, housing and community development.

Defining our priorities is more a matter of moral accounting than of cost accounting. The latter may help us determine what we are able to pay for, but it cannot help us decide what we want and what we need and what we are willing to pay for. It cannot help the five sixths of us who are affluent to decide whether we are willing to pay for programs that will create opportunity for the one sixth who are poor; that is a matter of moral accounting. It cannot help us decide whether beating the Russians to the moon is more important to us than purifying our poisoned air and lakes and rivers; that, too, is a matter of moral accounting. Nor can it help us decide whether we want to be the arbiter of the world's conflicts, the proud enforcer of a *Pax Americana*, even though that must mean the abandonment of the founding fathers' idea of America as an exemplary society and the betrayal of the idea of world peace under world law, which, as embodied in the Covenant of the League of Nations and the Charter of the United Nations, was also an American idea. These too, are matters of moral accounting.

• • •

Rich and powerful though our country is, it is not rich or powerful enough to shape the course of world history in a constructive or desired direction solely by the impact of its power and policy. Inevitably and demonstrably, our major impact on the world is not in what we *do* but in what we *are*. For all their world-wide influence, our aid and our diplomacy are only the shadow of America; the real America—and the real American influence—is something else. It is the way our people live, our tastes and games, our products and preferences, the way we treat one another, the way we govern ourselves, the ideas about man and man's relations with other men that took root and flowered in the American soil.

History testifies to this. A hundred years ago, England was dominant in the world, just as America is today. Now England is no longer dominant; her great fleets have vanished from the seas and only small fragments remain of the mighty British Empire. What survives? The legacy of hatred survives—hatred of the West and its arrogant imperialism, hatred of the condescension and the exploitation, hatred of the betrayal abroad of the democracy that Englishmen practiced at home. And the ideas survive—the ideas of liberty and tolerance and fair play to which Englishmen were giving meaning and reality at home while acting on different principles in the Empire. In retrospect, it seems clear that England's lasting and constructive impact on modern India, for example, springs not from the way she ruled in India but, despite that, from the way she was ruling England at the same time.

Possessed as they are of a genuine philanthropic impulse, many Americans feel that it would be selfish and exclusive, elitist and isolationist, to deny the world the potential benefits of our great wealth and power, restricting ourselves to a largely exemplary role. It is true that our wealth and power *can* be, and sometimes are, beneficial to foreign nations; but they can also be, and often are, immensely damaging and disruptive. Experience—ours and that of others—strongly suggests that the disruptive impact predominates, that when big nations act upon small nations, they tend to do them more harm than good. This is not necessarily for lack of good intentions; it is, rather, for lack of knowledge. Most men simply do not know what is best for other men; and when they pretend to know or genuinely try to find out, they usually end up taking what they believe to be best for themselves as that which is best for others.

Conceding this regrettable trait of human nature, we practice democracy among ourselves, restricting the freedom of individuals to impose their wills upon other individuals, restricting the state as well and channeling such coercion as is socially necessary through community institutions. We do not restrict the scope of Government because we wish to deny individuals the benefits of its wealth and power, we restrict our Government because we wish to protect individuals from its capacity for tyranny.

If it is wisdom to restrict the power of men over men within our society, is it not wisdom to do the same in our foreign relations? If we cannot count on the benevolence of an all-powerful Government toward its own people, whose needs and characteristics it knows something about and toward whom it is surely well disposed, how can we count on the benevolence of an all-powerful America toward peoples of whom we know very little? Clearly, we cannot; and, until such time as we are willing to offer our help through community institutions such as the United Nations and the World Bank, I think that, in limiting our commitments to small nations, we are doing more to spare them disruption than we are to deny them benefits.

Wisdom consists as much in knowing what you cannot do as in knowing what you can do. If we knew and were able to acknowledge the limits of our own capacity, we would be likely, more often than we do, to let nature take its course in one place and another, not because it is sure or even likely to take a good course but because, whatever nature's course may be, tampering with it in ignorance will almost surely make it worse.

We used, in the old days, to have this kind of wisdom and we also knew, almost instinctively, that what we made of ourselves and of our own society would probably have a lasting and beneficial impact on the world than anything we might do in our foreign relations. We were content, as they say, to let conduct serve as an unspoken sermon. We knew that it was the freedom and seemingly unlimited opportunity, the energy and marvelous creativity of our diverse population, rather than the romantic nonsense of "manifest destiny," that made the name America a symbol of hope to people all over the world.

We knew these things until events beyond our control carried us irrevocably into the world and its fearful problems. We recognized thereupon, as we had to, that some of our traditional ideas would no longer serve us, that we could no longer, for example, regard our power as something outside of the scales of the world balance of power and that, therefore, we could no longer remain neutral from the major conflicts of the major nations. But, as so often happens when ideas are being revised, we threw out some valid ideas with the obsolete ones. Recognizing that we could not help but be involved in many of the world's crises, we came to suppose that we *had* to be involved in every crisis that came along; and so we began to lose the understanding of our own limitations. Recognizing that we could not help but maintain an active foreign policy, we came to suppose that whatever we hoped to accomplish in the world would be accomplished by acts of foreign policy, and this—as we thought—being true, that foreign policy must without exception be given precedence over domestic needs; and so we began to lose our histoical understanding of the power of the American example.

The loss is manifest in Vietnam. There at least we have embraced the ideas that are so alien to our experience—the idea that our wisdom is as great as our power and the idea that our lasting impact on the world can be determined by the way we fight a war rather than by the way we run our country. These are the principal and most ominous effects of the war—the betrayal of ideas that have served America well and the great moral crisis that that betrayal has set loose among our people and their leaders.

The crisis will not soon be resolved, nor can its outcome be predicted. It may culminate, as I hope it will, in a reassertion of the traditional values, in a renewed awareness of the creative power of the American example. Or it may culminate in our becoming an empire of the traditional kind, ordained to rule for a time over an empty system of power and then to fade or fall, leaving, like its predecessors, a legacy of dust.

RADICALISM AND CONTEMPORARY AMERICAN SOCIETY

IRVING LOUIS HOROWITZ

CONVENTIONAL QUESTIONS ABOUT RADICALISM STILL EMANATE FROM the intellectual dark ages called the "proletarian thirties": from a time when talk about linkages between "American experience" and "Marxism" meant something in the way of social action, from a pristine past when talk about intellectuals, workers, and middle-class citizens as "vehicles for social justice" could be fused to a still vigorous labor movement; at a time when there was hot and heavy talk of managerial elites versus working class vanguards; at a time when gross categories such as Negroes, labor, poor, liberals, church groups, could be bandied about since there were few sociological studies distinguishing rich Negroes from poor Negroes, poor whites from poor blacks, labor gangsters from labor giants, marginal church groups from fundamentalist sects. If we now try to answer such a set of propositions in their gross terms, what we get are recipes for future behavior which reflect more on the moral sentiments of the proclaimer than on the facts of life proclaimed.

Let me address myself to the big issue, the question of substance and moment: Is a new radical movement possible in the United States? Of course, any movement called radical is possible. The burden of this question ought to be: Is a radical movement in this country imminent or feasible? Here the cliché answer is available:

From Irving Louis Horowitz, "Radicalism and Contemporary American Society," *Liberation*, 10:15–17, 30, May 1965. Copyright © 1965 by *Liberation*. Reprinted by permission of *Liberation* Magazine, New York in slightly modified form.

anything is possible—even the redefinition of events to prove that we are in the midst of a radical movement right now. Indeed, some social scientists even say that Americanism, socialism, and radicalism are united in a common enterprise to save the world from barbarism and/or communism.

The possibility of redefining events to suit either our idiosyncrasies or our ideologies is ever present. I will not attempt to answer whether a new radical movement in the United States is feasible but only indicate the sort of definition of radicalism which makes sense for the children of the sixties, and if we live that long, the generation of the seventies—a definition which starts with civil libertarianism and civil disobedience, but does not end there.

Classical American liberalism has no future. Not so much because liberal aims are dead in America. This is a conjectural matter. It was already so in the twenties—in the times of Mencken, Veblen, Dewey, and Bourne; although through a clever manipulation of words and symbols they were able to remain authentically American and liberal at the same time. This was generally true of pragmatism. But this domestic liberalism was made possible by the low stakes involved. If nativism, nationalism, and nervousness were always combined with radicalism in the past, this combination remained uncomfortable and disquieting, carrying with it a knowledge that such associations, like patriotism and flag-waving before them, were doomed to become symbols of the Right. This was inevitable, since it is always the authentic Right that is most adept at defending the national face and the national purpose. To be a radical is somehow to deny explicitly the existence of such a thing as a national purpose, and to repudiate face-saving as the basis of political decision-making.

There was always a suspect quality in the Left wrapping itself with the American flag. When the former head of the Communist Party, Earl Browder, pointed out that communism was twentieth-century Americanism—a statement uttered many times and in many forms—the communist movement surrendered its claims to radicalism. Its entire post-war existence was embarrassed by federal claims of communist un-Americanism, and absurd counter claims (supported by absurd academics) of its pro-Americanism. Perhaps radicalism is doomed to a minority status, an Olympian ideology of those who think; but it can never be entirely destroyed or eliminated, as can political movements staking a claim to bigger and better Americanism. The radical defends the person against the movement. The radical defends the dissenter against the conformer. Above all, the radical assumes the risks and the liabilities of his position. Neither the Communist nor those engaged in similar movements could ever do this. To the bitter end, Communists engaged in "coalition politics"—as if the major parties even gave a damn!

Even at its most prosaic level, radicalism, is tied to the future of the world rather than to the present of the United States. What separates the liberal from the radical is that for the liberal it is enough to demand a "war on poverty," while for the radical what is demanded is a concomitant "war on opulence." For the liberal, a call for a "revolution of rising expectations" is adequate, as if the economic world had an infinite elasticity and expensiveness in which all could gain and all could be content. The radical is less certain of this notion of infinite elasticity. In any event, he insists on a corresponding recognition of a "revolution of falling profits." In place of a consensus doctrine, the radical pushes for social demands with an assertion that some sector, group, some individual, must *pay* a premium for these social goods. In this sense, the radical posture is more tough-minded than that of the liberal. It insists that things desired have a price and a payoff; and that it is futile to disguise this fact in Pollyannaish phraseology, or in demagogic appeals to yawning masses.

While Marx sometimes defended the interests of one nation against another, of Poland against Russia, of Spain against France, of France against Germany, or of the North against the South in the American Civil War, the principicle was always the same—internationalism. It was the *rights of masses* against the *claims of classes*. This is one principle of Marxism that retains its full vitality. Support for the Third World, for Algeria against France, for Angola against Portugal, for the Congo against Belgium, for Ceylon against India, for Biafra against Nigeria, for Vietnam against the United States must remain genuine—but always qualified, always tempered by international needs. This is the ethics of Marxism as a humanistic outlook; a political ethic which permits the differentiation of nationalism without at the same time committing us to a celebration. Not to take such a standpoint, to insist upon either full allegiance to one brand of nationalism or to a textbook internationalism, is to betray reality—to serve up the living ethic of Marxism to the dead soul of Marx. And this indeed is precisely what has taken place. Marx has been drowned in Western Civilization programs—one more name added to "great books" courses. What is left after this process of intellectual castration is Marx the inept prophet, rather than Marx the radical violator of the sacred cows of western civilization.

What is radicalism today? In some measure it is an affirmation of negation, of stopping the machines. As Mario Savio, echoing the sentiments of Henry David Thoreau, put matters:

> There is a time when the operation of the machine becomes so odious, makes you so sick at heart that you can't take part; you can't even passively take part, and you've got to put your bodies upon the gears and upon the wheels, upon the levers, upon all the apparatus and you've got to make it stop. And you've got to indicate to the people who run it, to the people who own it, that unless you're free, the machines will be prevented from working at all.

What is Americanism today? In some measure it is the transformation of man into a fanatic nationalist and imbecilic purpose-finding patriot. As the President of the United States of America said in 1965, when addressing students from schools and colleges on a trip to Washington sponsored by the William Randolph Hearst Foundation: "I would like to see them [the students] develop as much fanaticism about the United States' political system as young Nazis did about their system during the war."

Perhaps someone astute in dialectical reasoning can synthesize these opposites of radicalism and Americanism. I cannot. Nor do I think the project worth undertaking. There is a limit to ecumenical sentiment; to sleazy efforts to liberalize Americanism and to conservatize radicalism. The history of the Soviet Union can be read as a gigantic contradiction between Marxism as a doctrine of liberation and Marxism as a metaphysics of enslavement. The choice in the U.S.S.R. was between radicalism and great Russian chauvinism. The Soviet leadership from Stalin to Brezhnev have chosen the latter. Can we for an instant imagine that the choice in the United States is somehow less urgent, or less significant? For an Evgenii Yevtushenko to become a radical meant for him to become a critic—ruthless and uncompromising—of Soviet life.

For a C. Wright Mills to have performed a similar role in American life during the faded fifties meant the same "un-Americanism": abstention from voting, rejection of the Cold War; the exposé of militarization of the country. This is not a question of the *quality* of radicalism in America—this is an advanced question to which we are not yet entitled to give answers. It is a question of the sheer survival of radicalism.

Any meaningful definition of radicalism must not simply be an affirmation of retreatism, but a set of propositions about the state of the world and what the individual ought to do about the world. It is an assertion that nations, like individuals, have the right to choose their own social system, whether they choose our way or not. It is a further assertion of the right of men to disaffiliate and dissociate if the original choice turns out to be sour. The first part is the tough part for the American ideology (and leadership) to accept; the second part is the tough part for the Soviet ideology (and leadership) to acknowledge.

The parameters of our modern world are not determined by either the words socialism or capitalism; but may just as readily be defined by the terms poverty-stricken and opulent, underdeveloped and overdeveloped, Christian and non-Christian, colored and white, etc. Such elements may be welded together at a critical moment in time, which is when revolutions are most likely to occur.

This appreciation of social change is still not radicalism. For a person to be radical means to deny the basis of his own superiority: to fight for blacks when he is white; to condemn Papal inaction when one is a Catholic; to urge land reform when one is a landlord, etc. That is why the poor and downtrodden can never be described as "radical"—what they do is "natural"—in keeping with their "interests." What the radical does is violate the canon of self-interest or national interest. He asserts a transcendent ethical principle. When Martin Luther King conducted a voter registration drive in Alabama he acted naturally; when he denounced anti-Semitism he behaved radically.

The rationalist Marx was a radical, not because of his description of historical tendencies, long run inevitabilities, majority interests (the downtrodden, the masses, the poor, etc.), but because at every critical moment he defended the ethics of internationalism against the facts of nationalism. The irrationalist

Nietzsche took radicalism a step further. He asserted the anti-historical character of a moral act. The ability to perform heroically means the ability to fight for what may be a losing cause rather than for that which is rising. Cervantes' *Don Quixote* was more of a radical than any downtrodden character in literature: because Don Quixote violated his class to gain justice; he abandoned his wife to restore his sexuality; because he acted against his *interests* in the effort to recapture his *manliness.*

Why is Joseph Conrad's *Secret Agent* so superior to Victor Hugo's *Les Miserables?* It is because the anarchist professor in Conrad's novel is endowed with consciousness—with an understanding of the police inspector as his externalized self. Jean Valjean can only run, can only be chased, can only be reduced to permanent enslavement since he searches only for permanent security. The radical alone can taste the abyss as he reaches for heavens. The radical alone can feel the shame of defeat at the moment of his triumph. This is why radicalism is a twentieth-century humanism. This is what transforms radicalism from sentimentalism, progressivism, liberalism, or any other fragmentary form of amelioration.

Thus it is given to the fortunate alone to behave radically, as distinct from those who behave naturally. As a white you can be radical, as Negro you behave naturally. As an American you can be radical in defense of Vietnamese independence, in Vietnam one behaves this way naturally. As a Christian or a Moslem you can be radical in defense of the Jew, as a Jew you can behave naturally only on the "Jewish question." As a rich man you can be radical with respect to land reform, as a peasant you can only behave naturally. To the extent then that self-awareness is a rare property in men, to that degree is radicalism doomed to a minority status, to an elite of those who transcend their particular egos. For every Evgenii Yevtushenko there are a thousand Ukrainian anti-Semites; and for every pacifist like A. J. Muste there are a thousand ready to take up arms. The search for radical politics has ended in collectivist demagogy. Politics to be radical must be anti-national, anti-Establishment, in short, self-negating—*antipolitique.*

It might be argued that this also defines reaction: the Negro who toadies up to white folks and uses chemicals to become white if possible; the General Khanhs who behave as if American troops should use napalm bombs on Vietnam villagers; the Jew who turns anti-Semite; etc. The answer to this is complicated: in a sense, such reaction does indeed deserve to be labeled radicalism. The radicalism of the Right and of the Left are logically coincident; however they are not coincident historically, or even in terms of psychological self-definition.

One never finds a Rightist using the phrase "radical of the Right." He howls to the contrary, that he is a good American, that Birchism is twentieth-century Americanism! There is no nobility in radicalism of such a posture. The Right is an appellation assigned to the Rightist, not one he wears. The radical of the Right is without consciousness of his extremism. He defends the "is," the present moment, even though this may mean a rolling back of time or a rolling back of other nations. The Rightist does not accept radicalism as a self-definition of the situation. Above all, the radical of the Right is not prepared to deny his interests in order to affirm his self. He is not prepared to empathize or to reverse roles. On the contrary, his is a position of pure egotism: of defending face, of saving territories that do not belong to him, etc. He has no transcendent principles. He perishes with his ego ideals in a final Götterdämerung of the American way.

The doubts that must plague those of us concerned with the future of radicalism cannot be settled by words alone. But at least we can underscore why it is one thing to speak of a radical man and quite another to speak of a political movement. We have too long institutionalized radicalism, and in this very process, castrated its meaning for individuals. The word radicalism can only be debased when it attaches itself to cheap political movements having ill-defined and prosaic ends. Look about the world and see how many absurdly conservative and historical political parties have employed the term "radical" in their titles. In such nations, the word itself creates a wry smile, like the word liberalism does in this country. Elsewhere in the world the notions of social action I have been talking of have had to run out from under the shell of the concept radicalism—and find new linguistic expressions.

In the United States radicalism is still a word which carries thrust. Let us keep it that way—let us not debase it by affixing it to a concept of Americanism, yahooism, or rah-rahism. The "image" of radicalism should never be allowed to be used as a protective covering for the worst infirmities of modern civilization. It should remain a term of *marginal use*, and in this way, retain its *central importance*. For a society per se to become, or to remain, radical would require of its main branches a flexibility and a willingness to appreciate its own inutilities rarely exhibited in a social system. Indeed the drive of a social system is toward structure and ultimately toward the maintenance of order. The same holds for political parties, whatever their ostensible persuasion or commitments. Individuals are better able to behave radically. They alone have the capacity to deny the necessity of what exists. They alone have the ability to call forth a scheme of the future as a judgment on the society of the present. Individualism has remained an exclusive preserve of the conservatives because Left-wing *politicos* have failed to face the fact that governmental bigness is an evil, and that solutions based on radical principles rather than radical people is a disease, and not a cure.

This account of radicalism does not imply the sort of thundering totalism and intellectual noisiness which has become standard in the writings of professorial oracles. There is no intent here to prove that radicalism is the one and only role a person can perform; only that radicalism is a significant role. The relation between radicals and revolutionists is a sorely neglected theme in political role performance. Rosa Luxemburg could perform as a revolutionist and as a leader of the *Spartacists*, of the German Left Socialist movement, but at the same time, she was able to function as a radical, as a critic of Lenin and of the dogma of proletarian dictatorship. This she did at a moment of revolutionary euphoria when serious thinking was at a premium. And it is her radicalism, after all, which is now best remembered. The same can be said of Eugene V. Debs, whose importance in the Socialist movement lay precisely in the fact of his being above the fratricidal struggles for control of the Socialist Party apparatus. Debs was the radical man who at the same time was quite powerless with respect to the organizational aspects of American socialism. He was far less concerned with organization than DeLeon. Yet, Debs alone emerged as the "ecumenical" figure for the Socialists. Examples of radicalism can be readily multiplied.

The point is clear enough. Radicalism entails a critique of organizational constraint. Yet, revolution can only be made in terms of a theory of organization. This is why the two roles of radical and revolutionary, while they may coexist in the same person, give rise to a considerable amount of tension within the person and between the organization and the individual. If revolutionary man is driven to join forces with other advocates for rapid change, the radical man is driven to point out how limited these changes are in practice. The revolutionist, upon completion of his aims, seeks the fruits of victory; the radical is charged with the chore of seeking new vistas to conquer.

This cerebral radicalism suffers the defects of its virtues: splendid isolation may result in a self-indulgent happy alienation from worldly problems, in an intensified isolation from political struggles which would leave the practical world to the least capable people. Precisely what it is to "act radically" or to "act naturally" may be differentially seen. A southern sheriff may see the struggle of Negroes for voting rights as the most "unnatural" thing in the world. And above all, this kind of radicalism, while "un-American," must appreciate the fact that a society exists which is flexible enough to absorb, if not to accept such un-Americanism. These are surely major difficulties in the position outlined, and they require treatment. For the time being, I can only say that the problems of this radical communion are certainly no more insurmountable than the problems posed by any other doctrine. Indeed, it has the singular advantage of at least not transforming its declarations into directives.

I should like to conclude on a cautionary note: radicalism is a posture, not a position. It may provide a style of life, but can never be a substitute for work. Radicalism cannot tell you the role of China vis-à-vis India in the developmental process of Asia. Radicalism cannot settle questions about the length of time it takes to make a transition from rural life to urban life. Radicalism cannot prove the merits or demerits of one or another form of economic investment. When radicalism is employed as a surrogate for social science it becomes fanaticism—an uncompromising effort to replace substance with style. These limits understood and expressed, radicalism can serve as a beacon light for measuring the distance between where we are and where we want to go —between the society and the utopia.

PART THREE

THE UNITED STATES AND
THE THIRD WORLD

THE UNITED STATES
AND THE
THIRD WORLD

INTRODUCTION

AMERICAN SOCIOLOGY HAS GENER-
ally been culture-bound in its restricted view of American society,
the West, capitalist and developed societies. This parochialism is
to be lamented in terms of its implications for the world; but it
must also be challenged for offering an intellectually stunted viewpoint. The study of man and society can hardly be adequate when
it confines its attention to a society which is industrialized, rich,
mostly Caucasian, primarily Christian, and which possesses the
peculiar constellation of cultural traits and institutions which are
manifest in the United States and the West. Furthermore, even
if one's focus were basically on American or European culture,
true insights flow from a historical and comparative framework.
Can one understand race as a variable in the United States without noting the history of slavery, the relations of the West to
Africa? Does the peculiar character of industrial development in
the West offer a context for understanding poverty in the Third
World and the relations between the rich and poor nations? Such
are among the questions rarely probed by sociologists.

While some might be tempted out of ignorance to argue that
one can explain America without looking at the rest of the world,
surely no one will claim that the world can be intelligently examined without viewing the role of the United States in the
world. Robert L. Heilbroner's thesis is that America has played
and does play a critical role in the world, a role which is contrary to some of its own history, and one which is condemned to
long-term disaster. His argument has been substantiated in a
variety of sources as outlined by Deutsch. The basic position is

that a form of economic imperialism, which is rampant within the American system, is characteristic of America in relation to the Third World.[1] The historical epoch of colonialism is past; yet, the economic and political vehicles of colonialism operate today in the international sphere, and it is argued that domestic structures are best seen in a similar vein.[2]

A radical sociology must be prepared to deal with the matter of the United States and the Third World. This means that sociology must face the dilemmas of intellectual acquiescence and servitude so characteristic of the past.[3] The basic forces which we have examined in previous sections in this book, which introduce strain in American society, also function to produce international strain. The distribution of power, wealth, and so on must be examined in the international system. Such analysis requires an intellectual framework for linking national and international systems, as Deutsch argues. Put very simply, if a radical sociology is to be relevant, it must transcend the particular features of the United States and must explain and deal with the majority of the world, which is poor, non-Caucasian, non-Christian, and non-capitalist.

We might have included a much larger number of selections in this section. In fact, one recent book of readings has come out presenting a radical framework for Latin America.[4] Yet, we are not so much attempting to offer a total framework, but rather to pose some questions which are appropriate for our quest as we have tried to indicate a perspective of radical sociology. The titles of the pieces themselves are indicative of these questions or perspectives. Hopefully, the reader will utilize this brief section to generate additional questions and add to an intellectual framework for viewing sociological issues from a radical perspective.[5]

---

[1] For example, John Gerassi, *The Great Fear*. New York: Macmillan, 1963. *Viet-Report*, April–May 1968, issue on Pre-war Latin America. David Horowitz, *Free World Colossus*. New York: Hill & Wang, 1965.

[2] See, for example, Dave Gilbert, *Consumptions Domestic Imperialism*. Ann Arbor, Michigan: Radical Education Project, 1968. *Viet-Report*, Summer 1968 issue on "Colonialism and Liberalism in America."

[3] This issue is examined in Irving Louis Horowitz (ed.), *The Rise and Fall of Project Camelot*. Cambridge, Mass.: MIT Press, 1967.

[4] Irving Louis Horowitz, Jose de Castro, and John Gerassi (eds.), *Latin American Radicalism*. New York: Random House, 1968.

[5] For an elaboration of this theme, see Steven E. Deutsch, "The Radical Perspective in Sociology," *Sociological Inquiry* (forthcoming).

COUNTERREVOLUTIONARY
AMERICA

ROBERT L. HEILBRONER

IS THE UNITED STATES FUNDAMENTALLY OPPOSED TO ECONOMIC DE-
velopment? The question is outrageous. Did we not coin the
phrase, "the revolution of rising expectations"? Have we not
supported the cause of development more generously than any
nation on earth, spent our intellectual energy on the problems of
development, offered our expertise freely to the backward nations
of the world? How can it possibly be suggested that the United
States might be opposed to economic development?

The answer is that we are not at all opposed to what we conceive economic development to be. The process depicted by the
"revolution of rising expectations" is a deeply attractive one. It
conjures up the image of a peasant in some primitive land, lean-
ing on his crude plow and looking to the horizon, where he sees
dimly, but for the *first time* (and that is what is so revolutionary
about it), the vision of a better life. From this electrifying vision
comes the necessary catalysis to change an old and stagnant way
of life. The pace of work quickens. Innovations, formerly feared
and resisted, are now eagerly accepted. The obstacles are admittedly very great—whence the need for foreign assistance—
but under the impetus of new hopes the economic mechanism
begins to turn faster, to gain traction against the environment.
Slowly, but surely, the Great Ascent begins.

There is much that is admirable about this well-intentioned

From Robert L. Heilbroner, "Counterrevolutionary America," *Commentary*,
43:31–38, April, 1967. Copyright © 1967 by *Commentary*. Reprinted by permission of the American Jewish Committee, New York.

popular view of "the revolution of rising expectations." Unfortunately, there is more that is delusive about it. For the buoyant appeal of its rhetoric conceals or passes in silence over by far the larger part of the spectrum of realities of the development process. One of these is the certainty that the revolutionary aspect of development will not be limited to the realm of ideas, but will vent its fury on institutions, social classes, and innocent men and women. Another is the great likelihood that the ideas needed to guide the revolution will not only be affirmative and reasonable, but also destructive and fanatic. A third is the realization that revolutionary efforts cannot be made, and certainly cannot be sustained, by voluntary effort alone, but require an iron hand, in the spheres both of economic direction and political control. And the fourth and most difficult of these realities to face is the probability that the political force most likely to succeed in carrying through the gigantic historical transformation of development is some form of extreme national collectivism or Communism.

In a word, what our rhetoric fails to bring to our attention is the likelihood that development will require policies and programs repugnant to our "way of life," that it will bring to the fore governments hostile to our international objectives, and that its regnant ideology will bitterly oppose capitalism as a system of world economic power. If that is the case, we would have to think twice before denying that the United States was fundamentally opposed to economic development.

But is it the case? Must development lead in directions that go counter to the present American political philosophy? Let me try to indicate, albeit much too briefly and summarily, the reasons that lead me to answer that question as I do.

I begin with the cardinal point, often noted but still insufficiently appreciated, that the process called "economic development" is not primarily economic at all. We think of development as a campaign of production to be fought with budgets and monetary policies and measured with indices of output and income. But the development process is much wider and deeper than can be indicated by such statistics. To be sure, in the end what is hoped for is a tremendous rise in output. But this will not come to pass until a series of tasks, at once cruder and more delicate, simpler and infinitely more difficult, has been commenced and carried along a certain distance.

In most of the new nations of Africa, these tasks consist in establishing the very underpinnings of nationhood itself—in determining national borders, establishing national languages, arousing a basic national (as distinguished from tribal) self-consciousness. Before these steps have been taken, the African states will remain no more than names insecurely affixed to the map, not social entities capable of undertaking an enormous collective venture in economic change. In Asia, nationhood is generally much further advanced than in Africa, but here the main impediment to development is the miasma of apathy and fatalism, superstition and distrust that vitiates every attempt to improve hopelessly inefficient modes of work and patterns of resource use: while India starves, a quarter of the world's cow population devours Indian crops, exempt either from effective employment or slaughter because of sacred taboos. In still other areas, mainly Latin America, the principal handicap to development is not an absence of national identity or the presence of suffocating cultures (although the latter certainly plays its part), but the cramping and crippling inhibitions of obsolete social institutions and reactionary social classes. Where landholding rather than industrial activity is still the basis for social and economic power, and where land is held essentially in fiefdoms rather than as productive real estate, it is not surprising that so much of society retains a medieval cast.

Thus, development is much more than a matter of encouraging economic growth within a given social structure. It is rather the *modernization* of that structure, a process of ideational, social, economic, and political change that requires the remaking of society in its most intimate as well as its most public attributes.[1] When we speak of the revolutionary nature of economic development, it is this kind of deeply penetrative change that we mean —change that reorganizes "normal" ways of thought, established patterns of family life, and structures of village authority as well as class and caste privilege.

What is so egregiously lacking in the great majority of the societies that are now attempting to make the Great Ascent is precisely this pervasive modernization. The trouble with India and Pakistan, with Brazil and Ecuador, with the Philippines and

[1] See C. E. Black, *The Dynamics of Modernization.*

Ethiopia, is not merely that economic growth lags, or proceeds at some pitiable pace. This is only a symptom of deeper-lying ills. The trouble is that the social physiology of these nations remains so depressingly unchanged despite the flurry of economic planning on top. The all-encompassing ignorance and poverty of the rural regions, the unbridgeable gulf between the peasant and the urban elites, the resistive conservatism of the village elders, the unyielding traditionalism of family life—all these remain obdurately, maddeningly, disastrously unchanged. In the cities, a few modern buildings, sometimes brilliantly executed, give a deceptive patina of modernity, but once one journeys into the immense countryside, the terrible stasis overwhelms all.

To this vast landscape of apathy and ignorance one must now make an exception of the very greatest importance. It is the fact that a very few nations, all of them Communist, have succeeded in reaching into the lives and stirring the minds of precisely that body of the peasantry which constitutes the insuperable problem elsewhere. In our concentration on the politics, the betrayals, the successes and failures of the Russian, Chinese, and Cuban revolutions, we forget that their central motivation has been just such a war *à l'outrance* against the arch-enemy of backwardness—not alone the backwardness of outmoded social superstructures but even more critically that of private inertia and traditionalism.

That the present is irreversibly and unqualifiedly freed from the dead hand of the past is, I think, beyond argument in the case of Russia. By this I do not only mean that Russia has made enormous economic strides. I refer rather to the gradual emancipation of its people from the "idiocy of rural life," their gradual entrance upon the stage of contemporary existence. This is not to hide in the smallest degree the continuing backwardness of the Russian countryside where now almost fifty—*and formerly perhaps eighty*—percent of the population lives. But even at its worst I do not think that life could now be described in the despairing terms that run through the Russian literature of our grandfathers' time. Here is Chekhov:

> During the summer and the winter there had been hours and days when it seemed as if these people [the peasants] lived worse than cattle, and it was terrible to be with them. They were coarse, dishonest, dirty, and drunken; they did not live at

peace with one another but quarreled continually, because they feared, suspected, and despised one another. . . . Crushing labor that made the whole body ache at night, cruel winters, scanty crops, overcrowding, and no help, and nowhere to look for help.

It is less certain that the vise of the past has been loosened in China or Cuba. It may well be that Cuba has suffered a considerable economic decline, in part due to absurd planning, in part to our refusal to buy her main crop. The economic record of China is nearly as inscrutable as its political turmoil, and we may not know for many years whether the Chinese peasant is today better or worse off than before the revolution. Yet what strikes me as significant in both countries is something else. In Cuba it is the educational effort that, according to *The New York Times*, has constituted a major effort of the Castro regime. In China it is the unmistakable evidence—and here I lean not alone on the sympathetic account of Edgar Snow but on the most horrified descriptions of the rampages of the Red Guards—that the younger generation is no longer fettered by the traditional view of things. The very fact that the Red Guards now revile their elders, an unthinkable defiance of age-old Chinese custom, is testimony of how deeply change has penetrated into the texture of Chinese life.

It is this herculean effort to reach and rally the great anonymous mass of the population that is *the* great accomplishment of Communism—even though it is an accomplishment that is still only partially accomplished. For if the areas of the world afflicted with the self-perpetuating disease of backwardness are ever to rid themselves of its debilitating effects, I think it is likely to be not merely because antiquated social structures have been dismantled (although this is an essential precondition), but because some shock treatment like that of Communism has been administered to them.

By way of contrast to this all-out effort, however short it may have fallen of its goal, we must place the timidity of the effort to bring modernization to the peoples of the non-Communist world. Here again I do not merely speak of lagging rates of growth. I refer to the fact that illiteracy in the non-Communist countries of Asia and Central America is increasing (by some 200 million in the last decade) because it has been "impossible" to mount an educational effort that will keep pace with population growth. I refer to the absence of substantial land reform in Latin America, despite how many years of promises. I refer to the indifference or incompetence or corruption of governing elites: the incredible sheiks with their oildoms; the vague, well-meaning leaders of India unable to break the caste system, kill the cows, control the birthrate, reach the villages, house or employ the labor rotting on the streets; the cynical governments of South America, not one of which, according to Lleras Camargo, former president of Colombia, has ever prosecuted a single politician or industrialist for evasion of taxes. And not least, I refer to the fact that every movement that arises to correct these conditions is instantly identified as "Communist" and put down with every means at hand, while the United States clucks or nods approval.

To be sure, even in the most petrified societies, the modernization process is at work. If there were time, the solvent acids of the twentieth century would work their way on the ideas and institutions of the most inert or resistant countries. But what lacks in the twentieth century is time. The multitudes of the underdeveloped world have only in the past two decades been summoned to their reveille. The one thing that is certain about the revolution of rising expectations is that it is only in its inception, and that its pressures for justice and action will steadily mount as the voice of the twentieth century penetrates to villages and slums where it is still almost inaudible. It is not surprising that Princeton historian C. E. Black, surveying this labile world, estimates that we must anticipate "ten to fifteen revolutions a year for the foreseeable future in the less developed societies."

In itself, this prospect of mounting political restiveness enjoins the speediest possible time schedule for development. But this political urgency is many times compounded by that of the population problem. Like an immense river in flood, the number of human beings rises each year to wash away the levees of the preceding year's labors and to pose future requirements of monstrous proportions. To provide shelter for the three billion human beings who will arrive on earth in the next forty years will require as many dwellings as have been constructed since recorded history began. To feed them will take double the world's present output of food. To cope with the mass exodus from the overcrowded countryside will necessitate cities of grotesque size—Calcutta, now a cesspool of three to five millions, threatens us by the year 2000 with a prospective population of from thirty to sixty millions.

These horrific figures spell one importunate message: haste. That is the *mene mene, tekel upharsin* written on the walls of government planning offices around the world. Even if the miracle of the loop is realized—the new contraceptive device that promises the first real breakthrough in population control—we must set ourselves for at least another generation of rampant increase.

But how to achieve haste? How to convince the silent and disbelieving men, how to break through the distrustful glances of women in black shawls, how to overcome the overt hostility of landlords, the opposition of the Church, the petty bickerings of military cliques, the black-marketeering of commercial dealers? I suspect there is only one way. The conditions of backwardness must be attacked with the passion, the ruthlessness, and the messianic fury of a jehad, a Holy War. Only a campaign of an intensity and singlemindedness that must approach the ludicrous and the unbearable offers the chance to ride roughshod over the resistance of the rich and the poor alike and to open the way for the forcible implantation of those modern attitudes and techniques without which there will be no escape from the misery of underdevelopment.

I need hardly add that the cost of this modernization process has been and will be horrendous. If Communism is the great modernizer, it is certainly not a benign agent of change. Stalin may well have exceeded Hitler as a mass executioner. Free inquiry in China has been supplanted by dogma and catechism; even in Russia nothing like freedom of criticism or of personal expression is allowed. Furthermore, the economic cost of industrialization in both countries has been at least as severe as that imposed by primitive capitalism.

Yet one must count the gains as well as the losses. Hundreds of millions who would have been confined to the narrow cells of changeless lives have been liberated from prisons they did not even know existed. Class structures that elevated the flighty or irresponsible have been supplanted by others that have promoted the ambitious and the dedicated. Economic systems that gave rise to luxury and poverty have given way to systems that provide a rough distributional justice. Above all, the prospect of a new future has been opened. It is this that lifts the current ordeal in China above the level of pure horror. The number of human beings in that country who have perished over the past centuries from hunger or neglect, is beyond computation. The present revolution may add its dreadful increment to this number. But it also holds out the hope that China may finally have been galvanized into social, political, and economic attitudes that for the first time make its modernization a possibility.

Two questions must be answered when we dare to risk so favorable a verdict on Communism as a modernizing agency. The first is whether the result is worth the cost, whether the possible—by no means assured—escape from underdevelopment is worth the lives that will be squandered to achieve it.

I do not know how one measures the moral price of historical victories or how one can ever decide that a diffuse gain is worth a sharp and particular loss. I only know that the way in which we ordinarily keep the books of history is wrong. No one is now toting up the balance of the wretches who starve in India, or the peasants of Northeastern Brazil who live in the swamps on crabs, or the undernourished and permanently stunted children of Hong Kong or Honduras. Their sufferings go unrecorded, and are not present to counterbalance the scales when the furies of revolution strike down their victims. Barrington Moore has made a nice calculation that bears on this problem. Taking as the weight in one pan the 35,000 to 40,000 persons who lost their lives—mainly for no fault of theirs—as a result of the Terror during the French Revolution, he asks what would have been the death rate from preventable starvation and injustice under the *ancien regime* to balance the scales. "Offhand," he writes, "it seems unlikely that this would be very much below the proportion of .0010 which [the] figure of 40,000 yields when set against an estimated population of 24 million."[2]

Is it unjust to charge the *ancien régime* in Russia with ten million preventable deaths? I think it not unreasonable. To charge the authorities in pre-revolutionary China with equally vast and preventable degradations? Theodore White, writing in 1946, had this to say: ". . . some scholars think that China is perhaps the

[2] *Social Origins of Dictatorship and Democracy*, p. 104.

only country in the world where the people eat less, live more bitterly, and are clothed worse than they were five hundred years ago."[3]

I do not recommend such a calculus of corpses—indeed, I am aware of the license it gives to the unscrupulous—but I raise it to show the onesidedness of our protestations against the brutality and violence of revolutions. In this regard, it is chastening to recall the multitudes who have been killed or mutilated by the Church which is now the first to protest against the excesses of Communism.

But there is an even more terrible second question to be asked. It is clear beyond doubt, however awkward it may be for our moralizing propensities, that historians excuse horror that succeeds; and that we write our comfortable books of moral philosophy, seated atop a mound of victims—slaves, serfs, laboring men and women, heretics, dissenters—who were crushed in the course of preparing the way for our triumphal entry into existence. But at least we are here to vindicate the carnage. What if we were not? What if the revolutions grind flesh and blood and produce nothing, if the end of the convulsion is not exhilaration but exhaustion, not triumph but defeat?

Before this possibility—which has been realized more than once in history—one stands mute. Mute, but not paralyzed. For there is the necessity of calculating what is likely to happen in the absence of the revolution whose prospective excesses hold us back. Here one must weigh what has been done to remedy underdevelopment—and what has not been done—in the past twenty years; how much time there remains before the population flood enforces its own ultimate solution; what is the likelihood of bringing modernization without the frenzied assault that Communism seems most capable of mounting. As I make this mental calculation I arrive at an answer which is even more painful than that of revolution. I see the alternative as the continuation, without substantial relief—and indeed with a substantial chance of deterioration—of the misery and meanness of life as it is now lived in the sinkhole of the world's backward regions.

I have put the case for the necessity of revolution as strongly as possible, but I must now widen the options beyond the stark

[3] *Thunder Out of China*, p. 32.

alternatives I have posed. To begin with, there are areas of the world where the immediate tasks are so far-reaching that little more can be expected for some decades than the primary missions of national identification and unification. Most of the new African states fall into this category. These states may suffer capitalist, Communist, Fascist, or other kinds of regimes during the remainder of this century, but whatever the nominal ideology in the saddle, the job at hand will be that of military and political nation-making.

There is another group of nations, less easy to identify, but much more important in the scale of events, where my analysis also does not apply. These are countries where the pressures of population growth seem sufficiently mild, or the existing political and social framework sufficiently adaptable, to allow for the hope of considerable progress without resort to violence. Greece, Turkey, Chile, Argentina, Mexico may be representatives of nations in this precarious but enviable situation. Some of them, incidentally, have already had revolutions of modernizing intent—fortunately for them in a day when the United States was not so frightened or so powerful as to be able to repress them.

In other words, the great arena of desperation to which the revolutionizing impetus of Communism seems most applicable is primarily the crowded land masses and archipelagoes of Southeast Asia and the impoverished areas of Central and South America. But even here, there is the possibility that the task of modernization may be undertaken by non-Communist elites. There is always the example of indigenous, independent leaders who rise up out of nowhere to overturn the established framework and to galvanize the masses—a Gandhi, a Martí, a pre-1958 Castro. Or there is that fertile ground for the breeding of national leaders—the army, as witness Ataturk or Nasser, among many.[4]

Thus there is certainly no inherent necessity that the revolu-

---

[4] What are the chances for modernizing revolutions of the Right, such as those of the Meiji Restoration or of Germany under Bismarck? I think they are small. The changes to be wrought in the areas of greatest backwardness are much more socially subversive than those of the nineteenth century, and the timespan allotted to the revolutionists is much smaller. Bourgeois revolutions are not apt to go far enough, particularly in changing property ownership. Still, one could imagine such revolutions with armed support and no doubt Fascistic ideologies. I doubt that they would be any less of a threat than revolutions of the Left.

tions of modernization be led by Communists. But it is well to bear two thoughts in mind when we consider the likely course of non-Communist revolutionary sweeps. The first is the nature of the mobilizing appeal of any successful revolutionary elite. Is it the austere banner of saving and investment that waves over the heads of the shouting marchers in Jakarta and Bombay, Cairo and Havana? It most certainly is not. The banner of economic development is that of nationalism, with its promise of personal immortality and collective majesty. It seems beyond question that a feverish nationalism will charge the atmosphere of any nation, Communist or not, that tries to make the Great Ascent—and as a result we must expect the symptoms of nationalism along with the disease: exaggerated xenophobia, a thin-skinned national sensitivity, a search for enemies as well as a glorification of the state.

These symptoms, which we have already seen in every quarter of the globe, make it impossible to expect easy and amicable relations between the developing states and the colossi of the developed world. No conceivable response on the part of America or Europe or, for that matter, Russia, will be able to play up to the vanities or salve the irritations of the emerging nations, much less satisfy their demands for help. Thus, we must anticipate an anti-American, or anti-Western, possibly even anti-white animus from any nation in the throes of modernization, even if it is not parroting Communist dogma.

Then there is a second caution as to the prospects for non-Communist revolutions. This is the question of what ideas and policies will guide their revolutionary efforts. Revolutions, especially if their whole orientation is to the future, require philosophy equally as much as force. It is here, of course, that Communism finds its special strength. The vocabulary in which it speaks—a vocabulary of class domination, of domestic and international exploitation—is rich in meaning to the backward nations. The view of history it espouses provides the support of historical inevitability to the fallible efforts of struggling leaders. Not least, the very dogmatic certitude and ritualistic repetition that stick in the craw of the Western observer offer the psychological assurances on which an unquestioning faith can be maintained.

If a non-Communist elite is to persevere in tasks that will prove Sisyphean in difficulty, it will also have to offer a philosophical interpretation of its role as convincing and elevating, and a diagnosis of social and economic requirements as sharp and simplistic, as that of Communism. Further, its will to succeed at whatever cost must be as firm as that of the Marxists. It is not impossible that such a philosophy can be developed, more or less independent of formal Marxian conceptions. It is likely, however, to resemble the creed of Communism far more than that of the West. Political liberty, economic freedom, and constitutional law may be the great achievements and the great issues of the most advanced nations, but to the least developed lands they are only dim abstractions, or worse, rationalizations behind which the great powers play their imperialist tricks or protect the privileges of their monied classes.

Thus, even if for many reason we should prefer the advent of non-Communist modernizing elites, we must realize that they too will present the United States with programs and policies antipathetic to much that America "believes in" and hostile to America as a world power. The leadership needed to mount a jehad against backwardness—and it is my main premise that only a Holy War will begin modernization in our time—will be forced to expound a philosophy that approves authoritarian and collectivist measures at home and that utilizes as the target for its national resentment abroad the towering villains of the world, of which the United States is now Number One.

All this confronts American policymakers and public opinion with a dilemma of a totally unforeseen kind. On the one hand we are eager to assist in the rescue of the great majority of mankind from conditions that we recognize as dreadful and ultimately dangerous. On the other hand, we seem to be committed, especially in the underdeveloped areas, to a policy of defeating Communism wherever it is within our military capacity to do so, and of repressing movements that might become Communist if they were allowed to follow their internal dynamics. Thus, we have on the one side the record of Point Four, the Peace Corps, and foreign aid generally; and on the other, Guatemala, Cuba, the Dominican Republic, and now Vietnam.

That these two policies might be in any way mutually incompatible, that economic development might contain revolutionary implications infinitely more far-reaching than those we have so blandly endorsed in the name of rising expectations, that Communism or a radical national collectivism might be the only vehicles for modernization in many key areas of the world—these are dilemmas we have never faced. Now I suggest that we do face them, and that we begin to examine in a serious way ideas that have hitherto been considered blasphemous, if not near-traitorous.

Suppose that most of Southeast Asia and much of Latin America were to go Communist, or to become controlled by revolutionary governments that espoused collectivist ideologies and vented extreme anti-American sentiments. Would this constitute a mortal threat to the United States?

I think it fair to claim that the purely *military* danger posed by such an eventuality would be slight. Given the present and prospective capabilities of the backward world, the addition of hundreds of millions of citizens to the potential armies of Communism would mean nothing when there was no way of deploying them against us. The prospect of an invasion by Communist hordes—the specter that frightened Europe after World War II with some (although retrospectively, not too much) realism—would be no more than a phantasm when applied to Asia or South America or Africa.

More important, the nuclear or conventional military power of Communism would not be materially increased by the armaments capacities of these areas for many years. By way of indication, the total consumption of energy of all kinds (in terms of coal equivalent) for Afghanistan, Bolivia, Brazil, Burma, Ceylon, Colombia, Costa Rica, Dominican Republic, Ecuador, El Salvador, Ethiopia, Guatemala, Haiti, Honduras, India, Indonesia, Iran, Iraq, Korea, Lebanon, Nicaragua, Pakistan, Paraguay, Peru, Philippines, U.A.R., Uruguay, and Venezuela is less than that annually consumed by West Germany alone. The total steel output of these countries is one-tenth of U.S. annual production. Thus, even the total communization of the backward world would not effectively alter the present balance of military strength in the world.

However small the military threat, it is undeniably true that a Communist or radical collectivist engulfment of these countries would cost us the loss of billions of dollars of capital invested there. Of our roughly $50 billions in overseas investment, some $10 billions are in mining, oil, utility, and manufacturing facilities in Latin America, some $4 billions in Asia including the Near East, and about $2 billions in Africa. To lose these assets would deal a heavy blow to a number of large corporations, particularly in oil, and would cost the nation as a whole the loss of some $3 or $4 billions a year in earnings from those areas.

A Marxist might conclude that the economic interests of a capitalist nation would find such a prospective loss insupportable, and that it would be "forced" to go to war. I do not think this is a warranted assumption, although it is undoubtedly a risk. Against a Gross National Product that is approaching ¾ of a trillion dollars and with total corporate assets over $1.3 trillions, the loss of even the whole $16 billions in the vulnerable areas should be manageable economically. Whether such a takeover could be resisted politically—that is, whether the red flag of Communism could be successfully waved by the corporate interests—is another question. I do not myself believe that the corporate elite is particularly war-minded—not nearly so much so as the military or the congressional—or that corporate seizures would be a suitable issue for purposes of drumming up interventionist sentiment.

By these remarks I do not wish airily to dismiss the dangers of a Communist avalanche in the backward nations. There would be dangers, not least those of an American hysteria. Rather, I want only to assert that the threats of a military or economic kind would not be insuperable, as they might well be if Europe were to succumb to a hostile regime.

But is that not the very point?, it will be asked. Would not a Communist success in a few backward nations lead to successes in others, and thus by degrees engulf the entire world, until the United States and perhaps Europe were fortresses beseiged on a hostile planet?

I think the answer to this fear is twofold. First, as many beside myself have argued, it is now clear that Communism, far from constituting a single unified movement with a common aim and dovetailing interests, is a movement in which similarities of economic and political structure and ideology are more than outweighed by divergencies of national interest and character. Two bloody wars have demonstrated that in the case of capitalism, structural similarities between nations do not prevent mortal combat. As with capitalism, so with Communism. Russian Communists have already been engaged in skirmishes with Polish and Hungarian Communists, have nearly come to blows with Yugoslavia, and now stand poised at the threshold of open fighting with China. Only in the mind of the *Daily News* (and perhaps still the

State Department) does it seem possible, in the face of this spectacle, to refer to the unified machinations of "international Communism" or the "Sino-Soviet bloc."

The realities, I believe, point in a very different direction. A world in which Communist governments were engaged in the enormous task of trying to modernize the worst areas of Asia, Latin America, and Africa would be a world in which sharp differences of national interest were certain to arise within these continental areas. The outlook would be for frictions and conflicts to develop among Communist nations with equal frequency as they developed between those nations and their non-Communist neighbors. A long period of jockeying for power and command over resources, rather than anything like a unified sharing of power and resources, seems unavoidable in the developing continents. This would not preclude a continuous barrage of anti-American propaganda, but it would certainly impede a movement to exert a coordinated Communist influence over these areas.

Second, it seems essential to distinguish among the causes of dangerous national and international behavior those that can be traced to the tenets of Communism and those that must be located elsewhere. "Do not talk to me about Communism and capitalism," said a Hungarian economist with whom I had lunch this winter. "Talk to me about rich nations and poor ones."

I think it is wealth and poverty, and not Communism or capitalism, that establishes much of the tone and tension of international relations. For that reason I would expect Communism in the backward nations (or national collectivism, if that emerges in the place of Communism) to be strident, belligerent, and insecure. If these regimes fail—as they may—their rhetoric may become hysterical and their behavior uncontrolled, although of small consequence. But if they succeed, which I believe they can, many of these traits should recede. Russia, Yugoslavia, or Poland are simply not to be compared, either by way of internal pronouncement or external behavior, with China, or, on a smaller scale, Cuba. Modernization brings, among other things, a waning of the stereotypes, commandments, and flagellations so characteristic of (and so necessary to) a nation engaged in the effort to alter itself from top to bottom. The idiom of ceaseless revolution becomes less relevant— even faintly embarrassing—to a nation that begins to be pleased with itself. Then, too, it seems reasonable to suppose that the vituperative quality of Communist invective would show some signs of abating were the United States to modify its own dogmatic attitude and to forego its own wearisome clichés about the nature of Communism.

I doubt there are many who will find these arguments wholly reassuring. They are not. It would be folly to imagine that the next generation or two, when Communism or national collectivism in the underdeveloped areas passes through its jehad stage, will be a time of international safety. But as always in these matters, it is only by a comparison with the alternatives that one can choose the preferable course. The prospect that I have offered as a plausible scenario of the future must be placed against that which results from a pursuit of our present course. And here I see two dangers of even greater magnitude: (1) the prospect of many more Vietnams, as radical movements assert themselves in other areas of the world; and (2) a continuation of the present inability of the most impoverished areas to modernize, with the prospect of an eventual human catastrophe on an unimaginable scale.

Nevertheless, there *is* a threat in the specter of a Communist or near-Communist supremacy in the underdeveloped world. It is that the rise of Communism would signal the end of capitalism as the dominant world order, and would force the acknowledgment that America no longer constituted the model on which the future of world civilization would be mainly based. In this way, as I have written before, the existence of Communism frightens American capitalism as the rise of Protestantism frightened the Catholic Church, or the French Revolution the English aristocracy.

It is, I think, the fear of losing our place in the sun, of finding ourselves at bay, that motivates a great deal of the anti-Communism on which so much of American foreign policy seems to be founded. In this regard I note that the nations of Europe, most of them profoundly more conservative than America in their social and economic dispositions, have made their peace with Communism far more intelligently and easily than we, and I conclude that this is in no small part due to their admission that they are no longer the leaders of the world.

The great question in our own nation is whether we can accept a similar scaling-down of our position in history. This would entail many profound changes in outlook and policy. It would mean the recognition that Communism, which may indeed represent a retrogressive movement in the West, where it should continue to be resisted with full energies, may nonetheless represent a progressive movement in the backward areas, where its advent may be the only chance these areas have of escaping misery. Collaterally, it means the recognition that "our side" has neither the political will, nor the ideological wish, nor the stomach for directing those changes that the backward world must make if it is ever to cease being backward. It would undoubtedly entail a more isolationist policy for the United States *vis-à-vis* the developing continents, and a greater willingness to permit revolutions there to work their way without our interference. It would mean in our daily political life the admission that the ideological battle of capitalism and Communism had passed its point of usefulness or relevance, and that religious diatribe must give way to the pragmatic dialogue of the age of science and technology.

I do not know how to estimate the chances of affecting such deepseated changes in the American outlook. It may be that the pull of vested interests, the inertia of bureaucracy, plus a certain lurking fundamentalism that regards Communism as an evil which admits of no discussion—the anti-Christ—will maintain America on its present course, with consequences that I find frightening to contemplate. But I believe that our attitudes are not hopelessly frozen. I detect, both above and below, signs that our present view of Communism is no longer wholly tenable and that it must be replaced with a new assessment if we are to remain maneuverable in action and cogent in discourse.

Two actions may help speed along this long overdue modernization of our own thought. The first is a continuation of the gradual thawing and convergence of American and Russian views and interests—a rapprochement that is proceeding slowly and hesitantly, but with a discernible momentum. Here the initiative must come from Russia as well as from ourselves.

The other action is for us alone to take. It is the public airing of the consequences of our blind anti-Communism for the underdeveloped world. It must be said aloud that our present policy prefers the absence of development to the chance for Communism —which is to say, that we prefer hunger and want and the existing inadequate assaults against the causes of hunger and want to any regime that declares its hostility to capitalism. There are strong American currents of humanitarianism that can be directed as a counterforce to this profoundly anti-humanitarian view. But for this counterforce to become mobilized it will be necessary to put fearlessly the outrageous question with which I began: is the United States fundamentally opposed to economic development?

AMERICA AND THE THIRD WORLD

STEVEN E. DEUTSCH

THE MOST ELEMENTARY ANALYSIS OF ANY SOCIETY WILL LIKELY focus on key components of the social structure and the institutional arrangements. Yet, as several writers have recently indicated, there is a tendency to psychologize much social analysis.[1] This leads to studies of life styles and attitudes of the poor, rather than studies of the structure of poverty. Such shifts in emphases tend to be more conservative, since they emphasize the individual and his deficiencies and maladjustments, and place relatively little stress upon the structure of society. C. Wright Mills observed this tendency among sociologists a quarter of a century ago.[2] It is the argument in this paper that a structural analysis is most appropriate for examining American society, and that there are useful parallels for extending the intellectual framework of American society into the industrializing and poor nations which make up the Third World.

THE AMERICAN SOCIAL STRUCTURE

A number of major sociological analyses have attempted to characterize American society. Some have ambitiously developed comprehensive social systems frameworks,[3] while other studies

[1] See George Homans, "Bringing Men Back In," *American Sociological Review*, 29 (Dec. 1964):809–818.
[2] C. Wright Mills, "The Professional Ideology of Social Pathologists," *American Journal of Sociology*, 49 (Sept. 1949):165–180.
[3] Robin M. Williams, Jr., *American Society: A Sociological Interpretation*. New York: Alfred A. Knopf, 1960.

have tapped particular modes of life, class life styles, community structures, or given institutions.[4] A few sociologists have documented the processes of social change within communities and have identified the historical patterns which seem to characterize a particular period, such as the Great Depression.[5] More recently, gross features of the American social structure have been "discovered." Michael Harrington's writings on poverty[6] were not treated with the same snobbishness as were the works of lay-sociologist Vance Packard.[7] The Kerner Commission report in the Spring of 1968,[8] along with the assassination of Martin Luther King, awakened many to the developing racial-class cleavages in the United States. In general, it can be argued that there have been several theoretical cross-currents in American sociology. For example, there are models of society which focus on its consentual aspects and others which focus on conflict.[9] Some debates, between sociologists are ideological as well as theoretical in nature, as, for example, those appearing regularly in the pages of the *American Sociologist*.[10] With the emergence of "action sociology"[11] has come an increasing use of structural analyses.

The framework for assessing the American condition, as it were, must not only identify social categories—such as that of the economically deprived within our economic-social structure—but it must also explain the nature of that social category and its relationship to other social groupings and institutions. This frame-

[4] W. L. Warner, *Yankee City*. New Haven: Yale University Press, 1963. Derek L. Phillips (ed.), *Studies in American Society*, 2 Vols. New York: Thomas Crowell, 1965, 1967.
[5] Robert S. Lynd and Helen Lynd, *Middletown*. New York: Harcourt, Brace, 1929 by the same authors: *Middletown In Transition*. New York: Harcourt, Brace, 1937.
[6] Michael Harrington, *The Other America*. New York: Macmillan, 1963.
[7] Vance Packard, *The Status Seekers*. New York: David McKay, 1959.
[8] *Report of the National Advisory Commission on Civil Disorders*. New York: Bantam Books, 1968.
[9] See Lewis Coser, *The Functions of Social Conflict*. Glencoe: The Free Press, 1956, note particularly the introduction.
[10] For example, Thomas Hoult, "Who Shall Prepare Himself for the Battle?" *American Sociologist*, 3 (February 1968):3–7. (See article in this book, p. 21.) Alvin W. Gouldner, "The Sociologist as Partisan: Sociology and the Welfare State," *American Sociologist*, 3 (May 1968):103–116.
[11] Arthur Shostak, *Sociology in Action*. Homewood: Dorsey Press, 1966; Alvin W. Gouldner and S. M. Miller (eds.), *Applied Sociology*. New York: Free Press, 1965.

work cannot be social-psychological or overly concerned with attitudinal and value dimensions, albeit these are important; the theories of culture and personality, character and social structure are important in their place.[12] The distribution of power in American society, the nature of the class structure and the distribution of work and economic opportunities, the distribution of educational opportunities, and the arrangement in coordinated institutions such as welfare—all need to be examined if one is to obtain a total picture of the United States as a social and sociological phenomenon. Thus, a structural account of American society will not only identify low-income persons, but will make poverty amid affluence understandable; it will not only identify the magnitude of the military establishment, but will permit a logical interpretation of the linkages between the economic and political apparatus. The poor in America are seen, then, not only as sociologically interesting specimens, but as the product of a particular kind of social structure. Similar interpretations can be applied to technologically displaced workers, unemployed black ghetto youth, and people in other social categories.[13] In fact, a structural analysis of poverty really tells the sociologist more about the affluent and about the total society, than it does about those who are poor.

THE CREATION OF UNDERDEVELOPMENT— CONCEPTUAL AND REAL

Although everyone knows that poverty exists, the social scientist faces the task of having to measure it. What level of income differentiates people who are poor from those who are not? Certain economic cut-off points have been used; for example, families with a yearly income of under $4000 are classified as poor, while those immediately above this mark but below the decent living

[12] For an overview of the culture and personality materials, see Anthony F. C. Wallace, *Culture and Personality*. New York: Random House, 1961. See also Hans Gerth and C. Wright Mills, *Character and Social Structure*. New York: Harcourt, Brace & World, 1953.
[13] For an analysis of problems related to particular social structures, see William A. Faunce, *Problems of an Industrial Society*. New York: McGraw-Hill, 1968.

standards level are labeled as deprived. This kind of measurement is utilized in international studies as well. Poor countries do indeed exist, and economists use particular cut-offs to measure relative economic position, often employing per capita national income as a device. The following discussion will attempt to indicate the parallels in analysis between an intra-national study of American society, and an inter-national perspective.

A number of intellectual traditions and theoretical viewpoints have considered the problem of underdevelopment. Political economists, applied anthropologists, and others have examined the processes of change and have attempted to deduce a general theory of development. Some theories have stressed the attitudinal or value components. Thus, writers such as McClelland and Hagen have argued that entrepreneurial attitudes, which they see as requisite for economic growth, are nurtured in particular kinds of child-rearing environments, and that cultures induce a personality type which is conducive to the potential economic development of that society.[14]

This theoretical school is somewhat analogous to those writers who discuss poverty in America as a subculture, with particular values engendered in low-income urban areas.[15] Yet, the cultural determinism implied in some of this work has clearly been refuted —or at least highly challenged[16]—and this viewpoint fails to account for the structuralist argument. While it is clear enough that some form of savings and investment—whether private or public, voluntary or induced (perhaps through taxes)—is necessary for economic growth, this does not mean that a particular form of personality must typify a society in order for growth to occur. Rather, this kind of argument smacks of a cultural chauvinism and absolutism: to become industrialized and economically advanced like the West, the underdeveloped nations of the world must follow the Western pattern. Such is indeed the implication of one writer, influential in government: W. W. Rostow, author of *The Stages of Economic Growth: A Non-Communist Mani-*

---

[14] Everett Hagen, *On the Theory of Social Change.* Homewood: Dorsey Press, 1962. David C. McClelland, *The Achieving Society.* Princeton: Van Nostrand & Co., 1961.

[15] Oscar Lewis, *La Vida: A Puerto Rican Family in the Culture of Poverty —San Juan and New York.* New York: Random House, 1966.

[16] Charles A. Valentine, *Culture and Poverty.* Chicago: University of Chicago Press, 1968.

festo.[17] Aside from its ideological character, it is apparent that this type of theory is of limited value in assessing the nature of the economic disparities in the world. The fact that Chicago ghetto residents have a different life-style than residents of luxury apartments does not adequately explain American social structure. Similarly, a theory which identifies varying value systems, some of which are associated with affluent world nations, does not offer an adequate overview.

Perhaps the case might be stated in bold and blunt terms: the existence of poor nations in the Third World can only be explained with an analysis showing the structural relationships between the rich and poor nations.[18] Most writers agree on categories: Europe, North America, Oceania (Australia, New Zealand), South Africa, and Japan represent largely capitalist, developed nations; Eastern Europe and the Soviet Union represent the industrialized socialist states, and the bulk of Africa, Asia and Latin America represent the poor, or underdeveloped nations, the Third World. While some might argue that the disparites might be explained in terms of the simple colonizer versus colony relationships which existed from the time of the Industrial Revolution to the present, such an explanation is overly simplistic. True, more than one-half of the 125 nations in the United Nations today have developed independence and national sovereignty since World War II. Yet, the international economic relationships must be seen in political terms. The capitalist states have not uniquely been colonial powers, nor have they alone pursued a neo-imperialist foreign policy. To argue differently would approach the statement that the position of black Americans today is solely the product of the history of slavery in the historical past—failing to assess the importance of racial discrimination; the relationship between race, education, technological displacement or unemployment; and the like.

If sociologists discern that poverty in America is more than a residual category, then they must understand how the distribution of income evolved into its present character, what the structure of the economic and social institutions are, and how change occurs, if at all. Similarly, the economic disparities in the world

---

[17] W. W. Rostow, *The Stages of Economic Growth: A Non-Communist Manifesto.* Cambridge: Cambridge University Press, 1960.
[18] For an argument for the rich-poor terminology, see Robert Theobald, *The Rich and the Poor.* New York: New American Library, 1961.

must be approached not only in the statistical terms which permit one to identify about 80 percent of the world's population as living in extremely poor countries with very low per-capita national incomes. To borrow the phrase from Paul Baran, we must examine "the roots of backwardness."[19] Underdevelopment is, to a considerable extent, the result of the colonialism and imperialism which emerged with the Industrial Revolution in Europe. Geographical and cultural factors alone do not adequately explain Japan's development starting in the late nineteenth century in contrast to the economic stagnation of China or India during the same historical period.

Just as the economic differentials between whites and blacks have increased in the United States during the past two decades of relative prosperity, so also have the gaps between the industrial and the underdeveloped nations grown. The Third World nations are beginning their ascent in a world which is largely industrialized and developed; whereas the West became industrialized in a very different milieu, starting two centuries ago.[20] Several basic differences obtain today which further alter the political context of economic development and social change. After the Industrial Revolution began in England in the mid-eighteenth century, it became increasingly clear that economic growth was related to political power and to the capacity of a society to compete internationally. It also became apparent that the pace of development, as well as its magnitude, necessitated the state's intervention in the private sector. The American government felt compelled to subsidize industrialization, expansion of the frontier, and the development of cross-continental railroads. In the colonial nations the economic system became virtually dominated by the colonial political apparatus; thus, bases for government intervention and a high degree of planning became institutionalized even before the time of national independence. Specifically, while the poor countries of the world are economically backward, they are not constrained by the traditional Western ideologies of private enterprise and laissez-faire. We shall say more about this shortly.

While the statistical evidence is considerable, it can be stated rather simply that the poor nations of the world are falling even

[19] Paul A. Baran, *The Political Economy of Growth*. New York: Monthly Review Press, 1957, Chapter 5, "On the Roots of Backwardness."
[20] Robert Heilbroner, *The Great Ascent*. New York: Harper & Row, 1963.

farther behind the rich, due to the structure of international economics.[21] The trade relations continue to operate against the poor nations which produce and export increasing quantities of raw materials, and in favor of the developed nations which produce more of the manufactured goods. The capital invested by the rich nations in the poor nations goes mostly into those industries which supply raw materials or petroleum products for their manufacturing industries, for such investments produce maximum return. Thus, the industrial nations are the greatest benefactors from their investment in the poor nations' economies. The new phenomenon of aid or assistance is very small in magnitude (less than one half of one percent of the United States' gross national product) and inadequate for coping with the structural problems of underdevelopment. In reality, the plight of the Third World is not that it exists as a residue of the developed and affluent nations of the world, but, rather, that it forms an integral part of the international political economy and that the current structure inevitably perpetuates international poverty. Where will the situation take us, and what are the guideposts for a sociological framework?

THE NATURE OF THE THIRD WORLD
ALTERNATIVES AND SOCIAL CHANGE

The precarious nature of predictions in the Third World is often pointed out. A few years ago a sociologist attempted to demonstrate the desirable democratic stability of multi-party systems and gave Nigeria as his illustration.[22] The tragic events in that country's recent history need no further commentary. Similarly, the illustrations of Ghana and Indonesia caution one against generalizing too far. Yet, some principles have emerged more clearly as sociologists and others have extended analyses from their own societies and made efforts to nuture viable theories of development.

To begin with, as suggested earlier, some particular relationships are structured by the international political economy. Many

---

[21] The discussion in the following paragraph relies heavily on Pierre Jalee, *The Pillage of the Third World*. New York: Monthly Review Press, 1968.
[22] William McCord, *The Springtime of Freedom*. New York: Oxford University Press, 1965.

of the African and Asian countries are new sovereign states, and their colonial past is significant in patterning their economic and social relations. While Latin American nations have a longer independent political history, their economic relations are closely allied with the United States, as has been documented in a variety of studies.[23] A structural analysis is necessary to cast into broader perspective the situation of most of the Third World. This context indicates that the underdeveloped nations are in their present economic situation not by some random and accidental happenstance, but due to their historical roles and present relations vis-à-vis the affluent nations—both capitalist and socialist.

There is increasing evidence that many Third World countries are rejecting the major models of development, the U.S. and U.S.S.R. Some countries are discerning that these industrial giants do not have the same dimensions as themselves, and these countries are searching for alternative models of relatively new nations with ethnically diverse or pluralistic populations, which have devised variant forms of economic and political structures for advancement. One such model is Yugoslavia, with its special mix of public and private sectors, the self-management concept, and its relative success in economic growth and cultural integration among its religiously and ethnically diverse population groupings.[24] The role of the state in the economy is on a priori grounds seen as different from that in the history of Western Europe and North America. At the same time, the anti-Stalinist tendencies have led to a more humanistic socialism with greater emphasis upon voluntarism and participation. This helps to explain the attraction of the Yugoslav model. In fact, the parallel with domestic sociological issues is striking once again; for a comparable ethos surrounds community organizations in ghetto areas which work for participation in poverty and educational decision-making and for a more human-oriented type of power structure which could produce economic betterment in the United States.

For sociological purposes, perhaps it is most useful to avoid

[23] Andre Gundar Frank, *Capitalism and Underdevelopment in Latin America.* New York: Monthly Review Press, 1967.
[24] See David S. Riddell, "Social Self-Government: The Background of Theory and Practice in Yugoslav Socialism," *British Journal of Sociology,* 19 (March 1968):47–75. (See article in this book, p. 130.)

characterizing the form of political structure, but rather to pin-point the social factors which appear most relevant in these alternative models of social change and economic development. The concept of planning is primary. Planning itself is hardly a revolutionary concept,[25] since it is axiomatic in systems analysis and efficiency planning in industrial enterprise. Yet, planning done by national political analysts with economic and social goals in the public sector is an extension of the development process in the West. Such planning calls for considerably more than the local community development efforts which have been a mainstay of this "development decade" promoted by UNESCO in the 1960s.[26] Full-scale planning must involve the integration of various cultural, social and economic sectors which comprise most Third World countries, and the commitment to socially desirable ends through a variety of coordinated means. Clearly this calls for experimentation and a variety of approaches.

The majority of developmental economists see the future in terms of American and Western European investment in the Third World. Most see this not in terms of political hegemony over the poor nations, but as a form of aid and assistance through capital advance, so that these poor nations can pull themselves up by the proverbial boot-straps. Yet, to begin with, most of the capital invested in the Third World countries of Asia, Africa and Latin America are monies derived from the contribution of these countries in the form of natural resources for the manufacturies of the Western developed nations. In a ringing indictment of social change and economic development theory, Frank states that

. . . where the development policy of this approach is ever more politically conservative and counsels others' gifts with open hands, an alternative policy for economic development and cultural change will have to be politically ever more revolutionary and help the peoples of the underdeveloped countries to take

[25] For an interesting analysis of this idea, see Bob Ross, "Is Planning a Revolution?" *Viet-Report*, Summer 1968, pp. 8–11, 61. (See article in this book, p. 217.)
[26] For study of community development and self-help projects in India, see Marshall B. Clinard, *Slums and Community Development: Experiments in Self-Help*. New York: The Free Press, 1966.

the destruction of this structure and the development of another system, into their own hands. If the developed countries cannot diffuse development, development theory, or development policy to the underdeveloped countries, then the people of these countries will have to develop them by themselves. These . . . modes of approach are the emperor's clothes, which have served to hide his naked imperialism. Rather than fashioning the emperor a new suit, these people will have have to dethrone him and clothe themselves."[27]

He is saying that the major modes of sociological theory of development are based upon a projection of a continuing model of diffusion from the advanced West into the Third World, both through the exemplary model of Western development and through Western investment in the poor nations. The last, Frank argues, is a mere gesture which obscures the reality that a poor nation's poverty is the product of national affluence elsewhere on the world scene.

This analysis of the Third World again should be observed in terms of the parallel with the domestic economic-social structure of America. Some critics of the Great Society[28] have essentially argued that federal poverty programs have disguised the growing affluence of those at the top of the economic ladder, who exploit the poor in a variety of forms, ranging from perpetual high rates of unemployment, to depressed wages, to inequities in the draft. There has been a move by some sociologists away from the social pathology perspective of the past, with its emphasis upon individual maladjustment, toward a more structuralist theory to explain societal problems such as mass poverty. This latter perspective denies the validity of simple theories of value change and adjustment which have sometimes been seen to underlie social problems. Similarly, social-psychological theories which posit that Third World citizens must alter their attitudinal structures to move out of economic backwardness, fail to comprehend and to deal with the structural realities in the world. As sociologists have by now reacted to early theories of social pathology, so should they re-

---

[27] Andre Gunder Frank, "Sociology of Development and Underdevelopment of Sociology," *Catalyst*, Summer 1967, pp. 73.
[28] For an overview, see Marvin E. Gettleman and David Mermelstein (eds.), *The Great Society Reader: The Failure of American Liberalism*. New York: Random House, 1967.

evaluate counterpart theories concerned with economic development and social theory. We need to take seriously what Robert
Heilbroner means by "counter-revolutionary America"[29] as we
generate and test theories of development.

[29] Robert Heilbroner, "Counterrevolutionary America," *Commentary*, 43
(April 1967):31–38. (See article in this book, p. 575.)

INDEX